The International City Management Association is the professional and educational organization for chief appointed management executives in local government. The purposes of ICMA are to enhance the quality of local government and to nurture and assist professional local government administrators in the U.S. and other countries. In furtherance of its mission, ICMA develops and disseminates new approaches to management through training programs, information services, and publications.

Managers, carrying a wide range of titles, serve cities, towns, counties, and councils of governments in all parts of the United States and Canada. These managers serve at the direction of elected councils and governing boards. ICMA serves these managers and local governments through many programs that aim at improving the manager's professional competence and strengthening the quality of all local governments.

The International City Management Association was founded in 1914; adopted its City Management Code of Ethics in 1924; and established its Institute for Training in Municipal Administration in 1934. The Institute, in turn, provided the basis for the Municipal Management Series, generally termed the "ICMA Green Books." ICMA's interests and activities include public management education; standards of ethics for members; *The Municipal Year Book* and other data services; local government research; and newsletters, *Public Mangement* magazine, and other publications. ICMA's efforts for the improvement of local government management—as represented by this book—are offered for all local governments and educational institutions.

Contributors

Douglas W. Ayres

Joseph N. Baker

Robert B. Burns

Stephen Chapple

Ronny J. Coleman

John M. Dionne

Douglas P. Forsman

John A. Granito

Thomas M. Hawkins, Jr.

Gerard J. Hoetmer

James R. Korom

Kenneth R. Lavoie

Leonard G. Marks

F. Patrick Marlatt

John Matzer, Jr.

Hugh McClees

Chester A. Newland

Don W. Oaks

James O. Page

Philip Schaenman

Jack W. Snook

David H. Teems

B. J. Thompson

Bruce J. Walz

Paul M. Whisenand

Municipal Management Series

Managing Fire Services

Second Edition

Published for the
ICMA Training
Institute

By the
International
City
Management
Association

Editors

Ronny J. Coleman
Fire Chief
Fullerton, California

John A. Granito
Fire and Public Safety Consultant

Professor and Vice President Emeritus
State University of New York

Municipal Management Series

Managing Fire Services

Effective Communication

The Effective Local Government Manager

Effective Supervisory Practices

Housing and Local Government

Local Government Police Management

Management of Local Planning

Management of Local Public Works

Management Policies in Local Government Finance

Managing Human Services

Managing Municipal Leisure Services

The Practice of Local Government Planning

The Practice of State and Regional Planning

Small Cities and Counties: A Guide to Managing Services

Library of Congress Cataloging-in-Publication Data

Managing Fire Services
  (Municipal management series)
  Bibliography: p.
  Includes index.
  1. Fire-departments—Management. I. Coleman, Ronny
J. II. Granito, John A. III. ICMA Training Institute.
IV. Series.
TH9145.M26 1988   363.3'7'068   88–6805
ISBN 0–87326–078–3

Printed in the United States of America.

949392919089
5432

Foreword

As this book goes to press, work is continuing on the final report of "America Burning Revisited," a conference sponsored in late 1987 by the U.S. Fire Administration to set its priorities for the future. Objectives of the conference were to reach a general consensus about the status of, and trends in, the U.S. fire problem; revisit the original "America Burning" report issued in 1973 by the National Commission on Fire Prevention and Control and evaluate progress toward its recommendations; and suggest guidelines for local, state, and federal efforts to reduce loss of life and property from fire.

Conference participants included representatives of all levels of government, the fire service, and fire-related industries and organizations, including the International City Management Association.

ICMA has had a presence in the field of fire service management for many years, since it published its first book on the subject in 1935. By 1967 that book, in its seventh edition, was entitled *Municipal Fire Administration* and had become one of the most popular of the "Green Books" in the Municipal Management Series. In 1979, reflecting changing times, ICMA published the first edition of *Managing Fire Services* in order to better serve the needs of fire service professionals, other managers in local government, and fire chiefs and managers in training.

Throughout the years, the fire service has been characterized by change—not only in the technology of fire prevention and suppression but also in the demand for services and the fiscal environment of local government. So-called "fire departments" are increasingly responsible for providing emergency medical services, planning for and responding to hazardous materials incidents and other emergencies, and enforcing local fire and building codes—as well as continuing their traditional suppression and prevention functions. Like other local departments, they often find themselves challenged to examine the cost-effectiveness of their programs and consider alternative means to achieve community fire protection goals. This new edition of *Managing Fire Services* reflects these changes that affect today's fire service while focusing as well on the constants that characterize sound management practice in a changing environment.

While fire protection is a highly technical field, this book is written from a managerial rather than a technical perspective. It seeks to identify and discuss the key managerial issues that face the fire chief and other departmental managers, the chief administrative officer, and local elected officials. While the book encompasses relevant theory and research, it does so primarily as background for practical management decision making.

This book, like others in the Municipal Management Series, has been published for the ICMA Training Institute. The institute offers in-service training specifically designed for local government officials whose jobs are to plan, direct, and coordinate the work of others. The Institute, sponsored by ICMA since 1934, has a training course to accompany each book in this series.

Many individuals contributed their efforts to the preparation of book. First and foremost are the the editors of this volume, Ronny J. Coleman, Fire Chief, Fullerton, California, and John A. Granito, fire and public safety consultant, and professor and vice president emeritus, State University of New York. Both made enormous contributions in conceptualizing the content, reviewing chapters, and writing original material.

The chapter authors deserve acknowledgment not only for their contributions but for their continuing assistance throughout the revision and editing process. And fire departments throughout the country contributed program descriptions, organization charts, and other materials to illustrate the text.

The National Fire Protection Association, Robert W. Grant, President, was helpful in providing photographs and other material and in reviewing portions of the manuscript for accuracy. We particularly wish to acknowledge the assistance of John R. Hall, Jr., Director, Fire Analysis Division; Thomas J. Klem, Director, Fire Investigations and Applied Research; and Robert Barr, Director, Fire Service Professional Qualifications Program.

Thanks also go to several persons currently or formerly with the U.S. Fire Administration, Clyde A. Bragdon, Jr., Administrator. Individuals who met with ICMA staff at the early stages of book development were Edward M. Wall, Deputy Administrator; James F. Coyle, Assistant Administrator for Fire Prevention and Arson Control; Roger P. Lanahan, Assistant Administrator for Firefighter Health and Safety; Harry J. Walsh, former Assistant Administrator. Also of assistance were Joseph L. Donovan, former Superintendent, National Fire Academy, and Michael P. Mitchell, former Deputy Superintendent, National Fire Academy.

Similarly, members of the staff of the International Association of Fire Chiefs, Garry L. Briese, Executive Director, provided assistance as the project progressed. Special thanks go to Ann L. Swing, Director, Management Information Center, and Harry Shaw, Operation Life Safety Consultant.

Other individuals who assisted in the preparation of this book include Colin A. Campbell, Association and Business Communications Consultant, Alexandria, Virginia; Steven Chapple, Assistant Attorney General for the Commonwealth of Virginia, who reviewed several portions for legal accuracy; Ann Copley and Jeffrey Counsell, von Briesen & Purtell, Milwaukee, Wisconsin, who assisted in the preparation of Chapter 12; Rebecca A. Geanaros, who prepared many of the illustrations; Dr. Harry E. Hickey, Chief of Fire Protection, Johns Hopkins University Applied Physics Laboratory, Laurel, Maryland, who helped review portions of the manuscript; Peggy Lilienthal Linden, Senior Education Specialist, Management and Education Branch, National Fire Academy; Venka V. Macintyre, who copy edited the manuscript; Charles H. Rule, Fire Chief, Manteca, California; Steven B. Rynecki, von Briesen & Purtell, Milwaukee, Wisconsin, who assisted in the preparation of Chapter 12; Alan J. Saly, Managing Editor, *Chief Fire Executive* magazine; Jim Sparr, Fire Chief, Fort Lauderdale, Florida; Gene Swearingen, Vice President, Participant Services, ICMA Retirement Corporation; Natalie Wasserman, Executive Director, Public Risk and Insurance Management Association; and Francis J. Yammarino, Assistant Professor, School of Management, State University of New York at Binghamton.

Finally, a number of ICMA staff members contributed to the project:

Barbara H. Moore, Director, Book Division, who had primary responsibility for working with the editors and authors to bring the project to fruition; Gerard J. Hoetmer, Director, Public Safety Programs, who wrote the chapter on alternative delivery systems and also provided assistance and advice throughout the project; Alice R. Markham, who provided research and editorial support; Dawn M. Leland, who supervised production; and Mary W. Blair, publications secretary.

William H. Hansell, Jr.
Executive Director

International City
Management Association

Washington, D.C.

Preface

Unless we have some belief that we can shape future events in the fire protection field, we tend to lose motivation, job satisfaction, and our sense of professionalism. Because of our high interest in improving community protection, we are constantly looking for ways to predict the future, to shape it, and to meet its challenge. We often use the words "future" and "challenge" together, and thus it is appropriate to introduce this book on fire service management with a comment on meeting the challenge of the future.

To discuss this challenge, several key issues must be addressed:

1. What is "the fire service," and how do we acquire our view of it?
2. What is meant by the "future," and how is the future of the fire service influenced?
3. How is the role of the fire service expanding?
4. What is being predicted for the fire service, and what can we do about it?

The fire service

At one time it was easy to define the fire service. For many decades, fire departments were either volunteer or paid units that were a part of municipal government or closely allied with it. The service provided was essentially fire suppression, and very few, if any, subsystems existed. If some kind of rescue service was needed, for example, it was provided by the regular "firemen." The federal government was not involved in any way with community fire protection and even state governments exercised little influence.

Of course, such a simplistic definition of the fire service no longer holds. Today, fire (or fire and rescue) departments may be public service agencies, and thus a full part of local government; privately owned corporations with a municipal services contract; units of a county, state, or federal agency; or part of an industry that provides its own protection. The fire protection group may be a not-for-profit corporation that provides free personnel for municipally owned equipment, or it may provide personnel, equipment, vehicles, and even fire stations for a contract price. Some fire suppression groups provide services only for property owners who pay an annual fee; others respond to any call but bill for services rendered. Other departments provide multiple services such as fire and police, or fire and emergency medical.

This diversity in the organizational design of the fire service is matched by a great variety of staffing patterns. There are volunteer departments, paid (career) departments, and combinations of the two. There are departments with part-time staff, on-call staff, "bunkers" who only remain at the station overnight, and firefighters who are employed full-time by the municipality but perform other types of duties as well.

As several chapters illustrate, departments now provide a multiplicity of services beyond fire suppression, ranging from emergency medical to building plan review to public education programs. In more and more cases, the title of fire department does not even come close to describing the services provided for the community.

Since the creation of the U.S. Fire Administration, of course, there has been a national agency providing co-ordination, research, data bases, and training. All of those efforts have exercised a strong influence on the fire service. So, too, has the Emergency Management Institute. Among the other organizations with nationwide influence are the International City Management Association, the International Association of Fire Chiefs, the International Association of Fire Fighters, the International Society of Fire Service Instructors, the National Fire Protection Association, and the Insurance Services Office. Several universities, notably the University of Maryland and Oklahoma State University, and the U.S. Department of Transportation (DOT) are very active, as well.

Fire protection and related activities have also increased significantly at the state level. Each state government has coordinating and training functions, some of which are highly developed. Joining with state fire marshals, many insurance companies and the International Association of Arson Investigators have been working to reduce fire loss. A great many public and private schools participate in "Learn Not to Burn," "Project Life," and related public education programs.

Widespread local and state legislation has developed in support of residential sprinkler systems, early detection systems, environmental monitoring systems, 911 reporting systems, public prevention and safety programs, hazardous materials programs, and the like. Numerous consulting firms offer their services, and many manufacturers and service

businesses—such as cable TV—are designing, producing, and marketing products related to fire safety. Consider, for example, the very large numbers of smoke detectors and home fire extinguishers that have been sold in the past decade. Almost every chapter in this book describes some facet of the expansion of the U.S. fire service. Today, we are also much more aware of fire problems in other nations. International travel to fire conferences is now common, and fire service periodicals and the media frequently report on foreign fire disasters.

To consider the future of the fire service is to contemplate interlocking and synergistic relationships of many organizations, the majority of which were not directly associated with community fire protection for many years. To view the fire service as anything less is to reduce our ability to predict the future, influence it, and successfully meet its challenges.

The future

In thinking about the future of the fire service, most of us tend to envision a scene of some future time, "after the changes have occurred and everything new is in place." We like to project ourselves to a point where a total package is all set and operating. In fact, of course, the future arrives in bits and pieces, each tomorrow following each tomorrow, and our attention is most often on the journey rather than the final destination—on the process and means rather than the end results. In a way, we may never sense that we have reached the future, since change continues and our vision itself turns into a "motion picture" that never really ends.

A very small example illustrates this phenomenon—the development and future of protective clothing, apparatus, and equipment. There has been steady progress in this area since firefighter health and safety became a national issue and it became evident that money would be spent by municipalities on better products. As technology advanced in several fields, from space shots to auto racing, the benefits of fire-safe materials, breathing apparatus, electronic alarms, and so on accrued to firefighters. Each year we see several advancements, along with the parallel development of robots and fixed extinguishing systems. The situation is always better, but constantly advancing. In fact, we will never reach an end.

This illustration also provides a view of how the future is influenced. Although certain global events may occur and reoccur outside of human influence, there is certainly overwhelming evidence that at least smaller-scale "futures" may be brought about by careful analysis, planning, and implementation of action plans.

The NASA space program, which in a few years took people to the moon and far beyond, shows the power of determination, commitment, leadership, knowledge, and resources. We know that these are key ingredients in shaping the future, but other factors are important, as in the continuing development of protective gear. There, as with the NASA projects, our ability to tap the advancements of other fields—other knowledge bases—is critical. Protective material (such as Nomex) was invented for other uses, and self-contained breathing apparatus stems from underwater SCUBA gear. Once again, we have used the technology of others to advance our own field.

Perhaps the best tool the fire service has for influencing the future is its ability to define problems and to invent workable solutions. "Flexibility and innovation" has long been the firefighters' motto. Consider, for example, that the fire service has begun to emphasize comprehensive fire prevention and public education in

its effort to lower fire loss statistics. Once the fire loss problem was clearly defined, and cost-effectiveness factored into the formula, the fire service saw that suppression efforts alone could never do the job. But even in the suppression field, it has added early detection and automatic reporting devices, more sophisticated fixed extinguishing systems, and escape plans, to name but a few.

Our willingness and ability to redefine major problems to more basic questions (how we can cause fires not to start, rather than how many hose streams will be needed) coupled with our flexibility and inventiveness will go a long way toward influencing the future.

The future of the fire service is also being shaped by the myriad other organizations with which it interacts. Many strong influences affect the fire service, and relatively few of them are particularly concerned with its long and proven history of dedicated public service, much less its future goals and objectives—be they mandated residential sprinklers or professional certification. Noble goals seldom bring automatic cooperation. To shape the future of community fire protection, the fire service must unify and become more proactive, more involved in strategic long-range planning, more conscious of its public image, and more knowledgeable about the power brokers.

The expanding role of the fire service

As fire protection professionals and community residents grow more aware of the dangers of modern life—from hazardous materials spills to heart attacks to earthquakes and floods in populated areas—the call for broader protection measures and more expert systems grows louder. Since almost all public safety incidents require quick response from trained, equipped, experienced, and highly organized personnel, it is natural that the most common agency of choice should be the fire and rescue department. Thus fire protection personnel find themselves involved in multi-hazard response work. In addition, now that elected leaders and the public are becoming increasingly aware of the high payoff value of comprehensive fire prevention and public education, many more of these activities are falling on the shoulders of fire departments. The service that thus far has placed the most strenuous demands on fire departments is, of course, emergency medical. The addition of EMS has already created both controversy and change in the traditional departments.

As suggested earlier, a parallel development to the demand for more services from the fire department—in some instances brought about by departments faced with declining fire suppression alarms—has been the entry into public protection by both nontraditional fire groups, such as private, contract departments, and by other types of agencies, such as environmental protection departments, DOT, and the Coast Guard. At the same time, the fire protection delivery system has expanded to include related local agencies such as EMS-designated hospitals; building, planning, and zoning departments; and the police and public works agencies. Organizations outside the fire departments that provide mutual aid as well as other types of assistance—such as the Red Cross and the National Guard—are also part of the system, as are the industrial groups that have created such systems as CHEMTREC. Added to these are the private organizations that can assist with prevention, training, and readiness programs, as well as the many organizations and businesses involved in public safety education, product development, and the marketing of items like detectors and concepts like EDITH (home fire

drills). The necessity of interrelating with these many organizations places new and additional demands on fire departments.

The technological advances that assist departments in conducting their work also call for new knowledge, skills, and attitudes. Automatic alarm systems, 911 reporting systems, and computer-aided dispatching serve as examples of what might be called "two-edged swords," the utilization of which requires change and effort plus new knowledge. The growing list of developments that have increased the ability to prevent fires and reduce their effect is impressive. Some of these, like smoke detectors, are reasonably new, while residential sprinklers, public education programs, and automatic defibrillation machines are improvements of older models. Nevertheless, fire departments have much more to learn. The number and complexity of relevant subsystems are growing exponentially. To deal effectively with these new subsystems and to direct their full benefits to the community may require alternative organizational structures and delivery systems. Two illustrations will suffice: Many departments report that public education and school programs are best conducted by experienced teachers oriented toward prevention work, rather than firefighters or inspectors oriented toward teaching. Thus we see increasing civilianization. Second, a variety of organizational and personnel structures are being used to deliver EMS, but it is still being housed within the fire department.

Almost all components of this fire protection delivery system are active and growing. Some have legal responsibilities and authority for aspects of safety; some are concerned with responding to pleas for help; some are there because of history, tradition, and a sense of duty; and some are in business to turn a profit. Whatever their purpose, each one expands the role of the fire service as the focus of community protection efforts.

Trends in community fire protection

Several concepts that have emerged in the 1980s are having a profound influence on the structure and operations of the U.S. fire service. These concepts and others described in the following chapters represent trends that will shape the future of fire protection:

1. Risk management, calculated risk, trade-offs, and decisions made by broad-based community groups, not just the "professionals"
2. Accountability and concern for cost-effectiveness
3. Local and regional planning, with fire protection but one element of an integrated emergency management system
4. Addition of related services to the delivery package
5. Comprehensive prevention, including anti-arson programs as a way to reduce fire loss
6. Fire protection leadership at and from the national level
7. Research, development, and increased data bases supported by enhanced management information systems and computerization, as significant aids to protection
8. Increased use of alternative organizational structures and nontraditional personnel in all aspects of fire protection work
9. Use of technology to improve protection and control costs.

These trends vary in degree from one part of the country to another, but are discernible to some degree almost everywhere.

Challenges

Even with strategic planning under way, every organization still has major tasks to perform if it is to prepare for the future. The U.S. fire service is no exception; goals and objectives present formidable challenges. Chapter 1 of this book outlines some major tasks that will have to be carried out if we are to reduce the fire problem. They are identified as external and internal challenges. External challenges include public education in fire safety, legal mandates for built-in protection, safer building design, protective clothing and gear for firefighters, safer transportation, better protection for the environment, and further development of fire-safe materials and products.

To bring about an effective movement toward these broad goals, the fire service must continue to improve its own effectiveness. The internal challenges lie in a number of areas: training, fire attack capabilities, productivity in such areas as prevention, management skills, affirmative action programs, and labor relations. Many of these as well as others are discussed in detail throughout this book. Each presents a continuing goal, with a higher level of attainment always possible. The current—and probably future—environment of the fire service provides great opportunities for meeting the challenges, external as well as internal. For example, while budgets are tight, public concern over disasters is at an all-time high, and hazardous materials dangers command more and more resources. Fire service leaders need to become more skilled in tapping available resources, and sometimes this means offering to expand services—into hazardous waste protection, for example—rather than threatening to reduce them.

In the future, the fire service can expect continued challenges. Economic pressures, pressures for more cost-effectiveness and productivity, and tight budget controls will undoubtedly remain. Calls for more service and the pressures from competing agencies will complicate the picture. Departments will undoubtedly continue to adjust their organizational structures and their staffing patterns to improve efficiency and effectiveness, and continue to push for the operational benefits of new and advancing technologies. Balancing the cost of protection with the difficulty of recruiting and retaining volunteers will require advanced management skills. The continuing demand by taxpayers and consumers for more professional and affordable protection service will focus increased attention on the certification and credentialing of personnel and very likely the certification of departments.

Each chapter of this book describes current and future concerns by the score, and their sum total presents fire service managers a challenge that is both large and exciting. To provide a safer total environment in a more complicated world, and in an affordable way, is indeed a professional's challenge. Those who lead in providing fire, emergency medical, and disaster protection for our communities must be aware of the political and economic climates, the importance of accountability and liability, the potential benefits of new technology and alternative organizational arrangements, and the necessity for continued training, education, and professionalism.

The challenges of the future will be met by the wise and sound management of today's fire service leaders and those of tomorrow.

John A. Granito
Ronny J. Coleman

Contents

Tables

Part one:
The context
of fire service
management

The evolution of fire services

Since the dawn of time fire has served as both a protector and an agent of progress. Uncontrolled, however, fire can unleash forces of destruction that are one of humankind's greatest curses. Learning to bring fire under control in order to modify the living environment has presented humans with one of their greatest challenges. In learning to control fire, the human race has had to learn to control itself. Had we not been successful in meeting that challenge, we would not have been able to inhabit most of the earth's surface. Controlled fire provides urban society with many conveniences that a good portion of the world's population now considers necessary. It also provides the means for the development of space-age technology to take us above and beyond the earth's surface.

Although great progress has been made in acquiring knowledge and developing the skills necessary to harness fire as a servant, fire frequently breaks out of control and becomes destructive. Nowhere is the toll of death, injury, and property destruction greater than in the industrialized nations. The United States itself has the worst record.

Most frequently, accidental fire results from either ignorance or lack of attention—in short, the human factor. For this reason, contemporary efforts to control fire must include education as well as research to determine new ways of controlling the complex physical and chemical processes of fire itself.

The origins

At some point before recorded history began, humans observed that fire set by natural forces such as lightning, meteorite impact, or volcanic eruption provided certain benefits. It drove game over cliffs or into natural corrals. Brush fires cleared forest of undergrowth so game could be better seen and hunted. Fire cleared other lands, which then produced better grassland, which, in turn, attracted more game.

Heat for warmth was, however, probably the first benefit of fire to be discovered. This heating was closely associated with the cooking of food. Early humans also found that they could use fire to destroy or protect against enemies—insects, beasts, and even other people. Eventually, through the centuries, the human race learned to fire pottery and bricks and to smelt metals. As great as many of these discoveries were, however, none was more significant than the art of firemaking itself.

Discovery of ignition sources

The first method used to ignite a fire deliberately is lost in antiquity. However, we may conclude that early humans probably observed such natural phenomena as the spark produced when flint strikes against pyrite, the "spontaneous ignition" of plant matter, and the friction of dry branches rubbing together in the wind. We do know that the friction method of ignition was commonly used by early peoples throughout the world.

The archaeological record   Archaeological studies have concluded that humans have known how to make fire for hundreds of thousands of years. The earliest evidence of this knowledge was found in France, near Nice, which may have been occupied as early as a million years ago. The antiquity of this site is exceptional. More abundant evidence of the ability to control fire does not appear until the Middle Pleistocene (approximately 500,000 years ago) at numerous sites in China and Europe. Indeed, the movement of people into these cold northern areas during interglacial periods would not have been possible without control over fire.

Peking Man, who inhabited the famous Choukoutien Cave some 40 miles from Peking about half a million years ago, is unquestionably the earliest clearly identified user of fire. "The unwholesome cannibal of this chilly, fire-heated den" is how Joseph Campbell describes him. Campbell also notes that "the remarkable thing about the Chinese find [of the cave] was the evidence of fire in the cave. For although a number of proto-human remains of this general period have been found elsewhere in the world, Choukoutien is unique in the evidence of fire."[1]

It was not until 30,000 to 10,000 B.C., however, that the "art of roasting" was invented.[2] So both Peking Man and—some 200,000 years later—Neanderthal Man were eaters of raw food, although they possessed fire. Campbell suggests that "the earliest hearths . . . could have been shrines, where fire was cherished in and for itself in the way of a holy image or primitive fetish. The practical value of such a living presence, then, would have been discovered in due time."[3] He goes on to point out that the hearth has remained significant in contemporary rituals surrounding home and marriage.

Friction, compression, and percussion   The most universal ancient method of firemaking was to convert muscular energy into heat through friction. A commonly used instrument was a fire drill, a wooden rod (or stick) resting in the hollow of a fire board, adjacent to tinder. The stick was rapidly rotated between the palms of the hands or with a thong looped around the stick. This ancient method of firemaking can still be found among contemporary preliterate people. It survived until recent years in peasant Europe. Mechanical fire drills were developed by the Eskimos, the ancient Egyptians, the Asians, and a few American Indians.

Other related friction methods include the fire saw and fire plough. Both of these were used in Indonesia, Southeast Asia, and Australia. The typical fire saw in Southeast Asia consisted of a piece of bamboo with a nick cut into the side. A thick, sharp-edged splinter was drawn back and forth in the nick until sufficient heat was generated to ignite the tinder. The fire plough consisted of a grooved board and a stick that was rubbed back and forth in the groove until the collected wood dust was ignited. It was commonly used in Polynesia and some parts of Africa.

An innovative device used in areas from Southeast Asia to the Philippines was the fire piston, which operated on the principle that heat is produced when gases in the atmosphere are subjected to pressure. It consisted of a cylinder (such as a bamboo tube) with a plunger. When sharply struck, the plunger was driven downward, thus compressing the air within the cylinder. This is the basic premise of the diesel engine today. Tinder placed at the base of the cyclinder was ignited from the heat generated from the compressed gases.

Percussion methods such as striking pyrite (a compound of iron and sulfur) were probably also invented in the early years of civilization. In the Old World the striking of iron on flint to produce sparks for firemaking was widespread from the beginning of the age of ironworking about 3,500 years ago. Much later, during the Industrial Revolution, after steel was invented, this principle was used to develop relatively lightweight firearms. The metal "strike-a-light" was an item greatly desired by American Indians trading with Europeans.

Preservation, borrowing, and perpetuation   Whatever the method of ignition, our early ancestors had to preserve fire carefully. As families, clans, and tribes moved away from their original habitat, they must have moved their fire with them. If the fire went out, they were at the mercy of the cold until a new fire was found. The easiest way to reignite was probably to borrow embers from a neighboring community.

Evidence of fire borrowing was found by Karl Weule, director of the Ethnological Museum in Leipzig, during a 1906 expedition to East Africa. In his early investigations he could not find any type of firemaking device. Each time he asked natives if he could see their firemaking devices, he was told they did not have any. After some observation it became clear that they simply did not start a new fire if they could help it. A dead tree trunk would be dragged to a convenient site and coals from somewhere else would be used to ignite the log, which would burn slowly and leave embers that would glow for many days. These embers were then used to light other fires. An African on a journey would carry along a glowing marrow or smoldering reed. Weule discovered that, although these Africans knew how to use a fire drill, they found it more convenient to "borrow fire."

All these early methods of firemaking were tedious and cumbersome. The invention in 1827 of the wooden match with a chemical head was thus of great significance. Attributed to John Walker, an Englishman, these matches contained phosphorous sulfate and were essentially the same as those used today. In 1855 safety matches were invented in Sweden and their use spread rapidly.

The modern technique of producing fire by introducing an electrical spark into a combustible gas-air mixture has been an even greater breakthrough as it made possible the internal combustion engine, which is used to power most of our modes of transportation and many tools and pieces of equipment.

Myths and rituals

Long before archaeologists discovered evidence of the early methods of making fire, humans had woven a fascinating web of myths to satisfy the mystery and doubt in their minds about the origin and power of fire.[4] Some centered on the sun. In Greek mythology, for example, Prometheus was the fire-giver who recognized the plight of humans without fire. Out of pity he stole fire from the sun's chariot and gave it to the human race. For this transgression Zeus ordered Prometheus severely punished.[5]

Many folktales identify animals as the first possessors of fire. In the stories of certain American Indian tribes, fire is passed along a chain of mammals, reptiles, birds, and fish, eventually going to the human race. The last carrier in the chain of fire bearers is often venerated and protected from death.[6]

Many cultures also imbued their deities with special powers related to fire. The Vedic god Agni protected humans against the mystery of darkness, and the Phoenician god Baal received human sacrifices by fire. The Roman god of fire was Vulcan, whose name survives today in the English verb *vulcanize*. The Aztecs of Mexico had Xuihtecutl, whom they worshipped with sacred flames.

Fire has also held a place in religious ceremony and in philosophy. Brahman households are still supposed to maintain a sacred fire for the worship of Agni, much as the virgin priestesses of ancient Rome watched over the perpetual holy fire at the temple of Vesta, goddess of the hearth. The Greeks called the same goddess Hestia and tended her fire in a public hearth in every city; they transported this fire with great care to kindle the fire on the hearth of any new colony.[7] The Greek philosopher Aristotle postulated that fire, earth, water, and air constituted the four essential elements of life and of all things. Plato believed that God used these four elements in creating the world, while Heraclitas declared fire to be the essential force behind creation.

Fire was indeed a potent force in myths and ritual and an even more potent one in real life when its power of destruction was unleashed.

The need for protection from fire

As the ability to ignite fire at will increased, respect for its power decreased. Since a watch was no longer needed to keep a fire from dying out, fires were often left unattended. Over the millennia many disastrous and tragic experiences have taught humanity the danger of this lack of attention.

Precautions, safety measures, and regulations to reduce the hazards of fire began to emerge as the characteristics of fire and various materials were discovered. People also found that they had to develop ways to protect themselves and their possessions when fire broke out of control or when fire ignited accidentally.

The first organized firefighting force that can be traced in history was established in Rome by Augustus Caesar around 23 B.C. Moved to action by a bad fire, Augustus established a body of 600 men belonging to the *familia publica*, "servants of the commonwealth," and had them stationed near the city gates.[8] As slaves, they had few rights in the society in which they were forced to live; moreover, they were often accused of being slow in responding to fires and of being reluctant to endure physical risk to save the lives and property of the Roman masters. Eventually, their work was supplemented by companies of volunteers, but these companies never enjoyed the favor of the government.[9]

After another bad fire in A.D. 6, Augustus formed a corps of professional firefighters known as the *vigiles* (watchmen). These were freemen, divided into seven battalions (*cohortes*) of 1,000 men each and commanded by the *praefectus vigilium*, a prefect of the equestrian rank who was directly responsible to the emperor (he is the direct ancestor of today's fire chief). The *vigiles* were distributed throughout the city. The cost of maintaining the corps was paid by the public treasury, and every fire prompted an official inquiry. When a fire was judged to be the result of negligence, the careless citizen was punished.[10]

Lessons from Rome

Through the centuries the story has been told of the cruel, obese, and truculent Emperor Nero who "fiddled as Rome burned." However true this description, Nero was apparently a man of vision and intelligence who fully recognized the dangers of unregulated construction. Before his reign, Rome had expended its wealth and resources on the construction of public edifices. Unfortunately, sound principles of construction were ignored in almost all other buildings. Tenements were built without any type of control and many collapsed before they were completed, maiming and killing workers by the score. Rome was, in fact, in a state of chaos just before the great fire of A.D. 64.

It is interesting to note that even before the great conflagration Nero had a master plan for the development of a new city. Immediately after the fire, reconstruction began. Nero's attitude toward conditions existing in Rome before the fire were well known, and accusations that he ordered the incineration have seemed well-founded to some historians. Nevertheless, Nero must be credited with reconstructing Rome in accordance with sound principles of construction, sanitation, and utility. From that time until the fall of Rome, both public and private building was closely regulated.[11]

Early building codes

The earliest known code of law regulating building construction is that of Hammurabi, founder of the Babylonian empire. Here is an extract from the code:

228: If a builder build a house for a man and complete it, that man shall pay him two shekels of silver per sar (approximately 12 square feet of house) as his wage.

229: If a builder has built a house for a man and his work is not strong, and if the house he has built falls in and kills the householder, that builder shall be slain.

230: If the child of the householder be killed, the child of that builder shall be slain.

231: If the slave of the householder be killed, he shall give slave for slave to the householder.

232: If goods have been destroyed, he shall replace all that has been destroyed; and because the house was not made strong, and it has fallen in, he shall restore the fallen house out of his own material.

233: If a builder has built a house for a man, and his work is not done properly and a wall shifts, then that builder shall make that wall good with his own silver.[12]

Early fire regulations

Throughout history, tragedies arising from holocaust and structural collapse have taught inhabitants—particularly city dwellers—how vulnerable they are to these forces of destruction. Most improvements in design, construction, public fire protection, and built-in safety features are directly related to experiences involving the loss of life and property; this explanation is known as the "catastrophe theory of reform."

Information is not complete regarding early efforts to combat and prevent fire after the collapse of classical Mediterranean civilization. There is only fragmentary evidence from areas as diverse as ancient India and China, the urban centers of medieval Islamic culture and the cities of sub-Saharan Africa, and the urban areas of Europe that emerged with feudal society. In view of the roots of American culture, however, it is interesting to look at some regulations found in medieval England.

Curfew, derived from the French for "cover fire," was adopted in Oxford in A.D. 872 requiring that fires be extinguished at a fixed hour in the evening. After 1066 a general curfew was established in England by William the Conqueror, who directed that a bell be rung in every community sometime between 7 and 9 o'clock each night. At this signal a metal fire cover was placed over the open hearth fires in each home to prevent sparks from igniting the rushes on which people slept. There is reason to believe that William had this law enforced not so much as a fire prevention measure but as a means of preventing revolt against his rule.

The first lord mayor of London issued an ordinance in 1189 requiring that new buildings have stone walls and slate or tile roofs, demonstrating that government officials were becoming concerned about the rapid spread of fire in the growing communities.

Richard I, who reigned during the last decade of the twelfth century, decreed that walls 16 feet high and 3 feet thick be erected between neighbors to prevent the spread of fire. Evidently he was not successful in enforcing this requirement since fires continued to spread and destroy large sections of London.

Possibly the first two fire protection enactments in England that dealt with occupancy instead of the buildings themselves were a 1566 ordinance in Manchester requiring safe storage of fuel for bakers' ovens and a 1583 parliamentary act forbidding tallow chandlers to melt tallow in dwellings.

The seventeenth and eighteenth centuries

The seventeenth and eighteenth centuries saw numerous fires and fire prevention efforts and the evolution of fire insurance companies.

Fire in colonial America

Hope for a new life, for freedom, and for personal ownership of property was a magnetic draw to the new world for courageous immigrants from England, France, Spain, the Netherlands, and Scandinavia.[13] In spite of the dangers in crossing a treacherous and relatively uncharted ocean, not to mention the threat of disease, hostile Indians, and famine, early colonists set sail by the hundreds.

As they landed they were forced to construct shelter hastily, and they chose the most expedient means available. Some carved caves in the sides of hills; others collected brush, tree limbs, clay, and grasses to build small cottages with thatched roofs. For protection from the bitter northeastern winters, the colonists built central fireplaces in these dwellings. They constructed the fireplaces of bricks and mud and the chimneys of brush and stalks, which they covered with a thick mixture of mud. These combustible chimneys, in combination with the thatched roofs, presented an even greater hazard than the natural elements or hostile Indians.

Many common commodities in the colonists' homes such as whiskey, brandy, and gunpowder contributed to the rapid spread of fire. To make matters worse, the colonists followed the European tradition of building structures up rather than out and clustered side by side. Although these closely built settlements were easier to protect from Indian attack, they greatly increased vulnerability to rapid fire spread.

Early conflagrations   The first permanent colony in the new world was founded in Jamestown, Virginia, in 1607. In 1608 it was devastated by fire, which destroyed most of the lodgings and provisions. Five years later Dutch traders landed near the mouth of the Hudson River to trade with the Indians. A few wooden huts were erected to form the first settlement on what is now Manhattan Island. One of the ships returned to Holland, and the remaining ship burned and sank, leaving the small crew isolated. Fortunately, the local Indians were friendly and helped to provide shelter. Because of this cordial reception and the Indians' interest in trading, the settlement of Nieuw Amsterdam was later established by the Dutch.

In 1620 a colony was settled at Plymouth, Massachusetts; three years later a fire spread out of control, destroying seven buildings and nearly all the provisions.

Boston had the dubious distinction of suffering the most frequent and most destructive fires in early America. One authority has pointed out that Boston had had nine serious fires before the Revolution, whereas Philadelphia and New York had not yet had one.[14] Flammable construction was undoubtedly a major factor contributing to Boston's poor fire record. Excellent building stone and material for making bricks were available in Nieuw Amsterdam (later to become New York City), whereas Boston's building stone was inferior. Consequently more wooden buildings were erected in Boston. Also contributing was the lax enforcement of fire prevention and building laws. In 1638, after numerous fires, Massachusetts passed a law prohibiting smoking outdoors, the first no-smoking law in America. Other colonial settlements followed this lead.[15]

Peter Stuyvesant and fire prevention   Nieuw Amsterdam might have experienced the same fire destruction as Boston had it not been for the strong personal leadership of Governor Peter Stuyvesant.[16] Recognizing the hazard of combustible chimneys, the governor succeeded in getting a law passed in 1648 that prohibited the construction of wooden or plaster chimneys. This was the first of many fire laws to be passed by the American colonists in efforts to prevent fire disasters.

Stuyvesant's next step was to appoint four volunteer fire wardens to enforce the law and inspect the chimneys to see that they were properly swept. These fire wardens were required to levy fines on owners of faulty chimneys. Such fines had become common in other colonies, and it became evident that measures had to be taken if the colonies were to survive. Much greater fines were imposed on the residents of Nieuw Amsterdam who were found guilty of negligently causing a fire. Assessing fines for such negligence was in keeping with the European tradition. Monies collected from the fines were used to purchase firefighting equipment such as ladders, 3-gallon water buckets, hooks, and swabs.

The greatest threat of major fire spread was presented by fires occurring at night while people slept. Gaining considerable headway before detection, as today, these fires became extremely difficult to control and extinguish. So many towns adopted a curfew and rang a bell at 9 p.m. to order all fires covered or extinguished until 4:30 a.m. An additional step was taken in 1658 by Stuyvesant when he appointed eight young men to roam the streets at night to watch for fires. These men, clad in long capes, carried a wooden rattle that was twirled to sound an alarm. The Rattle Watch soon grew from eight to fifty members

Figure 1–1 A member of the Rattle Watch in Nieuw Amsterdam.

and began to arouse opposition among the townspeople, who considered the Rattle Watch to be prowlers more than protectors. Resentment of the iron-fisted rule of Peter Stuyvesant helped lead to the British takeover in 1664.

The British renamed the colony New York and picked up where Stuyvesant had left off. An ordinance was soon adopted regulating the burning out of chimneys at regular intervals and forcing the use of chimney sweeps. Failure to comply resulted in a fine, proceeds again going to provide equipment. Other early laws made possible strict prosecution of arsonists. The first law relating to arson was passed in Maryland in 1638 and carried the death penalty.[17]

The Great Fire of London

The Great Fire of London in 1666 destroyed nearly two-thirds of that city. Some historians have stated that the destruction was more a blessing than a tragedy as London at that time was an unsanitary, crowded city consisting of low wood-frame houses and warehouses. Most thoroughfares had open drains that carried raw sewage, and household garbage was thrown into the streets. Dwelling units were overcrowded, sanitation was unknown, and epidemics were common. Plague had ravaged London for about a year prior to the fire with hundreds dying per week at its worst period.

Blessing or not, the London fire raged for five days and nights, destroying 13,200 homes, 87 churches (among them St. Paul's Cathedral), 20 warehouses, and 100,000 boats and barges and leaving 200,000 people homeless. Miraculously, only 6 lives were lost.

As a result of the fire, the English Parliament passed regulations called the London Building Act. However, it took two years for them to enact this legislation and then it applied only within the city boundaries of London. Sir Christopher Wren, architect of St. Paul's Cathedral, implored Parliament to enact laws requiring wider streets, green spaces, building setbacks, and the use of noncombustible materials in construction. His pleas were ignored and London was rebuilt in much the same style as before the fire. Wren is reported to have remarked, "The citizens of London have proved themselves unworthy of so great a fire."[18]

Other fire prevention efforts

Although London appeared not to have learned from experience, measures were taken in many other countries to prevent the recurrence of such a catastrophe. Probably the most advanced ideas in fire protection anywhere in seventeenth-century Europe were embodied in the fire ordinance of the German Empire passed in the 1670s. This required fireplaces and chimneys to be rebuilt with or enclosed by tile or stone, and to be large enough for a person to pass through and clean them. Other preventive measures pertained to the storage and handling of materials, even to the storage of fats and grease in subcellars by housewives.

Special equipment such as fire axes, water tubs, sledges, squirt guns, leather buckets, and long ladders had been developed and provided in German communities. Regulations in the fire ordinance specified their location and availability to maximize the effectiveness of their use.

In the American colonies, there were some attempts to legislate against the use of combustible construction. The Boston general court required all dwellings to be built of stone or brick and to be covered with slate or tile roofs. Obviously, this law was not enforced since Boston experienced several conflagrations in which combustible construction was a contributing factor.[19]

In a burst of fire consciousness, the Pennsylvania legislature in 1696 established a law prohibiting the smoking of tobacco on the streets of Philadelphia, punishable by a fine. No record can be found that the law was ever repealed.

Early insurance companies

Prior to the Great Fire of London, victims of fire depended on a traditional system of collecting donations from neighbors, friends, and sympathizers in other communities to restore their losses. Collections for victims of the London fire were insignificant, however, compared to their losses. The first fire insurance companies were formed in Europe to insure against loss, and the idea soon spread to the colonies. Apparently most, if not all, of the American companies failed rather quickly.

Benjamin Franklin is credited with founding the first successful American fire insurance company in 1752. A champion of fire prevention, his writings in his *Pennsylvania Gazette* had much to do with increasing public awareness of fire safety and with forming opinion on the importance of fire prevention. He had succeeded in convincing city officials to buy fire suppression equipment and to pass fire safety regulations. Franklin coined one of his most familiar epigrams, "An ounce of prevention is worth a pound of cure," in a letter warning the citizens of Philadelphia about the hazards of carrying burning firebrands or coals in a shovel from one room to another (he recommended using a closed warming pan) or "when your stairs, being in flames, you may be forced (as I once was) to leap out of your windows and hazard your necks to avoid being overroasted."[20]

In the beginning, Franklin's fire insurance company was named the Philadelphia Contributorship for the Insurance of Houses from Loss by Fire. Later the name was changed to the Hand-in-Hand Insurance Company.

Within a short time thereafter, several other insurance companies were formed. Since those early days, fire insurance companies have espoused support for fire prevention. Of course, they have a vested interest, but that interest has spurred the creation of many fire prevention regulations, improvements in structural conditions, increased safety in industrial processes, improvements in public fire protection, and the installation of built-in fire protection features and systems.

The nineteenth century

The nineteenth century was an exciting era for the United States.[21] The country expanded westward, thousands of immigrants swelled the population, American industry bourgeoned, and the merchant fleet and navy vessels began to gain international recognition. Along the Eastern seaboard cities and harbors were developing, older cities were expanding outward and upward. The century was filled with growth, enterprise, discovery, innovation—and fire!

Numerous major fires and conflagrations occurred in the United States during the nineteenth century, but the greatest happened after the Civil War. On July 4, 1866, in Portland, Maine, a firecracker went off in flammable material and ignited a wind-driven blaze that swept quickly through the heart of the city, leaving 10,000 homeless. Sympathetic citizens in many parts of the country organized public subscriptions to raise funds for those who had suffered severe losses. Rumors spread that many of the Portland insurance claims would not be paid because several of the insurance companies had been driven to bankruptcy. To quell these rumors, representatives from a number of insurance companies held an emergency meeting on July 7 in New York City and passed a resolution declaring that all Portland claims would be paid. The information was immediately made public in the newspapers.

A resolution passed during this critical meeting led to the founding of the National Board of Fire Underwriters on July 18, 1866.[22] This organization provided outstanding leadership in promoting fire prevention and fire protection until 1965, when it merged with two other organizations to become the American

Figure 1–2 The great fire of 1835 in New York City.

Insurance Association. Later this organization changed its name to the Insurance Services Office (ISO).

In the Midwest in 1871 two fires occurred the same day that were to leave a legacy of death and destruction in their wake. The Great Chicago fire, whether started by Mrs. O'Leary's infamous cow or not, burned for 27 hours, killed nearly 300 people, destroyed 17,500 buildings, and left approximately 100,000 homeless. The loss was estimated at $200 million, of which only $88 million was insured. Because of multiple bankruptcies of insurance companies, only $45 million was actually paid.

On that same day a forest fire in the area surrounding Peshtigo, a small lumbering community in Wisconsin, accelerated into a fire storm that swept through the town, destroying every building except for one home under construction. An even greater tragedy than the loss of property was the loss of nearly 800 lives. Being a lumbering town, Peshtigo was built of wood. Not only were the buildings and sidewalks constructed of wood, but sawdust was used on the roads to reduce dust. The fire moved so fast people could not flee. It was miraculous that over 950 members of the community survived the holocaust, which destroyed timber in an area covering 1,200 square miles.

Several other major fires occurred before the end of the century. The Great Boston Fire of 1872 claimed 13 lives and destroyed 776 buildings in an area of the business district approximately one-mile square. Boston's fire protection was inadequate at the time. Witnesses testified that hose streams did not go above the third floor, and many of the buildings were five and six stories high. The longest ladder reached only 40 feet. To make a bad matter worse, most of the horses were sick, so the heavy steam engines, ladder trucks and hose wagons had to be dragged to the fire by volunteers. Help came from 30 outside fire departments including those of New Haven, Connecticut; Portsmouth, New Hampshire; Biddeford, Maine; and Providence, Rhode Island.

Two obvious causes were recognized in these nineteenth-century conflagrations: combustible construction and ineffective fire protection methods. As Americans moved into the twentieth century they greatly reduced their vulnerability to conflagration through improved building construction and fire-resistive materials; increased water distribution capacity; powerful motorized apparatus with high-capacity pumps, aerial ladders, and elevated streams; and built-in fire protection systems and warning devices. One such system was the automatic fire sprinkler patented in 1872. The device has been credited to Henry Parmalee. The first sprinkler systems consisted of pipes with holes drilled in them. Parmalee's invention was a fusible link device that held back water under pressure.

Despite this and other advances, however, fire losses have continued.

The twentieth century

Technological and scientific advancements proliferated rapidly in the first part of the twentieth century. Even so, the most destructive fires in this nation, in terms of both life and property loss, occurred in this same era. The disastrous Hoboken waterfront fire of June 1900 with over 300 deaths and the Jacksonville, Florida, conflagration of May 1901 with a loss of 1,700 buildings were among the fires that have roared in this century, killing and maiming people by the thousands and destroying billions of dollars' worth of property.[23]

More sweeping conflagrations

Fire broke out in the basement of the six-story Hurst Building on Liberty Street in Baltimore, Maryland, in February, 1904.[24] Stored in that basement were highly combustible celluloid novelties. Within a few minutes the fire spread through an unenclosed shaft and burst from the top floor. It then spread onto nearby buildings with unprotected openings. From there the fire burned out of control. As the conflagration gained in intensity, the mayor placed urgent calls for help to several major cities. These cities responded by sending equipment and firefighters on flatcars. When out-of-town fire companies laid out their hose lines, however, they discovered that their couplings did not fit the Baltimore fire hydrants. Always resourceful, the firefighters dug up the cobblestone streets, built dams around the hydrants, and drafted water with their pumpers from the artificial ponds that were formed when the hydrants were opened. Mercantile property valued at $50 million had been destroyed in spite of the mutual aid efforts, and 50,000 people had been put out of work.

The great lesson, in addition to the hazard of unprotected vertical shafts and unprotected openings, was the need to standardize threads on hydrants, hoselines, and fittings. Virtually all cities throughout the nation have now adopted uniform couplings and threads.

Also as a result of the Baltimore fire, the Municipal Inspection and Grading System of the National Board of Fire Underwriters (NBFU) was established. Insurance companies were convinced that it was possible to contain fires more effectively. In 1904 a team of engineers was retained by the NBFU to survey congested centers of communities in all parts of the country. The engineers moved quickly, evaluating the potential for fire in many cities. As early as October 1905, an article in *World's Work* reported that 32 cities had been inspected and that several improvements had already been made in a number of evaluated cities.[25]

The insurance industry was responsible for most of the improvements in public fire protection at that time. In response to the underwriters' evaluation of the municipal fire defense, cities made countless improvements. The threat of higher insurance premiums and/or the reward of insurance savings had provided a large measure of the needed motivation.

A preliminary evaluation of the city of San Francisco was made by the NBFU fire prevention engineers in the fall of 1905. The resulting report pointed out the potential for disaster in this congested city with frame houses and difficult topography. Said the report:

San Francisco has violated all underwriting traditions and precedents by not burning up; that it has not done so is largely due to the vigilance of the fire department, which cannot be relied upon indefinitely to stave off the inevitable.[26]

On April 18, 1906, only six months after the inspection team had put out its report, an earthquake lasting only a minute and a half devastated the city and started the greatest conflagration in American history. The fire burned uncontrollably for two days, killed hundreds of people, and consumed 25,000 buildings on an area of 4.7 square miles. The estimated loss was $350 million to

Figure 1–3   U.S. fires and explosions with 50 or more deaths in nonmining structures, vehicles, or conflagrations, 1900–1987.

Incident	Date	Deaths
North German Lloyd Steamships, Hoboken, New Jersey	30 June 1900	326
Rhoades Opera House, Boyertown, Pennsylvania	12 January 1903	170
Iroquois Theatre, Chicago, Illinois	30 December 1903	602
S.S. *General Slocum* steamship, New York, New York	15 June 1904	1,030
R. B. Grover & Company shoe factory, Brockton, Massachusetts (boiler explosion)	20 March 1905	50
Earthquake and fire, San Francisco, California	18 April 1906	315[a]
Lakeview Grammar School, Collinwood, Ohio	4 March 1908	175
Forest fire, Bitterroot Mountains, Idaho	12 August 1910	85
Eddystone Ammunition Company, Eddystone, Pennsylvania (explosion)	10 April 1917	133
Semet-Solvay Company TNT manufacturer, Split Rock, New York	2 July 1918	50
Forest fire, northern Minnesota	12 October 1918	559
Cleveland School, Beulah, South Carolina	17 May 1923	77
Cleveland Clinic Hospital, Cleveland, Ohio	15 May 1929	125
Ohio State Penitentiary, Columbus, Ohio	21 April 1930	320
S.S. *Morro Castle*, off New Jersey coast	8 September 1934	135
Consolidated School, New London, Texas (gas explosion)	18 March 1937	294
Rhythm Club Dance Hall, Natchez, Mississippi	23 April 1940	207
Hercules Powder Company plant, Kenvil, New Jersey (explosion)	12 September 1940	52
Elwood Ordnance Plant, Joliet, Illinois (explosion)	5 June 1942	54
Cocoanut Grove nightclub, Boston, Massachusetts	28 November 1942	492
Ringling Brothers and Barnum and Bailey Circus tent, Hartford, Connecticut	6 July 1944	168
Munitions ships and depot, Port Chicago, California (explosion)	17 July 1944	322
East Ohio Gas Company, Cleveland, Ohio (explosion)	20 October 1944	136
LaSalle Hotel, Chicago, Illinois	5 June 1946	61
Winecoff Hotel, Atlanta, Georgia	7 December 1946	119
S.S. *Grandcamp* and Monsanto Chemical Company plant, Texas City, Texas	16 April 1947	468
St. Anthony's Hospital, Effingham, Illinois	4 April 1949	74
U.S.S. *Bennington* aircraft carrier, off Rhode Island	26 May 1954	103
Katie Jane nursing home, Warrenton, Missouri	17 February 1957	72
Our Lady of the Angels School, Chicago, Illinois	1 December 1958	95
U.S.S. *Constellation*, New York, New York	19 December 1960	50
Indiana State Fairgrounds Coliseum, Indianapolis, Indiana (gas explosion)	31 October 1963	74
Golden Age Nursing Home, Fitchville, Ohio	23 November 1963	63
Missile silo, near Searcy, Arkansas	9 August 1965	53
Beverly Hills Supper Club, Southgate, Kentucky	28 May 1977	165
MGM Grand Hotel, Las Vegas, Nevada	21 November 1980	85

Sources: National Fire Protection Association major incident files; National Security Council, *Accident Facts* (Chicago: National Safety Council, 1987); and James Cornell, *The Great International Disaster Book* (New York: Pocket Books, 1979).
Note: Incidents coded as "explosion" began with explosions;

some fire incidents had subsequent explosions and some explosion incidents had subsequent fires.
[a] Estimates of the death toll in the San Francisco earthquake and fire are quite varied, with some estimates as high as 800; no estimates separate fire from non-fire deaths.

Figure 1–4   Crowds line Sacramento Avenue to watch the progress of the San Francisco fire. This picture, taken by Arnold Genthe, was considered one of the best news photos ever taken.

Figure 1–5   The Cocoanut Grove fire in 1942.

$1 billion,[27] a sum equal to the aggregate of all of the large fires in the United States during the preceding fifty years.

Over 22,000 of the buildings destroyed had a wood frame. The lesson of combustible construction was not yet learned.

Chelsea, Massachusetts, had a district with numerous rag shops. A fire started in one of those shops one Sunday morning in April 1908, and was quickly driven to adjacent property by high winds. Within a few minutes it was whipped into a conflagration that ultimately destroyed about one-half of the improved area of the city. Monetary loss was estimated at $12 million, the insurance loss at $9 million. The hazard of combustible roofs and the vulnerability of ordinary buildings to sparks and embers were again emphasized. Despite that lesson, Chelsea experienced another fire almost identical in origin, spread, and fire control problems in October 1973.

Conflagrations occurred frequently in the United States during the first quarter of the twentieth century. In 1913 over 500 buildings were destroyed by fire in Hot Springs, Arkansas; 1,600 buildings were lost in 1914 in Salem, Massachusetts; in May 1917 Atlanta, Georgia, experienced simultaneous fires that destroyed a total of 1,900 buildings; 1,440 were consumed by fire in Paris, Texas, in 1924, and on the same day in Nashville, Tennessee, 650 buildings burned. The following day over 680 buildings in the center of Augusta, Georgia,

Figure 1–6   Over ninety students and three teachers died in the fire at Our Lady of the Angels school in Chicago in 1958. Fire prevention regulations, including fire drills, have since been more strictly enforced in schools throughout the country.

Figure 1–7   A fire in 1977 took the lives of 165 patrons and employees of the Beverly Hills Supper Club in Southgate, Kentucky. The club had no automatic sprinkler system.

Figure 1–8   The MGM Grand Hotel fire in Las Vegas, 1980.

burned. The most disastrous loss of life occurred in October 1918 as forest fires in Minnesota swept through 15 townships and claimed 559 victims, a sad reminder of the Peshtigo forest fire.[28] Thirty blocks in the center of Astoria, Oregon, were destroyed by fire in 1922 in the middle of a rain storm. A brush fire destroyed 640 dwellings in Berkeley, California, on September 17, 1923.

Major fires dwindled during the second quarter of the twentieth century as fire-resistive construction became more prevalent, fire suppression capabilities improved, and fire and building codes became more stringent and were more strictly enforced.

The potential for conflagration in the United States still exists, particularly in those parts of the country with large areas of combustible brush and forests. That was demonstrated in November 1961 when losses totaling an estimated $35 million resulted from roaring flames driven by Santa Ana winds into the exclusive Bel Air and Brentwood residential sections of Los Angeles, California. The firestorm consumed more than 450 homes, most of which had wood shingle roofs. Southern California has since suffered similar fires. The Sycamore Canyon fire in Santa Barbara and the Panorama fire in San Bernardino destroyed almost 1,000 homes. These had scenarios similar to the Bel Air fire. But the potential for catastrophic wildland fires is not unique to Southern California and the southwestern states that experience extreme weather conditions and have densely built, combustible dwellings. Between 1970 and 1980, the population in and around forests and other wildlands increased at a rate twice that of the population nationwide. The intermingling of high-value properties with highly combustible native vegetation in vast regions of the country is creating new potential hazards and challenges for the fire service responsible for protection of areas where the urban and wildland regions interface. In 1987, the United States experienced the greatest loss of natural resources in recent times. Devastating fires occurred from Alaska to Florida, from California to North Carolina, from Nevada to Minnesota. Strategies for protecting natural forest resources from fire were not designed with the idea that forests would also include numerous homes. The U.S. Forest Service, the National Fire Protection Association, and the U.S. Fire Administration have joined forces to focus national attention on this serious fire problem.[29]

Conflagration in confined areas

Large loss of life from fire and panic inside of buildings has also plagued the American public throughout the twentieth century.[30] The "fireproof" building of the Iroquois Theatre burned in 1903 with a loss of 602 lives. The lesson learned in this fire is that the absolutely "fireproof" building is far from safe when its contents are combustible. Soon after that tragedy, scores of regulations were passed throughout the nation requiring better exiting provisions in places of public assemblage: exit doors were to open in the direction of exit travel when released by a pressure-activated device, aisles had to be much wider, scenery and curtains were to be made of fire-resistive materials, lights were to be placed in caged-in compartments, and automatic sprinkler systems had to be installed.

Even so, disastrous fires continued to occur during the early part of the twentieth century. Eventually they stimulated an expression of public awareness and concern. Magazines and newspapers began to feature articles on fire safety in places of public assembly, factories, offices, and homes. Finally, many citizens were being taught the basic principles of fire safety and were becoming familiar with precautions that could be taken to prevent fires. But in spite of efforts in fire prevention education, the great losses of life in buildings and large property losses from major fires are written indelibly on the pages of twentieth-century history.

As the nation entered the latter half of the century, the fire service faced an ever-increasing range and magnitude of fire problems. High-rise structures, modes of transportation, industrial processes, highly combustible and toxic materials, all have demonstrated the urgent need for better fire protection training, organization, and equipment.

Other historical developments

Within the chronological evolution of the fire service, several other developments can be isolated, notably the evolution of firefighting apparatus and the evolution of volunteer departments.

Firefighting apparatus

Initially, the development and use of firefighting equipment in the American colonies was greatly influenced by fire control practices and inventions in Europe and England.[31] European conflagrations during the sixteenth and seventeenth centuries had led to the development of practical fire control methods. However, little attention had been given to the means of distributing water supplies for firefighting. Pumps and water systems had been used during the Egyptian dynasties and in the Roman Empire, but for whatever reason were forgotten until the early 1600s.[32]

Firefighting tactics in the early colonial days required the turnout of all available citizens, who would gather the town's supply of leather buckets and form two lines from a source of water, such as a cistern or pump, to the fire scene. One line would fill the buckets and pass them toward the fire, and the other line, usually women and children, would pass the empty buckets back to the water supply. These bucket brigades required fifty or more people for every 100 feet of distance from the water supply to the fire so their effectiveness obviously was limited.

Early improvements The first recorded reference to a fire engine in America appears in a 1653 agreement between the selectmen of Boston and Joseph Jynks (or Jenks). Jynks, an ironworker in nearby Saugas, was to build "ingines [*sic*] to convey water in case of fire."[33] These may have been hand-held water syringes, rather than pumpers. In any case, the Jynks engines did not prove

Figure 1–9   Firefighting in New York in the 1770s.

satisfactory. An early morning conflagration in Boston on November 27, 1676, destroyed about fifty homes and warehouses. As a result, the selectmen voted to buy the best fire engine London had to offer, which they put into service on January 27, 1678. It consisted of a wooden box approximately 3 feet long and 18 inches wide that stood on four legs and had handles at the front and rear so it could easily be carried to the fire. A hand-operated pump mounted inside the box fed a flexible snakelike nozzle, and a bucket brigade provided the water supply.

Manually operated fire engines improved considerably during the eighteenth century. An English manufacturer, Richard Newsham, built a fire engine superior to all others in the 1700s. His engines were constructed in six sizes. He claimed the largest could squeeze through a 3-foot passageway, a feat that no other fire engine could perform. Again, the engine consisted of a wooden box with a pump mounted inside and a swivel nozzle affixed to the top of the pump housing; the pump handles or "brakes" extended on each side. The four largest pumps were mounted on wheels, whereas the two smaller models had handles for carrying. It took three men on each side to operate the pump, which could deliver 30 to 170 gallons per minute at distances up to 120 feet. One of the major disadvantages of the Newsham engine was that the pulling handle did not pivot; to turn the rig from one street into another the firefighters had to pick up the engine and swing it around.

One improvement followed another as American craftsmen applied their ingenuity to designing these machines. In 1768 Richard Mason of Philadelphia devised a successful pumper with brakes extending from each end rather than the sides, making it easier for the bucket brigade to feed the cistern on the pump. The end-strokers were dubbed "Philadelphia-style" and won a large following, particularly because of the growing resentment toward British-made products.

Efforts to build rotary fire pumps were less successful. The coffee-mill engine had a side-mounted crank that turned an axle that rotated a gear with teeth, which in turn scooped water from the box and forced it through a mounted nozzle. A variation of this type of pump was the cider-mill, or windlass, engine. This model had long poles extending horizontally from the rotary pump, which were pushed by men on horses running in circles around the engine. Neither of these pumps enjoyed great success; rotary fire engines would not become practical until steam and gasoline engines could provide the power needed for effectiveness.

Around the beginning of the nineteenth century, three innovations greatly changed the methods and effectiveness of fire attack and reduced the number of volunteers needed to apply water to a fire: (1) the water mains system, (2) the fire hydrant, and (3) copper-riveted leather hose.

Prior to 1800 water for firefighting was drawn from wells, cisterns, and natural bodies. A major advance in firefighting technology took place in 1801 when Philadelphia opened its water mains system. Supplied by the Schuylkill River, the system consisted of hollowed logs beveled on the ends to fit together. Chief engineer of the Philadelphia Water Works Frederick Graff designed the first post-type fire hydrant the same year. It was a T-shaped hydrant with a faucet for drinking water on one side and a fire hose connection on the other.

New York installed a similar water system a little later, but did not install hydrants. New York firefighters had to dig down to the wooden water main, drill a hole in the pipe to fill their engines, then insert a wooden plug in that hole when the fire had been extinguished; hence the word *fireplug* evolved to describe a fire hydrant.

American firefighters in the early 1900s were able to improve leather hose by using metal rivets to bind the seams. The concept was first developed in Holland. Before then, leather had been sewn in the same fashion used for

Figure 1–10 This steam engine built by P. R. Hodge in 1840 began the era of self-propelled fire engines.

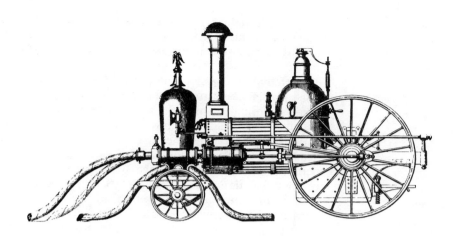

making shoes. The rivet method of construction greatly reduced leaking and made the hose strong enough to withstand the pressures produced by the large hand pumpers. The hose itself was made from the best cowhides, cut into pieces 3 feet long and formed into a tube; the ends and joints were riveted together. The hose lengths ran from 40 to 50 feet and together with the couplings weighed more than 80 pounds. In spite of the weight, leather hose became popular almost immediately and was soon available throughout the United States. Leather hose served well for over a quarter of a century in spite of the large amount of care required to prevent rot and cracking.

The hose wagon   Once a good water supply and fire hose were available, the hose wagon and hose reel became an important apparatus for the fire service. Companies using it could carry three times as much hose as the engine companies. A Philadelphia firefighter, Reuben Haines, conceived the idea of the hose wagon and formed the first hose company in 1803. Their rig was a four-wheeled box about 7 feet long with a 24-inch-deep hose bed. It carried 600 feet of folded hose (in short lengths) and cost $98. However, hose companies did not catch on as quickly in cities such as New York because of their poor water supply systems.

   The riveted hose made it more practical to pump water from its source to a fire some distance away. The engine company at the source would suction water into the apparatus, and the volunteers at the pump handles would then pump the water through their hose to the tub of the next engine, which, in turn, relayed the water on until the engine nearest the fire pumped the water at a strong pressure through the nozzle and onto the fire. Mayor Josiah Quincy of Boston remarked in 1825 that 100 feet of hose could do the work of 60 men with buckets. On one fire in New York, Chief Harry Howard counted thirty engines pumping in a line a mile and a half long from the water supply to the fire.

The steamer   Another important advance in fire suppression capability was the steam-driven fire engine. This powerful pumper could discharge as much water as six or more hand-operated pumpers, each of which required twenty or more men on the brakes. Furthermore, the steamer could pump as long as coal was fed to the firebox, whereas the volunteers on the hand-operated pumpers had to change crews every twenty or thirty minutes.

   However, the steam fire engines were not without problems: They were heavy, took a long time to build up steam pressure, and sent sparks flying from the boiler stack that could start additional fires or explosions. Although these engineering problems were soon resolved by improved designs and innovations, another major problem remained—the steamers failed to overcome the resistance of firefighters, who saw the steam-driven fire pumper, with its reduced manpower requirements, as a threat. Yet, it was the steam pumper that made the organization of paid departments feasible.

The chemical engine   The chemical engine was yet another innovation. In 1864 French scientists demonstrated that carbon dioxide gas would be released when sulfuric acid was added to a mixture of bicarbonate of soda and water. When the chemicals were combined in a closed container, enough gas pressure would build up to expel the water in a strong stream through an attached nozzle. This principle was quickly adopted and within five years the chemical engine company became a part of the American fire service. These engines could respond to a fire and start their attack while the steamers and hose companies were still hooking up. The chemical engine was also valuable in suburban and rural areas where water supplies were limited. Furthermore, it used a small-diameter hose and was ideal for extinguishing small fires with minimal water damage.

Hook-and-ladder and aerial ladder trucks   Hook-and-ladder companies also proliferated, but not as rapidly as engine companies and hose companies. These rigs carried ladders of varying lengths, hooks for stripping roofs and hauling down structures, axes, leather buckets, and other tools. As the ladder company evolved, this rig was to become a toolbox on wheels, loaded with salvage, rescue, and overhaul equipment.

Developing the capability for reaching upper floors of multistory buildings has always presented a problem for the fire service. The length of ladders was limited by weight and size factors. Both the ladders and the wagon carrying them had to be fairly short in order to turn corners in the narrow streets. The eventual solution was the apparatus-mounted aerial ladder, but early versions were flimsy and dangerous.

The first successful aerial ladder truck was built by Daniel D. Hayes, a machinist in the San Francisco fire department. Hayes patented his aerial in 1868. The wooden ladder extended 85 feet was raised by a single horizontal worm gear that was turned manually by a long handle. The aerial was operated by four to six men. Recognition for Hayes's invention came slowly, and it was nearly twenty years before his idea was widely accepted.

With the development of the aerial ladder truck, firefighters soon devised ways of placing a nozzle at the top rung so as to have the advantage of an elevated stream, since streams from the ground could not reach the upper floors of taller buildings. Another device used to elevate the stream was the water tower, which consisted of a base pipe mounted on a wagon deck with two extension pipes. The stream from the nozzle located at the top could reach 50 feet and could be directed and controlled by a rope held by firefighters on the ground. Other improvements quickly followed.

The fire horse   The weight of the steamers, chemical engines, and ladder trucks necessitated changes that inaugurated the next era of the American fire service. From the end of the Civil War until about 1923, American firefighters shared their stations with the fire horse. Although at first the fire fighters did not want to live in the same building with a horse, these animals soon became department pets and were bred, selected, trained, and matched to produce teams of superb strength and stamina.

Some fire horses were so intelligent and well trained that they could recognize the number of bells signaling their company and, when released from their stalls, could take their places in front of their rig without direction. The status of the horse in the American fire service at the time is evident from the fact that Philadelphia horses received annual vacations many years before the fire-fighters did.

Motorized apparatus The resistance of firefighters to having horses in the fire station was mild compared with their reaction to motorized apparatus, which began appearing on the scene shortly after the beginning of the twentieth century. In 1911 the Savannah, Georgia, fire department became the nation's first completely motorized department. Such a commitment at the time required a lot of courage on the part of the chief and demonstrated the faith of the community in the chief's judgment and in the future of the horseless engine. Within a decade, more than two hundred makers of motorized fire apparatus had entered the market.

Firefighting apparatus has improved rapidly since the demise of the horse-drawn steam engine, and corresponding innovations have been made in fire equipment. Perhaps the most important for the safety of the firefighter has been the self-contained breathing apparatus. But many others have also been significant, such as the mobile and portable radio, the spray nozzle, lightweight and large-diameter hose, remote and radio-controlled valves and engines, improved safety clothing, lightweight ladders, effective portable fire extinguishers, and water additives that reduce friction, penetrate deep-seated fires, and produce foam. The list goes on and on; these are only some examples of the kinds of innovations that have improved the ability of firefighters to do their jobs.

Figure 1–11   In 1890, during the era of the fire horse, a fireman on the truck is still struggling with his boots as children race alongside.

Evolution of the fire service

Until the mid-1800s, most firefighting was done by volunteers. The exception was Boston, where the selectmen not only purchased that first fire engine in 1678 but also established the first American firehouse to keep it in and hired a paid officer as captain of the rig.

Volunteer fire companies existed in cities up and down the Eastern seaboard, and their members became very tightly knit social groups in their various communities. Even today, volunteer fire companies constitute major social groups in certain parts of the United States. Many of the early companies were proud, exclusive, influential—and competitive. The rivalry became so intense in some areas that companies interfered with each other in responding to the fire scene and did not hesitate to start a fight or a riot whether on or off duty. Some volunteer fire companies even raced to the fire scene and used trickery to keep rival companies from beating them. It was considered a disgrace for one company to be passed by another while pulling its rig to a fire. To prevent such disgrace, a slower company might run a zigzag path down the narrow streets.

An even greater disgrace than being passed en route was to be "washed." As engine companies lined up to relay water to a fire, each company would pump to the tub of the next engine in line. The faster the water came into the tub, the faster the volunteers had to pump to keep their tub from overflowing. Tremendous competition arose as engine companies endeavored to overflow, or wash, the engine ahead of them, while desperately trying to keep the company below from washing their own engine. When a company was washed, it was not unusual for a black drape to be placed over the engine until the score was evened.[34]

Fistfights often broke out as companies battled for hydrants. History records that many buildings burned to the ground during these brawls, some of which turned into riots. In some cities thugs were hired to guard the hydrants. These "plug-uglies" would run ahead of their companies and, after locating the best available hydrant, fend off all comers until their engine arrived.[35]

Making matters even worse were the rewards and bonuses offered by insurance companies to the first company to get water on the fire of an insured building. In order to identify insured buildings, insurance companies placed their "mark" visibly on the structure. These marks, made of metal and wood, were very distinctive. For example, the Fire Association of Philadelphia used the outline of a wooden fire hydrant; the Philadelphia Contributorship for the Insurance of Houses from Loss by Fire issued a mark showing clasped hands.

Rivalry, indiscretions, riots, and disrespect for the law left citizens disenchanted with and even hostile toward the volunteers. Nevertheless, American cities were vulnerable to fire, and organized fire protection was essential. Until some means was developed to reduce the number of firefighters needed to combat a fire, it was economically impossible to change over to a paid department.

A fire in a Cincinnati wood-planing mill on a fall night in 1851 set into motion the events that led to the hiring of America's first professional firefighters. On that night, Western Fire and Hose Company No. 3 and Washington Company No. 1 began fighting; ten more companies joined the melee. These companies were joined by friends from across the river in Covington, Kentucky, who sighted the flames and came to lend their aid. The mill burned to the ground as the thirteen companies rioted.

The citizens were outraged. There had been 123 fires and several riots during the past year. Losses had doubled in one year, and insurance companies had raised their rates. The citizens demanded that city officials take corrective action. For quite some time, leading citizens of Cincinnati had been intrigued with the

Figure 1–12 The fire service has numerous traditions, yet it continually adopts new technology to replace the old.

possibility of designing a steam-powered fire engine. One steamer and a crew of three—the driver, the stoker, and the engineer—could produce as much water as six or more hand-operated engines with 120 to 200 men on the brakes. If such a pumper could be developed, the number of firefighters required to apply water to a fire could be greatly reduced, and a paid department could become a reality.

Within a short time after the mill burned, the city fathers signed a contract for the construction of a steam pumper, which was demonstrated on New Year's Day 1853. On March 10 the Cincinnati city council voted for a paid fire department.

The end of an era

Although the process was slow at first, within a decade of the advent of the first steamer in Cincinnati steam fire pumpers were rapidly acquired by major American cities, and great numbers of volunteers were no longer required.[36] Relieved from complete dependency on volunteers and tired of their abuses, one by one the major cities disbanded their volunteers and organized salaried departments.

The new paid departments were organized on paramilitary lines, a system that continues today. Titles for officers took on military connotations after the Civil War. The title of company foreman became lieutenant or captain; over several companies was a battalion commander or chief. A division commander was over the battalion chiefs and above the division commander was the deputy chief. The highest position in the department was given the title of fire commissioner, fire chief, or chief engineer.

Within a short period after it was organized, the New York fire department had a paid membership of 500 firefighters manning eighty-nine steamers, eleven hook and ladders, and fifty-four hose companies. The firefighters worked a twenty-four-hour shift for seven days a week, except for one twenty-four-hour day off each month. The organizational framework was set for what was to become the prevailing mode of paid fire departments.

It should be emphasized, however, that 800,000–900,000 volunteer firefighters are still providing fire protection for a large proportion of the nation's communities. The typical volunteers of today are dedicated to the protection of

The U.S. fire problem The following statistics, compiled by the National Fire Protection Association, indicate the extent of the fire problem in the United States. The statistics are for 1986 and show comparisons with 1985.

Fires: 2.3 million (down 4.2 percent)

Structure fires: 800,000 (down 6.9 percent)

Residential fires: 581,500 (down 6.5 percent)

Brush and grass fires: 502,000 (down 5.5 percent)

Civilian fire deaths: 5,850 (down 5.4 percent)

Civilian fire injuries: 26,825 (down 5.6 percent)

Property loss: $6.7 billion (down 8.4 percent)

Incendiary and suspicious fires (structures): 111,000 (down 5.1 percent)

Incendiary and suspicious fires (vehicles): 57,000 (up 25.3 percent)

Source: Michael J. Karter, Jr., "A Look at Fire Loss in the United States during 1986," *Fire Journal,* September/October 1987, pp. 36–46.

life and property from fire and are well trained in suppression tactics, unlike their late nineteenth-century predecessors.

Meeting today's challenge

Traditionally, the provision of fire protection in the United States has been a local responsibility. Officials in individual jurisdictions throughout the country have established the form, organization, and level of public fire protection considered adequate for their area. The fact that this responsibility rests at the local level has given rise to approximately 25,000 to 28,000 fire departments supported by over 1 million personnel. The U.S. Fire Administration estimated in 1987 that approximately 1,800 of these were fully paid fire departments with 190,000 members. The choice of organization (whether volunteer, part-paid, or fully paid) has been influenced by the extent of the local fire problem, the availability of personnel, and financial constraints.

Also central to the determination of alternative forms of fire protection is the scope of activities designated as responsibilities of the fire department. Such functions as fire suppression, emergency medical services, fire prevention, hazardous materials disclosure enforcement, fire safety education, building code enforcement, communications, disaster planning, regional coordination, data development, and community relations can all be included in a fire department's responsibilities today.

Through the years personnel in the American fire service have struggled to develop a fire defense capable of coping with the ever-increasing fire potential. Vastly improved fire apparatus and equipment, along with improved training, have greatly strengthened the fire attack; the adoption of building and fire codes has succeeded in limiting the threat of fire spread in some areas. The fire service has received considerable support from the insurance industry for strengthening the public defense as the threat of increased premiums and the potential for insurance savings have motivated public officials to make improvements.

America burning

In 1972 President Richard Nixon empowered a group to evaluate the American fire problem. The committee was called the National Commission on Fire Prevention and Control (NCFPC). The commission delivered its report, entitled *America Burning* to the President in <u>1973</u>. Chairman Richard E. Bland outlined several areas of concern:

1. There needs to be more emphasis on fire prevention.
2. The fire services need better training and education.
3. Americans must be educated about fire safety.
4. In both design and materials, the environment in which Americans live and work presents unnecessary hazards.
5. The fire protection features of buildings need to be improved.
6. Important areas of research are being neglected.[37]

To address these areas of concern the commission report made some specific recommendations to the president, Congress, state and local government, and the fire profession, both firefighting agencies and industry. It proposed that a U.S. Fire Administration be formed, which would

1. Develop a national fire data system to help establish priorities for research and action
2. Monitor fire research in both the governmental and private sectors, to assist the interchange of information, and to encourage research in areas that have been neglected
3. Provide block grants to states so that local governments may develop comprehensive fire-protection plans, improve firefighting equipment, and upgrade education of fire service personnel
4. Establish a National Fire Academy to train fire service officers and assist state and local training programs
5. Undertake a major effort to educate Americans in fire safety.[38]

Shortly thereafter, President Gerald Ford signed public law 90-438 creating the National Fire Prevention and Control Administration (NFPCA). The National Bureau of Standards increased its research in topics related to fire science, and a search began for a site for the proposed academy, which was eventually located in Emmitsburg, Maryland.

A great deal of time and effort were expended in creating the NFPCA and focusing national attention on the prevention and control of fire. Among the major accomplishments were the establishment of the National Fire Academy and the creation of a move toward built-in fire protection—smoke detectors and sprinklers. The effort also encountered major obstacles. Budget cuts were made in many staff positions and programs just as they were becoming effective. Organizational shifts occurred for several years. The NFPCA became the U.S. Fire Administration (USFA) with a change in administrations. Then the USFA was made part of the Federal Emergency Management Agency (FEMA) and the Fire Academy was made part of the National Emergency Training Center (NETC).

Despite difficulties, the U.S. Fire Administration initiated several programs that have had a significant impact on the current fire problem. Among them was the National Fire Incident Reporting System (NFIRS), which helps identify the fire problem; a public education effort; training and education of fire officers and arson investigators through the National Fire Academy; projects focusing on firefighter safety and health; and a series of projects involving smoke detector and sprinkler technology.

One of the major breakthroughs spurred by USFA research was the development of residential fire sprinklers by a team representing leading organizations with an interest in fire safety. The quick-response sprinkler technology was first field tested in Fort Lauderdale, Florida, in a series of hotel fire scenarios. Further tests followed in various parts of the country.

Starting with an ordinance in San Clemente, California, in 1978, a series of communities such as Cobb County, Georgia; Scottsdale, Arizona; and Greenburgh, New York, initiated "life safety" ordinances. A major test program, "Operation San Francisco," was cosponsored by the USFA, the International Association of Fire Chiefs (IAFC), and the Marriott Corporation. Its success led to the establishment of "Operation Life Safety," a consortium of the USFA, the IAFC, and the private sector. The goal of the program is to significantly reduce fire deaths and fire losses through public education and reliable use of smoke detectors and residential sprinkler systems.

In spite of these advancements, progress is still hindered by fiscal constraints. Costs for public fire protection (particularly for firefighters' salaries and benefits) have escalated so rapidly that many communities are being forced to reassess costs and to consider alternatives. Many towns have chosen to reduce staffing levels of fire companies, usually below what fire officials believe is safe or adequate. Some communities with paid employees have replaced them with auxiliary or volunteer personnel. Some areas have strengthened mutual aid agreements or contracted for fire protection with neighboring cities or counties. Other localities are exploring the possibility of forming larger fire protection districts or areas to take advantage of economies of scale and better distribution of fire companies. Others are making use of built-in fire protection to limit the fire problem. Some have resorted to fee schedules and cost recovery systems for certain services.

Central to these various alternatives are several fundamental questions each community must answer: What is an adequate level of fire protection? What are reasonable costs to the community and to builders and developers? Regardless of the approach taken, fire protection is a major consideration in every American city.

The phenomenal growth of this nation, in both population and building construction, has presented American fire service agencies with fire protection problems of such magnitude that their capabilities to prevent large loss of life and property have often been overtaxed. The external challenges that lie ahead with respect to the American fire problem are still legion. The most critical include

1. Educating the public in fire safety to combat the present ignorance, apathy, and indifference
2. Establishing laws, codes, and ordinances that will encourage built-in fire protection to limit the fire potential to the protection capability of the fire service agency
3. Designing and building structures that are fire safe for occupants of all ages and physical condition
4. Developing technologies in apparatus, clothing, and equipment that will provide firefighters with adequate protection in hostile environments
5. Reducing the potential for fire and explosion in vehicles, ships, and planes that transport people and hazardous materials
6. Developing means to better protect the urban-wildland interface of grasslands and forests through more effective laws, management, and fire control methods
7. Reducing the flammability of products such as clothing, furnishings, interior finishes of buildings, and personal commodities with which the American public is in constant contact.

In addition to these challenges, the fire service is faced with many internal challenges:

1. Improving training and education opportunities and delivery systems
2. Improving fire attack methods and capabilities
3. Improving productivity of fire resources in areas such as fire prevention activities
4. Improving management skills of fire officers in the area of planning, budgeting, organizing, leading, and evaluating
5. Developing successful affirmative action programs
6. Developing close cooperation between labor and management and better skills in labor relations.

As this chapter has shown, the fire service has come a long way over the course of its history. Slowly, people have come to better understand fire and to develop the technologies and organizational structures to prevent and control it. As this final section has suggested, the evolution of the fire service is ongoing. The chapters that follow discuss many of the changes that will mold it in the future.

1   Joseph Campbell, *The Masks of God: Primitive Mythology* (New York: Penguin Books, 1976), 361.
2   Ibid., 395.
3   Ibid.
4   For a broad survey of mythology, including references to fire, see Campbell, *The Masks of God: Primitive Mythology;* Joseph Campbell, *The Masks of God: Occidental Mythology* (New York: Viking Press, 1964); and Joseph Campbell, *The Masks of God: Oriental Mythology* (New York: Viking Press, 1962). For sun myths, see William Tyler Olcott, *Myths of the Sun* (New York: Capricorn Books, 1967); and Jean-Pierre Bayard, *Le Feu* (Paris: Ernest Flammarion, 1958), especially chap. 17, "Les Feux dans la Religion et dans L'Inde," 213–24.
5   Robert Graves, *The Greek Myths,* vol. 1, rev. ed. (Baltimore: Penguin Books, 1969), 144–45. For a discussion of fire theft in mythology in general, see Campbell, *The Masks of God: Primitive Mythology,* 277–81.
6   For general studies of totemic associations with animals, including fire-related aspects, see Sigmund Freud, *Totem and Taboo,* trans. A. A. Brill (New York: Vintage Books, 1946); and Claude Levi-Strauss, *Totemism,* trans. Rodney Needham (Boston: Beacon Press, 1963).
7   Edith Hamilton, *Mythology* (New York: New American Library, 1971), 35.
8   Henry Thompson Rowell, *Rome in the Augustan Age* (Norman, Okla.: University of Oklahoma Press, 1962), 116; Rodolfo Lanciani, *Ancient Rome* (New York: Houghton Miffin, 1888), 221.
9   Lanciani, *Ancient Rome,* 221.
10 Ibid., 222; Rowell, *Rome in the Augustan Age,* 116.
11 Robert E. O'Bannon, *Building Department Administration* (Whittier, Calif.: International Conference of Building Officials, 1973), 1/2.
12 Ibid., 1/8–9.
13 Except where otherwise indicated, the text in this section draws on Paul Robert Lyons, *Fire in America!* (Boston: National Fire Protection Association, 1976), 1–9. This material is used with the permission of the publisher.
14 Paul C. Ditzel, *Fire Engines, Firefighters* (New York: Crown Publishers, Inc., 1976), 16.
15 Ibid., 18.
16 Unless otherwise indicated, the material in this section draws on Ditzel, *Fire Engines, Firefighters,* 18–19. This material is used with the permission of Crown Publishers, New York.

17 Lyons, *Fire in America!* 6.
18 O'Bannon, *Building Department Administration,* 1/3
19 Lyons, *Fire in America!* 7.
20 Ditzel, *Fire Engines, Firefighters,* 29.
21 Much of this section is excerpted, with some editorial changes, from Lyons, *Fire in America!* chaps. 2–4. This material is excerpted with the permission of the National Fire Protection Association.
22 A. L. Todd, *A Spark Lighted in Portland: The Record of the National Board of Fire Underwriters* (New York: McGraw-Hill Book Company, 1966), 12.
23 Lyons, *Fire in America!* 113.
24 Much of this section is excerpted, with some editorial changes, from Lyons, *Fire in America!* chap. 5. This material is excerpted with the permission of the National Fire Protection Association.
25 Todd, *A Spark Lighted in Portland,* 44.
26 Ibid., 45.
27 Ibid., 46.
28 John V. Morris, *Fires and Firefighters* (Boston: Little, Brown, 1955), 383.
29 *Wildfire Strikes Home,* report of the National Wildland/Urban Fire Protection Conference, January 1987.
30 For background on two of the most serious of such twentieth-century fires, see Leon Stein, *The Triangle Fire* (New York: Lippincott, 1962); Corinne J. Naden, *The Triangle Shirtwaist Fire* (New York: Franklin Watts, 1971); Paul Benzaquin, *Fire in Boston's Cocoanut Grove* (Boston: Branden Press, 1967); National Fire Protection Association, *The Cocoanut Grove Night Club Fire* (Boston: National Fire Protection Association, 1943).
31 The major part of this section is excerpted, with some editorial changes, from Ditzel, *Fire Engines, Firefighters,* chaps. 3, 4, 7, 12, 15, and 17. This material is used with the permission of Crown Publishers, New York.
32 Lyons, *Fire in America!* 12.
33 Ditzel, *Fire Engines, Firefighters,* 21.
34 Ibid., 68.
35 Ibid., 66.
36 A major part of this section is excerpted, with some editorial changes, from Ditzel, *Fire Engines, Firefighters,* chap. 14. This material is used with permission of Crown Publishers, New York.
37 National Commission on Fire Prevention and Control, *America Burning* (Washington, D. C.: Government Printing Office, 1973), x–xi.
38 Ibid., 139.

2 Overview of the fire protection system

A system can be defined as a set of interacting elements that together form an integrated whole and are organized to accomplish a common purpose or goal. The systems approach was highly popularized by the monumental achievements of the space age, which enabled human beings to venture into outer space and then to land on the surface of the moon. C. West Churchman, a leading systems analyst, presented the concept in nontechnical terms in the 1960s.[1] The idea of an integrated approach to planning and managing any given problem was novel at that time. In the intervening years, numerous textbooks in the field of general management have refined the theory.

Beginning in 1973 with the publication of Harry Hickey's *Public Fire Safety Organization: A Systems Approach*, the concept became integrated into fire management techniques.[2] Subsequent work by Coleman and Brunacini and National Fire Academy courses further expanded the systems concept.[3] The idea that any system, including fire protection, consists of a variety of components that act together to achieve a common goal demands a generalist perspective.

Before moving on to discuss the systems approach, a word about definitions is in order. Many terms in the fire service have yet to be operationally defined and used consistently throughout the field. This chapter will use the term *fire protection system* to encompass the many elements internal and external to the fire department that contribute to efforts to prevent, suppress, and control fire and other emergencies.

The traditional approach to fire protection focused only on fire suppression. With the acceptance of the systems approach, however, fire protection came to be viewed in a much broader context that includes all elements relating to the *total* fire safety effort in a community.

A simple but complete fire protection goal could be ''to prevent and/or limit fire loss and property damage due to fire.'' This goal may be accomplished by enforcing codes that pertain to fire resistance and the modular design of structures, developing fire safety awareness among the citizenry, and maintaining an adequate, well-trained, and well-equipped fire suppression force.

The systems approach is based on the idea that many elements contribute to the goals established by and for the fire protection system. Figures 2–1, 2–2, and 2–3 illustrate three ways of viewing the components of the fire protection system. Figure 2–1 is a general diagram of an administrative system. Figure 2–2 suggests the complex relationships among the fire environment, the economy, legislation, management program elements, and actual incidents. Figure 2–3 shows the organizational components. As one element interacts with others, the system functions to achieve its goal or mission, which is to reach a consensus on the scope, objectives, and methods of providing community fire protection.

Traditionally, fire protection managers, particularly fire chiefs, have carried much of the burden of fire protection on their own shoulders and have not looked at fire protection as a total system. Today, the actors in each element of a system are likely to be aware of its role in the system and to accept responsibility for completing certain tasks. As the primary administrator of the total fire protection system, today's fire chief is responsible for identifying and working in the context of both the internal and external components or elements of the system. Internal components are those under the direct supervision of the fire department. External components are the other departments and functions of government and the private sector that can affect the activities of the fire service organization.

Within the systems context, it is important to remember that the local fire department operates first and foremost within the local community and must be responsive to its needs. Those needs are relayed in large part through the budgetary and policy decisions of the elected governing body. In many communities an appointed city or county manager works with the council to help implement these decisions. The fire chief and other department heads work with the manager in establishing levels of service, proposing new programs or improvements, and formulating budget requests, for example.

External components

The National Fire Academy has identified the following components of the fire protection system in a typical community: the city or county council and manager, the fire department, the emergency management organization, the building department, the engineering department, the water agency, the planning and zoning department, the police department, central services, general services, the municipal airport (and by extension other specialized facilities), and private developers.[4] To this list one might add federal and state fire and emergency agencies, industrial and private fire departments, and the insurance industry.

Functions of the components

Most of these components are external to the fire department itself, but all of them have roles in fire protection. An overview of the functions of the fire department is presented here to put the roles of the other components in perspective. A more detailed look at the fire department appears later in the chapter.

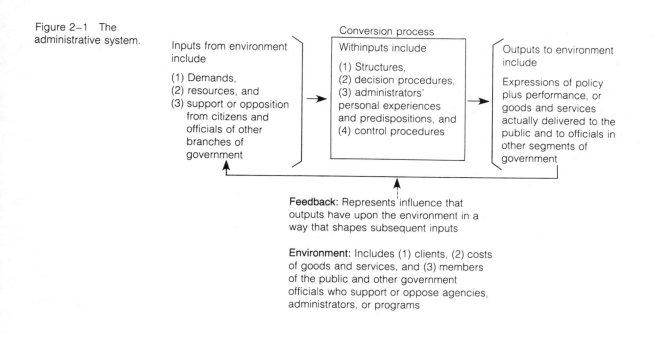

Figure 2–1 The administrative system.

Conversion process

Inputs from environment include

(1) Demands,
(2) resources, and
(3) support or opposition from citizens and officials of other branches of government

Withinputs include

(1) Structures,
(2) decision procedures,
(3) administrators' personal experiences and predispositions, and
(4) control procedures

Outputs to environment include

Expressions of policy plus performance, or goods and services actually delivered to the public and to officials in other segments of government

Feedback: Represents influence that outputs have upon the environment in a way that shapes subsequent inputs

Environment: Includes (1) clients, (2) costs of goods and services, and (3) members of the public and other government officials who support or oppose agencies, administrators, or programs

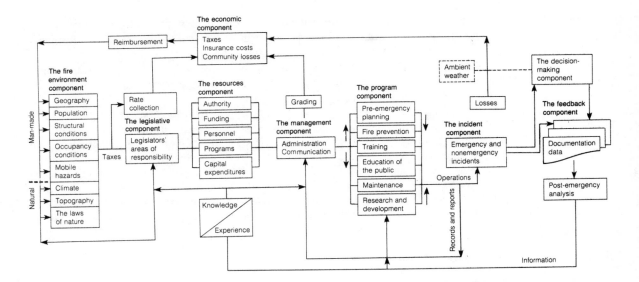

Figure 2–2   A fire protection system model.

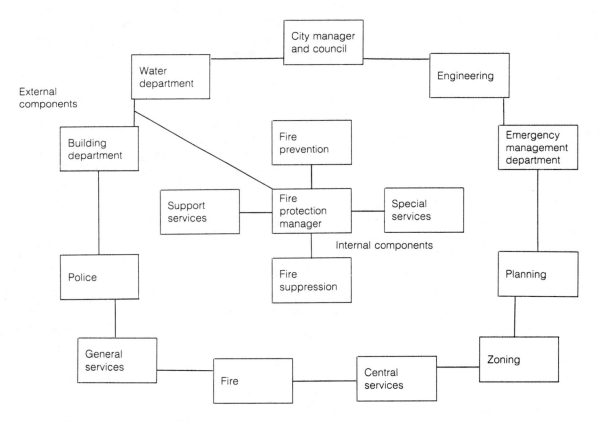

Figure 2–3   Typical fire protection components.

The city/county council and manager   As suggested above, the city or county governing body and appointed manager have the following responsibilities:

1. Receive recommendations from the fire department and determine the levels of 'service and resources to be provided
2. Allocate resources of the total local delivery system and determine local priorities relative to fire protection
3. Monitor the performance of all components of the system.

The fire department   The fire department performs the following functions:

1. Provides information and recommendations to the governing body for their decisions on community fire safety
2. Within budget limitations, maintains a well-trained and well-equipped fire suppression force for fire control
3. Coordinates and is responsible for public fire prevention awareness programs
4. Coordinates the community fire protection system
5. Provides periodic life-safety and fire hazard analysis, deficiency reductions, and code enforcement programs
6. Coordinates and provides community emergency medical services (EMS)
7. Conducts fire cause and arson investigations
8. Recommends ordinances and fire-safety laws to minimize loss of life and property by uncontrolled fire and maintains latest fire prevention codes
9. Reviews plans for new construction, fire-resistive construction, separations, built-in fire protection, hydrant layouts, and apparatus access in accordance with fire protection objectives
10. Performs related emergency services functions that may include the investigation and control of hazardous materials.

The emergency management organization   Emergency management is often a responsibility of the fire department, but it, too, involves many external actors. The emergency management organization

1. Coordinates the role of the fire service and other critical services within the entire emergency management system
2. Ensures delegation of authority for a wide range of disaster-level events
3. Provides all emergency personnel with opportunities for specialized education and training to certify professional performance in such areas as radiological monitoring, shelter management, mass evacuation and care, crisis relocation, and so on
4. Conducts tests and simulated exercises for the whole emergency management system
5. During emergencies, serves to establish a command post for the coordinated response of all critical services involved in the response.

The building department   The building department performs several functions relating to fire protection:

1. Enforces minimum building, plumbing, and electrical codes (to assure that modular levels of fire resistance are built into structures at the time of construction; the primary elements of this fire resistance are to provide for life safety, structural integrity, and reduction of fire hazard of built-in systems in structures)
2. Classifies occupancies and their required types of construction to ensure that the structure meets the fire- and life-safety needs of the occupancy
3. Issues occupancy permits that control changing occupancies, to ensure that the structure meets the fire protection and life-safety needs each time the occupancy changes

4. Recommends or requires the installation of fixed fire protection systems to meet fire safety performance objectives
5. Coordinates with emergency services on the assignment of street numbers, names, and requirements of posting of street numbers; approves numbering systems for multiple-occupancy developments
6. Provides rehabilitation programs that serve to correct structural deficiencies, including fire protection problems in older structures
7. Maintains up-to-date building codes.

The engineering department The engineering department, too, has several responsibilities in the area of fire protection:

1. Prepares preliminary layout of fire hydrants and water mains for new street development based on fire department and insurance company recommendations
2. Considers fire apparatus access (street width, turning radius, cul-de-sacs) during street development, based on recommendations from the fire department
3. Checks water system plans, prepared by private consulting engineers, for conformance to fire department and insurance company recommendations
4. Provides fire department with utility maps, including sewer system maps and storm drain system maps, for use in pre-fire planning and emergency operations
5. Maintains up-to-date city boundary and street system maps.

The water agency Needless to say, the water agency plays a vital role in fire protection:

1. Maintains water supply adequacy and reliability for use in fire suppression (fire flows)
2. Performs periodic inspections and maintenance of fire hydrant valves
3. Ensures that valving in mains is maintained so that maximum fire flow is available

---

Fire protection engineering Fire protection engineering is a discipline that contributes to virtually every aspect of the total fire protection system. Fire protection engineers apply the sciences of mathematics, physics, and chemistry; the engineering disciplines of statics, dynamics, fluid mechanics, strength of materials, and graphics; and specialized engineering education in codes and standards, the pyrometrics of materials, fire protection systems design, and fire modeling to the areas of fire prevention, fire protection, fire control, and suppression.

Fire protection engineering has been, and still is to some degree, a very limited field in which only a few fire-service-oriented personnel have chosen to labor. In the United States, only two schools, the University of Maryland and Oklahoma State University, have specialized in fire protection engineering. Other colleges have traditionally dedicated about four credit hours to fire protection systems. It is no wonder that fire protection engineering has received minimal acceptance in the public sector.

At the same time, fire protection engineers are needed increasingly to design fire detection and suppression systems. With large fire losses continuing, the insurance industry has begun to look seriously to preventive measures, and the demand for built-in protection systems has accelerated.

4. Maintains and repairs fire hydrants (this task includes flushing, painting, and flow testing)
5. Sends a representative to greater alarm fires to assist in water supply co-ordination
6. Maintains the records needed to meet insurance grading evaluations
7. Keeps fire department informed of hydrants and water mains that are "out of service"
8. Provides connections for private fire protection systems; inspects and maintains street valves to ensure uninterrupted water supply
9. Provides fire department with utility maps, including water system maps and water system pressure zone maps, for use in pre-fire planning and emergency operations.

The planning and zoning department   The planning and zoning department performs the following functions relating to fire safety:

1. Provides information that can be used to determine future fire protection needs
2. Controls the design of developments that affect access to buildings, separation of buildings, and open spaces (green areas) that serve as fire breaks
3. Considers fire protection resource needs in determining density and types of developments
4. Develops conservation and open space elements to identify potential hazard areas.

The police department   Of the police department's many responsibilities, the following are directly related to fire safety:

1. Provides traffic and crowd control at emergencies
2. Reports fire and fire hazards during patrols
3. Enforces no parking ordinances that protect fire protection facilities (fire hydrants, fire department connections, and access routes)
4. Assists the fire prevention division with fire investigations, especially those that involve the apprehension and prosecution of incendiary fire setters, and assists in handling and storing evidence
5. Enforces trespassing laws in designated fire areas
6. May maintain an aero squadron, which carries out air reconnaissance of mountain or canyon areas during brush fire operations and patrols canyons closed to the public in areas declared a high fire hazard
7. Maintains a communications center, which receives calls for assistance and dispatches appropriate personnel.

Central services   The office of central services contributes to local fire protection by

1. Reproducing written fire safety materials
2. Preparing and printing fire prevention information
3. Preparing and reproducing reports
4. Preparing transparencies and other visual aids.

General services   The fire safety functions of general services are performed by two units:

1. The shop division, which is responsible for preventive maintenance, emergency repairs, refueling and repairs at emergency scene, fabrication of equipment, repair and maintenance of power tools, and the preparation of apparatus and vehicle specifications.

2.   The building maintenance division, which maintains emergency generators, performs scheduled maintenance on fire department facilities, and provides advice on preventive maintenance programs.

Specialized fire protection   Airports, harbors, and other specialized facilities have the following fire-safety responsibilities:

1.   Within budget limitations, maintain a well-trained and well-equipped crash/fire/rescue force for specific emergencies
2.   During those hours when the facility is used, provide personnel to implement a second squad for suppression operations
3.   Provide specialized apparatus as needed.

Private developers   Fire safety is an important concern of all developers, who usually make every effort to

1.   Provide new construction plans for fire department review to ensure that all fire and life safety codes are being met and install fire protection systems as required
2.   Cooperate with the fire department in meeting local code requirements to minimize long-range effects of new construction
3.   Provide 8 × 10 readable plot plans on larger developments for fire department response books.

Other fire departments   In carrying out its work, the local fire department sometimes needs to coordinate its efforts with those of other departments. Federal and state agencies and industrial and private organizations often have responsibilities for incidents or properties in the local jurisdiction. Chapter 13 discusses the coordination of efforts for emergency response planning, and Chapter 17 examines private-sector fire services and their relation to other departments.

The insurance industry   The insurance industry is another element in the external system. The rates charged for insuring property against loss are affected by the industry's assessment of the risk that a loss will occur. In most states a rating organization develops advisory rates on behalf of insurance companies. Rates are determined for individual properties or for occupancy classes by considering building construction, private and public protection, hazards of occupancy, and loss experience. Public protection is judged by applying the

---

Insurance Services Office   Insurance Services Office, Inc. (ISO), is a non-profit corporation serving the insurance industry. Through a subsidiary, ISO assesses risks and sets advisory rates for fire insurance in most of the United States.

Using criteria listed in its Commercial Fire Rating Schedule, ISO surveys commercial properties, focusing on construction features, occupancy, exposure, and fire protection. It then determines specific fire rates and related underwriting information.

With its Fire Suppression Rating Schedule, it also collects information on community fire protection resources, including water supply and distribution; fire department apparatus, staffing, and training; and fire alarm receiving and dispatching. Each community receives a classification used in both commercial and personal property insurance rating.

The insurance industry often uses ISO information to set fire insurance rates.

grading schedule of the Insurance Services Office, which looks at such criteria as water supply, the fire department, fire service communications, and fire safety control.

Coordination of the components

These components exist in most communities, but many are not traditionally viewed as part of the fire protection system. A careful examination of each component, however, reveals its significance in community fire safety. For example, in many communities the building department is responsible for the enforcement of building codes and regulations. Most building codes are in some way related to the regulations affecting the fire department. Such elements as emergency egress, fire resistance of the structure, and fixed fire protection systems are specified by building codes. Since building officials are unlikely to have had direct experience with fire, it is important for the fire department to work closely with the building department as decisions affecting the fire service are made.[5]

Similarly, planning officials trying to attract new business and industry to the community must take into account the additional fire protection forces and equipment that will be necessary to protect those additional tax resources. The planning director then becomes a part of the fire protection system of that community.

These interrelationships create a need for careful coordination and communication among parts of the system. Codes, inspection procedures, water supply, and a multitude of other elements all come together in fire protection. Subsequent chapters detail the organizational means for achieving the necessary coordination.

Internal components

There is no single "best way" to organize or staff a fire department. The variation between small, medium-sized, and large fire departments is substantial, and the components of a volunteer or combination department differ somewhat from those of a fully paid department. But there are broad managerial and functional themes that apply to any department.

No matter how it is organized, a fire department has the following four functions: fire suppression, fire prevention, special services, and support functions.

Fire suppression

The evolution of the American fire service has been slow. Initially most fire departments were organized for the sole purpose of fighting fires. They did not spring into existence as full-blown organizations rationally dedicated to establishing a comprehensive fire protection system based on primary fire prevention activities, with a suppression subsystem designed only to be activated upon the breakdown of the prevention subsystem.

The traditional fire department structure has a fire chief at the head and various subordinate levels below that rank. These share many titles, based on historical development as a paramilitary organization: deputy chief, assistant chief, division chief, battalion chief, captain, lieutenant, engineer, and so on, with the choice being largely a matter of local preference.

Delivering firefighting capability is usually the task of teams of firefighters grouped together in fire companies. It has often been said that the individual fire company is the building block of the fire service. In some jurisdictions, the word *company* could designate an entire fire department. These companies could provide one or more pieces of motorized fire apparatus out of a single fire station. Larger fire departments, operating many pieces of apparatus out of several fire stations, may group clusters of such companies and stations under the supervision of one of the subordinate chiefs.

At times, these clusters are grouped in a way that will provide the supervising subordinate chief officer with a manageable span of control. At other times, fire departments may be more concerned with grouping their companies geographically. Each fire company or station may be under the command of an officer called captain, lieutenant, sergeant, foreman, or even senior firefighter.

Fire prevention

Fire prevention is less spectacular than suppression. It is also less expensive and is universally accepted as the most effective means of accomplishing the mission of the fire service. Traditionally, fire prevention has brought to mind the fire inspector, fire prevention bureau personnel, and, perhaps, the Smokey the Bear program of the U.S. Forest Service, the most intensive, long-term prevention program in existence. But prevention is much more than this. A well-planned fire prevention program includes inspection and code enforcement, public fire safety education, arson prevention programs, and fire and arson investigations.

The fire service has been a driving force in urging the adoption of legislation to require built-in fire protection systems—such as sprinklers—with proven track records of saving lives, property, and money. The fire service alone cannot achieve prevention, however. It is a joint effort by builders and developers, building code administrators, the public, and fire service personnel, who must also take responsibility for educating the others. Comprehensive prevention and code administration are discussed in detail in Chapter 15.

Inspection and code enforcement　Society operates by rules, regulations, and laws. With them we have a semblance of order and security; without them we would have chaos. In the fire service, the laws are fire prevention codes. These codes were established to provide minimum standards to prevent fires from starting and to limit the spread of fires that do start.

For enforcement purposes, most state statutes designate fire inspectors or fire marshals as the fire prevention and building code enforcement agents. As the most visible part of the fire service, the position carries with it a certain amount of prestige. Because the enforcement process is politically sensitive, the position also carries liability.

Fire inspectors conduct on-site inspections of business and industrial, public assembly, and other high-risk occupancies to identify risks and hazards, ensure compliance with code requirements, and record any existing violations. Usually they help educate occupants so that they can avoid routine problems and understand complex solutions. In the case of violations that require time to correct, inspectors return at a future date to check on compliance.

The monetary effectiveness of fire inspection programs is difficult to measure, as one large fire can cost more than many small ones. However, it is not difficult to see that fires increase when programs are cut back and that they decrease when those programs are expanded. We do know that, with an effective program, most fires can be prevented. Reduced fire calls represent direct financial savings to a municipality in that there will be less need to increase suppression forces and less loss of the tax base to fire.

Public fire safety education　Although in existence for many years, the delivery system for public fire education activities has changed. Previously public education was handled by inspections, consultations, or the fire incidents themselves. Now public fire education has become an organized network of information and consultation, picking up where codes and ordinances leave off. Chapter 15 discusses public education in further detail.

As statistics show, the greatest fire loss is in private homes. The fire service has therefore come to realize that codes and laws are not enough; the public must be taught to understand the risks and to cooperate in the area of fire prevention. Most U.S. fire departments do not have public education officers, and this function continues to be carried out by inspectors, investigators, and firefighters. The National Fire Academy and the National Fire Protection Association have made public fire education one of their primary objectives.

Some of the most successful public education programs have been those targeted at specific audiences. Programs designed for juveniles, such as "Stop-Drop-And-Roll," have specific targets. Others, including Operation EDITH (Exit Drills in the Home), are aimed at family populations. Some programs have been aimed at particular groups, such as school teachers, as in the Learn Not to Burn curriculum. Some programs have been designed for senior citizens, others for those with disabilities such as deafness, blindness, and reduced physical mobility.

If public education is to be effective, it must focus on citizen attitudes and behaviors in the community. The more diverse the demographics, the more diverse the program needs to be in reducing behavior that leads to either inappropriate use of fire or improper reaction to an incident.

A public fire education program has three major requirements:

1. It should be developed to achieve specific goals and objectives through well-organized lesson plans delivered by well-trained personnel.
2. It must have a competent staff to deliver the program. The staff should be well-versed in educational methodology and fire safety and should be large enough to attain the departmental objectives.
3. Its results should be measurable, whether by means of pre- and post-testing data, or other statistical data. Measured results are the only concrete evidence that will convince a locality of the effectiveness of the program. They show whether a public fire education program is viable.

Juvenile firesetter programs   In the past, juvenile firesetting was not seen as a fire service problem. Because a substantial proportion of all fires are set by juveniles, however, the manner in which these juveniles are handled has come under close scrutiny.

Traditional counseling for a juvenile firesetter consisted of someone, usually a firefighter or investigator, "talking" to the youngster, frequently using scare tactics. That counselor was not trained in interviewing or counseling techniques, nor was there any provision for guidance or education in fire safety for the child. As the need for improved juvenile counseling became evident, organizations such as the National Firehawk Association and the Federal Emergency Management Agency (FEMA) designed programs that could be implemented in individual fire departments. Every program is distinct in nature but all utilize education and counseling. Some programs use firefighters to work with the juveniles, whereas others use outside agencies.

An important factor to consider when working with juvenile firesetters is that the firesetting behavior is usually a symptom of a much larger problem. That is why trained professional counselors are essential in a well-developed program.

Another factor is that a juvenile firesetter often faces legal action and is taken through the juvenile court system, which has no fire safety education component. Clearly, juvenile firesetting is not a problem the fire service can handle alone; it requires assistance from mental health, juvenile justice, and perhaps other agencies.

Fire and arson investigations Fire investigations were begun by the National Board of Fire Underwriters at about the turn of the century. There was a need to identify causes in order to prevent fires in the future. Among the first to be identified were nonregulated construction standards and occupancy hazards. This was the beginning of standard and enforced fire and building codes.

The fire service of today has that same pressing need to determine why a fire started. The job is complicated by changing building standards and materials, the many new appliances and products available to consumers, and a greater population. The job is also complicated by intentionally set, or arson, fires. Arson fires are among the most difficult types of crimes to investigate, because the fire burns most of the materials an arsonist used to start the fire. Arson fires are sometimes set to destroy evidence of another crime, and the fire scene investigator must be able to read the scene accurately to determine what type of fire occurred.

Fire investigators routinely respond to the scene of an incident to systematically identify the factors involved in the cause and spread of the fire. This work involves both manual examination of debris and burned-out structural components and careful examination of the facts surrounding the incident. These facts may emerge from interviews with occupants, review of insurance records, and computer analysis of evidence. At each stage, investigators keep careful records and files of their findings. If the investigation uncovers evidence of arson, which is a crime, the investigator can become involved in the prosecution of the arsonist through the legal system. In many areas of the country law enforcement and fire service personnel work together to form arson investigation or "strike force" units, drawing on expertise from each of the disciplines.

Fire service investigators must constantly keep pace with technological advances in building construction and materials, energy sources, consumer products of man-made materials, and their impact on life safety by working with people such as fire protection engineers, architectural designers, manufacturing and industry representatives, and research laboratories. Fire and arson investigators also need to have a working knowledge of advances in forensic science to understand what they are looking for, how to preserve what they have collected, and how to use the results of the forensic laboratory examinations to determine the cause of fires.

Special services

In addition to the "traditional" services of suppression and prevention, the fire service has developed special services to meet evolving needs. Two major ones are emergency medical services (EMS), which are covered in detail in Chapter 14, and hazardous materials planning, which is a component of emergency management, covered in Chapter 13.

Emergency medical services The role of the U.S. fire service has expanded to meet community needs for improved emergency medical services. This development coincides with and is related to advancements in emergency medical technology and the modern philosophy of delivering basic and advanced life support services at the scene of a medical emergency and during transportation of the patient to a medical facility. The evolution of EMS also coincides with growing economic pressure to use the available time of service personnel more effectively.

The pressures of limited municipal finances and public demand for increased services are likely to continue, placing responsibility on local government to make cost-effective use of public employees. Use of fire department resources, including personnel, in the delivery of prehospital emergency care and transportation services is likely to increase as a result of these conflicting pressures.

Properly managed, the merger of EMS with traditional fire service responsi-bilites can contribute to a healthy future for fire departments. A new generation of fire service managers can be expected to emerge as personnel having a dual role rise through the ranks with broadened expectations and abundant practical experience in a total emergency service delivery context.

Hazardous materials planning and management Until the 1970s there were few regulatory provisions for the safe transport, storage, and disposal of haz-ardous and toxic materials. Agencies at the federal, state, and local levels did not want to become involved for fear of the potential shift in liability if hazardous materials were accidentally discharged. Manufacturers and transporters of toxic substances ignored regulations because of the high cost of safety equipment and of training employees in the proper use and handling of hazardous materials. Public sentiment and subsequent outcries were not yet strong enough to generate increased regulatory provisions.

Once the need for jurisdiction over the manufacture, transportation, storage, and disposal of hazardous and toxic substances was established, a barrage of regulatory provisions followed, such as the Toxic Substances Control Act en-acted by Congress in 1976, the 1976 Resource Conservation and Recovery Act, the Comprehensive Environmental Response, Compensation and Liability Act (Superfund) of 1980, and the Superfund Amendments and Reauthorization Act (SARA) of 1986. Fire service organizations are subject to these and many other regulations when committed to incidents involving hazardous materials.

Historically, fire service personnel were trained for quick response to accident scenes and immediate offensive tactics. After considerable loss of personnel and equipment, it became apparent that traditional fire service tactics needed to be restructured for hazmat operations.

Many fire service organizations, however, continue to perceive hazardous materials as a very low priority on their busy agendas. Because of the prepon-derance of federal and state regulations, little thought has been given to man-agement subsequent to the release of a hazardous or toxic substance into the environment. The complexity of regulations, the multiplicity of regulating agen-cies, and the increasing potential liability can become a nightmare that will tax the resources of the largest cities if greater priority is not given to proper planning and management of hazardous materials programs.

A few fire service organizations have developed stringent local ordinances for hazardous materials management, including the proper planning and man-agement of hazardous waste facilities. It is their intent to reduce the potential risk of accidental discharge of hazardous materials into the environment. De-partments with comprehensive emergency management plans often include haz-ardous materials incidents in those plans.

Support functions

In addition to the line functions of suppression, prevention, and special services, the fire department includes at least six major support functions: personnel administration (discussed in detail in Chapter 11), training (Chapter 18), in-formation services (Chapter 6), financial management (Chapter 8), public in-formation, and communications and dispatch.

Personnel administration Personnel costs usually take up more than 90 per-cent of a paid fire department's budget. In most medium-sized to large local governments, the authority for personnel management is divided between the fire chief and the central personnel agency. With increasing and conflicting demands being made on the fire service and, in turn, on management, it becomes all the more critical for a fire agency to become directly involved in personnel decisions. Therefore, it seems prudent for a fire agency to assign responsibility for personnel management to a particular unit or to a specific person or to divide it among a group of fire managers and/or supervisors.

Personnel administration consists of

1. Classifying the positions within the department
2. Creating detailed descriptions of the work to be performed by employees in each position, including promotional requirements
3. Administering the pay plan and benefits
4. Ensuring that the department does not discriminate in hiring, assigning, disciplining, or promoting employees
5. Recruiting potential fire department employees
6. Testing job candidates and candidates for promotion
7. Maintaining a system for performance appraisals
8. Creating opportunities for personnel development and training
9. Providing counseling and personnel referral services.

Training   Depending on the size of the department, the training function can be assigned to a single officer who also has other responsibilities, a full-time training officer, a part of a division, or an entire training division. The training function encompasses the following responsibilities:

1. Surveying employees' training needs through questionnaires or other means
2. Locating external training opportunities in community colleges, training academies, or other institutions
3. Monitoring technical and managerial changes to be certain that current training is relevant
4. Developing curricula for internal training programs (preparing lesson plans, visual aids, and tests or examinations)
5. Scheduling and delivering training sessions
6. Assisting and advising in the promotional examination process
7. Maintaining training records.

Information services   The computer has been described by some fire officers as the fourth major technological change to improve fire departments (the other three being the internal combustion engine, the centrifugal pump, and the radio). A computer not only increases the amount of information available to the fire officer, but also improves upon the quality of that information by making it more timely and more accurate.

If a department has fewer than 100 calls per year and can operate with information easily derived from hand tallies, it may not need a computer. However, if a fire service manager needs to have information processed in many different ways during the year, and it becomes time-consuming—and perhaps impossible—to retrieve the necessary information quickly, a computer should be used.

Information services include the following:

1. Collecting data from inside and outside the department on personnel, finances, incidents, schedules, equipment, inspections, and other aspects of fire protection
2. Maintaining information in easily accessible form
3. Creating reports periodically or on request to help department managers track their budgets, detect patterns of arson or other incidents, evaluate

the effectiveness of prevention and other programs, and perform other management tasks

4. Providing incident command information
5. Providing capability for computer-aided design of the fire protection system.

Financial management   Most local governments have a budget officer or finance director who coordinates and prepares the local government budget, monitors revenues and expenditures, and forecasts future needs and resources. In the fire department, financial management revolves around the departmental budget. Ultimate responsibility for the budget falls on the chief, but it cannot be prepared and executed without input from division heads and other managers. Financial management involves the following:

1. Projecting future needs for personnel, apparatus, equipment, and fire stations
2. Projecting the costs associated with these needs for the coming budget year
3. Proposing alternative means for achieving the local government's overall budget goals at various funding and service levels
4. Tracking expenditures during the year to be sure they remain in line with the budget
5. Projecting cost–benefit analysis between the public sector and the private sector.

Public information   Few fire departments have a public information office or a staff person who devotes full time to this function. Often the chief or another officer handles press inquiries, prepares an occasional news release, and arranges for publicity on programs provided to the public. No matter how it is handled, the public information function is increasingly important, particularly as the public becomes aware of the dangers of hazardous materials and other potential emergencies. The public information function includes the following:

Citizen information   The Glendale (Arizona) Fire Department has published a brochure called "After the Fire . . . We Continue to Serve" to help citizens adjust and recover after a fire loss. The brochure includes advice on the following topics:

Property insurance: Contacting the insurance company, removing valuables from the property, and handling uninsured losses

Relocating if the house is uninhabitable: Contacting the police, locating temporary housing, packing the necessary items, notifying those who need to reach you, and contacting utility services

Documents and records: Identifying documents that need to be recovered if at all possible, replacing those that are lost, and replacing savings bonds and cash

Salvage hints: Cleaning walls, furniture, carpeting, electrical appliances, cooking utensils, clothing, leather, and books

Food management: Determining which foods can be used and which should be discarded

Reference: A directory of organizations that can be of assistance, with their telephone numbers.

---

1. Publicizing the department's services, including prevention efforts and other programs designed to help citizens protect their lives and property from fire or recover after a fire has occurred. Publicity efforts can include flyers, brochures, posters, advertisements in local papers, and radio spots.
2. Developing a relationship with the media, providing information to reporters, and responding to their inquiries. See the accompanying sidebar on working with the media.
3. Providing public information at the scene of an emergency to explain what has occurred, what is being done about it, and, if applicable, what measures are being taken to protect citizens in the aftermath of the incident.
4. Explaining managerial and technological innovations that will improve the services provided by the department. Such innovations might include reorganization of programs and activities and acquisition of new apparatus or equipment.
5. Announcing major appointments or promotions of personnel and publicizing awards and other recognition of the department or its members.
6. Serving as a liaison with the private sector, the school system, and other actors in the total fire protection system to help educate them about the role of the department and secure their cooperation in prevention and other programs.

Media relations   The press plays an important role in the fire chief's relations with the community. It relays information from the fire department to the public on one hand and relays public opinion to the department on the other. Here are some guidelines for establishing and maintaining a good working relationship with the media— newspapers, radio, and television.

Establish a clear and systematic policy for press relations, coordinated by one person. This can be the chief or another designated officer, who should coordinate with the local public information officer to be sure all spokespersons for the local government are consistent in their responses to press inquiries.

Work with the press to set ground rules for restricted news coverage and to be certain you both have the same understanding of such terms as "off the record," "not for attribution," and "on background."

Take time to orient reporters to the department, and supply them with background material on complex issues.

Be sure information given to reporters is accurate and complete. If you do not know the answer to a question, do not bluff or refuse to answer, but offer to find out.

Practice a genuine open-door policy with reporters. Be available for interviews at times that will help them meet their deadlines. Return their phone calls promptly.

Handle news breaks among competing media as objectively and impartially as possible. Be sure you provide the same information to each reporter.

If a news story is inaccurate, do not hesitate to tell the reporter. But respect his or her news judgment and ignore minor inaccuracies.

Recognize the pressures on reporters: deadlines, limited time for checking statements, limited space or air time, and competition with other media. Learn to live with the skepticism that is built into reporters' professional backgrounds.

A specialized communication system The Life Safety System is a communication system designed to help local fire departments protect the life and safety of the elderly, handicapped, and medically at risk. The system features an in-home alarm system that automatically notifies the department in the event of a fire or medical emergency.

The Life Safety System is provided at cost to communities by the National Center for Life Safety, Inc., an independent nonprofit organization originally launched as a public service project of the International Association of Fire Fighters and the Muscular Dystrophy Association.

Three individual alarms protect users from unexpected emergencies. A *no-activity alarm* summons help if a subscriber fails to check in within a predetermined period of time. A *fire alarm* notifies the local fire department of the presence of smoke or fire in a subscriber's home. A *medical alarm* summons the local fire department when activated from a special remote control device carried by the subscriber.

To set up a Life Safety System, a fire department needs a central receiving unit and residential control units for the households that will be participating. Critical information on each user is stored in the receiving unit, and when a call comes in, the receiving unit shows the name, address, age, and medical profile of the user, as well as the names of physicians, relatives, and friends. The system uses existing fire department personnel and facilities to monitor and dispatch calls.

Among the communities that have installed the system are Pittsburgh, Pennsylvania; Orange and Anaheim, California; San Antonio, Texas; Topeka, Kansas; Montgomery County, Maryland; Phoenix, Arizona; Washington, DC; and Shaker Heights, Ohio.

Additional information is available from the National Center for Life Safety, Inc., 1015 Thirty-third Street, N.W., Suite 404, Washington, D.C. 20007. Telephone: 202-296-1873.

Communications and dispatch The basic requirements for a fire department communications center are three: the means of receiving an alarm, the ability to dispatch equipment to the proper location, and the ability to maintain contact with mobile units after dispatch. In addition, the dispatch and control function needs the ability to contact other departments for assistance and mutual aid and the ability to recall off-duty personnel. The communications center is often the link between the incident commander and preplanned information such as hazardous materials files or other data bases needed to support emergency operations. Components of the communications system can include telephones, radios, television, computers, and other media. Figure 2–4, on page 46, shows the major elements of a communication system for a large department.

Organizational structures

Fire departments deliver services through a bewildering variety of structures, and no overview of the fire protection system would be complete without a brief discussion of alternatives (these are covered in detail in Chapter 17).

Local pride and perhaps ignorance concerning the alternatives may lead a volunteer group of enthusiasts in a tiny unincorporated suburban housing tract

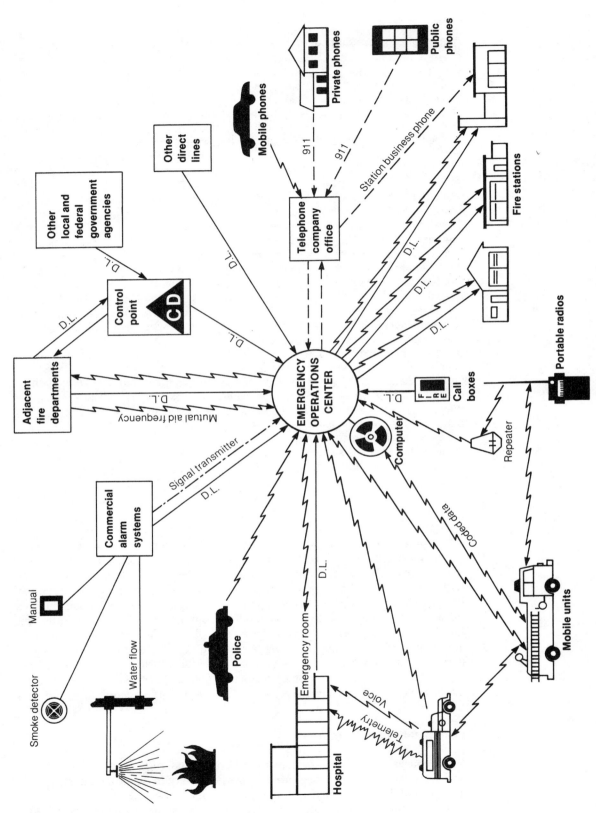

Figure 2–4   Communications system
elements, Fairfax County, Virginia.

to acquire a used gasoline tanker, fill it with water, and respond to highly informal requests for help, squirting water in the general direction of the flames without the protection of fire helmets, coats, or boots, and without such legal shields as incorporation or workers' compensation.

At the other extreme are sophisticated, professional organizations serving large metropolitan areas.

In between lie a variety of fire departments and agencies providing fire protection services through some combination of full-time and part-time paid and volunteer personnel. In addition, some jurisdictions receive fire protection from organizations whose full-time members are paid to perform dual functions, combining fire suppression duties with building inspection or police patrol. The latter type of organization is often called a public safety department or public safety organization.

In general, fire departments can be grouped into the following four categories (public safety organizations not included):

1. Volunteer (including jurisdictions that pay members token amounts but that employ no full-time fire protection personnel)
2. Mostly volunteer (full-time personnel make up less than half the membership)
3. Mostly paid (full-time personnel make up more than half but less than 100% of the membership)
4. Fully paid.

A local fire department may be tax supported by a municipality, a township, a county, or a special tax district. It may also be an independent not-for-profit corporation, funded either by donations (and some are funded quite well by this means) or by the contracting of fire services to other governmental jurisdictions, which raise the contract fees through taxation. A few fire departments are independent, profit-oriented corporations. Perhaps the best known private fire service organization is the Rural/Metro corporation with headquarters in Scottsdale, Arizona.

Summary

A fire protection delivery system is a complex structure, consisting of a wide range of components that have both traditional and nontraditional roles in achieving the objectives of reducing the loss of property and life from fire. The system includes not only the fire department but also the building department, the planning department, the water system, and other departments or subsystems that have an effect on the total fire problem. The absence of any one component of the fire protection system may weaken the fire defenses of a community.

The internal components of a fire department also represent many functions. In addition to its traditional function of fire suppression, the fire department is responsible for fire prevention, code enforcement, fire and arson investigation, public education, and such special services as EMS and hazardous materials planning and incident control. Prevention programs have proven to be successful, particularly when they include built-in automatic fire sprinklers, detection systems, and proactive structural conditions.

Fire protection is delivered through a wide variety of departmental structures and may be funded by taxes, donations, or fees.

This chapter has presented an overview of many subjects that will be covered in detail later in the book. The objective has been to create a framework for viewing the fire department in its total context and to emphasize the importance of the interrelations among the parts of the fire protection system.

1   C. West Churchman, *The Systems Approach* (New York: Dell Publishing, 1983).

2   Harry E. Hickey, *Public Fire Safety Organization: A Systems Approach* (Quincy, Mass.: National Fire Protection Association, 1973).

3   Ronny J. Coleman, *Management of Fire Service Op-* *erations* (North Scituate, Mass.: Duxbury Press, 1978); Alan Brunacini, *Fireground Commander* (Boston, Mass.: National Fire Protection Association, 1976).

4   National Fire Academy, *Fire Risk Analysis: A Systems Approach* (Emmitsburg, Md., 1984).

5   Ibid.

3 Organization and management

Like other organizations, a fire department is a complex system in which individual, interpersonal, physical, and technological elements come together for the purpose of achieving certain goals. Public administrators, including fire service managers, need to understand how organizations work in order to manage them effectively. That understanding comes from both theory and practice, and this chapter looks at both.

The chapter first reviews theories of organization and the management approaches suggested by each one. Then it examines basic organizational principles, including organizational design and structure, organizational culture, and power. Next it covers organizational change, focusing on organizational development and team building. Finally, it looks at the organizational characteristics of volunteer, combination, and career fire departments.

Management in private-sector organizations is often proposed as a model for managing in the public sector. However, many believe that management in the public sector is unique because of its relation to the democratic process, which is the cornerstone of U.S. society. Although private-sector organizations can concentrate on developing "efficient" systems, many believe that the methods used there cannot be directly applied to the public sector without appropriate modifications. They argue that accountability to citizens is different from responsiveness to customers.

Formal theories of public organization

Formal theories of organization can be grouped into several "schools of thought": the traditional "rational" or "scientific" model, the human relations approach, and several new approaches that draw on elements of both schools. The work of many early theorists provides a foundation for explaining the relationship between the work environment, the work force, and society. Their views provide a framework for understanding and appreciating diverse approaches to organization and management. At the same time, they provide a historical perspective on the effectiveness and ineffectiveness of various organizational structures and methods.

The traditional model

The traditional or "rational" model views management from a scientific or logical perspective.[1] The rational model tends to focus on the technical aspects of administration, particularly organizational process and efficiency. The work on "bureaucracy" by Max Weber (1864–1920) is particularly relevant as it relates to government. Weber's work focused on the effectiveness of government offices in Germany during the early 1900s. He believed large organizations

Portions of this chapter on team building were prepared by Jim Sparr, Fire Chief, Fort Lauderdale, Florida, and Peggy Lilienthal Linden, Senior Education Specialist, Management and Education Branch, National Fire Academy.

could be managed most efficiently by strict rules, clear and concise lines of authority, and a functional hierarchy linking various divisions of the organization. He advocated a high degree of job specialization and a strict separation between business and personal relationships. Weber considered the manager's job to be one of facilitating organizational goals through the application of these principles.

Elements of the "bureaucratic" approach certainly exist in the paramilitary structure of the fire service. Clear lines of authority, specific goals and objectives, and a functional hierarchy are useful principles when applied to the delivery of emergency services.

Frederick Taylor, who has been called "the father of scientific management," introduced a theory focusing on job processes—that is, the means to the end. His work in industry revolved around the idea that management knows little about the most efficient ways to manufacture goods. He maintained that detailed study is necessary in order to plan and organize work in the most efficient manner possible. He also recognized employee training as a critical component in improving efficiency. Equally important, he appreciated the need for labor's cooperation in developing the spirit of harmony required to improve long-term productivity. Current efforts in the fire service to develop new and more efficient procedures and operations are based on the principles derived from scientific management:

1. Evaluate the process by analyzing each step
2. Review data
3. Carefully look at various alternatives to current methods
4. Use efficiency as the criterion for judging a new process
5. Train workers to do the work, while management focuses on administration.

Another significant contributor to the rational model was Herbert Simon. His book entitled *Administrative Behavior* is considered by many to be its foundation. Simon argued that the role of the administrator is to make rational decisions based on objective and scientific analysis. He emphasized the need to distinguish between facts and values and argued that there was little point in trying to evaluate statements of value because they deal with how the world "should be." Instead, Simon concentrated on the observable world.

In 1950 Simon discussed the concept of the "administrative man," saying that individuals need to conform to the organization in order to experience "organizational success" within the hierarchy. This concept lies at the heart of the rational approach. From this perspective, organizational goals are of utmost importance, even at the expense of individual identity.

Henri Fayol (1841–1925) is often credited with formulating the first complete theory of management. Fayol's basic theory implied that management is definable and teachable. He specified five key functions of management: planning, organizing, commanding, controlling, and coordinating. This list was later altered by Luther Gulick to POSDCORB (planning, organizing, staffing, directing, coordinating, reporting, and budgeting). Today many managers seem to emphasize planning, controlling, organizing, staffing, and directing.[2] The components of Fayol's theory have been used as a foundation by fire service administrators. Planning is often considered to be deficient in the fire service, yet many managers now recognize that it is a critical element that will help the modern fire service organization keep pace with the challenges of the future.

In addition to defining management functions, Fayol worked extensively with organization charts and management principles. He identified the organization chart as being the appropriate tool for "explaining" the organization as a working unit. He also identified a number of principles that an organization must abide by if it is to be successful. Among the best known are the following:

1. Division of labor: Organizational units and employees should specialize in order to achieve maximum efficiency.
2. Unity of command: Each employee should have only one boss.
3. Chain of command: Organizational managers are ranked in a hierarchy of authority, from highest to lowest, and all communications must be from one manager to the person directly above or below.
4. Authority/responsibility: Each manager must have the ability and power to make decisions and give direction in order to get results.[3]

The traditional approach has influenced the structure and management of many organizations, fire departments included. Managers often set out to establish a "rational model" to direct the group toward a desired end. They normally do this by establishing organizational goals and objectives, on the assumption that employees will internalize organizational values and work to accomplish the objectives.

In the fire service, particularly in suppression and emergency activities, traditional principles have worked well. As the fire service assumes responsibility for such services as fire prevention and public education, however, the traditional model falls short, and managers need to borrow from other schools as well.

The human relations approach

The "Hawthorne" experiments and the work of Elton Mayo during the 1920s and early 1930s introduced a new and important theory of management encompassing human behavior—"organizational humanism," or the human relations movement. The research, conducted in the Hawthorne Western Electric plant, focused on the influence of various environmental elements on the work output of employees. As the experiments continued, it became apparent that there were other, nonenvironmental factors affecting employee performance and production. Mayo, using a series of elaborate interviews, determined that the employees responded to factors relating to them as individuals and to their individual needs. These factors included attention, recognition, and being listened to by management. This research acted as a catalyst for a shift of focus from the rational approach to managing people to a more "person-centered" one.[4]

The research resulting from Mayo's work propelled management theory into a completely new era—in which managers use behavioral science principles to view organizational behavior. The behavioral scientists looked in depth at organizational behavior, organizational and group structures, leadership styles, and how these interact with employee characteristics in affecting work output and efficiency. Work in this area included that of Abraham Maslow and Douglas McGregor.

Maslow is best known for his concept of the "hierarchy of needs," which he used to explain employee motivation. He classified needs in ascending order of urgency:

1. Physiological needs (including food and shelter)
2. Safety needs
3. Social needs (including friendship and social acceptance)
4. Ego needs (self-esteem and recognition)
5. Self-fulfillment or self-actualization needs (creativity, personal growth).

Douglas McGregor described two views of motivation: Theory *X*, which assumes that people dislike work, lack ambition, and need coercive direction, backed up by the threat of negative sanctions, to work toward organizational goals; and Theory *Y*, which assumes that people find satisfaction in work, seek responsibility willingly, and exercise imagination and self-direction when they are committed to organizational objectives.

The work of these two men provides fire service managers with valuable insights into such practices as team management and work scheduling. It also supports promotional and reward systems that create an environment focusing on the needs of individuals as well as the group and organization.

New approaches

As public organization theory has continued to evolve, several new directions are evident. Among them are the "new public administration" of the late 1960s and early 1970s, critical theory, and systems theory. A major theme in current thought can be characterized as "participative management."

The new public administration arose out of a concern that public organizations, particularly public bureaucracies, failed to mirror one of the major values of a democratic society—namely, *participation*. Proponents of this view argued that participation on the part of citizens was crucial to their personal fulfillment, and that this principle should be reflected in the organizations that serve them.[5] Public administrators thus have a responsibility, through their organizations, to set an example for society at large.

Proponents of the new public administration felt that traditional participative approaches were intended only to pacify rather than actually involve employees and clients.

The new public administration emphasized open organizational structures that are flexible and marked by constructive confrontation and exchange. They also sought to establish a hierarchy or structure within organizations that would provide for participation at all levels. The difficulty, however, became how to do this while still maintaining key elements of organizational structure, that is, chain of command, unity of command, span of control, and lines of authority and responsibility. Although the concept seemed attractive, proponents failed to find a viable means of implementing it in public organizations, where a hierarchy has traditionally been part of the system.

Robert Denhardt has done extensive work in an area called "critical theory," which is concerned with the premise that government, using the traditional rational approach, has become preoccupied with solving technical problems, at the expense of public participation in the democratic process. This "technical rationality," in its simplest form, is the use of the most efficient means to achieve a given end.[6]

The shift toward technical rationality as a basis for public administration causes significant problems in hierarchical organizations, including the fire service. The end result is that citizen input based on social values is replaced by bureaucratic decisions based on technical goals. Denhardt warns of the tendency to focus on the execution of specific tasks at the expense of the moral implications of actions. He believes that society can make decisions based on social values only by moving outside the system of regulation. He advocates broadening the "public sphere" in order to accomplish this—that is, restoring communicative interaction and emphasizing public input in making community decisions.[7]

Systems theories view the organization in the context of its external environment. Chapter 2 examines the fire service from a systems approach.

Today's fire service managers are borrowing from and utilizing various theories including those covered in this chapter. They are also borrowing from the private sector (as evidenced by the popularity of such books as *The One-Minute Manager* and *In Search of Excellence*[8]). Managers can expect the emergence of even more theories of management, which may change further the way they think about and deal with themselves, those they influence, and the organizations that they manage.

Historically, management theory emerged from a very autocratic, rule-oriented set of fundamental theories. Then for a time it was the process that seemed to make the difference in the efficiency of the organization. In the next phase of development, the human aspects of the work place seemed to be of utmost importance. Today, management theory is being viewed as a series of closely intertwined possibilities that must all be addressed and integrated if the manager is to be successful in an ever-changing environment. In addition, today's manager must be adept at solving problems, making decisions, and handling human relations and a host of other tasks. To meet this challenge, managers and those around them have to become more skilled. Education and learning need to be continuous and to take place both in the classroom and in the work place.

Approaches to management

It is very difficult to define approaches to management. One classification scheme closely parallels approaches to organization: traditional, human relations, human resources, and combinations. Figure 3–1 summarizes the major views.

A traditional approach to managing an organization—like McGregor's Theory X approach—might include significant emphasis on the process and the need to be efficient, with less emphasis on the human element, at least as it affects the output of the organization. This approach suggests management policies that prescribe close supervision and tight control of employees performing narrowly defined jobs, on the assumption that adequate performance will occur only if the manager is constantly alert and exercises tight formal control.

The human relations approach—McGregor's Theory Y—is best represented by such theories as Frederick Herzberg's "job enrichment" and the motivational positions of such theorists as Maslow. This approach prescribes some employee participation in decision making and assumes that employees will exercise self-control because they are essentially loyal and dependable if their basic social needs are fulfilled, if they feel they are important to the organization, and if their work is recognized by their superiors. A manager using this approach

Figure 3–1
Approaches to management.

Traditional	Human relations	Human resources
Assumptions		
1. People dislike work 2. Work only for money 3. Few capable of self-control or self-direction	1. People want to feel important 2. Want to be recognized 3. Want to be consulted	1. People want to contribute 2. Can exercise broad self-direction, self-control 3. Represent "untapped resources"
Policies		
1. Assign simple, repetitive tasks 2. Supervise closely—maintain tight control 3. Set rules and routines—enforce firmly but fairly	1. Manager should discuss plans—listen to objections 2. Allow self-control on routine tasks	1. Create climate where all can contribute fully 2. Develop full participation on *important problems* 3. Continually broaden area of self-direction and control
Expectations		
1. If closely controlled, people will meet standards 2. If firm but fair, people will respect supervisor	1. Participation increases satisfaction and morale 2. Subordinates will willingly cooperate	1. Direct improvements in decision-making and control 2. Satisfaction increases as "by-product"

would ensure that employees have opportunities for participation and would implement the kinds of controls that foster individual responsibility.

The human resources approach is similar to the human relations approach but focuses more on individual *contributions* than on recognition of individual accomplishments. The human resources approach assumes that employees represent an untapped resource that can be unleashed by the creation of a climate conducive to full contribution through participation.

The usefulness of any approach to managing an organization is directly related to the ability of the employees to respond to the approach. Moreover, various individuals will respond differently to each of the approaches outlined. The challenge for the successful manager is to assess the group and match the appropriate approach or combination of approaches to that particular group. To the extent possible, this matching should be extended to individual members to increase their performance and productivity. This approach has been called ''situational.'' The manager, after evaluating a situation and the individuals involved, needs to utilize an approach that will maximize the efforts of those involved.

The traditional organization

Traditionally, the fire service has tended to look at its structure as a means to an end, usually the single function of fire suppression. To perform this function,

Fire service management in 1933

In 1933 the career fire service was a pretty good deal, since secure jobs were hard to find during the depression. There were not the number of volunteer departments that there are today. The strength and influence of unions and of the human relations approach to managing people were hardly measurable.

Firefighting was not yet into its scientific period, and books and articles focused on "drills" conducted by "drillmasters." The work itself was seen as difficult, dirty, and dangerous, as indeed it was. Both vehicles and equipment would be considered primitive today.

If management means the way that superiors use people and other resources to accomplish sets of tasks, firefighters (then called "firemen") were organized in simple, military-type organizational structures and bossed by hard-nosed, autocratic officers who expected to see all feet leave the ground when they yelled "jump." More important, the fireman probably expected to be told to jump.

The techniques of scientific management were confined largely to time and motion studies and to how tasks should be organized and divided—the "division of labor." The old drill manuals of the 1920s and 1930s attest to the strong interest in such exercises as "two men advancing a hose line" and "three men advancing a hose line from a hydrant to the third story of a fire escape." Each step was carefully planned, and the minutes and seconds required were usually listed. Great pride existed in the division of labor, and competition—friendly and otherwise—was common between "engine men" and "truckies."

Fire department management then focused on getting jobs accomplished, and not on the feelings of the workers. Modern leadership theory would describe those fire chiefs as task-oriented rather than relationship-oriented. Most firemen would have been surprised at any other management style.

Source: Adapted from John A. Granito, "Trends in Fire Service Management," *Fire Service Today*, August 1983, 27.

the typical organization developed certain structural characteristics: recruitment of unskilled personnel, provision for training in the areas of physical tasks, emphasis on mechanical technology, direct cause and effect relationships, and clear, hierarchical authority relationships.

In many cases recruitment was accomplished by word of mouth. Firefighters would hear of an opening in the organization and encourage a friend to see the fire chief for a possible appointment. Typically, recruits had little or no experience in the area of fire protection. Many managers felt that knowing the character of the person being selected and having organization members as personal references outweighed the need for previous training or experience. Once a firefighter was selected, he was put into a recruit training program to learn the basic firefighting skills necessary to carry out fire suppression functions. In addition, most organizations spent considerable time teaching new members to operate the many types of firefighting vehicles utilized. Apparatus maintenance and mechanical aptitude were a big part of the training program. And suppression work required a paramilitary command structure.

Much of the success of the traditional organization was due to its simple function and structure. Because fire suppression was the primary service, it was relatively easy to organize resources and assign authority and responsibility. Efficient performance at the emergency scene was the criterion for success, and the organizational structure was designed to achieve it. Thus, the fire company became the basic building block of the fire service.

Personnel management was quite simple, particularly when most organizations were composed primarily of volunteer personnel. Record keeping was not required and little attention was given to formal promotional examinations or career development.

Today's organization

The organization that is emerging today, on the other hand, offers diverse fire protection services and requires a complex, multifaceted delivery system. Figure 3–2 shows how today's organization contrasts with the traditional one; it tends to have educated career employees; complex and intellectual tasks; electronic and other sophisticated technologies; recognition of multiple causes and effects; and a distinct overlap between workers and managers.[9]

The emergence of ''new organizations'' normally occurs when gaps in organizational performance indicate that structural or behavioral changes are needed. In addition to concerning themselves with physical and human resources and services provided, managers in the emerging organization generally spend con-

Figure 3–2 The traditional and emerging organizations.

The traditional organization	The emerging organization
Recruitment of unskilled personnel	Highly educated career employees
Physical task training	Complex, intellectual tasks
Emphasis on mechanical technology	Electronic and other sophisticated technologies
Direct cause-and-effect relationships	Multiple causes and effects
Clear, hierarchical authority relationships	Distinct overlaps between workers and managers

siderable time adapting to, and working in harmony with, the environment, which includes numerous political and social elements. They also tend to consider decisions, processes, and systems from a perspective of long-range social and economic impact, rather than from one that is technically sound and efficient but relatively short term.

Organizational principles

The need for people to form organizations to accomplish things has been around since the beginning of humankind. While at first informal in nature, groups became more sophisticated and formal to accomplish predetermined purposes. The formal organization provides a framework for establishing relationships among the component parts, assigning tasks to specific individuals and work units according to their skills and specialties, and coordinating activities of the component parts to accomplish goals.

Characteristics of the organization

Characteristics of the formal organization include authority and influence, responsibility, accountability, unity of command, span of control, and delegation.

Authority Traditionally, the establishment of authority has been viewed as a primary element in the formal organization. Further, many internal relationships are authority-based. Authority is often assumed to start at the top and filter down through the organization. In today's organization, however, considerable authority is shifting downward to lower levels with increased delegation.

Early theorists emphasized the role of formal authority to explain much of the behavior within an organization, and formal authority certainly is a major characteristic of the fire service. At the same time, many chiefs are utilizing informal lines of authority as well. They have discovered the need to influence the organization through such means as persuasion, suggestion, and motivational techniques.

In fact, managers now commonly use the word "influence" to describe their relationship with peers and subordinates. Traditionally, employees were "ordered" or "directed" to perform. Now, in an era of emphasizing employees, supervisors and administrators need to employ other kinds of influence. Many refer to this characteristic as "salesmanship." Whether it is accomplished through selling or influencing, the goal remains the same—to motivate employees to work productively to achieve the goals of the organization.

Responsibility Classical theorists believed that responsibility is commensurate with authority, but this principle has now been challenged. It seems that today's organization is placing emphasis on the manager's ability to go beyond the responsibilities spelled out in a job description and encourage innovative, creative behavior. This philosophy requires managers to utilize organization members in areas that are constantly expanding.

Accountability Accountability in government has been a focus of much attention, and the fire service has been no exception. Economic recessions and the increased cost of providing government services have brought with them a demand for administrative accountability when it comes to such things as capital expansion, staffing levels, levels and types of services offered, and future planning strategies and techniques. The renewed interest in accountability encompasses not only these broad concerns often vocalized by community members but also specific questions such as the processes by which employees report on the use of resources for which they are responsible.

Unity of command   Unity of command in most organizations is a by-product of organizational hierarchy. The principle implies that each member should report to only one person, both during routine operations and in an emergency situation. This enables supervisors to maintain necessary control as well as responsibility for the actions, safety, and welfare of those persons under their supervision.

Span of control   In addition to having unity of command, supervisors need to be assigned a group that is of manageable size. That is, each supervisor must have a reasonable ''span of control.'' A person's span of control is normally established on the basis of the nature and difficulty of the work, the skills and abilities of the persons being supervised, and the experience and ability of the supervisor. Normally, under nonemergency conditions most supervisors are expected to be able to supervise seven to twelve persons. Under emergency conditions, most experts recommend limiting the supervised group to three to five members.

Delegation   The successful organization is often the one that applies the principle of delegation. A manager who routinely passes considerable authority and responsibility downward is likely to benefit from developing employees' abilities, increasing productivity, and freeing top administrators to deal with long-term considerations, such as planning. Managers who find themselves behind in their work and unable to meet predetermined deadlines are often people who have failed to delegate work to others. Delegation, in addition to affording an organization the opportunity to accomplish more, provides growth opportunity to individual members. Work that might be routine for one individual might be creative and challenging for another. This challenge, when met, provides the foundation on which motivation can be increased through the use of recognition and reward.

Factors in organizational design

Several factors influence the overall design of public organizations. These factors include the purpose of the organization, the goals established by and for the organization, the size of the service area and the organization, the internal and external environment, and the technology used in providing necessary services.

Purpose   The purpose of a fire department, in general terms, is to provide public services. The level and kinds of services provided vary considerably among communities. Factors that influence the overall purpose include the geographic and demographic characteristics of the area served, the relationship and availability of services from other agencies, and the willingness and ability of a community to finance and support fire protection services. Often the purpose of an organization will be formalized in a mission statement.

Goals   Goals are developed to ensure that the organizational purposes are met. In addition goals provide the organization with internal direction, which facilitates both day-to-day management and long-term planning.

Size   The size of the service area and organization play an important part in the design of the organization. An organization that serves a large geographic area may need to be broad in scope in order to provide for adequate control. Similarly, as organizations grow larger there tends to be more need for specialization, with a corresponding need for new levels of supervision and management.

Environment   The internal and external environment also must be considered in determining the design of an organization. Internally, one looks at the relationships between labor and management, current binding contracts, and the capabilities and limitation of personnel. Externally, key considerations include the financial and political support of elected officials and the appointed administrator, other organizations with which relationships exist or must be developed in order to meet organizational goals, the extent to which the economic and political climate appears to be predictable and stable, the potential for growth or consolidation, and the overall attitude of the community toward the organization. Chapter 2 describes the external environment as part of the fire protection system.

Technology   The technology involved in delivering the service—that is, the state of the art in terms of human and technical capabilities—will dictate such things as availability of qualified personnel, the ability to add or change services offered, and the cost of changing or improving services as community needs or desires change.

Organizational structure

According to Peter Drucker, any organizational structure needs to provide for the following: clarity in position and assignments for employees, economy of effort in control and supervision, "direction of vision" toward ends rather than means, understanding of individual tasks and how they are related to organizational goals, effective decision making, stability and adaptability, and means for its own continuation.[10]

Determining what structure might work best for which organization can be quite complicated owing to the nature of the organizations themselves. For example, one service dimension of any fire department is emergency response in the form of fire suppression or emergency medical services. As noted earlier, managers have found that the traditional hierarchical structure seems to work quite effectively for managing people in these situations. Another dimension, however, is nonemergency services. This is where deficiencies become most apparent in the traditional structure. There seems to be a need to utilize human resources differently in order to solve problems, manage programs and projects, and handle the many nonemergency services and programs in a modern fire service organization. Administrators searching for a more effective means of utilizing people within the organization can consider drawing on several structural options.

Organization by function   One approach to organization is to examine what the organization is trying to accomplish and what resources are required to get the job done, then to group similar resources together according to the goals and objectives to be accomplished as well as the unique qualities, skills, and abilities of the personnel. This is referred to as "organizing by function" or "the functional approach to organization." Highly specialized organizations and small organizations concentrating primarily on the delivery of emergency services often rely on functional organization. Figure 3–3 shows a simple functional approach to fire department organization.

Advantages to this structure include

1. Technical efficiency
2. Clearly defined assignments that are commensurate with the individuals' experience, skill level, and authority
3. Maximized abilities through the careful assignment of personnel to positions

Figure 3–3   Functional
organization.

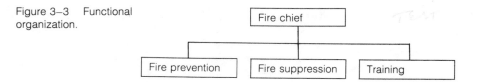

4. A clear sense of direction for members wishing to advance within the organization
5. Specialization of members within a specific function of the organization, which allows individuals to be trained to a high level and improve their efficiency
6. A reduction in internal and external confusion during emergency and non-emergency situations.

The result is a system that is comparatively simple to manage. Disadvantages include

1. A high level of resistance to change
2. A tendency to reinforce specialization so it becomes difficult to attract, train, and retain skilled technicians who have wide and varied abilities
3. Hampering lines of communication with unfamiliar terminology
4. Difficulty in distributing routine and regular work equitably among members
5. Losing track of the overall purpose or mission of the organization
6. A tendency to invest heavily in individual outcomes of work at the expense of overall organizational outcomes that are important but not directly related to what individuals currently do.

Organization by division   Owing to the nature of the services provided, the population served, or the size of the organization, it sometimes becomes necessary to further define the structure of the organization beyond that of function. A common means of further specializing resources is to organize by division (see Figure 3–4). The purpose of establishing divisions is to group resources according to internal relationships and related services. The manager can then assign specialists to oversee specific functions or services that have been designed. Common divisions within a local fire service organization include administration, communications, operations (including fire suppression, emergency medical services, and disaster planning), fire prevention (including public education, code enforcement, and investigation), personnel (including training), and maintenance.

Matrix organization   Matrix management was institutionalized as a result of the needs of many organizations, including the National Aeronautics and Space Administration (NASA). In the 1960s, NASA's goal was to place a man on the moon by the end of the decade. With this in mind, experts set out to devise a management structure that would allow technical *and* product development to proceed simultaneously. In addition, these developments would take place at various locations with little shared information because of national security requirements. If any component failed to meet time, financial, and quality control deadlines, the entire project would.

The resulting concept was ''matrix management.'' The underlying principle of this approach is to combine diverse resources in order to accomplish a specific predetermined goal or objective with little regard for the normal functional hierarchy. This approach is typically utilized for projects or tasks that have related technology but require special input from several persons or groups. In the case of NASA, the specialties were aerospace, automotive, and electrical.

Figure 3–4
Organization by division.

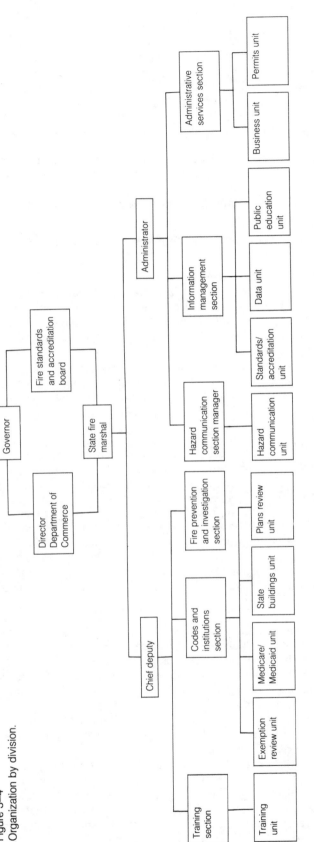

Figure 3–5   Matrix
organization.

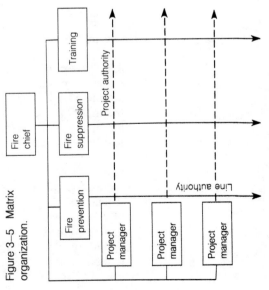

In this approach the group is brought together in order to accomplish a specific goal and once that goal is accomplished they return to their ''domicile'' position within the functional organization. A matrix organizational structure is illustrated in Figure 3–5. This approach has several advantages: it maximizes specialization, provides a forum for an interchange of concepts and ideas, develops an awareness of the ''big picture,'' and provides for individual recognition and growth. Disadvantages include difficulties in taking care of the routine work while members are assigned to a matrix project, temporary loss of unity of command, temporary gaps or overlaps in authority and responsibility, and difficulty in evaluating results unless the results are specific and measurable. In addition, employees have difficulty in understanding the concepts or procedures involved.

Examples Figures 3–6 through 3–12 show typical line organizations for departments of increasing size. In small departments, fire control personnel carry out prevention, inspection, training, maintenance, and other activities. As the department gets larger, specialized positions or divisions are added to the organization.

Organizational culture

Every organization possesses a culture or ''character,'' which is developed over a long period of time. An organization's character may reflect a high concern for service to the customer; it may place major emphasis on the skills and abilities of its employees; or it may encourage teamwork and participation. Another organization may discourage talented personnel; may emphasize longevity instead of performance; or may resist changes. Many factors affect the evolution of the organizational culture, including the example set by the organization's leaders; the kinds of authority, responsibilities, and expectations against which group and individual performance are measured; the methods used to select new employees; reliance or lack of reliance on standardized methods; the value placed on cooperation versus competition; and the general attitude of employees toward themselves, what they are doing, and the community they serve.

In a fire department, the organizational culture generally values strong leadership, use of established work methods, and a community service orientation. The chief and other managers can influence the organizational culture in a number of ways.

Leadership Many times leadership is thought to be important only at the top; yet successful organizations work hard at developing leadership throughout the organization and in as many activities as possible. This includes those ''informal activities'' that present themselves on a daily basis, whether it be around the fire stations or on the emergency scene. If an organization emphasizes leadership only at the top levels, employee morale and performance will suffer. At the same time, however, an organization that has leadership among the work force but lacks developed leadership skills at higher levels will also experience frustration and conflict, which can result in morale or attitude problems. The successful organization works hard at developing and recognizing leadership at all levels throughout the organization.

Expectations The organizational culture is also affected by expectations. Many fire department employees like to be needed and appreciated for their skills and abilities; they work hard at trying to identify their specific role in assisting with the accomplishment of desired organizational (and individual) goals and objec-

Continued on page 66

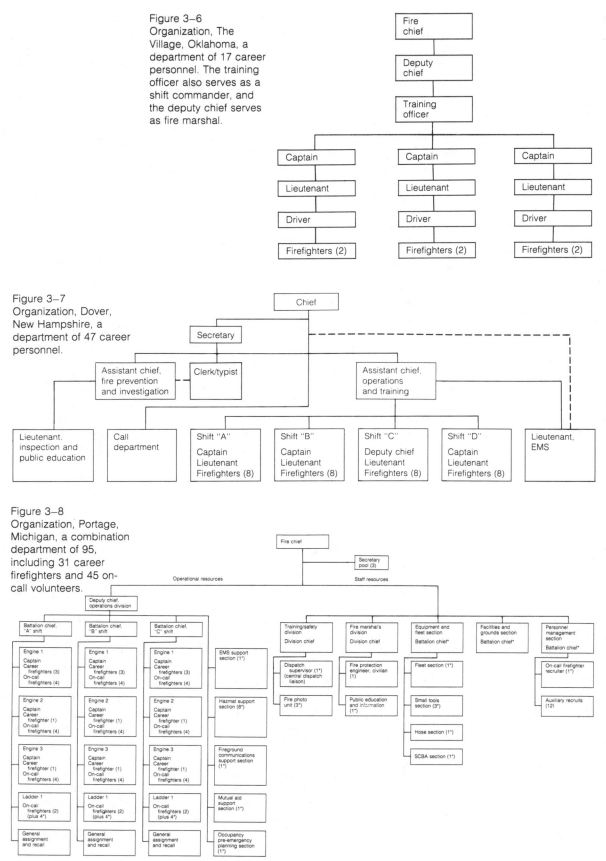

Figure 3–6
Organization, The Village, Oklahoma, a department of 17 career personnel. The training officer also serves as a shift commander, and the deputy chief serves as fire marshal.

Figure 3–7
Organization, Dover, New Hampshire, a department of 47 career personnel.

Figure 3–8
Organization, Portage, Michigan, a combination department of 95, including 31 career firefighters and 45 on-call volunteers.

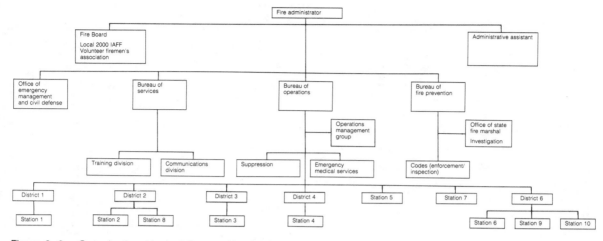

Figure 3–9   Organization, Howard County, Maryland, a combination department composed of 149 full-time and full-time equivalent personnel (of whom 127 are uniformed) and approximately 400 volunteers.

Figure 3–10 Organization, Wallingford, Connecticut, a department of 214, including 61 career and 150 volunteer personnel.

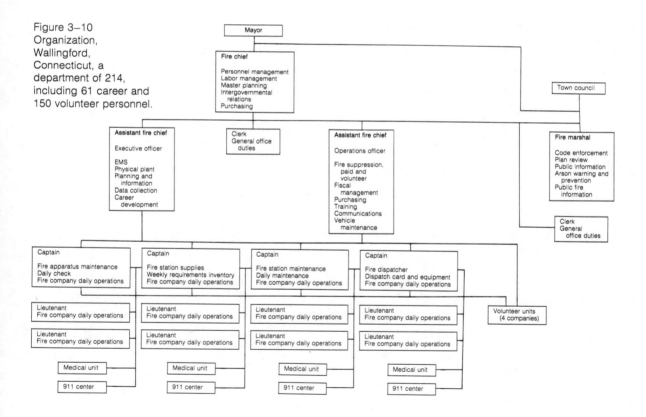

Figure 3–11
Functional organization,
Park Ridge, Illinois, a
department of 50 career
personnel.

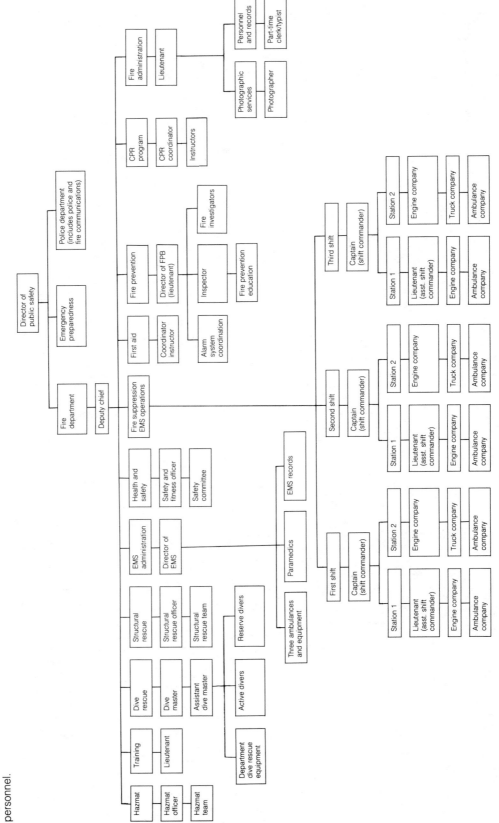

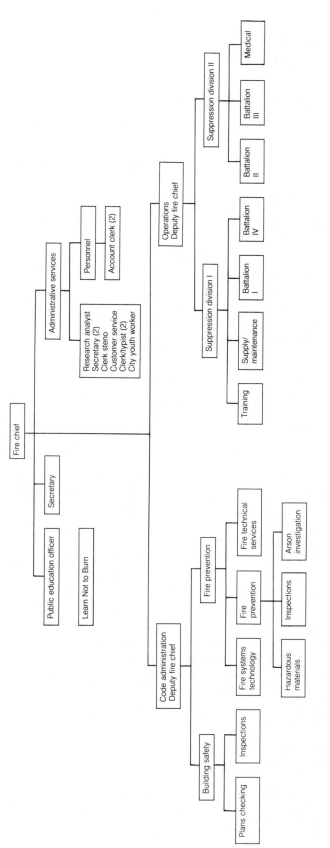

Figure 3–12 Organization, Tucson, Arizona, a department of 468 uniformed career personnel and 110 civilians.

Organizational culture   The simplest way to think about the culture of any group or social unit is to think of it as the total of the collective or shared learning of that unit as it develops its capacity to survive in its external environment and to manage its own internal affairs. Culture is the solution to external and internal problems that has worked consistently for a group and that is therefore taught to new members as the correct way to perceive, think about, and feel in relation to those problems. Such solutions eventually come to be assumptions about the na-

ture of reality, truth, time, space, human nature, human activity, and human relationships—then they come to be taken for granted and, finally, drop out of awareness. The power of culture is derived from the fact that it operates as a set of assumptions that are unconscious and taken for granted.

Source: Edgar H. Schein, "How Culture Forms, Develops, and Changes," in Ralph H. Kilmann et al., *Gaining Control of the Corporate Culture* (San Francisco: Jossey-Bass, 1985).

tives. Successful organizations usually have a high regard for and high expectations of their personnel. They challenge individuals' capabilities by assigning meaningful tasks, while communicating their expectations about results. Not only do these high expectations assist in developing the positive aspects of the organizational character, but they also help the organization meet the individual psychological needs of the membership.

Authority and responsibility   Clearly defined authority and responsibility not only represent a basic organizational principle, but they also assist the organization in developing the membership. Assigning authority and responsibility helps establish formal and informal lines of communication, functions as a yardstick in determining performance levels, provides growth opportunities for individuals and groups, and serves as a basis for recognition and reward.

Selection and recruitment   Organizations tend to attract and recruit persons with values similar to those projected by the organization and to reject those with conflicting values. Organizations that utilize a thorough and comprehensive recruitment and selection process (for both paid and volunteer members) normally receive a higher return on their investment—that is, higher levels of performance—than those organizations that do not have a quality staffing program. Once a recruit is selected, the organizational culture is a powerful force in molding his or her attitudes and performance.

Standardized methods   Standardized methods are important in many organizations. Standardizing the manner in which an organization operates, whether it be on the emergency scene or during routine daily operations, can reduce or perhaps eliminate undue stress and pressure on the individual or the group. Standardized methods are important to the volunteer organization because they reduce the time necessary to teach processes and procedures. The concept of standardization can be applied to something as simple as placing equipment on various vehicles, or as complex as organizational procedures or personnel policies and guidelines. In large organizations with paid personnel, standardization provides a way to administratively reduce the chances of conflict or confusion owing to time pressures and crisis situations.

Cooperation and teamwork   Organizations are often well served by fostering a reliance on cooperation and teamwork, but these characteristics may take a great deal of time and effort to develop if they do not exist. To do so requires a conscious change in individual and group behavior preceded by a change in knowledge and a change in individual and group attitudes. This can be accomplished through the development of a relationship based on a commitment to:

1. A common purpose
2. Predetermined individual and group goals and objectives
3. Emphasis on group achievement as a priority above individual achievement
4. Recognition of mutual interests
5. Understanding of special interests
6. Trust among organizational members, particularly between labor and management.

A key to developing relationships is to first improve communications, which in turn improves levels of understanding and appreciation; and second, provide an atmosphere that allows members to work together in achieving common objectives. The concept of "participative management" and the initiation of team building efforts have helped many organizations provide an environment conducive to the development of relationships that lead to cooperation and teamwork. (Team building is discussed in a later section.)

Employee attitudes   Attitudes are viewed as a key to the daily "climate" of the organization in terms of dealing with the "customer" (citizen) and in dealings of individuals with their work groups. Attitudes generally are developed as a result of an assumption or belief about a particular state of affairs. They can be as specific as an opinion about a person or directive, or can be as general as views regarding politics, a community, or society in general. Four specific factors that influence attitudes are

1. Values developed throughout life
2. The social position of the individual relative to his or her position in the organizational hierarchy
3. The experience of the individual and group as it relates to the issues at hand
4. The current "organizational atmosphere" surrounding the issues.

Some attitudes can be directly influenced by supervisors. This concept is compatible with an individual's desire to please those for and with whom they work. In the case of new recruits, they will look to formal and informal leaders for their "cues" and "behavior expectations." Because individual and group attitudes affect organizational behavior and performance they should be at the top of the list of elements for the manager to consider.

Organizational power

Power has been viewed as the ability to get someone else to do something or the ability to make things happen the way you want. The essence of power is control over the behavior of others, and the amount of "power" a person possesses within an organization is directly related to his or her ability to influence those others. Managers can acquire power through position or through personal relationships.

Positional power   Positional power has three primary bases: (1) reward, (2) coercion, and (3) legitimacy.[11] Reward power is utilized extensively in the fire service. Specific methods include promotions, pay and benefits, special assignments, special recognition, letters of commendation, compliments, or any action that the receiver considers to be positive and that acts as reinforcement for behavior or performance.

The power of coercion exists when someone with positional power is able to adversely affect another person, usually through punishment or the threat of punishment. Coercive power might be reflected in negative performance appraisals, reprimands, the withholding of a wage increase, the taking away of privileges, demotion, or, in extreme cases, termination. In most cases the true source of power lies in the threat of action rather than the action itself. The degree to which this power is used differs immensely from one organization to another. Its use, or lack of use, is often directly related to the manager's style, the character of the organization, and the relationship between labor and management. Most managers would agree that although coercive power is a legitimate source of power, it must be used sparingly and as a secondary power source if it is going to be a beneficial tool to the organization.

Legitimate power is derived from a member's formal position of authority within the organization. This power source provides a foundation from which procedures, policies, and practices are designed and implemented among organization members. The fire service has utilized legitimate power as a primary principle on which departments have organized themselves. A subordinate/supervisor relationship is necessary to function effectively during emergency operations. It is also important during daily operations among stations and teams of personnel.

Historically, most fire departments have emphasized legitimate power, derived from the organizational hierarchy and the need for authority during emergencies, and coercive power, derived from the fear of the consequences if one does not comply with the desires of superiors. Today much more emphasis is being placed on reward power and the ability of managers to influence others through extrinsic and intrinsic rewards. The key here is to be able to recognize the various types of position power and apply the right type of power to the given situation.

Personal power   Personal power is based on expertise and reference. Expert power is the ability to control another person's behavior by possessing knowledge, experience, or judgment that other persons or groups do not possess.[12] Expert power can also be based on the *perception* that a person has expertise. Expert power in the fire service is highly valued owing to the nature of the work performed and the need for accuracy during potentially critical situations. The difficulty, historically, has been in objectively analyzing the nature and degree of knowledge and wisdom derived from a given number of years of experience in the fire service. In addition, the question is commonly asked: To what extent do years of service affect a person's success in a supervisory position when the experience was gained as a technician? Such a question is difficult to answer, particularly when each case differs. As a source of power, however, there is little doubt that knowledge, experience, and judgment are helpful when working with and influencing subordinates in the fire service.

Referent power is based on a person's desire to identify with another person in a position of power. Persons possessing referent power are usually professionally competent people who have demonstrated their ability to get results. Others in the organization normally look at this type of person as a role model, from whom they would like to learn. As members continue their observations of this power, they begin to value the role model's perceptions, beliefs, and behavior and try to emulate them.

Referent power is usually associated with a relationship that has as an additional dimension—friendship. People tend to want to work and please their superiors because they like them. There is little doubt that referent power provides the supervisor or manager who possesses this type of power with a tool that helps to get more out of employees. The degree to which it can be utilized over a long period of time is directly related to the amount of expert power and legitimate power the person possesses, as well as the person's ability to use the power of reward.

Organizational change

Fire service organizations constantly face change caused by both external and internal forces. External forces include new technology, local budgetary cutbacks, and changes in the delivery system, the local elected leadership, or the composition or expectations of the community. Internal forces include personnel changes and the introduction of new programs or policies.

Change in an organization very often meets with resistance, either active or passive. Chapter 16 deals with the barriers to change and innovation in a fire department, suggests ways to create an environment for innovation, and provides a step-by-step blueprint for implementation of change.

Historically, managers have looked toward reorganization, job redesign, and temporary conflict reduction measures to handle the problems associated with change. More recently, however, fire chiefs have become aware of a whole array of techniques that can be employed to manage change.

Organizational development

The techniques used to help prepare for and manage change in the organization are collectively called *organizational development* (OD). This approach to "change management" reverses the traditional mandate approach and introduces a collective, collaborative process that, by its nature, tends to improve the organization by increasing the levels of trust and cooperation among the individuals and groups involved in providing fire protection to a community.

Organizational development techniques focus on several aspects of the organization:

1. Structure and policy, which may be addressed through such techniques as introducing management by objectives or other formalized management practices
2. Skills, which are addressed through technical training
3. Attitudes, values, and behavior, which are addressed by sensitivity training (teaching people to be more aware of themselves and others), managerial grid techniques (identifying and seeking to change the leadership style of the organization), team building (a popular approach that is detailed later), and various participative management methods.

OD focuses on four important organizational relationships: (1) the relationship between the organization and its environment, (2) intergroup relations (inside the organization), (3) the relationship between the employee and the formal organization, and (4) interpersonal relationships and their effect on organizational efficiency.[13]

The relationship between the fire department and its environment is important for several reasons. It depends on outside forces for financial support, in the form of budget approval; there is a need for community involvement in the determination of priorities, services, and programs offered by the organization; and there is a need for honest assessment and feedback relative to the quality and efficiency of the services provided. Most OD programs at some point emphasize the relationship between the organization and environment, and work hard at building and maintaining it.

Intergroup relationships are identified both formally and informally as part of a comprehensive OD program. The focus of attention stems from the need for input from all parts of the organization and the need for members to participate in the process to acquire a "vested" interest in the outcome. Formally, the organization will establish various systems to ensure that intergroup relationships are acknowledged and utilized. Methods might include committees, task forces, department meetings, officer meetings and reports, meetings with organized labor, or meetings or work sessions with support personnel. Informal intergroup relations can be developed through the use of quality circles, brain-storming sessions, and guided discussion sessions in fire stations. Thoughts, ideas, and questions derived from these activities can be followed up to ensure that two-way communication is occurring throughout the organization.

The interface between employees and the formal organization, once developed, will accomplish several important things. First, it will offer individuals many opportunities, both formal and informal, for input to the organization. Second, it will provide members with a sense of contribution. From the formal organization's perspective, the interface encourages input from all levels; ensures that input is representative of the whole organization; and provides a broader basis from which to identify, analyze, and utilize information.

OD encourages and develops interpersonal relationships, which are key to achieving maximum results within the organization. Before a relationship can develop, several things must be present: all parties involved must have some feelings about the issue or situation at hand; they must have a desire to invest time and energy; and they must be comfortable with their ability to perform in the environment selected as the forum in which the interaction will take place. An OD program will encourage members to strengthen their interpersonal relationships by providing multiple opportunities to utilize their skills and by recognizing and rewarding those who assist in improving interpersonal relationships. Other areas to be addressed during an organizational development program include motivational patterns, power relationships, the communication process, situation perception, organization values and norms, problem-solving procedures, goal-setting methods, and conflict resolution.[14]

Individuals may be motivated in a number of ways. Often an individual will behave in a manner that helps him or her become accepted by the group. Behavior will include agreement with group consensus, becoming involved with projects or activities that are popular with the group, and expending large amounts of time and energy in areas that are considered positive within the group or organization. In addition, the individual will associate with groups and activities that satisfy their needs for achievement, self-respect, understanding, challenge, recognition, and reward. These needs will be translated into patterns of behavior that should be observed and evaluated as part of a person's performance appraisal. Group motivational patterns are more vague and difficult to assess but may be more important to the manager. By observing these patterns the manager can get a good feel for those areas that are important to the group. Once these areas are identified, the organization can reinforce and build on the positive patterns and work at reducing or eliminating those patterns that are not in the best interest of the organization.

All organizations are affected by various types and sources of power—another important aspect of organizational development. Many processes or programs within an organization can be explained by the formal or informal use of power. The relationship between those individuals and groups possessing either position power or personal power can have a tremendous influence on the functioning of the manager. The manager must identify and work with those groups and individuals who possess power within the organization to ensure that existing power will be utilized to accomplish those goals and objectives the organization considers important.

The communication process is also important to organizational development. Both formal and informal communication systems must be developed and maintained. If the communication process is to be effective, the organization must ensure that the systems provide a multitude of ways for members to share information and ideas. The systems must be structured to encourage and solicit feedback about the effectiveness of the organization in meeting community needs, the quality and efficiency of the services provided, and the degree to which the organization is meeting group and individual needs as part of an employee development program.

Perceptions of the organization and its workings are important to the overall ability of the manager to improve the organization. A basic step in avoiding misperceptions is to ensure that the members of a department have accurate information about the state of affairs within a department by briefing all employees on a regular basis.

Organizational values and norms also play an important part in the development of the group. Not only must they be jointly developed, but it is also important to periodically check them against the expectations of the community and the basic philosophy of the department. This process is closely related to departmental evaluation and planning efforts, as described in Chapters 4 and 5: defining purpose, types of services to be provided, identifying priorities, and evaluating the degree to which the organization is productive. The manager must try to establish group consensus in the critical areas in order to provide a focus for measuring success during the OD process.

The establishment of a problem-solving process is essential to organizational development. Members of the organization must know what the process includes; the amount, type, and nature of the information utilized in making decisions; who is involved; and what criteria are used. The process includes identification of problems, generation and evaluation of alternatives, selection of solutions, goal setting, implementation of solutions, monitoring progress, and evaluation. Figure 3–13 outlines a problem-solving process in the context of organizational development.

Goal setting plays an important part in OD. Goals should be developed for at least four levels: the individual, the small group, the division, and the organization. Goals at any level should be directly tied to those of the levels immediately above and below. Specifically, individual goals should be consistent with and complement work group goals; work group goals should be consistent and assist in achieving divisional goals; and divisional goals should be designed to assist in the accomplishment of organizational goals. The ''linking of goals'' and participative goal setting that results in specifying difficult yet achievable goals tends to produce the highest levels of motivation and performance.

Conflict resolution processes are another part of the OD program. One approach to conflict resolution revolves around the manager. The process may begin with an informal meeting with the parties involved; then an informal session with another nonbiased individual; a formal meeting with a supervisor of the parties involved; and, if necessary, a third-party decision made by someone with higher managerial authority. Joint and participative conflict resolution

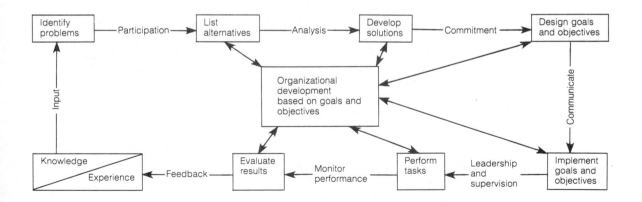

Figure 3–13   The problem-solving process.

approaches involving only the involved parties, with the manager in the background, are also widely used in OD.

Phases of OD can include

1. The diagnostic phase, during which the organization is analyzed and evaluated to determine strengths, weaknesses, and whether elements of OD are currently being utilized
2. The action-planning phase, which includes developing a comprehensive plan to create an atmosphere conducive to long-term problem solving and planning
3. The implementation phase, in which the plan is instituted
4. The evaluation phase, in which progress is monitored.

Many experts feel that the fire service is hampered in its endeavors to "develop the organization" primarily by its structure. As noted before, the hierarchical structure that is currently found in the fire service does much to satisfy organizational requirements.

The difficulty with this structure, however, is that it does not clearly convey to employees the overall organizational goals. This becomes a significant problem in large organizations with a significant number of paid stations and firefighters or in volunteer organizations where contact is infrequent or lacking in focus and purpose. Thus, the challenge in an OD program is great. As is the case with so many activities, OD is a "journey" and not an end result. OD is a continuous process—a process that involves many complex physical and human elements that must be integrated if they are to aid in the development of a mature organization.

Team building

As part of an organizational development effort, the purpose of team building is to help people who work together set goals and priorities and examine how they perform as a team, looking at their collective communication methods, their decision-making processes, and their personal relationships. The participants may be the top-level managers of the department, the members of a departmental work unit, the chief and other local government department heads, or other interdepartmental combinations such as police and fire officers who conduct arson investigations or leaders in departments with mutual aid agreements.

Team building consists of the following steps:

1. Diagnosis of current issues and problems, accomplished by frank exchanges of opinions and perceptions among group members. This step requires open communication and active listening by participants.
2. Group consensus or agreement on which problems deserve priority attention.
3. Recognition of the individual strengths (and weaknesses) of team members and how each can best contribute to the team's goals.
4. Agreement on an action plan that engages the efforts of all team members to solve a defined problem.
5. Implementation of the action plan.
6. Evaluation of the results.

Team building can be used to help solve organizational problems or as a proactive measure to prevent problems. For example, the following symptoms may indicate the need for team building:

1. Decreased output or loss of productivity by individuals
2. Increased grievances or complaints
3. Evidence of hostility or conflicts, suspicion, or distrust

4. Confusion over assignments, excessive competition, faulty communication, or unclear relationships
5. Apathy, indifference, or lack of initiative in solving problems
6. Ineffective staff meetings
7. High dependency on or negative reactions to authority
8. Complaints from the public about service
9. Poor interaction among work units
10. Low commitment to group objectives
11. High absenteeism or turnover.

On the other hand, team building may be employed under the following positive conditions:

1. When things are going well and the team wants to understand its present behavior
2. When a new group has been formed and needs to develop quickly into a working team
3. When several functioning units are being merged into a new unit
4. When the department or unit needs to be restructured because of a change in policy or technology.

A good time to initiate a team-building effort is when a new chief or division head is appointed, or when a change occurs in the city or county administration. Not only does the new appointee need to find out how the organization operates, but the other managers need to find out what this person expects and how he or she will lead and manage. Many old assumptions may have become inappropriate. The new person may have new priorities or an unfamiliar communication style, and the rest of the organization may face adjustments of behavior and attitudes. Team building can help the members of the organization establish structures and processes that will ensure a smooth transition and allow the work at hand to be accomplished effectively.

The fire service has several inherent characteristics that relate to team building. Probably no other local government service organization recognizes the importance of teamwork better than the fire service. Every fire company knows that suppression requires close coordination of efforts and fire command officers. Using the practices of teamwork in field operations as a foundation, the fire service should naturally accept team building in other areas, including fire department management. On the other hand, the paramilitary nature of the fire service organization, which facilitates teamwork on the emergency scene, also tends to make command officers focus on the *structure* of the organization rather than on its *processes*.

A team-building effort may be as informal as a series of meetings among the people involved. Frequently, however, fire service organizations turn to an external consultant to facilitate more formal team building. It is essential to get outside assistance if the organization has serious problems. The chief may get names of suggested facilitators from other organizations that have undertaken a similar effort. A consultant may then be hired on the basis of a phone interview or, if possible, a personal interview. It is imperative to check references. Characteristics to look for are suggested in the accompanying sidebar.

As a leader, the fire chief can promote team building by example. Forming a team of key fire management personnel that visibly reflects the chief's personal commitment to shared leadership can be a model for others in the department.

Organizations in the fire service

Organizations in the fire service are of three main types—volunteer, combination career/volunteer, and career. These types are discussed in Chapter 17, but a few of their organizational aspects are noted here.

Selecting a consultant Here are some characteristics to look for when selecting a team-building facilitator.

Experience. A consultant with public-sector experience, particularly in the public safety field, will have an immediate understanding of many problems facing your department. Private-sector experience may also be useful, however, as government departments become more "businesslike."

Communication skills. A facilitator must be skilled in two-way verbal and non-verbal communication and must be able to identify and break down barriers to communication.

Open-mindedness. The consultant should not be biased toward any particular organizational style and should not attempt to impose specific changes on the organization, unless the organization requests help in making changes.

Honesty and ethics. The consultant must be trustworthy so that no information about your department will be passed on to other organizations without the consent of those involved.

Track record. The chief should check references to be sure the proposed facilitator meets these criteria and can do the job.

The volunteer organization

The volunteer fire department has been an intricate part of fire protection in the United States for over 300 years. The key to its success seems to be directly related to the ability to manage by effectively recruiting, training, and maintaining volunteer personnel. Although many principles and concepts are relatively similar in career and volunteer organizations, other aspects differ, particularly as they relate to personnel and program management.

Volunteer organizations were built on four basic characteristics: pride, exclusiveness, influence, and competition. The early volunteer organization had a tremendous amount of pride in itself and the service it provided. It was exclusive in that only a select few were allowed to join (normally this was based on an election). It had tremendous influence, particularly in local political issues and elections. Volunteer organizations were in competition with one another primarily because of the number of volunteer companies in many communities and the lack of coordination among them.

The volunteer organization faces many challenges not found, or at least not emphasized, in the career organization. Being volunteer by nature, the organization must spend considerable time and effort in recruiting and maintaining its membership. The recruiting process must become one of "salesmanship." Thus, organizational principles such as hierarchy, unity of command, and span of control are initially placed on the back burner, while human relations and motivation are emphasized. Once individual needs have been met and the volunteer is a part of the organization, then organizational principles are taught and applied.

Managers encounter a number of difficulties in trying to utilize volunteers as the primary delivery system resource. These difficulties typically include availability (particularly during daytime hours), attrition or turnover, lack of available training time, limited availability of potential volunteers, and difficulty in certifying volunteers at higher levels.[15]

The lack of volunteer members presents several challenges. Organizing members into functional companies becomes difficult because of uncertainty about who will be able to respond to various alarms. On the emergency scene, unity of command and span of control become difficult to establish and maintain.

Normally volunteer organizations will use past experience to estimate the approximate number of members who might be expected to respond and will base the emergency scene structure on the expected norm. This task is much different and far more challenging than in an organization that relies on career personnel who are assigned to regular shifts and working hours.

Attrition is another major concern in volunteer organizations. Unlike the career organization, which offers its members extended employment opportunities, the volunteer organization must rely on meeting individual needs not already met in the volunteer's primary place of employment. Thus, the manager must continually develop and utilize methods and techniques designed to satisfy individual and group needs with primary emphasis being placed on the motivational aspects of the job and psychological rather than tangible rewards. Techniques and programs utilized to retain volunteers usually include thorough recruitment processes; quality training and educational opportunities designed to meet the needs of the individual; and a host of motivational techniques, including opportunities to be recognized, rewarded, and challenged within the scope of a volunteer position.

Lack of training time is an additional challenge for volunteer organizations. They are faced with the same expectations concerning types and levels of services as the career organizations; however, volunteer organizations do not have the time to train their personnel in all aspects of the job. Consequently, they must concentrate on the most important skills, with many areas not being covered adequately or at all.

The ability to recruit volunteer members is directly related to the number and availability of persons within the community who are capable of providing needed services, the overall relationship the organization has with the community, and the ability of the organization to systematically attract and recruit new members.

Because of constraints on training time, there seems to be a problem in certifying members at higher levels in programs such as EMS, officer development, driver certification, and fire prevention. Again, the time and levels of training required to accomplish these desired goals cause significant difficulties in volunteer organizations.

Organizational structure in volunteer departments is usually flat with broad areas of responsibilities assumed by persons in chief officer positions. Divisions usually include suppression and emergency medical services; fire prevention and public education; and an administrative division that coordinates other functions and services. Authority and responsibility are maintained at the upper level of the hierarchy for at least two reasons. First, it is often difficult to communicate and coordinate items of concern through several layers of the organization. Second, the time required to follow a multilayered chain of command is slow and cumbersome. Most volunteer organizations try to maintain a structure that provides for maximum flexibility.

Volunteer organizations tend to operate in a more informal manner than do larger career or combination organizations. This approach to managing people and systems seems to work quite well, particularly when dealing with volunteer personnel. It allows the membership to participate at a level that is both acceptable to the organization and comfortable to the individuals involved. This becomes important in meeting the needs of department members.

The combination career/volunteer organization

Combination departments are becoming increasingly common for several reasons. The physical size and population of communities served have grown, placing increased demands on volunteer organizations. In addition, many communities have required increased types and levels of services. This requires significant specialization. Combination departments normally use career staff to provide administrative services and special support services and functions. In addition, the combination department often uses career personnel to provide initial response to fire and medical emergencies. This approach makes it possible to respond rapidly, assess the situation, and implement a plan. The volunteer personnel will back up and fill in areas left vacant, assist in accomplishing the emergency plan established by the career personnel, and provide necessary support services. This approach of providing necessary staffing is widely considered to be the most efficient means of serving communities that need full services but cannot afford to keep a full complement of career personnel on hand for all emergency needs.

Career organizations

Organizations made up entirely of career personnel are normally found in larger urbanized areas with a population, financial base, and call volume that can support a paid department. A career organization usually provides for considerable specialization. A vertical structure is necessary to manage the many programs and activities normally associated with a larger career organization. Areas addressed usually include personnel management, research and development, administration, finance, fire prevention, code enforcement, cause determination and investigation, apparatus and building maintenance, support services, and the typical emergency operations found in other organizations.

Conclusion

In its early days, the fire service was a largely volunteer, suppression-oriented organization based on a military model of management. Today, it is a complex organization that provides diverse services, employs a new mix of personnel, and requires a more flexible management approach. While a paramilitary command structure works effectively for suppression and other emergency functions, it is less appropriate for such programs as public education. This chapter has provided an overview of organization and management principles, explaining their origins in theory, their usefulness in practice, and their application to today's fire service organization.

1   A summary of early organizational theories appears in Robert B. Buchele, *The Management of Business and Public Organizations* (New York: McGraw-Hill, 1977), 4–12.

2   Ibid., 7.

3   James A. F. Stoner, *Management* (Englewood Cliffs, N.J.: Prentice-Hall, 1978), 42–43.

4   Buchele, *Management of Business and Public Organizations*, 10.

5   Michael M. Harmon and Richard T. Mayer, *Organization Theory for Public Administration* (Boston: Little, Brown, 1986), 225–26.

6   Robert B. Denhardt, *Theories of Public Organization* (Monterey, Calif.: Brooks/Cole, 1984), 138, 168.

7   Ibid., 169–73.

8   Kenneth H. Blanchard and Spencer Johnson, *The One-Minute Manager* (New York: Morrow, 1982); Thomas J. Peters and Robert H. Waterman, Jr., *In Search of Excellence* (New York: Harper & Row, 1982).

9   Rosabeth Moss Kanter, *The Change Masters* (New York: Simon & Schuster, 1983), 42–43.

10   Peter F. Drucker, *Management: Tasks, Responsibilities, Practices* (New York: Harper & Row, 1974), 553–56.

11   John R. Schermerhorn, Jr., James G. Hunt, and Richard N. Osborn, *Managing Organizational Behavior* (New York: John Wiley & Sons, 1982), 478–79.

12   Ibid.

13   Felix A. Nigro and Lloyd G. Nigro, *Modern Public Administration* (New York: Harper & Row, 1980), 145.

14   Ibid., 145–46.

15   Jack W. Snook and Dan C. Olsen, *Recruiting, Training, and Maintaining Volunteer Firefighters* (Lake Oswego, Oreg.: Management Development Institute, 1983), 4.

4 Planning for community fire protection

Planning is a basic step in fire protection management. Texts on the subject universally list planning as one of the major management functions, usually the first.[1] Timely and dynamic fire protection planning provides the basis for systematic control of current and future fire risks and efficient and effective use of fire protection resources, thereby limiting fire losses and fire protection costs.

Most fire protection agencies are experiencing escalating demands for fire suppression and fire prevention services, fire safety education, emergency medical services, and hazardous materials control. However, the resources required to provide these services are limited or diminishing. To adequately meet these demands, a community—with the guidance of the fire department—must take the following steps:

1. Identify the nature and extent of the risks it faces

2. Establish the levels of service desired

3. Identify the most efficient and effective use of public and private resources to provide the established service levels

4. Implement a management and evaluation system that ensures the attainment and timely revision of service-level standards.

This chapter describes the planning process that encompasses all these steps as it applies to the community fire protection system. The fire protection system (its components are described in detail in Chapter 2) includes all public and private services that are available to protect people and property from fire. The following components should be included in the planning process:

1. The fire department. It enforces fire safety codes, provides fire safety education, provides rescue and emergency medical services, controls or suppresses fires, provides hazardous materials controls, determines the cause of fires, investigates arson, and supports arson prosecution.

2. The building department. It maintains and enforces building codes, a major factor in the establishment and control of fire risks and fire protection costs.

3. The planning or community development department. It regulates the use of land within a community through land use controls, such as zoning limitations, development density controls, height limitations, open space requirements, transportation systems, and utility system requirements. These factors influence the fire protection risks and the fire protection system requirements of a community. Community general plans, developed and maintained by planning departments, are the primary long-range planning documents for communities.

Portions of this chapter are based on ''Management and Planning for Fire Protection'' by John E. Steen from the 1979 edition of *Managing Fire Services*.

4. The water system. This component is essential to firefighting operations and to automatic sprinkler system design and performance. Fire protection requirements should be a key element in the design and construction of community water systems.

5. The public works or engineering department. This department is responsible for engineering and design related to utility systems, public roads, and traffic signal systems. Traffic circulation patterns, including road width, cul-de-sac length, maximum load capacity of road structures, and other factors affect the fire department's ability to respond to requests for service.

6. The police department. It investigates and assists in prosecution of arson, controls crowds at emergency incidents, reports hazardous conditions, and evacuates persons exposed to fire or hazardous materials risks.

7. The educational system. It plays a role in providing fire safety education. However, only a few schools have adopted a curriculum that requires fire prevention education.

8. Private-sector fire protection, including water companies, fire protection engineering firms, industrial or commercial emergency response teams (fire brigades), fire protection system manufacturers, contractors, and service companies.

9. Regional, state, and national organizations. Community fire protection efforts are frequently supported by regional, state, and national fire protection agencies, such as county fire departments, military fire departments, and state and federal emergency services offices. At the same time, state and federal legislation may place constraints on planning and managing local fire protection via preemption of authority in building code modifications, labor laws (e.g., Fair Labor Standards Act), safety practices, and hazardous materials reporting and control requirements.

An effective community fire protection plan cannot be developed without input from each of these components of the system. All organizations that have a major impact on the fire protection system should be involved so that their appropriate roles can be established and mutually agreed on.

The tangible end result of this planning process is a document, often called a community fire protection master plan. An even more important outcome of this effort should be a dynamic long-term planning process that can adjust to community demographics, land development patterns, and technological changes. This planning process should be integrated into the community management process. It is essential that the fire protection goals and standards that are developed within this plan be integrated into the community general plan.

The ability to project or predict future conditions that will affect the fire protection system is quite limited. Communities are dynamic. Changes with impacts on the fire protection system will occur. Therefore, the plan must be periodically revised and updated through an ongoing planning process that is coordinated with other community planning efforts such as general plan revisions, annual budget preparations, capital improvements programs, and utility system projections. As Peter Drucker has written: "Decisions exist only in the present. The question that faces the long-range planner is not what we should do tomorrow. It is: what do we have to do today to be ready for an uncertain tomorrow?"[2]

The rest of this chapter looks at the plans and planning processes used in the fire service, reviews the reasons for planning, and examines the systems concept in planning. It then presents a detailed examination of the planning process from the initial decision to plan through the process for updating a plan. The central theme is that good management is an essential part of planning. Although elected representatives often are the ones who decide how safe our communities will be by the enactment of the budget, sound policy decisions regarding priorities in expenditure cannot be made without objective and thorough planning, and decisions cannot be carried out as intended without effective, ongoing, professional management. This connection between policy-level decision making and planning and management cannot be emphasized enough.

A basic premise in fire protection planning is that no federal, state, or regional body or private-sector organization has yet developed fire protection standards that a community can adopt to meet its needs. What does exist is a series of laws, fire code standards, empirical data, and nationally recognized good practices that a community can use to determine its own levels of adequate service and acceptable risk. These are the major policy decisions which form the basis of fire protection planning. These actions are taken through the development and adoption of fire protection goals and objectives.

Types of plans

Planning—the creation of plans—is carried out on several levels. For fire protection, three levels might be identified: (1) long-range or master planning, (2) operational planning, and (3) tactical planning.

Long-range planning

Long-range or master planning is concerned with evaluating and changing the fire protection system to meet the needs of a changing environment. It is by nature policy-oriented, long range in time frame, and wide in scope, and it provides the major focus for this chapter. It strives to confront the technical, financial, operational, legal, legislative, and political aspects of fire protection.

Long-range planning is not a new concept. Industry has used it for many years (sometimes under the name of *strategic planning*) in developing and marketing products. Government, particularly the federal government, uses long-range planning, especially in technology-intensive areas such as space exploration. Long-range planning has also been used by the military, especially since World War II, to define the military threat and to define, develop, and acquire systems to protect against that threat. Long-range planning emphasizes anticipating conditions rather than merely reacting to them. In the past, long-range planning was not generally applied to service-oriented organizations, perhaps because the end product is not as visible as, say, a water system or a transit system.

To be useful to the decision maker, long-range planning must perform the following key functions: define the problem(s), identify the solution(s), and provide a scheme or plan by which to implement the solution(s). Since fire protection is a system of independent interacting elements, effective long-range planning has a high potential for improving efficiency and effectiveness.

In the 1970s, the National Fire Prevention and Control Administration (NFPCA; now the U.S. Fire Administration) embarked on a project designed to help local communities prepare fire protection master plans. NFPCA tested master planning procedures in numerous communities and produced several publications on the subject.[3] Subsequently, the master planning process has been used in other communities to develop effective long-range plans.[4]

Operational planning

Operational planning is done to make a system work on a day-to-day basis. It is primarily administrative in nature. It is exemplified by organizational planning, response planning, regional incident command and mutual aid planning, capital improvements planning, and so on. During the 1980s, for example, a great deal of emphasis has been put on general emergency planning for the community, as detailed in Chapter 13. Each of the four phases of emergency planning—mitigation, preparation, response, and recovery—requires continuous operational-level planning.

Tactical planning

Finally, tactical planning is detailed planning that focuses on achieving specific objectives. An example is pre-fire planning. Because of its technical nature, tactical planning is not discussed in detail in this chapter.

The need for planning

Why should a fire department or community expend the resources required to develop a long-range fire protection plan? In many communities, fire protection services are considered adequate by top management and elected officials. They receive fewer complaints about fire protection than any other service, and major fire losses are infrequent. Fire department budget requests often exceed the community's ability or willingness to expend funds, raising the question of whether the department is seeking to provide a level of service greater than that desired by the community. In addition, the community frequently is unaware of the direct and indirect impacts of fire losses.

The planning process can help confront such issues by

1. Establishing levels of service and risk that meet the needs and expectations of the community and fire department
2. Identifying the options and opportunities for controlling fire loss and cost within the public and private sectors
3. Defining fire protection standards that can serve as management criteria.

Public fire protection systems in the United States and Canada have developed in reaction to major fire incidents, with an emphasis on fire suppression. Typically, about 95 percent of paid fire department budgets are devoted to staffing for fire suppression activities. Few general plans contain community fire protection goals that establish acceptable levels of risk and cost for fire services in coordination with other development interests. Communities are frequently planned and constructed with little or no concern for the control of fire losses and fire protection costs, and many structures are built with minimal fire protection features.

For example, building codes are a primary factor in the establishment of fire risks and fire department operating costs. They establish allowable limits for building construction type, occupancy class, area, height, and building separation. Minimal automatic fire suppression systems are required for some construction types and occupancy classes. However, a growing number of cities and counties are enacting regulations that exceed these "minimal" requirements. The characteristics of buildings affect the work load of fire departments during fire fighting operations and prevention activities and consequently play a major role in determining resource requirements and expenditures. However, these fire protection impacts are rarely considered in the planning and development of building codes.

The fire protection elements of building and fire codes are primarily reactions to major fire disasters. For example, panic hardware requirements for public assembly occupancies were adopted only after the 1903 Iroquois Theatre fire in Chicago, Illinois, which resulted in 602 deaths. Flame spread requirements for public assemblages resulted from the Cocoanut Grove nightclub fire in 1942, which caused 492 deaths. Similar examples can be found throughout the codes.

Fire departments have little influence on the adoption and enforcement of "standard" building codes and frequently cope with codes and enforcement procedures that are counterproductive to efficient and effective fire protection. If a community desires to control fire losses and fire protection costs, it must limit the fire risks at the time buildings are constructed by incorporating building code provisions into its planning. Long-range planning emphasizes such prevention and control measures.

The lack of adequate planning and control with respect to new or increased service demands can be seen in the manner in which emergency medical services (EMS) and hazardous materials programs have evolved. These services are usually provided by fire departments, but not without significant organizational and economic impacts. For example, EMS demands can overtax volunteer fire departments owing to the volume of calls. Before such programs are initiated or expanded, a thorough evaluation needs to be performed to define work load and resource requirements and also to consider other methods that may be more efficient and/or effective. An established plan provides a method of conducting such analysis.

Fire protection planning also provides a means of evaluating the potential impacts of increased fire safety education, which is a major untapped resource of fire risk reduction. While some communities have developed effective communitywide fire safety education programs, most have not. A comparison of U.S. fire protection with that of other countries demonstrates the United States has consistently had the worst fire loss record in the world.[5] Although there are many contributing factors, the absence of comprehensive fire safety education stands out as a deficiency of U.S. fire protection in comparison with other industrialized nations.

The systems concept in planning

Systems analysis is a much used, much abused, and often misunderstood term. It has its genesis in the notion that large systems must be viewed as a whole, rather than as a number of integrated components, because these parts interact with a resultant effect on each other and on the system, and also because the system has an effect on the outside world (vice versa).

Systems analysis, in a general form, can be thought of as a closed loop feedback process, as illustrated in Figure 4–1.

The process begins with someone recognizing that a problem exists. This finding is usually expressed in a vague statement such as "We have a problem."

Figure 4–1
Systems analysis.

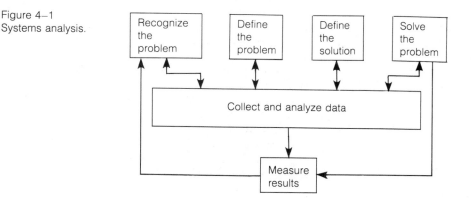

The first thing to do is to define the problem precisely. This may mean collecting and analyzing some pertinent data. Once the problem has been defined, an appropriate solution can be formulated. The next step is to choose an appropriate method of implementing the solution, consistent with the available resources. The preferred solution is then implemented and the results are measured by analyzing data. If the problem is not solved satisfactorily, the process is repeated, with changes in the level and or method of solution until the desired result is obtained. Fire protection master planning, or long-range planning, uses the techniques of systems analysis to determine the existing levels of service and risk provided by the community fire protection system and the concept of goal setting to establish the levels of service and risk desired in the future. (Again, note that there are no absolute requirements, in the legal sense, or in the form of national or regional standards that determine or establish the level of fire protection to be provided by a community.) The techniques of systems analysis are then used to formulate various ways and means of identifying, adopting, and providing the desired level of fire protection. These programs are analyzed and compared, and the best programs are selected. These programs—including an implementation program that defines authority, responsibility, and time frames—are consolidated into a fire protection plan.

The planning process

Long-range planning is a systematic process that has been used successfully in industry, in the military, and in the federal government. It is used in many communities throughout the country, not only for fire protection, but also for law enforcement, utility systems, parks and recreation, and other community services. It is applicable to any type of community—rural, suburban, urban—a county, a region (council of governments), or a state.

Cooperation and commitment

One of the most important ingredients of long-range planning is commitment. Long-range planning by its very nature requires commitment over a long period of time. Commitment is obtained through the cooperative involvement of the many community agencies that participate directly or indirectly in fire protection. The review and approval of interim planning products at various stages in the planning process enhances understanding and commitment. Cooperation is the key to commitment. To be successful, a plan must be understood and accepted by all who are to participate—in fire prevention and control, that is more or less everybody in the community. A plan frequently fails because some person or group was not committed to it, perhaps because of a misunderstanding. This process encourages negotiation and compromise among competing interests and produces a plan that obtains broad support throughout the community. When people are involved in a plan, they will identify with it, support it, and make it work.

It follows that commitment can best be achieved through the cooperation of all community organizations involved in fire protection. These would include the planning, building, and police departments; and in the private sector, merchants' associations, builders' associations, homeowners' groups, and industry representatives. The successful implementation of a plan depends directly on the extent to which the community is involved in developing the plan. The use of a planning team and advisory committee is intended to enhance cooperation and commitment.

Phases and activities

Planning is carried out in three phases or stages: preparation, planning, and implementation (Figure 4–2). Planning and implementation are iterative or repetitive, reflecting the fact that planning never stops, that implementation involves planning, and that planning is part of implementation.

A more detailed picture of the planning process is shown in Figure 4–3, which clarifies the major activities and their relations to each other. Here the iterative nature of the process is more apparent. Briefly, the primary planning activities are the following:

1. Deciding whether to undertake long-range planning
2. If a planning effort is to be undertaken, getting organized for it
3. Collecting and analyzing data to find out what the problems are
4. Defining goals and objectives (i.e., setting standards for service and risks)
5. Defining the programs and resources required to attain goals and objectives
6. Defining alternative programs, where appropriate
7. Comparing alternatives and selecting the best programs
8. Preparing a documented plan to implement and maintain the selected programs
9. Implementing and evaluating the plan (organizing, directing, and controlling)
10. Updating and modifying the plan.

At several points in the process, approvals are needed (see Figure 4–3). Approvals at interim stages of planning are necessary to maintain community awareness and participation and to obtain the commitments necessary to proceed to the next step in the planning process. Approvals of plan elements during the planning process are provided by management personnel, the planning team, or the citizens' advisory committee, as specified in the planning proposal. Final approvals are provided by elected officials.

Deciding whether to plan

The fire protection leadership in the community must make a conscious decision to embark on long-range planning. This is not to be made lightly: To be successful, planning efforts require a great deal of time and resources. In communities of 100,000 or less, one person should spend at least half of his or her time on managing the planning effort. Communities with populations of 100,000 or more should assign at least one person full time if possible.

Personnel time and some resources from other existing programs will be required to successfully complete this project. Furthermore, the climate has to be right before planning can exist in the community, since long-range planning is not necessarily acceptable to everyone. The decision to plan or not to plan should be made after stating and examining the reasons for and against it. Some reasons for planning might be an unacceptable level of fire deaths or property loss, the desire to stabilize or reduce public fire protection costs, the need to reduce duplicated or overlapping fire protection services, a desire to improve joint use of regional resources, or the need to increase fire protection as a result of the community's growth. Some reasons for not planning might be the existence of a satisfactory plan, or satisfaction with the status quo.

The decision to develop a fire protection plan should be outlined in a written proposal and presented to top management within the community (city manager,

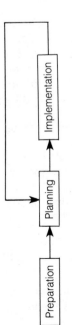

Figure 4–2   The three phases of planning.

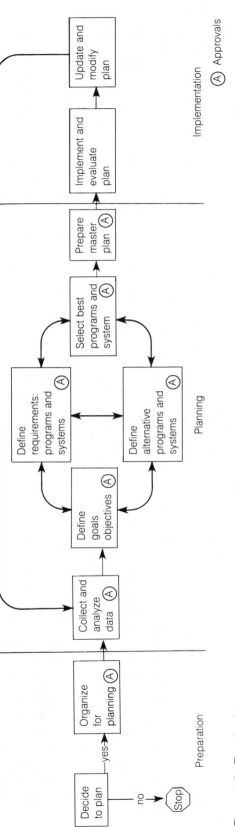

Figure 4–3   The planning process.

county executive officer, etc.). Since there will be substantial economic, political, and policy impacts from this decision, a formal written proposal should be developed for adoption by the elected governing body after it has been approved by top management.

The proposal might contain the following items:

1. A discussion of the need for a fire protection plan, such as high fire loss or anticipated rapid growth
2. The benefits potentially available from a plan, such as increased citizen awareness of fire risks and fire protection, control of fire protection costs and losses, increased private sector participation with resulting reduced public sector costs, improved fire department efficiency and effectiveness, and improved coordination between public agencies
3. Identification of the planning organization, including planning team leadership, membership and functions, advisory committee membership and functions, and the responsibilities of these groups
4. The budget and schedule, with milestones, for the planning work.

Organizing for planning

Once the decision to go ahead with planning has been made, the next step is to get organized. There are many things to do: select a planning leader and team, form an advisory group, and fund and schedule the planning as specified in the planning proposal.

Planning team   The planning team does the planning work. It is composed of a permanent cadre of a few planning and management-oriented professionals, augmented by resource persons as needed. Typical membership includes persons from the fire department, the planning department, the finance department, the building department, and the water department. The team is headed by a planning team leader whose functions are to assign tasks, provide guidance to the team members, coordinate the work, and report progress.

The planning team leader should also serve as the staff liaison with the advisory committee, if one is formed. The team members should be able to make decisions—to commit the group they represent—without having to obtain authorization. In other words, they have responsibility backed up by the requisite authority; this is very important—if it can be obtained. The planning team leader must be given the time and resources to manage this project.

Advisory committee   The advisory committee is an ad hoc group convened especially for the planning effort. It comprises community leaders who collectively provide guidance to the planning team so that the community is represented in the process. Typical membership includes representatives of the following bodies: major industries, the chamber of commerce, local financial institutions, major land developers, private water utilities, civic groups, educational institutions, labor organizations, news media, and similar groups.

Advisory committee members should represent the significant and influential community interests that will be affected by the plan and, like the planning team members, should be persons who are accepted as spokespersons for the groups they represent. Names of committee members should be proposed by the management or leadership of their respective organizations and submitted to the governing body of the community for official appointment to the advisory committee.

The role of the committee should be clearly identified. It should review the findings and proposals of the planning team and then make recommendations to the elected body. The primary function of the advisory committee is to ensure that the needs of a broad spectrum of the community are met by the plan. The advisory committee is intended to provide a forum for the resolution of conflicting interests. The result should be a compromise fire protection plan that has broad community support. The committee should be activated upon completion of the data gathering phase, as that part of the planning effort has proven to be time-consuming. It is important to maintain consistent progress in the planning process, with review and approval conducted in a timely fashion in order to maintain the interest and participation of the advisory committee.

The primary drawback to the use of a citizens advisory committee is the time and resources required to organize, coordinate, and support the deliberations of a committee. Successful master plans have been developed without an advisory committee. In general, however, plans developed with such committees have greater success in dealing with controversial issues and have a high rate of implementation of plan recommendations.

Using consultants Although fire protection planning must be done by those persons and organizations that constitute the fire protection system, fire protection consultants who are experienced in this process can provide technical assistance and serve as a catalyst in this process. If a community is unwilling to relieve a fire officer of a substantial number of his/her duties in order to manage this planning project, it may consider employing a consultant to perform some of the planning organization and coordination tasks.

Collecting and analyzing data

As soon as the proposal has been approved and the team has been authorized to proceed (in the form of a resolution by the governing body), the team starts the actual planning phase. The initial step is to collect and analyze data to determine the risks and problems. (For a detailed discussion of data collection and analysis, see Chapters 5 and 6.)

Data should be developed that identify the current and future fire protection risks, service demands (including EMS and hazmat) fire protection capabilities, financial requirements and revenues, and legal constraints. There is a tendency in this process to collect too much data or data that are ''nice to know'' but are not useful to planning. A good procedure to follow is to identify how each piece of information is used and what decisions will be made. If those questions cannot be clearly answered—don't collect the data.

The accuracy and thoroughness of the plan to be developed will depend on the quality of the data collected. This will be most evident later, when the time comes to measure progress toward the objectives that have been established for the implementation of the plan. In order to evaluate the results, it is important that the data be accurate and quantifiable. Most communities, however, discover that the available data are not adequate to support the planning process at the depth of analysis desired. The available information is frequently found to be incomplete, inaccurate, or in a form that is not readily usable in the planning process. Communities are therefore frequently forced to conduct the planning effort with incomplete data or stop the planning process while all efforts are put into data gathering.

If management decides to proceed with incomplete data, the planning team and advisory committee should review and approve this decision. It is acceptable to conduct planning with some incomplete data if the limitations are understood. However, this should be accompanied by a recommendation that an improved management information system be implemented as part of the plan.

If management decides to delay planning until *all* data are collected in the desired format, the planning process may be permanently postponed. Also if a major data-gathering effort is conducted without providing for the maintenance of the data (usually a computerized management information system) the same data-gathering effort may have to be carried out every year to measure the results of the implementation of the plan.

Experience has shown that it is more effective to proceed with some incomplete data than to delay the planning until *all* needed data are available. Again, this recommendation is based on the assumption that an improved management information system will be one of the outcomes of the plan.

Categories of data   The data required will probably fall into six general categories: demographic, geographic and physical, building and occupancy, organizational and functional (including fire incidence and loss, and EMS and other non–fire incident activities), financial, and legislative and legal. Specific data items can be identified within each of these categories. The subsequent analysis and planning cannot proceed without data on what has happened, what is happening, and what will probably happen. Insights into the future can be obtained from the historical and current data.

Demographic data   Demographic data can be related to fire incidence and emergency medical services. For example, U.S. Fire Administration studies indicate that age, sex, income level, ethnic background, educational level, and neighborhood can be correlated to fire incidence and loss.[6]

Geographic and physical data   The geography and physical characteristics of a community identify its existing and projected boundaries. These have a bearing on fire station locations, response times, and service demands, as do transportation networks, water systems, terrain and weather. Where brush or timber fires are a factor, the risk of the vegetation and climatic conditions should be identified. Natural disasters such as earthquakes, tornados, and floods influence emergency and rescue services and fireground operations.

Building and occupancy data   For most communities, the major fire risks result from and occur in the "built" environment (that is, in existing structures and occupancies). For this reason it is important to collect building and occupancy data that include the classification and location of occupancies, number of occupancies protected by alarm systems and sprinklers, age of buildings, and heights and areas of buildings. The relative fire risk of structures is frequently stated in terms of fire flow requirements, which identify a firefighting work load based upon building size, construction type, occupancy classification, height, fire resistance of roofing, building separation, and credits for automatic sprinkler systems. Corresponding fire department resources required to deliver this fire flow can be quantified.[7]

The types and densities of structures and occupancies that are allowed in the community's zoning ordinances also determine the current and future fire protection needs of the community.

Organizational and functional data   Data must be obtained on work loads in order to assess the allocation of current and future resources. These should cover fire prevention, pre-fire planning, and suppression activities; non–fire incident services; training activities; facilities and equipment maintenance; and public education. Where possible, work loads should be identified by personnel hours devoted to programs. The personnel hours should indicate the title of personnel assigned.

Fire prevention program data should identify the number and types of occupancies inspected, hazards found and corrected, fire safety education programs conducted and persons contacted, numbers and types of fire investigations, personnel time requirements by type of activity, suppression division resource allocations and activities in fire prevention, the measure of successful performance related to fire prevention programs (i.e., standard inspection frequencies, plan check "turnaround time," maximum allowable time for hazard correction), and citation program description.

Fire suppression data should include the numbers and types of incidents that occur by occupancy type and area of the community (these are most useful when expressed as rates); injuries and fatalities to citizens and firefighters; response times and distances (for first-due apparatus and full assignments); resource commitment to incidents (personnel hours and apparatus); mutual and automatic aid agreements, mutual aid resources available and frequency of mutual aid activity; communications system capabilities and equipment; and incident command system description.

The planning team also needs data on non–fire incident services such as emergency medical services and hazardous materials control. In many jurisdictions, emergency medical service responses account for the greatest proportion of the emergency service activities of the fire department. The extent to which a fire department is involved in these activities has major economic, political, and organizational implications. Data that accurately define these factors are essential to long-range community fire protection planning.

Training program data should include training and certification requirements for employment and promotion, records of skill maintenance training by task and personnel hours, career development training; and a physical fitness program description.

A facilities inventory should include the location, size, and age of fire stations and other facilities. A description of the adequacy of the facilities and projected relocations should be included.

Data related to fire apparatus and equipment should include an inventory of the number of vehicles by type, capacity, age, and general operating condition. Schedule replacement and maintenance programs should be defined. Records of maintenance costs and downtime should be provided.

The planning effort should also include data on fire protection functions that are or should be performed by other agencies, public and private.

Financial data Among the financial data required to conduct long-range planning are current and projected costs, current and projected revenues, limitations on revenues and expenditures, and optional revenue sources.

Operating and capital expenditures for the fire department for the past five years should be provided to assess current expenditure levels and to project future cost trends. In addition, in order to determine the *total cost* of providing fire protection services, expenditures incurred by other departments must also be considered. For example, certain expenditures by the water department (such as expenditures for water storage tank capacity and water pumps) directly or indirectly support fire protection, and certain expenditures by the police department (such as expenditures for traffic control and riot control) also support fire protection. The following are some other examples of cost data:

1. Operating budgets of community departments with expenditures related to fire protection (i.e., fire hydrant testing, maintenance, and repair by the water department)
2. Capital improvement budgets of other departments for items related to fire protection (water mains and fire hydrants, for example)
3. Private expenditures for fire protection (i.e., general costs of sprinkler installation and maintenance, alarm systems installation, maintenance, and operation, industrial fire brigades, rescue and ambulance services, and hospital emergency care and burn centers).

Data on current and projected revenues come from the operating budget, public revenues available by category (i.e., taxes, fees, grants, bond issues, and revenue projections related to future growth and/or redevelopment). Optional revenue sources, both actual and potential, also should be identified.

These include fees for service, augmented fire service availability fees, permit fees, fines related to citations, environmental impact report fire protection mitigation requirements, special district assessment revenue, and property tax increases for fire protection. Limitations on revenues include state-mandated tax or expenditure limitations, legal restrictions on use of funds, legal restrictions on collection of fees, and limits on bond indebtedness.

Legislative and legal data Many legislative acts and legal decisions affect the provision of fire protection, and an informed planner needs to keep in touch with these developments at the local, state, and federal levels. The data should include current legal decisions and legislation, and projected future actions. Examples of such data are Fair Labor Standards Act provisions and enforcement, hazardous materials transportation regulations, affirmative action plans, state fire marshal regulations, OSHA safety regulations for personnel, state emergency medical and rescue service regulations, and building or fire code provisions. Preemption of local authority to adopt and enforce safety requirements should be noted.

Sources of data When the required data are identified, the possible sources should be identified as well. Data will be obtained from sources both within and outside the community. Local sources include city departments (fire, planning, building, water, finance, public works, the administrative office, school administration, the attorney's office, the clerk's office), commercial businesses and organizations (insurance companies, merchants' associations), and industry. Other sources include county agencies, regional agencies (such as councils of governments and regional planning organizations), state agencies, and federal agencies.[8] A matrix of data required together with potential sources can be constructed. Figure 4–4 shows a simple example of this, and Chapters 5 and 6 outline further sources of data.

In addition to obtaining data from traditional sources, planners may need to collect some original data. For example, fire loss and incidence data may be obtained from fire department reports and insurance records—but these traditional sources will not indicate unreported fires or losses not covered by in-

Data source	Demographic	Geographic	Building and occupancy	Organizational and functional	Financial	Legislative
Fire department			X	X	X	X
Planning department	X	X	X	X	X	X
Building department			X	X	X	X
Water department			X	X	X	X
Finance department				X	X	X
Public works department		X		X	X	X
Administrative office	X	X		X	X	X
School administration	X			X	X	X
Attorney's office				X	X	X
Clerk's office	X	X		X	X	X
Commerce				X	X	
Industry				X	X	
County agencies	X		X	X	X	X
Regional agencies	X			X	X	X
State agencies	X			X	X	X
Federal agencies	X				X	X

Figure 4–4 Data required and sources of data.

surance. To complete the loss/incidence data, a survey of homeowners and businesses might be conducted. The survey could be carried out by mail (in water bills, for example), by telephone, or in person. Such a survey could be instituted on an annual basis and would ask respondents to evaluate community service expectations and the extent to which those expectations are being met.

Collection methods   When the data required and data sources are known, the data collection assignments should be made. Data collection will be performed primarily by the members of the planning team. As good a match as possible should be made between the collector and the source: For example, someone who is credible and known to the insurance industry will have a much better chance of obtaining insurance premium data than someone who is not. One person should be assigned to coordinate data gathering to ensure that information is complete, appropriate, and accurate.

Some persons or businesses may be reluctant to supply the data. In those cases, extra time will have to be spent on explaining the purpose of the project and use of the data, particularly to the private sector, as it is more likely to be reticent about supplying data. Confidentiality of data is all-important. Each data collector should be prepared to explain the data needed and how the data will and will not be used; the desired format should also be explained, and assurance given that confidentiality will be maintained.

There are many means of collecting the data; those employed will depend on the particular data desired. Building and occupancy data, for example, can be collected from building department records, fire inspection records, planning department zoning maps, county assessors' data, utility company records, and special surveys of the pre-fire plans of the fire department.

Previous planning reports conducted by local or regional agencies can provide valuable data. These include transportation system studies, utility system studies, and regional population and economic growth studies. Projections of future growth and development are particularly difficult. The local planning director can identify the best source of development projections. Fire departments should not attempt to develop such projections but should rely on the projections being used by other governmental agencies, especially the local planning departments.[9]

The data should be assembled as a report and displayed in graphic and tabular forms, where possible. Examples of the graphic display of information are shown in Chapter 6.

Analyzing data   When sufficient data are available, the next step is to organize and analyze the data to define the current status of the fire protection system—risk conditions and performance—and to identify existing or future problems.

Criteria for useful data   The analysis should be both quantitative and qualitative. Some questions that should be answered are

1. Do the data clearly and accurately specify conditions and problems?
2. Will the data selected enable managers to measure results (i.e., to determine when desired conditions or problem resolutions are attained)?
3. Do management personnel within the fire protection system and the advisory committee agree that the data are acceptable measures of results?
4. Can the data be readily maintained and updated to meet planning and management needs throughout the anticipated life of the plan?

After this analysis it may be necessary to conduct additional data gathering or to delete certain data. Two key points regarding the data gathering and analysis should be kept in mind:

1. These data will be the criteria used to choose the "best" programs.
2. These data will form the basis for measuring performance and the subsequent results.

Defining the situation   Fire risk and protection can be analyzed in several ways. One is to make a statistical summary of the structures and other risks in the planning area, including, for example, the distribution of building construction (type, area, and height), occupancy classification, and fire flow required. Such a summary will give a picture of what there is to burn and how it will change with time in the future (i.e., the fire risk).

A second method of analysis would be to summarize the fire and emergency medical response history within the community. For fire, such a summary might include, for each year, total responses, actual fires per 1,000 population, fires by type, fires by time of day, fires by occupancy, fires by source, fires by type and form of material, fires by ignition factor, civilian deaths by age and by cause, firefighter deaths by cause, civilian and firefighter injuries by type. Other information that might be included is property loss by occupancy and total property loss as well as the rate or percentage of incidents by type. For emergency medical services, useful data would be the number of responses by area of community, type of EMS calls, response times, types of service provided (basic life support or advanced life support). These fire and EMS histories can be extrapolated to the end of the planning period to obtain a projection of the fire and EMS experience for the near future.

A third means of analysis employs scenarios. A fire scenario is a sequential listing of the events and circumstances resulting in a loss, injury, or fatality. It can be used to link the type of loss with the events of a fire and to provide a description of the many elements of the fire problem in a concise form that is easy to comprehend.

Losses from fire are a direct result of a sequence of events embedded in a set of circumstances. If the chain of events should be broken or the circumstances altered, the end result—a loss—could be averted. Greater knowledge of the events and circumstances and of their causal relationships could help to prevent loss by indicating where to intervene in the chain of events or how to modify the circumstances.

The losses, events, and circumstances can be grouped into six categories: type of loss, type of occupancy, time of day, ignition source, item ignited, and direct cause of loss. Major constituent elements of each category can then be defined. (Figure 4–5 is an example of such a grouping.) A scenario can then

Type of loss	Type of occupancy	Time of day	Ignition source	Item ignited	Direct cause of loss
1. Death	1. Industrial	1. Day	1. Friction	1. Flammable fluids/gases	1. Smoke/gas
2. Injury	2. Commercial	2. Night	2. Flame	2. Furnishings	2. Heat/flame
3. Property	3. Public assembly		3. Matches/lighters	3. Structure	
	4. Institutional		4. Smoking material	4. Interior finish	
	5. Transportation		5. Electrical equipment	5. Apparel	
	6. Residential		6. Electrical wiring	6. Other	
	7. Independent of occupancy		7. Heating/cooking surface		
			8. Spontaneous		
			9. Arson		
			10. Other		

Figure 4–5   Fire scenario elements.

be formed by linking the elements, using one from each category (for example, death–residential–night–smoking–furnishings–smoke and gas.)

This scenario indicates that death occurs directly from smoke and gas emitted from burning furnishings, such as a mattress or a blanket, which were ignited by smoking materials, perhaps a cigarette that was carelessly handled, at night in a residence. It might be pointed out that this sequence of events, or scenario, represents perhaps the most common cause of fire-related death.

In general, the data needed to perform fire scenario analysis are obtained from fire incidence reports, which should contain the following information for each fire incident:

1.   The occupancy identification
2.   The time of day of the fire occurrence
3.   The source of ignition
4.   The spreading agent (item ignited)
5.   The direct cause of loss
6.   The loss(es).

Scenarios are by no means arbitrarily generated. They are derived by ranking fire incident data as follows:

1.   Losses ranked in order of frequency
2.   Occupancies ranked in order of frequency of each of the losses (death, injury, property)
3.   Time of day ranked in order of frequency for each occupancy
4.   Ignition source ranked in order of frequency for each time of day
5.   Item ignited ranked in order of frequency for each ignition source
6.   Direct cause of loss ranked in order of frequency for each item ignited.

Scenarios give a good idea of the causes of fire losses and the relative importance of these causes. This information can be used to devise intervention strategies such as educational programs, automatic suppression devices, and early warning devices, which would break the scenario chain of events and would thus prevent or reduce the loss. These events can be the subjects requiring action that have been identified as goals and objectives.

In order to use the scenario process effectively, a department needs an accurate data base containing a significant number of incidents. Fire departments that experience a low volume of incidents can use regional or statewide fire incident data where available. If data are unavailable, a department can develop a generalized scenario and identify effective intervention actions. Figure 4–6, for example, is a generalized scenario that indicates fire growth to flashover as compared with fire suppression response elements. The significant intervention is the activation of an automatic sprinkler system. These generalized scenarios are best displayed graphically rather than statistically. The result of this analysis should be a comparison of the fire control resources and fire risks as compared with current and projected fire protection resource capabilities.

Other methods of analysis that can contribute to planning are described in Chapter 6. They include detailed evaluations of comparative service levels and fire attack capabilities.

Defining goals and objectives

The next major step is to define goals and objectives that identify the purposes and results desired of the fire protection system. Together, goals and objectives establish the level of service to be provided in the community. The goals are policy statements of organizational purpose or intent. They describe ends toward which the department is working. Objectives, on the other hand, are specific interim results that are expected within a given time; in this sense they are

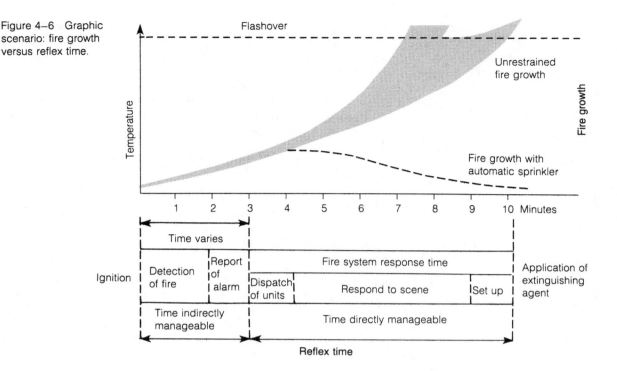

Figure 4–6 Graphic scenario: fire growth versus reflex time.

milestones. Goals and objectives should address the current status of fire and emergency medical services and outline measurable increments of change toward the desired status. Each time an objective is achieved, the level of service moves closer to a given goal. Goals and objectives should be as independent of the means of accomplishment as possible; they should state what to do, not how to do it. The "how" is addressed later in programs.

Mission statement The goals and objectives that come out of the planning process need to relate directly to the mission of the organization. If the department does not have a formal mission statement, the planning process is a good time to formulate one. The mission statement can be compared to the top of a pyramid—it is the capstone of the organization (see Figure 4–7). It states why the fire service delivery system exists and provides a structure for all of

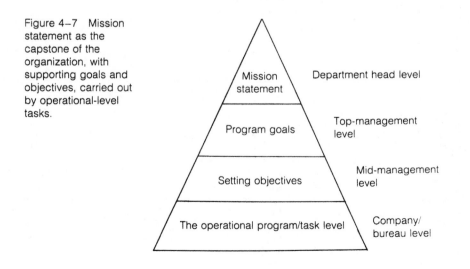

Figure 4–7 Mission statement as the capstone of the organization, with supporting goals and objectives, carried out by operational-level tasks.

the department's goals and objectives. It should look at the needs of the community as well. An example of a mission statement appears in Figure 10–2. Note that a mission statement should be closely linked with the enabling legislation that forms the overall organization.

Goals Fire protection goals define the levels of service and acceptable risks that meet the unique needs of a community. They form the basis for fire protection "standards," which are established as objectives. Here are some sample goals:

1. Provide adequate fire protection at acceptable cost
2. Reduce fire risks
3. Control fire losses
4. Achieve fire safety awareness at all levels of the community
5. Provide emergency medical life support services
6. Provide hazardous materials control services
7. Reduce overlapping services.

The fire protection system consists of subsystems, the goals of which may be in conflict. For example, the building department may prefer to modify building codes by submitting proposed changes to national building code organizations, whereas the fire department may consider local modifications to be more timely and effective. Resolving such conflicts is one of the primary purposes of the planning team and advisory committee reviews, deliberations, and recommendations.

Public fire protection policy is established when the elected body approves and adopts the goals. Although details of a plan are not normally reviewed with the elected officials during the development phase, a study session to review proposed goals would be an appropriate method of providing guidance to the planning team, since future steps in the planning will be based on the basic policies defined by these goals.

Objectives After goals have been tentatively adopted, the next step is to develop the objectives, which are then reviewed and approved by the advisory committee. Objectives define the standards for community fire protection (i.e., the levels of service) and are used to measure progress toward the attainment of goals. Objectives are used to develop specific fire protection system programs and resource requirements, to evaluate alternative programs and ultimately select the "best," and to evaluate the efficiency and effectiveness of programs that have been implemented. Guidelines for setting objectives appear in Figure 4–8. At least one objective should be developed for each goal. Here are some sample objectives:

1. The first-due engine will arrive within five minutes at 95 percent of the fire incidents.
2. All firefighters will attain and maintain Emergency Medical Technician certification with eighteen months.

Figure 4–8 Guidelines for setting objectives.

1. An objective should be consistent with authoritative goals (local government and fire department policy, charter provisions, and so on).
2. An objective should be stated in behavioral terms, as a guide to action. That is, it should clearly describe desired, observable results.
3. An objective should have intermediate targets and a specific completion date—in terms of the budget year or other time schedule.
4. An objective should include specific performance criteria, such as how many, what percent, which site, personnel levels, and costs.
5. An objective should be both challenging and attainable.

3. All hospitals and rest homes will be inspected semiannually by the fire prevention bureau.
4. A fire safety education program will be provided to all school-age children annually.
5. All apparatus shall receive a six-month preventive maintenance inspection, and no apparatus failures will result from a lack of preventive maintenance.

The accompanying sidebar gives examples of goals and corresponding objectives for the EMS component of a fire department plan.

Defining programs and resources required

After goals and objectives are set, planners need to determine what programs and resources are required to attain them. They need to answer the following questions:

1. What must be done to attain the objectives?
2. How will it be done?
3. When will it be done?
4. Who will do it (identified authority and responsibility)?
5. What resources (personnel, apparatus, materials, legislation, codes, etc.) are needed?

The programs proposed must meet the requirements of each objective. One program may provide the requirements for more than one objective.

Defining alternative programs

Often it is desirable to propose several possible ways to achieve a given objective. Each set of alternatives will be analyzed and the "best" program selected. A word of caution is in order here, however. While classical planning doctrine requires that two or more alternative programs be developed for each objective, attempts to do this can overwhelm and stall the planning effort. Develop alternative programs only when there are viable alternatives.

For example, here are alternatives to accomplish two objectives:

1. *Objective:* Inspect all commercial occupancies annually.
   a) Alternative 1: All inspections will be performed by fire prevention personnel.
   b) Alternative 2: Thirty percent of inspections will be performed by fire prevention personnel and 70 percent by suppression division personnel.
2. *Objective:* All fire apparatus shall recieve preventive maintenance inspections every six months.
   a) Alternative 1: Preventive maintenance will be performed by city shops.
   b) Alternative 2: Preventive maintenance will be performed by a qualified apparatus manufacturer.

The planning team then discusses alternatives to determine which ones are viable and deserve further analysis. The results should be reviewed with the advisory committee.

The planning team may be directed to evaluate major system alternatives as options (e.g., police-fire consolidation, contract fire protection, civilianization of certain divisions or positions, joint service agreements, volunteer/career staffing, and so on). These alternatives, which are discussed in detail in Chapter 17, can be evaluated effectively and unemotionally if the goals and objectives accurately and specifically define service level standards. It is recommended that a guideline be established that requires a proposed alternative system to meet *all* goals and objectives. It has frequently been found that some of the most controversial systems are able to meet documented goals and objectives only after major revisions to the basic concept.

EMS goals and objectives   For the fire department planning the development of an EMS component the following goals and objectives might be typical:

Goal I: Provide first-response and basic life support services in cases of medical emergency

Objectives:

1. Develop operational policies in co-ordination with hospital, medical director, police agencies, and ambulance services, by (*date*)
2. Design, purchase, and install radio and telephone communications equipment to permit public access to emergency medical services and to permit coordination between EMTs, public safety agencies, ambulance services and hospitals, by (*date*)
3. Equip designated apparatus and rescue vehicles with basic life support equipment and supplies, by (*date*)
4. Modify department training programs to provide continuing education of EMTs and maintenance of basic life support skills, by (*date*)
5. Train [*number to be inserted*] firefighters to level of EMT, by (*date*)
6. Initiate service, by (*date*).

Goal II: Provide advanced life support services and emergency ambulance transportation in cases of life-threatening medical emergency

Objectives:

1. Establish contractual relationship with medical control hospital for training of [*number to be inserted*] personnel as mobile intensive care paramedics and for continuing education, skill maintenance, and medical control functions, by (*date*)

2. Establish selection criteria and solicit paramedic training applications from among personnel previously trained to EMT level, by (*date*)
3. In coordination with medical control hospital, establish commencement date for paramedic training and arrange for appropriate staffing to replace personnel assigned to training program, by (*date*)
4. Establish specifications for mobile intensive care vehicles, equipment, and communications hardware and commence purchasing procedures, by (*date*)
5. Initiate paramedic training program, by (*date*)
6. Develop operational policies in co-ordination with medical control hospital, medical director, police agencies, and ambulance services, by (*date*)
7. Conduct community public education/orientation program in preparation for initiation of mobile intensive care service, by (*date*)
8. Take delivery of vehicles, equipment, and communications hardware and prepare for service, by (*date*)
9. In coordination with medical control hospital, medical director, and appropriate health-related agencies, prepare reporting instruments and procedures to facilitate ongoing evaluation of mobile intensive care program, by (*date*)
10. Conduct paramedic graduation exercises and initiate service, by (*date*).

The foregoing goals and objectives are not intended as a complete list of planning considerations for the respective programs; they merely illustrate the distinction between generalized goals and specific objectives.

At this point the viability of those alternatives would be identified and documented for analysis in the next task. Programs and program alternatives are reviewed and approved by the advisory committee.

Comparing alternatives and selecting the best programs

The planning team then analyzes the alternatives that have been identified and selects the ones that members believe will work best as components of the community's fire protection system. Alternatives should be judged against the quantifiable elements of the objectives as the selection criteria if at all possible. In some instances, however, qualitative analysis will be required. The results of this analysis also should be reviewed and approved by the advisory committee.

Preparing a documented plan

The planning document is prepared using the programs and/or systems selected in the previous step. The document should contain the following:

1. An executive summary, giving the highlights of the plan
2. A description of the reasons for conducting the plan, including a summary of the data analysis (a complete listing of data collected may be provided in an accompanying document)
3. A description of the planning organization, including acknowledgment of contributions to the planning effort, especially those of citizens, public agencies, and private sector organizations
4. Goals and objectives for the fire protection system
5. Requirements for achieving the goals and objectives
6. A summary of the alternatives and a description of the programs and systems selected
7. An implementation plan that specifically identifies the time schedule and management responsibility for the implementation of the programs
8. A budget for the forthcoming fiscal year
9. A long-range capital improvements plan
10. A community general plan element that incorporates the appropriate goals and objectives of the fire protection plan into the community general plan
11. Ordinances for adoption or modification of building/fire codes, zoning changes, fee schedules, and so on
12. A schedule for the periodic evaluation and revision of the plan and programs.

Implementing and evaluating the plan

The first step in the implementation phase is to have the plan approved by the governing body. The governing body should schedule study sessions and/or public hearings at which the community management personnel, the planning team leader and the advisory committee present the completed plan. The governing body will generally take the following actions:

1. Approve and adopt the plan in concept (this document is too large and dynamic to be formally approved and codified)
2. Approve annual budget
3. Approve capital improvements schedule
4. Approve revision of community general plan
5. Approve revised codes and ordinances.

After approval, the managers of the various departments and community agencies implement the plan as they assign program responsibility, establish resource allocation plans, and monitor the progress of programs that are part of the plan. Specific day-to-day management techniques are covered in other chapters.

An integral part of implementation is evaluating the results. Reporting and evaluation procedures should be established to ensure that the intended results of the plan are achieved. These evaluations should be conducted on a schedule to coincide with other reporting—for example, monthly activity reports, annual reports, and scheduled expenditure analysis. Again, it should be noted that most fire departments need to upgrade their management information systems to effectively monitor and evaluate the implementation of a long-range plan.

Updating and modifying the plan

The plan should be designed to respond to changing conditions in the community. It should be modified if projected or unexpected changes occur that affect the fire protection system or if the programs that have been selected as part of the plan are not producing the desired results (goals and objectives). These plan updates should become a part of ongoing management activities (i.e., annual budget preparations, capital improvements plan revisions, general plan amendments, and building/fire code revisions).

Some communities retain the advisory committee or planning team to review progress toward goals and to recommend plan modifications, but most find it preferable to integrate this process into the normal management functions of the organization.

The outlook

What trends in fire protection will affect the planning efforts of local communities? Perhaps the forecast might be:

1. Fire protection will focus less on suppression as a result of increased fire prevention activities.
2. Increased installation of automatic fire detection and suppression systems will continue to reduce fire losses.
3. Fire protection responsibility will continue to shift to the private sector.
4. The emergency medical service demands will continue to be a significant part of the fire protection system.
5. Fire departments will be expected to provide increased services in hazardous materials incident prevention and control.
6. Planning—along with organizing, implementing, and measuring—will continue to change the technician role of the fire service manager. He or she will increasingly need to assess future possibilities and plan to meet them rather than react to changes as they occur. An important criterion in assessing the effectiveness of the fire department will be the ability to manage change and innovation (see Chapter 16).
7. Funding for fire protection will continue to be limited. Reductions in available "public safety" funding will result from limited public financing and increased competition for the public safety dollar.

The need for long-range planning is evident and the methodology is available. Whether it can help solve some of the problems of providing fire protection will undoubtedly depend on how public-sector managers perceive the benefits and costs of initiating and implementing planning. There are definite costs or disincentives to planning. Foremost is the consideration that the planning should be participatory—that is, that planning is best done by the community, not by a small group in the fire department or by an outside consultant. Only through community participation, however, will the commitment and cooperation be forthcoming to support the programs in the plan. Many of the cities that have performed fire protection planning have discovered that the *process* of planning was as important as the end product. In many instances the planning project provided a unique opportunity for an interdisciplinary effort toward a common goal. The experience of working with members of other departments and with citizens gave fire department members a new perspective, which was just as important as the plan.

Another disincentive is a lack of planning expertise and experience. Many communities, especially small ones, feel that they have no personnel with sufficient planning and management abilities to lead or participate in a major planning project. A number of options are available to communities to meet this need:

1. Master planning guides developed by the U.S. Fire Administration contain procedures that may be used by any fire department or government official. These guides went out of print but are still valid if they can be obtained from a library or another source.
2. Training courses in planning procedures are available through some state fire academies.
3. A member of a local or regional planning agency may be recruited to serve on the planning team to provide expertise in planning methods.
4. Consultants with fire protection planning experience are available to provide assistance.

1 For example, Michael J. Jucius and William E. Schlender, *Elements of Managerial Action* (Homewood, Ill: Richard D. Irwin, 1965), 4–5, Peter F. Drucker, *Management: Tasks, Responsibilities, Practices* (New York: Harper & Row, 1974), 121–22; and Robert C. Ford and Cherrill Heaton, *Principles of Management* (Reston, Va.: Reston Publishing Company, 1980), 19.

2 Peter F. Drucker, *Technology, Management & Society* (New York: Harper & Row, 1970), 131.

3 National Fire Prevention and Control Administration, National Fire Safety and Research Office, *Urban Guide for Fire Prevention and Control Master Planning* (Washington, D.C.: Government Printing Office, 1977 and *A Basic Guide for Fire Prevention and Control Master Planning* (Washington, D.C.: Government Printing Office, 1977).

4 The U.S. Fire Administration lists 91 communities that contacted the administration for technical support and developed master planning documents. In addition, the following agencies are known to the author to have developed community fire protection master plans using the process developed in this chapter: Auburn, Washington, 1982; California State Fire Marshal, 1986; Clark County No. 5, Washington, 1985; Contra Costa County, California, 1981; Cowlitz County No. 2, Washington, 1983; El Segundo, California, 1983; Fresno County, California, 1981; Gig Harbor, Washington, 1984; Hanford, California, 1985; King County Fire District No. 20, 1979; Lake Tapps, Washington, 1985; Livermore, California, 1984; Morgan Hill, California, 1986; Palm Coast, Florida, 1985; Pleasanton, California, 1982; Sierra Vista, Arizona, 1985; and Vancouver, Washington, 1985.

5 See, for example, Philip S. Schaenman and Edward F. Seits, *International Concepts in Fire Protection: Practices from Japan, Hong Kong, Australia, and New Zealand* (Arlington, Va.: TriData, 1985); and Philip S. Schaenman, *International Concepts in Fire Protection: Ideas from Europe That Could Improve U.S. Fire Safety* (Arlington, Va.: TriData, 1982).

6 See, for example: National Fire Prevention and Control Administration, *The Human Factor in High Fire Risk Urban Neighborhoods: A Pilot Study in New Orleans, Louisiana* (Washington, D.C., 1976); *Highlights of the National Household Fire Survey* (Washington, D.C., n.d.); and *Fire Education Planning* (Washington, D.C., 1977).

7 National Fire Prevention and Control Administration, *Urban Guide for Fire Prevention and Control Master Planning*, appendices V and VI.

8 See, for example, National Fire Incident Reporting System (NFIRS), developed by the National Fire Prevention and Control Administration; the Uniform Fire Incident Reporting System (UFIRS), developed by the National Fire Protection Association; the California Fire Incident Reporting System (CFIRS); the Fire Incident Reporting and Evaluation System (FIRES), developed and used by the California cities of Huntington Beach, Seal Beach, Fountain Valley, and Westminster; and the Field Incident Reporting System (FIRS), developed by the Los Angeles Fire Department in the early 1960s.

9 A good reference on techniques of data gathering is: Carl V. Patton, "Information for Planning," in *The Practice of Local Government Planning*, ed. Frank S. So and Judith Getzels, 2d ed. (Washington, D.C.: International City Management Association, 1988).

5 Evaluating community fire protection

The current status of a community's ability to protect itself from fire is usually a top concern of professional managers, elected officials, and fire chiefs. Even when a serious fire has not occurred, this is often a pressing issue. It is always an urgent matter following a serious fire or other disaster that is considered the fire department's responsibility. To learn "where we stand," officials must evaluate the community's ability to protect itself against fires. Any kind of long-range or master planning requires that information as well.

To almost all lay people and to many fire officers, obtaining an orderly and comprehensive view of fire protection capabilities is a confusing task. What should be measured? How should it be measured? What is an adequate level of protection? Such questions appear difficult to answer, and the work involved in obtaining the answers often seems to exceed local capability.

In many communities, however, all or almost all of what is needed for a sound evaluation is at hand or readily available. It is often the case that local staff can collect the necessary data, arrange those data to illustrate the answers to key questions, and even interpret the answers so that they are most useful for local planning.

Outside assistance also can be helpful, of course, especially if local groups disagree over an issue and neutral outsiders can provide documented answers acceptable to all. Some communities, of course, prefer to use outsiders for individual projects and use local staff time for regular activities.

Whatever the background, the most useful evaluation reports involve local staff heavily. The judgments of outsiders, no matter how expert, seem more valid if extensive local input is used in formulating them.

The need for evaluation

Evaluation and planning (see Chapter 4) are interwoven, and each function is an extension of the other. Indeed, both must be ongoing if the community is to remain healthy. Of course, evaluation, like planning, is a *process*, and its value lies at least as much in its own activities as in the resulting document—the evaluation report or plan. Documents such as reports and plans tend to have short-term validity and usefulness. The process that has people discussing community safety goals typically has more value, but only if the process continues on an annual basis. It is sometimes said that the value of evaluation and planning is that these processes encourage people who typically don't talk together to communicate along common lines.

What makes community officials sense that an evaluation of fire protection is needed? There are many reasons, some more common than others. For example, a change in administration, especially when accompanied by charges of overspending, incompetence, laxity, or favoritism, will usually precipitate a move to change the fire department. Ideally, this is preceded by an objective evaluation.

Often, changes at the top level of fire department administration (or at the level of the fire marshal) also lead to an evaluation. Naturally, those newly arrived at the top positions may already have formulated their action plans. An objective and thorough evaluation of fire protection at the time will prove to the citizenry that the new official or officer has their best interests at heart.

Concern with fire protection capabilities also may stem from a single tragic incident. Each year brings examples of loss of life in a fire, the destruction of valuable commercial property, or the heartbreaking story of a home burned to the ground. Occasionally, some operational error by the fire department—a miscommunication, a refusal to cross boundary lines to respond to an emergency, a delayed response—generates a demand for improvement. There are instances, too, in which dissatisfied members of the fire department or their families demand an investigation, which may mean an evaluation. Whether the charge is accurate makes little difference, since the perception is that an examination must be conducted.

At the other extreme is a gradual change in fire loss experience. Whereas the dramatic incident typically prompts those outside the department to call for an evaluation, gradual change registers in the minds of fire department officials first.

Fire protection evaluation and planning may also be precipitated by a change in the size or configuration of the territory to be protected. Since fire suppression resources and capabilities are so often tied to geography, any change in the extent of the protected territory will likely result in plans to alter the capability level. Although resource increases and decreases are not always tied to enlarged or reduced responsibility, they frequently are. A loss in fire department resources may result in a reduction of territory or scope of service or in a change in organizational structure of the department in order to compensate. For example, the number of volunteers or part-time personnel may be increased because of an irreversible loss of full-time personnel. On the other hand, growth in territory, responsibility level, or scope of services to be provided also may result in a change in staffing practices, such as the transition to career personnel rather than all volunteer.

Other events in the community also may bring pressure for an evaluation of fire protection. These include the adoption of tax and expenditure limitations, reduction in the municipal tax base, loss of federal or state aid, and municipal bankruptcy.

Sometimes the pressure begins because something has occurred within the fire department itself or because it has brought public attention to itself. Internal quarreling, suspicion of criminal acts, public charges and countercharges, thoughtless public announcements and interviews, social events that get out of hand, and departmental involvement in local politics can all contribute to the type of unhappiness that leads to calls for change.

Many public officials, and fire department officers as well, long for the days when the only reason to examine the fire department came from the underwriting or insurance-rating organization. That simpler era appears to be gone forever.

Setting community goals

Fire protection may be evaluated against community goals as part of the large-scale planning for a master plan or smaller-scale planning for a "miniplan." Although the comprehensive master plan offers many benefits, most departments engage in less ambitious efforts because of time constraints, economic limitations, or political considerations. Miniplans are also useful evaluation tools.

The most useful evaluations and the plans that stem from them seem to come from communities that established their protection goals before the evaluative process began. Known goals provide the evaluation with a road map and make it possible to envision recommendations or alternatives more clearly. Community fire protection calls for a variety of goals and objectives (or parameters), including the following:

1. Acceptable level of risk of fire loss, averaged over a period of several years
2. Acceptable level of risk of loss of life due to fire, averaged over a period of several years
3. Types and scope of emergency services to be provided by the "fire department"
4. Number of suppression personnel constituting a first alarm assignment
5. Number and types of fire suppression vehicles constituting a first alarm assignment
6. Amount of elapsed time allowed between receipt of an alarm at the dispatch center and the arrival of the initial, or full first alarm assignment at the various zones within the district, and the various high hazard locations, such as schools and hospitals
7. Emphasis to be placed on comprehensive fire protection activities, including code development, enforcement, and administration, as well as public education
8. Type of staffing arrangements, especially for suppression services, including any volunteer or part-time paid personnel
9. Organizational structure and general administrative arrangements for the fire department and related support services.

For purposes of evaluation and planning, numbers 7, 8, and 9 above should be stated in terms of performance rather than simply what is in existence. For example, an objective under "administrative arrangements" might be to reduce the number of formal grievances. The evaluation might reveal that the number grows annually because there are no provisions to settle disputes at the first or second level of origin. That evaluative finding could lead to a recommendation for improved grievance procedures.

Designing an evaluation

Ideally, any evaluation will be more than an "audit" and will lead directly to an action plan. The best evaluations are designed at the same time that goals and objectives are being established and organizational structure is being conceived. That way, evaluations are much easier to conduct. For example, if a community installed a new dispatch and communications center with the understanding that emergency responses should be made within a three-minute time frame, then the necessary recording equipment could be installed and evaluation protocols could be implemented. If designed properly, the system could give reports and summaries, almost at the push of a button, to answer the evaluative question concerning speed of response. If none of this is thought of when the communication equipment is being selected, this particular evaluation becomes a much bigger task.

It is useful to have some sort of framework to help break down the vague concept of fire protection into elements that can be more easily analyzed. One kind of framework, created by Swersey and Ignall, appears in Figure 5–1. For purposes of evaluation, they suggest breaking down the events surrounding a fire into time periods, or intervals. The management issues that affect the events during each interval can be evaluated to see how each time interval can be shortened in the most cost-effective way.

Another framework for evaluation is the establishment of standards linked to the fire safety needs of the community. Chapter 17 describes an attempt in the state of Michigan to set standards for evaluating fire protection.

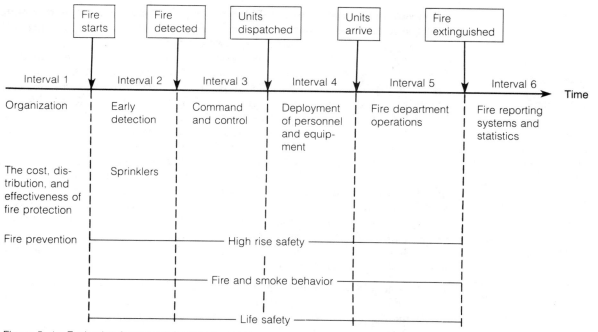

Figure 5–1   Evaluation framework for management options.

× *Defining the questions*

Ten questions need to be answered before the evaluation begins:

1. What are the purposes of the evaluation and for whom is it being conducted?
2. Which departments and services will be evaluated?
3. How much time is available for the evaluation?
4. Who will design it?
5. Who will be in charge of it?
6. Who will do the work, and will those who must provide information be reasonably cooperative?
7. Who will evaluate it?
8. How public will it become?
9. Is it part of a larger planning process to be conducted by someone else, and if so, do they want this evaluation?
10. Who will pay the costs associated with the evaluation?

Without acceptable answers to these questions, the process is not likely to go well. It is undoubtedly better to build for sensible arrangements in the very beginning, even though this may lead to a slow start. Otherwise, much more time will be wasted later.

A typical list of what communities want to evaluate includes: (1) relevant organizational structures; (2) scope of services provided and applicability of delivery systems; (3) management and staff support practices; (4) operating strategies and tasks; and (5) resource allocations, for example, for station locations and staff. To this list should be added (6) fire prevention programs, including public education; (7) relevant code administration; and (8) emergency service needs of the community, excluding law enforcement.

Any comprehensive evaluation of community fire defenses must include an evaluation of fire prevention as well as fire suppression capabilities. The code administration and enforcement program, the public safety education program, land use regulations, water supply, staffing levels and patterns, and other relevant aspects of fire defense must be evaluated as well.

In addition, the word *fire* should not be taken too literally, since most modern fire departments provide community defense against other dangers as well. Emergency medical, hazardous materials, and natural disaster services are commonly assigned to "fire departments." Evaluations, if they are to provide full benefit, must take into consideration two aspects of these other emergency services: (1) If the fire department is charged with providing other emergency services, how well is it providing them? and (2) If the fire department is not the service provider, who does provide them and how successfully?

Since an evaluation of fire defenses is being undertaken, the community might as well evaluate other related emergency services at the same time. It is surprising how interrelated the factors of service delivery are, and how synergistic. Indeed, even in a moderately well-developed department, an evaluation of fire defense capability takes in related services.

Another way of considering what could be the nature of an evaluation is to pose key questions such as these:

1. Are the goals and objectives of the department clearly stated, widely accepted, and appropriate to the community's projected future?
2. Is the department structured and managed in the most functional and cost-effective way?
3. Is a more comprehensive and extensive prevention and code administration program needed?
4. Do trained response crews, properly equipped, arrive at fire and other emergency incident locations within the recommended time frame and in sufficient numbers?
5. Are suppression and emergency management goals and tactics appropriate, safe, and effective?
6. Are the major functions of emergency management understood and operating?
7. Are all necessary levels and types of planning in place and functioning?
8. Is a balanced resource management program in operation?

Having a clear idea of the questions to be asked will help fire service managers explain the evaluation to the media, political leaders, active citizen groups, fire department personnel, unions and similar organizations, and other municipal departments. Experience indicates that a very fine line must be drawn between having the answers to questions at the time of announcement and having too many answers available before the evaluation even begins. Any indication that conclusions have already been drawn will make an objective evaluation very difficult or impossible. It is important to remember that the announcement of an evaluation will create anxieties for people inside and outside the department, and the most fruitful technique appears to be openness and honesty in all announcements and discussions.

Using consultants

Another reason for carefully defining the questions involves the use of outside consultants to conduct all or part of the evaluation. Consultants can assist considerably, but to do their job and to be cost effective to the community they need to know what the officials want of them and of the entire evaluation. Any request for proposals (RFP) should contain information about the purpose, scope, and other requirements of the evaluation, the breadth of the desired work, and the nature of the deliverables.

Very often, those individuals and groups that will be affected by action plans—or that perceive they will be affected—are asked to help formulate the RFP and to interview consultant applicants. Their cooperation is necessary for a successful evaluation and sometimes needs to be won. If an outside consultant is used, some knowledgeable and sensitive representative of the group requesting the evaluation needs to be put in charge of gathering the documents and data requested, arranging interviews, and providing transportation, office space, and other necessary items and services. That liaison representative should not accompany an outside consultant to the actual interviews.

If consultants are involved, media representatives will often seek to interview them while the evaluation study is in progress and also at its completion. It is best for the department to retain the role of liaison with the press, and agreements with the consultants need to be worked out beforehand. Reports and other deliverables are limited to those called for in the RFP.

The final design

Several approaches to evaluating fire defenses are available, and adaptations should be made to suit local circumstances and situations. An early decision is needed concerning how comprehensive the evaluation will be. Even though a comprehensive initial evaluation of fire defenses must include all aspects of fire prevention, including code administration, many officials want to focus only on suppression. Ideally, the evaluation will flow directly into the planning process. The sample analytical design presented below makes that connection.

If an initial evaluation—as a particular project to be completed within a given time frame—is to be conducted by fire department personnel, municipal personnel, and selected citizens (a common team), then the person with overall responsibility must allocate tasks so that personnel are not called upon to evaluate their own units and performance. The approach that uses only insiders needs especially careful planning, so that self-serving judgments are not made.

One possible design, which flows from evaluation to planning, contains seven steps:

1. A review of historical data relative to the department
2. A detailed examination and analysis of each subsystem of the fire protection delivery system and the interlocks and servomechanisms of that system
3. A review of any ISO or similar study, plus insurance rates
4. A review and analysis of components of the larger system (for example, city and county) within which the department lives, and their impact upon the department (this includes the financial resource base and funding parameters)
5. An objective assessment of progress, relative to contemporary plans, including possible future expenditure rates and the possible development of the most cost-effective protection plan
6. The development of action recommendations, possibly including action alternatives
7. The preparation of a report to named officials, containing details of the evaluation and any recommendations called for.

Data gathering

An extensive, comprehensive, and analytical initial evaluation should be based on a broad spectrum of data and information. Some can be obtained by examining documents, but much has to be gathered by interview. Those charged with evaluating services should not ignore input from citizens who use them.

Figure 5–2 shows a citizen questionnaire that is used to gather feedback. Chapter 6 also discusses sources and uses of data that may be relevant for purposes of evaluation.

Fire prevention data

Fire prevention effectiveness is difficult to judge, but there are relevant points that may be compared with earlier and following years.[1]

Figure 5–2　Emergency service questionnaire used by the fire department in Glendale, Arizona. The questions appear in Spanish on the reverse side.

GLENDALE FIRE DEPARTMENT
EMERGENCY SERVICE QUESTIONNAIRE

Your comments can help us to evaluate our emergency services. If you would take a moment to complete this questionnaire and mail it back in the attached self addressed envelope, we would appreciate it.

1. Do you feel the fire department arrived in a reasonable length of time?

   2-4 min.____　　4-6 min.____　　6-8 min.____　　10 or more min.____

   Comments:_____

   _____

2. Did you understand the actions taken by the fire department?

   Comments:_____

   _____

3. If this was a medical call, do you feel that the ambulance company provided a good level of service?

   Comments:_____

   _____

4. Do you feel that there are other ways we can improve our services?

   Comments:_____

   _____

Date and time service was rendered:_____

Your name (optional):_____

If you would like to personally discuss the services rendered, please contact the Administrative office at 931-5614.

Write additional comments:

THANK YOU FOR COMPLETING THIS SURVEY IT IS OUR INTENT TO PROVIDE THE HIGHEST LEVEL OF EMERGENCY SERVICE FOR THE GLENDALE CITIZENS. THROUGH YOUR ASSISTANCE WE WILL OBTAIN THIS GOAL.

1. Reported fire incident rates (annual)
   a) Number of fires per 1,000 population
   b) Number of residential building fires per 1,000 dwelling units, by type of unit
   c) Number of commercial/industrial/institutional fires per 1,000 occupancies, by type of occupancy
   d) Incendiary and suspicious origin fires per 1,000 population
   e) Number of fires in inspected properties per 1,000 occupancies, by type of occupancy
2. Number of estimated unreported fires per 1,000 population (annual)
3. Prevention activities
   a) Inspections
   b) Plan reviews
   c) Consultations
   d) Code administration activities
   e) Public education activities.

Fire suppression data

Fire suppression effectiveness may be judged by annual "loss-and-save" rates:

1. Dollar property loss per building fire, per capita and per $1,000 market value of property
2. Percentage of fires with significant spread of damage after arrival of initial attack units
3. Response time to fire call
   a) Average response time
   b) Percentage of responses taking more than desired time
4. Insurance rating of fire department and related systems
5. Fire-related deaths and injuries (annual)
   a) Number of civilian deaths (and injuries) per 100,000 (or other) population
   b) Number of civilian deaths (and injuries) per 1,000 fires
   c) Number of firefighter deaths per 1,000 fire employees
   d) Number of firefighter deaths per 1,000 fires
6. Work load (annual)
   a) Number and rate of service calls answered by type of call (e.g., fire or emergency medical response)
   b) Number of calls responded to per fire company
   c) Number and rate of fire prevention inspections
   d) Population protected per year (residential, work force, tourist, and other)
7. Suppression activities
   a) Alarm reports
   b) Personnel reports
   c) Alarm patterns.

EMS data

Emergency medical services may be judged by

1. Responses
2. Tiered responses
3. Personnel reports
4. Response pattern.

Financial data

Financial information will provide insights into the resources available to fund fire protection services:

1. Nonmunicipal income
   a) Restricted income
   b) Nonrestricted income
   c) Income for services rendered
   d) User fees
2. Municipal budget
   a) Income
   b) Expenditures
   c) Pension and other future commitments
   d) Patterns
3. Tangential benefits stemming from career, volunteer, or combination department depending on local history and the existing financial base.

Operations management data

Information on the effectiveness of operations management may be obtained from the following sources:

1. Mission statement
   a) Departmental goals
   b) Prevention goals
   c) Suppression goals
   d) Special service goals
   e) Administrative goals
   f) Summary of goals in specific performance terms
2. Fire protection committee of city government (role and appointments)
3. Fire department services (current and planned)
4. Organizational structure
   a) Administration
   b) Support services
   c) Prevention
   d) Suppression
   e) EMS
   f) Special services
   g) Training
   h) Civilianization
5. Demarcation of fire protection management areas
   a) Current boundaries
   b) Ability to meet expanded needs
6. Community fire risk analysis
   a) Past
   b) Current
   c) Future (changes in occupancy and/or development patterns)
   d) Special risks (waterfront, airport, hazardous materials)
   e) Nonfire risks
7. Relationships to other agencies (city, nearby fire agencies, nonfire agencies)
8. Suppression and disaster mutual aid
   a) Mutual aid
   b) Automatic response
   c) Stations
   d) Specialized/shared response

9. Staffing patterns
    a) Line and staff structure
    b) Job descriptions
    c) Use of paid civilian personnel
    d) Officer positions
    e) Special service positions
    f) Prevention positions
10. Stations and response
    a) Station location
    b) Response zones and times
    c) Station condition
    d) Relocation plans
    e) Vehicle assignments
    f) Planned shifting
11. Management information system
    a) Data topics
    b) Performance requirements
    c) Data collection systems
    d) Data storage systems
    e) Data retrieval systems
    f) Data usage systems
    g) Local, state, and national data collection requirements
    h) Computerization
    i) Annual reports
12. Incident and loss data collection and usage system as a special item
13. Comprehensive prevention program
    a) Public education
    b) Inspection programs
    c) Codes: safety, building, occupancy, etc.
    d) Code enforcement
    e) Early warning system
    f) Automatic extinguishing systems
    g) Cable TV or other monitoring
    h) Prevention unit structure
    i) Interface with other subunits and other agencies
    j) Staffing requirements
    k) Budget requirements
    l) Expected performance
    m) Arson prevention and investigation
14. Suppression program
    a) Station locations, expansion, funding
    b) Shared station concept, running times
    c) Apparatus: fire and special vehicles
    d) Apparatus replacement program and funding
    e) Staffing requirements
    f) Dispatching, including computer-aided dispatch
    g) Equipment needs
    h) Strategy and tactics, standard operating procedures
    i) Cost effective strategies and equipment
    j) Safety practices
15. EMS: need and response projections
    a) Locations
    b) Staffing and training
    c) Levels of service
    d) Arrangements

16. Hazardous materials response capability
    a) Structure
    b) Personnel and training
    c) Vehicles and equipment
    d) Backup and technical support
17. Disaster planning
    a) Disaster plans; hazard analysis and risk assessment
    b) Emergency management structure
    c) Needed resources
    d) Interagency cooperation
18. Special services
    a) Definition
    b) Goals
    c) Resources needed
19. Operating procedures manual
    a) Current scope
    b) Areas for expansion
20. Alarm and communications systems
    a) Current provisions
    b) Projected service requirements
    c) Solution options
    d) Cost analysis
21. Water supply
    a) Current services vs. demand
    b) Projected demand in city
    c) Projected demand under expansion mode
    d) Solution options and cost analysis
22. Vehicle and equipment maintenance
    a) Projections
    b) Options and cost analysis
23. Training program
    a) Goals
    b) Leadership
    c) Instructors
    d) Facility and equipment
    e) Curriculum(s) and special off-site courses
    f) Officer training and advancement program
    g) Budget requirements
24. Personnel practices
    a) Work contract projections
    b) Civilian projections
    c) Recruitment and hiring
    d) Physical and other testing programs
    e) Probationary requirements
    f) Career development
    g) Opportunities for women
    h) Performance evaluations
    i) Salary, fringe, and retirement projections; turnover; recruitment costs
25. Costs
    a) Capital budgets
    b) Operating budgets
    c) Measures of success and cost-effectiveness
    d) Shifting the costs from tax dollars
    e) Use of private protection
    f) Cost/service/risk trade-offs
    g) Pension plans and projected funding

26. The master plan
    a) Purposes
    b) Organizing for the design
    c) Time frame
    d) Measurements of good planning and plans
    e) Selecting the planning group
    f) Steering the group and the process
    g) Organizing a "drop a year/add a year" master plan
    h) Measurement of progress
    i) Approving the plan
    j) Implementing the plan
27. Working with elected and appointed officials, and with surrounding departments
    a) Managers
    b) Elected officials
    c) Similar departments
    d) Peer departments
    e) Service departments.

Data analysis

Analysis of the data may be accomplished by several approaches. First, the department may hire an organization specializing in computer analysis to provide the service. This may be expensive, but a computer printout lends credence to the conclusions and thus inspires confidence. An added benefit is that an outside or "third person" opinion has been interjected. This consideration could be significant if the plan is to be dealt with by an administration that is generally suspicious, justifiably or not, of anything the fire department proposes. Second, the department may hire a consultant. This may be less expensive than a full computer analysis, and although not as technologically elegant, it may also serve to quiet suspicions that the fire department is incurring unnecessary expense. Finally, analysis and projections can be done "in-house," using the tools at hand.

One of the first considerations in the analysis of data is its accuracy. An evaluation team that includes an experienced department member will have a distinct advantage over a team composed only of those with short-term exposure. Familiarity with the city planner or head of water resources, for example, will allow their perspectives to be taken into account and thus permit a more accurate interpretation of any information they might have provided.

Analysis of the data may provide new insights. It may only reaffirm what you already knew: Money, personnel, and machines are all in short supply. Even if no startling revelations burst from the pages, you should have a better idea of whether these problems are going to get worse in the future and possibly what new problems may be coming up. The planning process also should provide an opportunity to step back and ask some questions about the way things are being done. It is your chance to be innovative and to "think big."

Evaluating comparative service levels

As stated earlier, an evaluation is primarily concerned with comparative levels of service. The foremost question of interest is what mix of staffing levels and response times will provide the greatest suppression benefit for the lowest cost. A fairly simple method is available to answer this. Access to a personal computer will take some of the drudgery out of the number work and speed up the process.

The method

Step 1: If you have the data available, use a compass to plot on a map of the jurisdiction the response times in increments of one minute around each station (see Figure 5–3). If you don't have the data, determine average response speeds and, in proportion to the map's scale, use a compass to draw the one-minute gradients around each station.

The importance of accuracy In one plan development, the principal planners were assured by the community development office that a topographically isolated area of the city (Newnorth) would not have structures over two or three stories high for the next twenty years. The planner stated that another, older, section of the city (Oldnorth) would be where apartment buildings would be built in the foreseeable future. Although this seemed counter to common sense, the information had come from one of the primary people who determined what was built in the city, and where. The fire department planners did, however, check with the city planner to see if he would offer any contrary information. He did not, and even supported the CDO's contention that future multi-story development would be in Oldnorth.

The Newnorth area posed a special problem for the fire department because of its isolation, and also because its one fire station was so small that it could never accommodate more than one pumper and four firefighters. Since Newnorth was also developing rapidly, centrally located property was at a premium; moreover, the area contained about 25 percent of the total city population. The response rate for the unit was a moderate 350 runs per year. The information the planners had received led them to believe that a larger station would be required within the next five years, and so they recommended that the city acquire a parcel that would accommodate a larger station housing a pumper and space for an ambulance. With virtually no multi-story, multi-resident structures in the offing, they felt their major problem would be a stepped-up demand for EMS service

corresponding to population increases. Beefing up the numbers on the pumper could provide an attack and a simultaneous portable ladder operation. The planners knew the resources available for new stations were limited, and by proposing a smaller station that would not require aerial apparatus, they judged they could recommend a new station elsewhere in the city that would effectively consolidate two poorly located units.

After the plan had been finalized, but before it was presented to the city's governing body, the department learned that a development being planned at the extreme end of the Newnorth area included sixty wood frame apartment buildings, each four stories high. When approached about his previous information, the director of CDO responded, "Did I say that?" The city planner had already left for a new position. Fortunately, no firm steps had been taken to acquire a site, and a minipumper, quint, and ambulance concept replaced the pumper/ambulance configuration in the plan.

The message is clear: IF THE INFORMATION YOU HAVE RUNS COUNTER TO COMMON SENSE, DON'T IGNORE COMMON SENSE. At the very least, find out why the information doesn't seem right. In this case, the principal department planners were new to the jurisdiction; and when questioned, even members of the fire department with twenty years of experience would not dispute the officials. What became clearer after the fact was that the director of CDO and the chief executive both wanted new apartments for the economically disadvantaged in Oldnorth.

Step 2: Assign a numerical level of effectiveness to the varying staffing levels and response times. These numbers can be arbitrary, but must have some consistent relationship. For example, if we were to consider a six-crew engine company less than one minute away from a response location as very highly effective, we could assign this a "factor" of 10. Based on previous experiments with staffing levels, we might assign a five-crew engine company one minute away the factor of "8." A four-person crew would be assigned "5.2," and a three-person crew a "3.2." To account for various response times, you could project a reduction in effectiveness of 50 percent for each minute of increased response time. Therefore, a three-minute response is only 25 percent as effective as a response of one minute or less.

In judging the relative merits of several different scenarios, the consistent application of the factors becomes more important than the raw numbers assigned. Consequently, any numbers could be plugged into Table 5–1, although the factors used here are illustrated.

Using similar weighting for ladder units, you could assume that a very highly effective rating would require seven persons: one officer, and two each to handle

Figure 5–3 One-mile response time increments plotted on a map of the jurisdiction.

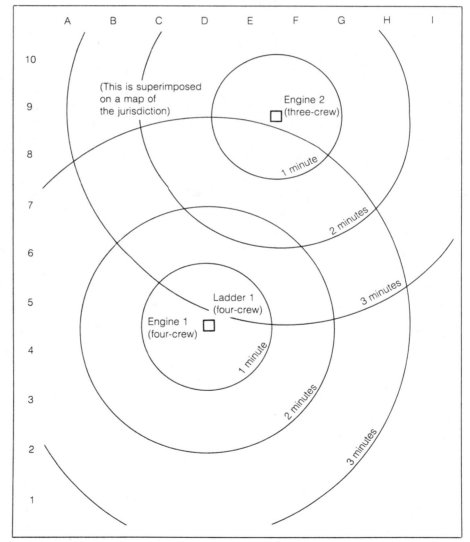

laddering, entry search, and roof operations. The resulting chart is illustrated in Table 5–2.

These weightings do not imply that engine and ladder contributions are similar or dissimilar when equally manned. That is a matter of opinion and judgment, and such evaluations will vary widely from department to department. Again, almost any values can be used as long as they have reasonable relationships and are consistently applied. For example, if you value an *existing* six-crew engine at 10 if it arrives within one minute, you must value a *proposed* six-crew engine that would arrive within one minute the same way.

Step 3: The factors developed in Step 2 are then projected using the response time circles drawn in Step 1 (see Figure 5–4). The map is divided into a grid—probably the most recognizable unit would be a block—and allowances are made for variations (e.g., an exceptionally large block would be considered two or three units, a smaller block one-half unit).

In Figure 5–4, assume that the shaded area—rows 6 and 7 in columns E, F, and G—are of particular interest for evaluation purposes.

The current resources are Engine 1 and Ladder 1 in row 5, column D; and Engine 2 in row 9, column F. Engine 1 and Ladder 1 are both four-crew units and Engine 2 is a three-crew company. When the question of how to best improve protection is examined, several suggestions emerge. We shall look at the following three:

1. Increase staffing of Engine 2 to four
2. Increase staffing of Engine 1 to five
3. Increase staffing of Ladder 1 to five.

Using previously given factors for the level of effectiveness for engine and ladder companies, construct a chart that lists the units, their assigned factors, and the percentage area in the box on the grid at which that level is provided. For example, in column F, row 6, Engine 1 and Ladder 1 are within two minutes of approximately 80 percent of the grid box and within three minutes of the remaining 20 percent. Engine 1 would be awarded a value of 2.6 for 80 percent, and 1.3 for the 20 percent. The ladder is credited with 1.6 and 0.8 for the 80 and 20 percent area, respectively. Engine 2 is within two minutes of 40 percent of the area, and within three minutes of the remaining 60 percent. Since Engine

Table 5–1   Level of effectiveness of engine companies by size and response time (10 = very highly effective; 0 = ineffective).

Size of crew	Response time in minutes		
	0–1	1–2	2–3
Six	10.0	5.0	2.5
Five	8.0	4.0	2.0
Four	5.2	2.6	1.3
Three	3.2	1.6	0.8

Table 5–2   Level of effectiveness of ladder units by size and response time (10 = very highly effective; 0 = ineffective).

Size of crew	Response time in minutes		
	0–1	1–2	2–3
Seven	10.0	5.0	2.5
Six	8.0	4.0	2.0
Five	5.2	2.6	1.3
Four	3.2	1.6	0.8

Table 5–3
Effectiveness of existing
protection, expressed
numerically.

Column and row	Engine 1		Ladder 1		Engine 2		Total factors
	Factor	Area	Factor	Area	Factor	Area	
E6	2.6	0.9	1.6	0.9	0.8	0.6	4.26
E6	5.2	0.1	3.2	0.1	1.6	0.4	1.48
E7	2.6	0.7	1.6	0.7	1.6	1	4.54
E7	1.3	0.3	0.8	0.3			0.63
F6	2.6	0.8	1.6	0.8	0.8	0.6	3.84
F6	1.3	0.2	0.8	0.2	1.6	0.4	1.06
F7	2.6	0.2	1.6	0.2	1.6	1	2.44
F7	1.3	0.8	0.8	0.8			1.68
G6	2.6	0.1	1.6	0.1	1.6	0.2	0.74
G6	1.3	0.9	0.8	0.9	0.8	0.8	2.53
G7	1.3	1	0.8	1	1.6	1	3.7
Total							26.9

Figure 5–4 Graphic
illustration of response
time evaluation.

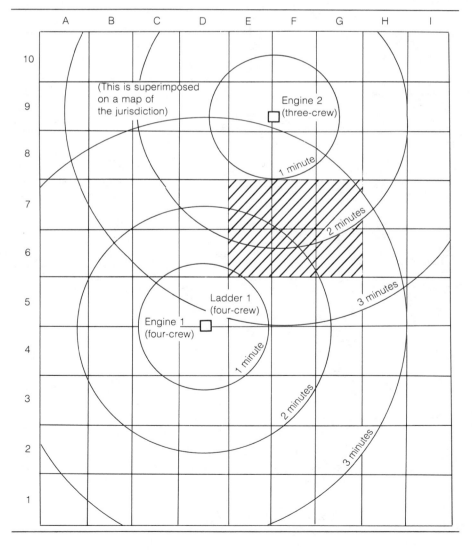

2 is a three-crew company, it is credited with 1.6 for the two-minute response area (40 percent), and 0.8 for the three-minute response area (60 percent). The factor and area would be multiplied for each column and row and the total added for all six grid boxes. The results are shown in Table 5–3, which gives a numerical indication of the effectiveness of the existing arrangement. The effects of each of the options are similarly computed in Tables 5–4, 5–5, and 5–6. Assuming that the cost of adding one firefighter per shift to any of the three units is the same, option 2 provides the greatest return by maximizing the contribution to the level of effectiveness.

Table 5–4
Effectiveness of option 1, increasing crew of Engine 2 from three to four.

Column and row	Engine 1		Ladder 1		Engine 2		Total factors
	Factor	Area	Factor	Area	Factor	Area	
E6	2.6	0.9	1.6	0.9	1.3	0.6	4.56
E6	5.2	0.1	3.2	0.1	2.6	0.4	1.88
E7	2.6	0.7	1.6	0.7	2.6	1	5.54
E7	1.3	0.3	0.8	0.3			0.63
F6	2.6	0.8	1.6	0.8	1.3	0.6	4.14
F6	1.3	0.2	0.8	0.2	2.6	0.4	1.46
F7	2.6	0.2	1.6	0.2	2.6	1	3.44
F7	1.3	0.8	0.8	0.8			1.68
G6	2.6	0.1	1.6	0.1	2.6	0.2	0.94
G6	1.3	0.9	0.8	0.9	1.3	0.8	2.93
G7	1.3	1	0.8	1	2.6	1	4.7
Total							31.9

Table 5–5
Effectiveness of option 2, increasing crew of Engine 1 from four to five.

Column and row	Engine 1		Ladder 1		Engine 2		Total factors
	Factor	Area	Factor	Area	Factor	Area	
E6	4	0.9	1.6	0.9	0.8	0.6	5.52
E6	8	0.1	3.2	0.1	1.6	0.4	1.76
E7	4	0.7	1.6	0.7	1.6	1	5.52
E7	2	0.3	0.8	0.3			0.84
F6	4	0.8	1.6	0.8	0.8	0.6	4.96
F6	2	0.2	0.8	0.2	1.6	0.4	1.2
F7	4	0.2	1.6	0.2	1.6	1	2.72
F7	2	0.8	0.8	0.8			2.24
G6	4	0.1	1.6	0.1	1.6	0.2	0.88
G6	2	0.9	0.8	0.9	0.8	0.8	3.16
G7	2	1	0.8	1	1.6	1	4.4
Total							33.2

Several precautions should be mentioned:

1. For simplicity, the example is based on a very small geographic area. It would be more appropriate, and more significant, to evaluate the city-wide effects of changes.
2. The key to the methodology is the relative values assigned to various units at various crew levels. Again, this is largely a matter of opinion and judgment. It is not "dark science," however, and if some reasonable thought is given to it, a value structure with rational relationships can be constructed for any jurisdiction.
3. The same methodology could be used to evaluate the addition of a new unit or the elimination of an existing unit. The cost-benefit relationship of such changes, or the increase or reduction of personnel requires the integration of the dollar value for the cost or saving of the strategy under consideration. Analysis should allow you to determine which will give you the most for the money.
4. The analysis can be as broad or as specific as you want. Engine 1 and Ladder 1 could be interpreted as covering 82 percent of the F6 grid box within two minutes and 18 percent within three minutes; or the major segment in each grid box could be considered to apply to the whole grid box (two-minute values for E1 and L1 in the F6 grid box). Another possible option is to divide response time into half-minute, or even fifteen-second increments.

Various other methods are available to assist a community in determining how best to locate suppression vehicles and crews, how large the crews should be, and what response patterns and alarm assignments should be incorporated. The aim is to attain a quick initial attack by sufficient firefighters, while still being cost effective. But fire losses, including lives lost, must be factored into the cost analysis. A project was conducted by the city of Tacoma, Washington, as early as 1976,[2] and national figures were collected following that by the International City Management Association and other participating organizations.[3] Several staffing studies have been conducted as well,[4] although a national study on this topic launched in 1980 was not completed because of a lack of funding.[5]

Table 5-6
Effectiveness of option 3, increasing crew of Ladder 1 from four to five.

Column and row	Engine 1		Ladder 1		Engine 2		Total factors
	Factor	Area	Factor	Area	Factor	Area	
E6	2.6	0.9	2.6	0.9	0.8	0.6	5.16
E6	5.2	0.1	5.2	0.1	1.6	0.4	1.68
E7	2.6	0.7	2.6	0.7	1.6	1	5.24
E7	1.3	0.3	1.3	0.3			0.78
F6	2.6	0.8	2.6	0.8	0.8	0.6	4.64
F6	1.3	0.2	1.3	0.2	1.6	0.4	1.16
F7	2.6	0.2	2.6	0.2	1.6	1	2.64
F7	1.3	0.8	1.3	0.8			2.08
G6	2.6	0.1	2.6	0.1	1.6	0.2	0.84
G6	1.3	0.9	1.3	0.9	0.8	0.8	2.98
G7	1.3	1	1.3	1	1.6	1	4.2
Total							31.4

Any method of analysis is a tool. If used intelligently, it has a definite advantage over "seat-of-the-pants" evaluation.

Alternatives

The process of evaluation implies that judgments will be made concerning the degree of satisfaction that a current arrangement provides. In fact, those doing the evaluating use some benchmark or model of whatever is being examined and cast the local situation up against that quality standard. To do this, either the local community must provide a description of what it believes is "right" for itself, or the evaluators must select their own standard. Often, the community has not thought about its goals in fire protection and expects the evaluation to spell out the goals and best arrangements for reaching them.

At some early point in the project, a few major alternatives will probably emerge. For example, there is always the "do-nothing" option. There will also be the "do-something" options, because there had to be some impetus to start the evaluation process in the first place. These will generally boil down to two or three that can be ranked from minimum to maximum in relation to cost, internal change, political ramifications, and so on. The facts of life tend to make the cost variable the predominant factor in the scale.

Feasibility

Once this ranking is developed, it is time to identify some of the key figures who will decide if the plan is going anywhere at all and determine what is feasible before too much time and effort are expended. If three options are (1) do nothing, (2) add one station, and (3) increase the staffing level citywide, approximate costs can be tied to each of these. If one of the principal determinants of feasibility is to be money, you have to find out early on which is acceptable. If the party controlling the purse strings is the mayor, the chairman of the board of finance, or the city manager, you have to have their input on the boundaries of the projected plan.

The key parties will vary from jurisdiction to jurisdiction, but will also vary with the significant elements of the plan. The firefighters union will probably not object to a new station or increased personnel; but if the new station is going to be minimally staffed and supplemented by paid-on-call personnel, the union will become a principal actor. If an element of the plan is to consolidate two stations, the elected or appointed representatives from the affected areas will have to be contacted early in the planning process. You may not be able to convince them that the municipality is better served by increasing response time to part of their district, but you may be able to get some feeling for the depth and direction of their objections.

In short, determine what elements from the evaluation that will survive politically, economically, and within any time contraints that may apply can be incorporated in the plan. Hours of long, arduous work on a technically competent plan will go down the drain if it has little or no chance of being implemented. Identify the people who will be key to the implementation, and don't forget those internal to the department itself.

Evaluating fire attack capabilities

Those conducting the evaluation need to be familiar with the spectrum of fire prevention activities, which range, for example, from special safety education programs for nursing home residents to the residential monitoring capabilities of cable television. Prevention programs are apparently better understood by elected officials and citizens than are the fundamental concepts of fire attack management. Nevertheless, a review of how progressive municipalities array and manage their suppression resources for fire attack at an ordinary residence illustrates what evaluations must consider.

A relatively high percentage of fire alarms are handled successfully by the first arriving suppression vehicle, provided it arrives quickly, has a sufficiently large crew, and does not have to perform multiple duties such as search and rescue or laddering as well as extinguishment. In one typical East Coast city, for example, 95 percent of the fire calls in 1985 were either false alarms or were handled by the first suppression vehicle to arrive at the scene. The remaining 5 percent required all first-alarm crews to handle the situation, sometimes with an additional pumper dispatched as well. Multiple alarms occurred much less than one in a hundred alarms. Early detection devices such as smoke alarms, sprinkler systems for automatic fire control or extinguishment, strong fire safety codes and continuing enforcement, and active public education programs all reduce the percentage of calls requiring sustained (and expensive) firefighting operations.

The problem for municipal officials, of course, is that some alarms do require multiple crews and sustained efforts. Smaller communities often suffer disproportionately large fire losses because of their apparent inability to maintain sufficient initial attack suppression forces. It is this dilemma of cost versus loss that makes careful evaluation and planning so important.

Research into fire indicates that temperature increases and fire builds during the first few minutes—typically three or four. If fuel (fire loading) and oxygen are sufficient, then localized free burning begins and continues for another brief time period. After four or five minutes, this unrestrained fire growth usually leads to flashover or ignition of the total contents of the room (or rooms, or building) of origin. This instantaneous fire spread is caused by superheated fuel and atmosphere and often occurs before the end of seven minutes.

Number of firefighters

Fire suppression operations have three basic functions: (1) rescue; (2) work involving the ladder, forcible entry, and ventilation; and (3) the application of water through hose lines. Rescue and ladder companies handle the first two, and engine companies the third. To raise ladders, ventilate, search, and rescue simultaneously takes quick action by at least four and often eight or more firefighters, each team under the supervision of an officer. The number of firefighters required to search and rescue should never be fewer than two and typically is at least four. The number of firefighters needed to advance and operate one hose line varies from two on smaller lines to four on large hand lines.

The standard formula for determining the volume of water needed and the number of hose lines to be advanced at a working structural fire is based on a minimum of two engine companies with at least eight firefighters. This formula calls for the discharge of three gallons of water per minute for every 100 cubic feet of involved fire area with typical fire loading. An area of 40 feet by 40 feet with 8-foot ceilings requires 384 gallons per minute. Two hose lines are needed to produce that flow, and a third line to cover the floor above. Exposure coverage and search and rescue are not yet taken into consideration, but already eight or nine hosemen are needed, plus the pump operators, plus the supervisor.

Various controlled and statistically based experiments by some cities and universities reveal that if about sixteen trained firefighters are not operating at the scene of a working fire within the critical time period, then dollar loss and injuries are significantly increased, as are the square feet of fire spread.[6]

As firefighting tactics were conducted for comparative purposes, five-person fire suppression companies were judged to be 100 percent effective in their task performance, four-person companies 65 percent effective, and three-person companies 38 percent effective; six-person companies are judged 20 percent faster than four-person companies.

Response time

A prudent response pattern needs quick response times as well as a sufficient number of firefighters for the immediate attack.

Officials need to establish a maximum response time following receipt of the dispatch instructions at the station. In some urban areas, one and a half minutes are considered a desirable maximum, whereas in other urban areas the number is set at two and a half or three. Obviously, the response time policy varies according to the fire danger, the ability of the municipality to locate stations and staff apparatus, and traffic speed. Average urban response speed is usually about 20 miles per hour. Once fire apparatus and personnel arrive at the scene, their initial activities require several more minutes.

Considering that the time required for flashover in structural fires with standard fuels is typically about seven minutes, the apparatus and firefighters must arrive and get operating very quickly. If it takes a resident two or three minutes to discover and report a fire and three minutes for the apparatus to be dispatched and arrive, the sizing up and initial attack need to be done in a minute or two, or the typical fire will have grown significantly in size. An unconscious person with depleted oxygen will typically suffer permanent brain damage after approximately four minutes. All of this needs to be considered within the context of multiple alarm fires and simultaneous alarms. Delayed response and understaffed response appear inevitable under those circumstances, unless planning is complete.

One task, then, in evaluating suppression ability is to determine how fast adequate firefighting forces can arrive at the scene of an incident and launch rescue operations, if needed, plus initial fire attack. Once the community or the evaluation team has determined satisfactory parameters for the size of the initial attack team and response time and has measured the local situation, it can judge how satisfactory the response is. Often the response time is longer than officials expected, especially if the time span is measured from the moment the alarm was received to the actual initial attack. Team size may not be satisfactory until several vehicles arrive, and this time delay must be considered as well. The efficiency of the attack team will be greatly diminished if an optimum number are not working at the scene.

Alternatives

Analysis of local attack capability may indicate that changes are needed, especially in view of the fact that simultaneous and multiple alarms will drain available forces. The importance of good attack force management leads many communities to examine alternative arrangements that could improve response capability without exceeding financial capability. These alternative arrangements and structures include regionalization of services, consolidation of fire departments or their supporting services, installation of built-in fire protection, automatic response from neighboring departments, contracting out for services, use of part-time or "call" employees, use or increased use of volunteers, use of civilians in place of more expensive uniformed personnel, and other possible measures described in detail in òther chapters, particularly Chapter 17. Obviously, changes that do not bring desired improvements or at least maintain current service levels at contained costs should not be implemented.

Another avenue of positive change stemming from the evaluation of suppression concerns equipment and tactics. Benefits may be realized from increased use of computers, improved fire attack equipment, selective dispatching, shifting the suppression companies' locations to provide increased coverage at critical times, using attack task forces, and other tactical advances. What may help— if, indeed, improvement is needed—can only be determined through a thorough and comprehensive evaluation of existing fire defenses.

Evaluating the water supply system

In evaluating fire attack capabilities and comparing service levels, the importance of water supply and its delivery to the scene of a fire must not be ignored. Since water is still the primary extinguishing agent, the ability of municipal water systems to supply sufficient quantities of water to fire department pumpers or fixed extinguishing systems, such as sprinklers, is basic and vital. Regardless of the speed of response or the number of firefighters available at the fire, without sufficient volumes of water delivered at working pressures, extinguishment will be difficult or impossible. Without municipal water supply systems (which typically consist of a reservoir of water, pumping stations, elevated water storage tanks, water mains, valves, and hydrants), water supply for firefighting will need to be drafted by pumps from streams, ponds, or other sources, or brought to the scene by tank truck.

Since water extinguishes fire by reducing the temperature (absorbing BTUs) it must be sprayed onto the burning material and surrounding heated atmosphere. A very effective way of doing this is to use fixed sprinkler systems installed in buildings. Since these systems are typically automatic, they require no personnel to activate them. Over the decades, their high degree of usefulness and cost effectiveness has been demonstrated many times. The second way to get water to the seat of the fire is to use hose lines and nozzles that take their pressure from fire pumpers and are advanced by firefighters. This is the most common method and assumes, of course, that a sufficient number of firefighters are available for the work as well as sufficient pumpers, hose lines, and water supply.

Since smaller fires are usually easier to extinguish, early arrival at the scene by enough firefighters to perform the work is essential to keep fire losses at a minimum. The major components in suppression systems that may be supplied by the municipality are:

1. Sufficient water supply at all locations to handle the type of construction and contents (called fire load) should ignition occur
2. Fixed, automatic fire control/extinguishing systems (usually brought about through building and fire safety codes)
3. Fire pumpers and other type vehicles and firefighting equipment
4. Sufficient firefighters for both initial and sustained firefighting
5. Station locations that permit a quick response to all parts of the district.

The details of municipal water supply systems and the formulas that provide guidelines for both sprinkler systems and the number of hose lines necessary for various types of construction and fire loading are available through a variety of technical sources. As already noted, fires are difficult to extinguish without sufficient volumes and pressures of water. Automatic, fixed extinguishing systems—such as sprinklers—are highly desirable and quite cost effective.

Presentation

Certain key people in your jurisdiction are involved in the political process. This may be the chief executive who heads the governing body or it may be the chairman of the powerful finance committee. Whatever the structure of your government, these key people will have a considerable effect on the extent to which a fire protection plan will become a reality. Consequently, it may be wise to offer them briefings before the formal public debut of the evaluation. Such prerelease briefings will help ensure that community leaders are not surprised or embarrassed by the findings. To announce that ''we are seriously underprotected in the east end of the city'' two days before the mayor kicks off his reelection campaign (even if this is true) may put your plan in the ''Titanic'' category. If the mayor is briefed prior to public announcements, he will find a way to cushion the political blow that such a statement could deliver. At the very least, such briefings will allow you to ''test the waters'' of feasibility. You should be alert to the feedback that you receive.

Because the evaluation will probably be dealing with some complex and technical aspects of the fire service, briefings provide an opportunity to clarify the fire service ''jargon'' that may appear in the document. A glossary should be included in the written plan—people aren't going to buy what they don't understand, and the field is loaded with terms that have vastly different meanings outside the profession—and a short list of definitions could be provided for the participants. You must make every effort to have these influential people understand just what the plan provides. The information that you're providing them now will allow them to ask significant and intelligent questions at the public presentation.

In all likelihood, the document will be formally presented in front of the governing body of the community. It will represent a significant juncture for your department, and you should put every effort into making it a success. Try to arrange a date, time, and location that will maximize public access. Attempt to depoliticize the event. The periods just before elections are particularly sensitive, and chances are that one or more provisions of the plan will be picked up and used as a political football. In the process, the plan will probably be twisted and exaggerated. The project as a whole will suffer.

Cooperation with the media is particularly important. Make every effort to accommodate them, and to ensure broad coverage. You should not ''leak'' all or part of the evaluation/plan in advance, but after the presentation you should make yourself widely available to the press. In this more informal setting, you will have a chance to address their particular concerns and make sure they are not misinformed.

The document that you present should be clearly and prominently labeled DRAFT COPY. The verbal presentation should emphasize the fact that the document is in draft form, and the intention is to make it available to members of the community and to the Chamber of Commerce, service organizations, and other groups. You cannot offer further opportunities for citizen involvement if it is presented as a final report.

If you have generated a reasonable, logical, justifiable evaluation/plan, you will have little trouble defending it. The statement must be looked at as an expression of the department's philosophy; not something that is carved in stone. The environment is too dynamic to allow most plans to continue unchanged for any period of time. The plan, of necessity, will have to be altered, so don't preclude citizen input.

Implementation

After the formal presentation comes the question of implementation. Government being government, it is unlikely to fix a target date on which the plan will become a full-blown reality. Depending on its elements and to a large extent the funding needed and what is available, a plan will probably progress toward fruition gradually, with short-range, medium-range, and long-range objectives. The day-to-day administration of the department must reflect the goals and objectives. If a new station is to replace one or two existing stations, for example, it will obviously be time to monitor anticipated expenses on the structures you intend to divest. Depending on the most likely time frame for completion of the new building, it may be possible to eliminate or curtail preventive or cosmetic maintenance. At the same time, the implementation scenario must incorporate the uncertainty of the future. The new station may be long delayed for any number of reasons, and it would be unwise to delay all work on the buildings. Some maintenance will be required to preserve resale value, and you have to maintain a habitable installation for your personnel. The bottom line is that the department may be occupying these buildings for the foreseeable future. A balanced approach that reflects a healthy respect for setbacks is mandatory.

In some cases, certain elements of the plan can be implemented with minor administrative changes. These should be addressed, and the necessary steps taken to bring them on line. Because implementation will probably take place by increments, there is no reason to hold off what is achievable just to wait for one final grandiose package. Accomplishing what can be accomplished with existing resources will illustrate confidence in the plan and its workability.

If reference has not been made to the tactics used in devising the plan it may well be appropriate to review them. What may be only too clear to the fire service manager may not be clear to the firefighter. Lest it be forgotten, their priorities aren't necessarily the same as the priorities of the manager, the department, or municipality. A major policy statement such as a reorganization or master plan is almost certain to contain points over which the difference in perspectives will become painfully obvious.

Several aspects of the initial evaluation need special attention, as activity begins to shift from analysis and evaluation to planning and implementation. As noted earlier, anxiety levels typically increase as both players and observers begin to speculate on why an evaluation is being conducted, what hidden agenda items are present, and what changes will be wrought as a result of the evaluation and the recommendations that usually spring from it.

Implementation can be hindered by a lack of agreement over what is "better" or what constitutes an "improvement." Often, assurances to various constituencies are offered, starting as far back as the time that the evaluation is first mentioned. Interestingly, people usually are much less anxious when a "planning" process is announced, as opposed to an "evaluation" process. In many communities, suspicions rise quickly and sides are soon drawn. Quite often, municipal officials, especially newly elected or appointed ones, and certain citizen groups are determined to reduce expenses—or at least to keep them at the current level. Under certain circumstances this perception will cause bargaining units in career departments to resist the entire process. Another group that is often concerned over resource limitations is composed of those who seek promotions and suspect curtailment of career opportunities.

Sometimes an evaluation is judged to be an attempt to eliminate one or more particular positions within the organization or to consolidate power. Since evaluations often examine consolidation of territory or of services—joint dispatching, for example—those with a vested interest, legitimate or otherwise, grow uneasy. Evaluations that lead to plans for addition (or deletion) of categories of personnel also may upset constituencies. Examples include changes in the number of volunteer firefighters or full-time firefighters, and the replacement of some uniformed personnel with civilian workers.

Equally important to implementation are the rising expectations that may develop once an evaluation is announced. Some, of course, nourish the hope that their favorite project will be promoted or that their own position will be enhanced. Others hope for the demise of programs they do not value. Many times the process will produce excellent suggestions that undoubtedly would improve community fire protection, but that cannot be implemented for one reason or another. Since no evaluation can serve all masters, some will be disappointed.

Bismarck is reported to have observed, ''Diplomacy is the art of the possible.'' Evaluations have the power to be exceedingly useful, but they cannot obtain what is not affordable, legal, or within the local value system. Moreover, outside consultants have limited power. Their evaluations must be objective and sound before they can be put to good use. And then the planning and the implementation must be the responsibility of the community. Open communication, mutual respect, honesty, and a lack of hidden agenda items will go far in leading all constituencies through the implementation phase.

Updating the plan

A good initial evaluation of fire defenses should provide the basis for an improved protection system for the community, and the process of evaluation should bring together for discussion a variety of people whose continuing involvement with the planning process is necessary. Further, a good evaluative study should stimulate discussion for continuing improvement. As the community continues to act on its plans, evaluation itself becomes an ongoing activity that charts the degree and quality of progress. Continuing evaluation is concerned with more specific types of activity than the initial broad evaluation, as the focus now is on particular projects only, and not all aspects of defense.

Provison must be made for updating the plan periodically to reflect steps toward completion, changes in the political or operational environment, goals that have to be identified as unattainable, and miscellaneous other changes.

A reasonable goal is to update on an annual basis. This strategy will allow you to add an ''out-year''—an additional year tacked on to the period the plan is designed to cover—to cover major new projects or to adjust for changing conditions. The update should include a critical look at the events of the past year that have affected the overall plan strategy. It should enumerate what has been accomplished, what is under way, and what has not taken place yet. Although it is not necessary to produce a formal document, this could be used as an opportunity to ''remind'' the chief executive and the governing body about the progress, or lack of progress, in meeting the plan's objectives. If a formal document is going to be prepared, provide more than just a list of what has and has not been done. A brief explanation of the reason or reasons for your various successes and failures should be included. Be specific and be honest. If the plan was presented as a statement of the department's philosophy, show how that philosophy applies.

It is much easier to report success than failure, but an honest assessment of progress is critical. The possibility of failure should have been planned for, and it is hoped that any damage to the plan will be minimal. Any project as complex as the one that you have undertaken can be expected to run into difficulty somewhere along the way.

Maintain a running list of factors that have affected or will affect implementation of plan elements. Keep the list in one place, preferably with the plan in a special folder or binder. When it is time for the update, they will be readily available.

A meeting of the principals involved in formulating the original plan may be a good idea. They were selected for the value of their input, so that a valid tactic now that will make your reappraisal more effective is to find out what has happened in their particular areas. It may be impossible to include everyone if your original effort was a full-scale master planning effort. If this was the case, you may have to select key individuals to become involved in the evaluation.

With annual updating, the evaluation/planning process becomes an ongoing part of the department's operations. It helps fire service and community leaders assess the current and future level of local fire protection capabilities, plan systematically for change, and implement improvements as time, money, and other constraints allow.

1 Portions of this material also appear in Philip S. Schaenman and Joe Swartz, *Measuring Fire Protection Productivity in Local Government: Some Initial Thoughts* (Boston: National Fire Protection Association, 1974), 15–17.

2 City of Tacoma, Washington, *A Fire Service Demand Charge Study* (Washington, D.C.: National Science Foundation, January 1976).

3 Research Triangle Institute, International City Management Association, and National Fire Protection Association, *Municipal Fire Service Workbook* (Washington, D.C.: Government Printing Office, 1977).

4 For example, John T. O'Hagan, "Staffing Levels: A Major New Study," *Fire Command,* November 1984, 16–19; idem, "Staffing Levels: Two-Story Apartment House Fire," *Fire Command*, December 1984, 24–27; and idem, "Staffing Levels: High-Rise Simulation," *Fire Command,* January 1985, 24–27, and February 1985, 36–38. See also Warren Y. Kimball, *Manning for Fire Attack* (Boston: National Fire Protection Association, 1969); Jan Chaiken and Edward Ignall, *Analysis of Fire Company Staffing Policies,*

concept paper (Santa Monica, Calif.: Rand Corporation, 1977); John C. Gerard and A. Terry Jacobsen, "Reduced Staffing: At What Cost?" *Fire Service Today,* September 1981, 15–21; Carl S. Smalley, "Fire Department Manpower," *Arkansas Municipalities,* June 1969; National Fire Academy, *Evaluation of the Impact of Response Time and Company Staffing on First Alarm Capability: A Decision Making Process,* research project for the National Fire Academy Executive Development III Program, Emmitsburg, Md., March 12–23, 1984; Alan Brunacini et al., "What Happens When Manpower Is Reduced?" *International Fire Chief,* January 1983, 17–23.

5 Christopher Niemczewski, "Fire Suppression Crew Size," *International Fire Chief,* January 1983, 12–16.

6 John A. Granito, "Evaluation and Planning of Public Fire Protection," *Fire Protection Handbook,* 16th ed. (Quincy, Mass.: National Fire Protection Association, 1986); and Robert W. Backoff, "Measuring Firefighting Effectiveness: Preliminary Report," School of Public Administration, Ohio State University, unpublished paper, 1986.

Part two:
Tools for
management

6 Management information systems and data analysis

Having good information that is readily available is <u>essential</u> to managing a fire department of any size. Good information is needed not only to help fire service managers make decisions, but also to back up those decisions with hard data that can stand the scrutiny of city managers, budget analysts, the press, and others. A fire service manager's career and the department's future depend on the ability to make and defend good decisions. Shooting from the hip no longer is enough in the competition for scarce resources. When other agencies and even public interest groups use management science to make the case for their priorities, the fire service manager must be prepared to do so, too.

In addition to supporting budget requests, good management information helps managers do the best possible job of reducing fires and related losses and providing other emergency services with the resources available. The range of problems facing fire departments today is formidable, and the amount of information they have to assimilate is huge. Even the smallest department can have any of ten thousand chemicals spilled at its door, or twenty-four types of arson committed, or hundreds of different tools and supplies to keep available for emergency medical service. No one can remember it all, and no one has to.

This chapter, written for the fire service manager who has only minimal familiarity with computers, outlines the basic principles of how to design and maintain a management information system (MIS). It discusses types of systems for organizing and processing information, types of information a department may collect and store, and computer models that are tailored to fire protection applications. It looks at policy decisions that guide the design of an MIS and practical considerations that influence the selection of computer hardware and software. The chapter then focuses on one of the most important but least understood uses of fire department data—fire incident analysis—and explains how to use and display data for policy planning, budgeting, and other management purposes. Finally, the chapter provides suggestions for controlling the quality of the data base and gives general recommendations for the fire service manager.

This discussion applies to fire departments of all sizes. The size of the system and the degree of computerization may vary, as may the sophistication of data analysis, but the basics are similar for all departments.

Types of management information systems

The fire chief has choices as to the type and capabilities of the department's management information system. The system can be manual, or it can be computerized at various levels of complexity and cost. The chief can store information in a simple set of files or use computers to store and retrieve data for analysis. The chief who is so inclined can use expert systems to support management decisions or can delegate the management information system to a good assistant chief—for a while.

Manual files

At the simplest level, the chief can have a set of paper files—one for financial information, one for rosters, one for personnel information, one for equipment status, one for maintenance history, and so on. The chief can gain access to these files either personally or indirectly through a secretary or aide, who finds the information in question. Similarly, the chief can process and analyze the data or have an assistant or a research section perform the analyses.

No matter how sophisticated the department's MIS, almost everyone still finds it useful to keep some manual files. Paper is transportable and cheap, can still be used in power failures, can be looked at in private, and does not take expertise to use.

Simple computer system with separate files

A computer can be used to imitate a manual system, except that the data are stored electronically in less space and can be recalled, displayed, scanned, and printed out much faster than with a manual system. Portable, battery-operated computers are relatively inexpensive and easily fit in an attache case. They can keep the daily calendar and a host of other information needed by the chief, and they are designed to require little expertise.

The simplest computer systems store the same sort of files that are stored manually—financial information, rosters, personnel—each one being independent of the others and accessed separately. The files can all be in one central computer owned and run by the department; they can be in a central computer operated by the municipality and accessible to the fire department via terminals; or they can be in one or more personal computers. But data are used from only one file at a time.

These simple systems have the capability to format the data into various tables and lists, to check or verify that the data are reasonable when they are input, and to do mathematical computations with the data.

There is a cost, and a considerable one at that, for using even this level of computerization. The cost includes data entry and maintenance of the files (to keep them up to date and to correct inaccuracies) as well as the cost of the computer hardware and software. Sometimes it is not worth the effort to com-

---

What is a management information system? A management information system is just what the name implies: a system for providing information needed to manage. Usually this formal name, management information system, or MIS, is employed when computers are used to store and process some or all of the information. The term sometimes refers to simple computerized systems that store separate files of information from which desired data can be retrieved. More commonly, it refers to more complex systems that allow data from several files to be intermixed. A more advanced MIS may use computer models to help in decision making, and may incorporate the logic and information of experts in the form of "expert systems" that imitate highly experienced advisors. Often the MIS is a collection of many programs that set up files, maintain the files, provide specialized analyses, and govern output report formats. In all, the MIS may consist of over a hundred separate programs, or several large ones that work together under an executive computer program. The system may be designed to be "user friendly" so that even chief executives with little training can interact with it directly, or it may be designed to be used by programmer/analysts or specialists trained in the use of the system, or both.

puterize. For example, most people still use a Rolodex or some other simple way to keep phone numbers rather than send the numbers to a computer center to be keypunched (people with personal computers or terminals at their desks, however, sometimes input such information directly into those computers).

Generally speaking, when a file involves less than several hundred records, paper is a reasonable alternative. A twenty-person fire department does not absolutely need its personnel files computerized. A department with less than a hundred runs a year can do a variety of tabulations of its fire incident information manually. However, even in these cases the number of data elements to deal with may be surprisingly large, especially when data are accumulated over time. For example, 100 fire incidents recorded in the National Fire Incident Reporting System format may have up to 6,000 data elements, not just 100, because there are up to 60 items to enter for each fire, and more than that in cases involving injuries. In five years, there may be 30,000 data elements, far beyond the volume that can be manipulated manually. Even for a simple alphabetized roster, a few names can be easily changed by pushing a button and a revised roster can be printed without retyping everything. Small computers provide convenience and simplicity for computerizing almost all such data.

Computer systems with advanced software

The next level of advancement in MIS is not through larger computers but through more specialized software for manipulating the data. Advances in software are moving in two directions. One is to make the computer easier to use— that is, to require less learning time and less expertise—and thus let more managers deal with their information systems directly. The other is to make the system more powerful—that is, able to store more data, process data more quickly, and produce a wider variety of analyses and reports.

Two developments in off-the-shelf software are data base management systems and financial spreadsheets. Data base managers can store a great number of data elements and allow the user to manipulate them in a wide variety of combinations. Spreadsheets store numerical data and allow the user to change various data elements to see their effect on other elements. It takes time to learn how to operate these powerful tools, but they can be used by programmers, managers throughout the department, and even by chiefs themselves.

The more advanced software packages are designed to use data from several files simultaneously. These are called relational data bases. For example, data on fires taken from the fire incident file for a particular building could be compared to the inspection history of that building taken from an inspection file. The user could analyze the frequency and severity of fires in buildings with up-to-date inspections versus buildings without recent inspections. The findings could be the basis for an evaluation of inspection programs or an argument for strengthening or changing them.

As new software increases the convenience and lowers the cost of data analysis, departments will do more of it. The payoff is much better information for decision making.

Expert systems

''Expert systems'' are a further advance for the MIS. The Center for Fire Research at the National Bureau of Standards is among the organizations that are researching expert systems for fire protection applications. In these systems the computer stores the decision processes of experts in a given field—what data they use and how they make their judgments. The user then can ask the computer to present the course of action the best experts would select collectively. For example, an expert system might be developed to help a chief decide on the optimal mix of fire prevention programs. The input would be the fire incidence profile of the community, the number of fire department personnel in various prevention specialties, socioeconomic profiles and trends, legal requirements for inspection and education programs, past experience with various prevention programs, and other data. The output might be the number of hours to commit to inspections, prevention education, and fire investigations by type of occupancy. The "recommendations" of the computer from such expert systems would not necessarily be adopted "as is" but rather would be a more advanced starting point for departmental decision making. These systems also permit the decisionmaker to see how the choices would change as assumptions about the environment change.

Types of information

The task of specifying the data to be collected and stored for an MIS can be approached from two directions: (1) by defining what information is required and then identifying the means of collecting it, or (2) by considering the readily available sources and the most that can reasonably be obtained from them. In practice the two approaches tend to converge. A few common sources provide much of the data needed for most of the uses that are described below.

It is useful to consider data in two groups: those collected by the fire department and those that come from outside sources. Fire department data come from incident reports, investigation reports, inspection records, lists of department resources and their status, pre-fire plans, and special studies. Data from outside the department include building and occupancy information from city planning and tax records, socioeconomic and demographic data from the U.S. Bureau of the Census or from local planning departments, and data on the performance of other fire departments, states, regions, and the nation.

Fire departments have much in common in the types of information they store. The differences lie in nomenclature, level of detail, and amount and organization of data. There are, of course, differences between paid and volunteer departments in personnel and financial data, and differences between fire-related data and data on other services offered by the department. But by and large the information requirements—though not necessarily the systems—are similar.

Management information systems in current use in fire departments typically include one or more of the sets of data described below. A computerized MIS can be dedicated to one of these areas; or can deal with several, with the others left manual; or it can deal with all of them. These are not complete lists but rather are meant to suggest the wide range of information categories that should be considered for a departmental MIS.

Personnel records

Most departments keep a great deal of information about their personnel. This is an area of strength in most departments, though the degree of automation varies. Typical personnel records include

1. Records for individual employees
   a) Personal data
   b) Medical history
   c) Career data
   d) Exposure data
2. Rosters
   a) Assignments to units
   b) Personnel on duty at the moment
   c) Inadequately staffed units (flagged)

3. Schedules
    a) Scheduled work days
    b) Schedules for inspectors, investigators, and companies
    c) Leave plans
4. Training and test records
    a) Certified skills
    b) Training needs
    c) Unit training records
    d) Unit training schedules
    e) Physical fitness records
    f) Promotion lists
    g) EMS recertification times
    h) Exam results
5. Recruiting
    a) Names of candidates
    b) Recruiting actions.

Despite privacy requirements, the amount of information stored on each person tends to increase. For example, two innovations are computerized baseline medical data for each firefighter (see accompanying sidebar) and records of on-the-job exposure to toxic substances. Exposure records indicate when a firefighter was exposed to a toxic substance, the type of substance, and some description of the time or extent of the exposure. There is not yet a standard for collecting such information, but it has important potential for understanding long-term health effects (by tracking shifts in biological measures and relating them to exposures) and for assisting in insurance and pension decisions (by providing data to distinguish effects of on-the-job exposures and accidents from other factors).

Building and inspection records

A second major class of information covers the characteristics, usage, and current inspection status of each building in the community.

Most fire departments inspect at least some classes of institutional and commercial occupancies. Some inspect much broader classes of occupancies, including residences. During each inspection someone usually documents the date, inspector, hazards found, hazards removed, and warnings or citations issued. The file on a building can include this information and also records of inspections prior to the occupation of the building, permits issued, and correspondence in connection with hazards and reinspections to see that hazards were removed.

In addition to this inspection information, some departments keep records identifying every structure in the community by street address. They also may have a subfile for each occupancy in the building. This building census is valuable for planning inspection policies, for computing risk by occupancy type, and for assessing hazards and needs as part of fire protection planning.

Baseline medical data   The Milwaukee Fire Department stores computerized data on every firefighter's normal heart and lung function. The same measurements can be taken at the scene of an incident and compared to the stored data in real time to help determine the need for hospitalization of the firefighter. It can save lives by indicating deviations from normal baselines, and avoid needless and expensive hospitalization by comparing any "redline" values to the firefighter's condition under normal circumstances.

In addition, many departments have detailed pre-fire plans of what apparatus would be needed and how a fire should be fought for large buildings, those with the greatest potential life loss, and those that are of most value to the community. These plans may include information on the location of hydrants, the existence of built-in fire suppression systems (especially sprinklers and standpipes), and special hazards or situations that firefighters should be aware of. These plans may also include a list of additional units that may be needed. All this information may be a part of the building file, too. This information may be transmitted by radio and may even appear on teleprinters or video displays in the apparatus on the way to the fire, depending on the sophistication of the technology available.

City records, such as building and construction permits, land use maps, and property tax records, can all help furnish information on the number of structures and the types of occupancies in each unit. Property tax records can be used as a starting point for estimating loss and for assessing property value at risk. But many types of property are not included on the tax records, or are not described in sufficient detail. "Walkaround" surveys by the fire department are generally the most thorough source. For some communities, maps of every local structure can be purchased from commercial firms, but these are not always kept up-to-date.

The data on individual buildings and occupanices not only provide immediate information during emergencies, but also are helpful in code administration. Examples of the various types of information that departments store on buildings are shown below.

1. Building characteristics (by individual building)
   a) Address
   b) Ownership
   c) Emergency contact
   d) Floor plans
   e) Construction type
   f) Floor space and volume
   g) Geocoding[1]
   h) Location of gas and electric shut-offs
   i) Fire protection features (sprinklers, detectors, standpipe locations, and so on)
   j) Deadend hallways
   k) Heating, ventilation, and air conditioning systems
   l) Underground floors
   m) Other hazards
   n) Vacant/abandoned status
2. Occupancy characteristics (for each occupancy per building)
   a) Name of business
   b) Type of establishment or use
   c) Names of owners/renters, managers
   d) Hazardous materials (location, type, typical quantity present)
   e) Other hazards (e.g., dangerous animals)[2]
   f) Presence and location of invalids or others needing special assistance (this file can be dangerous if it is not kept up-to-date; firefighters may continue to search for an invalid who is no longer in residence)
3. Inspection records, stored as part of the building/occupancy files or as separate files with data elements that allow linking the inspection records to the building/occupancy files.[3] Inspection records include review of plans for new buildings, legally mandated inspections, responses to complaints, and other inspections. Inspectors may want ready access to these files. Data elements include

a) New construction records
b) Plans review records (including for each plan the status of review, problems identified, responsible investigators)
c) Inspection history for existing buildings (dates, findings, inspection, enforcement actions, inspector or unit making the inspections)
d) Complaint file (citizen requests for inspections)
e) Violations pending
f) Court cases pending
g) Date for next inspection (tickler file)
h) Computerized notification system for letting building owners and managers know of inspections or violations, with sections of local ordinances stored for inclusion in letters when violations are found.

4. Fires and other incidents affecting building safety
a) Fire history of building (or the date of each fire and an incident number to allow access to fuller information in a separate incident file)
b) Floods, electrical overloading, false alarms, and other problems that resulted in calls

5. Permits
a) Outdoor burnings
b) Special equipment
c) Special events

6. Fee assessment (where fees are charged for routine or special inspections, reinspections, or permits).

Budgetary and financial records

Budgeting is covered in detail in Chapter 8, so coverage is abbreviated here. Among the records used are

1. Budget information
a) Current budget vs. expenditures to date

Data on building characteristics   The Tokyo and Osaka fire departments can transmit the floor plans of every commercial and high-rise building in real time to units on the fireground from a computerized file of the plan of every floor of every building. Larger storage capacities and the powerful graphic drawing equipment associated with modern computers make this possible. The same data can be stored manually, reviewed by someone in headquarters, and the information relayed by radio instead of sending the floor plans themselves.

Zurich, Switzerland, stores information on every chimney, fixed heating system, and major appliance in every building, residential as well as commercial. This information helps fire departments identify possible ignition sources and is used in the course of inspections and in determining the cause of fires.

A separate file of vacant or abandoned buildings may be kept to serve as a worklist for other agencies and an input to the arson early warning system. The Newark, New Jersey, fire department has kept such a computerized file of abandoned buildings, divided into those adjacent to inhabited buildings and those that are not. The file also indicates whether a vacant building is secured, and whether it is scheduled for demolition. Those buildings that are potential hazards to life safety are the prime focus of the department's efforts to get them knocked down, boarded up, or rehabilitated.

b)   Proposed budgets
c)   Supplementary data
2.   Purchasing records
3.   Fee collection records
4.   Fundraising information (particularly for volunteer departments, but also for paid departments that are turning to the private sector for some funds)
   a)   Donors' list
   b)   Canvassers' list
   c)   Pledge status (e.g., totals pledged, records of receipts vs. pledges)
   d)   Fundraising events.

Apparatus and equipment records

Apparatus and equipment records indicating date of servicing, type of servicing, and any improvements (for example, new pumps) are needed to keep inventories, prepare budget requests, determine maintenance schedules, and plan for new purchases. The length of time equipment is out of service is also important for assessing the efficiency of the department in keeping its equipment available and for evaluating different types of equipment and maintenance. These inventory and maintenance records commonly include

1.   Vehicle records
   a)   Equipment complement
   b)   Dates of purchase
   c)   Maintenance history (including total down time and time in shop for scheduled and unscheduled maintenance, nature of repairs, costs)
2.   Breathing apparatus records
   a)   Maintenance history (the same as for vehicles)
   b)   Refilling
   c)   Air quality tests
3.   Other personal protective equipment records
4.   Hose records
5.   Hydrant records
   a)   When tested
   b)   Status
6.   Other equipment

Incident and casualty data

One of the basic building blocks of a fire department MIS is the incident report filled out for each call. Most fire departments with computerized data systems use their state's fire incident reporting form, sometimes with modifications. Most states in turn feed the data into the National Fire Incident Reporting System (NFIRS), run by the U.S. Fire Administration. Most state forms are based on

---

Vehicle maintenance records   Little Rock, Arkansas, has a city-wide vehicle maintenance department that keeps detailed computerized records of each maintenance action to each vehicle, whether scheduled maintenance or repairs. In addition, the cost of the maintenance is recorded. This allows analyses of replace-repair strategies, and also provides data on productivity and on budgets. The same detailed records can be kept when maintenance is entirely within the fire department.

some version of the NFPA 901 fire reporting standard. The NFIRS Version 4 incident report, civilian casualty report, and fire service casualty report forms are shown in Figures 6–1 through 6–3.

The incident report captures a rich array of data, including the type of incident (whether it was a fire, false alarm, gasoline spill, rescue run, etc.); the number of personnel and types of equipment used at the scene; the times of arrival at the scene and of return to service; and the number of civilian and firefighter casualties. For fires it records the cause of the fire in terms of the source and form of the heat of ignition; the type and form of the material ignited and the ignition factor; the type of construction; the extent of damage and estimated loss; the existence of the fire detectors or sprinklers and whether they worked; the particular brand and model of equipment involved in the ignition; and related details.

A separate casualty report is filled out for each civilian or firefighter casualty, giving details of the reasons for the injury, the severity of the injury, where it was treated, and other information on the circumstances. For emergency medical services (EMS) runs, many departments have a different form with more details on the medical treatment rendered and the condition of the victim.

In any type of report to be filled out routinely, there is always a compromise between the level of detail to be collected on each incident and the burden placed on the firefighter who completes the form. Each person who thinks about

National Fire Incident Reporting System (NFIRS) The National Fire Incident Reporting System is a way of collecting comparable data on fires and other incidents for use at local, state, and national levels. The system is coordinated by the National Fire Data Center, which is one of the major program areas of the U.S. Fire Administration.

The basic idea in the system is to collect a core of reliable data—that recommended in the NFPA 901 Fire Reporting System—on a large enough sample of fires so that the local fire problem can be adequately assessed and fair and accurate information provided to the entire fire community.

The local departments send either incident and casualty forms or computer tapes containing the equivalent information to their state office responsible for statewide fire statistics; usually this is the state fire marshal's office. The state office uses the information in developing statewide fire reports, fire codes, inspection practices, and public education programs, and for answering questions raised by local fire depart-

ments, industry, elected officials, and other interested parties.

Most states provide each fire department participating in the system with a feedback report anywhere from once a month to once a year, and upon request. The states also send quarterly tapes to the National Fire Data Center, where they are used along with data from other sources to prepare estimates of the magnitude and characteristics of the United States fire problem. The information is also used to support legislation, to provide guidance to industry, to help set priorities in fire research, and to provide baseline information to local governments against which they can compare their own performance and help assess their own needs.

Participation by states in NFIRS is voluntary, though the goal is to get as close to 100 percent participation as possible. Within most states, participation of local governments in the state system is also voluntary, although most states have laws requiring the transmittal of at least some key information to the state on certain classes of fires.

what should be collected will come up with a slightly different idea. It is, however, extremely important that fire departments collect a common core of data, even though it will never be perfect for all purposes. Individual communities may wish to add additional items of interest to themselves that are not collected nationally. They may also wish to break out some of the elements in more detail than is done by the existing coding system.

Some local departments use a checklist format for their incident reports. Under each data element is a list of choices, and the person who completes the form checks one. Except in unusual cases, the only information that is written out is the name, telephone number, and other identifying data, and the narrative description of the incident. Checkoff forms are simple to use and do not require much consultation of manuals. But they may encourage firefighters to check one of the suggested choices instead of making the effort to fill out the "other" box when the checkoff list does not fit the situation. The checkoff format also requires a larger form and/or smaller print to accommodate all items.

Figure 6–1 Incident report form.

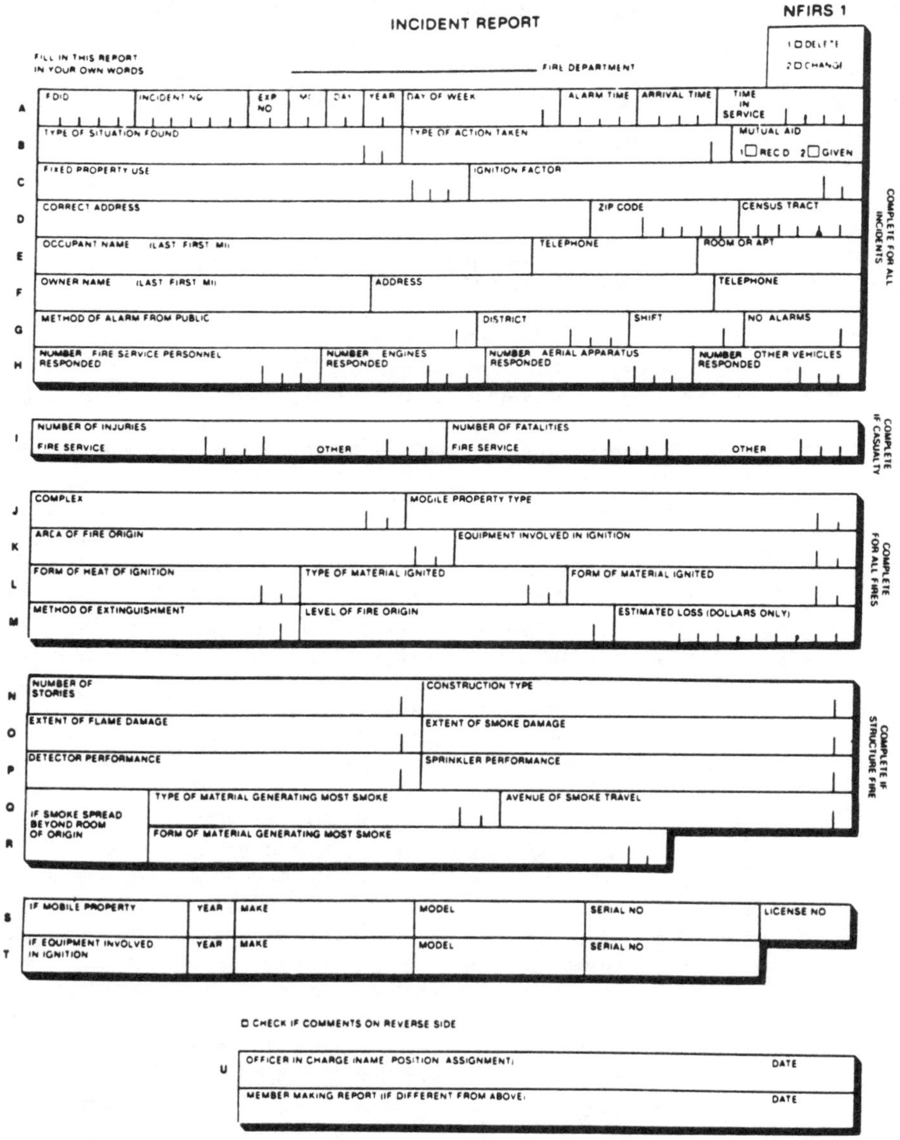
NFIRS 1

INCIDENT REPORT

1 ☐ DELETE
2 ☐ CHANGE

FILL IN THIS REPORT IN YOUR OWN WORDS

FIRE DEPARTMENT

A: FDID | INCIDENT NO | EXP NO | MO | DAY | YEAR | DAY OF WEEK | ALARM TIME | ARRIVAL TIME | TIME IN SERVICE

B: TYPE OF SITUATION FOUND | TYPE OF ACTION TAKEN | MUTUAL AID 1☐ REC'D 2☐ GIVEN

C: FIXED PROPERTY USE | IGNITION FACTOR

D: CORRECT ADDRESS | ZIP CODE | CENSUS TRACT

E: OCCUPANT NAME (LAST, FIRST, MI) | TELEPHONE | ROOM OR APT

F: OWNER NAME (LAST, FIRST, MI) | ADDRESS | TELEPHONE

G: METHOD OF ALARM FROM PUBLIC | DISTRICT | SHIFT | NO. ALARMS

H: NUMBER FIRE SERVICE PERSONNEL RESPONDED | NUMBER ENGINES RESPONDED | NUMBER AERIAL APPARATUS RESPONDED | NUMBER OTHER VEHICLES RESPONDED

COMPLETE FOR ALL INCIDENTS

I: NUMBER OF INJURIES: FIRE SERVICE | OTHER | NUMBER OF FATALITIES: FIRE SERVICE | OTHER

COMPLETE IF CASUALTY

J: COMPLEX | MOBILE PROPERTY TYPE

K: AREA OF FIRE ORIGIN | EQUIPMENT INVOLVED IN IGNITION

L: FORM OF HEAT OF IGNITION | TYPE OF MATERIAL IGNITED | FORM OF MATERIAL IGNITED

M: METHOD OF EXTINGUISHMENT | LEVEL OF FIRE ORIGIN | ESTIMATED LOSS (DOLLARS ONLY)

COMPLETE FOR ALL FIRES

N: NUMBER OF STORIES | CONSTRUCTION TYPE

O: EXTENT OF FLAME DAMAGE | EXTENT OF SMOKE DAMAGE

P: DETECTOR PERFORMANCE | SPRINKLER PERFORMANCE

Q: IF SMOKE SPREAD BEYOND ROOM OF ORIGIN | TYPE OF MATERIAL GENERATING MOST SMOKE | AVENUE OF SMOKE TRAVEL

R: FORM OF MATERIAL GENERATING MOST SMOKE

COMPLETE IF STRUCTURE FIRE

S: IF MOBILE PROPERTY | YEAR | MAKE | MODEL | SERIAL NO | LICENSE NO

T: IF EQUIPMENT INVOLVED IN IGNITION | YEAR | MAKE | MODEL | SERIAL NO

☐ CHECK IF COMMENTS ON REVERSE SIDE

U: OFFICER IN CHARGE (NAME, POSITION, ASSIGNMENT) | DATE

MEMBER MAKING REPORT (IF DIFFERENT FROM ABOVE) | DATE

Rather than use forms, some departments have the firefighter enter incident data directly into a computer terminal. The display screen may show a form, and the firefighter completes it directly on the screen. The firefighter needs to be familiar with the codes to use, or have the capability to call up definitions on the screen. In other systems, the firefighter is presented with a series of multiple choice questions, each showing the data element and the possible choices (as shown in Figure 6–4).

The computer may be programmed to screen each data element as it is entered to see if it is a legitimate choice. The computer may check further to see if it is a reasonable choice given the previous data entered. After a question is completed, the computer may branch to other questions. For example, if choice 1 is selected in Figure 6–4, the next screen may show a detailed menu for fires and explosions, and the user makes a further selection. Similarly, if injuries are reported, the computer may automatically call up the casualty report to be completed for each one.

Figure 6–2 Civilian casualty report form.

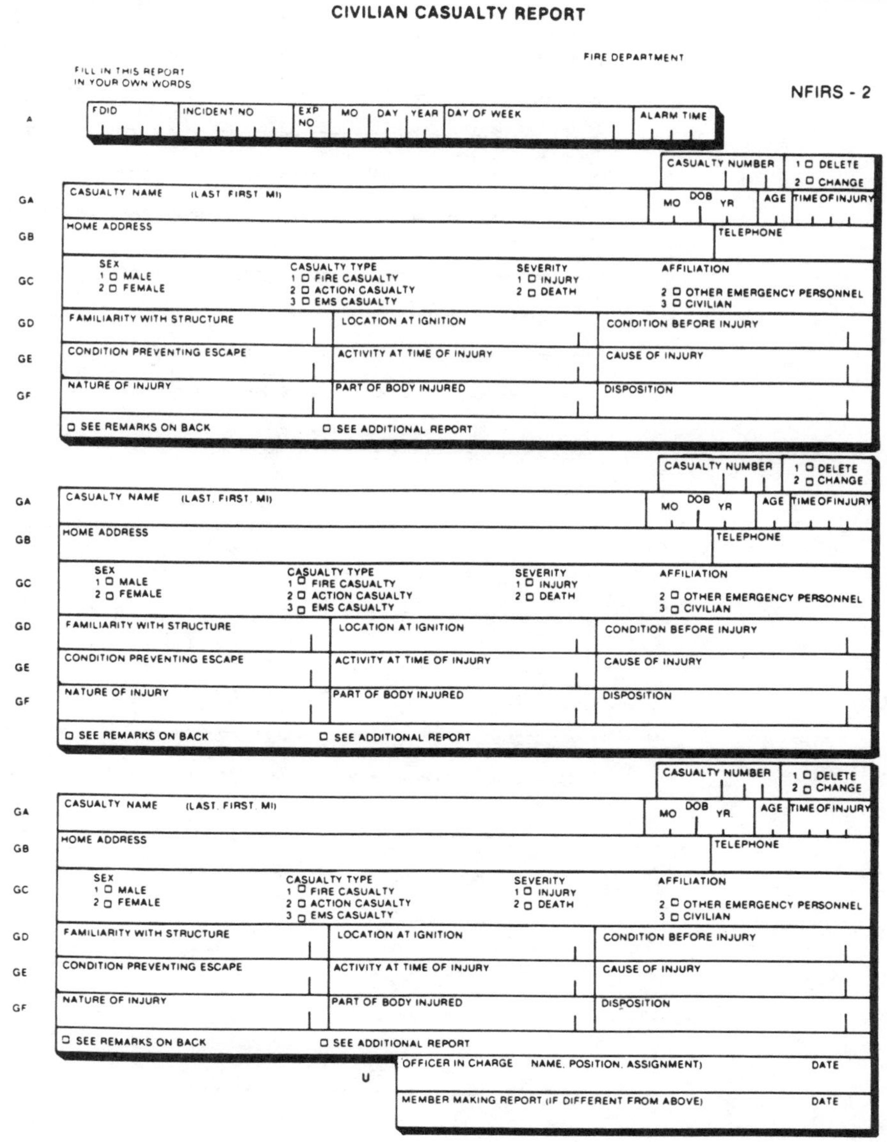

CIVILIAN CASUALTY REPORT

FIRE DEPARTMENT

FILL IN THIS REPORT IN YOUR OWN WORDS

NFIRS - 2

A FDID | INCIDENT NO | EXP NO | MO DAY YEAR | DAY OF WEEK | ALARM TIME

CASUALTY NUMBER | 1 ☐ DELETE 2 ☐ CHANGE

GA CASUALTY NAME (LAST, FIRST, MI) | DOB MO YR | AGE | TIME OF INJURY

GB HOME ADDRESS | TELEPHONE

GC SEX 1 ☐ MALE 2 ☐ FEMALE | CASUALTY TYPE 1 ☐ FIRE CASUALTY 2 ☐ ACTION CASUALTY 3 ☐ EMS CASUALTY | SEVERITY 1 ☐ INJURY 2 ☐ DEATH | AFFILIATION 2 ☐ OTHER EMERGENCY PERSONNEL 3 ☐ CIVILIAN

GD FAMILIARITY WITH STRUCTURE | LOCATION AT IGNITION | CONDITION BEFORE INJURY

GE CONDITION PREVENTING ESCAPE | ACTIVITY AT TIME OF INJURY | CAUSE OF INJURY

GF NATURE OF INJURY | PART OF BODY INJURED | DISPOSITION

☐ SEE REMARKS ON BACK ☐ SEE ADDITIONAL REPORT

CASUALTY NUMBER | 1 ☐ DELETE 2 ☐ CHANGE

GA CASUALTY NAME (LAST, FIRST, MI) | DOB MO YR | AGE | TIME OF INJURY

GB HOME ADDRESS | TELEPHONE

GC SEX 1 ☐ MALE 2 ☐ FEMALE | CASUALTY TYPE 1 ☐ FIRE CASUALTY 2 ☐ ACTION CASUALTY 3 ☐ EMS CASUALTY | SEVERITY 1 ☐ INJURY 2 ☐ DEATH | AFFILIATION 2 ☐ OTHER EMERGENCY PERSONNEL 3 ☐ CIVILIAN

GD FAMILIARITY WITH STRUCTURE | LOCATION AT IGNITION | CONDITION BEFORE INJURY

GE CONDITION PREVENTING ESCAPE | ACTIVITY AT TIME OF INJURY | CAUSE OF INJURY

GF NATURE OF INJURY | PART OF BODY INJURED | DISPOSITION

☐ SEE REMARKS ON BACK ☐ SEE ADDITIONAL REPORT

CASUALTY NUMBER | 1 ☐ DELETE 2 ☐ CHANGE

GA CASUALTY NAME (LAST, FIRST, MI) | DOB MO YR | AGE | TIME OF INJURY

GB HOME ADDRESS | TELEPHONE

GC SEX 1 ☐ MALE 2 ☐ FEMALE | CASUALTY TYPE 1 ☐ FIRE CASUALTY 2 ☐ ACTION CASUALTY 3 ☐ EMS CASUALTY | SEVERITY 1 ☐ INJURY 2 ☐ DEATH | AFFILIATION 2 ☐ OTHER EMERGENCY PERSONNEL 3 ☐ CIVILIAN

GD FAMILIARITY WITH STRUCTURE | LOCATION AT IGNITION | CONDITION BEFORE INJURY

GE CONDITION PREVENTING ESCAPE | ACTIVITY AT TIME OF INJURY | CAUSE OF INJURY

GF NATURE OF INJURY | PART OF BODY INJURED | DISPOSITION

☐ SEE REMARKS ON BACK ☐ SEE ADDITIONAL REPORT

U OFFICER IN CHARGE NAME, POSITION, ASSIGNMENT) | DATE

MEMBER MAKING REPORT (IF DIFFERENT FROM ABOVE) | DATE

Fire investigation data

Another major body of fire data comprises fire investigation reports. Most communities investigate incendiary or suspicious fires and fires involving deaths. Some communities investigate all building fires, all fires with severe injuries, and fires of special interest.

Fire investigation reports are an especially important pool of data because they are conducted by highly trained personnel and provide more details than do routine incident reports. Although traditionally used for special types of fires, in-depth investigations can also be used to obtain a better understanding of common types of fires that do not result in large losses but that collectively are important to life safety or property loss. They can be invaluable for planning remedial actions.

Figure 6–3 Fire service casualty report form.

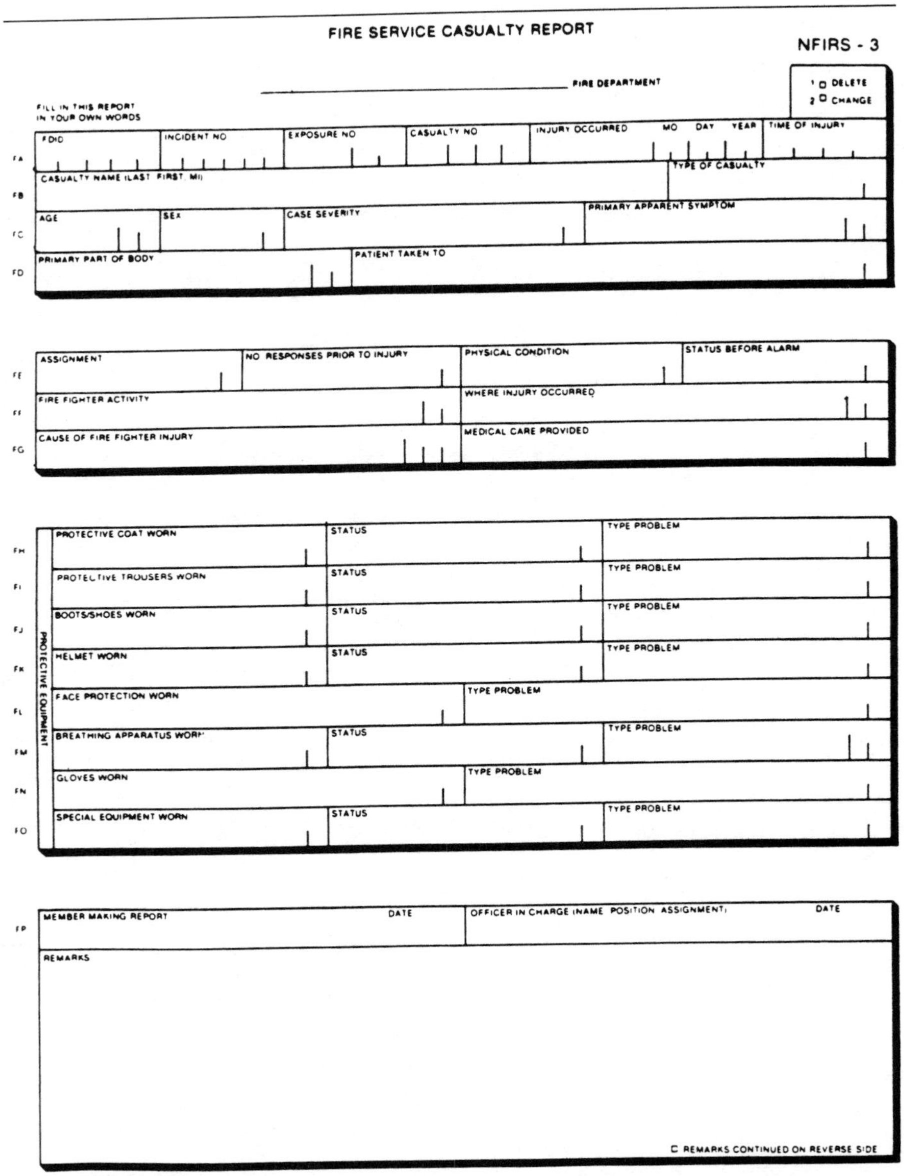

FIRE SERVICE CASUALTY REPORT

NFIRS - 3

FIRE DEPARTMENT

1 ☐ DELETE
2 ☐ CHANGE

FILL IN THIS REPORT IN YOUR OWN WORDS

FA: FDID | INCIDENT NO | EXPOSURE NO | CASUALTY NO | INJURY OCCURRED MO DAY YEAR | TIME OF INJURY

FB: CASUALTY NAME (LAST, FIRST, MI) | TYPE OF CASUALTY

FC: AGE | SEX | CASE SEVERITY | PRIMARY APPARENT SYMPTOM

FD: PRIMARY PART OF BODY | PATIENT TAKEN TO

FE: ASSIGNMENT | NO RESPONSES PRIOR TO INJURY | PHYSICAL CONDITION | STATUS BEFORE ALARM

FF: FIRE FIGHTER ACTIVITY | WHERE INJURY OCCURRED

FG: CAUSE OF FIRE FIGHTER INJURY | MEDICAL CARE PROVIDED

PROTECTIVE EQUIPMENT

FH: PROTECTIVE COAT WORN | STATUS | TYPE PROBLEM

FI: PROTECTIVE TROUSERS WORN | STATUS | TYPE PROBLEM

FJ: BOOTS/SHOES WORN | STATUS | TYPE PROBLEM

FK: HELMET WORN | STATUS | TYPE PROBLEM

FL: FACE PROTECTION WORN | TYPE PROBLEM

FM: BREATHING APPARATUS WORN | STATUS | TYPE PROBLEM

FN: GLOVES WORN | TYPE PROBLEM

FO: SPECIAL EQUIPMENT WORN | STATUS | TYPE PROBLEM

FP: MEMBER MAKING REPORT | DATE | OFFICER IN CHARGE (NAME, POSITION, ASSIGNMENT) | DATE

REMARKS

☐ REMARKS CONTINUED ON REVERSE SIDE

The format and definitions used for the fire investigation report should parallel those of the incident report to the extent possible so that the data on the basic incident file can be easily augmented.

Many departments fail to revise their incident reports to reflect new information from the investigation report. The most common change is from an original report of ''fire under investigation'' or ''cause undetermined'' to a final determination of the cause. Much valuable information about fires involving large losses and deaths never makes it to the incident files because people neglect to update them. Since the incident data form is the basis for so much management analysis, it is especially important to watch for this problem in an MIS. The system can be programmed so that updating will be done automatically; when an investigation report is entered, those data elements in common with the incident report can be updated.

Special fire department studies and bibliographies

Many fire departments conduct ''one-shot'' or occasional studies that provide useful information. Examples include estimates of indirect losses from fires, surveys of the attitudes of residents or businesses about fire department effectiveness, and detailed supplementary incident reports on certain types of fires. The MIS can keep a list of these reports, and a set of key words and a summary for each. The list can then be searched when a particular issue arises. For small departments a paper list may suffice. For departments of all sizes the MIS might also include the capability to access outside fire-related computerized bibliographic services.

Socioeconomic/demographic data

Much information on the characteristics of the people and property of a community is available from the U.S. Bureau of the Census, although the information may be almost ten years out of date just before a census is taken. To supplement the census data, the planning department often keeps information on population estimates, number of housing units by type, amount and location of substandard housing, amount of business, and so on. Much of the data will be tied to census tracts, which is one reason why it is important for fire departments to record the census tract on each incident report.

Figure 6–4 Sample computer screen showing menu of choices for type of situation found.

```
*****************************
*   TYPE OF SITUATION FOUND   *
*****************************

1) FIRE, EXPLOSION
2) OVERPRESSURE RUPTURE (NO COMBUSTION)
3) RESCUE CALL
4) HAZARDOUS CONDITION, STANDBY
5) SERVICE CALL
6) GOOD INTENT CALL
7) FALSE CALL
8) OTHER SITUATION FOUND


****************************
*   TYPE APPROPRIATE NUMBER   *
****************************
```

Fire departments may keep census data in computer files to analyze fire incidence by census tract. For smaller departments the census data in hard copy form should suffice.

Arson information

Management information systems for arson prevention and control have become highly developed.[4] Generally they serve two functions. First, they support the investigation of existing cases by keeping track of names and other data; identifying patterns and names that appear frequently in arson fires; and recording past fire history of buildings with suspicious fires. Second, the arson information management system can provide early warning of buildings ripe to be torched, based on their physical condition, tax arrears, violations, owner history, and other factors. Typical data files include the following:

1. Case data
   a) Offense reports and investigation data
   b) Arrest dispositions
   c) Master name indexes (all those involved in suspected arson; e.g., owners, occupants, lienholders, witnesses, subjects)
   d) Insurance coverage files (e.g., coverage limits, policy start and change dates, mortgages, names of insured)
2. Early warning data
   a) Property histories (properties with unpaid taxes, properties in poor condition, properties of failing businesses, etc.)
   b) Profiles of arson cases by time of day, day of week, month, dollar loss, etc.
   c) Incident maps (computerized pin maps).

Operations research models

Originally, the term *MIS* referred to a system that used a computer to model a corporate function or some area of its business, using simulations to test alternatives and devise optimal solutions. Such models have become feasible for some fire department decisions related to dispatch, fire station location, fire spread, firefighting operations, prevention, hazardous materials, and emergency management. Sometimes the computer is programmed to use decision algorithms (procedures) to help make decisions based on earlier analysis or wisdom. The computer decisions then are not the result of comparing alternative results from models but rather are a fixed set of rules.

Computer-aided dispatch

Commonplace today in fire departments, computer-aided or computer-assisted dispatch (CAD) systems often make the dispatch to a call automatically. Sometimes the computer presents a suggested dispatch for the dispatcher to approve or override, or the computer may be used to back up the manual dispatch, except in highly complex cases. Typically there is a manual backup system for the computer.

Computer-aided dispatch can be used not only to route apparatus to an incident, but also to route transport of victims to hospitals. Just as the typical CAD system keeps track of the status of each station and its companies, including specialized companies, an EMS-routing computer system can keep track of the status of hospitals in terms of available bed capacity and emergency room capacity, by specialty. Victims can be routed to the most appropriate hospital for them.[5]

Much valuable information is obtained in the process of receiving an emergency call and dispatching equipment to it. Dispatch records may be in the form of voice tapes, printed forms, informal notes, or computer files. Information associated with a dispatch often includes the nature of the call, the time of receipt of the call in the department, the time of arrival at the scene, the time the fire was knocked down, and the time the equipment was back in service. Of course the address and often the type of occupancy and the name of the person reporting the emergency also are recorded. This information is valuable for completing incident reports. The number of dispatches made can be used to check that incident reports are filled out for each call. The dispatcher also is usually the one who assigns an incident number to a call; that number becomes the key to coordinating various records on a particular incident.

In CAD systems the dispatcher enters much of the information directly into a computer during the course of a call. This information can be matched to other information on the incident provided separately by the officer at the scene; this system reduces the officer's paperwork and improves the reliability of the data.

Station location

Station location models are perhaps second only to CAD as an example of the widespread use of operations research techniques in fire departments. These models can compute the best locations for fire stations to meet various constraints such as specified response times. Detailed models use an actual street map of the community to compute response times and take into account the arrival of first due units coming from different stations.[6]

Fire spread

Fire spread models, which have been used for years to predict the evolution of wildfires, are now available for structural fires as well. They show how a fire and smoke will spread in a specific building as a function of the features and materials in the building, the status of various systems and openings in the building, and the location and nature of the fire's ignition. These models will become increasingly useful in making decisions about the safety design of buildings and how best to meet codes that specify desired building performance rather than the way to achieve it. They can be used in reviewing plans, in prefire planning, and in analyzing fire spread in past incidents that hold lessons for the future. As these models evolve, they take increasingly complex buildings and fire protection systems into account, for a wider range of building configurations. The Center for Fire Research at the National Bureau of Standards has sponsored and supported development of fire spread models.

Optimal firefighting operations

Large strides have been made toward developing models of optimal firefighting decisions, in work that is closely related to the use of the fire spread models. Fireground officers may some day be able to use models to predict in real time (that is, instantaneously), effects of such actions as ventilating a building in several places or activating built-in fire protection features.

Firefighting operations can already be assisted by tapping the department's MIS for data on the characteristics of buildings and their hazards. The information can be sent by radio link, either verbally or through printouts transmitted to a terminal mounted in the command vehicle. Traditionally, personnel have looked up characteristics of buildings manually in paper files or on microfiche.

As the process becomes more automated, it becomes useful for a wider range of fires, not only major ones but those in the incipient stage as well.

Optimal prevention management

True overall fire prevention management models are not yet available because of the difficulty in quantifying the effectiveness of alternative prevention strategies such as public education and inspections. Computer programs to assist in scheduling inspectors on inspections, speakers for public education talks, and other aspects of managing the work load are available and useful. But the more complex question of figuring out the best mix of prevention approaches remains elusive.

Hazardous materials response

In their simple form, the hazardous materials files for the MIS may be a purchased software package indicating in broad terms what to do for each type of hazardous materials incident, such as whether to evacuate the area and for what radius. Files may also be kept on experts such as chemical engineers available for consultation for various types of problems.

In more complex models, the amount of hazardous material spilled, maps of the area, wind and weather conditions, and other data can be fed into the computer in real time, and an "expert opinion" rendered on the best action or alternative actions. In the wake of federal legislation, hazardous materials response is receiving increasing attention in fire departments.

Integrated emergency management system (IEMS)

In large emergencies IEMS can help keep track of resources, victims, emergency forces on the scene, forces available for backing, and so on. The Federal Emergency Management Agency has supported the development of such management software and is a source for information on the emergency management software packages available. Similarly, the FIRESCOPE project in California tracks mutual aid resources and has a fire spread model.

Getting started: policy decisions

A series of questions must be answered when a fire department starts to design or improve a management information system. Basically they are the same questions that must be answered for developing a system in any organization, with modifications for the fire service.

The fundamental question, of course, is whether to use a computer at all. In some very small departments, or for some purposes, it may be more cost effective to keep files by hand. Assuming that the department needs computer capability, however, the key question is What is the purpose of the system? Getting past the generalities often is difficult, so it may be worth making two passes at this question. The sections below describe some of the other questions that need to be answered in developing an MIS. Ideally, one would start with objectives, then define the information needed to meet them and how to get that information. That is useful as a start. Realistically, what you get often depends on what you can get rather than what is most desirable. Therefore it is useful to sketch out what information is or can be collected, and how it can best be used.

Information to be stored

The information to be stored in the MIS might include fire incidents, inspection reports, investigations, building records, and the other types of files listed earlier in this chapter. For each type of input, additional questions have to be answered:

1. From what sources is the information to be obtained?
2. How will it be screened or checked before entry to ensure that the information stored in the data base is as accurate as possible? (This is discussed in a later section.)
3. How will the file be updated or corrected? For example, when the cause of a fire that was initially designated as "under investigation" is finally determined, how will that update be made, and how will the department ensure that it will be made?
4. How much historical data should be entered? This can be a large job not only because of the sheer volume, but also because data formats often change over time. For example, NFIRS switched from Version 3 to Version 4 in 1984. Firefighter casualty data changed considerably, as did some other data elements. To track ten-year trends that include 1984, an MIS has to store consistent data elements for the periods before and after the change, or earlier data must be translated into the more recent format.

Standard outputs and frequency of use

The fire service manager must define the reports that are to be produced routinely or periodically and a list of "standard reports" that are to be available upon request. Either category may include monthly activity reports, daily rosters, and annual trends in losses and causes, for example.

Timeliness is important, but a price is paid for producing data reports too often or not often enough. The frequency with which data should be generated depends on how fast the data are likely to change, how quickly remedial actions can be taken, and the tastes of the user. Fairly complete statistical reports are needed perhaps only once a year, as part of the annual budget process or departmental policy planning. At the other extreme, information on availability of personnel and equipment needs to be accessible continuously to identify the forces available to fight emergencies. In general, information will be required for the data system at one of the following frequencies: real time (instantaneously), daily, weekly, monthly, quarterly, annually, or upon request (but not instantaneously).

The frequency with which various types of information are generated may be influenced by the needs of those outside the city. For example, the state or federal government may require on a monthly or quarterly basis information that a local government needs only annually because of the small number of incidents it has and the difficulty in observing patterns over short intervals of time. But when the data are aggregated by the state for many small communities, patterns can be determined without waiting as long.

It is important to be realistic in setting requirements for the system and to avoid getting much more computer equipment and software than is needed, generating reports that never get used, and actually reducing usage by inundating users with too frequent reporting.

Flexibility for special reports and analyses

The range of special reports or information requests that are to be available from the system on demand (as opposed to scheduled reports) needs to be determined. So does the turnaround time and the constraints on requests. For example, it often is desirable to be able to generate a cross-tabulation of any two data elements on a fire incident report for all fires meeting a specified set of criteria. You might want the number of residential fires that caused casualties in the period 1980–85 according to the time of day when they occurred.

It is neither necessary nor possible to anticipate all uses of the MIS, nor to have an enormous set of predesigned reports. It *is* important to clearly define the data base and not build in barriers to its imaginative use. It is also important to maintain flexibility in the use of the data stored. This can be achieved by having a general purpose report generator that allows the user to select any elements in the data base conditioned on any other, so as to generate tables plotting *x* versus *y* conditioned on *a*, *b*, and *c*. Uses that were unforeseen at the time the system was designed may turn out to be among the most valuable ones.

Organization of data

There are two major viewpoints to consider when organizing data. One is the viewpoint of the potential users, and the other is the viewpoint of the programmer. As the system is being designed, a dialogue between the fire chief or other person assigned to oversee the MIS and the systems analyst/programmer is crucial. Often the user specifies needs first and leaves the organization of information within the computer to the programmer. The programmer may ask detailed questions about how the data will be used and how frequently.

As software and hardware become more powerful, it becomes easier to accommodate the user's requirements rather than have the organization of the system dictated by hardware or software.

Access to the system

Who will use the system? There are many potential users of the fire department's MIS, including the fire chief, divisional and battalion chiefs, and almost every officer in the department; the city manager and his or her staff; the city council; other city departments; budget personnel; the local media; industry; and the public. Some of the users are likely to use the system much more frequently than others. Some, such as the fire department's analysts, will be "primary" users who access the files directly, while other, "secondary," users (for example, the city manager or the local media) will use the data only after they have been analyzed.

It is important to identify these different types of users and the different ways in which they will be allowed or encouraged to interact with the system in order to choose the best language and output formats, to decide whether to spend the effort making the system easy to use for those with little computer training. For example, if the fire chief is expected to look at printouts, the formats and column headings should be as clear as possible. Even if the chief can read complex printouts, the time it takes to do so and the difficulty of showing them to anyone else may dictate a need for greater clarity than if the computer reports are to be used only by analysts. If departmental officers will be expected to request information directly from computer terminals, the system should be designed to present menus to guide them through the choices they need to make.

The cost-effectiveness of a data system can be ridiculously poor if its information is not used. Investing in clear output formats and ease of operation may increase the dollar cost of setting up the data system, but it can significantly improve the efficiency and effectiveness of the whole department in the long run.

Security requirements

The question of who has access to the MIS may well depend on the types of data involved. For example, the medical history of individuals would be closely held for privacy, and the status of an arson investigation would be closely held for security. But fire incident data might be accessible to virtually anyone. Coded key words and/or other controls to restrict access have to be part of the design of the system.

Accuracy requirements

There is no simple way to specify accuracy requirements, that is, how "good" the data need to be. Data must be accurate enough to answer with reasonable confidence the question being asked, so the requirements vary from question to question. For example, fire chiefs need to know exactly how many and which engine companies are available for dispatching at any instant. On the other hand, they can probably afford to miscount the number of fire calls each company has in a year by 2 or 3 out of 500, although they would not want to be off by 50, because then they would not know whether a 10 percent decrease in fire calls was due to successful prevention or to miscounting.

Fire chiefs not only need accurate data, but they also must be able to demonstrate the quality of their data publicly. Local officials need to believe the data are credible if they are to use them in making decisions. It is not enough to say that records are "as accurate as possible," or that data provided by the chief must be reliable because the chief is a reputable officer. Accuracy should be monitored regularly and quality control procedures, such as those discussed later in the chapter, should be in place.

On the other hand, too much precision can also be costly. For example, losses usually canot be estimated down to the last dollar. It is unnecessary to ask firefighters to be overly precise in estimating monetary loss, and it is counterproductive to spend more money appraising minor damage than the value of the damage itself.

Choosing a computer and computer services

A bewildering variety of computer hardware and software choices will have to be made when establishing a computer-based MIS.

Computer service is a highly technical field that is rapidly changing, as computer hardware and software capabilities improve and costs decrease. It takes someone in the computer field to keep fully abreast of these developments. Most departments should consider hiring a computer consultant to help them decide whether to acquire or improve computer services and select the most appropriate equipment and software for their needs and budget.

Basic decisions

Some of the basic decisions a department must make before selecting hardware and software are discussed in the following sections.

Purchase or lease? Among the basic hardware decisions is whether to buy or lease a computer specifically for the fire department, whether to rent access to a computer from a vendor or from another city or county department, or whether to use the community's centralized data processing department. In some local governments, all departments must use the centralized services, so the question is moot. Centralized computer departments are not always set up to deal with fast turnaround requests, and the advantage of using the computer versus doing analysis by hand decreases when the fire department does not have direct control over its use. Sometimes it is less expensive for the fire department to lease or purchase its own computer rather than use that of the city because of the peculiarities of local practices in billing and setting priorities on the computer, or because of personnel skills available, or for other reasons. The widely held belief in the economy of scale of large centralized computers no longer holds true for many situations.

On the other hand, owning a computer often brings new headaches to the fire department. Just as owning a car means providing for its maintenance, so does owning a computer. It is often more convenient and more economical overall to leave technical computer operations to a hired hand and use departmental technical expertise to work the fire problem.

Number and type of terminals   In designing the MIS, a second important consideration is the number and location of terminals. Computer terminals have keyboards for entering data into the computer, and a video screen or printer, or both, for getting data out. Terminals might be in a central location or in a few key locations such as the fire prevention bureau, central records, and the office of the chief. Or the terminals might be more widely distributed to battalions or even companies.

The trend is clearly toward allowing access at the dispersed, lower management levels as well as centrally. It is common to have remote terminals that allow access to a central computer data base from various offices and other locations. Less common but increasing in popularity are remote portable terminals installed in vehicles or apparatus, or, better yet, hand portable ones. Just as police officers in many cities are able to dial up auto license plate numbers from a foot officer's radio so it is possible to have a fire inspector dial up a building's investigation and fire history while making an inspection, and then update the file with the latest inspection results. Likewise, a firefighter could report incident data right from the scene or from a convenient location in the station to the MIS via a two-way portable computer terminal. The devices to do this already exist and are continually becoming lighter, cheaper, and more powerful.

Remote terminals can save firefighters time and paperwork and also provide a check at the source of the information being fed into the computer. A great deal of time is consumed by maintaining rosters, filling out incident reports, preparing monthly reports, and filling special information requests. Having input forms "built into" terminals to prompt the operator on what to fill in and having reasonableness checks applied to what he or she enters speeds up data entry and improves data quality.

The number and location of terminals depend on the flexibility and convenience needed in data manipulation, the importance of having immediate access to the data, whether the city or someone else sets priorities on use of a shared machine, and the need for confidentiality. The department should seek expert assistance in making these decisions.

Software decisions   A great deal of time is generally spent making hardware decisions because they represent immediate, tangible, out-of-pocket expenses. Too little thought is usually given to software, and even less to the department personnel time needed to provide inputs to the system, guide its development, and make use of it. In terms of dollars, software and personnel will probably account for the bulk of the costs.

A major software decision is whether the department should purchase standard software packages, develop its own software tailored to its own needs, or use some combination of the two. The answer depends on how comprehensive a data system is desired, the level of computer expertise that the department has, and how useful the department finds the existing software packages. Many departments have developed their own systems and many others use standard packages.

In making software decisions, consider compatibility with the hardware and software of other departments and with that of state fire agencies, for sharing software development investments. If each computer program in the MIS must be tailored to the department, programming costs will be high. On the other hand, packaged software is seldom just right either. The cost of customizing the software must be weighed against the inconvenience of using programs written by others without your particular setup in mind.

Compatibility is also important for other reasons. Compatibility with the department's own previous data systems makes it possible to track trends, and compatibility with existing or future systems of other departments makes it possible to share data. For example, it can be useful to link tax records to arson-related data, but to do so requires a common way of identifying buildings.

Implementation

A practical approach to answering these basic planning and design questions is to sketch out a list of requirements with several of the brightest members of the department, including some who are familiar with computers. Then visit or speak with a few other departments to see what they have done and what they would do differently if they could start over. Also find out how they have changed their system over time and how they are planning to expand it in the future. Then reconsider the list of requirements. Next, consult a computer professional for detailed advice, and modify the design again. Each department that has a computerized MIS will have a unique system tailored to its own needs. An example of the choices made by one department is shown in Figure 6–5.

It is wise to start modestly and build up from there unless money is unlimited and the department can hire a fleet of experts to design and operate the system. Many corporations and institutions have had difficulty getting a complex MIS to work properly. Starting modestly is easy with a modular system that can be upgraded over time. Get a piece working right before doing the whole thing.

It is important to recognize that the department will probably not realize cost savings in recordkeeping by starting an MIS. The main advantage is better information to make wiser decisions that will improve the cost-effectiveness of the entire department.

Fire incident analysis

By the time most officers rise to chief, they are familiar with a wide range of management data, although perhaps not within the context of a formal MIS. Most senior officers have learned to make use of personnel information, training and shift schedules, equipment maintenance records, inspections records, and other information needed for day-to-day management of people and equipment. It might seem natural to assume that fire incident data would be among these categories, but experience shows it is not. Although officers generate fire reports and use fire data for most of their careers, it remains one class of management information of which better use could be made.

There are perhaps two main reasons for the underuse of the rich array of elements in fire incident data. First, many of the details now recorded on fire incidents are relatively new for many departments, and they have not become accustomed to using them. Second, the details are most useful in guiding prevention programs, and they received less attention in the past before prevention began to rise as a priority in the fire service.

Figure 6–5 An example of the functions selected for the MIS in Prescott, Arizona.

Personnel management programs
EMS recertification dates—selected by name, engine company, shift, certification type, etc.;
Personnel roster—including hire date, emergency contact, blood type, performance rating, special skills, pager code, etc.;
Daily personnel status and activity report—including who is on duty, who is absent and the reason why, how many hours are spent on all required activities for each company, each day, etc.

Training records
Individual training record—selected by detail or summary report, including career total in each subject area;
Department training statistics—selected by company, shift, or a combination;
Training requirement report—including how well personnel are meeting the annual criteria set forth by the training officer.

Budget analysis
Budget summary report—including the percent of budget spent, encumbered monies, etc.;
Budget detail report—including a complete review of purchase orders, dates, and descriptions.

Inventory programs
Fire hose total inventory—selected by replacement date, location, size, type, test date, etc.;
Fire hydrant inventory—selected by test date, location, gpm, service availability, etc.;

Fixed asset inventory—selected by type, replacement date, location, etc.

Investigation programs
Fire investigation records—selected by occupants, suspects, witnesses, date, location, cause, and occupancy classification;
Name search reports;
Insurance master reports—relating policyholders to insurance carriers and fire histories.

Inspection records
Code enforcement status—reviewing occupancy inspections, rechecks, compliance rate, etc.;
Occupancy location reports—selected by address, business name, number of outstanding violations, etc.;
Forecast report—including work load indicator based on total numbers of inspections due for each month in a twelve-month period;
Master inspection report—summarizing all inspection activities, including violations, rechecks, and compliance dates.

Incident reporting program
Statistical reviews—selected by average response time by unit, by district, by incident type;
Response by unit—summarizing the activity of each piece of apparatus;
Incident summary report—analyzing all responses collectively, with the ability to narrow the parameters of the report by using multiple selection criteria.

This section explains how to analyze the fire problem from the top down, using NFIRS-like incident data. This information is at the heart of many aspects of prevention and suppression policy.

Although NFIRS data elements have evolved from what was called Version 3 in the late 1970s to Version 4 in the mid-1980s, the analysis here applies to the data from either version.

An example of the type of data the department would like to get from the MIS is shown in Figure 6–6, which is a map of fire incident rates per 100,000 population for each census tract in a hypothetical city, Community X. The darker shaded areas are those with the higher rates. The data have been averaged for a three-year period to reduce the effects of chance, which might cause individual tracts to be uncharacteristically high in any one year.

The figure shows that the highest incident rates are in two areas of the city: a cluster of tracts in the old part of the city, near the river, and a single tract in the east. The rates are medium in tracts adjacent to the high ones and relatively low elsewhere, with a few exceptions. (''Why are they different from their neighbors?'' one might ask.) The rates suggest which areas are most in need of help in preventing fires.

Figure 6–7 takes another cut at the incident data, showing the census tracts with the largest average number of fires per year. That information, coupled with more details on the severity of the fires and their time of day, can help

Figure 6–6   Fire incident rates by census tract: three-year average, 1985–87 (Community *X*).

Residential fires per 100,000 residents

- 600 and over
- 400 to 600
- 200 to 400
- less than 200

Figure 6–7   Number of fires per census tract: three-year average, 1985–87 (Community *X*).

Residential fires per tract

- Over 100
- 50 to 100
- 25 to 50
- Less than 25

managers decide where suppression forces should be located. It also indicates where the bulk of the fire problem lies. Note that the two figures present different types of information. To reduce the number of fires in the community by half, for example, it is not enough to know which tracts have the highest rates per capita (Figure 6–6) because they may contain only a small fraction of the local population. The most dilapidated and fire-prone area may have 20 percent of the population and its fire rate may be twice that of the rest of the city, but the majority of fires may occur elsewhere.

Identifying the fire problem

To identify its fire problem, every department should analyze the what, where, who, why, and when questions about its fires, casualties, and losses. Some of these questions and the elements needed to answer them are outlined below.

1. What burned?
    a) Type of property
        (1) Structures (by type of construction, number of stories, etc.)
        (2) Vehicles (e.g., cars, trucks, trains, planes)
        (3) Outdoor materials (e.g., forest, crops, trash)
        (4) Other
    b) Type of occupancy
        (1) Residential
        (2) Stores and offices
        (3) Institutions
        (4) Schools
        (5) Public assembly
        (6) Industrial
        (7) Storage
        (8) Vacant
        (9) Under construction
        (10) Other
2. Who suffered losses?
    a) Owners or occupants with dollar loss (by household income, age, race)
    b) Civilian casualties (by age, sex, race, ethnic group)
    c) Firefighter casualties (by age, rank, job assignment)
3. Where did the fire occur?
    a) Census tract or area
    b) Central business district versus residential and other business areas
    c) Neighborhood
4. When did the fire occur?
    a) Time of day
    b) Day of week
    c) Month
    d) Season
    e) Year
5. How did the fire, casualty, or loss occur (ignition and spread factors)?
    a) Cause of fire
        (1) "General" cause categories (e.g., arson, child playing, carelessness with smoking materials)
        (2) Ignition factor (e.g., incendiary, child playing, short circuit, discarded material)
        (3) Equipment involved in ignition (e.g., electric motor, television, blowtorch, stove)
        (4) Form of heat of ignition (e.g., spark, matches, cigarette)

    (5)   Type of material first ignited (e.g., wood, cotton, plastic, gasoline)

    (6)   Form of material first ignited (e.g., mattress, chair, cabinet, insulation)

b) Automatic detection or suppression effects

    (1)   Sprinkler performance

    (2)   Fire or smoke detector performance

c) Prevention factors

    (1)   Inspection history

    (2)   Relevant hazards outstanding

    (3)   Types of codes in effect

    (4)   Other

d) Reasons for spread

    (1)   Material contributing most to flame

    (2)   Material contributing most to smoke

    (3)   Avenue of flame spread

    (4)   Avenue of smoke spread

    (5)   Other

e) Suppression factors

    (1)   Response time of first unit

    (2)   Special problems encountered (e.g., equipment failure, blocked access, personnel shortage, water shortage, weather)

f) Casualty circumstances

    (1)   Immediate cause of casualty (e.g., exposed to fire products, fell, struck)

    (2)   Activity at time of injury

    (3)   Condition before injury (e.g., asleep, drunk)

    (4)   Other

6.   What was the extent of the losses?

   a) Casualties

    (1)   Number, severity, and nature of injuries

    (2)   Number of deaths

   b) Direct property loss

    (1)   Total dollar loss (structure, contents)

    (2)   Insurance payout

    (3)   Extent of smoke, heat, water, fire control damage (e.g., confined to object of origin, confined to room)

    (4)   Number of buildings destroyed

   c) "Indirect" losses

    (1)   Cost of medical, temporary lodging, food, and other expenses

    (2)   Person-days displaced from home

    (3)   Person-days lost from work

    (4)   Number of people displaced from neighborhood by fire

    (5)   Number of households with serious psychological problems resulting from fire

    (6)   Number of households with significant irreplaceable objects lost

    (7)   Number of pets killed.

Analytical judgment and an understanding of the community are needed to decide how to break out the above data most meaningfully. Some suggested cross-tabulations are shown in the figures and tables of this chapter. Once a few tables are prepared, questions will immediately arise as to why certain numbers are large or small. That is, the initial findings will themselves be highly suggestive of further questions. These questions and answers form much of the basis for planning (see Chapter 4) and evaluating fire protection (Chapter 5).

Much of the analysis of fire data consists simply of arranging the right data in tables and then looking for the large numbers; these indicate the big parts of the problem. All sorts of fancy statistical techniques can be applied to data, but many of the most important types of analysis are possible with a much simpler approach and the use of common sense. Some fire service managers have a fear of analysis, especially when tables appear as computer printouts. Yet many important analyses simply consist of finding the big number in a table and asking why it is big.

Top down analysis

Tables 6–1 through 6–6 illustrate the first steps in a "top-down" analysis of the fire problem. Only one table has been broken out by all three principal types of statistics—absolute numbers, rates, and percentages (Table 6–2)—but each of the other tables could be given similar treatment. The data shown for each table are hypothetical but realistic.

The analysis starts in Table 6–1 with the examination of the total number of calls received in one year by the fire department of Community X, by time of day. These calls are broken down into emergency and nonemergency calls. The emergency calls are further broken down into fires versus other calls. This shows the total work load of the department and the relative frequency of each kind of call. Most calls in Community X are not for fires but for emergency medical services (EMS). The breakout of calls by type, by time of day, and by weekday/weekend is useful for scheduling both personnel and departmental activities. For example, inspections, training, and equipment maintenance may be scheduled for periods of low activity.

Only the fire problem will be analyzed in the remainder of this discussion.

The number of fires and their losses in terms of deaths, injuries, and dollars are shown in Table 6–2 for the four major occupancy types: residential, nonresidential, mobile, and outside. Residential is further broken down into one- and two-family units, apartments, and other (for example, hotels and boardinghouses). This table gives an overview of the severity of the fire problem and the types of property where the problem is concentrated. All five measures (number of fires, civilian deaths, civilian injuries, firefighter injuries, dollar loss) are important. Firefighter deaths should also be considered when they occur.

According to Table 6–2, the greatest absolute number of fires in Community X occurs in outside properties, but for the most part, these fires are minor trash or grass fires and cause little loss. The greatest number of deaths and injuries occur in residential fires. The number of deaths is usually small (less than ten) for most communities, but may be high in any one year because of a single large fire. Therefore, the data may present a misleading picture if they cover only one year. Although a year of high injuries may also occur by chance, these tend to be based on a larger number of incidents and fluctuate less from year to year.

Dollar loss is highest for nonresidential structural fires in Community X, with over 10 percent of the total fire loss coming from one large industrial fire. Although this fire should be counted in the loss, it is useful to note the fraction of the loss from the one fire alone, especially if such fires are relatively rare.

Table 6–2 also shows that most fires in Community X are not in structures, but most losses are, and casualties are concentrated in residences, especially in one- and two-family dwellings. However, the *rate* of fires is higher for apartment dwellers than for those living in one- and two-family dwellings. That is, the life-safety problem is mainly in homes, but it may be more cost effective or more equitable to target prevention programs on apartments first, because they have a higher rate, with their residents suffering disproportionately higher casualty and dollar losses.

In addition to the current year's figures many departments show the previous year's figures and/or the change from the previous year for each data element. This can indicate improvement, or the reverse, from one year to the next. But

Table 6–1 Total fire department calls (Community X, 1987).

Calls	Weekday			Weekend (Sat./Sun.)			
	7 A.M.– 3 P.M.	3 P.M.– 11 P.M.	11 P.M.– 7 A.M.	7 A.M.– 3 P.M.	3 P.M.– 11 P.M.	11 P.M.– 7 P.M.	Total
Emergency calls							
Fires	1,040	1,310	700	460	490	300	4,300
EMS	4,130	3,500	2,370	1,200	2,890	910	15,000
False alarms	105	1,400	195	220	180	100	2,200
Good intent/scares	500	900	300	200	350	150	2,400
Other emergencies	25	125	50	50	50	100	400
Nonemergency calls	120	150	50	60	80	40	500
Annual total	5,920	7,385	3,665	2,190	4,040	1,600	24,800

Table 6–2 Fire overview showing losses by occupancy type (Community X, 1987).

Occupancy type	Fires	Civilian deaths	Civilian injuries	Firefighter injuries	Dollar loss ($000)
	Absolute number				
Residential	1,024	9	83	69	2,400
One/two family	752	6	54	45	1,700
Apartments	219	3	27	20	500
Other	53	0	2	4	200
Nonresidential	655	1	7	25	2,630[a]
Mobile	673	0	5	0	300
Outside	1,966	0	2	5	20
Total	4,318	10	97	99	5,350
	Rate (per 100,000 population)				
Residential	271	2.4	22	18	636
One/two family	256	2.1	19	N.A.	586
Apartments	288	3.9	36	N.A.	658
Other	N.A.	N.A.	N.A.	N.A.	N.A.
Nonresidential	174	3	2	7	697
Mobile	178	0	1	0	79
Outside	521	0	1	1	5
Total	1,111	2.7	26	26	1,418
	Percentage				
Residential	24	90	86	70	45
One/two family	17	60	57	45	32
Apartments	5	30	28	20	9
Other	1	0	2	4	4
Nonresidential	15	10	7	25	49
Mobile	16	0	5	0	6
Outside	45	0	2	5	0
Total	101	100	100	100	100

Note: Here, and in subsequent tables, totals are rounded.   [a]Includes one industrial fire with a $540,000 loss.
N.A.—Not applicable.

this year-to-year comparison may be misleading if any one year has an unusually small number of incidents or some other peculiarity. Another and perhaps better method is to compare the current year to the average number of fires or losses per year over a period of several years. Alternatively, the current year data can be put in tables and the longer-term trends can be shown in graphs as in Figure 6–8, where trends for similar communities are also shown. The figure shows that in Community *X* fires, deaths, injuries, and constant dollar losses have had an upward trend over the decade. The death rate is more irregular than the others because of the small numbers involved: one or two fires can significantly influence the rate in a given year. According to Figure 6–8, Community *X* shows a somewhat worse record than other, similar communities as regards total fires, deaths, and injuries and a somewhat better record on dollar losses.

Figure 6–9 carries the analysis of life safety in residences further by showing the general cause distributions for the different types of losses. The leading causes of deaths in residences in Community *X* are seen to be fires related to careless smoking, arson (incendiary/suspicious), and heating. For injuries, it is cooking, smoking, and heating. In terms of dollar loss, however, the leading causes are incendiary/suspicious fires and fires related to heating. Heating also is the leading cause in terms of the number of fires.

These cause profiles can help communitywide prevention efforts and can also suggest the need for special programs. Similar profiles can be developed for each census tract for more detailed guidance or for larger areas, such as counties, where fire incidence of individual towns is too low to provide statistically significant breakdowns.

More details on the leading causes of fire *deaths* in Community *X* are shown in Table 6–3. From the table it appears that the leading cause is cigarettes carelessly discarded or dropped on bedding, mattresses, or upholstered furniture.

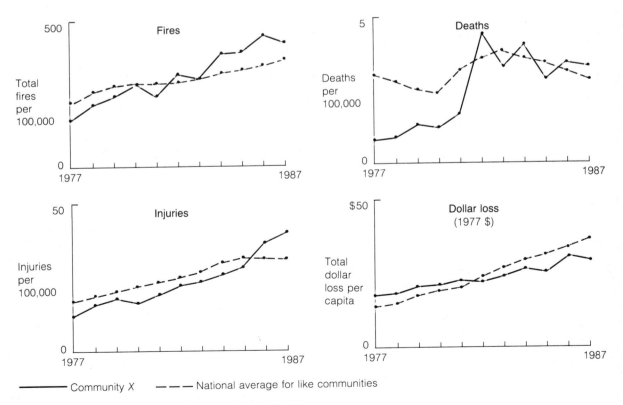

Figure 6–8   Trends in fire losses (Community *X*, 1977–87).

More details on the leading causes of *fires*, specifically heating fires, are shown in Table 6–4. From this presentation, the fire service manager can identify some potential problems: mechanical failure of central heating systems, misuse of portable heaters and water heaters, and faulty design, construction, and installation of fireplaces.

Heating systems could be further broken out in terms of fuel (gas, electricity, or oil) and even brands and models most frequently involved. More popular brands would be expected to show up more frequently, all other things being

Figure 6–9   Causes of residential fire losses (Community X, 1982).

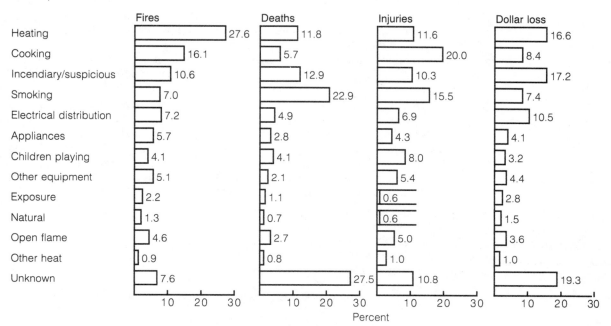

	Fires	Deaths	Injuries	Dollar loss
Heating	27.6	11.8	11.6	16.6
Cooking	16.1	5.7	20.0	8.4
Incendiary/suspicious	10.6	12.9	10.3	17.2
Smoking	7.0	22.9	15.5	7.4
Electrical distribution	7.2	4.9	6.9	10.5
Appliances	5.7	2.8	4.3	4.1
Children playing	4.1	4.1	8.0	3.2
Other equipment	5.1	2.1	5.4	4.4
Exposure	2.2	1.1	0.6	2.8
Natural	1.3	0.7	0.6	1.5
Open flame	4.6	2.7	5.0	3.6
Other heat	0.9	0.8	1.0	1.0
Unknown	7.6	27.5	10.8	19.3

Percent

Source: 1982 NFIRS (179,342 fires, 1,527 deaths, 7,263 injuries, and $1,200,779,000 in property loss).

Note: The figure reflects the actual distribution for the entire United States in 1982. It is typical of that for a small community.

Table 6–3   Details of fire deaths from careless smoking (Community X).

	Most common scenarios: deaths			
Percentage of cases	Type of smoking material involved in ignition	Form of material ignited	Type of material ignited	Ignition factor
25	Cigarette	Bedding	Cotton	Misuse of heat (discarded or dropped)
16	Cigarette	Mattress	Cotton	Same
15	Cigarette	Upholstered furniture	Various	Same
44	Other or unknown			

equal. But sometimes a particular product will appear much more frequently than its numbers in the community would lead one to expect.

What can fire managers do with this kind of information? Data on the types of residences having the most fires and the types of fires they have can be used to prepare public education programs for the particular groups with these problems. The same data broken out by area of the city can show where home-to-home inspections can have the greatest payoffs, or where homeowners' or tenants' associations ought to be contacted.

Table 6–5 illustrates an analysis of nonresidential structures showing the cause distribution of fires for each major nonresidential occupancy type in Community *X*. The largest numbers in the table suggest which causes might be considered first in targeting inspections for each occupancy type. Analogous tables showing absolute numbers for casualties and losses for each occupancy type would show the relative size of the problem among occupancy types, and would provide further information for deciding which types of occupancies should be the chief targets of a program.

In addition to providing information on where to concentrate inspections and public education programs, a series of increasingly detailed tables of causes of fires can be used to evaluate the success of a community's fire protection programs. For example, a program aimed at reducing the number of fireplace fires in single-family dwellings should be measured by its impact on that type of fire rather than on the total number of fires. It might be impossible to determine whether the program worked by looking only at total fires. On the other hand, a specific program may increase fire awareness in general, and the rates of many types of fires may go down as a result. But a downward trend in total fires after such a program is started does not necessarily mean that the

Table 6–4   Details of heating-related fires in residences (Community *X*).

Ignition factor	Central heating	Fixed local heating	Portable heaters	Chimney	Fire-places	Water heaters	Other and unknown	Total fires
Mechanical failure	58%	35%	23%	30%	10%	23%	36%	33%
Short circuit	11	4	11	0	0	2	9	5
Automatic control failure	12	7	3	0	0	3	7	5
Lack of maintenance, worn out	8	4	1	16	5	3	2	7
Part failure, leak, break	7	9	2	10	3	8	9	6
Other malfunction	19	11	6	4	2	6	9	9
Misuse or operation deficiency	28	38	63	25	25	71	42	37
Fuel spilled	2	2	1	0	0	9	4	3
Combustible too close to heat	3	3	8	1	1	9	0	4
Improper container or improper storage of flammable material	10	11	22	7	6	33	13	13
Other misuse of material ignited	4	4	1	4	9	4	7	4
Other operational deficiency	9	18	31	13	9	16	18	13
Design, construction, installation deficiency	8	19	8	40	56	4	18	23
Construction deficiency	1	6	0	10	25	1	0	8
Installed too close to combustible	4	7	6	15	11	2	13	7
Other	3	6	2	15	20	1	5	8
Other	2	2	1	2	2	1	2	2
Unknown	5	6	4	3	3	2	2	5
Percentage of fires	101	100	100	100	100	100	100	100

program caused the drop. Fires might be experiencing a downward trend in general, for unknown reasons. Separating the effectiveness of a particular program might require examining the fire experience of control groups of occupancies that were not exposed to the program.

Another type of analysis crucial to the fire problem is determining the reason for firefighter injuries, which make up a large portion of the total injuries from fire. Table 6–2 showed that firefighters had about the same number of injuries as civilians for fires reported to the fire service. Table 6–6 shows that 25 percent of firefighter injuries were due to smoke inhalation, recorded among injuries in the right-hand part of the table. Other firefighter injuries were relatively evenly distributed across various parts of the body, indicating that there is no obvious weak link. Their protective outfit, their safety training, and possibly their physical fitness may all need improvement.

Many other types of data analysis can be done; these examples are meant to be suggestive.

Table 6–5   Causes of nonresidential fires by occupancy type (Community *X*).

Cause	Public assembly	Education	Insti- tutions	Stores, offices	Basic industry	Manufac- turing	Storage	Vacant, construc- tion	Other	Total fires
Incendiary/suspicious	23%	55%	24%	19%	17%	7%	28%	71%	29%	29%
Electrical distribution	13	6	5	15	19	7	7	0.5	5	8
Open flame, spark	3	1	9	4	11	9	7	5	11	8
Smoking	8	13	33	9	3	6	5	2	3	8
Exposure	2	0.7	0.2	5	1	3	7	2	8	4
Cooking	24	2	4	2	1	2	0.6	0.3	0.9	4
Appliances	3	2	9	8	5	6	1	0	0.5	3
Heating	6	4	3	8	15	7	6	1	11	6
Flammable liquids	0.6	0.7	0.2	3	4	8	4	0.2	0.5	3
Children playing	1	3	1	2	0	0.6	10	6	11	5
Natural	2	2	1	1	3	8	4	0.3	2	3
Air conditioning, refrigeration	3	1	2	2	2	0.6	0	0.1	0.5	0.9
Gas	0.1	0	0.2	1	2	3	0.6	0	0	0.8
Explosives, fireworks	0.4	0	0	0	0	0	0.4	0	0.5	0.2
Other equipment	1	3	2	4	9	20	2	0.5	0.5	4
Other heat	3	2	1	4	3	5	4	3	2	4
Unknown	7	6	4	12	4	8	16	7	15	11
Total fires	100%	101%	99%	101%	99%	100%	103%	99%	100%	100%

Table 6–6   Nature of firefighter injuries (Community *X*).

Type of injury	No.	Percent	Part of body injured	No.	Percent
Smoke inhalation	25	25	Head, neck	12	12
Smoke and burns	4	4	Arm	9	9
Burns only	11	11	Body, trunk, back	11	11
Wound, cut, bleeding	17	17	Leg	10	10
Dislocation, fracture	3	3	Hand	11	11
Complaint of pain	6	6	Foot	4	4
Shock	1	1	Internal	31	31
Strain, sprain	17	17	Multiple parts	4	4
Other	13	13	Other	4	4
Undetermined	2	2	Undetermined	3	3
Total	99	100	Total	99	100

Displaying management information

Busy fire service managers and city officials tend to have neither the time nor the inclination to pore over detailed tables of numbers, however important that may be. Those who do have the patience and skill are still faced with the problem of conveying the information to their colleagues, their superiors, their staff, and the public. Thus, it is extremely important that the fire service manager not only ensure that the necessary information is produced but also that it is presented in such a way that the key results are understood quickly and clearly. This is doubly true when the results are to be presented in a speech or briefing rather than in a written document, because it is hard for the audience to grasp the significance of statistics presented verbally. Magazines, newspapers, television news, and even television commercials reinforce the fact that simple tables and graphics help get information across quickly. Good display may make the difference not only of whether or not a point is understood, but also of whether the information is even considered. Ideally, the analysts employed by the department should have access to a city graphics staff to help prepare graphs and maps showing important information for reports and presentations, and they should be encouraged to use it.

Some of the most basic and useful types of displays are illustrated in this chapter. Figure 6–9 is an example of a basic bar chart, in this case showing the proportion of fires that are due to different causes. The bar chart is very good for showing at a glance the relative size of each part of the problem.

Figure 6–8 illustrates simple trend plots of fires and losses over time. The inclusion of the line showing rates for "like" communities (of similar size, region, etc.) serves as a benchmark for comparison.

Figures 6–6 and 6–7 illustrate graphically how the fire problem varies from one part of the community to another. The darker the shading, the worse the problem. This type of display can be used to show the absolute number of deaths (or fires or dollar losses), the relative number per capita, or other data that vary geographically.

All the displays here would have been more effective in color. When color is available, it can help make an otherwise dull report exciting visually. If chosen well, color also can make it much easier to understand the major points.

Computerized MIS systems usually have at least some capability to generate graphs and charts from data in their data bases. These graphics can be generated quickly, without an art department. Many computer systems can generate the graphics in color, and some allow the user to prescreen the results before having them printed in hard copy. Some even give the choice of pictures or color slides. But the enhanced capability comes at greater cost, and many computer-generated displays are unattractive. Often it is possible to develop as good or better quality charts by hand, after carefully selecting the main points to be made and the best way to present them. As technology improves, computer-generated color displays will become more affordable and easier to use. But there is no need to wait for them to put key data into color graphics.

Using a management information system

Management information systems have a wide variety of uses, several of which have been discussed in the preceding sections. A more comprehensive summary follows.

Day-to-day department management

The minimum MIS in any fire department will need to provide information on the personnel in the department, what units they are assigned to, and whether they are on duty. Similarly, the system will need to keep track of what apparatus is available, what apparatus is in maintenance, what the backup is, what is currently deployed. This basic information tells the manager what is available for various missions and what is being used for calls in progress. This information is needed whether the system is all manual or whether it uses computer-aided dispatch.

A slightly more sophisticated MIS may not only indicate the current status of personnel and equipment, but also schedule resources, identify substitutes, and warn of resource-scheduling problems.

In addition to helping with day-to-day management of the total force, the MIS may provide information for managing prevention activities: for example, information on the various types of buildings in the community, whether they have had fires, when they were last inspected, and when their next inspections are due. The data may be kept in a way that makes it easy to match the causes of fires with the conditions discovered during inspections, so that the effectiveness of inspections can be assessed.

Day-to-day operational decisions

The MIS can furnish information that can aid suppression operations while they are under way. It can provide information from pre-fire plans on how to fight fires in particular places, special hazards that may exist, numbers of invalids, types of built-in suppression, and other data. The MIS can also furnish information useful for filling out the incident report on a fire, such as time of alarm, building value, building ownership, and construction. The MIS can help prevention operations in real time with information on violations outstanding and past suspicious fires associated with a property being inspected.

Policy planning

The MIS can provide information for planning both prevention and suppression policies. For example, it can tell whether the fire rate in the community is going up or down under existing prevention policies and, if it is changing, whether the change is in fire rates for apartments, single-family dwellings, or businesses, or some combination of occupancies. For occupancies with the greatest problems, either in absolute terms or in change over time, the causes of fires can be ascertained. For example, it might be found that the fire rate and losses in the community are rising almost entirely because of an increase in residential fires in four census tracts, with three factors leading: children intentionally setting fires, increased use of space heaters during recent severe winters, and lack of attention to food left cooking on stoves. These findings can suggest the need for starting a juvenile firesetters' counseling program and a public fire education program focusing on proper use of space heaters and on cooking hazards. If a communitywide program is not feasible, the program could focus first on the most severely affected areas.

For suppression, the MIS can show how well the loss per fire is being held down. The MIS also can provide information on response times to emergency calls in various areas of the community; frequency of fires; staffing levels used at various types of fires; and the times of day, week, and year when most fires occur. This information can help guide policies on the addition or relocation of stations, the relative advantages of variable versus constant staffing levels, and the need for new types of apparatus (as might be the case if highrise fires were on the increase).

Decisions regarding the best mix of volunteer and paid firefighters can be supported by such information as the number and types of fires, the number of paid and volunteer firefighters who typically work on the scene, the times of day when most fires occur, response times, and trends in losses.

Budget requests

The MIS can support budget requests by providing information on work loads, such as the number of calls by type of call, and upward or downward trends. For example, many departments have experienced sharp increases in EMS calls and may need additional rescue units. Some departments have experienced increases in multiple alarm calls and may require additional units or additional personnel per unit. The MIS may also show the existence of new hazards that require new equipment. An increased number of highrise fires, for example, may suggest the need for aerial apparatus or special highrise firefighting kits.

Detailed characteristics of the fires being experienced by the community may support budget requests for new services. For example, the knowledge that space heaters placed too close to combustibles is a major problem in the community, and that this problem caused twenty fires and $500,000 loss in the previous year, might be useful in arguing for the production costs of public service spots on radio or television to warn the local population of this particular hazard. The MIS can further support budget requests by general profiles of the fire problem that show the fire department is ''on top of things,'' and by program evaluations (discussed in the next section).

When the local government is attempting to cut costs, information may be generated to estimate the effects of potential budget reductions. Information on the frequency of multiple simultaneous calls and the relationship of losses to response time can be used to demonstrate the potential increase in the problem after various types of cutbacks.

Program evaluation

The data system can help managers assess the effectiveness of both newly instituted and long-standing fire protection programs. For example, it might provide data on firefighter on-duty heart attacks after institution of a physical fitness program, or firefighter head injuries after a change in helmet design, or firefighter smoke inhalation injuries after purchase of demand-breathing apparatus. It also might provide data showing whether serious fires have decreased after home inspection has been instituted in one part of the community, and, if so, whether the reduction was in types of fires that the program was aimed at or in all types of fires (indicating that the existence of the program rather than the particular content might be more significant).

Bargaining agreements

The MIS might provide information on whether productivity is going up or down, in support of wage or staffing level agreements. For example, the data system might indicate that an increasing number of calls was being handled by the same size force, which would imply that personnel were doing more work and therefore might be justified in seeking higher wages. On the other hand, a reduction in the number of fires after a period in which the force concentrated on prevention efforts might also be a reason for supporting a pay increase.

Other uses for data

The MIS also can provide information about structural configurations associated with the greatest fire spread and can identify problems requiring stronger codes or stronger code enforcement.

It can help identify consumer products repeatedly involved in fires; or, conversely, it may provide information showing that certain products being considered for regulation rarely are involved in fires.

Identification of the fire scenarios accounting for the greatest number of fire deaths, injuries, and dollar losses can help the local fire department, local university, or national organizations set research priorities.

Most MIS systems are frequently used to answer requests for fire information from industry, researchers, regulatory agencies, local officials, and others. Some of the requests may be for the purpose of supporting local decisions on particular items of legislation.

Finally, data for all these purposes also are of interest at higher levels of government. Data aggregated at state or national levels can provide baselines against which local governments can compare themselves. The data can help identify problems that may not be visible at the local level because of the relatively small number of incidents that may occur in any one jurisdiction. The data may help decisionmakers at all levels of government set priorities, select among programs, and measure progress over time. The most effective way to achieve these higher goals is to include the necessary data elements in local data systems in a form compatible with state and national reporting systems.

A final word

Although the list of proposed uses outlined here may seem somewhat intimidating, the same basic core of data serves most of them. Furthermore, the department does not have to put its data to use for all these purposes at the start.

Controlling the quality of the data base

"Garbage in, garbage out" is now a classic saying in data processing. If you put erroneous data into the fire data system, then it is difficult to get meaningful information out. Knowledgeable users with a clear understanding of the major sources of errors often can produce useful information from data with a great deal of error in them. But it is not prudent to count on this, and the fire service manager should build quality control into the MIS system.

Obtaining data

The first step in improving the quality of data is to train fire officers, investigators, and others who will collect and input data to the MIS on how to obtain that data accurately. For fire data this starts with being able to determine cause and other information as well as they can be established. Instruction on fire investigation and on filling out incident reports and other reports should be part of the basic training of fire officers, and perhaps all firefighters.

Supervisors can periodically monitor their officers' ability to obtain accurate data from investigations by occasional on-the-scene checking. Simulations can also be used to train and rate officers in investigating and reporting.

Recording data

The next step in ensuring accuracy is to be certain the information is recorded properly on the forms. Those filling out reports should understand the definitions of the various elements and the numerical codes to be applied to each. If the facts are accurate but miscoded, the effect is the same as if the investigation was incorrectly carried out in the first place. Fire officers therefore need training in filling out the paperwork correctly. The MIS design itself can influence the ability of the firefighter to correctly enter and code data by the simplicity of the system, by the clarity of training and instruction materials, and by the clarity of the forms to be filled out. Providing feedback to the data collectors on common errors and on their own errors also is important.

Error detection might be built into the system in several ways. A common method is to have supervisors check the reports made by their subordinates. For example, Columbus, Ohio, adopted a system in which company officers fill out incident reports in draft and battalion chiefs prepare the final copies; this means the latter have to review each form. Some communities also have a clerk in the central records office check each incident report or other record for completeness and reasonableness before it is keypunched.

When fire officers enter data directly into computer terminals instead of on paper, the computer can be used to check for valid codes and to cross-check different elements to see that all necessary elements have been filled out and that the values inserted are reasonable. This immediate check gives fire officers feedback on any suspected problems with the data while the data are still fresh in their minds.

Recorded data must be complete as well as accurate. Fire officers need to fill out all entries called for on each form and all forms for every incident. If, for example, the number of firefighter injuries is filled out on only 80 percent of the fires reported, it might be assumed by some that the remaining 20 percent of fires had no injuries. If there were 100 injuries during the previous year, the chief would want to know whether this year there were again 100, or 80, especially if the chief had instituted a special firefighter safety program or a physical fitness program. In the same way, if departments send in some unknown percentage of their incidents to their state reporting system, the state does not know whether the real fire situation has improved or worsened, or whether observed changes are due to changes in completeness of reporting. The amount of data provided for different types of calls may vary, but there must be some record for every call so that fire managers can account for the work load of the department, have records should legal questions arise, and understand the magnitude of the problem faced by the fire department and how it changes over time.

Processing data

The next factor to consider is the accuracy of data processing. Even properly and completely reported data are useless if they are scrambled when they are entered into the computer. Controls include verification keying in addition to the initial keying, careful design of input forms with an eye to making it easier for keypunchers to enter data, and possibly orientation on the intent of the system for the clerks who do the keying so that they can catch errors. A good keypuncher can be very proficient in doing this and can catch errors that will escape a computerized check.

After the computer checks the keypunched data for reasonableness, but before an incident is added to the master file, any problems noted by the computer can be reviewed by the keypuncher to see whether the information was omitted from the original form, was entered incorrectly, or was keyed incorrectly. If the fault was not in keying but in the original incident report, that report can be sent back for correction.

Errors may still get into a data base, even after a certain number of computer checks and human checks. Sometimes these errors are discovered in the process of using the data, when the information on a particular incident or a number of incidents seems unreasonable. Data collection problems should be relayed back to the training and retraining process.

Analyzing data

Another major consideration is the accuracy of data analysis. Poor analysis can distort information based on accurate data. For example, many communities have only a small number of fire deaths each year. Year-to-year changes might be caused simply by random fluctuations as opposed to real changes in the nature of the problem. A 10 percent reduction in the number of fires from ten to nine a year is more likely to be due to chance than is a 10 percent reduction from 1,000 fires to 900 fires. Fire service managers should be aware of (or get consultation on) the statistical significance of changes in their data so that they do not mistakenly change their policies because of random fluctuations from year to year. The more unreliable the input, the more important it is to have a competent analyst interpret the data and try to cope with the problems in the data.

Summary and recommendations

The computer has been described by some officers as the fourth major technological change to significantly improve fire protection, the other three being the internal combustion engine, the centrifugal pump, and the radio. The first change improved mobility and response time. The second improved the reliability and efficiency of providing water at high pressure. The third improved communications. The fourth major change—the use of the computer—can sharply improve the amount of information available to the fire officer and make it more timely and more accurate.

As computer processing costs go down and as computer hardware becomes smaller, less expensive, and more common everywhere, from the grocery store to the laboratory, the use of computer-based MIS in fire departments is likely. One computer expert, looking at the fire service, stated: "It is no longer a question of can or should fire departments of all sizes utilize modern computer and telecommunications techniques; the only question is when."

This chapter has been designed to give an overview of management information systems and data analysis for the fire service manager who is only slightly familiar with computers. In closing, here are some recommendations for successful implementation.

Use of data

The fire service manager should ensure that the data collected are analyzed and interpreted, and that key points are appropriately displayed. Too much information winds up in drawers, unused. Especially important is knowledge of the number and per capita rate of fires by occupancy and by cause. The data should be further broken down to detail the profiles and circumstances for injuries, deaths, and dollar loss. The key analytic technique is simply arraying data in tables and looking for the large numbers, which indicate the large parts of the problem. Upon finding the large numbers, the next step is to ask what caused the fire (or casualty) in successively deeper levels of detail to the limit of the data system.

Training and retraining

All personnel who actually collect or analyze fire-related data should be trained in collection techniques and thoroughly informed of the definitions to use. The same personnel should be periodically alerted to recurring errors and any changes in the data system. The training and retraining periods also offer a good opportunity to discuss the use of the system. An understanding of the ultimate purposes of the MIS can help personnel see the importance of the collection effort and increase their motivation to do the work completely and accurately.

Fire officers of captain rank or higher should, if possible, have sufficient training to be able to describe the fire problem at least in their own area. This is yet another type of training needed to improve the use of the MIS, in addition to training in investigation and reporting.

Controlling quality

The fire service manager should set up quality control procedures for the department's data regardless of community size. The procedures may include supervisory review of the incident reports of officers, communitywide reviews by a fire coding clerk, and computer screening of data as they are fed into the machine. Checks by hand or by computer can screen for valid codes, logical consistency among data elements, completeness, and consistency with information available from other sources.

Compatibility with state and national systems

Fire service managers should try to keep a core of data compatible with the format and coding used by state and national fire data systems, so that their department may contribute to the creation of the larger picture used for developing laws, standards, and research that ultimately affect their own community. The common core of data also will allow managers to accurately compare their community with others. Collecting data with standard definitions is especially important for smaller communities, where aggregation of data among like communities offers a chance to see patterns that an individual community cannot produce. Furthermore, keeping systems compatible will allow the local community to share software developed by others.

1   Geocoding is a method of systematically describing every location in a community so that the information in various data bases such as tax records, fire data, and police records can be brought together for any particular building or location using a standard format for each address. For a description of the geocoding used by one department (Alexandria, Virginia), see Peirce Eichelberger, "New Technologies and Old Friends: The Geographic-based Management Information System" *Fire Journal*, January 1985, pp. 39–43.

2   Kansas City, Missouri, was one of the first communities to keep a file of hazards that firefighters might encounter in an occupancy. Their favorite demonstration of the system for visitors was to call up on the computer an occupancy in which a pet lion was kept.

3   One of the first departments to computerize inspection records was Charlotte, North Carolina, which now has an extensive computerized history on each build-

ing. It can relate violations to types of fires by building. The system also can generate lists of occupancies due for inspection, by inspector, and also lists of inspections completed by inspector.

4   For a fuller discussion, see David Icove and M. Osama Soliman, "Computer-Assisted Arson Information Management," *International Fire Chief*, December 1983, pp. 28–31. Additional details can be obtained from the U.S. Fire Administration for the latest on their long-term program to improve arson information management systems, called AIMS.

5   Tokyo and some other large Japanese cities keep real-time records on the number of beds available in each hospital. They also track availability of special treatment facilities. Thus a burn victim or a person with a severe hand injury can be sent to the nearest hospital that has the capacity to help.

6   Public Technology, Inc. (PTI), Washington, D.C., is one source of information on the best of these models.

7 Resource management

Managing resources for the fire service involves a broad spectrum of management concepts and activities. Resource management encompasses human resources (people doing a job), material resources (things people need to do the job), and fiscal resources (money to pay the people and purchase the equipment). It also involves the effective use of time (priorities and schedules for both human and material resources).

Determining the level of resources required for fire, emergency medical, and related services is a complex task. As is the case in all service areas, a community must determine its needs in relation to the hazards in the community, the level of risk that is politically acceptable, and the level of service that is financially obtainable. Evaluating community fire protection, discussed at length in Chapter 5, is the basis for management policy and decision making in relation to the human and material resources required. Requirements are also set in the planning process through the establishment of community goals and objectives for fire and emergency services (see Chapter 4). Assessing resources and needs in this way is essential if the department is to establish a case for sufficient funding, as competition for funding in local government is often very keen.

In short, resource management includes

1. The implementation of community priorities, including perceived and determined needs
2. The implementation of departmental goals and objectives
3. A comprehensive analysis of hazards and work load
4. A determination of levels of funding required and available.

Although many books have been written on these topics, this chapter focuses on the issues most pertinent to the local fire department. It concentrates on human and material resources, while fiscal resources are covered in Chapter 8.

Managing human resources

Fire service activities are labor-intensive. As such, they rely heavily on the use of human resources to accomplish the tasks required. This is true not only for traditional activities but also for new and emerging fire department responsibilities. It is as true for volunteer departments as it is for paid departments. As is the case in nearly every labor-intensive activity, the quality of the organizational output is greatly influenced by the quality of the human resources engaged to accomplish the tasks. Human resource management is a matter of finding, developing, and nurturing these high-quality human resources.

Among the significant factors that affect the quality of human resources is the style of management used within the organization. Management styles have been explored in depth for years and continue to receive attention in an effort to name, qualify, quantify, and in general describe them. However hybrid the titles become, there are two basic styles on which managers build: authoritarian and participative.

The relationships between these styles of management are probably best described in the ''continuum of leadership behavior'' identified by Robert Tannenbaum and Warren H. Schmidt.[1] This now classic portrayal of the relationship continuum provides insight into the roles of managers and subordinates in a given system and defines the leadership styles of individuals or teams.

Much of the abundant literature on management and leadership styles advocates subordinate-centered leadership, or participative management, as a successful tool in managing human resources. The ''success companies'' in the private sector along with a few public sector examples provide some vivid portrayals of significant positive results when employees are allowed and encouraged to participate.[2]

As Chapter 3 points out, the quasi-military roots of the traditional fire service organization may make the implementation of participative strategies somewhat more difficult. However, the success of those fire departments that have implemented various of the strategies is a growing testimony to their effectiveness for the fire service.

Clearly, there are occasions when authoritarian postures are essential. During an emergency, for example, nearly all authorities agree on the need for strong leadership where decisions are made and announced by an incident manager or commander. Even in the incident management realm, there is room for important elements of participation in planning for emergencies. This is especially true in implementing feedback or input to the incident commander for making decisions.

The trend in human resource management styles is to give workers a greater role in the management process. The emergence and identification of the ''people-oriented excellence strategies'' is stimulating to many good managers and continues to improve the overall quality of human resource management in most fields.[3]

Although implementation may be slower and more cautious in the public sector, positive results will unquestionably be achieved and measured as the level of job satisfaction increases. Among the strategies employed by organizations are quality circles, sabbaticals, and employee development programs. They are discussed in detail in other chapters.

The work environment

A number of elements of the work setting affect the quality of work and the attitude of an organization's employees. Problems and/or programs in these areas may well affect employee recruitment and retention, productivity, operational costs, and many other areas of management responsibility. These areas include safety, quality of supervision, training, organized labor, and compensation and benefits.

Safety   A safe work environment is dictated by state and federal regulations and required by organized labor. It is also a requirement of a cost-effective operation. Although difficult to quantify precisely, the cost of job-related injuries incurred by employees in the work setting is a major contributor to the rising costs of pensions, workers compensation, and medical insurance.

As municipalities attempt to control personal service costs, the cost-effectiveness of a proactive safety program becomes readily apparent in both the public and private sectors. It is not uncommon to find evidence of 30–60 percent decreases in the direct costs of job-related injuries where a good safety program has been instituted.[4]

A major concern of fire service safety programs is the overall wellness of employees. The wellness concept encompasses not only physical fitness but also diet, tobacco and alcohol use, and stress management. In addition, fire service safety programs focus considerable attention on providing greater safety in the firefighting environment.

A wealth of research in practical application is under way in these areas. Research has developed significantly improved protective clothing for fire suppression personnel, hearing protection, eye protection, better guarding systems for equipment, stronger ladders, safer elevating mechanisms, better lighting systems, and so on. In addition to implementing these improvements, consensus standards organizations such as the National Fire Protection Association as well as the U.S. government have developed minimum standards for some procedural and hardware improvements that have increased firefighter safety.

No employee safety program is complete if it relies only upon hardware, however. As a management concern, safety must be reflected in every applicable procedure. Strong enforcement of well-written safety policies is likely to increase acceptance and awareness of those procedures and safety concepts among all employees.

A particularly effective way to encourage employees to participate is to have them become involved in developing and implementing safety procedures. Many organizations successfully use safety committees to develop procedures, conduct research, and test new products. However, the basic premise that safety is a management responsibility means that those concerns must be given constant attention by management.

Quality of supervision   The effectiveness of supervision is a key issue in developing employee performance and potential. To be most effective, supervisors must have an opportunity to help shape the organization's goals and objectives as well as oversee their implementation. *Team building* is an important tool in achieving this involvement (see Chapter 3). Regardless of the method used to foster unity of purpose, supervisors must be aware of the methods and be held measurable and accountable for them.

Several key checkpoints can be used to monitor supervisory competence. These checkpoints pertain to areas in which supervisors need some training and have room for growth:

1. *Competency in performance of subordinates.* Are employees performing to the expected levels and producing quality work?
2. *Organizational leadership framework.* Are supervisors, and consequently their employees, accomplishing what management perceives they should be accomplishing?
3. *Indicators of climate, attitude, and response to leadership.* Are employees accepting and accomplishing goals and objectives? Are they complying with safety procedures, work rules, and other policies?
4. *Comparison with comparable work units.* Are levels of productivity, satisfaction and policy compliance relatively comparable among comparable work units?[5]

Paramount to achieving good results from human resources is the "creditability" of an organization's leadership. Creditability is not an easily defined term. However, Ray Killian characterizes some of the elements of creditability in the accompanying sidebar.

Training   Fire department training efforts should focus on results. Particular emphasis should be put on producing competent human resources, competent work units, and a competent organization. Training toward these objectives requires quality programs that create and maintain excellence. Training is examined in detail in Chapter 18.

Many fire departments have been guilty of engaging in little or no training and producing almost no results. Others have engaged in disjointed programs for the sake of visibility, trendiness, or ill-perceived preparedness. The results of such misguided training efforts or lack of training are generally poor morale, poor performance, and organizational failure. Many fire service organizations have used and are continuing to use the performance-based training objectives specified by various organizations (i.e., the National Fire Protection Association and state training organizations) that set certification criteria. Standards developed by the National Professional Qualifications Board for the Fire Service, through the National Fire Protection Association, are extremely useful in focusing training on results-oriented objectives common to most fire departments. Standards are also available for many code enforcement activities through the model code agencies (see Chapter 15). Emergency medical service standards have been developed by a variety of sources.

Organizations that do not implement well-designed, results-oriented training will find it increasingly difficult to develop, motivate, and retain high-quality employees. Quality training will lead to career growth. This growth will contribute to employee satisfaction, good job performance, and the achievement of desired work outcomes.

Organized labor   Labor unions also exert a profound influence on the employees and management of an organization, especially in five basic ways:

1. Restrictions are placed on management's freedom of action.
2. Uniformity of treatment for employees is mandated.
3. Improved personnel policies and practices are required.
4. Generally, one spokesman is recognized for a group of employees.
5. Labor relations decision making is usually more centralized.[6]

These factors obviously have an effect on the human resources and management of a fire department. An essential role of management is to look after labor

---

A creditable leader

1. Clarifies what is expected and encourages its achievement by engaging in the activity

2. Gives access to information needed and establishes work guides, but permits freedom regarding how results will be achieved

3. Doesn't oversupervise, ask too many questions, or interfere as long as the job is being done in a satisfactory manner

4. Is tough enough to insist on results but permits others to be honest and staunch in their positions

5. Is consistent, does not change his or her mind too often

6. Insists that others be consistent by seeing that policies and rules are followed fairly and uniformly

7. Proves dependability by being available, keeping promises, and being willing to explain why

8. Is willing to fight the battle for the employee, when merited, regarding working conditions, pay, benefits, and promotions

9. Listens carefully and purposely and responds to the limits of his or her capability

10. Is a friendly human being with empathy and understanding rather than a boss devoid of reasonable compassion

11. Builds through every contact and activity a track record of trustworthiness and creditability.

Source: Ray A. Killian, *Human Resource Management: An ROI Approach* (New York: AMACOM, a division of the American Management Association, 1976), 149–50.

---

relations in the organized labor setting. Managing in the union environment is discussed in more detail in Chapter 12.

Compensation and benefits   Obviously, the level of compensation and benefits provided for employees can have a great impact on recruitment, performance, and retention. However, much research has indicated that compensation has less to do with job satisfaction than may have been perceived in the past. It is clear that the current generation of employees entering the work force value things other than money and are not nearly as cognizant of or concerned about financial rewards as were their predecessors reared during the 1930s and 1940s.

Motivation

All of these factors in the work place affect employee motivation. Motivation is a prime concern of all managers because it strongly affects performance. Thus, in the face of today's changing work force, new ways must be found to integrate organizational and employee goals. Changing work values, a diminishing work ethic, more guaranteed wages and benefits, decreased employee loyalty, adverse public opinion, and diluted management authority have been cited as some of the causes of declining motivation. Employee attitude surveys attribute worker dissatisfaction to changing worker attitudes, the job environment, demeaning and inept supervisors, authoritarian management, favoritism, poor communication, inadequate organizational policies, the nature of work itself, and peer and client relationships. Employee dissatisfaction is reflected in increased turnover, waste, absenteeism, accidents, sick leave, grievances, and disciplinary actions, which reduce productivity and increase costs and health and personal problems.

Many supervisors understand very little about what motivates their employees. Surveys continually show supervisors and subordinates disagreeing on motivators. Substantial evidence exists that employees are motivated by various factors, such as money, affiliation, a desire to achieve, a feeling of responsibility, recognition, power, and interesting work. Motivation is influenced by personality, physical and emotional states, organizational structure, policies and rules, the nature of the job, and interpersonal relations. Motivational strategies should be tailored to each employee's wants, concerns, interests, needs, and purposes and cannot remain static.

No single motivator works for all employees all the time. Motivators must be capable of satisfying the most intense employee needs. Individual differences mandate that a wide selection of motivators be devised and offered. Achievement-oriented employees are motivated by job enlargement and enrichment. For other employees improved compensation and benefits are key motivators. Power-oriented employees seek opportunities to direct work through others. Many employees respond to recognition.

Numerous techniques are available for motivating employees. These include job redesign, a full range of monetary and nonmonetary incentives, quality circles, quality of work life programs, labor-management committees, employee assistance programs, and employee attitude surveys. In selecting and using motivational techniques, fire service managers need to learn how contemporary workers think and what motivates them. Human relations skills need to be sharpened. Managers and supervisors can take a number of important steps in this direction:

1. Carefully define an employee's job and expected results.
2. Mutually establish understandable and acceptable job standards.
3. Involve employees in decision making.
4. Work with employees in setting work and career goals by encouraging

career development, pointing out opportunities for achievement, and providing assignments that advance career development.

5. Redesign and enlarge jobs to make them more interesting and to encourage better use of skills, knowledge, and experience.
6. Freely delegate the tasks that can be done effectively by someone else.
7. Engage in open communication with employees and give them continual positive feedback. Interact with employees on a regular basis.
8. Provide a satisfactory physical work environment.
9. Ensure that employees have adequate resources and equipment.
10. Give recognition, praise, and credit.
11. Provide training, technical assistance, direction, and guidance.
12. Remove organizational and supervisory roadblocks.
13. Match jobs with personal motives. Treat employees as individuals.
14. Offer a broad range of incentives.

Incentives

Incentive programs are techniques for rewarding employees on the basis of performance equal to or above preestablished levels. Local governments have used a number of monetary and nonmonetary incentive programs to increase motivation, production, safety, and efficiency.

Monetary incentives include merit increases, performance bonuses, safety awards, shared savings, attendance awards, competition and contest awards, suggestion awards, and education incentives. Such incentives, when based on objective, outcome-oriented performance criteria, can have significant positive effects.[7]

Nonmonetary incentives consist of job redesign and enlargement, team management, job rotation, job sharing, task systems, autonomous work units, alternative work schedules, service awards, career development programs, work standards, and performance targets.

Obstacles to meaningful incentive programs include legal prohibitions, restrictive labor agreements, labor opposition, and administrative, fiscal, and political constraints. Incentive programs are likely to fail because

1. They do not meet the personal needs of employees.
2. They are improperly designed and poorly administered.
3. They include standards that are difficult to achieve and are increased too frequently.
4. They do not provide meaningful rewards in a timely manner.
5. They do not provide benefits for supervisors.
6. They threaten the hierarchy within work groups.

Criteria for successful incentive programs include

1. Objective and attainable measures of work performance
2. Employee and union involvement in the design and implementation of the program
3. Frequent and diverse rewards
4. Administrative simplicity, including brief and understandable rules
5. Supervisory involvement in developing the program
6. Consideration of employee fears
7. Supervisory coverage in the program
8. An adequate budget
9. Promotion of the program
10. Appropriate monitoring and appeal provisions
11. Frequent redesign of the incentives to maintain interest.

Fire service managers can improve their operations and the level of job satisfaction and performance by recognizing the importance of motivation. Productivity improvement depends on managerial and supervisory understanding of the factors that influence employee productivity, including individual employee abilities and needs and formal and informal organizational conditions. Formal organizational factors affecting productivity consist of the elements described in the previous section, such as organizational structure, working conditions, management climate, communications, personnel practices and policies, and leadership style. Informal organizational factors include group dynamics and cohesiveness, and peer standards.

Locating human resources

The recruitment and selection of employees is discussed in greater depth in Chapter 11. However, in terms of resource management, there are subtle differences between recruiting for paid and volunteer firefighters.

Recruitment is particularly important to managing personnel needs in the volunteer fire service. The delicate balance between scheduling needs and availability often requires carefully planned recruiting efforts to ensure a level of coverage around the clock. Volunteers sometimes live in one location and work in another, and some volunteer organizations have different staffing during daylight and nighttime hours. The failure to recognize or fulfill specialized needs has caused severe staffing problems for many volunteer fire service operations in the past. Pressures on volunteer departments are discussed further in Chapter 17.

The problems of the paid force are different. One important factor in the recruitment and selection of employees for paid departments is the opportunity for lateral entry into many fire department staff and line positions. Another is the use of civilian personnel to perform staff functions. The decline of purely line-oriented entry and promotion systems has been a major step in increasing the professionalism of the fire service. In an increasingly competitive market for quality human resources, the fire service has broadened its utilization of nontraditional human resources and refined its use of traditional ones. The net result is a better-educated work force, more qualified managers, and the availability of more technical personnel who have varied experiences to draw on in the decision-making process.

This trend toward more lateral entry and professional mobility or transfers in the fire service will continue with increased interest in professional qualifications standards and increased pressure for quality management.

Scheduling

Scheduling fire suppression employees in fully paid departments is necessarily based on the premise that the basic level of service, the responding fire company, must be available at all times. Work schedules have evolved over many years into a range of average workweeks between 40 and 72 hours for line employees. With a myriad of scheduling options being utilized, a vast majority of career fire suppression personnel work within these parameters, with most working no more than 56 hours and less than 42 hours per average workweek. Figure 7–1 portrays some of the factors that influence scheduling choices.

Hours to be covered In most cases, 24 hours, 365 days per year, will need to be covered. However, in some situations where volunteer or paid on-call personnel are readily available during certain hours, coverage by these personnel may be an excellent option.

State and federal mandates Certain state and federal laws may affect scheduling by setting maximum hours for career personnel. The federal Fair Labor Standards Act requires that the U.S. Department of Labor periodically review average fire service workweeks and establish maximum allowable hours (at straight time compensation) in accordance with their findings.

Negotiated agreements Negotiations with organized labor will generally include the establishment of work schedules, especially the work cycle. Unions often attempt to decrease average workweeks.

Actual hours of productivity expected The actual hours of productivity expected from an employee have a major impact on scheduling. Although there may be many other advantages to a 24-hour shift, it is unrealistic to operate a scheduled shift of that length without planning for a significant rest period. These rest periods decrease actual productivity by creating periods of paid time when work is not being accomplished. The extent to which productivity is decreased depends on the number of occasions on which the rest period is interrupted for emergency or other activities.

Employee fatigue Fatigue affects not only productivity but also safety, morale, and general job performance. If long shifts are selected, fatigue must be managed. Fire suppression personnel should be in a reasonable state of physical and mental readiness at all times during their shift.

Number of funded positions All scheduling factors must be weighed against the number of funded positions. A reduction in work hours will typically mean that a corresponding increase in the number of personnel will be necessary to maintain predefined task group sizes or numbers. Although some compensation for work hour reductions may be generated by overtime funds, this strategy arrives at a point of diminishing returns very quickly. New full-time or part-time positions will almost always be the result of significant hour reduction for line or staff personnel unless there is a corresponding reduction in service levels.

Work load Examination of the work load in relation to differential scheduling schemes sometimes has bearing on the scheduling decision. This concept has been called "peak load" staffing. It consists of using nontraditional work assignments to put the maximum amount of personnel on duty when the work load is expected to be the highest. This theory has been applied primarily in the field of emergency medical services. It has been less successful in fire suppression. Some fire prevention bureaus have used it for handling special events.

Figure 7–2 outlines steps in the scheduling process.

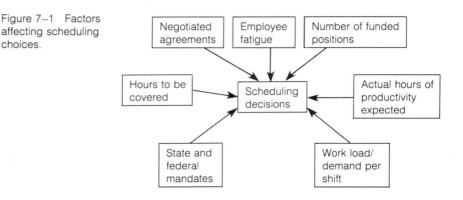

Figure 7–1 Factors affecting scheduling choices.

Deployment of human resources

Deployment of employees is a management decision, again based on a set of variables, that is keyed to cost-effectiveness in an organization. Figure 7–3 summarizes some of the major influences on deployment decisions.

Tasks to be accomplished Deployment decisions must be based on an analysis of all the tasks to be accomplished. Whether formal or informal, the analysis must define the elements of the overall task and the exact number of people required to do the tasks at an appropriate level. Fire suppression task analysis/resource relationships have been accomplished by several departments and or-

Figure 7–2 Steps in scheduling.

1. Identify shifts used in the schedule.
How many shifts are used?
What time does each shift start and end?
What are the shift lengths?
Do the shifts overlap?
Are personnel permanently assigned to a shift, or do they periodically rotate shift assignments? If they rotate, what is the shift rotation sequence?

2. Identify the duty cycle used in the schedule.
What are the lengths of the duty cycle and the week cycle?
Is the schedule locked? If so, the on-duty and off-duty periods of each group of employees must be analyzed separately.

3. Identify the schedule's on- and off-duty periods.
What are the maximum and minimum lengths of on- and off-duty periods?
How frequently do personnel have on- and off-duty periods of various lengths?
Are long (short) on- and off-duty periods grouped together or are they distributed throughout the week cycle?
Are long on-duty periods followed by long off-duty periods?
Are short off-duty periods preceded by short on-duty periods?
With what frequency are combinations of days of the week included in off-duty periods?

How many week-end off-duty periods are provided by the schedule?
How many off-duty hours are provided at each shift change?

4. Identify the groups of identically-scheduled employees using the schedule.
How many groups are used?
How many employees are assigned to each group?
What is the composition of each group in terms of personnel classifications and skill levels of group members?
To what extent does the schedule provide team integrity and unity of command?
Do the groups of employees constitute platoons?

5. Determine on-duty staffing provided by the schedule by time of day and day of week.

6. Determine whether Kelly days or payback days are used and how often they are given.

7. Determine the average work week.

Note: If more than one schedule is used, the steps should be performed for each schedule.

Figure 7–3 Factors affecting deployment of human resources.

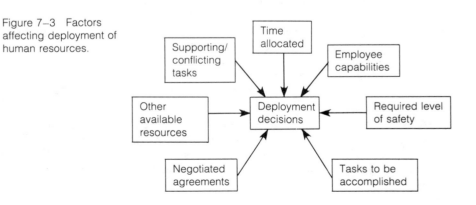

ganizations (Dallas, Texas, Fire Department; Seattle, Washington, Fire Department; United States Fire Administration; International Association of Fire Fighters) and will continue to be a central concern of management studies in the future. Task analyses for other fire service positions are readily available from many sources and have been used as a basis for the development of performance standards by the National Fire Protection Association and model code groups.

Employee capabilities Employee capabilities must be assessed in relation to the tasks to be accomplished. This means examining training levels, skill levels, physical ability, time management abilities, as well as other capabilities that affect an individual's ability to accomplish tasks.

Required level of safety It is easy to advocate total safety. However, in determining staff distribution, the manager must assess the level of acceptable risk. This risk management approach recognizes that although no environment is totally safe, particularly in the case of emergency fire service response, the level of safety will increase as a function of the amount of resource allocated to the task. Conversely, the risk will increase when the number of people assigned to a task (i.e., a fire company) decreases.

Time allocated for tasks Studies of fire company staffing clearly illustrate that the speed with which most fire service tasks are accomplished is significantly diminished as crew sizes are decreased. Yet there are no studies that establish the optimal staffing level. Therefore, the fire service manager must examine how much time is acceptable to accomplish the work and weigh the information heavily in decisions on staffing distribution. Many fire agencies rely on risk analysis and fire flow studies to help establish staffing levels.

Other available resources The availability of rapidly deployed assistance is an important consideration in the deployment of human resources. Mutual aid or automatic aid agreements or on-call supplemental forces are examples of useful management tools for increasing fire company strengths where circumstances permit. These concepts hold true in other areas as well, such as building and fire code enforcement, public education, and administrative functions. The deployment of personnel may also be influenced by the utilization of staff pools within given organizations. Manpower squads, multi-company stations, super-stations (large multi-company, multi-personnel stations placed in strategic locations), and specialty stations (where suppression personnel are assigned such other tasks as public education, planning, and so on) are examples of successful staff deployment alternatives.

Supporting/conflicting tasks The number and degree of conflicting tasks assigned to a given task group is another concern in deployment. Obviously, a fire company or an individual cannot be in two places at once. If the training program or public education activities are a priority, it is likely that the staff attached to these functions will have a diminished degree of availability for other concurrent tasks. Conversely, if no support tasks are assigned, organizational growth and productivity are both likely to decline.

Negotiated agreements Occasionally an employee bargaining unit will be successful in negotiating a minimum staffing clause. Deployment decisions are usually severely limited under these arrangements. In some cases minimum staffing clauses have forced fire companies to shut down and thus have affected response time.

⚹ *Allocation of human resources for service demand*

The allocation of human resources for service demand is really a combination of scheduling and deployment decisions based on the demand for services. Many approaches to the cost-effective utilization of staff have focused on defining the hours and geography of increased fire, emergency medical, inspection, and other work loads. Increasing (or diminishing) staff assignments according to demand has been a successful strategy in a number of larger cities and in "bedroom" communities. In large cities, statistical data have indicated that certain socioeconomic and building conditions drive fire and emergency medical service call loads upwards during certain hours, commonly in the evening, but sometimes in the morning. Staffing up for those situations (and only those situations) prevents devastating demands for normal resources all at once and allows a lower normal staffing level to be maintained during the rest of the work cycle. In bedroom communities, evidence supports the hypothesis that lower populations during the workday will generate less fire and EMS demand from 8 A.M. to 5 P.M. At the same time, the lower populations during the workday typically mean that fewer volunteer firefighters will be available.

In allocating emergency service personnel to meet varying levels of demand, basic information regarding the amount of work that can be accomplished safely by a given number of people must not be lost. Starting with an adequate number of employees to accomplish basic tasks and adding additional resources to meet peak load demands involves far less risk and is typically more cost effective than employing larger numbers of personnel and decreasing resources during low demand periods.

Managing volunteer and paid on-call human resources

There are some special concerns and issues in managing the human resources of a volunteer or paid on-call fire department. These individuals, who make up the vast majority of the U.S. fire service, must be selected, utilized, and rewarded properly in order to make an organization effective.

Most volunteers begin their fire service involvement with a high degree of commitment. Significant effort must be put forth to retain and nurture this commitment, or serious organizational and economic problems are likely to occur. The following paragraphs discuss areas that merit special concern in examining human resource management in volunteer fire departments.

There is often much pressure to make the selection and performance standards for volunteer firefighters lower than those for career fire service personnel. The volunteer fire service organizations that have recognized the necessity of maintaining equal standards have found not only a cadre of volunteer personnel willing to conform, but also a degree of resentment when the volunteer is asked to play a technically inferior role.

The National Fire Protection Association 1000 series standards, which address fire service personnel standards, do not differentiate between volunteer and career personnel. Although it is recognized that the time required to obtain training and to become certified at various levels may differ significantly among career and volunteer operations, the performance objectives are identical.

Volunteer personnel burnout and/or marginal participation are important management concerns, and one way to prevent burnout is to recruit volunteers with diverse backgrounds and interests. The resultant cadre of talented people is likely to represent many of the skills and abilities needed in an organization and, accordingly, allow for the spreading of work/organizational burdens to many participants. Use of some of the nonmonetary incentives discussed earlier will also aid in defusing polarization of membership and the resultant drop in activity level.

Like their career counterparts, volunteer firefighters have compensation and benefits needs. Monetary compensation, whether token or actually designed to offset expenses, may be worthwhile. However, compensation may serve to refocus volunteers away from a service orientation. If a monetary compensation package is utilized, it must be administered with total fairness and with regard for the value of members whose participation may differ but whose contribution to the organization may be equally valuable.

Many volunteer fire service organizations have chosen to provide a benefit program that is exclusive of any (or significant) direct payments. High-quality deferred compensation plans, paid training opportunities, participation awards, and excellent health insurance are but a few successful concepts. Many organizations sponsor controlled social events as well. However, if they fail to control the social environment, serious problems and negative community perceptions can arise. Policies allowing alcoholic beverages to be used in fire stations or at official business functions can have many negative ramifications that far outweigh any positive aspects.

Managing volunteer resources is a delicate and difficult task, and volunteer fire departments require every bit as much management skill and attention as do career organizations.

Managing material resources

Most paid fire service operations resemble businesses in that the major portion of their budget goes toward human resources. Further, the method used to plan, specify, and procure capital and other material resources can have a substantial impact on cost-effectiveness. This section covers the major components of material resource management: predicting future needs, deciding between new and rehabilitated equipment, purchasing procedures, capital improvements, utilization, and maintenance.

Managers and supervisors in local government have a high degree of accountability for the material resources entrusted to them. With accountability come responsibility and authority to see that those resources are utilized properly. Vivid examples of poor management in the area range from the petty pilfering of supplies for home use to the use (for profit) of fire apparatus to fill swimming pools.

Predicting future needs

Many of the small material needs of a fire department can be inventoried or purchased quickly. Examples include gloves, boots, hand lights, and medical supplies. However, major equipment such as fire apparatus cannot be purchased without careful research and planning. All fire service organizations should develop a needs assessment and amortization or replacement schedule for their major equipment in anticipation of growth or cutbacks, service life, obsolescence, maintenance costs, and so on. A rational replacement schedule is essential to sound resource management. Although guidelines for replacement of major equipment exist in broad terms, individual municipalities differ sufficiently to require their own needs assessment and replacement schedule. Figure 7–4 is a sample fire apparatus replacement schedule, and Figure 7–5 illustrates a supporting financial plan. Needs and material resources are also an important part of the budgeting process, which is discussed at length in Chapter 8.

Purchasing vs. rehabilitation

Often, a department with equipment needs can consider the value of rehabilitating older fire apparatus as opposed to purchasing new equipment. Generally

Figure 7–4 Fire equipment replacement schedule, from the annual budget, Champaign, Illinois.

```
━━━━━━━━━━━━━━━━━━━━━━━ ANNUAL BUDGET ━━━━━━━━━━━━━━━━━━━━━━━

    F I R E  E Q U I P M E N T  R E P L A C E M E N T  S C H E D U L E


                    FIRE EQUIPMENT REPLACEMENT GOALS

        QUANTITY          TYPE OF FIRE EQUIPMENT           MAXIMUM AGE

           1        Elevating Platform Truck (Snorkel)     25 Years
           1        Aerial Ladder Truck                    22 Years
           4        Front-Line Pumpers                     15 Years
           2        Reserve Pumpers*                       25 Years
           1        Utility/Rescue/Equipment Truck         10 Years


                   FIRE EQUIPMENT REPLACEMENT SCHEDULE

                                    YEAR OF      YEAR OF       YEARS OF
    DESCRIPTION                     PURCHASE     REPLACEMENT   SERVICE

    ELEVATING PLATFORM TRUCK (SNORKEL)
       L-111 FWD (85-ft)             1965         1988-89      24 years

    AERIAL LADDER TRUCK              1974         1995-96      22 years
       L-114 Seagrave (100-ft)

    FRONT-LINE PUMPERS:
       E-14 FMC 1500 GPM             1978         1992-93      15 years
       E-13 Emergency One 1250 GPM   1980         1994-95      15 years
       E-12 Pirsch 1250 GPM          1982         1997-98      16 years
       E-11 Pirsch 1250 GPM (Squirt) 1984         1999-00      16 years

    UTILITY/RESCUE/EQUIPMENT TRUCK:
       U-18 Ford                     1978         1989-90      12 years

    NOTE:  *When Front-Line Pumpers are replaced, they go on  reserve  status, with
           the oldest Reserve Pumper then actually being replaced.  One of the two
           Reserve Pumpers responds to "still alarm" fires.


━━━━━━━━━━━━━━━━━━━━━━ CITY OF CHAMPAIGN ━━━━━━━━━━━━━━━━━━━━━
```

speaking, this option merits serious consideration at the time of a needs assessment and then again when a purchase is due. Among the factors to be considered in the decision to buy or rehabilitate are

1. Return on investment. Will the interest income on the revenue saved sufficiently overcome the inflationary increase occurring when the apparatus is finally replaced?
2. Serviceability. Are the basic parts of the vehicle that will not be replaced readily available and will they remain so for the remainder of its service life?
3. Technology lag. Has a significant gain in technology been achieved, or will it be achieved, and would it negate the continued use of rehabilitated equipment?
4. Liability. Can the vehicle be brought up to current standards to limit liability to the agency in the event of an accident?

═══ ANNUAL BUDGET ═══

FIRE EQUIPMENT REPLACEMENT FUNDING

		ESTIMATED FIRE EQUIPMENT REPLACEMENT COST[1]	FIRE EQUIPMENT FUND REVENUES			
FISCAL YEAR	FIRE EQUIPMENT TO BE REPLACED		REQUIRED ANNUAL FUNDING[2]	INTEREST AND INVESTMENT INCOME[3]	TOTAL CITY FUNDING	PROJECTED YEAR-END BALANCE
1985-86	---	$ --	$ 78,000	$ 13,341	$ 91,341	$ 245,900
1986-87	---	--	81,900	19,500	101,400	347,300
1987-88	---	--	86,000	15,800	101,800	449,100
1988-89	L-111 Elevating Platform Truck (Snorkel)	456,000	90,300	33,700	124,000	117,100
1989-90	U-18 Utility/Rescue/Equipment Truck	161,000	94,800	43,000	137,800	93,900
1990-91	---	--	99,500	19,100	118,600	212,500
1991-92	---	--	104,500	15,900	120,400	332,900
1992-93	E-14 Pumper (1500 GPM)	201,000	109,800	25,000	134,800	266,700
1993-94	---	--	115,200	35,100	150,300	417,000
1994-95	E-13 Pumper (1500 GPM)	222,000	121,000	31,300	152,300	347,300
1995-96	L-114 Aerial Ladder Truck	517,000	127,000	42,700	169,700	0
1996-97	---	--	133,400	38,800	172,200	172,200
1997-98	E-12 Pumper (1500 GPM)	256,000	140,100	12,900	153,000	69,200
1998-99	---	--	147,100	24,400	171,500	240,700
1999-00	E-11 Pumper with Telescoping Boom	395,000	154,400	18,100	172,500	18,200
2000-01	---	--	162,200	31,000	193,200	211,400
2001-02	U-18 Utility/Revenue/Equipment Truck	275,000	170,300	15,900	186,200	122,600
2002-03	---	--	178,800	29,800	208,600	331,200
2003-04	---	--	187,700	24,800	212,500	543,700
2004-05	---	--	197,100	40,800	237,900	781,600
2005-06	---	--	207,000	58,600	265,600	1,047,200
2006-07	---	--	217,300	78,500	295,800	1,343,000
2007-08	E-14 Pumper (1500 GPM)	418,000	228,200	100,700	328,900	1,253,900
2008-09	---	--	239,600	125,400	365,000	1,618,900
2009-10	E-13 Pumper (1500 GPM)	461,000	251,600	121,400	373,000	1,530,900

NOTES:

1 - The fire equipment replacement cost estimates reflect a 5% annual increase for inflation.

2 - The required annual funding amounts include fire protection charge revenues and transfers from the General Operating Fund (or some other City Fund), and they reflect a 5% annual increase for inflation.

3 - The interest and investment income amounts reflect a 7½% annual interest rate, and assume that the revenue transfers would be made in full at the beginning of the fiscal years, while the required cash outlays for the replacement fire equipment would be made at the end of the fiscal years.

Figure 7–5   Financial plan for fire equipment replacement, from the annual budget, Champaign, Illinois.

Many organizations have discovered that their existing personnel can be utilized effectively in all or part of a rehabilitation project, thereby reducing costs and increasing the return on investment significantly.

It is extremely important to recognize a community's investment in its fire apparatus and equipment, whether rehabilitated or new. Decisions about this hardware should be made on the basis of cost-effectiveness, not cosmetics. A community should take pride in the appearance of its equipment, but that appearance should be a function of quality design and quality maintenance.

Purchasing

The term *purchasing* or *procurement* is generally used in local government to encompass locating, buying, distributing, storing, using, disposing, and paying for goods and services.

The procurement process includes setting standards and specifications, managing inventory, and taking procedural and substantive steps to award orders and contracts. The process summarized in the sidebar "The elements of purchasing" begins with the determination of requirements that are based not only on expenditures authorized by the operating budget but also on attempts to forecast both availability and anticipated use of materials and services. The process ends with physical receipt and distribution of goods or completion of contracted services. Purchasing is often accomplished through the finance department or through a separate purchasing department.

The elements of purchasing   The terms *materials management, purchasing,* and *procurement* are sometimes used interchangeably, but the term *procurement* is the most comprehensive for local government. Its elements include the following:

Requirements determination   Standards, specifications, classifications, cataloging, quantitative requirements.

Inventory management   Order quantities, stock levels, shelf life, physical inventories, computer models, order points.

Purchasing: preaward   Purchase procedures and records, sources of supply, bidding procedures, evaluation of bids, awards of orders and contracts.

Purchasing: postaward   Modifications of orders and contracts, receipt and inspection of deliveries, shortages and other discrepancies, payment procedures, audits.

Physical distribution   Transportation, receipt, storage, distribution, salvage, disposal.

Source: Abstracted, except for the first paragraph, from Harry Robert Page, *Public Purchasing and Materials Management* (Lexington, Mass.: Lexington Books, D.C. Heath, 1980), 24–26.

Purchasing policies vary widely among units of local government. Managerial latitude may be afforded at different levels or may be totally restricted. Among the policies that may vary are

1. Required bid vs. quotation (or open) purchasing
2. Bid and performance bond requirements
3. Number of bids and/or quotations required
4. Blanket order capabilities
5. Purchasing without requisitions
6. Affirmative action requirements
7. Plant visitation.

Establishing the purchasing policy is generally a managerial function of the finance department of the local government. Fire departments that operate as separate entities may carry out this function themselves. Input should be sought and offered by the principal operating departments, including the maintenance department.

The two largest material acquisitions of most fire departments are stations and apparatus. In the case of stations, the investment may be for a period of fifty years or more. In the case of apparatus, the purchase is affected by technological advances and operational needs, and the investment is for a shorter period. Apparatus purchases are more frequent, of course. Both kinds of purchases can be very large and for that reason are often open to much scrutiny and/or possible policy violations. Following are some guidelines for specifications, bidding, and contracts.

Specifications   Specifications for major capital purchases are of extreme importance. To create or determine specifications, it is necessary to decide on the type, configuration, durability, and cost of equipment that must last for many years. Personnel who are responsible for this job should examine existing equipment and model specs for applicability and should contact other fire service managers to learn of their experiences with similar equipment.

A primary source for developing fire apparatus specifications is the National Fire Protection Association's standard no. 1901 on automotive fire apparatus.

This consensus standard presents specification issues listing what is required for baseline performance and a number of options that can be added if needed. In addition, a number of other consensus standards have been published for fire and EMS equipment. Up-to-date standards can be obtained from the National Fire Protection Association, the American National Standards Institute, or the International Association of Fire Chiefs.

Sample specifications furnished by potential vendors usually include all basic features in equipment. However, the use of these documents may subtly exclude other vendors or open managers to criticism. Careful use of manufacturers' developed specifications may be desirable in cases where a particular product is to be specified because of positive experience or because it is compatible with existing equipment.

Although bidders will occasionally take exception to some or all portions of a specification and subsequently bid on an alternative product, this is not a practice to be encouraged. Specifications reflect what the purchaser requires and are not a leveraging tool for vendors to use against their competition or a fire service manager.

Bidding   The bidding process often begins with a request for proposals (RFP), which outlines performance standards for bidders. All bidding should be accomplished within the applicable state and municipal guidelines. The terms of bidding, especially timeliness and applicability, should be carefully stated in bid advertisements and in invitation sheets attached to the specifications. The rules of applicability must be observed to maintain the effectiveness of the bidding process. Bid bonds and performance bonds are controversial among purchasers and vendors. Bid bonds are generally accepted in the fire apparatus and large equipment business since bidding and contract execution periods are quite long and a fire department can be put at a significant financial disadvantage if rebidding is required.

Performance bonds are a hedge against the failure of a company to deliver a product by the end of the contract period. Since it takes a long time to manufacture fire apparatus and the costs involved are large, the bonds are recommended by most financial analysts. Managers should understand that the cost to the manufacturer of both bid and performance bonds is typically passed on in the price of the items purchased.

Contracts   For reasonably large purchases, a formal contract is a good idea. The legal staff available to the fire service organization should take a key role in finalizing this document. Key provisions of the contract will be the delivery date, bond execution date, inspection privileges, progress payments, and insurance and labor for equipment delivery.

Ethics   Because managers are in positions of public trust, they must observe certain ethical standards in purchasing items from vendors and negotiating with them. Every aspect of purchasing is watched closely by colleagues, suppliers, auditors, the governing body, and the general public.

Both the National Institute of Governmental Purchasing and the National Purchasing Institute have codes of ethics that state what they expect of their members. Four principles that appear in both codes serve as useful guidelines for the purchasing function in a fire department:

1. Accept and live up to the responsibilities that accompany a position of public trust.
2. Do not represent conflicting interests.
3. Do not misuse public or personal relationships for personal aggrandizement or profit.
4. Do not accept gifts or other items of value from suppliers.[8]

Capital improvements

Although the purchase of apparatus is a major expenditure for a department, it is a relatively short-term decision compared with the acquisition of buildings and land for fire stations and other facilities. A fire apparatus is mobile and replaceable. A fire station is a fixed asset that has both initial acquisition costs and ongoing expenses. Regardless of the methodology employed by a local agency, it is important to recognize that fire station location is a significant resource commitment.

Generally speaking, fire stations and other fire protection facilities—such as dispatch centers, training centers, and maintenance yards—are placed in the community on the basis of risk analysis and response time requirements, often with the help of computerized allocation models. Choosing the location of a fire protection facility involves several years of planning and the factors that need to be weighed are quite different from those considered in the acquisition of fire apparatus. In most fire protection agencies, fire station acquisition, like other capital improvements, must be studied carefully prior to approval.

One influence on fire station construction has been regionalization. In the past it was not uncommon for fire departments in adjoining jurisdictions to construct stations that had overlapping response areas. As a result of regionalization and functional consolidation of many services and the enactment of automatic aid agreements, the duplication of capital facilities has decreased.

To obtain adequate funding for these facilities, many communities have introduced ''impact fees'' assessed against new construction as it begins to increase the need for community fire protection. Such fees may be based on square footage and numbers of occupancies, for example, and can help offset the costs of providing service to a growing population.

Many elements of the actual construction of a fire station fall outside the fire department's authority. For this reason, the fire service manager must be reasonably familiar with the development process. In most departments, the fire prevention bureau's relationship to the building department provides a link to people who have a good grasp of these principles. However, some considerations fall outside the arena of strict code compliance.

For example, land acquisition is only the first step in constructing a fire station. Familiarity with the zoning process, the general plan of the community, environmental impact report requirements, and conditional permit use requirements are equally important.

A considerable amount of coordination is required between the fire service agency and the agency with responsibility and authority to deal with the community's development. Zoning, land use, and circulation have a real effect on fire station siting and utilization. In addition, citizens participate more and more in the fire station siting process. In many communities, the question of where to relocate fire stations has sparked a debate on two levels. Many people resist plans to move a fire station out of a high-risk neighborhood, because they perceive such a move as a reduction in service. On the other hand, citizens also tend to resist the placement of a new station in an established neighborhood, as it means condemnation of property and an increase in response activity.

One of the primary issues regarding construction of fire protection facilities is compliance with the existing codes imposed upon other general construction, and many fire departments have attempted to skirt local code requirements. It is critical that fire departments keep abreast of the ''state of the art'' with respect to construction. For example, many fire stations are now equipped with sprinklers, smoke detectors, and all the other life-safety devices required in other occupancies of public assembly.

Construction options Most fire departments have had direct experience with constructing at least one fire station. As fire protection agencies undergo tran-

sitions, i.e., growth and/or change in their mission, a number of construction options have emerged:

1. Remodeling of existing facilities
2. Utilization of portable facilities
3. Multiple use fire stations (fire station/public library)
4. Use of corporate headquarters (fire station headquarters located in conjunction with city hall)
5. Modular construction.

Each of these options can be incorporated into a resource management model, depending on the organization's needs. For example, if an existing fire station is located appropriately with respect to calls for service but fails to comply with the local code, it may be cost effective to remodel the facility to bring it up to code. This in turn may force the organization to use portable facilities in the interim. Portable facilities also have been found useful in communities where rapid growth has occurred but the demographics have not stabilized to the point where a definitive risk analysis can be performed. For example, many fire departments have used house trailers coupled with portable garages as temporary fire stations until a final site has been located.

The multiple use concept is not particularly new, but it has advantages in

---

Fire station location study   Ames, Iowa (population 46,000), has two fire stations to serve a 20-square-mile area. Residents in southeast Ames advocated construction of a third station to eliminate a perceived problem of high emergency vehicle travel time to their area. Therefore, the city needed a reliable method for (1) quantifying existing fire vehicle response time and (2) predicting response times from alternative locations of a third fire station or a relocated second fire station.

A request for proposal was distributed to fire management personnel in other communities, statistics professors, and others who had the expertise to help the city conduct a fire station location study. Two individuals were selected to serve as advisors.

The two advisors met with fire management personnel and other city staff for two days to initiate the study. A formula developed by the Rand Corporation was selected to predict fire vehicle response time. (It should be noted that this formula is a predictor of travel time, which is only one of four components of total response time, the others being dispatching time, turnout time, and setup time.)

The following were the chronological steps in the study:

1. A map of all streets accessible by fire vehicles was produced.

2. Land use and hazard potential were used to delineate 162 fire management zones.

3. The 162 management zones were designated as high, medium, or low on the basis of their hazard potential.

4. Travel times from each station to each of the 162 zones were determined on the basis of the Rand formula. This provided the average travel time to each zone for first and second responses.

5. The Rand travel time prediction formula was verified through analysis of actual run times. The Rand formula proved to be extremely accurate in predicting average travel time.

6. Several sites for a third fire station and a relocated station No. 2 were selected and tested for travel time response with the Rand formula. The travel times that were identified became the basis for comparing the

communities that are particularly sensitive to citizen involvement. A fire station is a visible facility. Therefore, stations have often been combined with recreational facilities and libraries, and in some cases have served as "mini-city halls."

Increasingly, cities are moving fire prevention bureaus and/or top administration of fire departments out of a headquarters facility into city hall. This arrangement offers many advantages in coordinating top-level functions in fire prevention. The primary disadvantage is that it disassociates the administration from the "combat" aspects of the organization. However, it seems to favor organizations that are heavily involved in fire prevention functions, such as fire protection analysis.

In communities undergoing rapid change, modular construction offers flexibility. Modularity means designing fire protection facilities in modules so that they may be expanded, remodeled, or otherwise reutilized as missions and/or organizational structures change over the years.

Trends in fire station design criteria   Initially, most fire departments in the United States designed their fire stations according to the needs of the volunteer fire department. The facilities quite frequently consisted of large apparatus rooms and relatively spartan living quarters. As fire departments began to

---

benefits of these alternative locations with the additional costs.

7. A detailed breakdown of the number of incidents and associated value loss was produced for all of the fire management zones in southeast Ames, which had the highest travel times. The incident and loss statistics, which covered a three-year period, were useful in further analyzing the costs and benefits of the station location alternatives.

The conclusion of the study was that no changes were required in the existing fire station locations. Surprisingly, none of the alternative sites for a relocated station No. 2 yielded superior overall travel times than the existing location of station No. 2. Also, the number of incidents, value loss, and travel times to southeast Ames indicated that the cost of a third fire station could not be justified. The study recommendation met with overwhelming support from the city council and the southeast Ames residents.

The fire management staff also realized other benefits as a result of the study:

1. Deployment practices were evaluated for the first time on a comprehensive basis. In several instances, it was determined that travel time could be reduced by switching the first response deployment to the other station. Fire managers and citizens can now be assured that travel times throughout the community are at the minimum possible.

2. Fire managers have the ability to quantitatively determine the impact of proposed changes in the street network upon fire vehicle travel time.

3. Fire managers can now better assess the impact of proposed annexations and land developments in the community on fire response time. The fire service has thus become more actively involved in the community's physical development.

4. The appropriate level of firefighting equipment and personnel to be deployed to a call can be better determined now because the level of hazard in each management zone has been identified.

5. Fire management has the expertise required to update this study as required by increasing growth and development in the community and to apply a proven method of selecting future station locations.

professionalize, it became clear that additional facilities such as adequate dormitories, communications facilities, and administrative offices were needed. Over the decades, the fire station design has tended to duplicate the floor plans of these early stations. However, various changes have started to affect fire station design.

First has been the need for dual facilities, as a result of having women in the fire service. Many fire stations being designed today incorporate dual facilities for restrooms, dormitories, and other amenities.

Second has been the growing use of the computer and the impact of electronic technology. The fire stations of today are wired and/or designed for the use of computers for general records management and for computer-aided dispatch. Many fire departments are using video cassette recorders in their training programs, and large training rooms and cable are being programmed into the construction of the station.

Third has been the influence of physical fitness programs. Many fire stations today have a separate room specifically designed to accommodate physical fitness equipment. Similarly, other changes in the mission or activities of the department—the incorporation of emergency medical services or hazardous materials responsibilities, for example—have significant implications for fire station location and design.

Utilizing material resources

Managing material resources includes not only planning, procurement, and station design and location but also utilizing those resources effectively. Decisions dealing with placement of equipment and fire stations often have political as well as cost ramifications.

The following considerations should be given particular attention in equipment deployment decisions.

1. Equipment resources should match the hazards protected and alarm frequency experienced. Are the properties to be protected within the performance range of the equipment provided? Although not all facilities can be addressed directly, the majority of properties or calls should warrant a ladder truck, brush truck, paramedic ambulance, and so on, if one is to be assigned to the given area.
2. Support resources should match the equipment assigned. Are sufficient water supplies available for pumpers carrying small quantities of water or should tanker shuttle equipment be provided? Are support hospitals available for paramedic teams or are only basic life support facilities available?
3. Basic levels of protection should be consistent. Is equipment distributed so as to provide a basic level of service on a reasonable scale?
4. Alternative resources should be identified and engaged. Are alternative equipment resources secured for areas that cannot be served effectively? The use of mutual aid can be an asset in protecting particularly remote areas within the boundaries of a given unit of government.

Maintenance program

A major part of resource management consists of carrying out a sound maintenance program. Especially in volunteer departments, maintenance has often been allowed to be "catch as catch can." Intermittent or poorly managed maintenance programs will have a high cost later in terms of repair dollars and downtime. A few important elements of a good maintenance program are

1. Regularly scheduled routine maintenance and inspection performed by fire service and/or fleet maintenance employees

2. Scheduled testing of major equipment such as pumps, engines, elevating devices, hose lines, and so on (testing procedures and standards exist for most major equipment)
3. A quality fleet maintenance or contract maintenance facility that is dependable and reasonably familiar with the equipment
4. Adequate stock of key parts required to maintain the equipment and keep it operable
5. Good maintenance records to form the basis of a reminder file and a record of recurring problems (these records should include complete shop manuals on as much equipment as possible).

Regardless of the quality of the original purchase or the maintenance, all equipment has an optimum service life. If this is exceeded, equipment will be down for long periods since parts will not be readily available and breakdowns will occur often.

For many years, the Insurance Services Office and its predecessor agencies specified the optimum service life for fire service vehicles and certain equipment. Although this is no longer the case (equipment that is tested and passes is considered to meet ISO criteria regardless of age), it is management's responsibility to be accountable for cost-effectiveness and to plan ahead to provide the quality of material resources desired by the community.

Productivity improvement

Among the most pressing issues for a fire service approaching the end of several decades of growth is productivity. When an organization is expanding, the issue usually does not arise. However, once a fire service organization stabilizes, it often has to compete with other governmental agencies for funds. The acquisition of resources, whether it be personnel, fire apparatus, or fire stations, is often tied to productivity. Having resources is one issue. Using them efficiently and effectively is another. Therefore, productivity is one of the greatest challenges facing the fire manager.

In local government productivity is generally defined as the efficiency with which inputs (resources) are transformed into outputs (desired programs and services). It is important for a fire service manager to understand these concepts as they relate to resource management. There are three ways in which an organization can increase productivity (see Figure 7–6):

1. Produce the same services and programs (outputs) with fewer organizational resources (inputs)
2. Produce more services with the same resources
3. Produce more services with fewer resources.

Figure 7–6
Management strategies for productivity improvement.

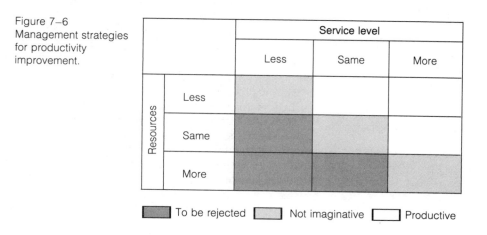

		Service level		
		Less	Same	More
Resources	Less			
	Same			
	More			

▨ To be rejected   ▧ Not imaginative   ☐ Productive

Productivity improvement efforts in government generally include actions to improve policies and services as well as operating efficiency. A variety of productivity indicators are discussed in other chapters of this book. Output measures include fire incidence data, work load data (including fire prevention assignments), response time measures for suppression and EMS calls, fire loss data, fire-related injury and death statistics, and input measures include dollar expenditures and personnel hours.[9] A related set of factors affecting the quality of work life is discussed earlier in this chapter.

Productivity indicators and the information they yield are useful only if they are employed to sustain excellent public service, reduce costs, and make improvements where possible. Three approaches to productivity improvement have been successfully followed in the public and private sectors: (1) capital and technological investment; (2) strengthened management and work redesign; and (3) work force improvement—working smarter and/or harder. These approaches are summarized here. Two other useful steps are also outlined in this section: (1) identification of obstacles to productivity improvement; and (2) a management audit of productivity improvement efforts.

Capital and technological investment

The greatest increases in output generally arise from investments in capital facilities and equipment incorporating science and new technologies. Four interrelated aspects of capital and technological investment merit the attention of managers: (1) relationship to labor costs, (2) technological redefinition of services and public expectations, (3) technological exchange and organizational impacts, and (4) unit cost savings and capital budgeting.

Historically, local governments have been extremely labor-intensive, with high work force costs. Where cost savings justify it, capital investment may help change that situation. In fact, advances and investment in fire service technology have resulted in productivity increases.

Capital investment typically results in the development of new products as well as the more efficient production of old ones. Until recently, local governments tended to focus only on the latter—on existing services or outputs. But the larger thrust of technological change is research and development that will lead to new processes and products to displace or add to old ones. In the private sector, such new product development is accompanied by market research designed to identify or change consumer demands. For many years little comparable activity occurred in government, except through technological transfer. Now, analysis of management and production systems in local governments may bring about such changes, including restructuring of citizen demand to reduce government costs.

Usefulness of technology depends on organizational size, structure, processes, and external linkages. The optimal size required to use certain technologies is simply not achievable in some governments. It makes no sense, obviously, to acquire firefighting equipment for high-rise structures in a jurisdiction with no buildings over three stories high. Technological transfer must be evaluated case by case, and improvements from other jurisdictions may or may not apply in a particular community. But, as a general rule, experience still supports technological exchange, transfer, and even shared use of capital equipment between jurisdictions to improve public service and reduce costs.

Cost savings through investment in capital equipment are the test of whether technological and other innovations should be made. If cost savings cannot be anticipated, capital investment probably is unwise. Savings resulting from a capital investment should at the very least amortize outlays by the end of its lifetime. For productivity improvement, it should also yield a net return on the invested capital (including an amount equal to or exceeding the interest). The point is that a fire department should go through systematic capital budgeting analysis before making investments aimed at productivity improvement. All aspects of costs need to be considered, including depreciation, interest charges, maintenance, and repair. Although the greatest increases in productivity in the U.S. economy have derived from capital investment, clearly not all such investments result in service improvements or cost savings.

Strengthened management and work design

The redesign of work processes was the thrust of productivity improvement in industrial and civil engineering during the early decades of this century, when professional management first became important in local government. At that time Frederick Taylor (see Chapter 3) offered two basic propositions that remain important: (1) work design can be engineered to enhance productivity; and (2) management is responsible for achieving that.

The time and motion studies of the early "efficiency experts" have mostly been surpassed by operations research and systems analysis. But periodic work design and redesign are essential in most production or service organizations for two reasons. First, numerous work processes are complex, with many sequential or parallel actions that are essential to service delivery *and* that are subject to improvement through analysis. Second, work arrangements tend to become obsolete, and those who are engaged in their routines easily miss new developments in citizen expectations and/or in work and delivery systems.

Management intervention to bring about essential changes may take many forms, discussed in Chapters 3 and 16. Internal and external management consultants are so commonly employed to assist with work redesign and other productivity improvement efforts, however, that they merit note here. Although many departments need to resort to outside assistance at times, internal managerial resources need to be regularly tuned to productivity improvement, service enhancement, and cost reduction. Many improvements may result from the efforts of those engaged in the work, given management encouragement. In-house consultants may also be employed to explore opportunities for change. Auditors who serve several jurisdictions should help their regular clients by suggesting exchange and transfer of technological and managerial developments, and cost-benefit analysis of auditing services should take into account whether they help introduce improvements that justify their cost. Even when a department relies on such sources, however, outside management consultants may bring new perspectives and ideas.

Work force improvement

Work force improvement efforts generally have taken two directions: improving the quality of the work force and securing increased effort. The productivity improvement measures discussed above—capital investment and work redesign—are aimed at helping the work force to "work smarter," as are actions to improve the quality of the labor force. "Working harder" is an alternative, and motivation approaches discussed earlier are aimed in part at achieving that. But to be useful the definitions of "working harder" and "working smarter" need to be deeper than those simple formula phrases. Producing more or producing better is generally the result of sound management in complex behavioral and situational relationships.

Obstacles to improvement

As a practical matter, managers may obtain useful results by periodically looking for and eliminating obstacles to productivity improvement, in addition to employing the approaches discussed above. Generally, workers and managers can recognize barriers to getting their work done, but they find it more difficult to discover or adopt new methods and systems. While many obstacles cannot be removed, others can be if they are identified and targeted for elimination.

Common obstacles to improvement in local governments are of four types: organizational constraints, resource limits, information deficiencies, and disincentives.

Organizational constraints Organizational constraints may be caused by political and legal frameworks that cannot be easily changed. Often, however, the limiting factors are structural and procedural and therefore managers have some control. A manager must strike a balance between one extreme of centralization and uniform prescription of rules and procedures and another extreme of dispersion of responsibility and differentiation of processes to suit every individual's wish. The manager can achieve control, especially with current information technology, without resorting to rigid and unchanging procedures. In addition, he or she can identify legal obstacles that are beyond change by management and bring them to the attention of officials for revision.

Resource limits Resource limits are common obstacles to productivity improvement. Managers need to inform citizens and officials of those constraints, but reallocations of money, people, equipment, buildings, or other resources may be justified by cost-benefit assessments to improve productivity in priority services or generally.

Information deficiencies Information is one resource whose deficiencies are most subject to managerial correction. Three practical questions may help identify and eliminate barriers: What data and analyses are needed? How is the information disseminated? How is it used?

Disincentives Finally, disincentives to productivity are common in governments. Although great attention is commonly given to motivation and incentives, often it is easier to identify and correct matters that turn people off, such as across-the-board budget cuts for both productive economizers and unproductive spendthrifts.

Self-audit for productivity improvement efforts

The self-audit presented in Figure 7–7 is designed to help managers identify and evaluate productivity improvement efforts in the organization.[10] The self-audit is organized around six basic questions:

1. What are the levels of interest in productivity improvement?
2. What measurement and evaluation criteria are used?
3. Are analysis techniques used for improvement?
4. Are high-potential improvement areas identified and acted on?
5. Are staff resources available to support improvement?
6. Are responsibilities for productivity improvement clearly defined?

Conclusion

Managing resources is a complex task that is key to the success of an organization. The proper use and development of people, things, and money will, to a great extent, determine the success of a fire department in achieving its goals and objectives. This chapter has addressed many aspects of resource management. In practice, however, the successful fire service manager must attain and

Figure 7–7 Self-audit for productivity improvement.

What are the levels of interest in productivity improvement?

1. *Do you devote sufficient time to productivity responsibilities?*
a) What percentage of time do you devote to
Reviewing the effectiveness of programs and services?
Reviewing operational performance?
Reviewing or developing new policies and procedures?
Other productivity issues?
b) Are policy, services, and productivity improvements regularly discussed in management staff meetings?
c) Do you specifically ask subordinates to improve productivity?
d) Do you follow up?
e) Do employees generally believe that you are interested in sustained excellent service and improvements?

2. *Are effectiveness, efficiency, and economy concerns reflected in clear goals and objectives?*
a) Are intended results—outputs and outcomes—clear?
b) Are intermediate work or service objectives used?
c) Is economical use of scarce resources practiced?
d) Are budgeting and other management support systems oriented to the performance and improvement of services?

3. *Are needs for excellence, improvement, and economy in services accepted throughout the organization?*
a) Is excellence in public service recognized and respected?
b) Are economizing behaviors common and are they recognized and respected?
c) Are employees regularly involved in improvement efforts?
d) What significant improvements have been made during the past year?

What measurement and evaluation criteria are used?

1. *What efficiency measures are regularly used?*
a) Are work force costs, total direct unit costs, or direct and indirect costs used as measures of input?
b) What outputs are used for efficiency measures?
c) Are records of resource uses (labor, time, equipment, etc.) regularly maintained for those outputs and reported to management?
d) Are data on input/output relationships analyzed? How is the information used?

2. *What effectiveness measures are used regularly?*
a) What performance indicators are used in day-to-day management?
b) Do those indicators distinguish between outputs and outcomes, and do they assess both?
c) Are quality standards used, and do they include such factors as timeliness, errors, and unique services?

3. *What measures are used to encourage economical use of scarce resources?*
a) Are there criteria for use of such scarce resources as water, energy, equipment, buildings, land, people, money, and things of historical importance?
b) What inventory controls and management systems are employed to maximize use of resources and to minimize costs?

4. *Is overall productivity assessed and reported?*
a) Are combined assessments made of effectiveness, efficiency, and economy?
b) Are selective, in-depth evaluations used?
c) Are performance and evaluation reports regularly prepared and reviewed with responsible persons?

Are analysis techniques used for improvement?

1. *Are methods and procedures frequently analyzed?*
a) Are managers currently informed about what others are doing in services and programs similar to theirs?
b) Are new technologies regularly assessed for possible use?

(continued on next page)

Figure 7–7
(*continued*).

c) Do employees and supervisors regularly make suggestions that are used for improvements?
d) Are staff specialists or consultants used to make improvement studies?

2. *Is employee use of time and resources regularly assessed?*
a) Is work distributed appropriately among employees?
b) Do employees have excessive nonproductive time waiting for assignments, equipment, preparatory operations, and so on?
c) Do peak loads create imbalances?
d) Are scheduling and/or production control techniques and systems used?

3. *Are employees motivated to perform well and help with improvements?*
a) Are employees informed about organizational and individual performance?
b) Is excellence valued, identified, recognized, and rewarded?
c) Is quality of employees' work life a managerial responsibility?

4. *Are outputs and intended results logical and realistic?*
a) Is the relationship between outputs and intended results valid?
b) Are performance targets regularly reviewed and revised as necessary?
c) Are alternative policies and service strategies regularly considered?

Are high-potential improvement areas identified and acted on?
1. *Have potential improvement targets been ranked in terms of available resources and impacts?*
a) Have available resources been assessed in terms of productivity potential?
b) How are activities ranked in order of improvement potential?
c) Is selection of improvement projects based on an assessment of overall government services and needs?
d) Are the potential cost savings and improvements in services calculated before significant efforts are initiated?

2. *Are problem areas periodically assessed?*
a) Are obstacles to excellent performance sought out and eliminated where possible?
b) Are persistent areas of deficient performance targeted for deliberate changes?
c) Are early warning systems employed and contingency assessments made to identify and deal with potential major problems before they occur?
d) Are unsuccessful and unneeded services and programs eliminated?

3. *Is excellent performance reinforced and expanded to other activities?*
a) Is high performance reinforced to sustain and enhance public service?
b) Are causes for high achievement determined and are the lessons used elsewhere, as applicable?

Are staff resources available to support improvement?
1. *Depending on government size, are productivity improvement functions staffed centrally, performed through general management, or supported from other sources?*
a) Is expertise in performance measurement and evaluation available to help managers?
b) Is assistance in management systems and procedures available to managers?
c) Is expertise in technology utilization and capital investment available to managers?

2. *Are varied expertise and disciplines among line managers utilized as staff resources?*
a) Do managers share their specialized expertise as needed outside their own departments?
b) Are they asked and encouraged to do that?

3. *Are central administrative staff personnel and organizations perceived positively or negatively as services, controllers, or both?*
a) Do central staff personnel work well with line organizations and vice versa?
b) Are administrative staff activities evaluated similarly to line operations?
c) How do administrative staff measure up in terms of service, control, or other criteria?

4. *Are training or other development opportunities for productivity improvement available to managers and employees?*
a) Are exemplary practices shared for potential use by others?
b) Are practices of other jurisdictions studied through professional meetings and networks?
c) Is special productivity improvement training effectively used?
Are responsibilities for productivity improvement clearly defined?
1. *Are productivity improvement responsibilities and authorities clearly identified for departmental supervisors and senior managers?*
a) Are managers held accountable for sustained excellence and improvements?
b) Do managers have authority commensurate with their responsibilities?
c) Are productivity improvement efforts coordinated?

2. *Are different responsibilities for effectiveness and operational efficiency separately identified but related?*
a) Is responsibility for effectiveness assigned to and carried out by senior managers?
b) Is responsibility for operational efficiency and performance assigned to and carried out by line supervisors?
c) Do managers recognize and act on distinctions and interrelationships among effectiveness, efficiency, and economy?

3. *Are central management responsibilities for improvement performed?*
a) Are central managerial systems clearly oriented toward excellence of public service and toward cost-effectiveness?
b) Are central procedures adequate to assure that productivity improvement responsibilities are accepted and carried out?

apply the skills required to balance needs with resources within the local government setting. Communities will continue to look toward their professional fire service managers to provide guidance to local government and to implement its priorities in resource management.

1   Robert Tannenbaum and Warren H. Schmidt, ''How to Choose a Leadership Pattern,'' *Harvard Business Review* 36, no.2 (March-April 1958): 95–101.
2   Thomas J. Peters and Robert H. Waterman, Jr., *In Search of Excellence* (New York: Warner Books, 1982), 3–26.
3   Ibid., 235–78.
4   University of Michigan, Survey Research Council, *Survey of Working Conditions,* for the U.S. Department of Labor, Employment Standards Administration, August 1971.
5   Ray A. Killian, *Human Resource Management: An ROI Approach* (New York: AMACOM, a division of the American Management Association, 1976), 148.
6   Dale S. Beach, *Personnel: The Management of People at Work,* 4th ed. (New York: Macmillan, 1980), 88–90.
7   John M. Greiner, ''Motivating Improved Productivity: Three Promising Approaches,'' *Public Management* 61 (October 1979): 5.
8   The complete codes can be obtained from the organizations: National Institute of Governmental Purchasing, Inc., 115 Hillwood Avenue, Falls Church, Virginia 22046; National Purchasing Institute, Inc., 201 Belt Line, Suite D, Cedar Hill, Texas 75104.
9   Philip S. Schaenman and Joe Swartz, *Measuring Fire Protection Productivity in Local Government* (Boston: National Fire Protection Association, 1974), 15–17.
10 This is adapted with major revisions from National Center for Productivity and Quality of Working Life, *Improving Productivity: A Self-Audit and Guide for Federal Executives and Managers* (Washington, D.C.: Government Printing Office, 1978).

Budgeting, finance, and cost containment

What is public budgeting? What do decisionmakers both inside and outside the fire department need to know about the elements that make up the budgetary process in their jurisdictions? How does the fire department fit into this process? What are the types of budget? How is an adopted budget controlled?

In the political and administrative climate of the late 1980s, these are questions that fire chiefs and other managers (and all those who aspire to such positions) must address if they are to be effective. Taken together, these questions—and some of the answers to them—form the basis of this chapter.

The chapter first reviews the local government budgetary setting and the theory and practice of public budgeting, then focuses on eight types of budgets and their strengths and weaknesses. The next section outlines and assesses the budgetary controls vital to successful management. The next sections discuss fire department revenues and expenditures, changing approaches to fire service budgeting, and cost pressures and cost containment related to liability, compensation packages, medical costs, and workers' compensation, followed by a review of retirement system budgeting. The chapter concludes with a discussion of budget preparation and presentation.

The budgetary setting

Public budgeting can be defined as the development and execution of a plan for effective use of financial resources in carrying out policies for a fiscal period. It is the expression in financial terms of the cumulative policies of the jurisdiction for that forthcoming fiscal period.

Elements in the budgeting process

Those with experience in this area might describe public budgeting as a strange combination of the political and the administrative, consisting of three seemingly disconnected but carefully intertwined elements: mechanical, analytical, and political:

1. Mechanical, or making sure that all the figures add up, are entered in the proper spaces in the correct forms, and are presented on time.
2. Analytical, or "massaging" the mechanically derived data to ensure that efficient and effective alternatives are chosen. Analytical tools include cost-benefit analysis, managerial analysis, alternative studies, reorganization plans, and other similar approaches.
3. Political, in which elected officials ultimately adopt a budget.

The budget cycle

The steps involved in preparing and executing a budget are commonly called the *budget cycle*. The cycle has several phases:

1. Preparation, when departmental units, department heads, and the local government manager or political executive estimate their resources and needs for the coming fiscal year. During this phase, the budget office estimates revenues, the chief administrator generally issues a policy statement indicating general budgetary directions, and the fire chief gathers and compiles budgetary data from throughout the department.
2. Adoption, when the budget is presented first to the chief administrator and then to the city council or county board for review and approval. The chief or the fire department staff generally makes these presentations.
3. Implementation, when the adopted budget is executed throughout the fiscal year.
4. Evaluation, when budgeted programs are reviewed throughout the year.

This chapter is primarily concerned with budget preparation and adoption, which are concentrated during the period known as "budget time." Implementation and evaluation are ongoing and are covered in other chapters.

Although the details and the scope differ, such is the setting of any—and every—budget system, no matter how small, or how large, the jurisdiction.

The theory and practice of budgeting

Anyone who has prepared a public budget knows that theory and practice do not always coincide. It is important to understand both.

Theory

Public budgeting theory holds that the purpose of the public budget is fourfold:

1. *To formalize policy*, which is expressed financially through the budget. The budget keeps score of priorities by dollar allocations to agencies or functions.
2. *To supply information* (*a*) to the policymakers so that they may more intelligently distribute available public dollars among competing governmental uses and (*b*) to the public so they will be informed of the priorities for their collective public assets and the services provided therewith.
3. *To supply specific data* to operational managers throughout the jurisdiction, so that they may fine-tune their operations as the fiscal year progresses. Such operational decision making, of course, presupposes that there is an accurate and timely budgetary accounting system with which to track revenues and expenditures as the fiscal year unfolds.
4. *To provide a mechanism for controlling objectives and expenditures*. The budget must show a balance between revenues and expenditures. Such a balance is much easier to achieve in "good" economic times than during downturns. When budgets are tight, controls tend to be emphasized.

Practice

Experience demonstrates the difficulty of operating a budgetary system on the basis of theory alone. The major reasons are the nature of the policy-making process, the requirements of budget control systems, and the inherent conflict between the two.

The policy-making process   The nature of the policy-making process is such that it is impossible to be entirely objective in deciding budgetary priorities.

Since the turn of the century various budgetary systems, approaches, and formats have been developed in the continuing quest for political objectivity by elected policymakers. It would appear that the very nature of democracy, which is based on representative elections and the "politics" associated with them, militates against objectivity in the usual sense. Budgeting could in addition be defined as a rational decision-making system working within a less-than-rational political process.

The management control system   The management control system ensures that monies are not expended for unintended purposes and objectives and that budget allocations are not exceeded. Most such systems are based on the assumption that strategically placed persons in the organization can control the behavior and the expenditure patterns of large numbers of persons and great sums of money. Thus, many budgets are almost solely control documents.

Conflicts between policy making and management control   Inherent conflicts exist between the policy-making process and the management control devices. A budgetary format or system that concentrates on the broad picture of programs and objectives usually lacks sufficient detail to be useful as a day-to-day management information and control tool. On the other hand, a financial decision-making approach that relies heavily on detailed data sufficient to meet operational needs usually invites "pencil counting" in the policy-making process, diverting elected officials from the overall objectives of public expenditures. Thus, any budgeting system is caught between these two conflicting needs and must be a compromise between them. Although these needs can be reconciled, such reconciliation is extemely difficult to accomplish and in fact seldom occurs. Fortunately, increasingly sophisticated computer systems are enabling governments to design and implement systems with both detailed data and policy summaries.

Types of budgets

Since the late nineteenth century eight basic budgetary systems or formats have been developed and, to a greater or lesser degree, installed in and used by governmental jurisdictions. Each represents an attempt to provide policymakers with sufficient information to make intelligent policy choices among competing priorities and to provide operational personnel with financial data on which to base day-to-day operational decisions.

The following discussion briefly describes each of the eight types of budget formats: the lump-sum budget, the line-item budget, the performance budget, the "classical" program budget, the planning-programming-budgeting system (PPBS), the cost-distribution program budget, the zero-base budget (ZBB), and the integrative budgeting system (IBS).

The lump-sum budget

Before the governmental reform movement, which began around the turn of the century, most fire departments were appropriated a lump sum of money considered adequate for their needs. The fire chief, who was usually politically appointed by the city council and its fire committee, would recommend the amount to the fire committee. The fire committee would review this recommendation and would, in turn, recommend an amount to the full city council. The finance committee of the council would add up all the amounts for all department committees and would adopt the budget and tax rate to finance the fire department and all other activities.

Department heads, subject to the general supervision of their committees, would dole out the money pretty much as they and the committee saw fit. Obviously there was considerable opportunity for mismanagement and diversion of monies. When such problems reached epidemic proportions, reformers sought major changes. One of these revisions was a strictly controlled budget, the line-item budget.

The line-item budget

By far the most common budgetary format, the line-item budget (Figure 8–1) is basically a listing of items of purchase and acquisition, by department, by agency, or, in some cases, by a smaller organizational unit. This type of budget concentrates on the object of expenditure (line item) in considerable detail and therefore tends to be a rather long document.

One feature of the line-item budget is that since dollars are appropriated for specific items, and failure to expend would be considered a lack of need for such monies, absolute expenditure of all appropriations is almost inevitable. If such monies are not spent, invariably the unexpended amount for the current fiscal year is lost, as is an equal amount for succeeding years.

Advantages The advantages of the line-item budget are simple. First, owing to the ease of adding up the lists of items to be purchased and services to be acquired, a budget total is easy to derive. When all such organizational monetary lists are added up and compared to total revenues, the amount ''out of balance'' or, rarely, the surplus, makes it relatively easy to ensure a balanced budget. (Historically, the difference was made up in property taxes, and the budget was ''balanced'' by calculating the out-of-balance amount in terms of cents per hundred dollars of assessed valuation.)

A second advantage is that it provides the level of operational detail needed by departmental supervisors for timing, revising, and controlling their internal day-to-day operations. Such detail is also vital to the preparation and justification of the next year's budget and as a base for estimating the cost of any modifications or additions.

A third advantage is that a line-item budget lends itself to budgetary (accounting) controls. The budget permits a direct linkage with the budgetary control accounting system, and since invoices and payrolls are recorded directly against specific line items, the chief is able to monitor spending item by item as the fiscal year progresses.

Disadvantages The line-item budget has major disadvantages—so many that most jurisdictions and budget theoreticians have at one time or another attempted to abandon it for another form. Most of the disadvantages are the ''flip sides'' of the advantages.

First, because the line-item budget is easy to balance, it may seem easy to make cuts. This is not the case, however, because a cut in one item may have ramifications throughout the budget. Furthermore, the budget gives no information on the operational implications of cuts, so arbitrary budget reductions may have unforeseen consequences.

A second drawback to the line-item budget is its emphasis on objects of expenditure (inputs) rather than on results of expenditure (outputs). Because the emphasis is on detail, most policy officials are tempted to ''cut out the fat'' of this budget rather than substantively explore alternative methods for using the budgeted dollars to secure the same objective. The profusion of detail also tends to reduce operational flexibility. Monies are appropriated for the specific

Continued on page 200

Departmental budget summary

Fund: 01	Program: Public safety	Function: 23	Department/Division: Fire		

				1985–86 Budget	
Classification	1982–83 Actual	1983–84 Actual	1984–85 Budget	Requested	Final
Salaries and wages	$1,442,790	$1,462,531	$2,080,427	$2,185,053	$2,182,553
Materials, supplies, and services	174,785	189,486	205,273	534,601	534,601
Equipment outlay	58,908	92,217	95,984	103,717	103,717
Departmental total	$1,676,483	$1,744,234	$2,381,684	$2,823,371	$2,820,871

Commentary

Primary purpose   To reduce the potential for, and the amount of, property damage and life loss resulting from emergencies such as fire, explosion, hazardous material, smoke, electricity, life-threatening medical, gas entrapment, and disaster by (a) developing and implementing a prevention program that adopts and enforces laws to control the magnitude of loss and educates the public, (b) adopting and implementing a program to respond to and mitigate the magnitude of property damage and life loss from emergencies.

Operational design   The Fire Department is divided into three operational divisions:
1. Administration, which provides the management needed to develop and direct implementation of policy, the budget, operational design, and analysis to cause effective operational alteration, secretarial, and clerical activities
2. Fire prevention, which provides management, supervision, fire and arson investigation, plan checking, public education, ordinance development, and public relations
3. Fire suppression, which provides management, supervision, emergency response for fire, rescue, explosion, specified medical, smoke, gas, hazardous materials, mutual aid and disaster incidents, limited nonemergency response to mitigate the cause and recommend repair and cleanup services, projects as assigned.

Divisions accomplish work through projects that are clarified by objectives identified in measurable terms. The objectives are specific tasks (units of work) that identify the completion of a project and its value toward achieving departmental goals. Projects are assigned to personnel (firefighters, fire engineers, fire inspectors) by supervisors who become project managers (coordinators). All projects are supervised daily and evaluated semiannually by managers.

	1984–85		1985–86 Budget	
Position title	Budget	Requested	Proposed	Final
Fire chief	1	1	1	1
Assistant fire chief	1	1	1	1
Battalion chief	3	3	3	3
Fire prevention manager	1	1	1	1
Fire captain	9	9	9	9
Fire prevention officer	1	1	1	1
Fire engineer	12	12	12	12
Firefighter	21	21	21	21
Secretary	1	1	1	1
Total positions	50	50	50	50

Figure 8–1   Line-item budget.

Salaries and wages	1982–83 Actual	1983–84 Actual	1984–85 Budget	1985–86 Budget	
				Requested	Final
Salaries, full time	$1,338,269	$1,340,197	$1,401,498	$1,443,584	$1,443,584
Salaries, overtime	19,929	33,446	25,000	35,000	35,000
Salaries, part time	2,900	6,097	7,500	7,500	7,500
Uniform allowance	7,725	7,340	8,500	8,500	8,500
Cash in lieu of benefits	15,904	15,469	34,260	33,309	33,309
Salaries, holiday pay	54,075	53,511	60,000	65,000	65,000
Overtime/callback pay	3,988	6,471	5,000	10,000	7,500
Fringe benefits	—	—	538,669	582,160	582,160
Total salaries and wages	$1,442,790	$1,462,531	$2,080,427	2,185,053	$2,182,553

Materials, supplies, and services	1982–83 Actual	1983–84 Actual	1984–85 Budget	1985–86 Budget	
				Requested	Final
Office supplies	$ 1,891	$ 3,162	$ 4,750	$ 4,893	$ 4,893
Office equipment maintenance	2,577	3,939	4,400	4,575	4,575
Printing and postage	1,981	3,644	7,150	5,720	5,720
Operating supplies	11,098	11,792	16,500	17,325	17,325
Dues and publications	1,286	1,486	2,650	2,650	2,650
Conferences and meetings	5,303	6,441	7,410	8,003	8,003
Auto allowance	1,125	1,800	—	1,800	1,800
Heat, light, power, water	7,825	6,882	7,275	8,730	8,730
Contractual services	7,049	21,420	10,000	9,000	9,000
Training services	7,380	12,960	15,730	15,730	15,730
Hydrant rental	818	685	1,200	—	—
Fire prevention	1,568	1,534	600	600	600
Minor firefighting equipment	4,695	13,300	3,900	4,173	4,173
Linen supplies	2,343	2,724	3,150	3,307	3,307
Information system services	—	—	—	35,936	35,936
Vehicle rental	104,791	85,898	105,373	123,442	123,442
Emergency preparedness	—	—	—	100,000	100,000
Insurance	—	—	—	34,071	34,071
Workers compensation insurance	—	—	—	137,010	137,010
Communications	9,555	7,355	10,285	12,136	12,136
Physical exam program	3,500	4,464	4,900	5,500	5,500
Total materials, supplies and services	$174,785	$189,486	$205,273	$534,601	$534,601

Equipment outlay	1982–83 Actual	1983–84 Actual	1984–85 Budget	1985–86 Budget	
				Requested	Final
Office	$ 5,364	$ 321	$ 7,900	$ 1,483	$ 1,483
Field	46,972	28,901	28,996	36,436	36,436
Motive	159	56,627	54,129	53,029	53,029
Buildings	1,486	1,809	900	950	950
Other than buildings	4,927	4,559	4,059	11,819	11,819
Total equipment outlay	$58,908	$92,217	$95,984	$103,717	$103,717

Figure 8–1   *continued.*

item: Should events change between preparation and execution, approval by a budgetary official or even the governing body is frequently needed to transfer monies among line items. Thus, operating officials may try to subvert the controls in order to secure greater flexibility in the use of appropriated resources.

Third, because the budget is easy to control, there is greater potential for overcontrol and for stifling innovation and enthusiasm. Furthermore, the obvious comparison of budgeted versus expended amounts ensures maximum spending of appropriations, whether such spending is needed or not.

The performance budget

Since the late 1920s, governmental budget analysts have periodically attempted in one way or another and with varying degrees of finesse to apply the scientific management principles of industrial engineer Frederick W. Taylor (see Chapter 3) to governmental operations and budgeting. The performance budget (Figure 8–2) is one example of such an application.

The performance budget has three features: (1) standards of performance are set for each organizational unit, (2) compliance is measured against those standards, and (3) those standards as units of work are divided by the dollars allocated and a unit cost is derived. The goal is to reduce, or at least to hold steady, the unit cost.

Advantages   The advantages of this budget system have to be viewed in historical perspective. As the line-item budget does not normally specify results or outputs, the performance budget system has introduced a major change in that results are at least considered. Goals are set in the form of desired outputs and a measurement system is developed to quantify the degree to which these objectives are reached. A jurisdiction changing from line-item to performance budgeting is automatically forced to look beyond the immediate dollar amounts in the line items and to attempt to see what the money is buying in terms of levels of service.

Continued on page 203

Fire department service levels FY's 1986–88

	1984–85 Expended	1985–86 Appropriated	1986–87 Proposed	1986–87 Recommended	1987–88 Proposed	1987–88 Recommended
Salaries	$3,390,004	$3,638,155	$3,874,878	$3,867,304	$3,913,834	$3,913,834
Benefits	1,309,350	1,455,525	1,524,408	1,522,852	1,543,523	1,543,523
Materials	488,395	624,788	700,488	696,588	649,269	649,269
Equip., noncapital	7,903	49,288	58,650	58,650	29,650	29,650
Capital	69,318	46,000	82,850	82,850	39,400	39,400
Total	$5,264,970	$5,813,756	$6,241,274	$6,228,244	$6,175,676	$6,175,676
Positions	112	112/1	114	113/1	114	114

Levels of service

Level one	1986–87	1987–88
Cost	$4,702,534	$4,643,787
Positions	83	83

Figure 8–2   Performance budget.

Operations   (five of seven stations staffed)

Suppression responses   Respond to commercial and residential areas and provide protection to structures from brush fires 75 percent of the time; respond to and assess hazardous materials incidents within the city and mutual aid areas 75 percent of the time; respond to life-threatening medical emergencies 70 percent of the time within the community; respond to calls for state-mandated mutual aid 100 percent of the time.

Maintenance   Provide ongoing minimal custodial upkeep of buildings, emergency repairs, when necessary, to fire-fighting equipment and vehicles and routine maintenance on 30 percent of hydrants and 100 percent of hoses once a year.

Inspections   Inspect commercial occupancies for fire prevention once every three years; answer fire-safety complaints within 72 hours; pre-fire plan 30 percent of those target hazards that present the greatest threat to life and property.

Training   Train new firefighter recruits only in structure and brush fire protection and hazardous materials incidents in order to provide basic firefighting skills, using station captains as instructors; provide time for personnel to be certified once a year in CPR and advanced first aid in order to maintain a minimum proficiency level for medical emergency responses; provide all personnel with ongoing rudimentary organizational training in order to respond to major emergencies; provide post-fire critique within 72 hours of fire.

Fire prevention/public education

Technical inspections   Technical inspections involving sprinkler systems, underground tank installations, certificates of occupancy completed within two weeks of request. State-mandated inspections of schools, hospitals, rest homes, halfway houses and all other state-licensed care facilities completed within 90 days of request.

Fire investigations   All fires will be investigated within 24 hours of time of occurrence.

Occupancy clearances   Forty percent of requests for occupancy clearances involving dance permits, clearances, second-hand dealers' permits will be completed within one month of request.

Ordinance and code development   Involvement in code and ordinance development accomplished through consultation only, with attorneys.

Fuels reduction   Fuels reduction program accomplished only in those areas where complaints are received.

Complaints   Complaints for life-threatening incidents will be responded to within 24 hours, non-life-threatening complaints followed up within one week.

New construction   Plan checks, ordinance and code development accomplished only on consultation basis for crisis issues.

Administration

Administrative organization   Develop policies and procedures for the basic organization in response to specific problems only; implement program planning in response to crisis situations only.

Personnel   Consult with personnel officer to resolve personnel matters; provide personnel assignments schedules in order to meet fire station manning requirements.

Finance   Consult with payroll division to resolve personnel financial matters; send purchasing requests to purchasing agent for processing; prepare departmental budget requests.

Level two	1986–87	1987–88
Cost	$546,872	$537,478
Positions	10	10

Operations   (six of seven fire stations staffed)

Suppression responses   Confine structure fires to the area of origin 73 percent of the time, to the buildings of origin 77 percent of the time, respond to and assess hazardous incidents 100 percent of the time and respond to medical emergencies of a life-threatening nature 85 percent of the time; respond to the most urgent public assistance calls.

Maintenance   Provide preventive maintenance to stations, firefighting equipment, and vehicles once a month and routine maintenance of 60 percent of hydrants once a year.

Continued on next page.

Figure 8–2   *continued.*

Inspections Inspect commercial occupancies for fire prevention once every two years; answer fire safety complaints within 48 hours; pre-fire plan 60 percent of those target hazards that present the greatest threat to life and property.

Training Provide a recruit academy for new firefighters only in structure and brush fire protection and hazardous materials incidents in order to accomplish standardized firefighting skills using the training officer as instructor with captain follow-up; certify personnel every other year in emergency medical technican (EMT) training in order to meet state-mandated requirements; provide all personnel with training in the incident command system for major emergency coordination; provide post-fire critique within 24 hours of fire.

Physical conditioning Provide time to all personnel for daily physical conditioning in order to reduce job-related injuries.

Indicators	1984–85 Actual	1985–86 Estimated	1986–88 (Annual)	
			Proposed	Recommended
Fires confined to area of origin	91%	90%	85%	85%
Fires confined to building of origin	97%	96%	95%	95%
Percentage of emergency responses performed without valid complaints from the public	100%	100%	99%	99%
Average number of hours spent in manipulative training on a department-wide basis per month	509	592	550	550
Percentage of building plans checked within 24 hours	75%	100%	100%	100%
Percentage of occupancy clearances processed within 24 hours	100%	100%	100%	100%
Percentage of time the department maintains the ability to respond with specialized equipment and specially trained individuals to hazardous materials incidents	90%	90%	90%	90%
Through public education and fuel modification, percentage of accidental fires confined to an area of less than 5 acres each	100%	98%	95%	95%
Through public education, maintain the percentage of dwelling units equipped with smoke detectors at or above	58%	58%	58%	58%
Formal fire safety education programs in schools (during school year) will be held at least	2×/month	8×/month	8×/month	8×/month
The percentage of the community reached through mass media presentations will be maintained at (1986–87)	70%	70%	70%	70%
The percentage of the community reached through mass media presentations will be maintained at (1987–88)	—	—	78%	78%
Number of senior citizen-oriented fire safety presentations delivered per month	N/A	1	3	3
Homeowner group post-fire incident safety awareness training will be conducted within two weeks following department-targeted incidents	100%	90%	90%	90%
An investigator for fire scene investigation will be available within 45 minutes	100%	100%	100%	100%
Initial fire scene fire investigations will be completed within 24 hours	80%	80%	85%	85%
Post fire scene fire investigations will be initiated within 9 hours of each department-identified incident in which criminal activity is suspected	85%	85%	85%	85%
12 hours	100%	100%	100%	100%

Figure 8–2 *continued.*

Disadvantages The major disadvantage of the performance budget is that the performance standards often are developed by a small group of "efficiency experts" who determine both what the appropriate unit of measurement for each work (budget) group will be and how many units of output should be secured. This imposition of standards can be self-defeating if there is little or no meaningful participation by those in the units whose performance is being measured.

Furthermore, personnel are needed to maintain the work statistics, creating a tendency to add personnel to count and control, thereby increasing both expense and employee resentment. Sometimes the measurement process ceases being a means and becomes an end in itself.

The task of maintaining statistics is further complicated by the difficulty of measuring performance in many of the less tangible local government services, particularly where quality as well as quantity is a requirement.

The "classical" program budget

Since the end of World War II jurisdictions have attempted to simplify the line-item budget process and to make it more conducive to goal setting and less subject to overcontrol at the line-item level. This approach to governmental fiscal priority setting at one time was loosely called program budgeting (Figure 8–3), a term that covers a multitude of approaches.

In so-called classical program budgets, most line items are either wholly abandoned or greatly reduced in number. Appropriations are by organizational unit, determined by supervisory responsibility. Within each program, appropriations are made by lump sums to major objects. These usually are (1) personal services (salaries, wages, and fringe benefits), (2) capital outlay for equipment or construction, (3) interfund transfers (an accounting term for shifting monies from one restricted "pot" to another), and (4) other services and supplies (everything not covered by 1, 2, and 3). Sometimes a few details are provided, but generally the thesis is that, without line-item detail as a distraction, goals and service levels can be discussed and decided intelligently.

Policymakers need to decide how much dollar analysis they wish to undertake for each program. Sometimes such decisions are difficult to make without some measurement of work load; in such a case some of the elements of the performance budget often are grafted into this original approach to program budgeting.

Advantages The major advantage of the classical program budget is the obvious concentration on programs and service levels rather than on the inputs of dollar amounts and line-item objects. Such an approach requires some analysis of the organization's supervisory pattern to determine budget units and, as a result, may promote reorganization to combine duplicating or overlapping programs.

By withholding minute budgetary details, a "classical" program approach tends to shift the focus of the budget process away from the control function and return the decision making to policymakers and departmental managers.

Disadvantages A major disadvantage of the classical program budget is that the term *program*, when used as a description of a budgeting system, becomes increasingly problematical the more precise one's definition of *program* becomes. A second disadvantage is the inherent loss of line-item detail. Operational experience has shown that this detail can be useful for day-to-day management decision making regarding the use of monetary resources. But, again, when such details exist, there is an almost irresistible pull toward the detailed decision making of the line-item budget and its strict controls. Simply put, it is easier to count pencils, axes, nozzles, and feet of hose used than to decide on service levels among competing programs. The conflict between policy-level information and operational data is particularly evident in the classical program budget approach to the division of available governmental revenues. This is why few such budgets remain and why "modified" program budgets exist.

The planning-programming-budgeting system (PPBS)

Much has been written about the planning-programming-budgeting system since it was adopted by the U.S. Department of Defense in 1962. Its quiet abandonment by the rest of the federal government in 1971 was not so well advertised.

PPBS is based on a chain of events. First, programs are identified and objectives are set. Alternative routes to reaching the objectives are catalogued and a centralized staff of independent analysts undertakes a cost-benefit study of each alternative. Ideally, the solution that proves to be the most cost beneficial

| Account: 300012 | | Department: Fire Department | | |
| Program: Fire Operations | | | | |
	FY 1984 Actual	FY 1985 Budget	FY 1986 Adopted	FY 1987 Projected
Employees				
Regular	126	126	126	126
Nonregular	0	0	0	0
Total employees	126	126	126	126
Expenditures				
Personnel	6,009,191	6,691,721	7,185,073	7,515,586
Services and supplies	65,097	70,046	72,345	70,215
Equipment	19,577	23,547	11,469	0
Total budget	6,093,865	6,785,314	7,268,887	7,585,801
Administrative services charges	771,902	750,274	728,484	744,908
Total direct program cost	6,865,767	7,535,588	7,997,371	8,330,709
Revenue				
Federal revenue sharing	435,141	423,500	0	0
General fund (unspecified)	6,413,577	7,082,088	7,980,371	8,313,709
Non-building licenses & permits (fire permits)	17,049	30,000	17,000	17,000
Total revenue	6,865,767	7,535,588	7,997,371	8,330,709
Performance data				
Respond to fire incidents	2,700	2,700	2,700	2,700
Respond to paramedic-related incidents	1,500	1,500	1,500	1,500

Program description　The Fire Operations program performs all duties related to preventing and extinguishing fires; responding to public and interdepartmental assistance calls; maintaining alarm boxes; and maintaining fire station apparatus, quarters, grounds, and equipment.

Programmatic changes　None.

Cost changes　The adopted budget for this program represents an increase of $483,573 or 7.1 percent from the prior year's appropriation. This change is primarily attributable to higher salary and benefit rates. The increase, however, was offset by a reduction of $100,316 in fire overtime.

Figure 8–3　Classical program budget.

is adopted by the policymakers and integrated into a multiyear plan. Each year of the plan is programmed into the current budget to ensure continuity of effort.

Advantages One major advantage is the systematic examination of a wide range of alternatives and another is the assurance of some year-to-year consistency in following an adopted plan to secure governmental program objectives. Thus, budgetary decisions are based on cost-effectiveness measures that provide the highest level of service for the lowest cost.

Disadvantages The disadvantages of PPBS have apparently outweighed the advantages, for few such budget systems remain, and most of these show signs of heavy stress and significant modification. Perhaps the most serious problem is the assumption that the elected representatives will choose the most cost-effective alternative. In practice, policymakers are influenced by political ac-

Account: 300020 Program: Fire Prevention	Department: Fire Department			
	FY 1984 Actual	FY 1985 Budget	FY 1986 Adopted	FY 1987 Projected
Employees				
Regular	8	8	8	8
Nonregular	0	0	0	0
Total employees	8	8	8	8
Expenditures				
Personnel	270,999	357,102	392,251	410,214
Services and supplies	7,977	8,847	12,189	12,189
Equipment	0	500	0	0
Total budget	278,976	366,449	404,440	422,403
Administrative services charges	3,517	33,467	27,055	29,493
Total direct program cost	282,493	399,916	431,495	451,896
Revenue				
General fund (unspecified)	282,493	399,916	431,495	451,896
Total revenue	282,493	399,916	431,495	451,896
Performance data				
Fire prevention inspections	5,500	5,500	6,500	6,500
Fire investigations	675	675	600	600
Brush surveys	1,500	1,500	1,200	1,200
Fire education presentations	2,600	2,600	2,600	2,700
Zoning inspections	0	0	2,000	2,500

Program description The Fire Prevention program provides for the review of construction plans, whether new or remodeling; issuance of permits as required by city codes; inspection of all occupancies within the city (except single-family dwellings); nighttime safety inspections in places of public assembly; weekend inspections of garage sales to assure compliance with permit procedures; annual brush surveys to help reduce fire hazards; filing of cases with city prosecutor to enforce compliance with city codes; investigation of citizen complaints; investigation of fires to determine cause and origin, including arrest and preparation of cases for prosecution; background investigations for firefighter, auxiliary firefighter, and paramedic applicants; public education presentations for schools (public and private), neighborhood groups, hospitals, retirement homes, industries, and high-rise occupancies; and all other required fire prevention activities.

Programmatic changes None.

Cost changes The adopted budget for this program represents an increase of $37,991 or 10.3 percent from the prior year's appropriation. This change is primarily attributable to higher salary and benefit rates.

Figure 8–3 *continued.*

ceptability and constituent/special interest group support in addition to considerations of economy and efficiency.

Yet another disadvantage of PPBS is that programs tend to be defined in such a way that they cut horizontally across supervisory lines, dividing program execution between operational officials and the budget office program analysts and creating a stalemate.

Critics of PPBS also point to the volume of cost-benefit analyses produced, the loss of operational line-item details in the drive for cost-benefit studies, the lack of adequate numbers of analysts, and the problem of untrained analysts, not to mention the mind-boggling problem of measuring every possible alternative to every possible governmental problem on which budget resources are spent or are proposed to be spent.

The cost-distribution program budget

In one modification of the program budget all costs, including indirect and "overhead" expenses, are summarized by program. Such "pure" program budgets are quite rare, owing, in great part, to the difficulty of constructing and maintaining an accounting system complex enough to distribute all such indirect costs to and among all direct operational programs.

Advantages The cost-distribution program budget has two major advantages. First, as is shown in Figure 8–4, when a program is considered, all costs (direct, one time, and indirect) as well as overhead are charged to the program through a cost-distribution accounting system. This means that the true and full cost of any change in service level is fully known. Such complete accounting does not allow hidden overhead and support expenses (which invariably rise with the enhancement of any direct governmental service effort) to accumulate.

A second, related, advantage is that such a budgeting system requires uniformity in determining true costs, to ensure that they are not arbitrarily applied, that all costs are equitably distributed across all operational programs, and that support and staff functions are adequately oriented to their support role rather than being solely oriented toward control. In other words, "overhead" costs and benefits are uniformly distributed to the benefit of those serviced.

Disadvantages A significant disadvantage is that management must be able to tolerate a certain openness if it is to place operational responsibility and flexibility in the hands of "program" managers, whereas many governmental organizations are too control-oriented to permit, much less systematize, such decentralized authority to match assigned responsibilities.

The other disadvantage is obvious—the requirement for a comprehensive cost-distribution accounting system. With the advent of low-cost computers, neither hardware nor implementing software is the problem; only the willingness to design and implement complete cost-distributional systems inherent in pure program budgeting is lacking. No uniform cost accounting methodology exists for fire department management.

Zero-base budgeting (ZBB)

No discussion of governmental budgeting systems would be complete without some discussion of zero-base budgeting. First developed by industry, zero-base budgeting was later applied to several jurisdictions and then to part of the federal government.

The basic steps in ZBB are (1) identifying decision units (programs) within the jurisdiction and combining them into decision packages, (2) analyzing each decision unit in the decision package, (3) evaluating and ranking all decision packages, and (4) preparing the detailed operating budget on the basis of the approved decision packages.

A decision package consists of several parts: (1) a statement of purpose and objective; (2) a description of proposed actions; (3) costs and benefits of the package and the proposed actions; (4) work load and performance measures; (5) alternative means of accomplishing the objectives; and (6) various levels of effort, (*a*) current level of activity, (*b*) increased level of activity, (*c*) reduced level of activity, or (*d*) elimination of the program. Increases and decreases are usually expressed in percentages; for example, decision packages may include a program costed at a 10 percent and a 15 percent increase in level of effort, and at a 10 percent and 15 percent decrease.

Advantages   One advantage of ZBB is that it calls for a complete and orderly review of all governmental efforts, which are then ranked according to their priority as determined by current beliefs and needs. Furthermore, it encourages policymakers to find new ways of accomplishing old objectives and fosters decentralization of authority and decision making.

Disadvantages   Despite scant experience at the local level, several disadvantages have been identified. One significant problem is the inherent subjectivity in the ranking process. What one person with one view might rank as high, another person with a different view and orientation might rank as quite low or even eliminate.

Another disadvantage is that decision units are difficult to define. The questions here, as in classical program budgeting, are: What is the composition of the program as defined? Are all costs included therein or are some cost elements centralized elsewhere and not distributed across the programs (decision units)?

Zero-base budgeting is designed to ensure that there is continuing, adequate review and rejustification for operations already in existence. Unless the fire service manager using ZBB is firm about what constitutes adequate and up-to-date justification, all current operations will probably be justifiable, but some subsidiary employee duties and line-item expenses may well not be defensible in detail.

The integrative budgeting system (IBS)

Several jurisdictions have taken an eclectic approach to governmental budgeting and have devised their own systems, choosing from other systems those elements that seem to work. This approach to public priority setting is known as an integrative budgeting system.

Essentially line-item based and computer-driven, the IBS approach uses only three major objects—personal services, maintenance and operation, and capital outlay and improvement—within each program to formulate policy and determine level of service. Detailed line-item budgets are for operational use only and can be used to develop the "totals" for program budgets. The totals are appropriated without detailed control and are subjected to post-audit and critique. A diligent and self-critical management review is needed in selecting the "best" alternative when such a post-audit review takes place.

Under this system, programs are defined at the lowest level of supervision or responsibility; they are aggregated upward, with all overhead and support costs distributed across all programs. Performance "indicators"—not cut-and-dried measurements—are established with the participation of program managers, but are used only by the program managers for self-measurement purposes. Cost-benefit principles are adapted from PPBS, but are applied only where preliminary study indicates that the effort would be both productive and

Fire Department

This department controls and extinguishes injurious or dangerous fires; protects life and property from fire risks by inspecting buildings for fire hazards and enforcing laws relating to fire prevention; carries on a fire prevention educational program; investigates suspected cases of arson; and provides rescue service, salvage service, and emergency medical service.

Expenditures and appropriations	Budget appropriation, 1986–87	Expenditures 1984–85	Estimated expenditures 1985–86
Salaries			
General	$ 10,274,043	$ 6,897,230	$ 8,200,000
Firefighters	119,787,422	106,055,040	109,200,000
Firefighter bonuses	804,055	2,870,254	2,950,000
Civilian ambulance employees	14,098,459	10,967,767	12,500,000
Unused sick time	2,037,413	1,377,616	1,843,000
Civilian ambulance employees' bonuses	276,551	226,804	235,000
Overtime—general	77,203	128,985	90,000
Overtime—firefighters	954,438	1,094,124	850,000
Overtime—constant staffing firefighters	28,962,451	19,823,574	25,000,000
Overtime—civilian ambulance employees	28,853	254,901	70,000
Overtime—constant staffing civilian ambulance employees	2,471,528	1,376,752	2,400,000
Total salaries	$179,772,416	$151,073,047	$163,338,000
Expense			
Printing and binding	$ 198,832	$ 145,191	$ 193,500
Traveling expense	17,094	20,800	25,000
Construction materials	169,884	140,049	122,000
Contractual services	1,232,169	796,182	1,110,000
Contract brush clearance	416,000	314,487	400,000
Field equipment expense	1,600,979	1,346,418	1,316,000
Investigations	6,258	500	4,400
Petroleum products	677,268	865,587	734,000
Rescue supplies and expense	323,904	186,437	222,000
Transportation expense	500	70	150
Utilities expense private companies	676	—	650
Governmental meetings	942	347	300
Uniforms	1,010,064	627,404	817,000
Water control devices	354,272	426,951	327,500
Office and administrative expense	376,001	233,389	325,500
Operating supplies and expense	795,901	505,443	698,500
Total expense	$ 7,180,744	$ 5,609,255	$ 6,296,500
Equipment			
Furniture, office and technical equipment	$ 133,151	$ 115,292	$ 93,000
Transportation equipment	1,585,153	1,245,540	4,280,000
Other operating equipment	64,461	24,710	20,500
Total equipment	$ 1,782,765	$ 1,385,542	$ 4,393,500
Special			
Equipment lease acquisition	$ 2,150,360	$ 85,000	$ 1,972,000
Total special	$ 2,150,360	$ 85,000	$ 1,972,000
Total fire	$190,886,285	$158,152,844	$176,000,000

Figure 8–4   Cost-distribution program budget.

Source of funds	Budget appropriation, 1986–87	Actual 1984–85	Estimated 1985–86
General fund	$190,886,285	$157,578,018	$176,000,000
1984 Olympic Games trust fund	—	574,826	—
Total funds	$190,886,285	$158,152,844	$176,000,000

Supporting data

Distribution of 1986–87 appropriations by program

Program	Salaries	Expense	Equipment	Special	Budget
Arson investigation	$ 1,396,891	$ 11,204	$ 448	$ —	$ 1,408,543
Fire prevention	9,721,417	588,394	7,289	—	10,317,100
Fire suppression	132,578,931	1,695,138	594,612	2,150,360	137,019,041
Emergency ambulance service	16,278,436	445,903	792,956	—	17,517,295
Technical support	15,049,498	4,036,583	387,460	—	19,473,541
General administration and support	4,747,243	403,522			5,150,765
	$179,772,416	$7,180,744	$1,782,765	$2,150,360	$190,886,285

Distribution of 1986–87 total cost of programs

Program	Authorized regular positions	Budget	Support program allocation	Related costs	Cost allocated to other budgets	Total cost of program
Arson investigation	26	$ 1,408,543	$ 169,385	$ 925,858	$ —	$ 2,503,786
Fire prevention	208	10,317,100	1,064,710	5,413,739	—	16,795,549
Fire suppression	2,436	137,019,041	20,026,695	108,933,583	—	265,979,319
Emergency ambulance service	351	17,517,295	3,363,516	5,985,115	—	26,865,926
Technical support	282	19,473,541	(19,473,541)	—	—	—
General administration and support	121	5,150,765	(5,150,765)	—	—	—
	3,424	$190,886,285	$ —	$121,258,295	$ —	$312,144,580

Figure 8–4 *continued.*

politically acceptable. Controls are limited, being primarily behavioral in nature, and are not predicated upon any authoritarian control system.

Elected officials have the opportunity to set definitive levels of service by viewing the specific data/dollar match-ups provided by the IBS.

The IBS system has been shown to work best in conjunction with a true merit pay plan for management personnel and in an organization that has a history of limited political priority swings. The existence of data limits the ability of elected officials to be arbitrary and capricious.

Advantages A major advantage is the proven nature of those elements that have been incorporated into the integrative budgeting system. The flexibility that comes from the computerization of the entire system and the reliance on nonauthoritarian controls can also be numbered among the good points.

Disadvantages IBS also has significant disadvantages, however. Primary among these is that behavioral controls rest on the techniques of management by objectives (MBO) and organizational development (OD)—techniques that are time-consuming and may threaten some managers or management systems. Furthermore, the entire budgetary accounting system must be completely rebuilt and computerized. This requires a complex schedule of centralization, redesign, training, and decentralization concurrent with the MBO/OD efforts. Three years, optimally, would be required to design and implement the IBS approach for public budgeting in any specific jurisdiction.

An equally important drawback is that the system supplies information that requires policy officials to make hard decisions regarding service levels, which is something that many, if not most, policy officials find difficult to do.

Budget controls

Budget controls are necessary to ensure that adopted policy objectives, spending priorities, and appropriations are adhered to. In fact, the term *control* has become almost synonymous with the word *budget*. Those controls applied to public budgets can be divided into two broad categories—traditional controls and behavioral controls. Behavioral controls, which are covered in other chapters, include motivational techniques, management by objectives, organizational development, job enrichment, and other management strategies. Traditional budget controls are covered here. They include line-item accounting, budgetary accounting reports, percentage deviation reports, allotments, position controls, purchase order and contract award review, performance statistics review, and review of other specific expenses.

Line-item accounting

Line-item accounting control is the essence of and the reason for line-item budgeting. Each and every payroll, purchase order, contract award, and invoice is charged against the appropriate budget item, and the amount remaining available in that specific line item is reduced by the amount encumbered by the payroll entry, purchase order, or contract award. If no encumbrance system is in place, the reduction is made at the time an invoice is received.

The burden is on operating personnel not to exceed their spending authority for each specific line. These people, in turn, depend on the timeliness and accuracy of the budgetary accounting system and its timely and accurate monthly reports. In that sense "control" is out of their hands even while they are held responsible for not spending over appropriations. If the monthly reports are not received within two or three weeks and are not accurate within 2 percent, then there is no true control. Additional deviations from these standards of time and accuracy act to exempt department personnel from budget control and responsibility.

Budgetary accounting reports

Budgetary accounting reports provide operating personnel, as well as the budgetary control person or group, with monthly reports showing the balances remaining unexpended and/or unencumbered in each account. These reports are usually line item in nature, as they are of great utility to operating personnel in such format. Sometimes the control group or person will require strict adherence to the dollar limits of each line item and either will not permit monetary transfers between items or will require extensive justification or even the approval of the governing body. Such tight dollar controls may force the operating official to subvert the controls to achieve the financial and operational flexibility to "get the job done." As noted earlier, this almost forced subversion may be the greatest flaw in line-item budgeting.

Percentage deviation reports

Although percentage deviation reports are helpful budgetary management devices, they are subject to the same overuse and misuse as line-item and budgetary accounting reports. Percentage deviation reports provide operating personnel—and budget controllers—with line-item data of two kinds: (1) dollar amount expended or encumbered to date and (2) a comparison of that amount against the "normal" monthly rate of expenditure (e.g., 33 percent for four months, 50 percent for six months, 67 percent for eight months). Assuming an even flow of expenditures over the budget year, these reports show where overspending and underspending could be occurring. In practice, however, fire department expenditures do not all fall within neat calendar patterns. Some expenditures are cyclical, such as overtime during vacation periods or heavy fire seasons. This can lead to the next control.

Allotments

An allotment system subdivides the budget for each unit into quarterly or monthly (usually the former) allotments. That amount cannot be exceeded for the time period. To further complicate matters, allotment systems have to be predicated on seasonal differences in expenditure rates. When coupled with line-item controls, allotments can almost force an operating official to spend more time on the budget management and control system than on the primary public service responsibilities of the operating unit.

Position controls

Position controls are essential in that most governmental jurisdictions expend from 60 percent to 90 percent of their budgets on personal services in the form of salaries, wages, and direct fringe benefits. For this reason, controlling the number of positions and their salary levels (by means of position classification and, within that system, by the steps between minimum and maximum salary) limits budgetary expenditures. It is probably equally important to ensure that there is some equity and consistency between organizational units, both as to pay ranges and as to number of personnel by classification category. Budgeting a lump sum for personnel without such limits would openly invite favoritism, cause organizational morale to deteriorate and eventually create enormous budgetary difficulties.

Part-time positions are usually budgeted and controlled by the number of hours of service permitted for each part-time classification. Overtime and fringe benefits can only be controlled by dollar limits through the budget system.

Purchase order and contract award review

In the "normal" course of events after a budget has been adopted, the fire chief can requisition any approved item directly from the purchasing office as the item becomes necessary. But in some agencies the routing system for requisitions requires that the central budget office re-review and reapprove the specific item or contract *before* it can be received by the purchasing office for acquisition. Thus, a conflict arises between the requisitioning fire agency and the budget controllers as they renegotiate the need for the item or service. A disadvantage of this control is that it inevitably separates the responsibility for operating results from the authority to expend the amounts appropriated to achieve those results. If the budget office denies purchasing authorization, the operating person may be tempted to undermine the operations of the department and assign blame to the controllers. Such assignment of responsibility very likely would be justified.

Performance statistics review

Performance statistics review is another budgetary control used especially where units "produced" lend themselves to division into amounts budgeted or expended, resulting in a unit cost. Those who use such controls must take into account the flaws in reporting (1) "production," (2) seasonality of outputs and expenditures, and (3) time lags. Such control devices should be approached cautiously and used only after all elements and data input have been verified.

Review of specific expenses

Travel and subsistence expenses are often singled out for special justification and control, largely because such expenses are frequent targets for political attack and because abuses in the form of "junkets" are particularly visible and galling to taxpayers. Some control systems go so far as to require prior approval by the governing body for trips. Expenses for training, dues, and subscriptions also may be singled out for special attention, requiring the fire chief and other officers to spend time and effort justifying their requests.

Cost recovery for hazardous materials spills In Modesto, California, the potential for hazardous materials incidents is exacerbated by chemicals and by-products used by the agricultural industry. These materials are constantly in transit to and from the city airport, on railroads, and on interstate highways in and near the city. Over the years hazardous materials have been spilled on streets and freeways and have been found on properties during fire department inspections.

To relieve the fire department—and ultimately the taxpayers—of the costs of cleanup and abatement, the fire chief recommended, and the city council adopted, a cost recovery ordinance.

The ordinance, consisting of an addition and an amendment to the city's municipal code, reads as follows:

"*Deposits of Hazardous Materials: Cleanup or Abatement: Liability for Costs.* (a) The Fire Department is authorized to clean up or abate the effects of any hazardous material de-

posited upon or into property or facilities of the City; and any person or persons who intentionally or negligently caused such deposit shall be liable for the payment of all costs incurred by the Fire Department as a result of such cleanup or abatement activity. The remedy provided by this section shall be in addition to any other remedies provided by law.

"(b) For purposes of this section 'hazardous materials' shall be defined as any substance or materials in a quantity or form which, in the determination of the Fire Chief or his authorized representative, poses an unreasonable and imminent risk to the life, health or safety of persons or property or to the ecological balance of the environment, and shall include, but not be limited to, such substances as explosives, radioactive materials, petroleum or petroleum products or gases, poisons, etiologic (biologic) agents, flammables and corrosives.

"(c) For purposes of this section, costs incurred by the Fire Department shall include, but shall not necessarily be

Changing approaches to fire service budgeting

It is easy to manage when there is a surplus of money. When money is in short supply, management becomes more challenging. Several changes have affected fire department budgets in the 1980s. Public financial stresses have sometimes resulted in budget reductions, while the addition of emergency medical services and hazardous materials disclosure ordinances to fire department responsibilities has caused work load increases. Faced with such changes, fire service managers have become creative in looking at alternatives for service delivery and focusing their budgetary resources on decreasing fire losses.

Resources for budgeting

It is axiomatic that annual revenues must at least equal—and should usually exceed—budgeted appropriations and the expenditure of public monies at the local level. Paid fire departments have usually not generated monies sufficient for their own direct support; rather, fire protection has been regarded as a communitywide service supported by the general fund of the local government. Departments have usually expended monies in proportion to available total local revenue. Data on expenditures in individual cities are published annually by the International City Management Association in its *Municipal Year Book*.

Like other local government departments, fire departments have been affected by the tax and expenditure limitation movement symbolized by the adoption of

---

limited to, the following: actual labor costs of City personnel, including workers' compensation benefits, fringe benefits, administrative overhead; cost of equipment operation, cost of materials obtained directly by the City; and cost of any contract labor and materials.

"(d) The authority to recover costs under this section shall not include actual fire suppression services which are normally or usually provided by the Fire Department."

Routine firefighting costs are not included in the responsible party's bill from the city; only costs incurred in abating the hazardous materials portion of the incident are charged. Thus, the city has eliminated the possibility that a responsible party could charge the city legitimately with discrimination.

After an incident occurs, the fire department notifies the city attorney's office, which immediately notifies the appropriate responsible party they are "on notice," and will be expected to reimburse the city for the actual costs.

When all facts have been gathered, the fire department reports to the finance department, specifying the exact time each piece of apparatus was utilized during the incident and the exact amount of time each individual involved spent at the incident. The police department follows the same procedure. The finance department costs out labor, fringe benefits, equipment use, and indirect costs.

The fire department then submits all facts and costs to the city attorney's office, which follows up its initial notice with a bill for the actual costs of the incident.

The city attorney's office pursues a vigorous collection policy, concentrating on written communications rather than court actions. The follow-up efforts are persistent; funds have been collected for incidents up to two years old. A court trial is reserved as a last resort if the responsible party fails to pay.

This procedure has proven effective in recovering the city's costs of hazardous materials cleanup and abatement.

Proposition 13 in California. Such voter initiatives have created increased competition for already scarce governmental financial resources. As a result, fire departments have become more entrepreneurial in generating their own sources of revenue and recovering costs. Some departments charge fees for such specific services as fire inspection and plan checking. These fees are intended to support the services that regulate hazardous occupancies, materials, and processes. Fire departments have also considered, and some have implemented, emergency medical service (EMS) fees for both basic and advanced life support calls and transportation, augmented fire service availability (AFSA) fees for protection of large buildings with greater than average service demands, and charges for salvage work at fire scenes and for fires caused by hazards that existed through the neglect of owners or occupants. Some departments also have instituted ambulance subscription or membership programs that help offset the costs of providing EMS. And in local governments with a hazardous materials management plan, permit fees and fines for violation of the local ordinance can augment fire service budgets.

Instituting a cost recovery system

When a department is called upon to do more than its traditional duty with a budget that has not increased, one way out is to institute a cost recovery program for additional services—and to handle increased demands by billing for services rendered.

Many incidents qualify for cost recovery. Convictions of arson or false alarms often include a provision that the fire department be reimbursed for suppression services. Routine standbys at public events and ambulance transports from free-standing medical clinics are candidates for cost recovery. Unusual or special services, especially those that benefit a business, also qualify.

Hazardous materials incidents are the newest drain. Departments that have organized Level II and Level III response teams have lost expensive encapsulated suits and other equipment after just one incident. This is a special problem on interstate highway incidents where the damaged equipment is not being replaced by the transporter. The shipper and receiver are not in the community and do not plan to replace the equipment. One incident could destroy specialized clothing and monitoring equipment valued in thousands of dollars, leaving the response team unable to handle future incidents. In addition to the loss of specialized equipment, the required service time greatly exceeds traditional fire department service times.

The foundation of a cost recovery program is to determine the value of the services you provide. This service value should be approached the same way a business owner figures the cost of providing his or her goods. There are no "free" services.

To determine the value of your employee's service, take the gross pay and add the additional costs of maintaining that position (health insurance, workers' compensation, retirement, etc.) to determine the department's cost of providing that firefighter's position. The cost of that position could be up to 150 percent of the employee's gross pay.

In combination fire departments, count your qualified volunteers just as career staff. Departments with objective job descriptions (apparatus operator, company officer), or those that utilize the NFPA 1000 series in a certification program can easily justify the value of volunteer firefighters. Most paid-on-call firefighters are provided a token payment; determine their value as full time employees.

Delivery alternatives

Chapter 17 looks in detail at alternatives for fire service delivery—volunteer, fully paid, and combination departments, private-sector fire services, and consolidation, for example. In budgeting, particularly in using a zero-base approach, the fire service manager can examine the full range of alternatives in various decision packages, weighing the cost of each against the cost of potential fire losses. For each alternative, the chief can identify the cost and the potential results.

Fire loss management

Creative thinking by fire department managers also has been directed at managing fire losses. As early as the 1960s and 1970s, fire chiefs were among the early proponents of local ordinances requiring that automatic sprinkler systems and smoke detectors be installed in new construction and that some kinds of

---

All-volunteer departments have several options. If a paid or part-paid department is near your community, use its personal service costs in figuring yours. A second approach is to establish your costs through your local police department's service cost. The cost of a police officer is identical to that of a firefighter in many urban areas. If you have no local police, then compare your costs with the state police.

The goal is to determine the hourly cost of service. Beyond hostile fires and medical emergencies, much of the work fire departments perform can be considered as a "cost of doing business" for many of the people we assist. You may be surprised at the positive results of your looking at "the business of protection."

Equipment that is depleted, damaged or destroyed on an incident can also be recovered with an itemized list. Vehicle costs are a little more complex. Vehicle costs are composed of three sections; maintenance, operating and replacement.

The key to successful cost recovery is to pre-plan your billing process. Determine before the emergency occurs what your department considers new services. This requires a review of local and state regulations before making up the bill format. Have a policy on when the bill is presented to the responsible party. Hazardous materials certified transporters have to carry insurance to cover the clean up expenses for any accidents. Some Pennsylvania fire companies have sent their bill to the county-authorized clean up company for inclusion with their bill to the shipper.

Pre-planning the cost recovery program also helps your major incident paperwork, since much of the same information is required by the federal, state and local offices.

A benefit of using a cost recovery program is that the chief fire executive sees where the resources are going. It can work both after a major incident and while looking at the regular services you give. An analysis of what services your department provides may give you some ways of recovering those costs so you can continue to provide specialized services (hazmat, EMS) and invest that money into handling fires.

Source: Michael J. Ward, "Recovering Costs for Better Service," *Chief Fire Executive*, May/June 1987, 41–43, 77. The article includes detailed examples of cost determination methods.

older structures be retrofitted as well. Early ordinances governed large buildings, since the idea was to reduce the size of potential fires. This attack on the maximum size of fires represented a strategic shift in emphasis from measures of technical *efficiency* to measures of *effectiveness* in fire loss management.

Concurrent with this shift has been a focus of fire department resources on fire prevention and public fire education. If the size of fires is reduced through sprinkler systems, the required fire flow is also reduced and fewer fire companies are needed for fire control. Similarly, if smoldering smoke is detected early, people are able to rescue themselves in the early stages of the fire cycle and call the fire department while the fire is still small and relatively easy to extinguish. In short, fire prevention programs reduce the cost of providing fire suppression.

Fire loss management is cost effective for the community at large. The community pays for fire losses directly, through insurance premiums, or by supporting the preventive efforts of the fire department. A loss that never occurs is intangible, but it can be viewed as a form of revenue generated (or saved) by the fire department.

The importance of allocating resources for fire suppression should not be neglected, of course. An industrial economy depends on large concentrations of combustible materials, and suppression forces must be adequate to control fires and to satisfy the requirements of insurers. The budget needs to support management of the total fire problem rather than react to individual fires.

Cost pressures and cost containment

Like all local government budgets, fire department budgets are pressured by rising costs of liability coverage, compensation packages, medical insurance, and workers' compensation insurance coverage. The following sections describe these costs and suggest strategies for cost containment.

Liability

In past years, the concept of sovereign immunity protected the fire department from liability claims. The courts have gradually set aside this immunity, leaving local governments and their component departments increasingly vulnerable to lawsuits. This change, combined with a tendency by juries to award large settlements when the government, with its ''deep pockets,'' is to pay, has created a liability crisis for local governments.

Some efforts have been made to control this trend. The state of Washington, for example, passed a law that provides exemption from civil liability to managers and participants in government-operated emergency medical systems when they are engaged in official acts of delivering services. Some jurisdictions also have placed caps on awards for economic and/or noneconomic damages, such as ''pain and suffering.''

In the meantime, the increased vulnerability to lawsuits has resulted in a rise in insurance costs. The department can help protect itself by a sound risk management program. Through self-insurance or higher deductibles a local government can reduce the cost of insurance premiums and retain more of the risk itself. To control costs, it can direct its legal staff to fight unreasonable claims and seek prompt settlements on reasonable ones.

A department's best defense against lawsuits is a prevention program that minimizes the department's exposure to tort liability, combined with careful documentation. Two major elements of such a program are training and safety programs. It is the responsibility of the department to train personnel in departmental procedures, safety practices, and prudent use of equipment and vehicles. The public expects, and has a right to expect, its firefighters to be fully trained professionals. Training is discussed in detail in Chapter 18. Departments also need to establish defensible safety policies. Some departments, for example, restrict the speed of all but the first engine company responding to a call until the need for additional companies is established.

Compensation packages

Labor relations, discussed in detail in Chapter 12, have a major effect on the budget in the form of negotiated wage and compensation settlements. The concept of labor relations implies an ongoing exchange of money in the form of salaries for personal services. Salary is usually defined in terms of a monthly or hourly wage. In fact, however, the financial cost of the wage settlement includes everything in the compensation package. Many organizations now establish wage increases as "total compensation."

Typically, salaries are the beginning point of the compensation package. It is necessary to add the cost of paid leave for vacations, holidays, scheduled time off, bereavement leave, and sick leave. (Each week of paid leave is worth about 2 percent of compensation.) In addition to salary and paid leave, the compensation package may include group medical, dental, and vision insurance; retirement for service or disability; continuation of retirement allowances to survivors; and retroactive retirement benefits for past service. Benefits are discussed further in Chapter 11.

The compensation package can be put together in many ways to meet the needs of the organization and the individuals, but for budgeting purposes it is important to keep in mind that each of these benefits has a cost to the department and that the total package determines the true cost of a negotiated salary scale.

Medical costs

Rising medical costs have affected compensation by increasing the cost of health insurance. In response, local governments have built cost containment provisions into their group health plans. The employer, for example, may require the employee to share insurance premium costs in some ratio, set a cap or ceiling on certain insurance benefits, or structure the plan to encourage outpatient and preventive care. Still another cost containment feature is the use of increased deductibles, which pass along a greater portion of medical costs to the employee.

Workers' compensation insurance

Workers' compensation insurance rates are set on the basis of loss experience on a statewide basis, and local governments may believe they have little control over them. In fact, however, any steps the fire department takes to reduce the risk of accidents and injuries in the work place can ultimately help reduce those costs. In the fire service some risks must be taken and the consequences suffered, but through loss prevention or physical fitness programs, personnel can learn to reduce risks in necessary activities and to avoid unnecessary risks. Most injuries to firefighters occur in and around the fire station. In addition to training in the proper use of safety equipment and procedures, loss prevention in this regard includes maintenance of the well-being of personnel through health programs and the provision of safe and comfortable quarters.

Retirement systems budgeting

Fire service employees participate in numerous retirement systems. These retirement systems must provide the monies, when needed, for a number of retirement benefits, which normally include retirement after a specific number of years of service (such as twenty, twenty-five, or thirty years) or at a specific age (such as fifty or fifty-five).

Most retirement systems also provide benefits for service-connected or non-service-connected disability and allowances for surviving spouses and children after service-connected or nonservice-connected death of the employee before retirement or death after retirement. The monthly premiums for retirement programs may be paid entirely by the employer or jointly by the employer and employee. The employer contribution rate for current service is part of the total compensation package, discussed earlier.

All retirement systems involve two kinds of costs: (1) benefits paid to retirees and survivors and (2) administrative expenses of operations and investment counsel. Most boards of trustees of retirement funds have been established by local or state laws and many include persons with limited expertise in money management. Experts in fund investment management should be obtained on a contractual basis with an annual retainer. The contract should be reviewed every few years to ensure prudent management of these trust funds. Retirement funds are fiduciary in nature and the employer should provide for a prudent level of security and management. Security can be achieved by insurance and by custodial possession in large banks. Regular independent audits and actuarial evaluations are an absolute necessity.

In a *defined contribution* retirement plan, the employer is obligated only to make contributions, and the level of benefits depends on the performance of the retirement investments or funds during the years of contribution and retirement. In a *defined benefit* plan, the retirement system is obligated to pay out a guaranteed amount in vested benefits. To be sure that the necessary money will be available when due, it is essential to plan for decades into the future. Again, expert assistance is mandatory and is easily obtained by employing an actuary, who can calculate the probable cost of the benefits by determining the many variables associated with the members of the retirement system (and their dependents), such as ages of entry, exit, death, and/or disability. The actuary evaluates and analyzes the assets on hand, the estimated interest rates, and the estimated payments to determine the necessary rates of future contributions to fund the estimated costs for the current and future vested benefits.

Other aspects of budgeting for retirement system costs include consideration of personnel management. Some provisions of modern retirement systems provide for early vesting of benefits earned to date, instead of postponement of

---

Elements of a risk management program

Assign someone to be responsible for risk management and give that person the support of top management.

Establish formal policies and procedures, including a system for tracking losses and implementing corrective measures.

Identify risks and determine which losses are most costly in terms of frequency and/or severity.

Implement risk management approaches:

1. Avoidance, or reduction in programs that present hazards (this may not be an option in a fire department)

2. Prevention of accidents through health and safety programs, fleet safety standards, and emergency procedures

3. Loss reduction through claims investigation and attention to recurring problems

4. Risk transfer through purchase of insurance or indemnity contracts

5. Risk financing through self-insurance, intergovernmental risk sharing pools, or other alternative mechanisms.

vesting to the actual date of retirement. Thus, dissatisfied employees do not need to stay in their jobs only for the purpose of receiving their benefits.

The age of entry into a retirement plan is limited in most fire and police department retirement systems. Fixed entry age is a historical accident that has the effect of inhibiting personnel transfers and career mobility among local agencies and from local to state to federal service. Early vesting of benefits and reciprocity of retirement credits among retirement systems—local, state, and federal government programs and private academic systems—can help encourage professional career mobility. Unified and integrated systems also help avoid "double dipping" and increase the efficient and effective use of personnel.

Retirement systems may become underfunded if increased benefits are granted retroactively to the date of entry for current employees. This creates an "instant" unfunded liability. Provisions for fully funding these "actuarial debts" are calculated by the actuary. Funding is usually in effect over a long term such as thirty or forty years, consistent with the life spans of the members and dependents who receive these retroactive benefits. These current monthly contribution rates are termed *prior service* when attributed to unfunded prior services and are in addition to the contribution rates for current service. Prior service costs are an expense to the employer but are not normally considered as part of the compensation package of the current employee. These costs are incurred by agreeing to a benefit for which neither employer nor employee has made any contribution to the retirement fund in the years of prior service covered. Thus the employer agrees to make the greater payments for both the benefits and their required funding, but in the future.

Unfunded liability may also result from long-term inflation, which affects the benefits to be paid in the future. Long-term inflation at relatively high rates has high costs. Contribution rates must be adjusted to provide for the required monies so that financial chaos and bankruptcy are avoided in the future.

Budget preparation

The fire chief is responsible for preparing the budget, which will reflect the financial requirements to provide services. Usually a staff person is assigned to gather the specific information needed to begin the process. The budget process involves the following steps:

1. Review the budget for the current fiscal year and compare expenditures with budgeted amounts
2. Talk with division heads to establish goals and priorities within general guidelines regarding inflation, cost of living, and available revenues (guidelines are usually set by the city manager, mayor, or other executive early in the budget cycle)
3. Determine the number of personnel required to maintain certain levels of service by calculating work schedules, paid leaves, and estimated use of disability and sick leave
4. Make an inventory of physical needs: supplies, utilities, professional services, repairs to vehicles and equipment
5. Determine requirements for capital outlays: vehicles, large items of equipment, and new buildings
6. Transmit through channels the proposed operating budget plus requests for capital items to be included in the overall capital budget for the city or county.

As these specific line items are categorized and accumulated into larger subtotals and totals, the budget outline is augmented until it becomes a definitive set of data that reflects the resources needed for the program. As part of this process, consideration of alternative service levels will require various subsets of costs to provide differential levels of service. For example, each engine company requires a number of personnel and fringe benefit costs and tools at a total cost for that engine company. To consider alternatives, it is necessary to calculate the costs of having more and less personnel on that engine company. The actual budget that the fire chief recommends is based on providing the optimal level of services consistent with the available financial resources.

Since municipal officials and, indeed, all citizens are concerned with the cost of fire insurance—and thus the "class" or ISO rating of the local fire department—it must be factored into budget planning and development. The fire rating schedule should not determine the budget, but since fire insurance premiums are part of the total cost of fire protection and indemnity to the community, a cost analysis will determine the advantages of budgeting additional resources to improve the ISO rating.

As the dollar amounts are accumulated into programs, they should be related to specific public safety needs. As stated above in the section on fire loss management, sprinklers and smoke alarms enable the public to discover and extinguish fires at an early stage of development. While public fire safety education helps in preventing fires from starting, early alarm and built-in extinguishment capability will reduce the overall costs for fire protection. At the same time, the public demand for paramedics and EMTs makes it possible for communities to use the same personnel for two types of services.

Budget presentation

After the budget is prepared by the department, it is presented to the city manager or chief elected official for incorporation into the overall local government budget and then to the council. The chief often makes both of these presentations, sometimes with assistance from other officers.

The budget presentation needs to focus on the fire department's mission and show how the proposed budget will help accomplish that mission efficiently and effectively. The manager or mayor and council have both a monetary and a political interest in the fire department budget. They need to be persuaded that the budget provides cost-effective fire protection services—that the department has examined possible economies of scale and alternative delivery methods in arriving at its recommendation. At the same time, they need to be convinced that public needs are being met in a timely and effective manner. If the fire department fails in its mission to protect the public, it will have failed in its mission to provide public safety. Local decisionmakers take public safety needs very seriously, and they will decide the level of protection to be provided to the public.

The budget presentation must explain how the recommended amount of money will enable the fire department to deliver this level of service. The specific details can often be related in simple terms of unit costs, units of service, aggregate costs and per capita costs displayed on charts and bar graphs (see examples in Chapter 6). These charts should also explain the distribution of protection services across geographical areas. This can be easily done by obtaining a map from the engineering department and displaying the main travel routes of the city, geographical obstacles (such as rivers, bridges, and other choke points that restrict travel routes), travel distance, and the average speed of vehicles.

In sorting through and preparing the mountain of data needed for a budget presentation, the chief may be tempted to make assumptions or "guesstimates" or even to modify the numbers in order to present the best possible argument for the budget. Sometimes it is necessary to use reasonable estimates if no data are available, but if data exist—if distances can be measured, for example, or if response can be timed—the actual numbers should be used. Nothing undermines the credibility of a department as quickly as the suspicion that its budget numbers are erroneous or that its chief is deceitful.

None of this suggests, however, that the chief may not argue persuasively for the budget. The chief is expected to be an advocate for the department and may legitimately appeal to the manager and council on its behalf.

Summary and conclusion

This chapter has provided a basic overview of the budgetary process in local government. All who have worked in local government will recognize that budget-related matters take up a great deal of staff time and effort throughout the fiscal year—and more so in times of fiscal pressures and public disenchantment. Professional managers both in and outside the fire service should be aware of, and prepared for, these pressures if they are to provide effective and professional service, and if they are to maintain their department's position in the current scramble for scarce resources.

The chapter represents a starting point. Like generations of their predecessors, individual fire service managers will find that there is no substitute for real-life experience in grappling with the specifics of a fire department in a particular community with its own economic, social, and political characteristics.

9 Legal aspects of fire department management

Local government officials, including fire service personnel at operational and managerial levels, are both empowered and limited by law. Second only to the production of nuclear power, local governments may be the most regulated industry in the United States. The legal system under which local governments operate is in every way as complex, and sometimes convoluted, as the managerial and operational framework for the allocation of manpower and equipment to provide comprehensive fire prevention and suppression and emergency medical services to a large city. Levels of need and responsibility, gradations in quality, maintenance of the integrity of the firefighting system, simple or devastating system failures, and the obligation to provide one of the truly essential public services are all standards that are as familiar to a local government attorney as they are to the fire chief and his or her deputies.

In fact, many of the skills that make a good fire chief or other manager in a major local government department are the same skills needed to oversee the legal needs of the organization. These skills include an overall understanding of the organization and its goals, an awareness of the legal framework under which it operates, and a recognition of the need for expertise, either to anticipate or to address particular problems as they arise.

Overview

This overview discusses some of the fundamental legal principles that managers in general, and fire department managers in particular, must keep in mind in operating their departments or divisions. In addition, it briefly shows how these principles apply to various aspects of fire department management. The remainder of the chapter examines the important role of each employee and manager in the fire department in fulfilling the legal obligations of the city or county by careful contemplation, use of risk management and risk reduction techniques, and adherence to the management and policy goals of the local government. Several topics of substantial interest to fire service personnel, such as negligent inspection and ambulance service, are also covered.

The legal principles applicable to general-purpose local governments—cities, counties, townships, and the like—are quite similar in most states. Special-purpose districts and authorities often operate under more restrictive state legislation, and these differences are noted where they apply. To assist the reader, a glossary of legal terms appears at the end of the chapter.

Fundamental obligations

This section focuses on five obligations that appear to crosscut all other responsibilities of local government managers and department heads. There are, of course, many more crosscutting responsibilities, but attention to the following will increase the likelihood that the employees and managers of the department are acting in compliance with legal principles.

Awareness of legal developments and issues   It is standard advice that managers must be aware of new developments that might affect their work. In the legal context, this advice is particularly important. Most court decisions are effective the day they are decided; some are retroactive at least to the time period covered by the statute of limitations found in the law under which the case was decided. Consequently, if the state supreme court decides that local governments in the state are no longer entitled to sovereign immunity for their acts, or that a state statute limiting the amount of damages for negligent acts by local governments is unconstitutional, cities and counties may, from that day forward, be liable in money damages for those acts.

When the U.S. Supreme Court decided, in February 1985, that the federal Fair Labor Standards Act (FLSA) provisions on hours, wages, and overtime

---

A case sampler   The law applying to fire service officials is constantly changing as courts hand down new decisions. The following sampling of cases decided in 1986 provides a "snapshot" of case law at the time and reinforces the importance of awareness on the part of the chief.

Ayres v. *Indian Heights Volunteer Fire Dept.*   The Supreme Court of Indiana overturned a lower appellate court ruling which had held that the volunteer company was an "independent contractor" which was not protected by Indiana's local government immunity statutes. *Ayres* involved allegations that the fire company had improperly fought a vehicle fire by allowing it to spread to and destroy a garage. On appeal, the state supreme court held that volunteer fire companies in Indiana are "instrumentalities of local government" and that the Indian Heights company was protected from liability. (493 N.E.2d 1229 [Ind., 1986])

Helman v. *County of Warren*   Following a fire in his motorcycle shop, Helman sued a volunteer fire company for improper firefighting methods and the county for negligence in the 911 telephone system's delay in processing the call for assistance. His suits were dismissed on grounds that neither the company nor the county had undertaken any duty to Helman from which liability could arise. When the order dismissing the county as a party was appealed to the New York Court of Appeals, the dismissal was affirmed. (501 N.Y.S.2d 325 [N.Y., 1986])

Lawhon v. *City of Smithville*   In an action for negligence in fighting a fire that destroyed his restaurant, Lawhon argued that the city had waived its immunity by purchasing liability insurance and therefore fell within a statutory waiver of immunity to the extent that its activities were covered by insurance. The court held that regardless of the waiver of immunity, the city could not be liable because it had no legal duty to any individual to fight a fire. Rather, the duty was owed only to the public generally, so no individual could claim damages for any failure of the firefighters to use proper standards. (715 S.W.2d 300 [Mo. App., 1986])

Kenevan v. *City of New York*   Kenevan and four other firefighters responded on Engine 228 to a report of an abandoned vehicle fire. The pumper was driven past the burning car about 15 to 30 feet and parked with its warning lights on and slightly protruding into westbound traffic. While three firefighters extinguished the fire, the captain walked behind the fire scene with a hand light to watch and warn oncoming traffic of the fire operations. One car approached at a high speed and hit the firefighters, despite the captain's warning. Kenevan died two days later.

Kenevan's estate brought suit against the city, both the captain and driver of Engine 228, and the driver of the car that hit them. The specific allegations were negligence in the failure of the city to remove the abandoned vehicle, negligence by the captain in failing to

Continued on next page.

could be applied to government employees,[1] the city's or county's liability for wages and scheduling began as of that date. In the case of FLSA, Congress subsequently took action that minimizes the managerial dilemma created by the original decision.[2] Similarly, in 1986 Congress eased local government burdens on the forced retirement of uniformed officers under the Age Discrimination in Employment Act, which allows for the application of fair, mandated retirement systems until the early 1990s.[3]

Actions by Congress and the state legislature can have an immediate effect on a departmental budget, plan, or mode of operation. When Congress eliminated General Revenue Sharing in the fall of 1986, departments that had factored the anticipated amounts into their budgets had to make rapid adjustments. Effects of such decisions are particularly devastating when the federal, state, and local governments have overlapping fiscal years and the current budget of one governmental entity is subject to the planning budget of another entity on a different cycle.

---

establish fire lines, and negligence of the apparatus driver by parking the apparatus improperly. The case went to jury trial, which found all four defendants negligent in varying degrees.

On appeal, the court overturned the jury award against the city and the two firefighters. Since the abandoned vehicle was lawfully parked, the court held that there was no duty on the part of the city to remove it, and hence, no liability for failing to do so. New York case law was cited by the court in its holding that both the driver and captain of Engine 228 were "exercising their professional judgement" and were not liable for errors of judgement in firefighting activities. The court held that the car driver must bear full responsibility. (507 N.Y.S.2d 193 [A.D. 2 Dept., 1986])

Zern v. *Muldoon*   A fire began in a restaurant operated by Muldoon and owned by Zern. The building suffered extensive damage, and Zern and other tenants filed suit against Muldoon, who joined Citizens Fire Company of Palmyra (Pennsylvania) as an additional defendant. Citizens claimed immunity from suit as a local agency. After reviewing case law and extensively researching the history of firefighting in Pennsylvania, the court held that volunteer fire companies are governmental agencies which are protected by governmental immunity. (516 A.2d 799 [Pa. Cwlth., 1986])

Weaver v. *Union City Volunteer Fire Dept.*   The court held that a firefighting training exercise was within the scope of public firefighting duties, and the fire company was not liable for damages caused by the spread of a training fire to an adjacent barn. (518 A.2d 7 [Pa. Cwlth., 1986])

Sierra v. *City and County of Denver* An exception to immunity in almost all jurisdictions is for injuries resulting from the negligent operation of a motor vehicle. In this case the plaintiff claimed that she was injured when she was stricken by a fire hose that was being dragged across her yard by a pumper. (The opinion does not make clear whether this was a supply line being laid in or what precise evolution was involved.) The Colorado court held that her claim was sufficient to go to trial under the motor vehicle exception to immunity. (730 P.2d 902 [Colo. App., 1986])

Barth by Barth v. *Board of Education* A Chicago student was injured at a public school while playing kickball at about 10:40 A.M. After he became sick in the principal's office, a school employee dialed 911 at 11:00 A.M. and told the dispatcher that an injured boy needed to be taken to the hospital. The dispatcher took the name and address of the caller and said he would take care of it. At 11:30 and again at 11:45 additional calls were made to the 911 emergency center and again the dis-

Actions by federal and state regulatory agencies can also have immediate and unanticipated effects on operations and budgeting. Major initiatives regarding the removal of asbestos from buildings or the mandated installation of sprinklers or other built-in fire protection can directly affect the work and budgets of fire departments.

State and national organizations representing local governments and professionals are some of the best sources of the information needed to maintain sufficient levels of awareness. The State and Local Legal Center of the Academy for State and Local Government deals with Supreme Court issues, and the U.S. Conference of Mayors, the National League of Cities, and the National Association of Counties track legal issues on the local level. Finally, the International Association of Fire Chiefs, the National Fire Protection Association, and the International Association of Fire Fighters, AFL-CIO, are resources for specific inquiries regarding problems directly related to firefighting and management of fire departments.[4] As indicated below, however, ongoing attention

---

patcher indicated that the matter would be taken care of. Fire department records indicated that an ambulance was dispatched at 11:48, reached the school two minutes later, and arrived at Holy Cross Hospital, which was directly across the street from the school, at noon.

Suit was filed against the school board and the city, alleging negligence and willful and wanton misconduct. Immunity claims were denied and the case proceeded to jury trial. At trial, expert medical testimony established that the delay of one hour in transporting the injured student to the hospital allowed a blood clot to grow from the size of a walnut to the size of an orange before it was surgically removed. The physician also testified that permanent physical and intellectual function damage resulted, which would not have occurred had treatment not been delayed. The jury awarded $2.5 million to the student, assessing half the liability to the board and half to the city. On appeal the Illinois appellate court affirmed the lower court decision that the city was not immune for the actions of the 911 operators. (490 N.E.2d 77 [Ill. App. 1 Dist., 1986])

Steiner v. *City of Pittsburgh*   The court upheld dismissal of a complaint against the city which alleged willful, wanton, and malicious conduct against a 911 operator for failing to send aid to a caller. Unlike Illinois, the Pennsylvania immunity statute immunized the city for intentional harm caused by its employees. (509 A.2d 1368 [Pa. Cwlth., 1986])

Lewis v. *Estate of Smith*   Two people were injured in an apartment fire in the city of Blackfoot, Idaho. Among others, they sued the city, claiming that the city had inspected the apartment prior to the fire and failed to have known fire code violations corrected. While the state has governmental immunity for "discretionary" functions, the Idaho Supreme Court held that operational activities not involving discretion are not immunized and must be performed with due (ordinary) care. The court held that the city's failure to provide regularly scheduled inspections due to funding cuts was "discretionary" and thus immune from liability. However, the court held that the city's failure to abate known fire code violations after inspections were conducted may have been a breach of a nondiscretionary duty which was established by the city's own ordinance, and ordered that the case be returned to the district court for additional proceedings. (727 P.2d 1183 [Idaho, 1986])

Source: Adapted from D. Michael Craley, "Update of Liability Cases Involving Firefighting Activity," *Chief Fire Executive*, September/October 1987.

to the daily flow of information received from citizens, newspapers, magazines, and other media, along with an effort to correlate that information with the daily workings and problems of the department, will go a long way toward anticipation of problems.

The city or county attorney is an indispensable ally in maintaining this awareness. The Supreme Court has ruled that most public officials can be immune from legal damages for violations of rights if they can show that even through "due diligence" they could not have known that their actions were illegal.[5] Consultation with the city or county attorney can be cited in court as an indication of such diligence. (Further discussion of this issue appears in the section on civil rights.)

Nondiscrimination   Government service is a public trust. Throughout the following sections, particularly those on civil rights and conflict of interest, a recurring theme is the fair and open treatment of citizens, neighborhoods, and employees in all activities—from the provision of fire suppression or emergency medical services to the allocation of resources, such as the location of new fire stations, in the city.

The U.S. Constitution and all state constitutions provide explicit and enforceable protections that say, essentially, that a government of the people must be fair to all of the people. Many states have broad "government in the sunshine" (open meeting), freedom of information (open records), and competitive bidding laws designed to ensure responsiveness to the citizenry and to guarantee that the conduct of the public's business is undertaken in the best public interest. Penalties for violations of constitutional and statutory duties can be substantial, ranging from criminal sanctions to the awarding of damages against the personal assets of intractable officials.

The principles are fairly simple. Favoritism is not allowed; personal dealing for profit or advantage will be punished; and discrimination on the basis of race, age, creed, sex, or religion will not be tolerated. Local governments and their officials have been found liable for the misallocation of resources between predominantly white and predominantly black neighborhoods in the provision of sewers, or the curbing of streets, or in the building of schools.[6] There is little doubt that the same nondiscrimination rules would be applied in a case involving fire prevention or suppression.[7] Local government officials with personal interests in contracts have found themselves in jail and subject to enormous civil damages. Local government officials who have treated employees unfairly on the basis of age or sex or race have found themselves and their employer liable for damages, for back pay, and for other remedial relief.

Later, this chapter discusses notions of due process, equal protection, and simple fairness under the law. This overview only means to stress that a manager's instinctual notions of fairness and fidelity to duty may be the best guides to fulfillment of the public good. After all, managers of the public interest have achieved that status by serving the public interest. There can be no better guideline.

Use of the city or county attorney   Just as the fire chief and deputy chiefs keep pace with developments in the fire service, the city or county attorney follows new legal developments that can affect the activities of local government. The manager's basic rule should be *When in doubt, ask!* For example, an important distinction in the law is drawn between the "discretionary" and "ministerial" functions of local government officials. The distinction is particularly important in basic public-safety areas such as police or fire protection. A deputy chief's final decision to condemn or close a building as a fire hazard after a full investigation and finding of facts, for example, may well be ministerial; courts can require officials to perform ministerial acts. However, the decision-making process by which the building is condemned, having to do with the hazards posed by faulty wiring, deteriorating gas lines or inadequate fire protection equipment, presents the official with a number of discretionary decisions; courts are hesitant to second-guess the expertise of professionals over discretionary decisions.

This distinction is fraught with difficulties, however. The fire inspector, for example, can demonstrate an expertise in the dangers posed by certain building conditions. Can that inspector show similar expertise in the management of people in his or her decision to terminate or discipline an employee? In the latter case, the expertise of the personnel manager is essential, as is the expertise of local counsel in assuring that the steps to be taken in the firing or disciplining are properly sorted out between the fire inspector and the personnel manager. Attorneys invariably would rather put an hour of time into the assessment process than have to spend a year in litigation over the appropriateness of a decision.

Intergovernmental obligations Local governments operate in an enormous web of overlapping, contradictory, and conflicting governmental rules and standards. This is even true of basic operating departments like police or fire where large capital outlays may have been supported by federal funds such as General Revenue Sharing, or where tax-exempt bonds were issued in conformance with state financing and federal tax laws.

Intergovernmental programs and service delivery often mesh federal funding with state authority and supervision and local implementation. Each level of government has its own rules regarding personnel, finance, accounting, budgeting, record keeping and the like. Even with the best advice, it may be impossible to adhere to all these rules. Furthermore, the rules are flexible, subject to ongoing review and always subject to new interpretations by federal or state courts or by any one of the levels of government involved in the process.

This complexity takes on additional importance in times of budget reductions and fiscal restraint. Even if the fire department's budget is fairly sacrosanct—regarded by elected officials and citizens as being beyond most budget cuts—fire departments can still be buffeted by reductions in other departments. For example, a city's inability to maintain a full force of building inspectors may mean that fire hazards are increased. Similarly, the inability of a local government to find adequate insurance may decrease the fire department's ability to allocate rescue or fire suppression resources in the community.

The legal consequences of intergovernmental cooperation can hardly be overestimated. Fire departments find themselves in a web of protective services over numerous jurisdictions and with responsibilities under state and federal law. Each interagency agreement, as discussed below, creates significant legal obligations. Similarly, grant and contract agreements that were workable with full funding become difficult to maintain when the funding scheme fails. As discussed below, a fundamental legal problem arises when a governmental agency has promised a given level of service, delivered it, and created a reliance on the part of the public that the service will be continued. Consequently, operational cutbacks, mandated by budgetary restraints, create a potential for liability. Local government fire officials should be constantly alert to the legal relationships mandated by the intergovernmental system.

Anticipation, prevention, and reduction of risks Since the 1970s much attention has been paid to the role of risk management and reduction in local government. The International City Management Association has provided survey data and publications on the subject and in 1978 organized the Public Risk and Insurance Management Association (PRIMA) to bring together the professional risk management activities of local governments. This emphasis on risk management and reduction is particularly rewarding in the legal forum. While

managers and attorneys cannot predict with certainty the final outcome of legislation, regulations, and court decisions, they can predict potential results. Just
as an attentive manager can anticipate potential problems in his or her department, an attentive city or county attorney is familiar with the implications of
pending cases or legislation.

Fire agencies, more than almost any other department in a city or county,
are capable of providing and encouraging realistic and workable risk reduction
strategies. In fact, a major responsibility of the fire department is prevention—
through better inspections, public education, and so. The theories underlying
risk reduction are not complicated and can be applied on a human scale in
neighborhoods or throughout whole cities.

In terms of internal management, staff training and the improvement of
systems for purchasing, personnel, and safety can all serve to minimize legal
vulnerabilities. The local government attorney should be an essential actor in
the design and implementation of departmental risk management programs.
These efforts, and the accompanying analyses, will help managers predict their
budgetary needs and insurance costs and will, in fact, substantially reduce the
possibility that departmental errors or oversights will lead to lengthy and costly
litigation.

Application to staff functions

This section and the one following explain how the obligations outlined above
apply to various areas of activity commonly undertaken by fire departments.
"Staff functions" are generally defined as the activities—such as personnel
management, planning, and budgeting—that must take place before the department can deliver "line" services, such as fire suppression, fire inspections,
and emergency medical services.

Personnel management and labor relations   The legal problems surrounding
personnel management and labor relations are enormously complex and often
confusing. Legislation at both the state and federal levels, along with a spate
of civil rights suits involving public employees, has further complicated the
general turmoil in the field of personnel management.

The courts have been quite generous in sustaining congressional actions that
impose duties on local governments in their relations with employees. In *Garcia*
v. *San Antonio Metropolitan Transit Authority*, decided in 1985, the Supreme
Court found that the mere fact that federal agencies (here, the Department of
Labor) were imposing their rules on traditional activities of local government
(i.e., police and fire services) in no way implicated the "sovereignty" of the
states or their local governments.[8] This decision was later modified somewhat
by federal legislation, but the implications are clear: Local public employers
must abide by federal regulations in personnel management, unless Congress
legislates otherwise.

The net result of *Garcia* is that Congress and the federal regulatory agencies
will feel that they have a much freer hand in defining relationships between
local governments and their employees. It is possible that legislation concerning
public-sector pension plans and public employee labor relations will be introduced and passed in the wake of *Garcia*. Similarly, in three 1986 cases the
Supreme Court upheld the application of the Age Discrimination in Employment
Act, which generally prohibits mandatory retirement prior to age seventy, for
most government employees; this rule was to be applied to uniformed safety
officers such as police officers and firefighters.[9] However, these decisions also
were adjusted by Congress. In the Age Discrimination in Employment Amendments of 1986, the age seventy was eliminated; for most employees, mandatory
retirement is no longer legal. In making this change, however, Congress also
allowed the reimposition of mandatory retirement for police and fire officials.[10]

The Supreme Court and the lower federal courts have been somewhat more sympathetic to the needs of local government managers in the control and discipline of the work place. At least two cases have held that public employees' First Amendment rights to speak freely were not violated when the employees were disciplined for abusive or disruptive on-the-job activities. Although the employees' complaints had some features that might warrant protection, the negative effect on the efficiency and smooth operation of the work place was sufficient to justify disciplinary action.[11]

Finally, of course, the obligation to be fair and nondiscriminatory arises on a daily basis in public employment. State and federal courts have been diligent in enforcing statutes designed to ensure that factors such as age, sex, race, national origin, religion, and handicap are not considered in decisions on the hiring, promotion, retention, or compensation of employees. The advice of local counsel in these areas is critical. Very difficult questions arise over equal pay for equal work, pregnancy-related discrimination, affirmative action goals, compliance with a quagmire of federal, state, and local laws, and "comparable worth." The premise underlying comparable worth is that the salary discrepancies often found between jobs traditionally held by women and those traditionally held by men (for example, nurse or secretary versus firefighter or truck maintenance officer) are the result of long-standing societal biases that undervalue the jobs performed by women. There is much litigation around this theory.

Planning, program design, and finance The potential legal questions in planning, program design, and finance range from differential provision of public services to neighborhoods[12] to the imposition of liability for failure to comply with local fire codes. Planning and finance (or budgeting) are among the easiest areas for the early recognition, intervention, and reduction of legal risks facing the city or county.

Clearly, the creation of a fire inspection system imposed on buildings throughout the jurisdiction will help minimize the risks faced by the fire department, in terms of the number of fires, the knowledge of the standards applied, and the equipment in operation in a building that has caught fire. Effective budget oversight will ensure that resources are allocated fairly and that authorities recognize the need for new equipment, additional facilities, and the maintenance of existing equipment and facilities.

Purchasing and contracting out The principles outlined above, particularly regarding fairness and openness in dealing and the general principle of protection of the public treasury, have generated a significant body of law and regulation over local government procurement. The requirement for competitive bidding is almost universal among governments and usually includes very detailed steps that require strict compliance with the law to ensure the validity of contracts.

Federal budget reductions, combined with various state and local tax limitation measures, have forced many local governments to look to the contracting out or "privatization" of some services. This is particularly true for services that require significant initial capital investments—for example, the development of solid waste disposal plants. Fire departments sometimes contract out for ambulance services, and in a number of jurisdictions there is a constant struggle between the fire department and private ambulance companies as to which of them should provide either 911, twenty-four-hour emergency services and/or routine patient transportation. These programs are fraught with legal difficulties. See the accompanying sidebar on the ambulance dilemma.

Advice of counsel in such areas is critical, particularly since these programs represent new and innovative techniques for the provision of public services by private parties that are subject to a constantly changing matrix of laws.

Application to line functions   Just as the manager must attend to the dictates of the law in overseeing service delivery, equal attention must be paid to the impact of the services actually delivered. From basic services, such as fire suppression on a neighborhood basis, to the enormously complicated task of running communitywide emergency and fire suppression facilities and services, all activities are subject to scrutiny in the press, in the political arena, and in the courts. The principles remain the same, however, and the sections below provide fire department managers with additional information on which to base their decisions within several aspects of the law.

Civil rights obligations under Section 1983

The incredible proliferation of lawsuits against local governments and officials under the Federal Civil Rights Act of 1871 (42 U.S.C. Section 1983) makes

---

Affirmative action in fire services   In 1986 and 1987 the U.S. Supreme Court handed down six very important cases regarding affirmative action—including disputes over numerical goals designed to correct imbalances in work forces and the application of traditional affirmative action remedies to discrimination against women. Litigation has been going on for years over the propriety of using affirmative action goals and timetables at all stages of employment, from hiring to retention, promotion, dismissals, and budget-enforced layoffs. Various claims of favoritism and "reverse discrimination" have been made.

The Court is slowly evolving a workable set of standards for the applications of affirmative action. Notably, the dominant factor seems to be the extent to which an employee has "property" interest in his or her position. The second substantial factor is the amount of overt racism or sexism that can be shown. The Court will support very specific, hard-nosed remedies where it can be shown that there was blatant racial discrimination in the past that has seriously skewed the current racial makeup of the work force. See *Local 28, Sheet Metal Workers International Association* v. *EEOC*, 106 S.Ct. 3019 (1986).

The "property interest" analysis seeks to ensure fairness in all employment practices. When an employee actually has a position, he or she has some property interest in maintaining that position, and the government should not be allowed to discriminate in such a way that the employee's vested rights in his or her job are jeopardized. Accordingly, in both hiring and promotion decisions, affirmative action is proper to attempt to ameliorate the effects of past discrimination; new applicants for jobs, or people seeking promotions, have no real vested interest in the *new* position, so affirmative action activities can be implemented with little danger of interfering with the property rights of existing employees.

For example, in *Local No. 98, International Association of Firefighters* v. *City of Cleveland (Vanguards)*, 106 S.Ct. 3063 (1986), the Supreme Court approved a court order designed to enforce an agreement between the city and a minority employee organization that included a race-conscious promotion plan. The Supreme Court approved of the agreement despite the fact that it might benefit employees who were not actual victims of the city's past discriminatory practices.

In layoffs, however, the rules change. In *Wygant* v. *Jackson Board of Education*, 106 S.Ct. 1842 (1986), the Court held that it was improper under the Equal Protection Clause for a school board, following a collective bargaining agreement, to lay off nonminority teachers with more seniority than the

awareness of this area essential for local government officials. Knowledge of Section 1983 and interpretive court rulings regulating local official actions and decisions is essential to avoid or minimize liability under the statute.

Section 1983 states that "every person who, under color of any statute, ordinance, regulation, custom or usage of any state or territory" deprives anyone of "rights, privileges, and immunities secured by the Constitution and laws" of the United States shall be liable to the injured party.

Elements of a civil rights violation under the law

Among the "rights, privileges, and immunities" cited in Section 1983 are the due process, equal protection, and privileges and immunity clauses of the Constitution. These protections are made available to all citizens and most residents of the United States under the Fourteenth Amendment to the Constitution.

---

retained minority teachers even given the goal of alleviating the effects of past societal discrimination. The Court essentially found that the senior nonminority teacher had a property interest in his or her job that could not be eliminated even given the important goals the school board was pursuing.

In *Johnson* v. *Transportation Agency, Santa Clara County*, 107 S.Ct. 1442 (1987) the Court found that the county could consider gender among other factors in promoting a woman under a voluntary affirmative action plan. The Court found that the plan was designed to eliminate a "manifest imbalance" in a "traditionally segregated job category." The case indicates that it is proper to employ affirmative action even where there is no showing of actual past discrimination, at least where such efforts are directed to hiring or promotion. Notably, the case applies the same standards and remedies to suspected societal discrimination against women as it applies in cases alleging discrimination based on race.

California Federal Savings & Loan v. *Guerra*, 107 S.Ct. 683 (1987) held that a California statute which mandated generous pregnancy leave benefits was not preempted by the Federal Pregnancy Discrimination Act. The Court supported this differential treatment on the ground that it is permissible in the pursuit of the goal of achieving equality of employment op-

portunities and removing barriers that favor identifiable groups of employees over other employees.

Finally, overt discrimination will still be subject to specific remedies. In *United States* v. *Paradise*, 107 S.Ct. 1053 (1987), the Court considered a challenge to a race-based promotion plan for state troopers and concluded that a court-ordered affirmative action plan establishing a one-for-one racial quota for promotions was permissible in light of the employer's long history of excluding blacks from employment. Any such plan has to be "narrowly tailored" to achieve the goal of remedying proven and continuing discrimination and should at least demonstrate some flexibility and an attempt to achieve fairness.

The basic goal, then, should be to seek affirmative action plans and programs that serve the essential purposes of the integration of the work force for minorities and women, but that only minimally affect the *existing* employment relationship enjoyed by current workers. Again, this area is most complex, and managers are encouraged to work closely with the city or county attorney in designing or implementing affirmative action programs.

The guarantee of due process protects a broad range of activities including the essential civil rights safeguards of requiring notice of charges, a hearing, and an opportunity for one to defend his or her rights and to confront accusers in a neutral forum.

The equal protection clause ensures uniform treatment of individuals in similar circumstances. Equal protection challenges have involved claims of unequal treatment in employment classifications, wage standards, and the provision of public services.

A Section 1983 action may be brought against a local government for depriving a person of rights guaranteed by federal statutes as well as by the Constitution. The Supreme Court has concluded that "laws" under Section 1983 encompass federal statutes such as Social Security and environmental acts in addition to civil rights statutes.[13]

Public official liability

Since 1978, Section 1983 has been broadly interpreted by the U.S. Supreme Court against both municipalities and their local officials. This attention has turned to deep concern about the increased costs of litigation and potential liability of public officials.

Public officials can be found *personally* liable under this section for nominal, compensatory, or punitive monetary damages. Officials are subject to liability for official acts performed under color of state or local law if those acts violate the established constitutional or statutory rights of an individual. Although the statute covers a wide range of protected rights, the federal doctrine of official immunity ultimately determines personal liability under Section 1983.

Ambulance services A number of interesting legal questions concerning the provision of ambulance and emergency medical transportation services arose in the early 1980s when cities were being sued under Federal antitrust laws. A notable case was *Gold Cross Ambulance Service* v. *City of Kansas City, Missouri*, 705 F.2d 1005 (8th Cir. 1984). The following discussion draws on several cases and the problems they presented.

Essentially, it appeared that ambulance services could be broken into two segments: emergency (911-EMS) medical transportation and trauma care; and routine, predictable ambulance service provided on a scheduled basis. The 911 services were very expensive since they had to be provided on a twenty-four-hour basis and required that the personnel operating the vehicle had to have more specialized and advanced medical training. Of course, there was little predictability as to how frequent or how extensive the use of

this service would be. Mere transportation, on the other hand, was a profitable enterprise; the skills and training needed were not great; and there was certainty as to the daily provision of the service.

The cities in these cases had ordinances regulating the provision of ambulance services. More often than not, it was recognized that the transportation service would effectively subsidize the 911 service and that such regulation, by providing a virtual monopoly to one or two companies, could also mandate that twenty-four-hour services would be available. In several of these cases, the cities received no acceptable bids for the services and, consequently, decided to provide these services out of the public treasury. These decisions, of course, required substantial equipment and training outlays by the cities.

When it first appeared that the antitrust laws might be used to challenge the

All municipal officers and employees have some immunity from personal liability for damages under Section 1983, depending on the scope and type of duties performed.

There are two types of official immunity, absolute immunity and qualified immunity. State and local legislators and judges are entitled to absolute immunity from damages in Section 1983 actions. Most other state and local officials have only a qualified immunity from damages in their exercise of administrative, ministerial, or executive powers.

The scope of qualified immunity was clarified in the 1982 U.S. Supreme court decision *Harlow* v. *Fitzgerald*.[14] In *Harlow*, the Court specifically held that "government officials performing discretionary functions generally are shielded from liability for civil damages insofar as their conduct does not violate clearly established statutory or constitutional rights of which a reasonable person should have known."

Applying this test, a public official is required to be familiar with clearly established law governing his or her conduct. Thus, a public official will not be granted the benefit of qualified immunity if he or she knows or reasonably should have known that certain conduct could violate an individual's civil rights. The difficulty with the "qualified" standard is that it has not yet evolved into a comprehensive test that allows an individual to identify clear constitutional or statutory rights that must be protected as he or she performs official acts on behalf of the government.

It is important to reemphasize here that a public official is more likely to be protected by qualified immunity if he or she has consulted the city attorney when in doubt as to the propriety of proposed actions. Moreover, if the attorney's advice is coupled with other evidence that the official followed departmental procedures and regulations, he or she should be immune from liability.

---

cities in making these choices (see *Community Communications Corp.* v. *City of Boulder*, 455 U.S. 40 [1982]), private ambulance companies began to ask cities if they could provide the routine transportation services while leaving the more expensive, 911 services with the cities. The cities, of course, objected, arguing that the mere fact that they were helping subsidize their EMS services out of transportation services did not make them "competitors" for purposes of antitrust review.

The dilemma was that the cities, having tried to provide these services, and having incurred truly substantial expenses in doing so, were now being challenged as having "assumed" a private role in a private market. In litigating these cases, the cities maintained that they had pursued the public interest in first designing appropriate EMS facilities and that the public investment should not now be wasted only to meet some private entity's current notion that it wanted the business and thought it could make a go of it. The cities argued that the importance of these services to the public welfare was such that they could not be left to the whim of the private marketplace, particularly in light of the public investment.

By and large, the cities were successful in defending these cases, although much of that success came only after lengthy and expensive litigation. Finally, in response to these and other equally perplexing cases, Congress adopted a statute that substantially protects local governments from antitrust attack (P.L. 98–544, 15 U.S.C. Section 35) and the Supreme Court realized that governments acting in the public interest should not be considered antitrust violators (*Town of Hallie* v. *City of Eau Claire*, 105 S.Ct. 1713 [1985]) and *Fisher* v. *City of Berkeley*, 106 S.Ct. 1045 [1986]). Still, the questions presented by these cases—positing both economic and legal problems—will no doubt continue to be litigated.

Local government liabili

State and local officials   not the only ''persons'' that can be sued under
Section 1983; the Suprem   ourt has determined that municipalities are included
in the definition of perso   Local government units have no protection under
the absolute or qualified   nunity defenses. As a result, municipal liability is
absolute when a federall   uaranteed right is violated. Even if a municipal
official can establish persc   or official immunity, that immunity will not shield
the local government fror   bility for Section 1983 violations. In the wake of
Supreme Court decisions   al governments are in effect strictly liable for acts
or policies that violate ar   lividual's civil rights.

Liability for official poli

When can a city be sued under Section 1983? The law holds the city liable for
conduct of its officials performed ''under color of any statute, ordinance, regulation, custom or usage of any state or territory '' This language has been
interpreted to include all acts that reflect an official custom or policy of the
municipality. Customs or policies include formal statements, such as ordinances
or resolutions, as well as any unwritten policies or practices that, through
continued usage, take on the force of law.

Although it is often difficult to determine what constitutes local custom or
policy, a single act of official misconduct usually is not enough to establish
municipal liability. In extreme circumstances, however, the Supreme Court has
held cities liable for single acts.[15]

Similarly, mere *negligence* by employees is not sufficient to create municipal
liability under Section 1983. Rather, it must be shown that the employee had

---

**Civil rights issues affecting fire
departments** Most of the reported
cases regarding firefighters and departments based on Section 1983 involve employment relations. For
example, in *Owen* v. *City of Independence*, the Supreme Court held that a
police chief who was dismissed without
a hearing or written specifications of
the charges against him, and an opportunity to rebut those charges, was
denied due process. *Owen* is important
because the Court held that even
where the officials were entitled to a
qualified immunity, as discussed in the
text, the city itself could not claim the
benefits of that immunity; thus municipalities can be held strictly liable for
the illegal acts of their officers.

In *Burnley* v. *Thompson*, the court of
appeals upheld the dismissal of a probationary firefighter who participated in
an illegal strike. The court also found
that the city was not obligated to provide a termination hearing given the
emergency circumstances the city was

facing and its immediate need to replace strikers so as to restore fire services to the city. *Owen* and subsequent
cases may have eroded this rule, although it is likely that a post-termination
hearing would be sufficient to meet due
process standards.

In *Klupt* v. *Blue Island Fire Department*,
a district court ruled that allegations by
a discharged fireman that other firefighters met with supervisors to deprive
him of his job on antisemitic grounds
stated a sufficient claim of conspiracy
that he could sue under Section 1983.

Very few reported cases have to do
with the regulatory and fire suppression
activities of fire departments, but a
great many cases involve the regulatory and coercive activities of other municipal employees, such as police
officers and building inspectors. Given
the veritable explosion in Section 1983
litigation against municipalities, it would
not be surprising to see additional suits
based on a number of theories filed

express or implied municipal authorization for the official misconduct. If the city or county deliberately ignores official misconduct once it is put on notice of acts or probable acts that deprive an individual of civil rights, the government may well be liable. Such a challenge must allege that the municipality is responsible for the local official's disregard of known facts or gross negligence pertaining to a Section 1983 violation.

Liability for the conduct of subordinates

A municipality cannot be held liable under Section 1983 simply because of the employer-employee relationship between the city and its employee. There must be evidence that the employee's impermissible conduct was based on a municipal policy or custom or on indifference.

Although an official cannot be held liable for the acts of subordinates on this *respondeat superior* theory, an official may be liable if he or she directly participated in an alleged civil rights violation. Moreover, courts have found officials liable for subordinates' acts in cases where they have shown any direct or indirect approval, participation, sanction, promotion, or knowledge of a subordinate's misconduct resulting in a civil rights violation.

Liability for damages under Section 1983

Municipalities are often the subject of Section 1983 civil rights suits since they are perceived to have "deep pockets." Section 1983 damage awards against local governments and their officials can be quite substantial, but the U.S. Supreme Court has established limits on the amount of municipal liability. A

---

against fire officials. First, at the point at which fire regulations require expenditures that are disproportionate to the value of a building (e.g., mandating the installation of a sprinkler system in an old building where the capital expenditures for sprinklers are unjustifiable given the life expectancy of the building), the building owners may claim that the remaining useful life of their building has been "taken" by the city or county, thereby entitling them to compensation.

Second, fire agencies have significant investigatory powers, particularly in cases of suspected arson. Failures to acquire adequate search warrants, or unwarranted intrusions on the privacy of individuals, could well lead to Section 1983 claims as abuses of governmental power.

Third, the failure of a fire agency to provide equal or roughly equal services to all parts of the community may result in civil rights actions. In several early

cases, plaintiffs living in largely black communities were able to show that the community was making disproportionate expenditures of public funds to white areas of the community. Decisions regarding the allocation of fire stations or the allocation of equipment and personnel to given communities could provide grist for the Section 1983 mill.

It is important to remember that these civil rights claims exist with regard to both staff activities (personnel, individual firefighters, budgeting) and line activities (fire inspections, fairness in dealing with neighborhoods). Again, the solution is to provide fair and unbiased forums for the resolution of internal disputes and to recognize the special relationship that local governments have with their citizens, which, if nothing else, requires that they be treated equally.

city may be subject to liability for nominal and compensatory damages only; punitive or exemplary damages cannot be awarded against a municipality under the statute, although they can be awarded against individual officials who violate the law.

Attorney's fees

Although local governments cannot be held liable for punitive damages, Section 1983 litigation can be made even more costly by an award of attorney's fees under the Civil Rights Attorney's Fees Awards Act of 1976.[16] The statute provides that the court at its discretion may award reasonable attorney's fees from a local government, or its officials personally, to a prevailing plaintiff. The courts have been generous in awarding attorney's fees to Section 1983 plaintiffs, even where the damage award is nominal, or where simple injunctive relief is given.[17] Moreover, a plaintiff may be considered a "prevailing party" and awarded fees by means of a favorable settlement or success on significant issues. Decisions on the awarding of attorney's fees for defendants have not been so generous. To the contrary, the Supreme Court has held that a defendant can obtain attorney's fees only when the plaintiff's claim is "meritless" or "frivolous."

⚜ Local government tort liability

Understanding tort liability is particularly important given the nature of fire services and the role of the fire department in the overall local government operation. In the 1970s and 1980s there have been an increasing number of court decisions requiring local governments to pay large damage awards because some fault or failure was ascribed to the municipality. This section focuses primarily on the tort liability of fire department managers and employees as well as the municipality's liability for wrongful acts or omissions.

Introduction to tort principles

Liability arising from the activities of fire departments, including suppression, prevention, and inspection, results from a failure of duty. In order for an individual or municipality to be found liable, the injured party must prove negligence. Generally, municipal officers acting within the scope of their authority and without negligence are not personally liable for damage resulting from their acts. However, employees and officials are responsible for negligent or improper acts committed during the performance of their duties.

To prove negligence, the plaintiff must show that the officer or employee had a duty to the public and to the particular injured party and that the failure to perform that duty with the required care and skill was the cause of the plaintiff's injury.

Public officers and employees have duties that are defined by federal, state, and local statutes. Each of these statutes regulates, to some degree, the facilities and services provided by the fire department, so that the department has a duty to operate within established legal guidelines. Tort liability is an area governed almost completely by state law. The extent to which specific legal tort doctrines apply to specific acts varies from state to state, so the following discussion is general.

Once legal duties have been established or created, either by internal departmental custom and policy or by statutory standards, fire department personnel have to act with reasonable skill and care.

A breach of these duties may occur in two ways:

1. The improper performance of an act
2. A failure to act (e.g., if the city decides to reduce services on the basis of fiscal cutbacks, the subsequent failure to provide services may result in tort liability).

When the municipality takes action that encourages reliance by the public or an individual, and thereby creates a duty relationship, a breach of that duty may cause injury to the plaintiff and give rise to tort liability.

The amount of damages that a plaintiff may recover can have a significant impact on the budget of a city or county that is already financially burdened by the increased costs of essential services. Therefore, it is extremely important for the fire chief to work closely with the city or county attorney in handling damage claims against the city. The attorney can provide advice as to the nature and extent of the city's liability and may suggest precautions to avoid actions in the future.

Liability for negligent inspection   A number of state courts, notably in Florida, have found local officials and governments liable for failure to inspect or for "negligent inspection." This doctrine holds all of the prerequisites for the finding of tort liability: There must be a duty to the citizens generally and individually, and there must be a breach of that duty resulting in injury. Most of these cases have arisen with regard to building inspections.

The scenario, in the context of fire services, might be something like this:

1. In adopting fire ordinances and codes requiring sprinkler systems, use of fire-retardant building materials, smoke detectors, and the like, the municipality has created a duty of fire safety that it owes to the public.

2. As a result of budget reductions, the municipality is not able to conform its inspections for fire services to the standards set out in its ordinance. Or, as a result of significant new construction in the municipality, it could provide adequate inspections only if it added new fire inspection personnel.

3. A building that was not inspected, or only cursorily inspected, catches fire, which leads to the loss of life and substantial property damage. As a result of the loss, the building owner is virtually bankrupt and the estates of the deceased are seeking a defendant with the funds to pay for their loss.

4. The estates sue the building owner *and* the municipality on the theory that the city failed in its duty to provide proper inspections; that if the municipality's ordinances had been enforced, the deaths would not have occurred; and that the municipality is therefore responsible for the deaths.

Much like the antitrust problems local governments faced in the early 1980s, this theory blossomed for a while. Finally, the Florida Supreme Court, reviewing the opinions of the state's lower appellate courts propounding this theory, invalidated the theory on the ground that the duty owed by local governments is a duty to the public at large and not to individual members of the public who happen to be injured.

It can be expected, however, that this theory or similar theories will arise again. Part of the risk reduction program of the community should be a full assessment of the duties created by state law or local ordinance along with an analysis of the extent to which the community is committing sufficient resources to comply with those duties.

Municipal liability

The great variation in state tort law makes it difficult to list all the circumstances under which, and the extent to which, municipalities may be held liable for the acts of their employees.

The scope and extent of local government liability depends on the circumstances under which a governmental entity is immune from tort liability in the particular jurisdiction. All state and federal jurisdictions have some form of sovereign immunity under specific circumstances. In some states, municipal liability is the rule and immunity is the exception. In other states, however, immunity is the rule and liability is the exception. Ultimately this means that state law may impose liability on the basis of whether the act is a *governmental* or a *proprietary* activity of the city.

Although the governmental-proprietary distinction is quite difficult to describe, liability and immunity for local government tort actions are often based on it. It is important to remember that immunity and liability may appear to be hopelessly intertwined, but are two separate and distinct issues.

The standard for liability for negligence by a municipality is the same as that for an individual: The plaintiff must show that the city or county had a duty to the injured person and that it failed in its duty and, thereby, allegedly caused the injury.

Unlike civil rights liability, tort liability frequently results under the doctrine of *respondeat superior*: The municipality is accountable to an individual who suffers a direct injury caused by the negligence of a municipal employee acting within the scope of his or her employment.

A primer on legal terms The following definitions and explanations are designed to clarify legal terms used throughout this chapter.

Damages Legal damages generally refer to the payment of money to a prevailing plaintiff for several purposes, including the compensation of victims, the punishment of wrongdoers, and the creation of a deterrent to behavior that might injure people. In civil rights and tort cases, public officials can be held *personally* liable for their actions, and the prevailing plaintiff can be awarded money from the personal assets of the official, including his or her bank accounts, capital assets, wages, and savings. Personal damages can even be awarded against a supervisor or someone other than the actual wrongdoer, but first some personal hostility or indifference to problems generally has to be shown.

Damages, actual Actual or compensatory damages are meant to compensate the plaintiff for his or her financial losses. Generally they include out-of-pocket expenses along with anticipated losses such as lost wages. For example, an employee who is wrongfully discharged may sue for back wages, reinstatement, reestablishment of seniority, and other actual monetary losses if he or she can demonstrate that they resulted from the discharge.

Damages, compensatory See Damages, actual.

Damages, exemplary See Damages, punitive.

Damages, punitive Punitive or exemplary damages are designed to deter behavior that is unacceptable by punishing the wrongdoer. Under civil rights laws, local governments themselves cannot be held liable for punitive damages, but the standard for imposing punitive damages on individual officers and employees is quite lax.

Defendant The defendant, in litigation, is the party charged by the plaintiff with

Municipal officer and employee liability

The liability of an employee is separate from municipal liability. Generally, municipal officers are immune from individual liability when acting in good faith, without negligence, and within the scope of their authority. Under many state and local statutes, however, municipal officers and employees can be held personally liable for damage or injury resulting from public work performed if the injury resulted from negligent or improper performance of the work.

This admixture of "official" liability and liability in one's "personal capacity," when played against the potential liability of governmental entities themselves, creates vexing problems in litigation and in the defense of lawsuits. As all of these areas are in a substantial state of flux, public officials should always consult with the jurisdiction's lawyers whenever litigation seems a possibility.

Conflict of interest

Local government officials and employees are required to act with the utmost good faith, fidelity, and respect as fiduciaries of the municipality and the public trust. This duty mandates that public officials must maintain a high degree of propriety in the performance of their obligations. They must be mindful of the appearances of, or actual, conflicts that might arise from their actions. A conflict of interest may occur in a variety of forms relevant to holding public office or a public job. This includes outside employment interests, private financial interests, personal relations, acceptance of gifts, and abuse of office or position.

---

responsibility for some wrongful or inappropriate act or failure to act. This is the party that will be liable for damages if he or she loses the case. Generally the plaintiff has the "burden of proof"; that is, he or she must demonstrate that the action of the defendant was the cause of injury.

Discretionary/ministerial functions
Discretionary functions are those in which an official may use personal judgment in making decisions; in such a case, he or she is generally protected from litigation questioning those decisions. Ministerial functions are those in which the official may not use personal judgment, and a court may order him or her to act. The distinction is used to evaluate government officials' responsibility for various actions. It is based on the theory that government officials should be free, whenever possible, to make decisions that improve the public welfare. For example, building officials may have discretion in deciding the types and qualities of materials that can be used in construction.

However, once a contractor has complied with all state and local regulations and has complied with the building permit in constructing a facility, a building inspector has no discretion in issuance of an occupancy certificate; this is a ministerial function.

Fiduciary Fiduciary means based on trust. The law recognizes that when one individual (including a governmental entity) has a relationship with another, certain circumstances require that extraordinary standards be imposed on the relationship based on the need for trust and fidelity. For example, because public officials have unique powers over individuals (such as police or taxing powers), they have a fiduciary relationship with citizens and are subject to the highest standards of behavior to ensure that they do not violate the public trust placed in their hands.

Governmental/proprietary actions
Governmental actions are those carried
Continued on next page.

Many of these conflict-of-interest areas are governed by state or local statutes or charters. The most familiar application of the conflict-of-interest prohibition is in the area of municipal contracts. Generally, state law prohibits public officials from contracting with an agency they represent or from having a private interest, direct or indirect, in city contracts. Because of their public positions, municipal officers are held to a strict standard of accountability when dealing on the city's or county's behalf. The interest of an employee or officer in a public contract may be a financial one, which benefits the officer either directly or indirectly. Here is an example of a direct conflict: A managerial-level fire department officer authorizes the signing of a contract with a private company to purchase new uniforms and protective equipment for firefighters. If that manager receives a commission as a result of the awarding of the contract, the contract can be held void and unenforceable as against public policy.

Similarly, an indirect conflict would arise if the contracting official is related to an officer or director of the private company or is financially interested in the company as a stockholder. In addition to invalidating the contract, a violation of the conflict-of-interest requirements may result in removal from office, liability for all profits received, and possible criminal prosecution and fines. This prohibition of an officer's personal and financial interest extends through all stages of contract negotiation and performance.

Public officials must avoid not only private interests in public contracts, but also situations that *appear* inconsistent with the proper performance of their duties. Awareness of potential conflicts is essential; even the most innocent or harmless situations may be tainted with the appearance of self-interest or self-dealing. These general principles apply in the following four areas:

---

out by a government and its officials when they are acting under their governmental powers in fulfillment of their public obligations. Proprietary actions are those carried out by a government or its officials when they are acting as private parties. When carrying out governmental activities (providing police services, for example), officials are generally protected from ordinary lawsuits and penalties. When carrying out proprietary activities (providing limousine service to the airport in competition with the private sector, for example), they are subject to the same standards as any private party. It has become increasingly difficult to draw clear lines between governmental and proprietary activities, because the definition of "public purposes" has expanded dramatically.

Immunity   Immunity means protection from suit or liability. Immunity is frequently granted to governments and their officials on grounds that the business of government is so important that officials who are acting in good faith

and within the scope of their duties should not be vulnerable to suits.

Immunity, absolute   Under federal law, certain officials, in the exercise of their official duties, have absolute immunity from suit. This includes prosecutors and judges. They generally enjoy such immunity only when acting in their official capacities.

Immunity, qualified   Under federal law, an official who acted reasonably and could not have known, through due care, that he or she was violating someone's rights, may have immunity for actions taken under those circumstances.

Immunity, sovereign   Sovereign immunity, derived from the ancient dictum that "the king can do no wrong," provides governments with immunity from suits. It has been substantially eroded in recent years. Many states have abolished it, and others have set dollar limits on the amount that can be awarded in suits against the state.

1. *The receipt of gifts, commissions, or bonuses*. The receipt of anything of value that may directly or indirectly influence a public official in his or her actions is clearly illegal and is easily traceable.
2. *Interest in the contracting corporation*. The ownership of stock or the holding of office in a corporation with which an officer contracts on behalf of the public, either directly or indirectly, is prohibited. The general rule includes ownership or holding of office not only by the public official but also by the spouse or other immediate family members of the public official.
3. *Personal relationships*. Public officials must avoid situations in which their actions may be affected by personal relationships. Family and personal ties that interfere with an official's obligation to pursue the public good or that create an appearance of special interest are forbidden.
4. *Political contributions or considerations*. An officer must refrain from making or receiving contributions or considerations that benefit his or her political interests or the interests of someone with managerial or political authority over the official. This area is closely regulated by federal and state statutes.

Conclusion

Despite a great deal of anxiety over municipal and individual liability, fire department managers can take action to help protect themselves, their employees, and their departments. As this chapter has shown, managers need to follow several guidelines:

Ministerial   See Discretionary/ministerial functions.

Negligence   Negligence is failure to do something that a reasonable person, guided by the considerations that ordinarily regulate human affairs, would do, or doing something that a reasonable and prudent person would not do.

Plaintiff   The plaintiff, in litigation, is the person who brings an action, the party who complains or sues.

Proprietary actions   See Governmental/proprietary actions.

Relief, equitable   Equitable or injunctive relief is action by a court to compel an official to act or to prevent the official from acting. For example, a court might order a city or county to reallocate its fire service resources to benefit parts of the jurisdiction that have received inadequate services in the past. In so doing, the court implies that the wrong that is being committed, or would be committed, is so substantial that the court should use its powers to implement or to end the activity immediately.

Relief, injunctive   See Relief, equitable.

Respondeat superior   Literally, *respondeat superior* means "let the master answer." In modern terms, it means that an employer, such as a local government, can be held responsible in certain cases for the wrongful actions of its employees.

Tort liability   Tort liability is responsibility for a private or civil wrong or action, a violation of a duty imposed by law or by the nature of the relationship between the parties involved. Three elements of a tort are (1) existence of a legal duty on the part of the defendant toward the plaintiff, (2) breach of that duty, and (3) damage as a result. Torts may be intentional (assault or battery, for example) or may arise from a negligent act or failure to act (unsafe operation of an automobile, for example).

---

1. Be aware of actual and potential legal developments that affect their work
2. Adhere to strict principles of nondiscrimination, openness, and public welfare in the performance of their duties
3. Consult with the city or county attorney when in doubt about anything with possible legal implications
4. Anticipate, manage, and reduce risks wherever possible.

To help managers ask the right questions, this chapter has presented a primer on civil rights obligations, general tort liability, and conflict of interest issues. Knowledge of these basics, combined with conscientious application of the guidelines listed above, will go a long way toward reducing the chances of time-consuming and costly litigation.

1   Garcia v. San Antonio Metropolitan Transit Authority, 105 S.Ct. 1005 (1985).

2   On November 7, 1985, Congress passed the Fair Labor Standards Amendments of 1985, P.L. 99–150, signed by President Reagan on November 13, 1985. The act represented a compromise between state and local government representatives, labor groups, and Congress. Among other things, the act amended the FLSA to allow state and local employers to grant compensatory time in lieu of paid overtime at a rate of time-and-a-half as of April 15, 1986. The application of the overtime standards to local police and fire agencies was particularly troubling given the traditional on-off scheduling problems of twenty-four-hour emergency services. Most of these problems have now been ameliorated—managers are urged to consult with local counsel on the applicability of the Fair Labor Standards Act.

3   Age Discrimination in Employment Amendments, P.L. 99–591, signed October 31, 1986: see also note 10.

4   Addresses: State and Local Legal Center, Academy for State and Local Government, 444 North Capitol Street, Washington, D.C. 20001 (202-638-1445); U.S. Conference of Mayors, 1620 Eye Street, N.W., Washington, D.C. 20006 (202-293-7330); National League of Cities, 1301 Pennsylvania Avenue, N.W., Washington, D.C. 20004 (202-626-3010); National Association of Counties, 440 First Street, N.W., Washington, D.C. 20001 (202-393-6226); International Association of Fire Chiefs, 1329 18th Street, N.W., Washington, D.C. 20036 (202-833-3420); National Fire Protection Association, Batterymarch Park, Quincy, Mass. (617-770-3000); International Association of Fire Fighters, 1750 New York Avenue, N.W., Washington, D.C. 20006 (202-737-8484).

5   Harlow v. Fitzgerald, 457 U.S. 800 (1982): In 1985 the Supreme Court returned to the "qualified immunity" questions raised in *Harlow* and handed down a case that should provide substantial guidance to local government lawyers in advising public officials: Mitchell v. Forsyth, 105 S.Ct. 2806 (1985). In *Mitchell* the Court essentially held that these "qualified" immunities are really immunities from suit, not just from liability; consequently, if the official reasonably believed he or she was operating within the law, he or she and the government should be able to escape even having to go to trial for alleged violations. See, also, Commuter Transportation Services v. Hillsborough County, 801 F.2d 1286 (11th Cir. 1986).

6   See, Johnson v. City of Arcadia, Florida, 450 F.Supp. 1363 (N.D. Fla. 1978).

7   See, generally, McQuillan, *Municipal Corporations,* 3d ed. (1984), Chapter 45, Fire and Police Departments.

8   See *Garcia,* note 1.

9   Local 98, International Association of Firefighters v. City of Cleveland, 106 S.Ct. 3063 (1986); see also Wygant v. Jackson Board of Education, 106 S.Ct. 1842 (1986) and Local 28, Sheet Metal Workers International Association v. EEOC, 106 S.Ct. 3019 (1986).

10   Age Discrimination in Employment Amendments of 1986, P.L. 99–591, signed October 31, 1986. The act essentially provides a seven-year grace period for state and local governments in mandating retirement for uniformed officers at a certain age. This includes supervisory personnel who used to be uniformed officers. The act also sets standards for maximum hiring ages. A municipality is allowed to use the ages for entry and retirement that it had in force on the date of the Supreme Court decision in *EEOC* v. *Wyoming,* March 3, 1983. The effective date of the act was January 12, 1987; claims pending on that date continue to be valid, but are still subject to claims that the age was a bonafide occupational qualification. Finally, the act mandates that a study including representatives of both employers and employees be conducted under the auspices of the Department of Labor and the Equal Employment Opportunity Commission to assess whether there exist, in fact, viable medical tests that can demonstrate the physical competency of given individuals to perform the work required of a police officer or firefighter.

11   Connick v. Myers, 461 U.S. 168 (1983); see also Pickering v. Board of Education, 391 U.S. 563 (1968), Perry v. Sindermann, 408 U.S. 593 (1972), and Branti v. Finkel, 455 U.S. 507 (1980).

12   See the case cited in note 6.

13   Monell v. Social Services Department, City of New York, 436 U.S. 658 (1978); see also Owen v. City of Independence, 445 U.S. 442 (1980).

14   See the case cited in note 5.

15   Pembauer v. City of Cincinnati, 106 S.Ct. 1292 (1986), and City of Oklahoma City v. Tuttle, 105 S.Ct. 2427 (1985). In *Pembauer* the Court found that an official who has policy-making authority on behalf of the local government can make a single decision that violates individual constitutional rights. In this case, a district attorney authorized police officers to chop down the door to a doctor's clinic in violation of his rights. However, in *Tuttle,* the Court found that a single bad decision by a line police officer could not be used to impose liability on the city.

16   42 U.S.C. Section 1988.

17   See, e.g., City of Riverside v. Riviera, 106 S.Ct. 2686 (1986), which sustained an attorney award in an amount of about seven times the actual damages awarded against the city.

10 Program management

The effective management of programs or projects is particularly important to the success of public fire service organizations. Many services provided by these organizations are difficult to assess on a short-term basis, and ineffective day-to-day management often destroys support for what are essentially good programs. Program or project management is a well-known concept in the field of business and industry. It consists of planning techniques, scheduling tools, establishing control, developing communication skills, and employing an evaluation process that allows an organization to make changes as a program or project unfolds.

In simple terms, program management refers to the application of good management techniques to any given program. Those unfamiliar with the concept may imagine that program management is merely maintaining control over a well-defined but often complicated task. At its most sophisticated, it is a complex concept expressed by mathematical formulas and extensive matrices, charts, and graphs by some authors. For the fire service manager, the truth is somewhere in between.

Although the terms *project* and *program* are often used interchangeably, even by authorities on the subject, a technical distinction can be made. Ongoing activities that flow from the department's mission statement and directly accomplish goals and objectives articulated by that statement (e.g., the maintenance of a fire prevention or public education activity) may be labeled "programs." Typically, training, maintenance, pre-fire planning, and other ongoing activities are called programs. Any short-term activity that will not be repeated and typically results in a tangible end product, such as a new fire station or a task force report, may be labeled a "project." Typically, projects result in expansions or other modifications to programs. Whereas the term *program management* is often used in a general sense to describe both program and project management, the term *project management* refers more specifically to the use of management concepts introduced in the late 1950s and emphasizes detailed charting of activity, progress, and events at various stages of a specific capital project.

It may be helpful to view programs and projects not as different entities, but rather as points on a continuum. Traditional management tools such as planning, organizing, staffing, directing, coordinating, reporting, and budgeting (POSDCORB) would be used primarily at the program end of the continuum. Charts, graphs, computers, and specialized scheduling and cost prediction methodologies and evaluation techniques would be used more at the project end. All the tools and techniques, however, are used to some extent throughout the continuum.[1]

In this chapter, program management encompasses both programs and projects. The discussion opens with a brief description of the environment in which program management takes place and then turns to three dimensions of program management: (1) setting program objectives (deciding what to do); (2) implementing them (getting it done); and (3) evaluating the results (determining how well it was done).

The environment of program management

Many fire officers have spent most of their careers in a physical world of fighting fire, providing medical aid, and reacting to danger. They have often been portrayed by an admiring public as classic heroes standing in the ashes—resolute and valiant. When fire officers are promoted to management positions and are asked to oversee competing programs or to complete complex projects, they need to view the community and the political environment differently. Their background provides them with only a few obvious tools to accomplish these tasks.

The political environment

In a fire department, service levels, project funding, and program implementation all require political action. In most cases of resource allocation, the fire department is just one of many competitors for limited funds. Fire service programs and projects are not abstract entities in the political environment; they are real fire stations, training facilities, and fire prevention or public education programs that may or may not be funded.

Most fire protection is provided by local government, which is at least to some extent a political arena. The fire service program manager's sphere of operation is part of that political arena. To some, the term *politics* may imply favoritism and special treatment, influence peddling, and back-room deals. In its more neutral sense, however, the term refers to the relations that exist among individuals and groups.

It is imperative that the fire service manager understand the political environment. This understanding begins with an analysis of the community's power structure. Power flows from intangibles, which together constitute the community's political base. Fire service program managers are distinguished from most other political figures in that they are the recipients and ultimately the users of this power, which is entrusted to them through the chief administrative officer, codes and ordinances, and the allocation of budget resources.

The political base may be defined differently in each community because it varies with the demographics of the community—the combination of people, organizations, attitudes, and relationships that together produce the particular character of the community. To get to know and understand that political base, the manager must look at certain indicators such as geographical features, economic trends, the mix of business and industry, growth trends, climatic conditions, the age of the community, demographics (the age spread of inhabitants, the distribution of ethnic and income groups), political attitudes (conservative/liberal posture), and revenue base.

Data on these indicators may be found in news reports, census publications, and local government records. The relative influence of each component will, of course, vary from community to community, issue to issue, and time to time. On the basis of this knowledge, the chief or program manager must do a good job of selling the department and its services to the community. A department that is professional, active, and highly visible will achieve a strong level of local support. That support can be considered a form of positive political pressure since local authorities will be reluctant to reduce a service that clearly benefits the entire community. A chief who maintains ongoing cordial relations with local leaders will find the political climate favorable for departmental requests and programs.

The fire service program manager must know what individuals, groups, and organizations might influence programs or projects. They must analyze, for any given scenario, the view these individuals or groups have of the department.

For example, before the chamber of commerce can materially assist the department in getting a new code program implemented, chamber members must have confidence in the department and its managers. Do they view the staff as professional? If the staff presents data at a public meeting, do they believe that the material has been obtained through extensive research or do they suspect that figures may have been pulled from thin air? If a conflict goes to appeal, do they believe that the staff will analyze the issue with an open mind, or that they will become defensive and inflexible? What kind of relationship does the staff have with chamber members or with someone else in the business/industrial community? Is it positive or negative? Questions like these may be asked about each element of the political base.

If the answers to such questions are positive and reflect a confidence in the department, the group in question can help the department achieve its goals. Securing such assistance may be as simple as asking the Rotary Club to write a letter to the city council in support of the department's proposed affirmative action outreach program. It may also be more involved. You may have to secure funding to purchase smoke detectors for those who cannot afford them before adopting a code mandating the devices throughout your community; you may have to obtain funding for sophisticated hazardous material monitoring equipment before forming a hazmat response team; or you may want the health department to change its requirement for redundant backflow-prevention devices before proposing a comprehensive automatic fire sprinkler ordinance. In each case, the need must be communicated.

If the answers to the political questions are negative and reflect a lack of confidence, the department may face an uphill struggle to obtain the resources it seeks. In that case, the chief needs to take the lead in finding a way to reduce the negative view. Here, the role and relationships and the image of the chief

---

Program management strategies

Where should the program manager begin? Here is a checklist of strategies that may be helpful at the outset:

1. Listening

2. Doing seedwork for future projects

3. Having visibility within the organization—but not too much

4. Conducting yourself with openness and honesty; building trust

5. Giving credit to others even if it's your own idea—especially in the media

6. Giving prompt positive feedback

7. Taking reasonable risks

8. Relaying sincere compliments publicly

9. Observing protocol

10. Being aware of implied power

11. Seeking win-win vs. win-lose situations (managing the situation so that everyone comes out with something positive)

12. Sharing ownership

13. Working with line people

14. Information sharing before taking action steps

15. Being open to alternative suggestions.

Source: James L. Mercer and Susan W. Woolston, "Science and Technology Networks," in *Public Technology: Key to Improved Government Productivity*, James L. Mercer and Ronald J. Philips, eds. (New York: AMACOM, a division of the American Management Association, 1981), 249–50..

---

are central to the community's confidence in fire service programs and projects. Community leaders need to be persuaded that the chief will take every opportunity to further the objectives of fire protection. Most important, they should believe that the chief's goals and objectives are consistent with those of the chief administrative officer and the interests of the community at large.

With the proper tools, a program manager can become an "artist," recognizing and, where necessary, creating an atmosphere for the success of departmental programs.

The organizational environment

The program manager also needs to be aware of the internal organizational environment (see Chapter 3). Many projects and programs represent a change in the status quo, and the program manager should anticipate some negative reactions, especially in the early stages, to the idea of change in the organization. Barriers to innovation and suggestions for smoothly implementing programmatic changes are outlined in Chapter 16.

The public sector environment

Program managers in the public sector differ from those in the private sector in a number of ways:[2]

1. Their work is influenced by pressures from many diverse interests in the community.
2. They must function in an organizational environment of great diversity.
3. They are judged not so much on financial results as on intangibles such as efficiency, which can be difficult to measure.
4. They work in a "goldfish bowl" and are visible to the media and the community, who may or may not understand the complexities of the job.[3] No one could fail to appreciate the impact of a visible catastrophe such as the fire in the MGM Grand Hotel in Las Vegas. The mandates immediately placed upon the local fire chief, after such a fire, often are emotionally charged, poorly conceived, and without option. They may, in addition, be impossible to perform.
5. They often are expected to show results in less time than corporate managers are allowed (for example, managers in California had to respond to Proposition 13 within one fiscal year cycle).
6. They are expected to produce results in an environment characterized by stability and reliability, which tends to make employees efficient but disinclined to take risks in order to be effective and innovative.
7. As a result of their public role, they are expected to demonstrate strong individual leadership, sometimes to the point of not delegating authority or relying on others in the organization.

An often debated issue relating to the fire service and other public services has to do with productivity. The question is how to define and describe it. Clean windows are no less a product for a service company than a bushel of potatoes is for a farmer, and no less a product than a gross of new computers or widgets. In the public sector well-lit streets; acceptable arrest, conviction, and recidivism rates; and reasonable fire safety and service levels are the products of good government. This productivity can be measured by programs subordinated to and flowing from properly established community/department goals and objectives.

Management basics

Program management boils down to balancing the three classic concerns of public administration—getting the right things done (effectiveness), accomplishing them in the right ways (efficiency), and limiting the use of scarce resources (economy).

Performance- and results-oriented management

The most commonly prescribed general approaches to management today are oriented toward performance and results. One such approach, management by objectives (MBO), was popularized by Peter Drucker in 1949, and it came to be widely used by governments when people saw what successful managers actually do. Techniques of results-oriented management have varied with changing times and circumstances, but, given the present understanding that this approach must be applied situationally, the summary in Figure 10–1 sets forth common elements of effective management. One reason for the popularity of results-oriented management is that it is functionally oriented and adaptable to the varied management needs of the department.

The technique of focusing on expected and actual results can be used both on organizations as a whole and on individual programs, projects, and employees, as long as the different needs of varied parts of the organization are respected. It is especially suited to managing managers, but it is also useful for managing nonsupervisory personnel. *Program results* may be analyzed as *outputs* and *outcomes*. The distinction is important in practical management. Outputs are what a department does; outcomes are the consequences of that action (or inaction). Results-oriented management requires that outputs be tangible and quantifiable: for example, in terms of number of inspections completed, number of calls answered, and so on.

Organizational planning is generally a key aspect of results-oriented management. Objectives for a given year need to be related to past results and long-term goals. Planned courses of action may be for any period, perhaps three, five, or seven years. In general, plans should be relatively uncluttered, but they should include alternative goals plus various strategies for accomplishing selected goals. Chapter 4 discusses planning in detail.

Outcomes—the consequences of departmental action—are harder to define, but they need to be taken into account by management. They tell whether or not a program accomplished what was intended in the community. For example, completing inspections may or may not result in reduced incidence of fire.

Figure 10–1
Performance- and
results-oriented
management.

Formulate policies
1. Set goals, objectives, and priorities in terms of available resources and results to be accomplished in a given time.
2. Develop plans for accomplishment of results.

Implement plans
3. Assign responsibilities, delegate authority, and allocate resources.
4. Use functionally oriented management systems to coordinate organizational resources and performance.
5. Involve people in productive activity through shared performance targets and work processes and through training and reinforcement of positive job-related behaviors.
6. Track productivity indicators and progress toward end results.

Evaluate results
7. Evaluate outputs and outcomes in terms of effectiveness (including quality), efficiency, and economy.
8. Generate and implement improvements in objectives, results, and administrative processes (to increase productivity through improved technology, better utilization of people, and so on).

Requiring smoke detectors in homes may or may not result in reduced fire loss. But the actual results, intended or not, convey important information.

Decision making

Decision making is a management function that extends throughout the planning, implementation, and evaluation phases of a project. In general, decision making is not something done at any given moment but is the cumulative effect or product of a complex and sophisticated process generally extending over a considerable period of time.[4] The decision-making process does not occur in a vacuum. It is systematically interwoven with the organizational structure and mission, the specific program objectives, and the political and other environmental influences. No "device"—whether flipping a coin, working three-dimensional decision trees, or using state-of-the-art computers—can produce effective decisions unless all these influences are considered.

Setting program objectives

The program manager must make certain that two sets of activities take place during the policy formulation or planning stage (see Figure 10–1):

1. Goals, objectives, and priorities must be set in terms of available resources and results to be accomplished in a given time.
2. Plans must be developed for accomplishing results.

It is useful to distinguish between *goals*—expected long-term results in three, five, or seven years, for example—and *objectives* of a shorter operating period, such as a quarter of the current budget year.

Program goals and objectives must be related to other organizational priorities. That is, they must be consistent with the general mission of the department, key service areas in which particular results are expected, and indicators of accomplishment. Then changes or new programs may be clearly related to ongoing services.

A mission statement describes why a department or other government unit exists and how one knows whether it accomplishes its generally intended purpose.[5] For example, a fire department mission statement might read as follows: "To contribute within appropriate authority to the maintenance and improvement of the quality of life in the jurisdiction through fire prevention, fire suppression, rescue, special service and fire alarm communications to all who live, visit, work, or invest here." Another example is shown in Figure 10–2.

Key service areas generally define where time, money, and other resources are to be invested, and they should relate directly to the departmental mission. These might be fire prevention, fire suppression, emergency rescue, and so on, with intermediate measures, outputs, and outcomes expressed in terms of specific indicators of effectiveness. In the case of fire suppression, for example, an intermediate measure might be "average response time." An output might be "fire loss in dollar replacement value limited to a given amount." An outcome might be "reduced community fire insurance rates."

Before objectives can be properly set, it is essential to clarify the outputs and outcomes expected. Evaluation approaches and criteria are discussed in some detail later in this chapter and in Chapter 5. The important point to note here is that they must be identified and understood before implementation begins if objectives are to be accomplished.

Goal setting

One school of thought that advocates "scientific" techniques argues that "rational" models derived from the disciplines of economics and engineering

Figure 10–2
Departmental mission
statement.

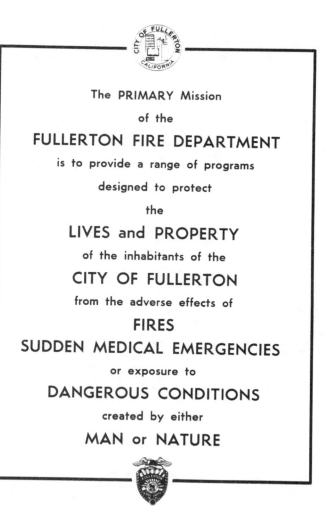

The PRIMARY Mission

of the

FULLERTON FIRE DEPARTMENT

is to provide a range of programs

designed to protect

the

LIVES and PROPERTY

of the inhabitants of the

CITY OF FULLERTON

from the adverse effects of

FIRES

SUDDEN MEDICAL EMERGENCIES

or exposure to

DANGEROUS CONDITIONS

created by either

MAN or NATURE

should be adapted for management programs and that emphasis should be on quantitative, empirical data and non-normative measures of alternatives. This school places great importance on goal setting not only to establish the desired end result but also to identify the stepping stones (objectives) by which to reach that end. This view usually is summarized as "If you don't know exactly where you are going, how will you know when you get there?"

Another school of thought argues that some factors are simply not quantifiable. Rather, goals and objectives should be set on the basis of an iterative process with emphasis on continuing feedback from the community and others involved. According to this school of thought, purely rational models cannot be effectively constructed for any but the simplest actions and are, therefore, not only of little value but may well be dysfunctional, as they create the false impression of being effective because they look complex and sophisticated.

In fact, elements from both schools of thought must be blended in the fire service if a manager is to be effective. An analysis without any quantified standards leaves the program manager not knowing what the results are to be measured against. But any cost-benefit analysis that does not constantly monitor informal inputs is probably without value.

Ideally, efficiency and effectiveness will result when the goals and objectives of the organization are the same as those of the individual. Early management texts for the fire service emphasized the importance of having the employee internalize the goals and objectives of the organization. Goals were therefore considered fixed, perfect, and immutable. The implications were clear. The employee had to conform to these stated goals, and the manager's role was to bring about this internalization by the employee.

Today's brand of goal setting is based in large measure on mutuality of self-interest. Grounded in MBO, goal setting is viewed as negotiations leading to a contract. The organization has goals and objectives that provide the general framework for this negotiation process. The individual employee has personal goals grounded in self-interest. The manager's role here is to communicate the organization's goals to the individual, help individuals articulate their own goals, and then align the goals of both so that the organization and individual will be able to engage in a contractual relationship.

The key to successful goal setting for the program manager is a clear and fundamental understanding of the organization's goals and a willingness to cooperate, coordinate, adjust, and adapt within the negotiation process.

Setting objectives

Objectives need to be stated in terms of expected behavior, a specific final result, dates for tracking accomplishments, and necessary resources and limits. For example, an objective related to an intermediate measure might be "To reduce average response time to fires from eight to seven minutes by the third quarter of this year, within present work force and budget levels." An output-oriented objective might be "To reduce residential fire loss by 10 percent during this budget year, within present work force and budget levels."

Typically, the local chief administrative officer and the fire chief share responsibility for formulating specific objectives, and the details are handled by those responsible for accomplishing them. Two-way communication is essential.

Developing action plans

The program manager develops action plans to determine how to achieve specific objectives. The following steps might be proposed to accomplish the objective of reducing response time: (1) identify causes of late arrivals, (2) select causes that are easiest to eliminate, (3) develop alternative solutions, (4) test alternatives, and (5) routinely implement workable actions.

In action planning, as this example shows, management has to make two initial determinations: (1) the sequence of actions required to achieve objectives, and (2) related time schedules. Tentative plans may have to be tested and revised prior to full-scale commitment to action. Operating-level managers must be directly involved in these determinations.

Scheduling

The tools and techniques used by project management since approximately 1950 have been developed through a multidisciplinary effort. The field of engineering has made the greatest contribution, the most visible of which is "networks," the mathematically supported graphic displays of event interdependencies. These networks provide a structure for project planning, scheduling, and controlling. The best examples of these were originally developed by the U.S. Navy to monitor the Polaris Project. They are known as PERT (program evaluation and review technique) and CPM (critical path method).[6]

The key element of PERT is planning. It is simple and straightforward. You think through the entire project, itemize every critical task necessary to accomplish the objective, think about how and when these tasks will be done and what implications one task may have for another. After thinking through the project, the manager is able to construct a network of relationships and inter-dependencies.

The mechanical part of PERT is a graphic display of the network of various tasks and their relationships and calculation of the interdependent values. The network, thus displayed, provides a "skeleton" of project management.

In a PERT diagram (see Figure 10–3), the circled letters represent events that must occur before a project can be completed. The arrows between the events represent the sequence of events and the relationships among them. Although arrow length is unimportant, for display purposes it helps to scale and proportion the overall chart. The number on the arrow represents units of time required for the activity between events.

In the example, time is noted in weeks. It takes two weeks to complete the activity between A and B, for example. The longest path through the network is the critical path (CP), and for this network it is A–B–D–E–F, for a total of 7 weeks. Since all other paths through the network take less time, the critical path is the one that determines the earliest date for project completion. The CPM method is particularly useful for charting major capital projects.

PERT and CPM network techniques apply to both large and small projects. The value increases, of course, with the size of the project; at the same time, the probability of efficiency and effectiveness with the intuitive approach decreases. For purposes of illustration, it may be appropriate to view the single-engine emergency response to an unknown condition as a small project, and the multijurisdictional major wildland incident that goes on for days or weeks as a large project.

No manager, regardless of skill and experience, could be expected to bring the large incident under control efficiently and effectively without formal planning and utilization of predetermined control mechanisms. A combination of just such mechanisms is the Integrated Emergency Management System (IEMS). Although there may be some doubt as to whether IEMS should be considered a "project," it clearly includes the elements of project management: setting goals and objectives, determining roles, scheduling, controlling, and feedback.

The value of PERT/CPM in scheduling is that a scarce resource can be allocated according to a timetable. More often than not, the critical scarce resource is personnel, but it can be tools, dollars, equipment, space to work, or many other things. Management can also use PERT/CPM for planning and controlling. The project manager remains a planner, literally, until the project is history. Each planning modification, of course, implies changes in scheduling. As the project proceeds, the planned, scheduled network is compared with actual performance, and any deviation can be flagged immediately.

Administrative procedures

Once action plans are made, it is necessary to allocate resources, establish essential administrative rules and procedures, and assign formal responsibility and authority. Accountability is thus fixed, since someone has been identified to make sure that steps are taken and objectives are accomplished. In results-

Figure 10–3 PERT diagram (units are in weeks).

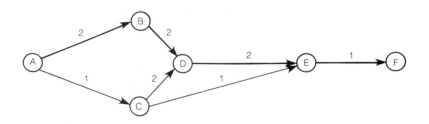

Program management tools Among the most important methods of program and policy implementation are PERT, CPM, and MBO. PERT involves mapping out the sequence of steps necessary to carry out a program or project. It also permits comparisons among different paths of action, each of which has a different "margin of safety" available in its projected resource requirements. The path with the smallest margin of extra resources is the *critical path*. Despite the sophistication of PERT and CPM, much of the calculation depends on human judgment, thus leaving its accuracy somewhat uncertain. MBO represents a fairly flexible approach to setting long-term and short-term goals while monitoring actual programmatic results and effectiveness. Among its potential benefits are helping administrators recognize conflicting objectives and deal with them, providing opportunities for employee participation in defining objectives, and providing feedback and measurement of organizational accomplishment.

Source: George J. Gordon, *Public Administration in America* (New York: St. Martin's Press, 1982), 474.

oriented management, these administrative procedures are designed to help accomplish results rather than to provide negative controls over people and their actions. In short, administrative procedures are expected to provide frameworks oriented toward results, not bureaucratic barriers to accomplishment.

Among the many failures that are possible at this stage, three are common. First, managers sometimes err in forcing a centralized "one best way" on operating levels, without allowing flexibility. Such rigidity may promote failure. Second, managers may require excessive or overly complex paperwork and documentation, even where flexibility is encouraged. Third, managers may violate the purposes of results-oriented management by tying it too closely to individual performance reviews and compensation. What is most needed is informed organizational leadership and management systems consistent with that. MBO is one of several such systems. But MBO does not serve well as a general management system if it is used primarily for individual performance appraisal and compensation determination, although it may be useful for those purposes after it is well established.

Implementation

The actual accomplishments of a project or program depend in large measure on implementation activities. In addition, means of accomplishment—the problems and processes of implementation—must be considered in the initial planning stages. In the end, getting the objectives accomplished—implementation—remains at the heart of management responsibility.

Four managerial activities contribute to getting objectives accomplished (see Figure 10–1):

1. Assign responsibilities, delegate authority, and allocate resources to individuals or teams.
2. Use functionally oriented management systems to coordinate organizational resources and performance.
3. Involve people in productive activity through shared performance targets and work processes and provide training and reinforcement of positive job-related behaviors.
4. Track productivity indicators and measure progress toward end results.

Communication is the essence of these four managerial functions. Taken together, they are designed to maintain departmentwide exchange of information.

Responsibilities, authority, resources

The program manager's most important activities are to assign responsibilities, delegate authority, and allocate resources. In practice, however, some contradictions underlie these functions. Subordinate managers and nonsupervisory personnel need clear job assignments and authority to carry them out; yet responsibilities often overlap, programmatic boundaries blur, and authority can be in flux. In a contradictory organizational environment, the manager attempts to create and maintain workable relationships. That requires an understanding of organizational structures and processes. It also requires active leadership to balance the requirements of stability and change.

In the assignment of responsibilities, two concepts are generally workable starting points:

1. Functional specialization and organizational grouping are the most commonly accepted bases for the assignment of responsibilities. For example, education programs are generally a matter for the fire prevention bureau.
2. Authority to act needs to be consistent with responsibilities for accomplishing the objectives of the program or project.

Continuity and stability are usually possible at operating levels because, in an ongoing organization, most functions can be assigned on the basis of past practice and experience. The chief does not need to make organizational changes when established routines work reasonably well and new functions readily fit existing patterns.

Often, however, old patterns do not fit new responsibilities or even some established ones. If fire prevention is a priority, for example, some of the functions necessary to accomplish it may lie outside the department—inspections may have to be undertaken by the building department, curriculum materials may have to be the responsibility of the school system, and apprehension of arson suspects may rest with the police. Because of such complexities, "matrix forms" of program management may sometimes work best. The structure of a project may be based on the skills and expertise needed for such activities both inside and outside the organization, irrespective of hierarchy. There are practical limits to such complexity, however, if desired outputs and outcomes are to be accomplished.

In short, two guidelines should be followed in assigning responsibility and delegating authority: (1) maximize functional expertise and (2) minimize organizational and administrative complexity. Once responsibility is assigned, the manager must see that the resources needed to perform the job are allocated: money, personnel, plant and equipment, and information.

Management systems

Management systems must be functionally oriented if they are to coordinate organizational resources and performance for implementation. Far more is required than merely managing by results.

First, the chief should see that intermediate productivity controls, related to functions, are established so that progress can be monitored and potential failures can be identified before they become crises. Second, the chief must keep an eye on the maintenance and development of the department as a whole, often using trade-offs and balancing priorities among different units. Otherwise, competition for resources among programs may become destructive to the department. In short, attention must be focused on management processes, as well as on final results.

Work rules and performance targets

Controls are also necessary at the service delivery level. Firefighters and other employees who actually perform services and supporting functions must be motivated to accept performance targets and work processes through the reinforcement of positive job-related behavior. Controls are particularly important in three areas of service delivery: work rules, performance targets, and work processes.

Work rules Explicit work rules that establish standards for behavior are generally necessary to meet both the legal and the technical requirements of the department. If they are not clearly established by managerial leadership, they will emerge through practice and can become binding in fact. Here are four points to keep in mind in developing work rules: (1) They need to be kept current; (2) there should not be too many; (3) they should be functional; and (4) whenever possible, they should be guides to behavior (which can be evaluated later), not limits on action.

Performance targets Performance targets are most useful when applied to work groups. When applied to individuals, they may indicate training needs, provide motivational and disciplinary feedback, and be an effective basis for reward systems. When applied to individuals, however, performance targets can lead to counterproductive behavior and place limits on managerial discretion.[7] Unions generally seek to control performance levels when quantified work standards are applied to individuals for compensation purposes, and workers then tend to work to the rules, becoming relatively rigid and conflict oriented.[8]

Work processes Work processes are generally defined largely by those who perform the work. Routine production work may be engineered more uniformly by management. In either case, three factors must be considered in establishing work processes: (1) government functions, (2) the workers and their skills and needs, and (3) the people affected by the activity. Here, too, managers should focus on work modules (such as an engine company) and work groups (such as the fire prevention bureau or the training division) rather than on discrete units of work and individual workers. In short, as with performance targets, work processes need to be considered from the perspective of functional organizational management, not individual employee control.

Tracking progress

Another important aspect of implementation for program managers and for the chief is tracking progress in terms of periodic productivity measures and progress toward end results. Automated information systems can help, but relatively simple paper and oral reporting systems may serve just as well. For example, a calendar marked with target dates may be adequate to track some timetables.

Tracking activities and results must be a sustained managerial activity, regular but not merely routine. Figure 10–4 shows examples of quarterly reports used for this purpose. Periodic reports are a classic monitoring device. Monitoring needs to be visible except when security or privacy rights are involved. Whenever possible, the information gained from tracking should be available to all concerned managers. Tracking can then serve as a positive organizational management mechanism rather than as a negative control.

Evaluation of results

Evaluation can be defined as the regular collection of data and analysis of information about the efficiency, economy, and effectiveness of departmental services and other activities. The purposes of evaluation are to help managers (and elected officials) improve the implementation of programs, allocate scarce resources, and choose among programs and levels of various activities.

Principal evaluation activities are

1. Internal management evaluation, which focuses on resource utilization, operating methods, and work load accomplishment
2. Performance measurement, focusing on outputs and outcomes
3. Policy and program evaluation, a general management assessment of implementation, results, and alternatives.

In practice, the distinctions among these kinds of evaluation are not so sharp, and they need not be separated except to ensure that each kind of evaluation is accomplished. Performance measurement and program evaluation are discussed here.

Performance measurement

Performance measurement, like internal management evaluation, is an ongoing, day-to-day management responsibility. Department records often contain the information needed to measure performance by creating ratios of output to input. Chapter 6 discusses the kinds of data that fire departments commonly collect: inspections (output) per staff day (input), or employees trained (output) per $1,000 spent (input). Sometimes, however, measures of unit cost may be needed, and those are expressed as ratios of input to output (for example, dollars per employee trained). Unit costs are especially useful in evaluating the cost implications of a proposed change in service level, and they are often used to justify budgets. Whichever ratio is used, reliable output and input data are needed.

Output indicators   Output indicators must meet several requirements. First, they should be comprehensive enough to cover all major work loads. Second, they should not mix apples and oranges. Third, they should be quantifiable and related to work load. That is, an output indicator should be a measure of something that is a direct result of an activity.

Input indicators   Three types of input indicator can be used. First, if the activity is labor-intensive, the only indicator may be labor cost—that is, employee hours and personnel dollars. Labor cost is the productivity measure used by the U.S. Bureau of Labor Statistics, and it is the easiest for most departments to use. The drawback of this simple measure is that it fails to account for capital investment or technological and managerial inputs, which are often the greatest contributors to improved productivity.

A second input indicator is all direct production costs—labor, capital equipment, and supplies. It is highly useful except when allocation of capital equipment costs is complicated.

A third input indicator is total costs, which include direct costs and indirect or overhead costs. Except in externally funded projects, measuring total cost may be an unnecessarily complicated procedure.

Efficiency comparisons   Efficiency analysis based on output and input information generally involves four types of comparisons: (1) over time, (2) among internal organizational units, (3) with external organizations, and (4) with a standard. Efficiency data are most commonly used to compare past and present ratios of output to input (or vice versa) or to compare similar organizational units, such as bureaus or projects within a department. Local activities cannot be compared with similar activities in other governments or in private business without data from other organizations, nor can they be compared with a standard unless a standard has been established. If records are available, historical standards provide the easiest reference points for measuring change over time. Engineered standards are the purest, but they can only be set by specially trained personnel. Estimated standards arrived at by persons knowledgeable about the work of the department may also be used.

Quality measures   In many local government activities, quality is measured by citizens' perceptions of service. (For example, citizens often complain of delay, inaccuracy, discourtesy, or general absence of helpfulness in governmental activities.) In the fire service, some objective measures of quality also are possible; response time is one example.

Figure 10–4 Quarterly reports used for tracking progress.

FLAGSTAFF FIRE DEPARTMENT

ONGOING PROGRAM

2nd & 3rd QTR _____ YEAR

DIVISION/SECTION Resource Management

PROGRAM Hose Inventory and Maintenance

GOAL To maintain an accurate hose inventory and condition status, and conduct semiannual hose maintenance. (Spring pressure testing and fall flushing)

OBJECTIVES THIS QUARTER	HOW WE DID THIS QUARTER
1. Test all hoses	1. 42,200 ft. tested; 600 man hours invested
2. Update computer account #'s	2. 100% complete
3. Recouple all Pacific Coast threads to National Standard threads	3. Hose coupler is inoperative-- steps taken to acquire new one, with hardware.
4. Build air powered hose testing manifold	4. 20% complete
5. Remove destroyed hose from computer	5. 100% complete

NEXT QUARTER OBJECTIVES:

1. Finish air powered hose testing manifold
2. Build hose rack for Station #3
3. Rewrite procedures for hose
4. Recouple damaged hoses
5. Acquire new hose coupler
6. Put "Damaged Hose Cards" in service

Program evaluation

The difference between ongoing performance measurement and in-depth program evaluation is largely a matter of focus and degree. The chief generally is responsible for in-depth program evaluation, whereas performance is measured by all the managers. Chapter 5 discusses program evaluation in detail.

Conclusion

The art of management is based on a body of knowledge that is the result of evolution rather than revolution. The tools and skills have been added slowly and have been tested through time and use against a matrix composed of mathematical, technological, and human factors. The new approaches that have

---

FLAGSTAFF FIRE DEPARTMENT

ONGOING PROGRAM

DIVISION/SECTION Emergency Medical Service   2nd & 3rd QTR _____ YEAR

PROGRAM _____ EMS Continuing Education

GOAL Provide direction and assistance to members involved in EMS to

maintain the proficiency level required by the state.

OBJECTIVES THIS QUARTER	HOW WE DID THIS QUARTER
1. Certify 2 members as EMT's	1. Completed
2. Recertify 5 members as EMT's	2. 4 completed, 1 in recertification class
3. Recertify 4 members as IEMT's	3. Completed
4. Verify all FFD personnel on DHS computer bank	4. Completed
5. Schedule 4 hours hospital client time per quarter for all ALS personnel	5. Procedure written

NEXT QUARTER OBJECTIVES:

1. Certify 3 members as EMT's

2. Recertify 3 members as EMT's

3. Add new members to DHS computer bank

4. Ensure basic life support C.E. is being provided on duty to all personnel (B.L.S. and A.L.S.)

emerged over the years—management science, management by objectives, strategic planning, quality circles, and so on—have had the effect of both building up and blending the existing body of management knowledge, thereby increasing and strengthening that understanding.

This book contains fundamental principles of fire service management drawn from an existing body of management knowledge. More particularly, its chapters explain the techniques and technologies that many managers will be using in the fire service for the next decade. These pertain to all areas of program management: organization, planning, evaluating fire protection, management information systems, and resource management.

Chapter 17 provides an especially valuable review for the program manager, particularly in the discussion of privatization and its impact on the program/ project team. The greying of the distinctions between the public and private sectors is manifested in the proliferation of private consultants specializing in managing government projects. Many fire departments are hiring nonuniformed administrative aides to supervise major programs and projects.

Fire departments have increasingly taken advantage of commercial and industrial innovation and progress during recent years and the expectation is that this trend of technology transfer will continue.

The successful program manager needs to understand the role of the computer in society and in the organization. Computerization offers a great opportunity to management in general and to program/project management in particular. The fire chief will surely benefit from the reduced cost of both computer hardware and software and from the pure volume of software that has become available since computers were adopted by business and industry.

Many management practices may be used by a responsible fire officer to enhance excellence of fire and other emergency services. Most of the management approaches presented in this chapter are generally applicable, but imagination and initiative are required to adapt them to the specific needs and environments of different situations. That is the exciting challenge of fire service management: searching out and applying tools and processes that facilitate improved organizational performance in the ever-changing environments of emergency services.

1   Ira Sharkansky, *Public Administration* (Chicago: Markham, 1970), 174.

2   William B. Eddy, *Public Organization Behavior and Development* (Cambridge, Mass.: Winthrop, 1981), 7–10.

3   George J. Gordon, *Public Administration in America* (New York: St. Martin's Press, 1982), 22–23.

4   Ibid., 35.

5   Thomas K. Connellan, *Management by Objectives in Local Government: A System of Organizational Leadership*, Management Information Service Reports, vol. 7, no. 24 (Washington, D.C.: International City Management Association, February 1975).

6   For an introduction to PERT/CPM, see Melvin Silverman, *The Technical Manager's Survival Book* (New York: McGraw-Hill, 1984).

7   See Robert F. Mager and Peter Pipe, *Analyzing Performance Problems; or, You Really Oughta Wanna* (Belmont, Calif.: Fearon, 1970).

8   Chester A. Newland, "Labor Relations," in *Productivity Improvement Handbook for State and Local Government*, ed. George J. Washnis (New York: John Wiley, 1980), 503–29.

11 Personnel management

Public personnel management is in a state of flux because of shifts in traditional employment relations. Work force demographics, attitudes, labor law, and employee expectations are changing. Employees are questioning authority, seeking meaningful work, participating in decisions affecting them, and looking for personal recognition. They place more value on leisure and personal affairs. Public organizations are striving to match the need for human resources with the new needs of the work force. Performance pay (merit pay), employee motivation, productivity bargaining, affirmative action, sex discrimination, participatory management, the Fair Labor Standards Act (FLSA), Occupational Health and Safety Administration (OSHA) regulations, drug abuse and drug testing, and the impact of technology are just a few of the personnel-related pressures confronting fire service managers. In response to these and other issues, existing personnel activities are changing as new techniques are being developed.

Fire service managers and supervisors and other local government officials need to be informed about changing personnel issues and techniques. They also need to be aware that volunteer as well as paid departments are subject to many legal provisions regulating personnel practices. Productivity improvement, increased job satisfaction, improved labor-management relations, and more effective service delivery all depend on how well managers utilize their human resources. Both traditional and new personnel management techniques can help managers utilize their personnel more effectively.

This chapter provides an overview of personnel management for the fire service: organizing for personnel management, position classification and job analysis, total compensation, human resource planning, equal employment opportunity and affirmative action, recruitment, selection and assignment, performance appraisal, and personnel development. Some other topics that are often treated as a part of personnel management—the work environment, motivation, and incentives—are covered under human resources management in Chapter 7.

Organizing for personnel management

The basic framework for organizing the overall local government personnel function is usually set forth in state statutes or local charters and ordinances. Personnel organizational structures usually include the independent civil service commission, the executive personnel system, or some combination of both. Civil service commissions may have only advisory powers, or they may be responsible for the direct administration of the personnel function. Common functions of civil service commissions include establishing qualification standards, approving classification standards, overseeing salary schedules, developing internal standards for promoting personnel, serving as an adjudicator for appeals, and approving personnel rules.

Reform efforts in personnel administration are directed at improving personnel systems in accordance with common merit principles. Basic elements of reform include the creation of centralized personnel management systems separated from quasi-judicial activities; decentralization of such personnel activities as recruitment, examinations, and position classification; development of objective job-related performance evaluation and merit pay systems; establishment of career executive programs; and creation of broad job classes.

The size and scope of the local government personnel program depend on the form of government, the number and diversity of functions performed, and the number of employees. Some local governments have personnel departments headed by full-time personnel professionals, whereas others assign personnel management to officials who have other responsibilities. Some fire departments that operate as independent governmental agencies have personnel functions supervised by a fire officer or a civilian administrative assistant.

In most medium-sized and large local governments, authority in the area of personnel management is divided between the fire chief and an independent central personnel department or agency. The traditional role of the central personnel department is to provide technical expertise in the management of personnel resources and to ensure the preservation of the merit system. Large personnel agencies employ a number of specialists in such areas as classification, testing, pay, training, and labor relations (in some instances labor relations is a separate function).

The central personnel department ensures that personnel practices are consistent and that municipal employees are not treated arbitrarily. In addition, it is supposed to eliminate duplication of personnel activities among departments. Even when principal responsibility for overall personnel decisions is centralized, fire officers should be prepared to make recommendations and offer assistance as appropriate to ensure sound personnel decisions affecting the department.

The effectiveness of the personnel system depends on its legal basis, staffing, financial resources, and political environment. Personnel resources available to fire service managers therefore vary among local governments. For this reason, fire officers should become familiar with their personnel system and its capabilities. This involves reading those sections of the law establishing the personnel system and the written policies, rules, and regulations that have been prepared for administration of the system. Fire officers must also be aware of state and federal law on labor relations, affirmative action, equal employment opportunity, and employee safety. Such information along with discussions with those responsible for personnel will acquaint fire service managers with the types of personnel services available to them and the constraints under which they must operate.

Human resource planning

Human resource planning, which is discussed in detail in Chapter 7, includes the development, maintenance, and utilization of the skills of actual and potential members of the fire department. It addresses the basic question of how many actual and potential employees ought to be selected, trained, and utilized. Human resource planners have a major responsibility to have the right number of qualified people available and deployed at the right time. Human resource planning has two parts. The first is staffing the organization, and the second is providing career development guidance to incumbent personnel.

To establish needs, the manager needs to be able to forecast employee attrition, estimate specific fire protection requirements, and predict the availability of qualified personnel. No simple model or rule of thumb exists to help the manager accomplish these tasks. And human resources needs differ considerably among local governments. Even in cities and counties of similar sizes and populations, the number of employees required to deliver appropriate fire services will differ. A few of the reasons for such variations are type of land area, density, degree of industrialization, amount of property to be protected, number and types of fire risks, level of risk elected officials are willing to live with, average number of working hours per week, arrangements for recall of off-duty personnel, type of personnel (paid vs. volunteer), and citizen expectations of the fire service.

Staffing has taken on new significance because of the substantial costs connected with fire service employees. Many local governments have been compelled to modernize their equipment, improve their methods, and streamline their operations in order to increase productivity. An important question that invariably arises is how many fire service personnel and what ratio of full-time paid personnel, reserves, and civilians are required to provide an adequate level of service.

Human resource decisions were significantly affected by changes in the applicability of the Fair Labor Standards Act (FLSA) in 1985. Until then, FLSA did not apply to employees of state and local governments. In February 1985 the Supreme Court ruled, in *Garcia* v. *San Antonio Metropolitan Transit Authority*, that state and local workers were to be included in the FLSA, and that employers must comply with minimum wage, overtime, compensatory time, and record-keeping requirements. Compliance initially threatened to disrupt schedules, eliminate certain traditional practices, and increase wage costs. In late 1985, however, a legislative solution emerged that retained basic coverage of public employees by FLSA, but made accommodations to decrease the cost burdens of complying with the statute's overtime requirement and clarified the status of volunteers.[1]

Position classification and job analysis

Position classification is the foundation of personnel systems. It serves as the basis for pay, selection, promotion, performance appraisal, and training. Position classification is a system of grouping similar positions under common job titles on the basis of the kind of work, the level of difficulty and responsibility, and the qualifications required. A position comprises a group of duties and responsibilities assigned to one employee, whereas a class is a group of

---

Civilianization The civilianization of traditional fire service positions has increased for several reasons, the primary one being economy.

Administrative procedures and needs have become so complex, and many staff support functions have become so specialized, that fire suppression personnel do not always have the skills necessary to manage new systems effectively.

Civilian employees in the fire service are frequently hired for clerical work, data management, emergency communications, vehicle maintenance and repair, code enforcement and public education, emergency medical services, emergency preparedness and planning, buildings and grounds maintenance, and certain training functions. Many fire service personnel prefer shift work to the five-day, eight-to-five week. Civilians may be attracted to the fire service for economic reasons. Public safety pensions, for example, can be considerably more attractive than civilian pensions.

On the down side, uniformed personnel may not accept civilians as "one of us," and civilians may resist the quasi-military management style of the fire service and may tend to change jobs at a more rapid rate than career-minded uniformed personnel. These differences can create conflict within the department.

positions that are similar in duties and responsibilities, require approximately the same qualifications in education and experience, can be filled through similar testing procedures, and can be assigned the same job title and salary. A class description is the specification of the duties, responsibilities, and qualifications of positions in the class. The classification plan includes all the classes and class titles that have been established, the specification of each class, and the procedures for maintaining the plan. Fire service managers should become acquainted with the position classification plan of the entire department and the job descriptions for positions in their areas of responsibility.

A position classification plan is based on a job analysis, which consists of gathering and evaluating facts about jobs, including the tasks involved, methods or tools used, services produced, qualifications needed to perform the job, and the level of performance required of the worker. Job analysis is a means of identifying the skills, behavior, knowledge, and abilities employees need to perform a job successfully. Direct observation, interviews, and questionnaires are employed in job analysis. Job analysis is time-consuming and expensive and requires skilled and experienced analysts. Nevertheless, it is the cornerstone of a reliable personnel structure and process.

Information gathered in a job analysis will help the fire service manager gain a clear understanding of what makes up a job, what an employee is responsible for, and what an employee needs to do in order to perform the job well. The analysis also provides the basis for establishing job-related tests for selection and promotion.

Fire officers have an important role to play in position classification. They and their employees may be involved in the mechanics of classification by completing questionnaires, participating in work audits, and serving on committees to review job factors and their importance. Strong management support is required to make the classification effort successful. Fire service managers should impress on their employees the importance of cooperating in classification studies. They should constantly review the integrity of the classification system by checking to see if their employees believe the system is equitable. Job descriptions should be periodically reviewed to determine whether they accurately define the physical and environmental characteristics of work performed. Classification plans also need to be reviewed periodically to ensure that they reflect the changing nature of work, the need for new skills and qualifications, changes in organizational structure, and changes in the scope and level of services provided.

Total compensation

With the increasing weight and cost assigned to deferred compensation, health insurance, retirement plans, and vacations, among other benefits, it is no longer possible to depict employee earnings accurately by looking only at wages and salaries. For this reason, the term *total compensation* often is used to indicate that pay and benefits make up one package. Equitable and competitive pay/ benefit plans are essential in ensuring a high level of performance and in attracting and retaining good employees. The concept of total compensation is increasingly common, and employee organizations can no longer claim that their wages are too low while ignoring a generous pension plan.

Pay plans

A pay plan lists all the position classes together with the pay rates or ranges assigned to each class. The orderly grouping of positions resulting from the position classification plan enables management to develop a systematic and equitable salary structure. A local government pay plan generally includes a series of different pay ranges of three to seven steps between minimum and maximum steps. The range structure should be realistic, with an adequate spread between minimum and maximum pay to differentiate between performance levels.

✗ Formal policies and procedures should exist to guide managers in implementing the pay plan. These policies will cover such matters as placement of newly appointed or promoted employees on the salary schedule and periodic salary adjustments. Other matters covered include appointment within the salary range, recognition for outstanding service, education-incentive pay, overtime, longevity, pay for part-time and temporary employees, and pay-rate adjustments for transfers, promotions, demotions, severance, and cost-of-living changes. Fire service managers should carefully review the pay plan and policies pertaining to its administration. They should also identify and document pay problems associated with employee recruitment and turnover.

✗ The purpose of merit pay is to link pay adjustments to superior individual performance. Performance appraisals provide the basis for merit increases. (Performance appraisal is discussed later in this chapter.) Merit pay should motivate employees, recognize and reward quality performance, and help retain employees. Linking pay to performance is difficult and emotional both for supervisors and for employees. A merit pay system is not suited to every organization. There must be strong commitment, proper system design, and adequate communication and training. Merit pay systems often fail because there are no criteria to measure performance, supervisors are reluctant to use the system, financial and top management support are inadequate, and the rewards are poor.

✗ A major pay issue is equal pay for work that has comparable value. Pay equity, or comparable worth, is based on the idea that men and women whose jobs make equivalent demands on them and call for comparable skills or are considered of comparable worth to the employer should receive equal pay. The concept of comparability is being studied in several states and cities to see if existing job classification systems involve sex discrimination. Job or evaluation studies examine established job classes and evaluate the skills and education required and the related salary ranges as they affect men and women. Some of the new evaluation studies use complex scoring systems based on mathematical formulas that assign worth points to components found in most jobs such as knowledge and skills, mental demands, accountability, and working conditions. Critics say comparable worth is an arbitrary and subjective standard. Proponents contend that the object of the studies is to provide a means of overcoming generations of discrimination in the way salaries are set.

Benefits — Biggest Headache

Employee benefits are part of compensation. Employee benefits are growing in number, dollar value, and complexity because of collective bargaining and the desire of employees to increase personal security. Benefit packages are changing to meet different needs, which vary with age, financial and family position, attitudes, and life style.[2] Trends in the 1980s have shown that there is considerable interest in alternative work schedules, more holidays, longer vacations, personal counseling and assistance, early retirement, payment of unused sick leave, and deferred compensation.

Deferred compensation is a valuable benefit because of the deferred income tax liability. Many local governments make it possible for employees to participate in deferred compensation plans such as those offered by the ICMA Retirement Corporation and the U.S. Conference of Mayors. These plans provide a way of sheltering income and planning for retirement. Although some tax-deferred accounts are subject to IRS restrictions, they are a benefit option that should be explored.

Health insurance programs are being expanded to include treatment of mental illness and drug dependency, maternity benefits for unwed mothers, and dental and vision plans.

Some jurisdictions have employee assistance programs to help employees with personal problems. These programs provide direct service or referral for substance abuse problems, psychological or marital counseling, physical fitness or weight loss counseling, financial planning, or other needs.

Flexible benefit plans are another innovation that offers choices of benefits. Several types of plans are available. Under a "cafeteria" plan, all employees may have minimum levels in each of several benefit areas in addition to a choice beyond the minimum coverage. A "buffet" plan provides employees with the option of retaining the same benefits they previously had or choosing lower benefits and obtaining credits that may be used to purchase other benefits. An alternative "diner's" plan creates sets of benefit packages that are offered to target groups of employees such as single employees and single parents.

Flexible benefit plans help to shift some of the benefit costs to the employee and serve as a method of introducing new benefits. Such plans also aid in improving employee relations and attracting and retaining personnel. Flexible benefit plans are likely to be complex and costly. They involve considerable administration and record keeping and generally require computers. Specialized counseling and training are necessary to explain the complex options and eligibility requirements. Unions are usually cool to such plans because they fear some employees will decline benefits that they need.

Fire service managers should keep up with new developments in fringe benefits and should closely monitor employee complaints and concerns relating to benefit administration. Current employee handbooks and annual benefit statements that show the type and value of the benefits earned by each employee are valuable employee relations tools.

Equal employment opportunity and affirmative action

So much of personnel management is affected by explicit affirmative action requirements that this subject deserves a separate discussion. Indeed, many fire personnel managers find nondiscriminatory hiring, assignment, discipline, and promotion procedures to be the most perplexing and frustrating of their administrative responsibilities. Most fire service organizations have developed active support for equal employment opportunity—as have firefighter unions. In many cases this active support has been genuine and persistent, although in a few instances it has taken the form of cosmetic slogans with very little substantive progress.

Equal employment opportunity refers to the right of all individuals to compete on an equal basis for a job without regard to race, color, religion, sex, national origin, or (since 1967) age. Affirmative action, as defined in the Code of Federal Regulations, refers to "all actions appropriate to overcome the effects of past or present practices, policies, or other barriers to equal employment opportunity."[3]

In the main, four federal laws have championed the affirmative action cause: Section 1981 of the Civil Rights Act of 1866; Section 1983 of Title 42 of the U.S. Code, based on the Civil Rights Act of 1871; the Fourteenth Amendment to the U.S. Constitution; and Title VII of the Civil Rights Act of 1964, as amended by the Equal Employment Opportunity Act of 1972.

Title VII has become the modern civil rights tool. Along with Constitutional guarantees, Title VII prohibits public employers from discriminating on the basis of race, color, religion, sex, or national origin in all employment practices (including hiring, promotion, firing, compensation, and various other terms and conditions of employment). In 1964 the U.S. Equal Employment Opportunity Commission (EEOC) was established to investigate violations of the Civil Rights Act of 1964. EEOC standards apply to public employers.

Equal employment laws, policies, and practices were originally promulgated to eradicate intentional and unethical acts of job discrimination. Nevertheless, Title VII recognized that much discrimination emanated from routine, frequently unbiased employment practices. Many practices have in fact unintentionally perpetuated discrimination against minorities and women, and these practices have been challenged in the courts. Both court decisions and employment laws have clearly stated that the status quo must change and that minorities and women will not only be employed but will be actively recruited and appropriately selected. Anything to the contrary will be permissible only upon clear evidence that a particular person is incapable of performing validated job-related tasks.

Conflicting signals

The initial thrust of the equal employment legislation was primarily to eliminate unfair and discriminatory job practices where minorities were concerned. As a reaction to this emphasis some members of the majority have charged "Reverse

---

Hiring procedures Rather than wait until it was forced to provide an objective hiring process including an affirmative action program, the Altamonte Springs (Florida) Fire Department put in place a process that would decrease the possibility of discrimination cases against the department. The working model was designed so that any individual could carry it out with minimum assistance.

Through nationwide research, the department located organizations that had had contact with the federal court system and were under court order to establish and maintain job-related, nondiscriminatory hiring processes. These hiring processes varied a great deal even though they were based on the same federal guidelines.

For the most part, the departments used an initial screening process to determine individual certifications and qualifications. Next came more extensive background checks and examination procedures. The examinations varied greatly depending on regulations set by the federal government.

A particular concern was how to hire the best applicants for the position and yet conform to equal employment op-

portunity and affirmative action guidelines. Existing written and practical exams were changed to include specific job-related items. The exams were then validated in-house and tested over two years of hiring before they were used as hire/no hire indicators. The exams were broken down into subject areas in order to determine each applicant's strengths and weaknesses, which were charted and eventually turned over to supervisors to identify training needs when the applicant was hired.

After completing the process, each applicant was placed on an eligibility list in order of predicted success as indicated by examination scores. This list was split into two categories—the first showing all candidates in order of predicted success and the second showing protected classes in order of predicted success. Every third person hired came from the second list if a person in a protected class did not fall into the top three of the first list.

This process has proven itself over time. Those hired have met the department's minimum standards, and the turnover rate for recruits has dropped dramatically.

266 Managing Fire Services

discrimination!'' The most outstanding illustration of this was the 1978 case *Regents of the University of California* v. *Bakke*, in which the plaintiff, a white male, gained admission to the university after challenging a program that allowed a less-qualified minority person to be admitted ahead of him. The case raised questions that are exceedingly complex: What is the meaning of equal opportunity? How much help should any person or race receive from the government to atone for past disadvantages? Can any citizen be held back so that others can catch up?

Further questions were raised by court decisions relating to layoffs as local governments began to feel economic pressures on their budgets. Impending layoffs force municipalities to ask the question, ''Who should be laid off—recently hired minority firefighters or more senior white firefighters?'' After contradictory lower court rulings, the U.S. Supreme Court tackled the issue in *Memphis Fire Fighters Local Union No. 1784* v. *Stotts* (1984) and *Wygant* v. *Jackson Board of Education* (1986). In *Stotts* the city had a ''last hired first fired'' rule. Minorities who had been hired under a consent decree would be most affected. The Supreme Court held that it is not unlawful for an employer to differentiate between employees based on a bona fide seniority system and held that a court could award competitive seniority *only* when the beneficiary of the award ''has actually been a victim of illegal discrimination.'' In *Wygant*, the Court struck down a voluntary affirmative action plan which provided for the layoff of more senior nonminority teachers prior to the layoff of less senior minority teachers in an effort to maintain a balanced minority student-teacher ratio. The Court stated that societal discrimination alone was not enough to justify a racial classification; there must be some showing of prior discrimination by the governmental unit involved before allowing limited use of racial classifications. These cases indicate that, at least as to layoffs and the removal of a specific person holding a specific job, it is important to show actual discrimination that affected the individuals seeking retention.

In *Johnson* v. *Transportation Agency, Santa Clara County, California, et al.* (1987), the U.S. Supreme Court ruled that the employer did not violate the prohibition against sex discrimination in Title VII by taking into account (among other factors) the sex of qualified competing applicants for promotion and promoting a woman over a man. Other cases involving affirmative action in the fire service are discussed in Chapter 9.

Women in the fire service

One of the most emotional equal opportunity issues to face the fire service has been whether or not women can perform fire suppression activities.[4] The major question has been whether women can perform as well as men on physical tests, since women in the United States often have less opportunity and encouragement than men to develop physical strength. When women apply for firefighter positions, their progress through the selection process will be watched closely by existing employees to make sure the standards are not lowered and that performance is ensured; by special interest groups to ensure that the system is fair; and by the news media looking for a story. Their performance appraisals likewise will be scrutinized for evidence of subjectivity.

Needless to say, the testing and appraisal processes must be fair and job-related. Women applicants, like all others, must be monitored carefully to ensure that testing, recording of results, and ranking of candidates can survive a challenge from either side of the issue. The sexism issue is fueled when poorly qualified women are hired or promoted.

After a woman is selected and serves a probationary period, the management of the fire department must continue to ensure that discrimination does not occur. Fire officers must assume the responsibility for the transition that takes place when women move into the fire station and must be sure that the company officers and firefighters are prepared to deal with this break with tradition.

The transition has both practical and psychological aspects. Practical questions surround accommodations—sleeping, bathing, and toilet facilities. With preparation, the department can find simple solutions:

1. A dress code in the bunk room (T-shirts and gym shorts or jump suits, for example)
2. Private rooms in new fire stations and partitions in older station bunk rooms
3. Toilet facility doors with locks or a reversible sign, with "men" on one side and "women" on the other
4. A "first come, first served" policy for showers.

The issue of personal privacy in the fire station has been a perennial problem for the fire service. Women have brought it to the surface again.

One psychological aspect of the transition involves harassment. It is traditional in the fire service that rookies will be a victim of some form of harassment, meaning they have to "prove themselves." Any department needs written rules prohibiting the kinds of horseplay and pranks that can cause physical injury. When women are included among rookie firefighters, sexual harassment becomes a real danger, and rules and policies must include it as well.

Discrimination in volunteer departments Several discrimination suits have been brought against volunteer fire departments, long thought immune from such actions. Typical of these was a Department of Justice suit charging the volunteer fire department in Cambridge, Maryland, with refusing to accept blacks and women as members.

The suit named the city, city commissioners, mayor, fire department, fire department president, and fire chief as defendants. It charged the officials with violating the public facilities section of the Civil Rights Act of 1964 and the Revenue Sharing Act of 1972 by allowing the fire department to use city facilities and acquiescing in the department's "intentional policy of discriminating on the basis of race and sex."

The suit said the fire department was organized in 1882 and all members had been white men until the Justice Department notified the city of the suit in September 1985. Since then, the fire department had formally changed its policy of excluding blacks and women and had accepted two blacks as members. However, the suit said, the fire department had refused to publicize its new nondiscrimination policy or take adequate steps to ensure that the policy would be carried out.

The suit said that no more than 75 of the department's 400-plus members were authorized to serve as firefighters. It said further that the fire department occupied most of the first and second floors of city hall and included recreation rooms for members and guests.

The suit added that membership applications were not available to the public and that applicants had to be sponsored by members. In instances where one black and one woman were sponsored, the applicants were rejected.

The suit asked the court to enjoin the defendants from denying blacks and women equal access to city facilities and from excluding blacks and women from participating in the firefighting and recreational activities of the department. The suit also asked the court to require defendants to devise a plan to eliminate the alleged discriminatory practices.

Source: Adapted from *International Fire Chief*, January 1986, 7-8.

Harassment lawsuits can be filed against individuals, the fire chief, and the jurisdiction. The chief should ensure that employees are well aware of what constitutes harassment. The EEOC defines sexual harassment as ''unwelcome sexual advances, requests for sexual favors, and other verbal and/or physical conduct of a sexual nature.'' Sexual harassment is illegal and supervisors must know that

1. An employer is responsible for the conduct of its employees with regard to sexual harassment when it knew or should have known about the acts.
2. An employer may be responsible for such nonemployees as salespeople or the public with respect to sexual harassment if the employer knew or should have known and failed to abate it.
3. The EEOC has said that employers should act to prevent sexual harassment by all available means. Communication, organizational policy, and training must be used to emphasize this issue. Enforcing sanctions and day-to-day adherence by all top management personnel are mandated.[5]

Failure to understand the seriousness of sexual harassment in the work place could cause costly employment and civil litigation. It is the victim's interpretation and not the intent of the harasser that makes points in court. As in fire protection, prevention must be the goal of management.

Another issue connected with the employment of women is that many fire personnel resist accepting women in the fire service, particularly in fire suppression. External problems may surface in the form of jealousy from other firefighters' wives, husbands, and boyfriends. The officers and personnel in the department may adopt a fatherly role and be overly protective, or they may subject female firefighters to subtle and overt pressures that eventually make employment impossible. The chief needs to take the lead in ensuring the fairness of departmental procedures vis-à-vis all employees and in establishing standards of behavior for all the personnel in the department.

Age discrimination and mandatory retirement

In 1983, in *EEOC* v. *Wyoming*, the U.S. Supreme Court found that state and local governments are bound by the Age Discrimination in Employment Act of 1967 (ADEA). The case involved a supervisor who was involuntarily retired at age fifty-five, as required by state statute. The Court held that the statute violated ADEA and that ADEA could legally be applied. The case had serious implications for fire departments with mandatory retirement ages.

In the Age Discrimination in Employment Amendments of 1986, Congress exempted firefighters and police officers from the ADEA until 1993, allowing a city or county to set maximum hiring and mandatory retirement ages. The legislation also required the Department of Labor and the EEOC to study whether tests can be used to establish the physical ability of a firefighter to work beyond a given age.

Test validation

At the heart of equal employment opportunity questions lies test validation. EEOC guidelines on employment selection procedures require that employees using a test of any kind be able to document that the test does in fact examine for job-related skills, knowledge, and abilities and job behavior (SKA/JB) These are established in the process of job analysis described earlier. Selection criteria, methods, and instruments have been challenged in the courts; in other words, the validity of the tests used in selecting, assigning, and promoting employees is under close scrutiny. The question of validity may be stated as follows: Does the test in reality measure what it was intended to measure? Associated with

Pregnancy and discrimination The Department of Justice established that pregnancy cannot be used as a basis for discrimination by obtaining a consent decree that required the Fallbrook (California) Fire Protection District to compensate six present and former employees who were denied payment for pregnancy-related expenses. The decree resolved an employment discrimination suit filed against the district in late 1985. The suit charged the district with violating the Civil Rights Act of 1964 and the Pregnancy Discrimination Act of 1978 by administering a group health insurance plan that discriminated against employees on the basis of sex. The Justice Department said the plan excluded from coverage certain pregnancy-related medical expenses.

Source: Adapted from *International Fire Chief*, July 1986, 8.

the concept of validity are the equally important subjects of job task analysis and cultural impartiality. The identification and preparation of relevant and valid tests requires considerable specialized skill, and fire service managers need to work with personnel specialists to locate appropriate testing devices.

Those responsible for testing have an obligation to strive for reliability, validity, objectivity, and job relatedness. Obviously, any culturally biased tests or test items must be excluded if a validation is to be technically sound and socially fair. A nonessential minimum height requirement is a case in point; if set too high, it would tend to adversely affect female, Hispanic, and Oriental applicants. Also, certain words and language usages may have different connotations for different groups. It should be borne in mind, as well, that physical testing should encompass only those activities and abilities that are required on the job. It is important to emphasize, however, that in the end, only the courts can validate a test.

Recommendations for increasing representativeness

Programs designed to make a fire agency more representative are best adapted to the particular characteristics of the department, the governmental jurisdiction, and the community it serves. The recommended steps that follow will be useless unless management makes a sincere and sustained effort to ensure that the agency is an equal opportunity employer. The following steps are recommended:

1. All job announcements should state that the agency is "an equal opportunity employer."
2. The affirmative action responsibility should be assigned to a particular individual of management rank and authority.
3. Specially trained recruitment task forces should be developed and put into operation.
4. Referral sources (e.g., colleges, military services, other government agencies, ethnic organizations) should be identified and continuous liaison with them should be maintained.
5. Full use of the media should be sought.
6. Walk-in recruitment counseling plus site visits to colleges and also to neighborhood centers should be provided by each fire station.
7. The time period from recruitment to selection should be kept to a minimum.
8. All tests should be validated and based on the SKA/JBs, as determined by periodic job analyses.
9. All fire personnel should participate in in-service training programs that develop their understanding of the need for representation and that elicit their involvement in the course of this.

Recruitment

The fundamental goal of recruitment is to attract qualified individuals to serve as firefighters. The term *qualified* denotes persons who possess, or can acquire through entry-level training, the required skills, knowledge, abilities, and job behaviors to perform the tasks/duties of a firefighter effectively. Sometimes recruitment is difficult—especially when the fire department is having trouble with its image, salaries and fringe benefits are low, few people have existing or potential qualifications, residency requirements are a constraining factor, or administrative procedures are complicated.

Fortunately, the fire service is thought to perform a highly important community activity—it protects life and property. Thus, any potential limitations on a successful recruitment program may be offset by the following incentives: a purposeful job, a stimulating set of responsibilities, a collegial working environment, reasonable pay and benefits, opportunities for career advancement, and job security. The point is to attempt to attract the *most qualified* candidates for the next phase of the hiring process—selection. The quality and effectiveness of the fire service, then, starts with recruitment.

Sources of candidates

Those responsible for recruiting may find potential applicants through a variety of sources, including current fire service employees and other employees, walk-ins and write-ins, educational institutions, employment services, and consultants and professional recruiters. Affirmative action efforts may include special recruitment techniques to make sure the department reaches potential minority and female candidates.

Attractive, imaginative, and current literature and application forms should be available at all times. This initial contact is important because it can either motivate an individual toward a career in the fire service or discourage that person from competing in the selection process. Clear and appealing brochures and other handouts should be readily available from the personnel office and from all fire stations and fire personnel, even when no jobs are currently open. (Such material can also help to augment fire/community relations.)

Interaction with candidates

There are a number of ways to make contact with potential firefighters, such as posted and mailed job vacancy announcements; advertising (newspapers, radio, and television); recruitment task force teams; visits, displays, and open houses; work-study programs and internships; cooperative recruiting efforts; and professional associations. These techniques are equally applicable to recruiting for entry-level, supervisory, and management personnel. Printed information should not only be attractive, but it should clearly specify minimum job requirements, the duties/tasks of a firefighter, the nature of the work environment, and other relevant employment conditions and expectations.

The management responsibility

The recruitment and selection of personnel for the fire service is a basic responsibility of management. This responsibility can no more be delegated than can management's responsibility to organize, plan, or budget. To do so is to abdicate a management function that is crucial to the proper operation of any organization.

Selection and assignment

Fire personnel selection means choosing human talent for the fire service in accordance with the tasks/duties of the job. As suggested earlier, the selection process actually begins with recruitment. The succeeding stages are examination, certification, and assignment (placement). Traditionally, emphasis falls on examination. The primary purpose of an examination or test is to identify those applicants who possess or are likely to possess the highest degree of SKA/JBs needed to fulfill the job requirements. (It should be remembered that tests throughout the recruitment sequence—both before and after the training or academy program—must be validated and must be planned in relation to the training skills taught.)

Testing

Fire agency personnel may undergo four types of tests: (1) entry-level (for new employees); (2) lateral entry (for experienced fire personnel acquired from other fire agencies—for the same position and for promotion); (3) promotional (open or closed to external competition); and (4) specialized assignment (e.g., fire prevention and arson). As noted before, test validation is essential.

Assessment centers are one instrument that is used to help identify candidates for selection, promotion, assignment, or development. Briefly, an assessment center is a carefully planned simulation of particular work conditions. Candidates are placed in job-related situations and asked to perform a series of tasks designed to evaluate their ability to perform the tasks necessary for success in the job. Assessment centers employ group and individual exercises, including written tests, interviews, role playing, leaderless group discussion, problem analysis, and in-basket, speech, and nonverbal exercises. Exercises, which can be designed to cover a one- to three-day period, simulate the job environment.

Executive mobility/lateral entry
Opportunities for executive mobility through lateral entry have increased for individuals wishing to advance their professional careers. Usually, the position for which outside candidates are recruited is that of fire chief, but it is not unusual to see positions open for managers and some certified firefighters and emergency medical technicians.

Lateral mobility can bring new ideas and better qualified personnel to the fire department. It provides an opportunity for individual advancement by young, competent personnel who may be limited by the size of their departments, the lack of promotional opportunities, or stagnated leadership. Employees who know that their departments will advertise on the outside rather than relying on seniority or patronage to fill vacancies may be motivated to upgrade their skills.

Among the disadvantages to lateral entry can be nontransferability or vesting requirements of local and state pensions. In addition, outsiders do not have a base from which to work and can inherit severe local problems, with hidden political implications and consequences on which they have not been briefed completely or accurately. Similarly, they may bring problems of their own.

The existence of lateral entry may tempt cities to advertise on the outside with the intention of hiring from within, and may tempt outside candidates to apply with no intention of accepting employment if hired.

With the significant changes occurring in local government, opportunities for lateral and upward movement within the fire service are almost certain to increase.

Skills often measured in an assessment center include writing skills, creativity, stress tolerance, motivation, interpersonal skills, verbal ability, sensitivity, flexibility, tenacity, initiative, independence, problem analysis, planning and organizing, judgment, decisiveness, use of delegation, management control, and risk taking. The accompanying sidebar describes the exercises in a typical assessment center.

The steps involved in setting up an assessment center are job analysis, selection and training of assessors, design of exercises, observation, feedback, evaluation, and validation. The success of the assessment center method depends in particular on the use of trained assessors and adequate feedback.

Assessment centers have both advantages and disadvantages. Although they show how candidates perform in job-related situations, they are costly and take time to to set up.[6] They are seldom used for positions at levels lower than middle management.

Performance appraisal

Once a firefighter is hired, he or she must be continually evaluated and given feedback about performance. Few personnel topics receive more attention than performance appraisal systems, which are usually the basis for decisions concerning pay, promotions, discipline, transfers, training, and employee development. Appraisals can help improve motivation and productivity and assist in career development.

There are several performance appraisal systems. The narrative or essay appraisal system consists of written statements prepared by supervisors, employees, peers, or some combination of these. The statements vary in length and content and identify strengths, weaknesses, and the potential for development. However, such systems lack the quantified information required for personnel decisions, tend to be unstructured, and depend on the appraiser's writing ability. Essay appraisals do offer an opportunity for a two-way exchange between supervisor and employee and are used in jobs requiring abstract knowledge and skills. They are most effective if related to performance standards.

Graphic rating scales or report card ratings are widely used. They consist of a set of statements or factors that call attention to certain traits such as quality of work, attitude toward job and others, initiative, cooperativeness, loyalty, dependability, appearance, and judgment. Adjectival or numeric scales are used to rate the employee according to such categories as unsatisfactory, below average, average, above average, and superior. Provision is usually made for written comments by the rater. These systems are easy to develop and use for a broad range of jobs and are more consistent than essay appraisals. Several pitfalls are associated with the graphic rating scale, however. One major weakness is that they are based on ambiguous terms. Supervisors tend to be lenient and allow judgments on one element to influence all others. Graphic rating systems are highly subjective and have little to offer in the way of feedback and training. Most supervisors resist commenting and tend to give "satisfactory" ratings. In some cases raters are instructed to force ratings into a normal or bell-shaped curve.

In a forced-choice system, the rater completes a form, choosing from a set of statements the one that best describes an employee. The statements of behavior represent poor to outstanding performance, but the terms in each set are matched so that they appear equally favorable or unfavorable to the rater. The rater does not know what the scoring weights are for each statement. Trained specialists construct the appraisal instrument. A third party interprets the results of scores and explains them to the rater, who in turn explains the results to the employee. It is difficult to provide constructive feedback, counseling, and advice on career development under this system because the ratings are interpreted by someone else. Forced-choice rating systems are expensive to use. Such a system is usually limited to middle- and lower-management positions.

Behaviorially anchored rating scales employ statements that are developed by job knowledge experts to describe incidents typical of successful job performance. Job analysis and statistical analysis are used to identify those kinds of behavior that distinguish effective from ineffective performance. Employees are rated on a numeric or adjectival scale to measure the frequency with which they engage in each kind of behavior. Examples of statements for a supervisor include "explains why the change is necessary," "discusses how the change will affect the employee," and "listens to the employee's concerns." Each supervisor would be rated on a scale such as

almost never   1   2   3   4   5   almost always.

Behaviorially anchored systems are costly and time-consuming to develop. Not all performance dimensions can be reduced to specific kinds of behavior, especially when the position involves the exercise of judgment and discretion.

Assessment center exercises

1. *Assigned role group discussion.* In this leaderless group discussion, participants acting as department heads of a hypothetical city must allocate revenue sharing money in the time allotted or make other judgments on the varying proposals offered. Each participant is assigned a role (point of view) to sell to other team members and is provided with a choice of projects to back and the opportunity to bargain and trade off projects for support.

2. *Nonassigned role group discussion.* This exercise is a cooperative, leaderless group discussion in which four short case studies dealing with problems facing the city are presented to the group of participants. The participants act as consultants who must make group recommendations on each of the problems. Assessors observe each participant's role in the group and the handling of the content of the discussion.

3. *In-basket exercise.* Problems that challenge middle and upper-level executives in local government are simulated in the in-basket exercise. These include relationships with department superiors, subordinates, peers, representatives from special interest groups, executive and legislative branches, the public, and the news media. Coming back from vacation, the participant must deal with memos, letters, policies, bills, etc., found in his or her in-basket.

After the in-basket has been completed, the participant fills out an extensive form concerning his or her handling of the various items.

4. *Speech exercise.* Each participant is given a written narrative description of a policy, event, situation, etc., and specific situational problems related to the narrative that require a response. The participant is required to make a formal oral presentation, based upon the background narrative description (before the city council, at a news conference, before an employee group, etc.).

5. *Analysis problem.* The analysis problem is an individual exercise. The participant is given a particular problem and a considerable amount of data about it. He or she must then analyze the problem and make a number of management recommendations. The exercise is designed to elicit behaviors related to various dimensions of managerial effectiveness. The primary area of behavior evaluated in this exercise is the ability to sift through data and find pertinent information to reach a logical and practical conclusion.

Source: Adapted from Debbie Cutchin and David Alonso, *Solving Personnel Problems through the Assessment Center*, Management Information Service Reports, vol. 13, no. 2 (Washington, D.C.: International City Management Association, February 1981), 8.

In a critical incident–based system, the supervisor and employee identify incidents critical to successful job performance. Raters match actual incidents against a predetermined critical incident scale to which numeric values can be assigned. The process is time-consuming and costly if technicians are used to identify critical incidents; furthermore, job analysis is essential to the development of the system. A less formalized approach has supervisors keeping records of actual incidents of positive and negative behavior. This information is used in discussing performance with employees, but has limited application with respect to future performance.

Another approach is to appraise performance by means of comparative rankings. Individuals in a given category are compared with others doing the same job. Under paired comparison, each employee is compared with every other employee. Every possible combination of everyone being rated is presented to the rater. An employee's relative position in the final ranking is determined by the number of times one individual is preferred over another. Weaknesses of this approach include the large number of ratings that must be made, possible bias toward specific employees, and difficulties in distinguishing degrees of difference between employees rated.

Alternation ranking consists of deciding who is most valuable and who is least valuable until a rank order list is established. Ranking systems are simple to use but can be easily manipulated and they score low in reliability and validity. Little insight is provided about the intervals between ranked individuals. Ranking techniques are useful for making decisions about employees where multiple judgments are used.

Each appraisal technique has strengths and weaknesses. Selection of a technique should be related to the desired objective and the unique characteristics of the organization. Some techniques are appropriate for making pay decisions, whereas others are better suited for career counseling, organization development, and motivation. Effective performance appraisal systems have most of the following characteristics:

1. The system is based on a job analysis.
2. The purpose of the system is clearly defined.
3. The system is based on job-related behavior and clearly defined performance standards.
4. Appraisals are conducted on an ongoing basis.
5. Appraisers receive extensive training in the use of appraisal techniques and in counseling employees.
6. Provision is made for appraisal discussion and positive feedback. Performance strengths and weaknesses are clearly spelled out along with a clear plan of action of what is needed to correct faults and improve performance.
7. There is a clear link between good performance and a reward system.

Whatever system is selected, it is imperative to document all appraisal efforts to ensure fairness to employees and to avoid inviting grievances.

Appraisal systems frequently produce disappointing and unsatisfactory results. Fire service managers therefore need to know not only about the different types of appraisal systems but also about the pitfalls associated with them. Obstacles to effective systems include the lack of a clear idea of what the system is supposed to do and failure to plan for ways to meet supervisory resistance. Many systems measure what employees are doing instead of results. Job requirements may not be defined in terms of desirable performance. In some cases, supervisors are not adequately trained and do not properly communicate with their employees. Employee performance may not be documented in clear behavioral and job-relevant terms.

Improved employee motivation and productivity depend on appraisal systems that provide for continuous feedback. Attention should be directed not only toward past performance but also toward future career development opportunities. Fire service managers must develop and establish performance standards as a basis for measuring progress toward results. They need to monitor the appraisal process closely to determine its workability. Even without an appraisal system, evaluation will still take place. Supervisors inevitably form judgments about their employees.

Personnel development

A personnel development program essentially integrates recruitment, selection, training and education, career planning, career counseling, performance appraisal, and other human resource considerations (health, safety, etc.) into a single system and unit. As a consequence, the traditional responsibilities of the department manager are expanded to encompass managing personnel development. In addition, the area of personnel might include a careful program of management development for top decisionmakers. This area is also of vital significance, especially in the fire service.

The goal of personnel development is not only to improve the performance of incumbent personnel, but also to create a pool of personnel qualified for the positions of advanced generalists, specialists, supervisors, managers, and executives. Personnel development integrates the concepts of career development and management development.

Many departments have developed and distributed "career development guides" to their employees. These documents provide all personnel with a single source of information on preparing for examinations, testing procedures, prerequisites, and methods of selection. They provide personnel with a sense of perspective on their own career choices and provide the organization with a framework for career counseling and succession planning. When prepared and used carefully, a career development guide can produce better candidates for promotion and simultaneously improve the fire protection agency as a whole.

A major component of personnel development, of course, is training, which is discussed in detail in Chapter 18. Another is internships in other local government departments or private-sector organizations. Internships or officer exchange programs create an opportunity for individuals to observe the management and operation of agencies facing problems similar to their own. Such an exchange of personnel is beneficial on any level, but perhaps most helpful to specialists and managers.

No one can develop judgment and learn how to make good decisions except by making decisions. One way to develop this ability is to serve on management committees and boards. Such an opportunity to examine incidents from management's viewpoint has been found to broaden a participant's perspective.

The benefit of rotating personnel for training and development is well known in private organizations and to a lesser extent in the public service. This helps new employees broaden their perspective of the entire fire service and agency and introduces them to the type of fire service work they particularly like.

One increasingly popular aspect of personnel development is health and fitness programs. More than most other local government jobs, firefighting makes physical demands on employees. In addition, firefighters are subject to injuries that can be prevented if physical strength and endurance are maintained. To ensure that personnel maintain the level of fitness required for their work and their overall health, many fire departments have instituted mandatory physical fitness programs designed to improve and maintain strength, cardiovascular endurance, and flexibility; to discourage smoking; and to promote weight control. A typical fitness program has the following components:

1. A written policy explaining the rationale, purpose, and scope of the program
2. Medical screening to ensure that each individual has the physical capacity to engage in an exercise regimen
3. Assessment of current weight, blood pressure, heart rate, and physical abilities (situps, pushups, jumps, handgrip, bench press, distance walk/run) and establishment of individual targets for each employee
4. An individual or group exercise program designed to help individuals reach and maintain their targets
5. Enforcement of minimal fitness levels through counseling and disciplinary procedures.

Health and fitness programs may be conducted in association with local hospitals or other health organizations. They also may provide written manuals that give employees additional health information and guidance on safe and effective exercise practices.

Conclusion

Fire department personnel managers are being confronted with decisions that must be made in the context of cost reduction, increased service demands, public unions, equal employment opportunity, changing case law, new management techniques and tools, political pressures, and intergovernmental relations. Although there is nothing new about these issues, the demands, constraints, and intricacies that affect decisions on these issues are changing. In the future, adaptation, innovation, and commitment will become three important bywords among fire chiefs and those responsible for fire department personnel management.

1   *FLSA: What It Means, What to Do* (Washington, D.C.: International City Management Association and National League of Cities, 1986) explains the provisions of the law, helps department heads plan work schedules, and provides checklists for monitoring compliance with FLSA.

2   Kenneth A. Kovach, ''New Directions in Fringe Benefits,'' *S.A.M. Advanced Management Journal* (Summer 1983): 63

3   Title 29 CFR 1608, 1979.

4   For an overview of data involving women in the fire service, see Michael S. Waters, ''The Recruitment and Retention of Women in the Career Fire Service,'' *International Fire Chief*, May, June, and July 1986.

5   Richel Raines, Trudy Sopp, and Yvonne Williams, ''Sex and Power in the Work Place,'' *Western City*, June 1983.

6   For a description of assessment centers in local government, see Debbie Cutchin and David Alonso, *Solving Employee Problems through the Assessment Center*, Management Information Service Reports, vol. 13, no. 2 (Washington, D.C.: International City Management Association, 1981).

Labor-management relations

Background and training in labor-management relations are becoming increasingly important for public-sector managers, including fire chiefs. The cost of personnel—salaries and benefits—is one of the largest single expenditures in the fire department budget, and the labor-management relations area is one place where the chief can play a significant role in minimizing labor costs and increasing efficiency. Furthermore, an explosion of legislation affecting labor relations in the fire service has caused drastic changes in practice and requires increased understanding and knowledge of labor relations law.

It is impossible to give definitive guidelines on labor relations for a "typical" fire chief. For one thing, each state has its own regulations governing public-sector labor relations. On the local level, fire departments vary greatly in size, use of volunteer versus paid firefighters, and other characteristics. Moreover, the personalities and the levels of assertiveness, training, and sophistication on both sides of the labor-management relationship have a significant effect on practice.

This chapter covers the aspects of labor-management relations that are of most importance to the chief—organizing efforts and procedures, scope of bargaining, negotiating the collective bargaining agreement, impasse resolution, typical contract clauses, grievance processing, and employee discipline. Throughout, it seeks to help the chief better understand the implications of court decisions, specific contract language, and various actions by employers and employees.

Background

Labor-management relations in the public sector have evolved from unionism and collective bargaining in the private sector. Legislation in the private sector began with the judicial protection of management's interests, then moved to statutory protection of unions' interests, and finally to a careful balancing of the interests of management, unions, and individual employees. The history was not lost when public-sector laws were drafted. Many adopted the language of these private-sector laws and, presumably, the balance these laws were designed to achieve.

Collective bargaining in the public sector

The trend toward granting collective bargaining rights to public employees began in 1951, when a court case (*Norwalk Teachers' Association* v. *Board of Education*)[1] signaled the end of a general denial of public-sector bargaining rights.[2] Eight years later, Wisconsin became the first state to enact a public-sector labor relations statute.[3] That measure covered only municipal employee relations, but Wisconsin later extended its statutory coverage to include state employees as well as police and fire employees.[4]

Today, public-sector bargaining is widely accepted, with nearly half of all full-time state and local government employees belonging to unions in 1980, six times the percentage organized in 1968.[5] Table 12–1 shows the percentage of employees who are unionized in selected state and local functions. Local fire protection has a 70.6 percent level of unionization, the highest on the list. Table 12–2 shows levels of unionization in several selected states.

States vary widely in their statutory recognition of public-sector bargaining. Twenty-five states and the District of Columbia had comprehensive collective bargaining statutes as of 1985 (see Table 12–3). Twenty-three of these states also engage in formal negotiations with state employees.[6] Fourteen states have statutes that partly govern collective bargaining with public employees. The remaining eleven states have no statute governing such bargaining.

The state statute determines the answers to three questions for the fire officer:

1. Am I legally obligated to negotiate with the representative of my employees?
2. If so, if we fail to reach an agreement, can my employees legally strike?
3. If strikes are not an option, is there another way that the union can force a result in bargaining that I may not agree with (such as binding arbitration)?

The answers to these questions will be primary factors in setting labor relations policy for the department.

Table 12–1
Percentage of full-time employees in selected state and local government functions who belong to an employee organization, October 1980.

Function	State and local government	State government	Local government
Total	48.8	40.5	51.9
For selected functions			
Education	55.4	29.6	61.3
Teachers	64.9	36.1	67.9
Other	38.1	26.4	44.4
Highways	45.0	52.9	37.6
Public welfare	41.8	41.2	42.4
Hospitals	40.0	49.8	29.4
Police protection	52.7	51.8	52.8
Local fire protection	70.6	00.0	70.6
Sanitation other than sewerage	40.2	00.0	40.2
All other functions	39.4	41.4	38.3

Source: U.S. Department of Commerce, Bureau of the Census, *Labor-Management Relations in State and Local Governments,* (Washington, D.C.: Government Printing Office, 1981), 7.

Table 12–2 Percentage of employees unionized in selected states.

State	Total number of employees	Percentage organized
California	1,005,005	61.8
New York	896,224	81.9
Texas	654,029	25.9
Pennsylvania	448,699	65.1
Illinois	472,778	48.0

Source: U.S. Department of Commerce, Bureau of the Census, *Labor-Management Relations in State and Local Governments* (Washington, D.C.: Government Printing Office, 1981).

Major differences from private sector

Public-sector labor legislation is different from the traditional private-sector model in several major ways.

First, the "scope of bargaining" in a jurisdiction has a profound impact on a department's labor relations policies. The subjects over which management is legally obligated to bargain determine whether it can unilaterally take action in a certain area, or whether it must first discuss this action with the chosen representative of its employees. Statutes with a broad scope of bargaining generally restrict management flexibility, while statutes with a limited scope of bargaining allow greater flexibility to carry out management goals.

The second significant difference between public- and private-sector labor relations is the treatment of impasses. In the private sector, if the employer and union are incapable of resolving their differences, they resort to the economic weapons of strikes, lockouts, and the replacement of workers. This economic struggle is viewed as counterproductive—a "failure" of the labor relations process. In the fire service, however, public safety is at stake. A firefighters' strike could cause loss of life and millions of dollars of property damage. Consequently, most states prohibit strikes in the fire service and offer some alternative impasse resolution mechanism such as binding arbitration or an advisory fact-finding procedure. The fire chief should become familiar with the particular impasse resolution procedures available to public safety employees in the state.

Table 12–3 Statutory recognition of public-sector bargaining.

Full coverage	Partial coverage	No coverage by state statute
Alaska	Alabama	Arizona
California	Georgia	Arkansas
Connecticut	Idaho	Colorado[b]
Delaware	Indiana	Louisiana
District of Columbia	Kentucky	Mississippi
Florida	Maine[a]	New Mexico
Hawaii	Maryland	North Carolina
Illinois	Nevada	South Carolina[b]
Iowa	North Dakota	Utah[b]
Kansas	Oklahoma	Virginia[b]
Massachusetts	Tennessee	West Virginia
Michigan	Texas	
Minnesota	Washington	
Missouri	Wyoming	
Montana		
Nebraska		
New Hampshire		
New Jersey		
New York		
Ohio		
Oregon		
Pennsylvania		
Rhode Island		
South Dakota		
Vermont		
Wisconsin		

Source: Calvin William Sharpe, *Introduction: The Ohio Public Sector Bargaining Law*, 35 Case W. Res. L. Rev. 345, 348 (1985).
Note: See 1 Pub. Employee Bargaining Rep. (CCH) 1661–2241 (¶600 for each state deals with coverage) (1978).
[a]Maine fails to mention county employees.
[b]Grievance procedure for public employees.

The third difference between the public and private sectors is a practical one. In the private sector, the "bottom line" in labor relations is the effect on the profitability of the enterprise, either in terms of efficiency of operation or total cost of labor services. In the public sector, however, the political dimension tends to predominate. If firefighters can mobilize public opinion in their favor on a particular labor relations issue, "cost" often becomes a secondary consideration.

Organizing efforts and procedures

Unionization is a legitimate concern for all fire chiefs, even in states without a public-sector bargaining statute. The International Association of Fire Fighters (IAFF), the Service Employees International Union (SEIU), the Teamsters, and many other labor organizations represent increasing numbers of public-sector employees, including firefighters.

The organizing process

Statutes that authorize public-sector collective bargaining usually specify procedures for determining the exclusive representative of certain employee groups. These procedures are designed to determine, through an election, whether an appropriate group of employees wants union representation and who that union representative will be. The union representative is then "certified" as the exclusive bargaining representative and is charged with the responsibility of negotiating for that employee group. "Exclusive" representative status is retained unless a rival union or a group of employees files a decertification petition, asking for the incumbent union's exclusive status to be terminated.

The typical procedure for determining exclusive representative status begins with the union approaching the employer and requesting voluntary recognition without an election after offering proof of majority status, usually in the form of signed union authorization cards. If the employer reviews those cards to determine whether a majority of the employees have indicated a desire to have the union represent them, the employer may be bound to recognize the union without the opportunity for an election. Therefore, if departmental employees are not currently represented and a union makes a demand for voluntary recognition, it is usually best to return the authorization cards or other proof without reviewing it, and the union should be directed to file a petition for election.

Once a petition for election is filed, the state agency will determine an "appropriate unit." Units incorporating all firefighters, excluding the chief, are common. Some units exclude other command officers or such classifications as fire mechanics and dispatchers. Finally, certain employees are entitled to statutory exclusion from the bargaining unit because they perform confidential labor relations duties, supervisory duties, or administrative duties.

After an appropriate unit is defined by the state agency, an election date is set. Both the union and the employer then have an opportunity to communicate their views on unionization to the employees. After this "campaign," the election is held and the state agency will certify the results of the election. If the majority of the votes are for "no union," the union may not call for another election for the next calendar year. If a majority elects a public sector union, the union is "certified," and the duty to bargain begins.

Campaigning

During the campaign, most state statutes prohibit improper pressure, such as increases in wages or other economic benefits, from either side. Moreover, supervisors must be careful not to violate employee rights to free choice during this election. These prohibitions include "surveillance" of union activities, making promises based on the outcome of the election ("if you vote no, you will get a big raise"), interrogation of employees about their preferences or union activities, and threats concerning the outcome of the election ("if the union is elected, layoffs will occur").

Management *is* permitted to communicate its thoughts and ideas about the unionization process and to predict the effects unionization may have on labor-management relations in the community. But this campaign must be conducted very carefully. If the employer wishes to conduct an aggressive anti-union campaign, a management consultant or labor attorney should be consulted at the earliest possible opportunity to decrease the possibility of legal challenges later.

A variety of "causes" may lead employees to seek unionization, including poor management, unequal treatment, employee dissatisfaction over economic or other benefits, or simply a desire to follow the example of the employees in a neighboring community who may be unionized. Each employment relationship is different, and the reasons for unionization in any particular community are unique.

Scope of bargaining

Once a union is certified, the department has a legal duty to bargain. Even in states without public-sector collective bargaining, the city or county may be presented with a list of demands by an informal employee association or group. This section defines those subjects over which public employers should be prepared to negotiate.

✓ *Negotiability*

The National Labor Relations Act (NLRA), which governs labor relations in the private sector, served as a model for many public bargaining statutes. The NLRA defines the phrase "to bargain collectively" as "the performance of the mutual obligation of the employer and the representative of the employee to meet at reasonable times and confer in good faith with respect to wages, hours, and other terms and conditions of employment." Subjects encompassed by the phrase "wages, hours, and other terms and conditions of employment" are said to be "negotiable" or "mandatory" subjects of bargaining.

The question of negotiability, or what is bargainable, can be grouped into three categories:

1. *Mandatory* subjects of bargaining, over which labor and management *must* bargain
2. *Permissive* subjects of bargaining, over which labor and management *may* bargain
3. *Illegal* or prohibited subjects of bargaining, over which labor and management *cannot* bargain.

An employer's duty to bargain is limited to mandatory bargaining subjects; in the case of permissive subjects, the employer may choose to bargain but is not required to do so. Even when the subjects of bargaining are mandatory, the duty to bargain does not compel either party to agree to any proposal, nor does it require either party to make concessions. The only requirement under the law is that each party must meet at reasonable times and confer in "good faith" over mandatory subjects of bargaining.

The definition of mandatory subjects of bargaining is not uniform but varies by state. Some states have closely tailored their negotiability provisions to those of the NLRA, while others have branched out on their own. The three most common approaches to negotiability are

1. The NLRA model, which is the broadest approach, fashioned after the negotiability analysis used in the private sector
2. The balancing test, which balances the legitimate interests of employees to bargain over the subject against the employer's interest in setting important public policies without union interference
3. The laundry list, which is a specific enumeration of negotiable (or non-negotiable) topics that appears in the state statute.

Familiarity with the approach used in the jurisdiction will help the fire service manager understand what topics must be discussed with the union.

Common topics of bargaining

A few topics of interest to all fire chiefs generate a fair amount of litigation. Here is a review of some of these important topics.

Minimum staffing Minimum staffing requirements are often sought by the union because they ensure a stable level of employment; management, on the other hand, avoids such requirements because they interfere with the chief's ability to control the departmental budget.

In a New Hampshire case,[7] the Public Employees' Labor Relations Board determined that the city did not violate its bargaining obligation by establishing new staffing levels without bargaining after the expiration of a contract providing for minimum staffing levels. The commission held that staffing levels are a permissive bargaining subject because of a statutory provision granting the chief exclusive rights to determine the department's organizational structure and number of personnel and to select personnel.

Likewise, the Wisconsin Employment Relations Commission held that a firefighter union's proposal concerning minimum staffing for fire trucks sent to official calls was permissive, where the relationship between the number of personnel assigned to each unit and safety was merely theoretical and thus was insufficient to overcome the relationship between service-level concerns and management prerogatives.[8] Other states have determined that the number of firefighters aboard each piece of firefighting apparatus responding to first alarms was not a mandatory bargaining subject. A major case to argue this issue was *City of Bangor* v. *Bangor Firefighters Association.*[9]

In contrast, when a connection between safety levels and minimum staffing can be established, minimum staffing is considered a mandatory bargaining subject. For instance, in an Oregon case the union presented evidence demonstrating that the assignment of fewer than three officers per firefighting company would result in increased frequency and severity of injuries. On the basis of the evidence, the court found that the union's proposal directly affected employee safety and was therefore a mandatory bargaining subject.[10] Work load and safety have been linked in other states as well.

Civilianization Management often wants to use civilian personnel because they have technical expertise or because they are less expensive. Unions, on the other hand, want to protect what has historically been the work of their members. Thus, if the chief wants civilian employees to perform work traditionally performed by firefighters, the question of whether these civilians should be included in the bargaining unit becomes important.

The inclusion of civilian personnel in firefighter bargaining units is generally covered in the appropriate public-sector labor statutes. In Connecticut, for example. a statute requires firefighting bargaining units to consist of those employees serving in either a "uniformed or investigatory" capacity. Since the job duties of civilian dispatchers included neither of those responsibilities, dispatchers were properly excluded from the bargaining unit, even though they had traditionally been included.[11]

In contrast, full-time and regular part-time dispatchers employed by a fire district in Illinois have been found to constitute an appropriate unit for bargaining purposes.[12] Although dispatchers did not belong to a formal union, they did meet the criteria for inclusion:

1. Employees met among themselves for purposes of negotiating with the employer.
2. Employees submitted written proposals, which the employer met with a counteroffer.
3. The organization was governed by bylaws.
4. Employees voted on acceptance of the employer's proposal.
5. The employer indicated it would participate in further negotiations once an audit was completed.
6. The employer deducted dues from dispatchers' wages for the employee organization.

Public safety officers   The negotiability of the decision to use public safety officers (personnel who perform both fire and police functions) has been examined in Wisconsin,[13] where the employment relations commission held that the city's decision to create a new public safety officer (PSO) position was a management prerogative, and thus a permissive bargaining subject; the city did not violate its duty to bargain by creating the position. The commission also held that, although the city was not required to bargain with the police union over its *decision* to create a PSO classification, if it selected employees for this position and established wages, incentive pay, and other terms and conditions of employment, it would be acting illegally unless it bargained with the union first. Therefore, *some* aspects of the PSO program concerned mandatory topics, and were bargainable. Accordingly, the commission found that the city was required to reinstate the status quo, and bargain with the union over mandatory aspects of the PSO classification.

Subcontracting   Subcontracting of some fire services can be a method of saving money, but it may be negotiable. The Washington public employment relations commission held that a city's refusal to bargain over its decision to subcontract firefighting duties after negotiations broke down was unlawful.[14] The commission found that the transfer of bargaining unit work to non-unit employees was a mandatory subject of bargaining.

In another case negotiability of the subcontracting decision was found to depend on past bargaining practices.[15] The board there held that the city did not violate its bargaining obligations by unilaterally assigning work on fire alarms to nonunion employees following the retirement of the two employees in charge of this work. Up to then the work had been performed by the superintendent and assistant superintendent of fire alarms, both of whom were included in the firefighting unit. Moreover, all alarm work had been shared by unit employees, police department employees, and private electrical contractors. Under such circumstances, the city's assignment of fire alarm work to nonunion employees was consistent with past practice, and as such, did not violate its bargaining duty.

A commission in Michigan, on the other hand, found that the city had violated its bargaining obligation by unilaterally subcontracting ambulance services previously performed by members of the firefighters' unit, while the city and union were actively engaged in contract negotiations. The commission found that, even though the contract with the ambulance service had slightly improved the method of financing the service, it did not change the fundamental method of providing service except to replace union employees with those of an outside contractor.

In each of these cases, the chief tried to take certain actions to improve service or reduce costs, and the unions opposed the action. Whether the decision was negotiable was a key issue in whether the chief was successful.

Union activities   Another question that may arise is whether employees in a bargaining unit may use paid work time to participate in such activities as negotiations, grievance processing, testimony at unfair labor practice hearings, or attendance at union international conventions or union-sponsored training sessions. The general rule is that such activities must be undertaken on non-working time, but the collective bargaining agreement could be construed as permitting the use of paid time for these activities, or, alternatively, to require the granting of unpaid leave time.

Negotiating the collective bargaining agreement

After determining which subjects the employer is obligated to discuss at the bargaining table, the next step is to determine how best to bargain. The process is usually regulated by a public-sector bargaining statute administered by a state agency. Although each state differs, there are several common approaches under the law.

The "good faith" requirement

In general, management has an obligation to bargain "in good faith"—to meet with the bargaining representative of the employees and to discuss mandatory subjects of bargaining, with the intention to reach an agreement if possible. If unions are dissatisfied with the results of negotiation, they may allege that the employer bargained in bad faith. Many states are authorized to judge cases in which the duty to bargain in good faith has been violated. For example, if the state agency determines that a strike was caused by the bad faith bargaining of the employer, the agency may have the authority to order reinstatement of striking workers.

Certain actions are typically found to violate the duty to bargain in good faith, whether or not that was the intent of the employer. These "per se" violations are considered serious, and should be avoided if possible.

1. *Unilateral changes in mandatory subjects of bargaining.* During negotiations, the employer must maintain the "status quo" and must make no changes in mandatory subjects of bargaining. Although there are several exceptions to this general rule, it is important to note that even *improvements* in mandatory subjects of bargaining constitute a per se violation. Unilaterally granting a wage increase or other new benefit, as well as taking these benefits away, could subject the employer to claims of bad faith bargaining.

2. *"Bypassing the representative."* Bargaining directly with individual employees without dealing with the bargaining representative is a per se violation. Sometimes the employer will try to subvert the legitimate interests of the union representative by meeting with assembled groups of employees and encouraging a voluntary settlement on the employer's terms, thus weakening the status of the union representative. But even sending letters to employees on the status of bargaining could be deemed a violation of this principle. Except in rare cases, communication to individual employees about bargaining is best left to the union.

3. *Failure to execute a written contract.* Once an agreement is reached, the employer is generally obligated to reduce that agreement to writing and sign it. Cases where this obligation is not met are rare. However, questions arise about the practicalities of "signing off" on a tentative agreement during bargaining. In so doing, the employer may be obligated to live up to that tentative agreement, even if no agreement is reached on the remaining issues. Therefore, the employer should make clear at the outset of negotiations that all tentative agreements are subject to agreement on all issues in dispute.

4. *Refusal to meet at reasonable times.* The bargaining process requires face-to-face contact between the negotiators and an opportunity to resolve the problems between them. Thus, requiring the union to bargain by mail or to submit proposals in writing without a face-to-face meeting is commonly prohibited.

5. *Insisting on discussion of nonmandatory subjects of bargaining.* Certain issues of interest to one party may constitute a permissive subject of bargaining. If either party insists that a permissive subject be resolved before other issues are even addressed, a per se violation of the duty to bargain in good faith may have occurred. For example, minimum staffing is considered to be a permissive subject of bargaining in many states. If the union refuses to continue negotiations unless the employer first agrees to provide certain minimum staffing guarantees, a per se violation may have occurred.

Most unfair labor practice charges stem from a claim that the employer was simply "going through the motions," and did not enter negotiations "in good faith." To avoid these charges, employers should document the interchanges during bargaining to show a neutral third party that they entered negotiations with the intent to reach an agreement if an agreement was possible. This should include all written proposals and a summary of each side's position on the issues, emphasizing any management concessions.

Creating this "paper trail" may be difficult. Court cases focus on the "totality" of the parties' conduct throughout negotiations as an indication of whether good faith was present, but this is a very subjective approach. They examine such factors as the scheduling and timing of negotiations and the length of the negotiation sessions. In one private-sector case, for example, the parties met thirty-seven times over a ten-month period. Some of the meetings occurred at close intervals and were very long, but the great majority were of short duration (about two hours) and the lags between were considerable. On the basis of the scheduling of these meetings, the NLRB found the employer was not bargaining in good faith. Finally, although state laws do not require an employer to make a concession on any specific issue, the failure of the employer to modify its position on any particular issue could be construed as evidence of "bad faith."

To avoid charges of bad faith bargaining, employers should keep in mind the following guidelines:

1. When developing initial proposals, make sure there is enough room for maneuver between the initial proposal and the "bottom line." This means that the employer can still depart from the initial proposal on a particular issue without compromising his or her ultimate goals in bargaining.
2. Avoid a "take-it-or-leave-it" approach or phrases such as "this is my last offer."
3. Always be available to meet. Although an employer's schedule, and that of the negotiating team, will dictate some limitations on this rule, indicating a willingness to meet on the union's terms could help avoid claims that the employer refused to meet a reasonable number of times.
4. Be sure someone takes careful notes on all bargaining sessions and other communications between the parties. These notes will form the foundation of the employer's argument that steps were taken to accommodate

the employees' interests, movement was made on each issue on the table, and that the employer intended to reach an agreement.

The final point to note about the duty to bargain in good faith concerns the definition of "impasse." When the parties legitimately reach their last offers, and neither party is willing to move any further on the issues remaining, impasse is reached and the employer is relieved of the duty to meet with the union. But whether a bargaining impasse exists is difficult to judge. Many public-sector decisions cite a private-sector case that sets forth the following test:

The bargaining history, the good faith of the parties in negotiations, the length of the negotiations, the importance of the issue or issues as to which there is disagreement, the contemporaneous understanding of the parties as to the state of negotiations, are all relevant factors to be considered in deciding whether an impasse in bargaining existed.[16]

Because this test is so ambiguous, it is risky to assume than an impasse exists. If the employer refuses to meet with the union because the parties have reached an impasse and the state later determines that no impasse existed, the employer will have violated its duty to bargain in good faith. When in doubt, the chief should be prepared to meet with the union even if it appears that an impasse may exist.

Some states have established a procedural mechanism to determine whether an impasse exists. If either party believes that an impasse exists, statutory mechanisms can be requested to verify that fact. These systems can be used to avoid the risk of guessing wrong on this important issue.

Practical aspects of collective bargaining

It is difficult to describe a typical or advisable bargaining strategy. The best approach to negotiations is the one that works for the bargaining team, consistent with the policies set by local elected leaders. Nonetheless, some common threads appear in most bargaining strategies.

As contract negotiations approach, the individuals in charge of those negotiations will begin communicating with elected leaders or the city or county manager to discuss overall policy and strategy in the bargaining process. This is an important first step. The political and personal interests of the various people on the employer's side of the table may not clearly indicate the employer's goals and strategies in the bargaining process. Thus, at the outset, the entire management team should be involved in formulating management's overall philosophy toward the bargaining process.

Selecting the negotiating team   Once the general bargaining goals and strategies are defined, a negotiating team is assembled and asked to prepare proposals. A good negotiating team usually relies on several important resource people, including the fire chief. He should be prepared to provide information on how the department is run and the potential effect of changes in contract language on day-to-day operations. The chief's contacts with chiefs in nearby municipalities will help determine how others handle particular problems. Finally, the chief will have daily personal contact with the individual members of the union's bargaining team, and may be able to provide valuable information on their attitudes toward specific topics.

The negotiating team should also include an expert in local government finances. During the later rounds of negotiations, when economic items are ordinarily discussed, the ability to calculate the costs of the various economic proposals, as well as the ability to analyze a fire department or city budget, is indispensable.

The employer should also consider using a professional negotiator. In many cases, the city or county has on staff a labor relations professional whose primary responsibility is to oversee negotiations with all local government employees. Alternatively, outside consultants, attorneys, and professional negotiators are readily available. The union's negotiating team will almost certainly include a professional negotiator, as well as a finance expert (from the *union's* point of view).

The negotiating team should not ordinarily include any individual who has the authority to make a final decision on the contract settlement. In the heat of negotiations, a decisionmaker might say or do things inconsistent with the overall bargaining goals and strategies of the negotiating team. Furthermore, the union's bargaining team will often focus its efforts on the decisionmaker, undercutting the authority of the rest of the negotiating team. Finally, the union's "decisionmaker" (namely, a ratification vote by the entire membership) is not at the bargaining table, and the employer should retain the same ability to recommend a settlement that must be accepted by others.

The absence of the decisionmaker does not relieve the team of its obligation to negotiate an acceptable contract. It is important to establish the limits of the bargaining team's authority at the earliest opportunity and to maintain frequent and consistent contact with the decisionmaker to reassess those limits.

Gathering information   Before proceeding to the bargaining table, the negotiating team should gather relevant information. Many sources, both in-house and external, will be invaluable in preparing proposals, as well as assessing negotiation goals. Useful information that can be gathered within the organization includes

1. Bargaining history for the fire union, including initial proposals, subsequent proposals, and final offers for each of the past several rounds of negotiations
2. Grievance history in the firefighters' bargaining unit, including a list of grievances that were lost, won, or settled
3. A survey of supervisors, asking what common operational problems they have faced during the term of the previous contract, what contract language is troublesome from their viewpoint, and what they believe are the union's goals and strategies in negotiations
4. Analysis of other bargaining units or unrepresented groups of employees within the city, including an assessment of their benefit package in comparison with that of the fire unit
5. A budgetary analysis of the city's overall financial health, as well as the history of the fire department budget.

Information from external sources is more varied. It includes evidence of national, state, and local economic conditions; cost-of-living information; local unemployment figures; census data; and budget data from other communities. The most important data will be the economic and noneconomic benefits enjoyed by firefighters in "comparable" municipalities. Analysis of "comparability" involves two steps. First, "comparable" jurisdictions must be defined. Second, the overall wage and benefit package enjoyed by firefighters in those communities must be carefully and critically assessed and compared with the local package.

As a practical matter, defining comparables is a job for an advocate. Both the employer and the union negotiator will use their versions of the comparables as a factual basis for their demands. The union negotiator will attempt to show that the department lags behind, while the city negotiator will attempt to show that local firefighters do well compared with those in similar jurisdictions. Thus, the selection of comparables is not entirely objective but depends upon the demands each side is making at the table. The chief's negotiator will select a list of comparable communities in which the overall economic and noneconomic benefit package is lower than in the local community. The union negotiator will do the opposite.

Nonetheless, in the selection of comparables, certain physical characteristics cannot be ignored. Size, region of the country, and type of community (suburban, rural) are commonly used to develop the "comparables." But a variety of other factors might be applicable in the right case. For example, Figure 12–1 shows one method of making a comparability determination. This exhibit, actually used in litigation, shows the variety of information that might legitimately be relied upon to support a position of comparability. To develop this exhibit, the employer gathered data in eight areas, and ranked each possible comparable.

The second task in the comparability analysis is to assess the overall wage and benefit package enjoyed by firefighters in those communities. Figure 12–2, also used in litigation, shows an analysis of every economic benefit enjoyed by firefighters in various jurisdictions. Hours actually worked are used to calculate an hourly figure that can be said to represent the overall hourly economic benefit package enjoyed by the firefighters in those communities.

The last step in comparability analysis is to examine recent contract settlements. Even if a community has a better economic package than other local communities, observers (such as arbitrators) are likely to assume that economic settlements should be roughly the same in percentage terms. Thus, if surrounding communities are awarding 5 percent wage increases, city or county negotiators should be prepared to follow that pattern.

Developing specific proposals   The final step in preparing for negotiations is to develop specific contract proposals. Of course, analyzing the data discussed above will help fire chiefs assess the possible economic and noneconomic goals they should be setting. Then, in light of the legal duty to bargain, they should

City	Changes in major GF revenue sources	Relative tax effort	Changes in population	Growth in housing units	Per capita income growth	Changes in state equalized valuation	Per capita income	Changes in unemployment	Raw score	Rank
1.	18	20	11	6	1	11	2	2	71.00	6[a]
2.	1	13	6	5	15	2	9	1	52.00	1
3.	7	12	5	2	16	12	1	4	59.00	3
4.	4	19	6	3	2	4	12	6	56.00	2
5.	8	22	1	1	4	15	7	10	69.00	4[a]
6.	5	8	10	9	3	13	15	8	71.00	6[a]
7.	2	7	2	14	20	1	18	12	76.00	8
8.	3	21	4	4	17	5	5	21	80.00	9[a]
9.	12	11	19	12	3	8	6	9	80.00	9[a]
10.	6	10	7	7	22	6	19	11	88.00	11[a]
11.	13	4	9	8	13	15	13	13	88.00	11[a]
12.	16	18	15	11	5	10	10	16	101.00	15[a]
13.	9	16	13	10	6	9	11	18	92.00	13
14.	14	17	19	17	7	14	4	5	97.00	14
15.	17	15	18	19	9	17	3	3	101.00	15[a]
16.	15	1	16	13	12	18	20	13	108.00	17
17.	11	6	22	22	11	20	3	20	115.00	18
18.	19	14	12	15	21	7	22	14	124.00	20
19.	21	2	14	18	18	19	17	13	122.00	19
20.	22	3	17	20	9	21	16	17	125.00	21
21.	10	9	8	16	8	3	8	7	69.00	4[a]
Target city	20	5	21	21	19	22	21	22	150.00	22

[a]Identical average.

Figure 12–1 Sample comparability analysis.

City	Base wage	Bonuses/allowances						Insurance					Pension contri-bution	Total compen-sation	Hours worked	Vaca-tion	Sick leave	Pers. days	Holi-days	Net hours worked	Hourly wage
		Lon-gevity	Food	Educa-tion	Shift premium	Holiday	Total	Health	Dental	Life	Optical	Total									
1.	25,224	600	503	350	0	1,098	2,551	2,976	168	92	0	3,236	6,054	37,065	2912	240	168	0	0	2504	14.80
2.	27,664	480	400	0	0	500	1,380	3,435	0	139	0	3,574	6,919	39,537	2912	276	144	0	0	2492	15.87
3.	26,739	638	688	0	737	376	2,439	3,384	521	126	0	4,031	13,281	46,490	2621	400	156	0	0	2065	22.51
4.	23,846	1,236	432	0	0	0	1,668	2,262	500	204	0	2,966	7,439	35,919	2912	168	288	0	0	2300	15.22
5.	25,448	200	360	200	0	664	1,424	2,640	204	180	0	3,024	4,782	34,678	2808	216	136	24	96	2432	14.26
6.	26,724	1,069	550	2,138	0	1,644	5,401	2,329	337	233	100	2,999	9,781	45,306	2912	288	288	48	0	2288	19.62
Target city	26,580	360	350	1,500	0	619	2,829	1,966	288	222	0	2,476	9,284	41,169	2912	288	192	0	0	2432	16.93
7.	28,665	1,426	525	500	0	1,653	4,104	2,321	237	54	30	2,642	8,835	44,246	2621	240	288	24	4	2065	21.43
8.	28,131	350	625	1,458	0	1,407	3,840	2,666	455	91	0	3,212	3,702	38,885	2808	264	216	0	0	2328	16.70
9.	24,793	480	546	480	0	605	1,931	3,387	406	86	0	3,879	4,071	34,854	2621	168	192	24	0	2237	15.50
10.	25,822	300	200	400	0	926	1,826	2,448	0	0	0	2,448	775	30,871	2621	216	144	0	0	2261	13.65
11.	25,916	560	425	0	0	605	2,111	1,738	230	105	0	2,073	7,085	36,664	2808	216	288	0	0	2280	16.08
12.	27,310	400	550	500	0	1,366	2,816	3,012	300	221	36	3,569	7,472	41,167	2912	264	216	24	0	2408	17.10
13.	29,474	1,179	400	0	0	1,312	2,891	2,833	570	180	0	3,583	6,862	42,810	2808	288	144	24	125	2227	19.22
14.	29,030	1,161	250	2,600	0	1,489	5,500	2,911	781	124	93	3,909	5,690	44,129	2808	224	0	48	4	2532	17.43
15.	29,142	1,000	410	0	0	1,681	3,091	2,900	450	130	40	3,520	7,519	46,269	2912	360	288	36	0	2228	20.77
16.	28,146	600	425	2,842	0	1,530	5,397	3,699	378	134	0	4,211	5,965	43,719	2912	312	288	0	0	2312	18.91

Figure 12–2 Sample comparison of wage-benefit packages.

put in sufficient additional proposals to enable them to "trade" at the bargaining table and thus engage in good faith negotiations.

Input for bargaining proposals should be obtained from frontline supervisors, the department's grievance-processing history, analysis of its collective bargaining agreement by a professional labor relations consultant, as well as from the elected leaders and administrative staff outside of the fire department. Initial proposals should coordinate the department's negotiation strategy with that used by other city or county departments, and should also take into account the ongoing negotiations in fire departments outside the community. Finally, when developing an initial set of proposals, err on the side of including too many proposals. They can always be dropped later.

Negotiations   The negotiations process can be divided into three relatively distinct phases. The early stages of negotiations include the initial meeting(s) and several followup meetings at which each party's goal is to receive and understand the other party's proposals, offer facts in support of their own proposals, and assess the other side's weaknesses. In this stage, each side will be attempting to guess which of the proposals are merely items the other side would like to have, which proposals are items the other side feels strongly about, and which proposals are part of the other side's "bottom line." Accurate conclusions on these points will be invaluable in trying to predict the other side's bargaining strategy.

In the second phase of negotiations, both parties begin to drop those proposals that they feel are not necessary for a complete package. Both parties also begin to reduce their initial demands on "bottom line" items. Finally, both parties may begin to "package" proposals. For example, the union may offer to drop three of its proposals *if* the city agrees to do the same. Throughout this phase, the issues become narrowed to a handful of important items both parties need to ensure ratification of a contract.

The final stage of negotiations is the time when both parties make hard choices. The discussion will be narrowed to a handful of important issues, usually including wages. If agreement cannot be reached at this stage, post-negotiation impasse resolution mechanisms come into play. In those states with a strike option, the union's political and economic strength must be assessed before the city or county "gives in" on any of the important economic items. Where binding arbitration is available in some form, both parties' strengths and weaknesses in that process must be assessed before any movement on the major economic items is contemplated. Finally, even where no binding arbitration or strike option is available, care must be taken to assess the union's local political muscle before making any final decisions that might precipitate an impasse.

Many practical suggestions for negotiations are covered in the books cited in the bibliography to this chapter, and the accompanying sidebar summarizes many of them.

In the final analysis, negotiation is a human process. The ability to understand, anticipate, and deal with the human problems that arise in the negotiations process is invaluable. The techniques, rules, and legal considerations discussed above are important components of the process, but understanding the human condition makes a negotiator, and the negotiations process, successful.

Impasse resolution

If negotiations are unsuccessful and the parties reach impasse, various options may be available. Strikes, legal or illegal, may occur. Binding arbitration may be available. Or, the employer may be able to implement its last offer without argument. This section explores those options.

The strike

Most American jurisdictions, including the federal government, have adopted laws establishing public-sector collective bargaining similar to that in the private sector. Unlike the private sector, however, only a few jurisdictions allow any sort of public-sector strike. Since 1912, federal government employees have been statutorily prohibited from participating in strikes against the federal government.[17] Strikes by state employees are illegal in all but ten states,[18] and strikes by government employees are illegal in many jurisdictions.

This analysis, of course, applies only to the public sector. Employees of private fire services may be permitted to strike even if their public-sector counterparts may not. Nevertheless, comments about union liability for damages caused in a strike, as well as the practical limits of the strike option that follow, apply with equal force to these employees.

The notion that public-sector strikes are incompatible with the proper functioning of government is based on two premises. The first premise is that government is sovereign. This premise argues that "the people" delegate sovereignty to the government, which must therefore employ people to carry on its vital tasks. Government employees are thus different from private-sector employees. They are agents of the government and serve the public welfare and not a private purpose. The second premise is that public-sector strikes distort the democratic process. This premise argues that if public-sector employees had the power to strike, they would possess a disproportionate share of power in the American political process.

Although courts have recognized that the First Amendment guarantees public employees the right of association and of free speech, they have consistently upheld prohibitions against public-sector strikes.[19] Courts have held that strikes are subject to reasonable regulation and that an absolute prohibition against public-sector strikes is constitutional.

Guidelines for negotiations

1. Enter into negotiations with concrete and positive objectives.

2. Anticipate the issues to be raised by the other side.

3. Spend adequate time selecting the bargaining team and preparing your position.

4. Designate only one spokesperson.

5. Learn as much as you can about the members of the other team.

6. Keep in touch with the city manager or mayor and the elected council and don't recommend anything unless you know they will agree to it.

7. Ask for important things early in the negotiations, but don't ask for anything that is already your prerogative.

8. Don't accept in the beginning any demand that you plan to refuse in the end.

9. Do not engage in piecemeal bargaining.

10. Identify your final offer and go no further; don't bluff.

11. Try to trade little things for big things.

12. Try to keep open all channels of communication, both with the other side and with your own side.

13. Do not become angry unintentionally.

14. Limit your discussions to problems, not personalities or principles.

15. Reduce all agreements to writing.

As of 1987, ten states had granted some of their public employees a limited right to strike. They were Alaska, California, Hawaii, Illinois, Minnesota, Montana, Oregon, Pennsylvania, Vermont, and Wisconsin. Typically, the statutes in these states permit public-sector strikes only if such strikes do not endanger the public health, safety, or welfare—a rationale commonly used to limit firefighters' right to strike. The statutes generally prohibit strikes by employees in police and fire protection services, correctional facilities, and health care institutions. In some instances, statutes provide binding arbitration as a trade-off for prohibiting the right to strike.

Practical limits of the strike option　The effectiveness of the strike option is a practical matter, not just a legal one. For example, even in states outlawing public-sector strikes, public-sector unions can strike illegally and at the same time exercise economic and political control over the outcome of negotiations. During a firefighters' strike, even an illegal one, citizens may feel that their safety, and the safety of their homes, is jeopardized and may insist on an end to the strike at any cost. At the same time, the unavailability of a trained work force to replace the striking firefighters, and the lack of quick access to the courts, may limit the city's ability to end the strike except on the union's terms.

On the other hand, even in states where public-sector employee strikes are authorized, those strikes may not affect the outcome of negotiations. If a municipality is able to enlist the support of surrounding communities through mutual-aid agreements, or hire adequately trained replacement workers to assist with firefighting, or use state guard troops, a firefighters' strike may not have the intended effect. Moreover, if the elected leaders of the community support the employer's position at the bargaining table, a legal strike may not affect the outcome of negotiations. Therefore, it is not enough to know whether a firefighters' strike is "legal." Other factors also determine whether such a strike would be effective in controlling the negotiations process.

Union liability　In the event of a strike, it is inevitable there will be losses to the employer, to nonunion members, and possibly to third parties. In some situations, these losses can be compensated through a lawsuit against the union.

According to private-sector laws, a union cannot be held liable for illegal acts (such as violence) that occurred during a legal strike, unless the injured parties can establish that the union gave express or implied authorization for the conduct, or that the union ratified the conduct after it occurred. If the violent conduct was instigated by an authorized agent of the union, then the union may be held liable for that activity. Thus, acts of violence by individual union members while on strike are generally not considered to cause union liability unless a union official commits the act.

"Clear proof" is required to establish that an activity was "authorized" by the union. This requirement may be met without express authorization by the union *if* it can be proven that the union, by its conduct, supported the strike. For example, in the case of violence by a picketer, the union's overt aid to the individual who performed the acts of violence against the employer may result in union liability.

In the case of public-sector strikes, few state statutes expressly provide for damage actions by public-sector employers. Nevertheless, public employers and third parties have successfully sued for recovery of damages against public-sector unions.

Finally, an employer may be entitled to damages for a union's violation of a no-strike clause in the collective bargaining agreement. The compensatory damages recoverable in such a lawsuit are the actual loss sustained by the employer as a result of the breach. Obviously, it is difficult to prove exactly what losses are attributable to the union's actions.

Possible management responses Public-sector strikes are a reality, and public employers must respond to them. The best preparation is the strike contingency plan. The existence and implementation of a complete, realistic strike contingency plan can mean the difference between success and failure for the employer in the event of a strike.

Every public jurisdiction should prepare a plan covering the following topics:

1. Providing fire services
   a) What services to provide
   b) Sources of manpower
   c) Training and equipment
2. Beginning appropriate legal proceedings
3. Political considerations
   a) Communications with the press
   b) Communications with the public
   c) Communications with the union
   d) Communications with other city or county employees
4. Effects on other operations
   a) Safety of employees who choose to cross a picket line
   b) Protection against vandalism, damage, and sabotage
   c) Ensuring safe, uninterrupted delivery of services
5. Establishing a strike committee to spearhead all local government efforts.

A complete strike planning manual should contain a section on the legal remedies available to a public employer in the event of an illegal strike. In some cases the employer may be able to get an injunction against illegal public employee strikes or may be able to sue for damages caused by such a strike. Relief may be available if the striking union pickets the residences and/or places of business of elected officials. The legal ramifications and possible responses to all these activities should be considered *before* they happen.

Binding arbitration

Many states have statutes that provide for ''binding interest arbitration'' as an impasse resolution mechanism, often as an alternative to the strike option. Binding arbitration takes many forms and may differ from state to state on several important points:

1. The employee groups covered
2. Pre-arbitration impasse procedures
3. Selection of arbitrators
4. Final offer submission deadline
5. Method of selection between the final offers of the parties.

Alternative approaches Three examples are presented here to show the major differences between states. In Wisconsin, if either party believes impasse has been reached, the Wisconsin Employment Relations Commission (WERC) is notified. An investigator from the WERC staff attempts to mediate the dispute, and if unsuccessful, certifies that impasse has been reached. The investigator then asks both parties to file a final offer, which cannot be changed thereafter. A list of arbitrators is sent to both parties, and both parties alternate in striking names from the list until one name remains, who is designated as the arbitrator. That individual sets a hearing date, and has the power to mediate if requested by both parties. If mediation is unsuccessful, a hearing is held. Both parties present testimony and evidence in support of their final offers. The arbitrator then selects one party's final offer on all the issues addressed therein, pronouncing one a clear ''winner'' and the other a ''loser.''

Michigan's process is slightly different. There, if either party feels impasse has been reached, the Michigan Employment Relations Commission (MERC) is notified. MERC certifies that an impasse exists (without mediation) and forwards a list of arbitrators. Each party strikes names from the list until one person remains. Each party then appoints an arbitrator of its own to form a three-person arbitration panel. That panel sets a date for hearing. Both parties submit "preliminary" final offers, which form the basis for the evidence at the hearing. *After* the hearing, both parties submit "final" final offers, which may not be changed, and file briefs. The arbitration panel can choose either party's final offer on *each* of the economic items in dispute, and may choose either party's final offer or mandate some other resolution of the noneconomic items in dispute. Here, there may not be a clear "winner," since both parties could "win" on several issues.

Finally, the Iowa system begins when either party notifies the state agency that they believe an impasse exists. The state agency, the Iowa Public Employment Relations Board (PERB), investigates to determine whether the parties are at impasse, and the investigator attempts to mediate the dispute. If unsuccessful, a list of factfinders is sent to the parties, whereupon both parties alternate in striking names from the list until one remains. The factfinder then sets a date for the hearing, and both parties submit evidence on the issues in dispute as defined by the parties' "preliminary" offers. The factfinder does not have the authority to issue a binding resolution of the dispute, but may issue a factfinding "recommendation." If either party chooses to reject the factfinder's recommendation, a list of arbitrators is sent to the parties. After both parties strike names from this list, the remaining name is appointed arbitrator, who will attempt to bring about a binding resolution of the impasse. The parties must submit final offers before the arbitration hearing, and the arbitrator may choose the employer's final offer, the union's final offer, or the factfinder's recommended resolution on each of the issues in dispute.

The most significant distinguishing characteristic of binding arbitration is that the parties must submit an unchangeable final offer, and that the decisionmaker is limited to choosing between the parties' final offers, whether on a total package basis or issue by issue. In Wisconsin, the final offers must be submitted very early in the process, and the arbitrator is restricted to a total package final offer. In Michigan, final offers are not submitted until very late in the process, and the arbitrator enjoys considerable flexibility in choosing either party's final offer on each issue in dispute.

Factors considered by arbitrators   In each state, the arbitrator will be guided by statutory factors in making a decision. These statutory factors form the basis for the evidence to be developed in anticipation of the arbitration hearing. The list of factors used is relatively universal, and is exemplified by the list of factors contained in the Michigan statute:

1. The lawful authority of the employer
2. Stipulations of the parties
3. The interests and welfare of the public and the financial ability of the unit of government to provide for them
4. Comparison of the wages, hours, and conditions of employment of those involved in the arbitration proceeding with the wages, hours, and conditions of employment of other employees performing similar services and with other employees generally:
    a) In public employment in comparable communities
    b) In private employment in comparable communities
5. The average consumer prices for goods and services, commonly known as the cost of living

6. The overall compensation currently received by the employees, including direct wage compensation, vacations, holidays and other excused time, insurance and pensions, medical and hospitalization benefits, the continuity and stability of employment, and all other benefits received
7. Changes in any of the foregoing circumstances while the arbitration proceedings are pending
8. Other factors that are normally or traditionally taken into consideration in the determination of wages, hours, and conditions of employment through voluntary collective bargaining, mediation, factfinding, arbitration, or otherwise between the parties, in the public service or in private employment.

Of these factors, "comparability" is often given the greatest weight. Thus, each party's case in arbitration centers around analysis of the wage and benefit package received in comparable communities by similar employees. As noted earlier, parties generally disagree over which communities are considered "comparable," as well as the method for analyzing the value of the wage and benefit packages.

Of the other statutory factors, perhaps the most hotly contested is the so-called ability-to-pay argument. This argument, raised by the employer, argues that a particular wage settlement demanded by the union is unacceptable because the city or county does not have adequate funds to meet that demand.

This argument is frequently misused. It is generally not sufficient for an employer to focus on the fire department budget to support its claim of inability to pay. An astute arbitrator will look beyond the departmental budget to determine whether adequate funds truly do exist to meet the union's demands. First, the employer should be prepared to show declining revenues from sources at all levels—federal, state, and local. Second, the employer should be prepared to demonstrate that it has made substantial efforts to eliminate all unnecessary expenditures from the budget. This aspect of the ability-to-pay argument causes the most difficulty, since the arbitrator will be making independent judgments about budget cuts decided upon in the political process. Having an "outsider" tell the city or county that it should cut one program in order to fund wage increases for the fire department often leads to cries of "loss of local control," and "carpetbagging." In addition, the employer should be prepared to show that the burden of wage freezes or low wage increases has been shouldered by all employee groups, including the management staff. It is difficult to make an ability-to-pay argument when high ranking management employees have received substantial wage increases. Finally, other facts should be developed to show that efforts were made to increase revenues wherever possible and that the taxing authority of the city has been used to its fullest.

Arbitrators' views of the ability-to-pay argument vary. Some view this as a "black-and-white" issue, believing that if the employer has enough money to pay the wage demands, the impact on other community services is irrelevant. Others weigh the effect of the union's wage demand to determine whether other important and necessary services will be adversely affected. Some arbitrators, even if they conclude that the city or county is unable to pay, weigh the other factors more heavily. And finally, some arbitrators avoid awarding a wage freeze except in the most serious circumstances. But in general, arbitrators view the employer's inability to pay as rare and will scrutinize the budget very carefully to ensure that the argument is a legitimate one.

The local economy is often cited as a basis for reduced wage increases by the employer, especially where public sector wage settlements are higher than local private sector settlements. Even though the statutes generally require the arbitrator to consider the local private-sector economy, comparisons are usually made in the following order:

1. Comparability with firefighters in comparable communities
2. Comparability with other public-sector employees who are subject to binding arbitration (usually police officers) in comparable communities
3. Comparability with other internal city or county employee groups
4. Comparability with local private-sector groups.

Employers should keep this hierarchy in mind when preparing their strategy for binding arbitration.

"Cost of living" also has engendered substantial argument over the years. Indexes of the cost of living, usually the Consumer Price Index, can present varying pictures of local and national economic health. Moreover, when the Consumer Price Index is high, unions tend to emphasize it. The opposite is true when the Consumer Price Index is low. In either event, arbitrators usually rely upon comparables to a greater extent than cost of living.

The final important factor used in binding arbitration proceedings is the role of the status quo. Most arbitrators, in one fashion or another, adhere to the view that the party demanding a change from the parties' historic practice bears a "heavy burden" to justify a need for the change. Thus, if the union is proposing a modification to contract language or a new economic benefit, it will generally be required to show substantial support for the change among the comparables, as well as some unique local reasons why change is necessary. Similarly, if the employer wishes to insert a new contract clause or eliminate a benefit, it carries the same heavy burden. On the issue of wages, the comparability pattern will usually establish the norm, with both parties required to show some justification for deviation from that pattern. Of course, any definition of the "comparable pattern" is subject to argument.

Conclusion   Statutory binding arbitration procedures have been criticized by management advocates for many years. Loss of local control, insensitivity to local issues, and escalating benefit packages have been blamed on binding arbitration laws. Whether or not these are legitimate criticisms, state legislatures apparently believe these alleged ills are more than offset by the "labor peace" that results from avoiding public-sector strikes. For this reason, public-sector bargaining statutes, despite these criticisms, are very likely here to stay.

Typical contract clauses

Once the collective bargaining process is successfully concluded and a new agreement is signed, the task of administering this agreement falls to the chief. This task is very complex and sometimes requires specialized interpretation skills. In analyzing and administering a contract, the first step is to understand what it says. There are several key clauses in almost every collective bargaining agreement that must be analyzed carefully to get a true picture of the chief's rights and obligations when taking action in the department. Beyond these clauses, there are some commonly accepted "rules" of interpretation that can be applied to contract language. The following sections discuss various clauses typically contained in collective bargaining agreements and the frequency with which favorable and unfavorable language is found in collective bargaining agreements nationwide (based on a survey of firefighter contracts).

Management rights clause

Every day fire chiefs make decisions that affect fire department employees but are not specifically covered by the collective bargaining agreement. A key to whether the chief's contemplated action will be upheld against union challenge may be found in the wording of a management rights clause. Although the language of the contract is clearly important to the chief, negotiations are often more concerned with economic issues than with the wording of such items as the management rights clause. The result may be an acceptable economic package for the local government, but it may also mean a corresponding reduction in the power of the fire chief. This section gives fire chiefs a framework for evaluating a management rights clause that can be used to assess their ability to function as effective decisionmakers.

The doctrine of "residual rights" is key to understanding management rights clauses. It holds that management retains all rights except those specifically given to the union through the collective bargaining process. Thus, some advocates argue that no management rights clause is necessary or that a very general clause is all that is required. Others feel that a more detailed and specific clause is preferable, because it will help convince an arbitrator that the union has bargained away its right to contest certain actions taken by the chief. If the chief takes some action not specifically covered by the collective bargaining agreement and the management rights clause is silent on the issue, an arbitrator may be more likely to "second-guess" the chief's decision. If the management rights clause specifically covers the area in question, reserving to the chief the right to make a decision in a specified area, arbitrators will often side with the chief. Similarly, if the union challenges the chief's decision by alleging a violation of a duty to bargain over the issue, many state agencies will search for the existence of a specific waiver of the right to bargain. If the employer can point to a specific grant of power to take the challenged action in the management rights clause, the state agency is more likely to find that the union waived the right to bargain over the issue.

For purposes of this section, management rights clauses have been divided into five main types, each with its own strengths and weaknesses. The frequency with which each clause appears nationally has been established by a survey of 102 firefighter collective bargaining agreements from across the country conducted in conjunction with the National League of Cities.[20]

Strong management rights clauses A strong management rights clause has three main features:

1. It specifies the concept of residual rights by indicating that any action not specifically mentioned in the agreement is reserved to management. It might say, for example, that management rights are vested "exclusively in the city . . . except as specifically defined in other articles of this agreement."
2. It contains a specific list of rights covering those areas most important to effective fire department administration, such as the rights to subcontract, discipline, make job assignments and transfers, lay off employees, develop or change work schedules (including overtime and shift changes), establish rules and regulations, evaluate employees, and create, combine, or eliminate job classifications. This specific list should begin with a phrase such as "Management's rights shall include, *but not be limited to*, the following: . . ." The word "reasonable" weakens the management rights clause (e.g., "the right to invoke reasonable rules") and can invite challenges from the union.
3. It clearly indicates that the exercise of some or all management rights is not subject to review under the grievance arbitration procedure.

Management rights clauses including these factors exist in approximately 10 percent of the collective bargaining agreements surveyed.

Comprehensive management rights clauses The comprehensive clause, like the strong management rights clause, typically contains an extensive list of specific rights reserved to management and clearly specifies the residual rights doctrine. The main difference is that it contains no language that prevents a grievance over the exercise of management rights from being pursued under arbitration.

Omitting the no-arbitration language from a management rights clause does not destroy its value. If the chief takes an action that is challenged by the union through unfair labor practice procedures, specific mention of the right to act unilaterally in the management rights clause may still be construed as a knowing waiver of the right to bargain by the union. A similar challenge through contractual grievance arbitration procedures may be unsuccessful under either the strong or comprehensive language, but the comprehensive language increases the chance of a loss for the chief. In any case, the absence of language specifically giving the arbitrator the right to review management's action is preferable to the use of the term "reasonable."

Comprehensive clauses are found in approximately 13 percent of the collective bargaining agreements studied.

General management rights clauses   Like the comprehensive clause, the general management rights clause specifies the residual rights doctrine, contains a specific list of management rights, and is silent on the arbitrability of the exercise of management rights. The critical difference between the general clause and the comprehensive clause is that the general clause typically lists fewer and less important specific management rights.

While the difference in value between a general clause and a comprehensive clause tends to be a judgment call, a clause without some of the following rights might be termed a general rather than a comprehensive clause.

1. Creation, modification, or deletion of rules and regulations
2. Subcontracting
3. Change in departmental structures or reduction in the workday or workweek
4. Work assignments
5. Scheduling of employees
6. Increasing or decreasing the size or composition of the work force.

Some contracts that contain a general management rights clause may specifically grant particular management rights in other clauses in the contract. For example, the grievance arbitration clause may preclude the arbitrator from passing judgment on the exercise of certain management rights. Alternatively, an hours-of-work or layoff clause may grant critical rights allowing the employer to act in those areas. The entire contract should be examined to determine the full extent of management's rights.

General clauses are the most common, existing in 36 percent of collective bargaining agreements studied.

Residual rights clauses   This type of clause is relatively short. It simply states that the employer retains the right to manage its affairs unless specifically covered in other articles of the collective bargaining agreement. As mentioned above, some advocates prefer this type of clause to a specific enumeration of rights, because, by *including* certain items on this list, an arbitrator can conclude that the parties meant to *exclude* certain others.

The main weakness of a residual rights clause is that it is seldom considered a waiver of the union's right to bargain over an issue, and many state agencies require a specific waiver in the case of a mandatory subject of bargaining. Where the fire chief wishes to reduce hours, for example, a duty to bargain arises unless the contract specifically grants management the right to reduce hours. If the fire chief's decision is challenged through the unfair labor practice procedure in this example, the result could be a reversal of the chief's action.

Residual rights clauses were found in 13 percent of collective bargaining agreements studied.

Weak management rights clause "Weak" management rights clauses are typified by language that specifically grants to the union the power to challenge management decisions through the arbitration procedure, duty to bargain procedures, or both. While such clauses may rely on the residual rights doctrine and/or list specific management rights, they often contain a provision that states: "Nothing contained in this section shall be deemed to deny the right of any employee to submit a grievance with regard to the exercise of such rights." Alternatively, the clause may indicate the exercise of management rights "does not preclude employees from bargaining or consulting with the employer concerning wages, hours, and other terms and conditions of employment." The former wording specifically grants the arbitrator the power to review the chief's action, while the latter allows the union to file an unfair labor practice charge for failing to bargain with the union over a mandatory subject of bargaining. A weak management rights clause is also typified by liberal use of the term "reasonable."

Clauses of this kind were found in 6 percent of departments surveyed.

Grievance procedures clause

Although a greivance procedure should allow, or even encourage, open and frank discussions between the chief and officers concerning changes in fire department operations, that grievance procedure should not permit the union or dissatisfied employees to prevent necessary changes from occurring. To avoid this result, fire chiefs should examine the grievance procedure to determine whether it is too easy for dissatisfied employees or the union to effectively challenge their decisions.

Definitions The first step in clarifying the chief's decision-making authority is to settle on an appropriate definition of grievance. The definition, when read in conjunction with limitations on the powers of an arbitrator (discussed below), may prevent an arbitrator from ruling on certain disputes that fall outside the definition. For example, if the definition of a grievance excludes disciplinary decisions, the arbitrator will have no authority to rule on a grievance on that subject. Arbitrators generally assume that a matter can be treated as a grievance unless the parties clearly exclude it from coverage under the grievance procedure.

All but 6 percent of the collective bargaining agreements surveyed had some definition of a grievance. The definitions can be described as "narrow," "limited," or "broad."

A "narrow" definition, which is most desirable from management's point of view, defines grievances as disputes over the "interpretation and application of the *specific* terms of this collective bargaining agreement." This language places the burden on an employee or the union to point to a specific clause or article that has allegedly been violated by the chief's action. A narrow definition also exempts specific areas from the grievance process. For example, it may exclude such actions as the following:

1. Disciplinary actions
2. Departmental operations
3. Matter subject to resolution under state civil service provisions

4.   Promotions
5.   Creation of departmental rules and regulations.

A narrow definition was found in approximately 11 percent of collective bargaining agreements studied nationwide.

The "limited" definition, which appears in 43 percent of all collective bargaining agreements nationwide, is similar to the narrow definition but does not exclude specific subjects from coverage under the grievance procedure. Thus, a limited definition may provide "Only matters involving the interpretation, application or enforcement of the terms of this agreement shall constitute a grievance." Because specific rights are not reserved to management in certain key areas, the chief may be challenged in an area critical to the efficient operation of the department, and an arbitrator may reverse the chief's actions, or the chief may back down for fear of union challenge.

Broadly defined, a grievance is a dispute that involves the interpretation or application of the collective bargaining agreement, departmental rules and regulations, personnel rules, state and federal statutes, or any dispute over conditions of employment. Forty-two percent of all agreements nationwide were of this kind.

Since arbitrators tend to presume that a matter is grievable unless the parties specifically exclude it, a broad definition invites dissatisfied employees to challenge unpopular decisions by the chief on grounds that they violate departmental rules or regulations, applicable state or federal statutes, or other documents. As arbitration approaches, the existence of these additional restrictions may have the effect of making management's case appear weaker and the union's case appear stronger.

Some collective bargaining agreements contain a compromise between the broad definition and narrow definitions. The parties agree that grievances will cover the areas traditionally included under a broad definition, but then exempt certain key decision-making areas from coverage under the grievance procedure.

Time limits and "mousetraps"   Most collective bargaining agreements will have a series of steps for grievance procedures and a time limit at each step. In larger departments, more steps are common. In smaller departments, where most employees have direct access to the chief, fewer steps are generally used. Regardless of the number of steps, the parties should be aware of time limits.

The first key time limit applies to when the grievance must initially be filed. A shorter time limit will prevent stale grievances, reduce the amount of potential back pay (especially in a discharge case), and generally force disputes into the open early, rather than allow them to fester beneath the surface. Alternatively, a longer time limit for bringing the initial grievance may convey an impression of openness and willingness to listen, which can have its own beneficial effects.

The clock should begin running when an employee knows or *should have known* of the event giving rise to the grievance. This will prevent some grievances by employees who, through negligence or inaction, do not become aware of a certain situation. For example, if the chief issues a new departmental rule and posts it on the bulletin board, but the employee fails to check the bulletin board, an arbitrator could infer that notice of the existence of that rule was given on the day it was posted.

A critical time limit in the grievance process is the number of days a grievance may be held at the last step before the union must proceed to arbitration. Unions frequently allow a series of grievances to accumulate "waiting for arbitration," appeal several grievances to arbitration all at once, and then attempt to pressure management into resolving one or more of the issues in favor of the employees, even though some of the grievances, when considered separately, are without merit. Thus, rapid grievance processing, including going to arbitration, may be desirable.

A "mousetrap" provision specifies what happens if either party fails to act on a required time limit. Such provisions are critical. If a contract does not specify a penalty, arbitrators will generally be lenient when either party misses a time limit. Thus, if management denies a grievance at an early stage of the process and the union fails to appeal to the next step in a timely manner and later requests arbitration, the arbitrator may allow the grievance to be heard.

A common type of mousetrap provision provides that, if either party misses a time limit contained in the grievance procedure, the grievance will automatically be appealed to the next step. Another provides that if either party misses a time limit in the grievance procedure, the grievance will be deemed settled on the basis of the last decision of management. This type of provision acts against the union and forces members to actively process grievances. While unions are generally averse to such a clause, some employers have been successful in getting unions to agree on the theory that it is the union's grievance procedure, not management's. If a grievance is not meritorious enough to process rapidly under the contractual time limits, the union should not be overly concerned if it is resolved against the union because of its own failure to act.

A few mousetrap provisions specify that the grievance is sustained if management does not act in a timely manner in any step of the grievance process. If such a clause exists, the chief and other local officials must be especially alert, since they do not process grievances every day and often do not have systems designed for handling grievances under strict time limits. Chiefs also should be alert for attempts to introduce such provisions into an existing contract.

A number of contracts include clauses permitting employees to process grievances on department time. While granting a certain amount of time per week or month for union stewards to process grievances is a policy decision that communities should make independently, such a provision may encourage the filing of grievances where none may otherwise exist if employees prefer to process grievances rather than perform their regular duties.

The final step in the grievance procedure Depending on the size of the department, historical practice, and various other factors, the final step in a department's grievance procedure might be binding arbitration, advisory arbitration, final review by a representative of management, final review by a union/management grievance committee, or final review by a civil service board or some other individual or body agreed upon by the parties. For various reasons, unions have traditionally sought, and have been able to obtain, binding arbitration of grievances in most collective bargaining agreements. The study of collective bargaining agreements nationwide found that approximately 80 percent of these agreements required binding arbitration.

Because binding arbitration is relatively common, the best strategy for management is to seek other clauses that restrict the arbitrator's decision-making authority by defining its scope. There is no "magic language" in this area, but here are some examples of the key phrases that might be included in the clause:

1. The arbitrator shall be bound by the specific language of this collective bargaining agreement.
2. The arbitrator shall expressly confine himself to the precise issues submitted to him by the parties.
3. The arbitrator shall have no authority to consider any issues not specifically submitted or not covered by the specific terms of the collective bargaining agreement.
4. No decision, or part of a decision, surpassing the limits on the arbitrator's power shall be binding on the parties.

Another alternative, as in the narrow grievance definition, is to list specific areas outside the arbitrator's authority. Again, although the arbitrator may be able to rule in various areas, management can reserve the right to act in certain sensitive or key decision-making areas. These areas may depend on the specific problems that may exist in each department.

A final consideration in the area of grievance arbitration is the availability of a "loser pays" provision. Although rare, such a clause may have some merit. It prevents the union from pushing grievances without merit to arbitration, in which case members would have to pay for the entire arbitration proceeding. On the other hand, such a clause may encourage the arbitrator to "split" an arbitration decision to prevent a clear "winner" from emerging. The benefits and problems of this particular clause should be discussed in detail with the negotiator before it is proposed for inclusion in an agreement.

The right to set staffing levels

The chief should be able to determine the number of employees needed in the department. This includes the right to determine staff levels on a given day or week, the right to lay off and recall employees as needed, and finally, the right to subcontract.

Minimum staffing levels Some states treat minimum staffing levels as a mandatory subject of bargaining. In this case, contract language that restricts or freezes staffing creates several problems. First, it can hamper the employer's ability to introduce technological changes or to respond to changing economic circumstances. Second, it can block an employer's attempts to reduce staff where desirable. Finally, it may require an employer to incur overtime obligations when some employees are absent and others are needed to meet the minimum staffing levels.

Minimum staffing requirements come in a variety of forms. Some establish a minimum number of employees that must be maintained in the department. Others define where or when those employees must be assigned. For example, some contracts specify that a certain minimum number of firefighters must be stationed in each station on each shift.

If the city has successfully avoided contractual minimum staffing requirements, management's negotiators should seek an affirmative contractual right to determine staffing levels. This right can be established in two ways. First, the contract may *explicitly* state that decisions concerning staffing requirements are reserved solely to management. Eight percent of collective bargaining agreements studied nationwide contain such language. Second, the contract may implicitly reserve staffing decisions to management. Twenty-three percent of the collective bargaining agreements studied contain such language. Typical "implicit" clauses give management the right to determine "the methods, means and personnel" by which operations are to be conducted. They may be strengthened by additional language in the contract (usually in the management rights clause) reserving to management the right to "hire, assign, retain, or relieve" employees from their duties. Determining whether a contract meets this test is complex, however, and creates difficulty even for experienced practitioners.

Sixty-six percent of contracts studied nationwide contained *no reference* to staffing requirements. Even in these cases, arbitrators may defer to the employer and uphold the chief's staffing decisions if the altered schedule does not create safety and health hazards or an "excessive" work load for the remaining employees.

One other problem should be noted. Although one part of the collective bargaining agreement may specifically reserve to the city the right to set staffing levels, that right may be restricted by contract clauses (or departmental rules and regulations) that require a certain amount of overtime, a certain number of firefighters on each piece of equipment, or some other limitation on establishing staffing levels.

Layoffs and recall   The first thing the chief must consider before adjusting the size of the work force through a layoff is whether the contract limits the reasons for the layoff. According to one standard, used in 15 percent of the collective bargaining agreements studied, staff reductions must be "necessary" before layoffs may occur. Although this term *seems* relatively harmless, arbitrators have frequently required the employer to demonstrate that *no other alternatives* to layoff exist. Thus, the argument that cost savings would be achieved or that departmental efficiency would increase because of the layoff may not be adequate.

Forty-two percent of the collective bargaining agreements studied placed some other limits on the reasons for layoff. For example, some allow layoffs for "lack of work, lack of funds, or departmental reorganization," requiring the employer to justify the layoff in light of those reasons.

The chief's negotiators naturally should avoid clauses that restrict management's ability to determine when and under what circumstances a reduction in force will occur. However, if the bargaining process or the city's political leadership requires the chief to make some concessions on the reasons for a reduction in force, any compromise language should include the phrase "or for other legitimate reasons." With this language, the chief improves the chances of winning an arbitration case if the union later challenges a reduction in force.

Unions also favor a strict seniority layoff system. Such a system generates a number of problems, including an avalanche of bumping, placing unqualified or underqualified employees in critical jobs, and moving employees from one classification or division to another where such movement is not administratively desirable or feasible. In spite of these problems, 35 percent of all collective bargaining agreements studied call for seniority as the exclusive criterion for the order of layoffs.

An ideal clause from management's point of view allows the chief to determine which employees will be laid off "on the basis of such criteria as the chief deems appropriate." Such open-ended language would almost certainly be opposed by the union, however, and other measures of an employee's qualifications may be suggested. These could include "demonstrated ability, competency, skill, the needs of the department, experience, or training." As a last resort, the chief may be willing to consider using seniority as one, *but only one*, of these factors. The impact of seniority could be further limited in these situations if this criterion was used only when all the other factors are "equal" or "relatively equal."

If seniority cannot be avoided as one criterion for layoff, the chief may wish to consider preserving existing organizational or operational units of the department. Seniority should only apply within those units, thus preventing massive realignment of personnel in each organizational unit of the employer after each layoff (through bumping).

From the chief's point of view, the order of recall, like the order of layoff, should be based on qualifications. Considerations that could be used by the chief include "work requirements, efficiency and conduct of individual employees, length of service, and the recommendation of the chief." Alternatively the order of recall could simply follow the order in which the employees were laid off. This system should be overlaid with some contractual language requiring that the returning employees be "qualified" to perform the duties to which they are being recalled.

The language of the collective bargaining agreement should also consider the *mechanics* of recall, including the length of time employees retain recall rights, how employees who are being recalled must be given notice, the length of time that employees have to respond to this notice, and provisions for loss of recall rights for failure to respond in a timely fashion.

Subcontracting Subcontracting has traditionally had a limited role in fire department labor relations, possibly because of the long-standing belief that subcontracting is not feasible owing to the unique nature of the duties, activities, and responsibilities of firefighters. However, many public employers now realize that trained firefighters may be unnecessary in many areas of administration involving a clerical or other supportive role.

If the collective bargaining agreement does not address management's ability to subcontract services, an arbitrator may be called upon to review a subcontracting decision. In making a decision, arbitrators often rely on some or all of the following factors to determine the "good faith reasonableness" of the employer's action:

1. Past practice. Has the employer subcontracted unilaterally in the past?
2. Impact on the bargaining unit. How many bargaining unit employees are affected?
3. Effect on unit employees. Will subcontracting merely result in a transfer to new duties or will affected employees be displaced?
4. Justification. Can the employer present convincing economic or operational reasons to justify subcontracting?
5. Availability of appropriate equipment or qualified employees. Is this a situation where the employer *cannot* perform the work in-house?
6. Job security provisions of the collective bargaining agreement. Does the contract contain clauses that protect employees' job security, bargaining unit work, or hours?
7. Negotiation history. Can the union demonstrate that a mutual understanding exists concerning limitations on the employer's right to subcontract?

Answers to these questions will determine, in large part, whether the chief's subcontracting decisions will be upheld.

The right to subcontract may be explicit or merely implied. Language that *implies* the right to subcontract may state that management retains the right to "establish standards and methods, to hire civilians, to transfer work, or to otherwise perform work as required by the demands to maintain the efficiency of public operations."

Sometimes more than one clause may determine whether management has the right to subcontract. Statements indicating that management determines the "manner in which the city's fire prevention activities are to be conducted," that the city has "statutory and charter rights and obligations in contracting for matters pertaining to municipal operations," and that the city reserves "all rights concerning the management, organization, and duration of the fire department" might be read together to establish an implicit right to subcontract.

A clause granting an implicit right to subcontract usually states that management reserves the right to determine "the methods, means, personnel, and policies by which departmental operations are to be conducted." In one case, the arbitrator determined that this wording implied the employer could staff a new "911" communications system with civilian employees.[21]

Many collective bargaining agreements *explicitly* reserve the right to subcontract. Nonetheless, some limits still exist. If an employer makes a subcontracting decision, but the impact of that action is so extensive that the bargaining status of the union is completely eliminated or significantly impaired, an arbitrator may hold that management has gone too far and may reverse the action.

No-strike clauses

Many state statutes define "strike" in a way that may not prevent the union from applying economic pressure during a labor dispute. Under a literal reading of many state laws, unions may be able to engage in a slowdown, refuse certain overtime or job assignments, or refuse to cross the picket lines of other unions without violating state statutes. The impact of such action on the chief's ability to run the department is obvious.

 A strong *contractual* no-strike clause employs a broad definition of the term "strike." To cover as many situations as possible, this definition should include the following actions:

1. Concerted failure to report for duty
2. Concerted absence of employees from their positions
3. Concerted stoppage of work
4. Concerted submission of resignations
5. Concerted abstinence in whole *or in part* by any group of employees from the full and faithful performance of their duties
6. Participation in a deliberate and concerted course of conduct that adversely affects the services of the employer
7. Picketing in furtherance of such work stoppage
8. Engaging in a sympathy strike.

Second, a strong no-strike clause contains contractual provisions that help force the end of the strike. Disciplining strikers, up to and including discharge, may be effective in reaching this end. Forty percent of collective bargaining agreements studied nationwide specifically allowed employers to discipline employees for engaging in strike activity. It is also advisable to ensure that the employer has the authority to *selectively* discipline employees. If such language is included in the agreement, the employer will not be forced to discharge or otherwise discipline *all* striking employees, but may be permitted to discipline only the "leaders."

Another provision that can help force the end of a strike is a requirement for the union to take some sort of affirmative steps to end it, whether the union has officially authorized the strike or not. To prevent the union from working behind the scenes to encourage or assist striking employees, specific clauses should be included in the collective bargaining agreement requiring the union to take some of the following acts:

1. Publicly disavow the strike or work stoppage
2. Request, in writing, that all employees return to work (a copy to be supplied to the city)
3. Notify the city or county of the measures taken to end the strike within a limited period of time.

Such requirements can be backed up with provisions that make the union legally responsible for damages, fines, or other penalties in the event of a strike.

The final important provision in a strong no-strike clause is some limitation on an arbitrator's authority. A provision stating that the only question a grievance proceeding may consider is whether a strike occurred should allow the chief to unilaterally determine the discipline or other penalties to be assessed.

Zipper clauses

A zipper clause "zips up" the collective bargaining agreement. In its most basic form, a zipper clause contains two provisions. First, the clause states that the terms and provisions of the agreement constitute "the entire agreement between the parties" and "supersede all previous communications, representations, or agreements, either verbal or written, between the parties.'' This type of provision prevents a union from relying on a past practice or some other ''understanding'' that may have existed before the contract was signed.

The second major provision commonly found in a zipper clause states that the parties waive their right to bargain during the term of the contract. In most jurisdictions this waiver must be ''clear and unequivocal.'' This provision might be worded as follows:

> The employer and the union, for the life of this agreement, each voluntarily and unqualifiedly waives the right, and each agrees that the other shall not be obligated to bargain collectively with respect to any subject or matter referred to, or covered in this agreement, or with respect to any subject or matter not specifically referred to or covered in this agreement, even though such subject or matter may not have been within the knowledge or contemplation of either or both the parties at the time they negotiated or signed this agreement.

In many jurisdictions, the language cited above will constitute a waiver of the union's right to bargain over an issue not discussed in the collective bargaining agreement. Thus, if the chief wishes to implement change in an area not covered by the agreement, the chief is not required to bargain first. Although many jurisdictions do not consider a zipper clause alone to be a ''clear and unequivocal'' waiver, when the zipper clause is read in the light of other clauses in the contract, especially a strong management rights clause, the state agency may find a ''clear and unequivocal'' waiver of the right to bargain by the union. Thus, when read in conjunction with other provisions of the agreement, the zipper clause can strengthen management's case in both grievance arbitration and for an alleged refusal to bargain. However, when read in the light of a past practice clause or some other pro-union provision, the zipper clause may be ineffective.

Duration/reopener clauses

When the parties sign a collective bargaining agreement, it is often difficult to determine what economic circumstances will exist when that contract expires. Often, it is to the employer's advantage to allow the collective bargaining agreement to renew itself automatically, but the opposite may be true where the department is faced with dwindling economic resources or troublesome and unworkable contract language.

A common duration provision states that the agreement will automatically renew itself after a certain date if the parties are unable to negotiate a new agreement, or if either party fails to terminate the agreement in a timely fashion. Here is a typical example of the wording used in this kind of clause:

> This contract shall be effective as of the first day of July, 198___, and shall remain in full force and effect until June 30, 198___, and shall automatically be renewed from year to year thereafter, unless either party notifies the other in writing not later than January 1, 198___, that it wishes to modify this contract.

The automatic renewal provision can work to the employer's advantage or disadvantage. If the union fails to give the required notice, the employer is protected from changes for an additional year. On the other hand, if the city or county fails to give proper notice, it may have given up the opportunity to renegotiate troublesome clauses. In addition, certain ''automatic'' provisions of the collective bargaining agreement may continue in effect unless the contract is terminated. Most typical in this area is the COLA (cost-of-living adjustment) clause, which still appears in many collective bargaining agreements across the country.

Even if a contract automatically expires on a given date, it may allow for reopening negotiations before that date on a specific issue, such as wages, or may permit each party to raise a limited number of issues in the reopened negotiations.

One final provision often included in a duration or reopener clause is a "savings clause," which typically provides that "if any article or section of the agreement is held invalid by operation of law or by any tribunal having jurisdiction, the remainder of the contract shall not be affected thereby." Many clauses go on to indicate that the parties must enter into immediate negotiations to replace the invalid article or section. Such a renegotiation clause is not desirable from a management point of view, as various "side" issues are often introduced into the negotiations.

Maintenance of standards

Since the parties cannot foresee every problem that may arise during the term of a collective bargaining agreement, it is important to include some language that addresses unforeseen events. Contracts with a strong management rights clause will reserve to management the right to effectuate necessary changes, provided the specific terms of the contract are not violated.

In many cases, however, a union will insist on a maintenance of standards (or "past practices") clause that preserves existing employee benefits, even though those benefits are not specifically spelled out in the agreement. If such a clause exists, it may prevent the employer from making changes. Thus, two specific issues should be addressed when negotiating any maintenance of standards clause:

1. The scope of the areas in which change is prohibited
2. The steps management must take to implement change in those areas.

Scope   About one-fifth of collective bargaining agreements studied nationwide contained maintenance of standards clauses that applied "across the board" to all benefits. A typical example would be worded as follows:

It is understood and agreed that all employees' rights and benefits which are presently enjoyed but not specifically covered in this agreement shall be maintained.

Arbitrators routinely apply such language to *all* existing rights and benefits, no matter how minor. For this reason alone, this language should be avoided.

If some kind of maintenance of standards clause must be agreed to during negotiations in order to reach a contract, it may be advisable to limit its application to a specified number of issues, as illustrated in the following example:

The city shall maintain its existing policy with respect to _____
_____, but all remaining areas shall remain solely within the discretion of the employer to modify, establish or eliminate.

If the areas governed by this clause are carefully drawn, the chief will retain the necessary power to implement change.

Steps for change   Some maintenance of standards clauses allow no change in existing conditions or benefits, while others allow changes with prior negotiation and mutual agreement with the union. Clauses of these two types appear in approximately 38 percent of all collective bargaining agreements studied nationwide.

On the other hand, 13 percent of collective bargaining agreements allow change in existing conditions if the employer meets with or consults the union before making the change. In addition, 14 percent indicate changes may be implemented if the union receives prior notification of the change. The advantages of such a clause are obvious.

Rules and regulations clause

A clause discussing management's rights and authority to change existing rules and regulations or implement new rules and regulations appears in approximately 77 percent of collective bargaining agreements. These provisions generally revolve around three main issues:

1. The union's role in the creation of new rules or regulations or modification of existing ones
2. Discipline for violation of rules and regulations
3. Availability of grievance and arbitration procedures for review of departmental rules and regulations.

The union's role Some collective bargaining agreements reserve to management "the exclusive right to manage and direct the department, including the right to formulate departmental policy, rules and regulations." Only a few prohibit the establishment of new rules or regulations without the union's consent.

Between these two extremes is a middle ground that parallels the "meet and confer" or "notification" requirements found in maintenance of standards clauses. Some agreements merely require the employer to notify the union of changes in rules and regulations, and others require both notice and consultation with the union. Since notice needs to be given in any case if a rule is to be effective, a notice requirement is not a substantial intrusion into the employer's rights. Similarly, the requirement to "consult" with the union still leaves management the right to make a unilateral change in existing rules or regulations.

Discipline Consistent with the rule that employees must "work now and grieve later" and thus not refuse to obey a rule even when that rule may be "wrong," arbitrators typically require employees to observe the employer's rules and regulations and uphold discipline for violation of those rules and regulations. However, in the course of a discipline or discharge case it is not unheard of for an arbitrator to review the appropriateness of a newly promulgated rule or regulation even if the union has not contested it. Thus, if an employee is subsequently discharged for violation of that rule, the arbitrator may have jurisdiction to determine whether the rule is appropriate, and whether violation of that rule should appropriately lead to discharge.

Arbitral review The final issue discussed in rules and regulations clauses relates to the availability of review through grievance and arbitration procedures. Many agreements that specifically deal with the employee's right to grieve rules and regulations apply a "reasonableness" standard, allowing employees to grieve "unreasonable" rules. Unless the contract specifically discusses the grievability of employer rules and regulations, an employee will probably have access to an arbitrator to review the appropriateness of a new rule or regulation. Although arbitrators differ on this issue, they tend to view their jurisdiction as broad.

Several collective bargaining agreements place a time limit on the right to grieve new rules or regulations:

The association shall have the opportunity to grieve the promulgation of any new rule or regulation thirty days after the promulgation and furnishing the same to the association as to the reasonableness or propriety of said rule or regulation.

Such wording will prevent the union from challenging the applicability of a particular rule or regulation after thirty days. Under such language, if an employee is subsequently disciplined or discharged for violating a challenged rule, the union may have waived its right to contest the reasonableness of the rule, and the only issue before the arbitrator is whether the rule was violated.

Duty to bargain concerns

As indicated earlier, the legal duty to bargain does not end when the contract is signed. Rather, it is an ongoing obligation that the chief should carefully assess whenever making changes that depart from the status quo. This does not mean that the chief should avoid change, but only that the chief must take additional steps to ensure that the changes will not be subject to later challenge by the union. When a change is contemplated, the contract should first be analyzed to determine whether it specifically authorizes or specifically prohibits the action sought.

Many actions will not be directly addressed by the contract. In those situations, the union has two grounds for challenging the chief's decisions. First, the union could file a grievance claiming that a clause of the contract—which by inference covers the topic—has been violated. Second, the union could claim that the contract does not cover the subject, and thus that a unilateral change constitutes a violation of the duty to bargain in good faith. In either event, it is usually wise to notify the union of management's intentions and give them an opportunity to discuss the issues. If the union fails to respond and a grievance is filed later, the employer can argue that the union was put on notice of the intended change and raised no arguments against it. Similarly, if the union fails to respond to the notice and later claims the employer violated the duty to bargain in good faith, the employer can argue that the union has waived the duty to bargain by its silence.

Some might view this approach as asking the union's "permission" to make changes in the fire service. A more realistic view is that, since the employees elect an exclusive bargaining representative, they are a legitimate force in the decision-making process. For this reason, notice and an opportunity to discuss the issues relevant to the firefighters are statutorily mandated, and an important first step in the chief's decision-making process.

Grievance processing

The grievance procedure is one of the key clauses in the collective bargaining agreement. This procedure makes it possible to address disputes over the interpretation of the agreement. Therefore, it is important to deal with the grievance procedure proactively to minimize challenges to the chief's legitimate decision-making authority while maximizing the communication that is so important to a successful labor-management relationship.

The typical grievance procedure begins by obliging the frontline supervisor and the affected employee to discuss the problem in question. The grievance will eventually be put in writing and processed through various steps, culminating at the chief's level. Thereafter, the grievance may be appealed to the city or county manager or elected body, followed by appeal to binding arbitration in many cases.

The roles of union and management representatives are similar. Both parties wish to draw out the other side's legal positions and the factual bases for those positions at the earliest stage possible without restricting themselves to a limited number of facts or arguments. Thus, at each step in the process, each will be asking the other party to submit a factual basis for its position and its interpretation of the disputed contract language.

To achieve this goal from the management point of view, several questions should be asked at each step in the grievance process. The supervisor should already have some idea of what the grievance is about and should have done some preliminary research into the facts and circumstances surrounding the grievance. When questioned by the union, the supervisor should avoid saying that those are the *only* facts the employer relies on, or the *only* interpretation the employer believes is supportable. Rather, there may be a variety of facts and arguments yet to be discovered that may be useful later in the grievance process.

The supervisor should also be prepared to ask the union to describe all relevant facts, contract language, and arguments that the union relies upon. The supervisor should also ask the union to inform the city of any new facts or arguments that may later come to light. This will avoid "surprises" at a later stage in the grievance procedure, especially during the arbitration hearing. During each step, arguments with the union should be avoided as they will do little to resolve the conflict. Thus, after gathering sufficient facts and arguments, the supervisor should indicate that the union will be given an answer shortly.

Another important management goal is to avoid permitting the union to process untimely grievances or to process disputes that do not meet the contractual definition of a grievance. However, arguments of timeliness and arbitrability must be raised at the earliest possible moment, or an arbitrator may later reject them. Therefore, at each step of the grievance procedure, the supervisor should ask whether the grievance is timely and whether it meets the definition of a grievance.

In the answer to the grievance, these other arguments should be raised. On the merits of the grievance, it is enough to simply say "grievance denied" without detailed explanation. By explaining the reasons in detail, the employer may be limited to defending only those reasons in arbitration, and not be permitted to raise new facts or arguments that may come to light after the answer has been submitted.

By following the above steps, the city or county should have a good idea of what the grievance is about before binding arbitration begins. This is important for several reasons. First, a clear picture of the union's view of the grievance will be invaluable in preparing the case. Second, by raising jurisdictional arguments early, the employer is more likely to prevail on those arguments before the arbitrator. In the arbitration process, both parties will have an opportunity to present their cases and facts before the arbitrator, followed by a decision that is generally considered binding.

Appeals of arbitration decisions are generally unsuccessful.

Employee discipline

Successful discipline or discharge of public employees is very difficult and complex in the labor relations field. Each state has a store of statutes, regulations, and procedures governing the disciplinary process. However, this complex process can be simplified by an understanding of "just cause," which is applied by most arbitrators to a discipline or discharge case.

Just cause

Many collective bargaining agreements contain a short clause stating that no employee shall be disciplined or discharged except for "just cause." Innocuous as this provision seems, it is highly frustrating because just cause defies absolute definition. Fortunately, the basic elements of just cause that arbitrators recognize can be reduced to seven simple tests:

1. Notice. "Did the Employer give to the employee forewarning or foreknowledge of the possible or probable consequences of the employee's disciplinary conduct?"
2. Reasonable rule or order. "Was the Employer's rule or managerial order reasonably related to (a) the orderly, efficient, and safe operation of the Employer's business, and (b) the performance that the Employer might properly expect of the employee?"

3. Investigation. "Did the Employer, before administering the discipline . . . , make an effort to discover whether the employee did in fact violate or disobey a rule or order of management?"
4. Fair investigation. "Was the Employer's investigation conducted fairly and objectively?"
5. Proof. "At the investigation, did the 'judge' obtain substantial evidence or proof that the employee was guilty as charged?"
6. Equal treatment. "Has the Employer applied its rules, orders and penalties even-handedly and without discrimination to all employees?"
7. Penalty. "Was the degree of discipline administered . . . reasonably related to (a) the seriousness of the employee's *proven* offense, and (b) the record of the employee in his service with the Employer?"[22]

Notice   A fundamental component of the just cause standard is that employees must be told what kind of conduct will lead to discipline—especially if the penalty is discharge. In addition, the requirement of notice means the employer must let employees know what kinds of conduct will lead to discipline and what sort of discipline will result. Notice of the penalty is particularly important; employees guilty of conduct they know or should have known is unacceptable have sometimes been put back to work because they were not forewarned that the penalty could be discharge. Thus, the final warning should state, "Future misconduct could lead to discipline up to and including discharge."

Reasonable rule or order   One of the most common areas of dispute concerning the reasonableness of a rule or order is personal grooming. Arbitrators generally agree that an employer may adopt dress and grooming rules dictating employees' personal appearance, provided these rules serve a reasonable business purpose. For both dress and grooming rules, business purposes typically relate to three considerations: company image, safety, and sanitation.

The problem is illustrated in a case in which two firefighters were disciplined for failing to comply with a grooming code.[23] The city stated that its directive, which called for short hair, neat mustaches, and no beards, was reasonable and a proper exercise of managerial authority. The city contended its prohibition against facial hair was safety-related because bushy mustaches or beards interfere with the proper functioning of the face mask and also affect giving mouth to mouth resuscitation. The city also cited the need for uniformity of appearance and the departmental image. The union, on the other hand, argued that the city's safety and image concerns were meritless, and that the real issue was a difference in tastes between the older fire executives and the younger men.

The arbitrator held that the city cannot be given, *carte blanche*, control over its employees' personal appearance and hairstyles. Beside finding that the rules would be unreasonable in the absence of a safety justification, the arbitrator noted that arbitrary hair codes have been declared unconstitutional. The arbitrator added, however, that a city *may* successfully document its safety contention in some future case, but had failed to provide sufficient facts in this case.

Investigation   The investigation requirement was discussed in another case.[24] The chief was notified that an employee had been in a fight. He talked to an investigating officer and read the officer's report. He then discharged the employee. The investigation consisted solely of reading the arresting officer's written report and interviewing one officer. The arbitrator determined this "investigation" was insufficient, and reinstated the firefighter.

Fair investigation   If the investigation is to be useful, it must be carried out in an objective manner. Someone from management, usually the chief, must make certain that all available evidence is collected and analyzed from a disinterested third party's perspective. A supervisor may be too caught up in defending his own view to be a reliable source of evidence, especially in a heated case.

A "wrong" decision is likely to result if a single supervisor has the ultimate authority to function as witness, prosecutor, and judge. Without the possibility of intervention, or a second opinion from higher management, the employee is susceptible to a single supervisor's prejudice, animosity, ignorance, or mistake. Thus, the chief should carefully review the decisions of subordinates, and should seek a second opinion before making a final decision.

Proof   Once the employer has thoroughly investigated the facts, the question is whether sufficient proof exists that the employee misbehaved. "Proof" must meet three basic criteria:

1. The charge must be tailored to the facts, it must be known by the employee, and it must be reasonably clear and specific.
2. The employer must prove what is charged and not something else.
3. Proof must exist at the time of discharge.

A common proof problem—excessive absenteeism—is illustrated in another case.[25] Here, the chief disciplined an employee for excessive absenteeism by halting the accrual of sick leave and requiring that a physician's letter accompany any future illness.

The arbitrator noted that the discipline imposed indicated that the employer believed the employee was using sick leave when he was not actually sick. The employer admitted that no attempt had been made to investigate the absences, claiming it lacked the resources to do so. The employer then conceded that every one of the employee's absences was legitimate but argued that the absences were higher than the department average, and thus "excessive."

The arbitrator found for the employee, and concluded the employer had the ability to limit use of sick leave to genuine illnesses. It could use any reasonable means of investigation available, and the employee would have a duty to cooperate in the investigation. Thus, the employer may not assume "abuse" by proving "excessive use" of sick leave.

Equal treatment   This test is simple, but nevertheless is commonly violated. The union will rely on situations similar to the one being litigated to argue that similarly situated employees were treated differently. To avoid the problem, the chief should review all prior cases involving similar situations before making a decision on the proper penalty. This does not mean that all penalties must be the same for a particular offense, but that differences must be explainable on a rational basis. Further, if the union produces new examples of unequal treatment, the chief should consider modifying the penalty accordingly.

Penalty   The last of the seven just cause tests pertains to whether the penalty was reasonably related to (a) the seriousness of the employee's *proven* offense, and (b) the record of the employee in service with the employer. For example, in a Tucson case,[26] a paramedic who used fire department vehicles and drugs to treat his dog for grand mal seizures was given an eight-day suspension, one-year probation, and three-month assignment to a fire suppression company before being allowed back to paramedic work. He was also denied a 2.5 percent merit increase, since he was ineligible for any merit increases while on probation.

The arbitrator found that the penalty was appropriate, because the paramedic willfully took the unit out of service, which he was not allowed to do, and in doing so, he put personal concerns ahead of professional duties—and thus committed an act of insubordination. Moreover, in using the squad's drugs, the paramedic not only circumvented the inventory process, but rendered the drug box incomplete.

The penalty issue is often difficult. Arbitrators may try to "split" their decision by upholding discipline, but reducing the penalty. In response, some chiefs "double" the penalty, which makes reduction even more likely. Although assessing the penalty is not a scientific process, experience and good judgment, as well as following the other six steps of "just cause," will help ensure that the penalty will be upheld.

Constitutional due process

Not all public-sector employers are aware that the constitutional protection of "life, liberty and property" applies to public-sector employees, including firefighters. These protections have produced an explosion in the number of lawsuits filed in the federal courts over discipline of public employees. Because chiefs are generally at the forefront of disciplining firefighters, it is useful to periodically review the basic elements of due process protections in the employment law context.

Property interest in the job   Federal courts have held that public-sector employees with an expectation of continued employment enjoy a property interest in their jobs that entitles them to constitutional protections before that property right is taken away. Thus, when a tenured public employee is disciplined or discharged, certain constitutional due process protections apply.[27]

Before an employee's property interest can be taken away through discharge, due process protections must be given. Historically, these protections have included the right to notice of specific charges against the employee, notice of the evidence supporting those charges, the opportunity for a hearing, the opportunity to face and cross-examine witnesses, be represented by counsel, and have the charges decided by an impartial decisionmaker. Until the decision in *Cleveland Board of Education* v. *Loudermill*, discussed below, these constitutional guarantees were typically fulfilled by a hearing *after* the discharge before a Civil Service Commission, city council, or arbitrator.

Liberty interests   Even where employees have no expectation of continued employment, they generally have a constitutionally protected "liberty" interest in their right to search for other work within their chosen profession. If an employee is discharged for reasons that might harm the employee's "reputation," if those reasons are "publicized," and may prevent the employee from securing other employment, an employee's liberty interest to search for another job may have been compromised, and some due process protections will be required.

The protections that employees should receive for violation of a liberty interest are similar to those required for violation of a property interest. If the employee requests, a "trial-type hearing" must be given so the employee has an opportunity to "clear his or her name." For example, if a fire department discharges a nonunion probationary employee (with no property interest in continued employment), if the reasons for the discharge include allegations that the employee is a liar, a cheat, and a crook, and if these allegations are somehow made public (even "through the grapevine"), the employee would be entitled to an opportunity to prove that he or she is not a liar, cheat, or crook. If only the city council and the discharged employee are aware of the reasons for discharge, the reasons have not been "publicized" and there is probably no need for a hearing. Furthermore, no hearing is required if the employee does not dispute the truth of the allegations.

The* Loudermill *case A 1985 case, *Cleveland Board of Education* v. *Loudermill*,[28] is very important because it modifies historical due process requirements by requiring that employers give employees the opportunity for a hearing *before* termination. *Loudermill*, issued by the U.S. Supreme Court, consisted of two companion cases. In the first, plaintiff Loudermill was discharged from his position as a security guard for lying on his employment application; he indicated that he had never been convicted of a felony, but his employer later learned that he had been convicted of grand larceny. Loudermill appealed to a Civil Service Commission and lost. In the second case, plaintiff Donnelly was discharged from his position as bus mechanic for failing an eye examination. Donnelly also appealed to the Civil Service Commission, and was reinstated without back pay. Both filed suit in federal court in separate actions, and both cases found their way to the U.S. Supreme Court.

The defendants in both cases contended that whatever property right plaintiffs had, the procedures for terminating that right were defined by state law, which merely guaranteed appeals to the Civil Service Commission after discharge. The Supreme Court disagreed, finding that the procedures for deprivation of a property right are spelled out under the Constitution; *both* constitutional and state procedural rules must be followed before the discharge will be effective.

The court stated that "some kind of hearing" is required *before* terminating a property right. The Supreme Court did *not* spell out the details of that hearing. At various points in this decision, the Court indicated there should be "some opportunity for the employee to present his side of the case," "a meaningful opportunity to invoke the discretion of the decisionmaker," and "an opportunity to respond" to allegations of misconduct. It also indicated that the hearing may be "something less" than a full evidentiary hearing; the hearing "need not definitively resolve the propriety of the discharge"; "it should be an initial check against mistaken decisions"; the hearing should determine "whether there are reasonable grounds to believe that the charges against the employee are true and support the proposed action"; it should include "the opportunity to present reasons, either in person or in writing"; the employee should receive "oral or written notice of the charges against him, [and] an explanation of the employer's evidence"; and finally, "the formality and procedural requisites for the hearing can vary, depending on the importance of the interests involved and the nature of the subsequent proceedings."

This case gives very little guidance on the precise boundaries of an appropriate pre-termination due process hearing. All that can be safely said after reading this case is that, where a full blown hearing is available *after* the termination (such as grievance arbitration or civil service commission review), the employer is nonetheless obligated to notify the employee of the charges against him, briefly review the evidence, and give the employee a chance to present his or her side of the story, all *before* the decision to discharge is made.

Conclusion

In addition to the restrictions found in Civil Service statutes, just cause provisions of applicable collective bargaining agreements, and departmental rules and regulations, communities and fire chiefs must comply with due process requirements before disciplining or discharging employees. The discipline process is very complex. The interplay of the just cause and constitutional due process protections discussed above will be affected by local civil service statutes, the provisions of the city charter, and a myriad of other federal, state, and local statutory protections. It is difficult to generalize in this complex area. Nonetheless, if constitutional due process protections and the just cause standard can be met, the employer will have a strong argument that an employee's discipline or discharge was proper and justified.

A final word

Public-sector labor relations is a complex area. This chapter is designed to give the fire chief a legal and practical framework for understanding the process. However, it is difficult to find a substitute for experience in this very difficult field. Overall, the chief who is successful at labor relations is the one who understands the concepts addressed in this chapter, but moreover, understands the personnel in the department. Whether the resulting process is cooperative, conciliatory, or dictatorial will depend on the ability of the fire chief to work in both the legal and the interpersonal environments.

1   Norwalk Teachers' Association v. Board of Education, 138 Conn. 269, 83 A.2d 842 (1951).
2   See Calvin William Sharpe, *Introduction: The Ohio Public Sector Bargaining Law*, 35 Case W. Res. L. Rev. 345, 348 (1985).
3   *Id.; Developments in the Law: Public Employment*, 97 Harv. L. Rev. 1611, 1678 (1984).
4   *See* Wisconsin Statutes Annotated §111.70–.97 (West 1978).
5   Sharpe, *supra*, at 346.
6   H. Tanimota and G. Inaba, *State Employee Bargaining: Policy and Organization*, 108 Monthly Lab. Rev. 5, 53 (51) (1985).
7   IAFF Local 1088 v. City of Berlin.
8   City of Fond du Lac (Fire Department), Dec. No. 22373.
9   City of Bangor v. Bangor Firefighters Association, Decision of MLRB, 9-2-83.
10 City of Salem v. IAFF Local 314, 684 P.2d 605 (1984).
11 City of Waterbury, Decision No. 2472 (4-8-86).
12 Northland Fire Protection District, III. SLRB (10-23-85).
13 City of Eau Claire, WERC 5-22-80.
14 City of Kelso, PERC 12-20-84.
15 City of Stamford (Connecticut SBLR 3-18-84).
16 Taft Broadcasting Company, 163 NLRB 475, 64 LRRM 1386 (1967).
17 5 U.S.C. §7311 (1976). Employees of the federal government are statutorily prohibited from striking. An individual is prohibited from holding a federal position if he ''participates in a strike, or asserts the right to strike against the government of the United States.''
18 Donald A. Dripps, ''New Direction for the Regulation of Public Sector Strikes'' 60 N.Y.U.L. Rev. 590, 591 (Oct. 1985).
19 United Steelworkers v. University of Alabama, 430 F. Supp. 996, 1001 (N.D. Ala. 1977), *aff'd.*, 599 F.2d 56 (5th Cir. 1979).
20 Steven B. Rynecki, Douglas A. Cairns, and Donald J. Cairns, *Firefighter Collective Bargaining Agreements* (Washington, D.C.: National League of Cities, 1979).
21 *See* City of Jamestown, CCH 72-2 ARB. N. 8392.
22 Adolph M. Koven and Susan L. Smith, *Just Cause: The Seven Tests* (San Francisco: Coloracre Publications, 1985).
23 City of Detroit, 61 LA 645.
24 In the Matter of Arbitration between City of Ardmore and IAFF Local 1881, PSAA 830017.
25 In the Matter of Arbitration between Clark County and IAFF Local No. 1908, PSAA 818160.
26 In the Matter of Arbitration between City of Tucson and IAFF Local 479, 1983.
27 Board of Regents v. Roth, 408 U.S. 564, 92 S.Ct. 2701, 33 L.Ed. 2d 548 (1972).
28 Cleveland Board of Education v. Loudermill, 470 U.S. 532, 105 S.Ct. 1487, 84 L.Ed. 2d 494 (1985).

Part three: Managing special services

Emergency management

The art of fire service management can be boiled down to two tasks: managing the department today and preparing it for tomorrow. The fire service manager can help meet both responsibilities by working to improve the community's emergency management capabilities. Improvements in emergency management not only prepare the department to cope with tomorrow's disasters, but also improve the management of day-to-day operations. These investments can also lead to improvements in working relations with other agencies and with other jurisdictions. By taking a leadership role in emergency management, fire service managers protect the public, their response personnel, and their own professional reputation. Thus, time and resources invested in emergency management can pay them current and future dividends.

Accordingly, fire service managers, both career and volunteer, should review their options to see how taking initiative in emergency management planning can help them meet the needs of today's and tomorrow's fire department. The purpose of this chapter is to help fire service managers examine their department's emergency management responsibilities in light of the changing missions of the fire service, the change in demand for traditional services, and growth in the hazards facing the community; and to give a practical overview of emergency management options and suggestions for improving a fire department's emergency management efforts.

Drawing on lessons learned from disaster response operations, the chapter discusses the role of the fire service in emergency management, the evolution of federal emergency management policy, and the options available to fire chiefs for mitigation, preparedness, response, and recovery. Like the rest of the book, this chapter focuses on the *management* aspects of emergency programs, rather than day-to-day tactical operations, which are covered in numerous other books for the fire service.

The fire service role

The fire service role in emergency management appears to be expanding. For one thing, the risks threatening our communities have increased and changed. In addition, there is a clear trend for fire departments to take on new missions, such as emergency medical services and hazardous materials response. When a department assumes the lead-agency role in one of these new missions, it increases the department's emergency management preparedness and response activities. Furthermore, it can be cost effective to assign emergency management responsibilities to an existing department instead of establishing a separate unit. Decisions of this nature must be based on the problems faced by the jurisdiction.

The growing risk

Experts predict that for the foreseeable future disasters will occur more frequently, will be more destructive, and will require better and more coordinated response than ever before.

National trends affecting emergency management

1. Shift from a federal focus to state and local governments. In the recent past, the long-term growth of a federal presence at the state and local levels has been curbed. State and local governments are not equipped to fill the many voids created by cuts in federal programs. On the other hand, there has been an increase in the quality of expertise found at the state and local levels.

2. Shift in demographics. The nation's elderly are clustering in areas that have never experienced such concentrated human settlements. Some of these areas are flood-prone and others will be demolished by hurricanes. Many of the nation's elderly are building retirement homes in canyons. And an increased number of Americans prefer mobile homes. Do we have even an estimate of the number of people residing in such dwellings who have operative warning systems and access to nearby shelters?

3. Shift in definitions of casualty and negligence. Liability has become a matter of concern for many emergency management professionals.

4. Shift to multi- or integrated hazard management. Although complex, the IEMS concept holds much promise. The manner in which IEMS will be implemented will affect the nation's security, as well as the lives of those at risk today because of choices made regarding where to build a house.

5. Shift from structural mitigation to experiments with nonstructural approaches. The National Flood Insurance Program, for example, illustrates an emerging philosophy that has recast the question of flood prevention. Rather than continue with the basic flood-mitigation approaches of dam builders, we must now ask: "What is the most efficient use of flood-prone lands?"

6. Shift in professional expectations. A new group of emergency management professionals is emerging. As in other occupational groups, this rising professional ethic will bring new levels of expertise, and important political pressures, into the emergency management arena.

Source: Abridged from Thomas E. Drabek, *Some Emergining Issues in Emergency Management*, National Emergency Training Center Monograph Series, vol. 1, no. 3 (Emmitsburg, Md., 1984).

First, increasing numbers of citizens are exposed to chemical and technological dangers. Industries using hazardous substances are often located in close proximity to residential areas, and hazardous materials are transported through densely populated communities by highway and rail. Some chemicals are relatively new, and measures for their containment and control are not yet tested.[1] Second, the social and economic interdependence of today's complex metropolitan areas increases the potential for disasters with regional and even national reverberations.[2] Third, floods and hurricanes threaten new, high-risk developments at the seaside and on floodplains.[3] Finally, antisocial behavior presents new dangers. Experts predict a growing threat from domestic terrorism. Product tampering that began with the "Tylenol murders" suggests just one path that domestic terrorism can take. In our increasingly interdependent society, we grow more vulnerable to threats and the consequences of such actions. Communities ill-prepared to deal with the consequences of these acts may have to pay a very high price indeed.

Although local officials may view disasters as too rare to be worth the investment in time and energy, survey data indicate otherwise:

1. Over half of the jurisdictions responding to a 1982 survey conducted by the International City Management Association reported that they had experienced a disaster in the past twelve years.
2. In the same survey, local governments reported over $16 billion in property losses, 2,490 deaths, and 9,161 injuries from disasters since 1970.[4]
3. In an earlier survey 40 percent of the responding fire chiefs indicated that a disaster had caused activation of their disaster plan. Winter blizzards, water disasters, wind storms (hurricanes or tornadoes), and hazardous materials incidents were the primary disasters that caused the local plan to be activated.[5]

Clearly, local governments are at risk and can expect disaster to strike sooner or later.

The changing fire service

Managing today's department typically means managing more than one mission. Fire departments practicing only the art of fire suppression are now rare. In their place are departments performing an ever-widening array of services, including emergency medical response and transport; light, heavy, and specialty rescue; specialized extrication; and hazardous materials response. In fact, these make up the bulk of many departments' responses, while the traditional service, fire suppression, has slipped to a lower percentage of total responses.

Although the number of fires may be declining, however, the fire suppression mission itself has become more complex in the face of new and greater risks. High-rise structures have become increasingly common. Technology has changed the way buildings are constructed and how they are furnished. As the MGM Grand fire in Las Vegas demonstrated, fires in modern, high-tech structures can grow to disastrous proportions. Firefighting tactics have changed to better manage the heavy resource demands and allow for a more coordinated approach to the high-rise fire problem.

Increasingly, small and rural departments face the responsibility of protecting large developments and even high-rise structures. These incidents show why all departments should be prepared to move smoothly from a routine response mode to one requiring large-scale, multi-agency incident management.

Many fire departments have also assumed lead-agency responsibilities for hazardous materials response. Incidents such as Bhopal and Mississauga warn fire departments that have accepted the leadership role in handling hazardous material incidents how significant a challenge these materials pose. Planning and response may require coordination from twenty or more local, state, and

---

It can happen here   The typical U.S. community faces a major disaster about once every twelve years. This means that a chief of average tenure may never have to activate the emergency management plan. On the other hand, a department may face multiple disasters in a few days. Under a newly elected chief, the Bullhead City (Arizona) Volunteer Fire Department undertook the following in four days: fought a major brushfire (which almost trapped eighty firefighters when the winds shifted back on their fire lines); re- sponded 50 miles to bring the first arriving mutual aid units to a hazardous materials incident (BLEVE) in Kingman, Arizona; responded to a multi-alarm casino conflagration in Loughlin, Nevada; battled a fatal gasoline tanker truck explosion; and controlled a multi-alarm shopping center fire. Although this is an extreme case, the point that it makes is sobering: No fire chief, even in small communities or in remote areas, can afford to say, "It won't happen here."

federal response agencies. Even after a minor spill law enforcement agencies may have to control traffic and crowds, public works agencies may have to provide essential supplies such as sand and heavy equipment for cleanup and debris removal, and health agencies may have to check for environmental damage. In more complex incidents, the roadsides leading to the scene can clog with vehicles as responders from other jurisdictions, state agencies, federal agencies, voluntary agencies, the media, public officials, and private industry descend on the scene.

The changes in the nature of the hazards and the requirements for effective, coordinated response mean that fire departments have to improve day-to-day operations in a number of missions. Although the range of missions differs from department to department, most missions share common requirements: effective techniques to manage complex emergency incidents, coordination with other organizations, and skill in communicating with all segments of the community (including the public, the private sector, voluntary agencies, and the media). These improvements enable the department to assume a greater role in emergency management. In short, many fire departments already have in place the systems and resources necessary for that role, even though large emergencies

---

The nature of disasters Disasters are qualitatively different from smaller emergencies.

During disasters, organizations are forced into more and different kinds of interactions with other groups. For example, businesses may be required to interact with social service agencies for the first time during crisis periods. Local private groups may be required to coordinate their activities with remote and/or unfamiliar governmental bureaucracies. There is little time to adjust to the blurring of interorganizational boundaries, or the informal sharing or pooling of personnel, tasks, and equipment.

During disasters, organizations lose some of their autonomy. The freedom of mobility within the community, for example, may be restricted by police barricades or an evacuation order. Or, during disasters involving chemicals, site control may be vested in an outside agency such as a state or regional hazardous materials response team or FEMA.

During disasters, performance standards for organizations may change.

For example, while standard operating procedures for fire service professionals require a swift response to emergencies involving structural fires, firefighters respond differently to fire-related emergencies involving unidentified chemical substances or materials whose properties are not thoroughly understood.

During disasters, the boundaries between public and private organizations may be crossed, and a more cohesive relationship between public and private sectors is required.

In short, a disaster is not simply a large-scale accident or emergency. Organizations must recognize that during crisis situations the environment changes quickly and drastically and that their disaster preparedness planning and response strategies must give consideration to this important fact.

Source: Abridged from Enrico L. Quarantelli, *Organizational Behavior in Disasters and Implications for Disaster Planning*, National Emergency Training Center Monograph Series (Washington, D.C.: Government Printing Office, 1984).

and disasters require nonroutine responses. The fire department is involved in emergency management even when the direct responsibility lies elsewhere.

Responsibilities under SARA

In 1986 Congress passed the Superfund Amendments and Reauthorization Act (SARA). This law, which is directed toward the nation's hazardous materials problem, establishes significant planning requirements for states and localities. Every person in the fire service is affected by the requirements set forth in SARA, and it is very important that fire officers review the requirements and participate in local planning committees.

Here are the major features of the law:

1. Each governor must appoint a state emergency response commission, which is required to designate local emergency planning districts, appoint a local emergency planning committee for each district, supervise and coordinate the activities of these planning committees, review emergency plans, receive chemical release notifications, and establish procedures for receiving and processing requests from the public for information and/or copies of emergency response plans, material safety data sheets, and EPA's list of extremely hazardous substances.
2. SARA identifies the types of organizations that should be included in the emergency planning committee. The fire department is identified as one such group.
3. Facilities are subject to specific requirements for planning and notification of a release if a substance on EPA's list of extremely hazardous substances is present at the facility in an amount in excess of the threshold planning quantity for that substance.
4. Facilities must notify the emergency planning committee of a representative who will be the facilities emergency coordinator.
5. Local facility owners and operators are required to provide necessary information to the local emergency planning committee.
6. If a release occurs the legislation requires that the community emergency coordinator be notified.
7. October 1988 was set as the deadline for completion of an emergency plan by the local planning committee. Local state planning committees can provide the additional specific requirements of the local planning committee.[6]

It is important that local officials prepare themselves to deal with this legislation. Since hazardous materials are an integral part of a fire department's response, initiation of plans will be extremely beneficial.

Lessons for fire service managers

In meeting this challenge in emergency management, fire service managers should bear in mind the lessons learned about emergency management practices and needs from U.S. disasters in the recent past. These lessons include the following:

1. The most frequent problems encountered in responding to the disaster are problems in coordination and communication.
2. Managers "cannot expect to manage major emergencies with the same clear boundaries between public agencies and the community that normally exist."[7]
3. Postdisaster critiques reveal underutilization of available resources, particularly in the private sector and voluntary agencies.

4. Response must be as close to day-to-day procedures as possible.
5. Plans must be tested.
6. The chief administrative officer should take an active leadership role in the planning.
7. Emergency management is seldom a high priority among citizens—until a disaster occurs.

The challenge confronting the fire service manager in applying these lessons bears out the words of H. G. Wells: "Human history becomes more and more a race between education and catastrophe."

The evolution of federal emergency management policy

Emergency management concepts at the federal level have changed in response to the growing challenges from natural and technological disasters and continual innovations in disaster mitigation and response. Federal emergency management policies have evolved significantly since the Second World War. During the 1950s, the federal government's thrust was toward local civil preparedness for wartime emergencies. During the 1960s and early 1970s, policies were adopted to make civil defense resources available for dual use: preparation for both wartime emergencies and peacetime disasters. With the creation of the Federal Emergency Management Agency (FEMA) in 1979, congressional policies fostered hazard-specific planning for a range of disasters, including peacetime and wartime nuclear disasters, earthquake, hurricane, and floods. In 1981, FEMA began to adopt an all-hazards approach to provide a "single, flexible system capable of adjusting to many kinds of hazards."[8]

Comprehensive emergency management

The long-term goal that FEMA adopted to achieve this all-hazard approach is known as comprehensive emergency management (CEM)—the capability at each level of government to

1. Coordinate with other levels
2. Carry out activities effectively in the areas of mitigation, preparedness, response, and recovery
3. Deal with all types of potential hazards.[9]

The CEM approach is based on the premise that each phase of emergency management—mitigation, preparedness, response, and recovery—is a building block for dealing with the next phase (see Figure 13–1).

Mitigation　Mitigation activities are those that reduce the probability or limit the effects of a disaster. They often take the form of regulations, ordinances, and similar initiatives that achieve mitigation through engineering, enforcement, or education. Restricting wood shingle roofing in wildfire-prone areas is one example that illustrates how local governments can act to mitigate hazards.

Preparedness　Preparedness activities include planning how to respond in case an emergency or disaster occurs. This phase also includes increasing the resources available and improving their effectiveness. Preparedness activities are designed to help save lives and minimize damage by preparing people to respond appropriately when an emergency is imminent. To properly respond, a jurisdiction must have a plan, trained personnel, and necessary resources.

Response　Response activities include warning, rescue and other on-scene operations, and evacuation. Response activities are designed to provide emergency assistance to victims, protect property, and reduce the likelihood of secondary

Figure 13–1   The four phases of comprehensive emergency management.

Definitions	General measures
Mitigation: actions taken to eliminate or reduce the degree of long-term risk to human life and property from natural and man-made hazards; mitigation assumes that society is exposed to risks whether or not an emergency occurs	Building codes Disaster insurance Land use management Litigation Monitoring/inspection Public education Research Risk mapping Safety codes Statutes/ordinances Tax incentives/disincentives
Preparedness: actions taken in advance of an emergency that develop operational capabilities and facilitate an effective response in the event an emergency occurs	Continuity of government Emergency broadcast system Emergency communications Emergency operations centers Emergency operations plans Emergency public information materials Exercise of plans/systems Hazards analysis Mutual aid agreements Resource management Training response personnel Warning systems
Response: actions taken immediately before, during, or directly after an emergency occurs to save lives, minimize damage to property, and enhance the effectiveness of recovery	Emergency plan activation Emergency broadcast system activation Emergency instructions to the public Emergency medical assistance Staffing the emergency operations center Public official alerting Reception and care Shelter/evacuation Search and rescue Resource mobilization Warning systems activation
Recovery: activity to return vital life-support systems to minimum operating standards and long-term activity designed to return life to normal or improved levels	Crisis counseling Damage assessment Debris clearance Decontamination Disaster assistance centers Disaster insurance payments Disaster loans and grants Disaster unemployment assistance Public information Reassessment of emergency plans Reconstruction Temporary housing

damage. The local fire department, police department, rescue squad, public works personnel, emergency medical services, and other emergency support services are primary responders, but the response phase includes all services that reduce casualties and damage and/or speed recovery.

Recovery   Recovery consists of both short-term and long-term activities. This continues until all systems are returned to minimum operating standards. Short-term activities include restoration of vital services, such as food supply, temporary shelter, and utilities. Long-term recovery from a disaster may continue for years until the entire disaster area is completely redeveloped, either as it was in the past or for entirely new purposes that are less disaster-prone. For example, flood-prone areas can be rezoned and the area turned into open space or parkland. This illustrates that during recovery, opportunities to mitigate future disasters arise. Recovery planning should include a review of ways to avoid future emergencies and to improve preparedness and response.

Comprehensive emergency management requires a partnership among local, state, and federal governments. This strategy is built upon the principle of teamwork—strong coordination and cooperation between agencies and jurisdictions.[10] Previously, the federal emphasis on war-related planning obscured this partnership. The fact that the title of civil defense director has changed in many communities to that of emergency management coordinator or emergency program manager reflects the position's prime responsibility: to coordinate the planning for and response to all types of disasters that could affect the locality. Emergency services managers have become more sophisticated in their approach to coordinating the response to major incidents.

This evolution in federal policy has brought it into a more realistic alignment with local priorities. By preparing for all hazards, natural or man-made, fire departments and other local agencies are encouraged to play a far more active role in all four phases of emergency management.

Integrated Emergency Management System

The Federal Emergency Management Agency adopted the Integrated Emergency Management System (IEMS) as the basic strategy for achieving comprehensive emergency management. CEM is the goal and IEMS is an approach. The IEMS process is outlined in Figure 13–2. The cooperative integrated approach to disaster management is not a new concept at the local level. Many local governments have used elements of the strategy to prepare for natural and man-made disasters for many years, and these governments are currently incorporating IEMS concepts into their own emergency management systems. Basically, the premise of IEMS is that all organizations plan together for the various disasters that could occur in that locality. Then, when a disaster occurs, all agencies can react in a coordinated manner. IEMS is designed to develop all the capabilities required to perform the functions common to all types of disasters.

IEMS recognizes that the size and scope of the emergency spectrum ranges from isolated events, like explosions and fires, to wide-area disasters, like tornadoes, hurricanes, earthquakes, conventional war, and nuclear war. Different as their threats are, their management requires the same tools and procedures: direction and control, population protection, communications, resource coordination, medical care, and public information.

While IEMS emphasizes these functional similarities, it also recognizes unique aspects of each type of hazard. The importance of each function and the levels of resources required will vary from incident to incident. For example, the problems associated with a catastrophic failure at a nuclear power plant will require special attention and will require greater federal involvement.

Thus, IEMS is a management strategy for developing, implementing, and operating a community's emergency management system. The IEMS strategy specifically consists of

1. Addressing all the potential hazards faced by a community
2. Establishing an emergency management program that is tailored to the specific requirements of each community
3. Developing plans that consider the functions common to all types of disasters (e.g., warning), as well as the activities unique to specific emergencies (e.g., radiological monitoring)

4. Incorporating existing personnel assignments, operating procedures, and facilities into the disaster response plan (to the extent possible)
5. Establishing a full partnership among federal, state, and local governments (with provision for flexibility at the different levels of government) for achieving common goals
6. Integrating emergency management planning into the mainstream of overall state and local government policy making and operations
7. Including all local government agencies, (e.g., law enforcement, public works, finance, etc.) together with the private sector (e.g., the American Red Cross) as appropriate in the emergency management process
8. Addressing all four phases of emergency management: mitigation, preparedness, response, and recovery; this includes the development of a general plan with special "annexes" to cover agency-specific, or disaster-specific needs.

When implemented, IEMS provides a systematic approach to comprehensive emergency management. It seeks to provide citizens with a response capability that is reliable, predictable, coordinated, and effective.

Any community approach that addresses these elements—whether it is called IEMS or something else—will inevitably help improve the community's emergency response capabilities.

Reviewing options

Assessing current capabilities for effective emergency management requires, first, an understanding of the relationship between emergency management and fire protection and, second, a determination of what policy options should be pursued. Fire protection master planning and emergency management planning are quite similar in their approach to making strategic choices. Emergency management, like fire protection, requires a systems approach.

The four phases of emergency management—mitigation, preparedness, response, and recovery—have rough parallels in terms more familiar to the fire

---

Figure 13–2 The IEMS process.

1. Hazards analysis. Identify potential hazards to the community and the possible impact of each hazard on people and property.
2. Capability assessment. Measure current capabilities against FEMA's standards and criteria for basic emergency management functions to identify local weaknesses.
3. Emergency operations plans. Develop a plan applicable to all potential hazards, with separate treatment of specific hazards.
4. Capability maintenance. Keep plans up to date, equipment in good repair, personnel trained, procedures tested.
5. Mitigation efforts. Take steps to eliminate or reduce hazards and to limit their potential effects.
6. Emergency operations. Employ current plans to meet any emergency that arises, and use it as an opportunity to test existing capabilities under real conditions.
7. Evaluation. Analyze the outcome of emergency operations to further assess capabilities and identify the need for future mitigation efforts.
8. Capability shortfall. Note the areas where current capability falls short of FEMA standards and criteria.
9. Multi-year development plan. Prepare a five-year plan addressing the shortfalls and outlining steps toward reaching the desired level of capability.
10. Annual development increment. Determine the next year's goals and the financial and technical assistance needed to accomplish them.
11. State/local resources. Use state and local resources as appropriate to make the designated improvements.
12. Federal sources. Use FEMA's Comprehensive Cooperative Agreements with states as the vehicle for funding FEMA-approved activities.
13. Annual work increment. Revise emergency operations plans and multi-year development plans to reflect the improvements achieved each year.

service: prevention, training, response, and return to service (see Figure 13–3). Because it is important to consider options in all four phases of the comprehensive emergency management system, the following sections take each emergency phase in order and point out options for the fire service executive to consider.

A thorough review of the community's emergency management status is likely to reveal a number of potential areas for improvement. Most departments will benefit from a careful assessment of what steps can be taken immediately and over the long haul to improve the community's readiness.

The first step in improving emergency management is to review the department's current responsibilities. This should be done at least annually. A department currently responsible for emergency management has a different set of considerations than a department without this responsibility or one that is about to assume it. Whatever the degree of current responsibility, a complete size-up would include a thorough review of the community's emergency management or disaster plan,[11] a review of potential hazards and current capabilities, and a determination of which options can be pursued with high confidence of success.

On the basis of these initial reviews and consultation with other community organizations, as appropriate, the fire service manager should formulate an action plan that specifies what options will receive priority attention. This action plan could be narrowly focused or comprehensive. At one extreme the review could lead to actions as simple as hosting a meeting with counterparts in other agencies or drafting a memo to the jurisdictions' CAO outlining options for improvements. On the other hand, the review could result in a decision to undertake a wholesale review of all emergency management policies. The option selected is less important than its probability of success. Given emergency management's historically low priority in most communities, options that produce tangible results in a short time at low risk should receive prime consideration.

Mitigation options

Fire and building codes and sprinkler ordinances are examples of disaster prevention through mitigation activities. The fire service can consider other options as well. Floodplain management and other aspects of land use planning are areas for greater fire service involvement. By taking part in land use planning decisions, the fire service can influence actions that will later determine the risk to the community from man-made and natural hazards as well as the capability of the department to protect the community from these hazards.

Hazardous materials is another area in which increased mitigation is likely. Like fire prevention, mitigation in hazardous materials storage and transportation means increasing safety and reducing excessive risks; educating the public as well as those directly involved in handling hazardous materials; and enforcement, which may include restricting and monitoring storage and shipment. Because of the number of public and private sector interests in this field, Superfund legislation requires special local planning bodies to determine how best to prevent and control hazardous materials emergencies.

Preparedness: emergency management planning

Preparedness includes planning, training, team-building and improving any aspect of the community's ability to respond. History provides some important lessons about preparedness:

1. At the heart of preparedness is sound planning.
2. Activities that are not normally thought of as part of the conventional planning process are the key to creating an effective plan.
3. Plans that address only governmental resources will be ill-prepared to deal with forces in the community (such as the public) and outside it (the national media, volunteer resources), and these difficult-to-control forces can create the "disaster after the disaster."
4. Teamwork is essential in designing the plan and building the system.
5. Plans cannot be tested in the files; they must be tested in the field through training, drills, and exercises.

The main obstacle to emergency management preparedness does not appear to be the lack of a written plan, as most local governments have such plans.[12] It is far more likely that the plan was developed without sufficient input from all parties with a stake in emergency management, has not been improved through regular review and exercise, and fails to anticipate postdisaster events.

The remainder of this section describes a logical process for emergency management planning, and the bibliography for the chapter cites a number of resources that can guide managers through the process. In brief, the steps include

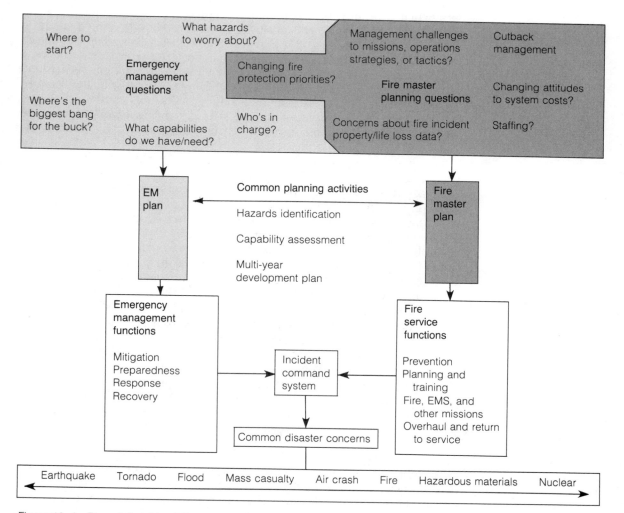

Figure 13–3 The relationship of fire protection and emergency management planning activities.

1. Getting political commitment
2. Building a planning team
3. Identifying hazards and assessing capabilities
4. Coordinating with other agencies, both public and private, that should be involved in emergency preparedness, response, or recovery to determine the status of their capabilities, requirements, and resources
5. Developing the basic plan, based on a review of existing plans; selecting and outlining the functional annexes and the hazard-specific appendixes for review by the planning team
6. Developing the fire and rescue functional annex
7. Gaining official approval by the governing body
8. Maintaining and updating the plan through regular, communitywide disaster drills, table-top exercises, and multi-agency critiques of special incidents.

Getting political commitment

No emergency management plan will work unless the political leadership of the community supports it. The plan depends on the chief administrative officer (city manager, mayor, or other executive) for approval of the planning process, designation of an interdepartmental planning team or task force, and approval of budgetary requests for staff positions and other resources.

City managers, mayors, and members of local governing bodies may not perceive emergency management planning as a priority. They often face issues that they consider more urgent and immediate than a planning process whose payoff appears to be at best distant and uncertain. Many communities have never experienced a major disaster, so political and administrative leaders may not envision the consequences of neglect. Similarly, owing to lack of experience, they may believe the community is better prepared than it actually is, or that somehow it can "muddle through."

It is the responsibility of the fire chief to promote the importance of emergency preparedness. The means of doing so depend on the state of emergency management planning in the community and the official role of the fire department in the process. At a minimum, the fire service manager can take an active role in improving the planning process and lobby other organizations (public and private) to join in the planning effort.

The chief can go further by making formal presentations to the governing body and by engaging other organizations through workshops or exercises. Typically, local elected officials are not well versed in the risks facing their community or the role comprehensive emergency planning can play in reducing that risk. A specially tailored presentation to the elected body often secures official approval for the planning process. Workshops provide an ideal opportunity for public and private organizations to begin to work more closely together in the planning process.[13] They are particularly effective as a kickoff for a large communities or where a number of jurisdictions may want to consider joint planning or resource sharing. A large-scale fire disaster exercise can drive home the need for interagency planning. By inviting senior policymakers, other agencies, the media, and private volunteer agencies to take part, the chief can demonstrate the need for interagency planning.

The goal of such initiatives is to receive a mandate for some specific action, be it as large as a complete remake of the community's plan or as limited as an exploratory task force to review options. Sometimes conditions are such that only a limited step can be taken. Nevertheless, taking that single step is important. Indeed, where resistance is high and confidence is low, taking a piece-meal approach is almost always better than waiting for conditions to change sufficiently to support a comprehensive program. Anything that builds teamwork among organizations contributes to preparedness. The step itself or the sequence in which steps are taken is less important than the fact that one or more steps can be identified as success stories. Attacking the problem by breaking it down into smaller tasks is as valid around the planning table as it is on the fireground.

Building a planning team

Once the backing of political leaders is obtained, the next step is to organize a team to carry out the plan or improvement. The size and composition of the planning group must meet local needs and the project's scope. In principle the planning team needs to represent all the public and private sector interests that can play a role in developing the community's preparedness, but then it might be too large to actually perform the planning. Therefore, it is customary to use an advisory council to provide the representation and a smaller core group to undertake the detailed planning. It is best if the core group consists of at least one individual who can be assigned to the project full time. Without this commitment, the planning process can lose momentum or be sidetracked by the urgent press of other duties. Full-time assignments might last for several months to a year or more, depending on the scope of the planning activity.

Membership in the core team should consist of the chief administrative officer or his or her designee and key emergency response agencies such as fire, rescue, police, public works and utilities, in addition to those with direct emergency management responsibilities.

Any local volunteer fire department should be represented on the disaster planning team. Volunteer departments often are the first to respond to an incident, the first to begin operations, and the first to establish an incident command system. How they react will in some situations determine the severity of the incident. In addition to their personnel, facilities, and equipment, volunteer departments often have access to critical resources in the community at large. These resources should be identified and utilized as appropriate.

Despite the difficulty that some volunteer departments have in finding the time and resources to take part in preparedness activities, such as planning and disaster exercises, every effort needs to be made to see that they play an active role. As a minimum, volunteer chiefs should meet with local officials to ensure that the department will be adequately represented during the planning process and that it will be committed to the plan once it is in place.

When planning is multi-jurisdictional, it is more likely to result in implementation than planning undertaken by a single jurisdiction. The reason may be "peer pressure"—that is, participating jurisdictions seem to strive to keep the planning process on track and see the results implemented, rather than be seen as the first partner to renege on a multi-jurisdictional agreement.[14]

It is likely that the most frequent form that multi-jurisdictional emergency planning will take is countywide planning. This may involve the participation of a number of incorporated and unincorporated areas. Multi-jurisdictional planning obviously takes even more organization. Because commitment has to be obtained from a number of jurisdictions, this option is often overlooked or dismissed as being too difficult. Before communities come to a decision, however, they should weigh both the pros and the cons of this approach. A multi-jurisdictional approach is appropriate if there has been a track record of successful multi-jurisdictional efforts for similar activities, resource limitations within the jurisdictions make "solo" emergency planning impractical or undesirable, or emergency response practices commonly call for jurisdictions to respond together.

Identifying hazards and assessing capabilities

Next in the emergency management planning process is a comprehensive identification of potential hazards facing the community and an assessment of the community's capabilities to deal with those hazards. Once shortfalls have been identified, the community can begin to estimate the time and other resources needed to develop and maintain a desired level of emergency management capability.

The Federal Emergency Management Agency has prepared a planning tool to help cities and counties begin this process. Known as the Hazard Identification, Capability Assessment, and Multi-Year Development Plan (HICA/MYDP), the planning tool outlines a logical process for determining priorities and scheduling activities to improve emergency management.

Local governments receiving Emergency Management Assistance support (sometimes referred to as civil defense matching funds or Comprehensive Co-operative Agreement [CCA] funds) are required to submit HICA/MYDP data to FEMA annually. FEMA encourages jurisdictions to convene a group of local officials involved in emergency management activities to participate in this planning process that identifies hazards and assesses capability using a standard workbook.[15] Local fire officials should logically take part in any local team that develops or reviews the HICA/MYDP materials.

FEMA provides feedback to each participating jurisdiction in the form of a local data report. Fire officials not familiar with the HICA/MYDP workbook results and the local data report can check with local emergency management officials.

The HICA/MYDP process is not designed to be the only tool used in developing the community's comprehensive emergency management plan, but it does facilitate a description of hazards, capabilities, and development plans.

Coordinating with other agencies

Turf battles and ambiguity over authority are not uncommon in a disaster. One reason is that during disasters local governments are forced to deal with many forces over which their control is limited—the media, voluntary agencies, and the public at large, for example. Another reason is that the boundaries of power among various public agencies and levels of government are far from clear in the unusual circumstances surrounding a disaster. Questions such as "Who's in charge in a hazardous materials incident on a highway" or "What agency, under what conditions, can order a hospital to be evacuated?" are difficult enough to determine in advance of an incident. Waiting for a disaster to occur before resolving these and similar role conflicts can make disaster control, which is never easy, impossible. The consequences can include improper resource utilization, fractured policy decisions, a tug of war for control at the scene, and negative publicity when the critique begins. Therefore, sorting out these and similar turf questions ahead of time is the only responsible course of action.

The secret to stopping turf battles is a joint examination of each agency's or government's potential roles, written definitions of those roles for each type disaster, and explanation of role definitions to all key players in advance. In practice, this requires an understanding of local, state, and federal regulations. Statutory provisions will often dictate who has the ultimate responsibility and who should be in charge at the scene. Agencies that do not have statutory authority will be less likely to try to usurp the authority of another agency if they understand both the legal requirements and how their responsibilites can be safely and effectively discharged under the provisions of the statute. In many instances the question of who is in charge will come down to a judgment call to be settled by the chief elected or appointed local official.

Another common thread that seems to run through many disaster critiques is the question of why existing resources were not used more effectively. In part the explanation lies in the assumptions and expectations of nonemergency workers. By virtue of their professions, librarians, recreation workers, and land use planners, for example, are not expected to think of potential disasters. But each may have a role in certain disaster scenarios. The librarian is essential in the classification of historical documents that could be used to rebuild a community. Recreation workers may be mobilized to provide activities for evacuees or their children as part of shelter planning. Planners must recognize floodplains, ground faults, and other natural problems when developing a land use plan. Many times persons without emergency experience are unaware that they might have a role to play in emergency management. Unless they are involved in an ongoing preparedness program, including disaster exercises, other agencies may not understand their responsibilities.

Developing the plan

The emergency management plan consists of three major elements:

1. The basic plan, which outlines the jurisdiction's approach to emergency management, including broad policies, plans, legal authorities, and procedures that "will be relied upon to alert, notify, recall, and employ emergency response forces, warn and protect citizens, protect property, and request aid/support from other local communities, the state, and/or the federal government."[16] The basic plan should assign responsibilities to all organizations and designate a lead agency that will have primary operational control for each type of disaster and will coordinate emergency operations center activities with the incident command system.
2. Functional annexes, which are a series of annexes that address activities and responsibilities common to most emergency response and recovery operations—e.g., communications, public information, direction and control, emergency organization, alerting and warning, population protection (evacuation and sheltering), contamination monitoring and control, emergency support services (fire and rescue, law enforcement, etc.), resource management, and continuity of government.
3. Hazard-specific appendixes, which contain technical information, details, and methods for use in a specific emergency, e.g., earthquake, nuclear facility accident.

Figure 13–4 illustrates the relationship of these three components in an emergency management plan.

The basic plan   The bibliography lists several documents fire service managers can consult in developing and reviewing a community's basic emergency management plan. Below is a checklist of features commonly omitted from a community's basic plan that disaster research has shown should be addressed.

1. Establishing emergency equipment rate and use agreements with contractors/industry
2. Establishing communication link to a major area radio/TV station, such as protected phone line or dedicated radio channel
3. Installing rotary phone connections and establishing staff procedures to operate a citizen emergency information phone bank (other than 911)
4. Training citizen members of Block Watch or other neighborhood-based groups for emergency self-help
5. Developing warning systems for all elements of the population
6. Establishing agreements with Radio Amateur Civil Emergency Service (RACES), CB, or other radio amateurs for assisting city staff in an emergency or warning situation
7. Establishing a location and staff responsible for a "media information center" at which reporters will be given frequently updated information during an extended emergency

Figure 13–4
Components of an
emergency operations
plan.

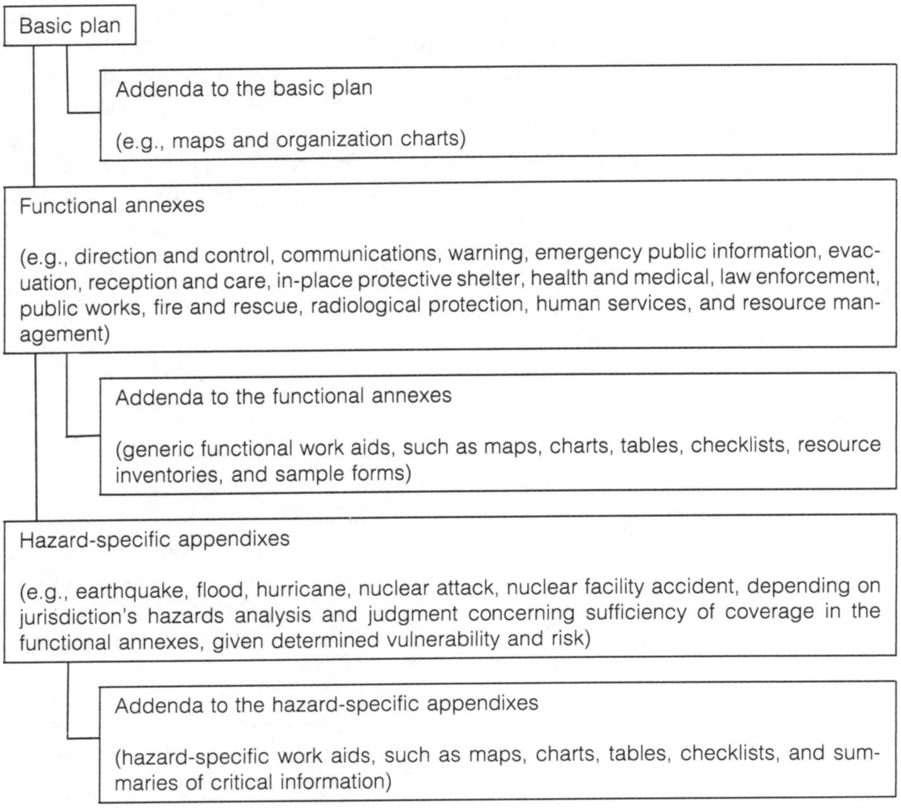

Basic plan

Addenda to the basic plan

(e.g., maps and organization charts)

Functional annexes

(e.g., direction and control, communications, warning, emergency public information, evacuation, reception and care, in-place protective shelter, health and medical, law enforcement, public works, fire and rescue, radiological protection, human services, and resource management)

Addenda to the functional annexes

(generic functional work aids, such as maps, charts, tables, checklists, resource inventories, and sample forms)

Hazard-specific appendixes

(e.g., earthquake, flood, hurricane, nuclear attack, nuclear facility accident, depending on jurisdiction's hazards analysis and judgment concerning sufficiency of coverage in the functional annexes, given determined vulnerability and risk)

Addenda to the hazard-specific appendixes

(hazard-specific work aids, such as maps, charts, tables, checklists, and summaries of critical information)

8. Designating and training city staff to take responsibility for organizing untrained citizen volunteers who may show up in a major emergency
9. Establishing a procedure (multiple casualty incident plan) with hospital and ambulance managers for coordinating the reception of casualties in a major emergency
10. Establishing open purchase orders or other means for city departments to make and document necessary emergency expenditures
11. Designating specific methods and staff trained to make public evacuation warnings, other than fixed outdoor sites
12. Designating usable vehicles and drivers to carry transit-dependent and mobility-impaired persons during an evacuation of a neighborhood or institution
13. Designating voluntary group or agency responsible for housing citizens temporarily evacuated from a hazardous area
14. Establishing an incident command system that designates staff who will provide needed command post services in a multi-agency emergency response (joint communications, food, media relations, etc.)
15. Providing for ''canned'' emergency ordinances and procedures (curfew, rationing, forcible evacuation, and other emergency measures).[17]

Functional annexes For each functional area, the functional annex specifically defines the responsibilities, tasks, procedures, and operations to be performed before, during, and after an emergency. Responsibilities should be analyzed to ensure there is no overlap or unclear responsibilities, and procedures for augmenting resources should be covered. Some of the operational actions identified in the annex may be hazard-specific, but the majority will be common to most types of disasters.

Some functional annexes like fire and rescue and law enforcement are likely candidates for development by a single agency. Others, such as command and control or communications, are likely to benefit from development by a multi-agency task force.

Hazard-specific appendixes   As necessary, hazard-specific appendixes must be developed and added to the functional annexes. The appendixes contain the special procedures for other hazard-specific incidents to deal with the unique requirements of various disaster types. Hazard-specific incidents that may need special procedures developed for them include major fires, terrorist incidents, hazardous materials, aircraft, rail (passenger and freight), floods, snow emergency, tornado, hurricane, water shortages, nuclear incident, war emergency, and any other emergency identified in the hazard analysis. A direct concern to fire departments is the fact that the specifics for managing a conflagration would be dealt with in the hazard-specific appendix for major fires. The appendix identifies what steps will be pursued when the event continues to escalate. For example, escalation may cause warning sirens to be sounded or mutual aid agreements to be enacted. More specific details that indicate what is to be done by the first units to arrive may be included by reference to the department rules, regulations, standard operating procedures, or policy statements.

A hazard-specific appendix needs to be developed for multi-casualty incidents. For example, a community's basic plan together with its functional annexes and mass casualty-specific appendix should enable responders to cope with a multi-casualty event on a highway complicated by inclement weather, hazardous materials, or special access/rescue problems.[18]

Multi-hazard evacuation plan   Green River, Wyoming, a city of about 15,000 in the southwestern corner of the state, is prepared for multiple dangers that could require evacuation of citizens. A major interstate and a railroad pose the possibility of hazardous materials accidents, and a dam 42 miles upriver poses a flood threat.

The city had an emergency operations plan that outlined separate evacuation procedures for these and other hazards, but it became clear that the plans had much in common and that one multi-hazard evacuation plan could be used instead.

Working with the county and with state emergency management agencies, local emergency planners identified the problem and the potential dangers the plan would address. They found that the following emergencies could be handled with one evacuation plan: (1) hazardous materials incidents, (2) flood or dam failure, (3) major fires, (4) health-related emergencies, and (5) nuclear war.

Next, the planners listed local reception and shelter areas, staging areas for buses, and evacuation routes. They counted the number of available city first responders and investigated the length of time necessary for call-out of off-duty personnel.

Faced with the question of how to notify the citizens, the city purchased and installed an outdoor warning system. This system is tested once a month in conjunction with the local emergency broadcast radio station. In addition, local police and fire equipment public address systems are available.

After taking these steps, the city contacted the county and state emergency management agencies for assistance in putting together a plan. Following meetings and several rewrites, Green River's Multi-Hazard Evacuation Plan was formalized.

In January 1988 the Chemical Manufacturers Association recognized the City of Green River Emergency Services group for its outstanding efforts toward improving Green River's emergency response capabilities.

A number of other appendixes merit the fire department's consideration. For example, an earthquake-specific appendix might be needed to explain that in such an event apparatus would have to be moved out of stations to keep it from being trapped inside in case of a structural failure.

Developing the fire and rescue annex

Beyond contributing to the basic plan and other functional annexes, fire departments will need to take the lead role in developing the fire and rescue functional annex and hazard-specific appendixes for the community's emergency operations plan.

This annex should outline the general policies, procedures, and responsibilities for fire prevention, fire suppression, and search and rescue under potential disaster conditions. The annex becomes a part of the operations or procedural manuals and should be available to all personnel. If search and rescue are not fire department responsibilities, they can be addressed by the appropriate agencies in a separate annex.

Even the smallest volunteer fire department should have a functional annex. Special considerations such as the need to coordinate the schedules of volunteers make it imperative for volunteer departments to work through this requirement. Many volunteer fire departments find this assignment is best delegated to a volunteer who is not currently active as a responder and thus has the time to complete this task.

The fire department annex should be compared with the other annexes of the plan to determine compatibility. Conflicts between agencies should be identified at the review stage, not at the incident site. Potential "turf battles" and other conflicts can be settled through this process.

The key provisions of a fire department functional annex include a description of the department's incident command system (ICS) and the establishment of a uniform ICS for all agencies that may be involved in disaster response, a system for recalling personnel to active duty, physical arrangements for emergency personnel and their dependents, and debriefing procedures.

Establishing incident command systems   A fire department's disaster response should be based on an effective incident command system. That is to say, when a normal fire operation expands to a major incident, there should be a specific procedure to follow. The incident command system should include specific definitions of responsibilities for both line and staff functions, formalized in an organization chart that depicts the relationship between staff and line operations. As the incident escalates, the system should permit an orderly buildup of resources.

The system used by the fire department must work in concert with the community's overall incident command system. If other agencies have a different approach to incident command or no approach at all, conflicts and misunderstandings will hurt performance at a most critical time. Other local government agencies should at least be familiar with the incident command system used by the fire department, but it would be even better if other emergency response agencies (police, public works, utility, and others) adopted a common system. A common system makes common sense and minimizes role conflicts; it need not mean the compromise of command or loss of control.

The same principle holds true for regional mutual aid systems. The fact that a particular jurisdiction has developed its own incident command procedures may mean it works well locally, but falls apart when mutual aid departments unfamiliar with it come to assist. Large counties, for example, usually have numerous local departments and each can practice independence to a fault. Common sense dictates a single countywide incident command system.

When an incident is confined to a single jurisdiction, incident command remains with that jurisdiction. When an incident involves more than one jurisdiction, a unified command system calls for joint decision making, but individual jurisdictions remain responsible for command within their own boundaries. At the same time, however, mutual aid chiefs may be required to become subordinate officers to a host jurisdiction's command structure. This situation may call for the utmost tact and professionalism, yet is necessary to reach the common objective of protecting the public. ICS is discussed in more detail later.

Obtaining additional resources   The functional annex also needs to provide for emergency recall of personnel. Most career fire departments work a schedule that allows two-thirds of the employees to be off duty at any one time. A specific process for calling those off-duty resources back to duty in an emergency is an essential element of the functional annex. This comprehensive recall or notification system must work reliably given the community's expected range of disasters. That is, it should work when activated as the command system dictates or when conditions warrant. It should also be capable of notifying the appropriate people quickly and accurately. Providing for the delayed release of on-duty personnel is another technique that can provide "surge capacity."

Volunteer departments must develop a call-back system that can be relied on to turn out sufficient members to meet major emergencies. In a volunteer department, the number of members available may vary greatly. Typically, however, the large number of active and inactive members provides a potentially large pool. Each organization should have an idea of how many people can be assembled at any given time.

Although only some of the members will serve as emergency responders, others can provide a wide range of support activities, from providing reserves to providing food, drink, and warm clothing to front-line fire and medical personnel. Other volunteers can maintain the fire station as a staging point, a supply point, or even, perhaps, as an evacuation center. Establishing a way to obtain sufficient response deserves forethought. Discussing the need to call back volunteers with local employers may prove beneficial. Many are willing to allow volunteers time off during a disaster or a pending disaster situation.

It is sound practice for both career and volunteer departments to test their recall procedures periodically.

Providing for needs of personnel and dependents   Sometimes emergency operation plans overlook the arrangements needed to assist families of those who are required to work during a disaster. The dependents of fire personnel and other emergency workers may be subjected to the same dangers and disruptions as others in a disaster area. Department members should be encouraged to work out a plan of action for their family members in the event of disaster. The department should also establish procedures to determine the well-being of dependents and assign specific personnel to coordinate this activity. These two steps can do much to relieve needless anxiety and increase the ability of emergency personnel to concentrate on their immediate responsibilities. In their planning, departments may wish to consider such special arrangements as evacuation centers for family members. For extended operations, a communication system with dependents must be anticipated. As soon as it is feasible, on-duty personnel should be able to receive messages from family members.

Crisis debriefing   What happens to firefighters or EMS personnel after all the victims of a disaster have been treated and transported to medical facilities? What happens to these same people weeks after the event? A growing body of evidence suggests that emergency workers can become silent victims of critical incidents through post-incident or post-traumatic stress.

Researchers have documented post-traumatic stress following the serious injury or death of a co-worker or a small child, and following mass casualty incidents, such as the Hyatt Regency skywalk collapse in Kansas City. Crisis debriefing is a way of helping emergency workers understand and cope with their reactions. Failure to provide debriefing and follow-up treatment as necessary could result in alcoholism, drug abuse, or other manifestations of an emergency worker's inability to cope with a traumatic event.

Either the basic plan or the fire and rescue functional annex should outline a crisis debriefing procedure. Experts in the field recommend that stress debriefing should begin as early in the incident as practical. Therefore, it should be an integral part of both the response and recovery phases. Psychologists, mental health workers, ministers, and others must be trained and organized in advance to help with the debriefing process.

Gaining official approval

It makes good legal as well as political sense to submit all policy-related decisions to the local governing body for debate and approval. This makes such decisions "discretionary," "planning," or "legislative" rather than "ministerial" acts.[19] As Chapter 9 explains, ministerial acts are far more open to challenge in any subsequent liability suit.

Since disaster plans by their very nature involve decisions and approvals at all levels, attention should be paid to which decisions need to be coordinated with or approved by other departments or governmental bodies.

Maintaining the plan

Because of the nature of disasters, it is unlikely that a formal plan, no matter how complete, can anticipate all the critical problems that will arise. Virtually every after-action report repeats this lesson. This does not mean plans are a wasted paper exercise; it means that plans are necessary, but not sufficient.

The interagency working relations developed through the planning process are the most effective vehicle for maintaining the plan and improving it through practice. Both periodic exercises and the lessons learned from local incidents and disasters elsewhere can provide the basis for updating and improving the plan.

Research has documented what communities do to prepare for the next disaster after they have suffered a major one. The results are worth noting:

What is interesting is that recent [disaster] experience does not change the effort put into traditional plan updates and exercises all that dramatically. What does increase dramatically is participation in the activities that push separate agencies into a dialogue with each other and with the governing body concerning how the system really works. Three of these activities are 1. multi-agency critiques after routine or moderate local emergencies; 2. regular meetings of a multi-departmental planning body; and 3. at least annual reviews of emergency roles with elected officials.[20]

These are exactly the kinds of activities that often fail to gain support before a real disaster tests local abilities. They are activities that build a capacity for collaboration.

Staff meetings   If the community's chief executive is willing to support it, holding a monthly emergency management meeting for all agencies and organizations involved can provide a long-term vehicle for improving preparedness. As the accompanying sidebar relates, a major benefit is the improved day-to-day working relationships among attending agencies. While the agenda may focus on emergency management topics, the relationships that are nurtured by the regular meetings help officials work together to resolve other operational problems.

Exercises and training   Training and exercise plans are the next logical step after the plan is revised and approved. The paradox here is that the need for exercises is well understood, but all too seldom acted upon. Consider these facts from a survey of local governments: Although nearly nine out of ten jurisdictions said that disaster preparedness training is needed in their community, only 58 percent of cities and 72 percent of counties actually test their plans annually.[21]

Even where plans are tested annually, local officials may point out that the exercise was not a true test of the community's emergency management capabilities.

To be effective, therefore, training must be realistic and include roles for senior management, policymakers, media, and the public. Table-top exercises can test many aspects of disaster preparedness and should be a part of an annual program to improve local and regional emergency management capability. State and federal emergency management officials can provide for both information and expertise in developing full-scale scenarios.

Some parts of a disaster plan may need to be tested more frequently than others and may be checked independently of other systems. Call-back procedures, for example, should be tested periodically, particularly for volunteer organizations. Volunteer chiefs cannot count on optimal staffing at any given point but must make projections. Time of day, day of week, season of the year, weather conditions, and other factors will affect the availability of volunteers. Call-back tests, like other disaster exercises, provide the framework for building an effective network of disaster response resources.

Response options

In the response phase, the capability gained through preparedness is tested by the requirement to react effectively to an emergency with the appropriate resources. This section describes three ways that communities can build bridges between day-to-day operations and disaster response capabilities:

1. Improving incident command for the fire department and for other agencies

---

Monthly emergency management meetings   In Prince William County, Virginia, the county executive hosts a monthly meeting of key departmental staff and representatives of nearby jurisdictions, federal and state agencies, and other groups with an interest or involvement in emergency management.

The meetings began after the director of fire and rescue service recognized that the support of the county executive was key to developing a strong emergency management system. Together, the two attended a seminar at the National Emergency Training Center. The county executive came away committed to action and appointed an emergency management services committee that became the core of the county's IEMS.

The meetings have been credited not only with improving emergency preparation but also with strengthening communications and working relations among all agencies, both in IEMS matters and in everyday operations.

Source: Excerpted from Joyce C. Eaby, with Robert S. Noe, Jr., and Selby C. Jacobs, "Starting a Fire at the Top," *International Fire Chief* 51, no. 10 (October 1985): 20–22.

2. Improving the effectiveness of the emergency operations center and integrating incident command with emergency operations center activities
3. Expanding mutual aid programs.

Improving incident command

As suggested earlier, one of the best ways to build an effective emergency management network is to build an interagency incident command system.[22] Many fire departments have adopted some form of fire incident command system. Fire officials should seek to expand the system until it can be used for all hazards, by all local response agencies, and with the response forces of neighboring jurisdictions.

The ICS is an integrated set of personnel, policies, procedures, and equipment linked together within a common organizational structure to perform a specific mission—usually the management of resources assigned to an incident.

The ICS concept was initiated in 1973 as a way to manage operations at large brush fires. It was developed by a team of individuals representing the major wildland firefighting agencies in California in a project that became known as FIRESCOPE. ICS proved so successful that it has been adopted by numerous federal, state, and local authorities. ICS was originally designed for use in multi-jurisdictional situations; that is, when resources of several jurisdictions (e.g., cities and counties) are working together on a given incident. These resources may be from a single discipline (e.g., law enforcement) or a number of different disciplines working together; such as fire, law enforcement, and emergency management.

The ICS consists of the following components:

1. Common terminology for personnel, facilities, equipment, organizational positions, and operational procedures
2. A common organizational structure for the entire incident; this structure normally includes: command, operations, planning, logistics, and finance functions. If the incident crosses jurisdictional boundaries, a unified management team is formed to represent the interests of all affected jurisdictions
3. A modular organizational framework that is built from the top down and tailored to meet the specific type and quantity of resources needed for a particular incident (this unified organizational structure brings all agencies within a common structure built to fit the needs of the incident: establishing the command positions first, then appointing operations, logistics, and planning, and financial positions only as they are needed)
4. Written or oral action plans to accomplish stated incident control objectives
5. Integrated facilities used, as appropriate, by all participating agencies and jurisdictions
6. Integrated communications providing inter-agency, interjurisdictional communications capability.[23]

ICS concepts will work for practically any agency or situation. In part, this is because ICS is based on sound organizational principles such as span of control, management by objectives, and operations research. It is also due in part to the fact that these organizational principles were tested and refined through a decade of large-scale wildfire operations and other major incidents.

Even though ICS was designed to manage large-scale incidents, it can be effectively used for routine incidents as well. In fact, experience has shown that agencies that use the ICS for routine work are more effective in their day-to-day operations and in major emergencies.

Agencies can practice ICS on a day-to-day basis by encouraging first-arriving officers to think of themselves as the incident commander. As such, they are responsible for overall command as well as operations, logistics, planning, and finance. Of course, in practice, the need for logistics, planning, and finance is usually so minor that it can be handled by the officer in charge. For most incidents, the only responsibility that may have to be delegated is operations. This happens when a battalion chief assumes overall incident command and assigns an engine company officer to manage the fireground operations of the engine, ladder, and rescue companies on the scene. This leaves the battalion chief free to size up the overall incident, plan the response, and coordinate it with the response of other agencies, such as the police.

Improving the emergency operations center

Many local government plans call for the activation of the emergency operations center (EOC). Although ICS can and should be used for lesser incidents, typically, EOCs are fully staffed in the event of a major emergency. For these situations, policy needs to be formulated, resources organized, and the needs of the responders in the field coordinated.

How can field incident management and EOC activities be effectively meshed? Various models have been designed to show the potential organizational structure at an emergency operations center. Most models were developed during the era when nuclear attack preparedness was in vogue. Many communities have adopted these configurations to meet other potential hazards. Jurisdictions in the emergency planning zone of nuclear power plants have adopted procedures with a high degree of centralized command and control similar to the military model. This appears appropriate in light of the threat, the high level of public information generated by a nuclear incident threat, and the evacuation requirements.

Another EOC incident management model can work in areas with or without a highly developd EOC.[24] The model used is very simple. Personnel assigned to respond to the EOC are divided into three groups: policy, coordination, and operations. Each group functions in a specific role. The policy group sets policies required during a disaster. To carry out the policy, the coordination group ensures that the necessary resources are acquired and coordinated. Field command is the responsibility of the operations group. Normally, the policy and coordination groups are physically separated and operate from different areas of an EOC. If necessary, these groups could even function in separate facilities. In fact, the operations groups could operate out of an alternate EOC or even at an incident command post in the field.

The policy group is composed of senior elected and appointed officials. Mayors, council members, city managers, and department heads are the main team members. The policy group, as the name implies, tackles such questions as whether and when to evacuate a community in a hurricane track. Other policy issues might include disaster declarations, goal setting, resource allocation and priority setting, communicating with the public, rationing, curfews, and related legal and political decisions. Indeed, the policy group can consider policy options associated with any economic, political, legal, and social implications of the disaster.

Often disasters require decisions for which policymakers need the advice of key department heads. Because both policymakers and managers are in the group, these decisions can be made more effectively. Participation by elected officials will vary according to the type of government. Department heads such as the fire and police chief should always be members of the policy group to advise elected and appointed officials. Their input on policy decisions should be from two viewpoints. First, they must review proposed policies and offer their assessment of how the policies under consideration might affect all aspects of the community. Second, the professional knowledge each member brings to the group should be brought to bear during deliberations about alternative courses of action. A fire chief not only has to be prepared to point out how a particular policy might adversely affect fire operations, but also, how the policy might affect other aspects of the community. At times such advocacy may require expressing a minority opinion. And although final decision making power rests with the mayor, city manager, or elected body, the responsibility to provide candid professional opinion rests with the fire service executive.

Once the policy group has arrived at a decision, the coordination group ensures orderly implementation of policy. The coordination group can be made up of assistants, deputies, and second-ranking staff of organizations represented on the policy group. As their name implies, their responsibility is to coordinate the actions of local agencies. For example, if the policy group establishes that a curfew needs to be imposed, the coordination group would ensure that the procedure involved in operating a curfew was coordinated with and could be followed by all organizations. Each agency, under the incident commander, would then be responsible for implementing its part of the curfew policy. As even the most complete plans cannot provide for every contingency, the co-ordination group can make and coordinate on-the-spot decisions as the need arises.

The operations group directs the use of the response resources in the field as coordinated by the coordination group under policies set by the policy group. For large incidents, this group is responsible for directing the operations of the various agencies and departments in the field. Agency supervisors at the battalion or assistant chief level, for example, would make up this group at the emergency operations center. In smaller operations each agency's senior operations officer in the field would have this responsibility under an overall incident command mechanism.

Operations personnel may be part of an incident management team or located at special department operation centers. For example, during a severe snow storm, the public works department may activate its own operations center, as other agencies may not need to become involved in responding to the emergency.

The advantages of this system are well proven in practice. First, policymakers are separated from operational decisions so they can concentrate on policy issues. Second, because all agencies are linked for the express purpose of ensuring that operations are coordinated, fewer operational problems will be encountered in managing the necessary resources. Third, this model can be activated with reasonable speed and can function for extended periods. Fourth, this division of effort means the right people are assigned the right responsibilities with reasonable work loads. Policymakers are not being asked to make operational decisions and those assigned to coordinate are not bogged down trying to implement operational plans.

Integrating incident command with EOC operations

The fire department incident command system should not conflict with the emergency operations center operations established by a locality. The only way to test their working relationship is to conduct drills and exercises in which all parties from politicians to private contractors participate.

To ensure smooth interaction between the incident commander in the field and the emergency operations center, the command and control system needs to be an outgrowth of day-to-day incident management practices. It is counterproductive to maintain a day-to-day system and then switch to a different incident management system for a major event.

The fact that the major problems reported in disaster response are poor coordination, communication, and utilization of resources makes clear the need for the effective meshing of policy, resource coordination, and incident command. Incident command combined with effective EOC operations reduces the disorganization that wastes resources, hinders operations, and threatens effective, efficient response.

Expanding mutual aid programs

No community can bank on being able to handle a disaster without outside assistance. It is the community's responsibility to manage that outside assistance and to be ready to give assistance when called. This is the essence of mutual aid.

Mutual aid usually takes one of two forms. The first and most common is a written agreement among two or more departments to respond to formal requests for assistance under specified conditions. The second is an automatic aid agreement, which, as the phrase implies, permits dispatchers to send the nearest available unit automatically, regardless of jurisdictional boundaries.

Mutual aid is one of the fire service's oldest and finest traditions. The concept began as informal understandings among fire departments that they would respond to one anothers' calls for assistance. Later, neighboring departments formalized these agreements in writing. Thus, for a major fire, personnel and equipment from surrounding areas can be asked to respond to the affected jurisdiction. The extra people or equipment are used at the scene or at empty fire stations. Under such agreements it is typical for command to remain with the host jurisdiction and for each department to assume responsibility for its own personnel and apparatus.

Mutual aid lies at the heart of integrated emergency management. Mutual aid functions so effectively that today, in states such as California, task forces from one jurisdiction may travel hundreds of miles to respond to calls for assistance from other jurisdictions. What makes this sytem work is that the aid is truly mutual; that is, it is reciprocal. To achieve true reciprocity, however, it is necessary to avoid what is sometimes called the "Robin Hood syndrome." The Robin Hood syndrome is often cited by large-city policymakers when opposing a regional mutual aid pact. They fear, sometimes with reason, that the smaller communities will become dependent on the resources of the larger community—that the resource-poor jurisdictions will "steal" from the resource-rich one. What is less frequently realized is that in the event of a major catastrophe it may be the large jurisdiction that is in need of assistance. For example, in California brush fires, the big cities have used substantial resources from smaller cities. As a solution, some jurisdictions have developed creative payback mechanisms; the aid is mutual, but one type of aid is exchanged for another.

Automatic aid agreements An example of automatic aid is the Northern Virginia Interjurisdictional Response Agreement, formed in 1974 by the counties of Arlington and Fairfax and the city of Alexandria. Firefighters from the jurisdictions respond according to the location of the incident. Command at the scene rests with the host jurisdiction, and firefighters work as a cohesive response group. For example, Fairfax County has a high-rise district located very close to the Arlington and Alexandria border. If a structural incident occurs in that area, all three jurisdictions would respond with an engine company. Despite the doubts of early critics, the system proved successful. Among the modifications that have evolved are a specific radio frequency dedicated to multi-jurisdictional incidents and an arrangement whereby all participating jurisdictions' employees have the same work schedule.

For example, one department provides training resources in exchange for response coverage.

Automatic aid has one distinct advantage over on-call mutual aid. Since it is practiced daily, both command and operational personnel gain the necessary experience and confidence to use it to the utmost advantage in a major emergency. For both types of mutual aid, the fire and rescue functional annex should identify the process for activating the mutual aid agreements.

If fire departments have already developed effective mutual aid arrangements in their area, fire department officials may take the lead in explaining the concept and benefits to officials in other departments. Fire chiefs can use their experience with such agreements to encourage others, such as public works departments, to develop mutual aid agreements. The concept of mutual aid is as valid for public works as it is for fire. Police agencies, despite many legal constraints, also have demonstrated the benefits of effective mutual aid agreements.

Where traditional mutual aid is not feasible for geographical or other reasons, the department may explore other options to increase its response capability. For example, civilian fire chiefs have entered into mutual aid agreements with their military counterparts, securing access to military personnel during a major event. Correctional facilities, job corps camps, and recreational areas may provide sources of staff that can be used in specific situations. Of course, in the case of correctional facilities, the cooperation of prison officials is necessary because various safeguards are required. Some jurisdictions have met their peak seasonal demands by training volunteers drawn from seasonal work forces. These short-term volunteers receive rudimentary training in basic firefighting or support skills. Advance planning and careful selection are the secrets to tapping nontraditional sources of usable talent.

Recovery options

Recovery is the final phase of emergency management. During this phase, work begins to return the disaster area to predisaster conditions or to better than predisaster conditions. Fire department responsibilities do not end with the response phase. In addition to the housekeeping chores required to return the personnel and equipment to normal operational fitness, the fire department can play a number of roles in rehabilitating the community and mitigating future disasters.

The recovery period is characterized by predictable problems. With good reason, public officials who have experienced a major incident call the recovery period the "disaster after the disaster." Typically, the fallout from large-scale disasters includes these realities:

1. Returning to routine service, closing shelters, and otherwise returning to "normal"
2. Dealing with the media and with groups of visiting dignitaries and other officials
3. Documenting expenditures and attempting to obtain reimbursement, principally from local, state, or federal sources
4. Supporting the public's efforts to recover
5. Facing litigation (the courts, the public, and policymakers are all coming to expect higher levels of professional performance and record keeping from emergency services personnel)
6. Providing public information on disaster recovery status
7. Providing critical incident stress counseling services.

Dealing with these additional burdens is particularly difficult given the emotional and physical letdown that usually follows a major incident, but planning for them and including them in practical exercises can decrease their potential for disrupting recovery.

The actual role of the fire department during this phase will vary according to the incident. By learning from disaster case studies, fire service managers can prepare contingency plans for their department's role in the recovery phase.

The postdisaster recovery phase offers a brief opportunity for fire service managers to obtain changes in building, fire, and other codes and to lobby for other needed improvements in legislation and resources. Pleas that may have fallen on deaf ears before are far more likely to receive a sympathetic hearing. Likewise, when disasters strike other jurisdictions, fire service managers with initiative will also take advantage to press policymakers for improvements.

Conclusion

To prepare today's department for the future, the fire service manager has to take time and resources away from current concerns. This challenges the managers to try to forecast future needs. How will the community change? How will the department need to change to meet these new challenges? How will it need to function? Where will the people, funds, and information come from to make these transitions?

Long-range departmental planning, like fire protection master planning, is likely to foresee a need for interagency and interjurisdictional systems to cope with even more complex and deadly incidents.

Fire service managers will need to work with other agencies in the community to cope with these complexities. And most critically, fire service managers can provide the management insight and leadership needed to prevent and respond to these types of incidents. Since fire departments control needed resources and personnel and, what is most important, have special expertise to handle various situations, their leadership in emergency response is not just desirable, it is essential for optimal performance.

Failure of the fire department to be a responsive participant could create an ineffective disaster response. The fire chief must be ready to accept this new challenge.

The success of an emergency management program can be judged only over time, but it appears to work best when

1. The community has incorporated the lessons learned from the past and from others
2. The plan is kept updated and the people prepared
3. The plan's precepts are practiced in day-to-day operations
4. The plan's special conditions are practiced regularly in a realistic, "all-parties-involved" exercise
5. The network of working relationships among all resources (public agency, private sector, voluntary agencies, media, and the general public) are maintained.

Given the importance of emergency management, the fire service executive has little choice but to become vigorously involved in its improvement. This chapter has sought to show that the fire service executive does have a wide range of options to pursue.

In emergency management, the fire service executive can become a front-line risk manager for the community, reducing risks and turning liabilities that threaten the community into opportunities to improve the working relationships among its agencies and neighboring jurisdictions. The situation is clear: Every day that passes brings the community one day closer to the next disaster. The challenge for the fire service manager is clear as well: to manage the department today and prepare it for tomorrow so that it can win the race (in H. G. Wells's words) "between education and catastrophe."

1 Roger E. Kasperson and K. David Pijawka, "Societal Response to Hazards and Major Hazard Events: Comparing Natural and Technological Hazards," *Public Administration Review* 45 (January 1985, special issue), 17.

2 Enrico L. Quarantelli and Kathleen J. Tierney, *Disaster Preparedness Planning* (Columbus: Ohio State University, Disaster Research Center, 1979).

3 Claire B. Rubin, *Managing the Recovery from a Natural Disaster*, Management Information Service Reports, vol. 14, no. 2 (February 1982), 2.

4 Gerard J. Hoetmer, *Emergency Management*, Baseline Data Reports, vol. 15, no. 4 (April 1983), 2.

5 International Association of Fire Chiefs, *Fire Service Emergency Management Handbook* (Washington, D.C., 1985), 145.

6 National Response Team, *Hazardous Materials Emergency Planning Guide* (Washington, D.C.: Environmental Protection Agency, 1987).

7 Jack Kartez, "Adaptive Planning for Community Disaster Response: Learning from Experience Is Not So Easy for Local Government," paper presented at the national planning conference of the American Planning Association, Los Angeles, 9 May 1986, 4.

8 Louis O. Giuffrida, *Emergency Management: The National Perspective*, vol. 1 (Emmitsburg, Md.: National Emergency Training Center, 1983).

9 The comprehensive emergency management concept was developed by Hilary Whittaker under a grant from the Defense Civil Preparedness Agency, a predecessor of the Federal Emergency Management Agency.

10 International Association of Fire Chiefs, *IEMS Presentation Kit*, 3.

11 For further assistance in identifying strengths and weaknesses in the emergency management plan, see International Association of Fire Chiefs, *Fire Service Emergency Management Handbook*; Federal Emergency Management Agency, *Guide for the Review of State and Local Emergency Operations Plans: Interim Guidance*; and *Local Government Disaster Protection: Final Technical Report*, prepared for FEMA by Lisa Stevenson and Marie Hayman (Washington, D.C.: International City Management Association, 1981).

12 Hoetmer, *Emergency Management*, table 6. Among respondents to a survey, 83 percent of cities and 93 percent of counties reported formal emergency management plans.

13 A workshop planning kit is available from the Emergency Management Information Center, National Emergency Training Center, Emmitsburg, Maryland.

14 Harvey G. Ryland, *Multi-Jurisdictional Master Planning* (Emmitsburg, Md.: Federal Emergency Management Agency, 1979).

15 Federal Emergency Management Agency, *Hazard Identification, Capability Assessment, and Multi-Year Development Plan* (Emmitsburg, Md., 1985), II-1.

16 Federal Emergency Management Agency, *Guide for the Review of State and Local Emergency Operations Plans*, 2-2.

17 Adapted from Jack Kartez, *Emergency Management Planning Profile* (Pullman, Wash.: Environmental Research Center, Washington State University, 1986), 7.

18 For information on mass casualty incident command procedures, see: *Multi-Casualty Incident Operational Procedures*, available through the Los Angeles County Chapter of the California Fire Chiefs Association, 600 Montebello Boulevard, Montebello, California 90640.

19 Jon A. Kusler, "Liability as a Dilemma for Local Managers," *Public Administration Review* 45 (January 1985, special issue), 121.

20 Kartez, "Adaptive Planning."

21 Hoetmer, *Emergency Management*, 7.

22 The National Fire Academy, 1600 South Seton Avenue, Emmitsburg, Maryland 20727, has a course on the Model Incident Command System; see also Alan Brunacini, *Fire Command* (Quincy, Mass.: National Fire Protection Association, 1985).

23 International Association of Fire Chiefs, *IEMS Presentation Kit*, 34.

24 This model for EOC operations is based on the system used in the Comprehensive Emergency Management Course taught at the Emergency Management Institute in Emmitsburg, Maryland. The institute trains a local government's key decision makers, challenging them to resolve problems presented in disaster scenarios specific to their communities.

14

Emergency medical and rescue services

Accompanied by a lengthy debate in the 1970s and early 1980s about whether emergency medical services (EMS) were an appropriate activity for the fire service, EMS has become a reality for the majority of fire departments in the United States. Today, from half to three-quarters of the emergency incidents handled by a typical fire department are EMS-related.[1] In general, the fire chief no longer faces the question of whether or not to embrace EMS as a fire department function and, if so, how to implement it. Nonetheless, the management of emergency medical and rescue services remains complex and challenging, particularly in the light of changes in the economics of local government and of health care.

Those who agree that the fire service should provide EMS have pointed out several benefits of this arrangement. For example, productivity increases when cross-trained employees are able to perform two essential public safety tasks (fire protection and emergency medical services). Furthermore, the structure and stability of the fire department and the paramilitary discipline and training of firefighters are compatible with EMS responsibilities. In the aftermath of tax-limitation measures, loss of federal revenue-sharing funds, and relentless efforts to reduce the cost of health care (including medical transportation), EMS has acquired a new potential: By providing ambulance transportation or advanced life support on a fee-for-service basis, many fire departments can generate revenues.

The character and scope of EMS are still influenced by federal initiatives of the 1970s.[2] At that time, the concept of a comprehensive EMS system was established in federal law. It was defined as a multifaceted system encompassing such components as citizen access, transportation, personnel training, communications, trauma center designation, public education, critical patient transfers, and patient rehabilitation. Despite the subsequent withdrawal of federal funds and regulations, state and local governments regard EMS in much the same way. The role of the fire service in the system is generally limited to the *prehospital* phase, which is often shared by other local government employees (most often police officers) and various private-sector groups (such as ambulance companies).

Against that background, this chapter analyzes EMS from a managerial perspective—that is, from the viewpoint of key decisionmakers inside and outside a local fire department. First, it presents an overview of EMS—its historical development, new services and improvements, and a preview of the management challenges for the fire service. It goes on to look at planning for EMS, then describes six operational profiles for EMS in a community. Finally, it examines the management challenges of direction and control, coordination, and program evaluation. The purpose of the chapter is to provide tools that the fire service manager can draw on to fashion a chain of command and an implementation process appropriate to the community. As with other program areas in the fire service, there is no "one best way" to implement EMS; it must be tailored to the managerial, political, and administrative realities of a specific jurisdiction.

Overview

Fire department participation in EMS varies greatly throughout the United States. Its activities can range from maintaining and operating a dispatch and communications facility to training personnel in first aid or basic life support; operating first-response units (including pumper or ladder companies), basic life support units (with or without patient transportation), and advanced life support units (staffed by either firefighter or civilian paramedics); and providing public education, including blood pressure screening programs and training of citizens in the technique of cardiopulmonary resuscitation (CPR).

Historical background

How did this involvement come about? Fire service involvement in EMS has evolved gradually. As early as 1928 a few fire departments began to provide first aid services to citizens suffering from breathing difficulties and heart attack symptoms. Primitive resuscitator-inhalator devices used by fire departments to assist firefighters in cases of smoke inhalation became the standard equipment for aiding the public in medical episodes. By 1930 fire departments had begun to develop special vehicles for this function; these often included heavy rescue and extrication equipment for specialized rescue and firefighting situations.

Equipment, medical aid training, and operational procedures changed very little over the next three decades. In the early 1960s, however, new techniques in artificial breathing and circulation were devised, leading to the technique of CPR. (Some fire departments actually adopted this technique even before it

---

Glossary

Ambulance: A vehicular conveyance designed and operated for transportation of ill and injured persons in a prone or supine position, equipped and staffed to provide for first aid or life support measures to be applied during transportation.

CPR (cardiopulmonary resuscitation): A combination of artificial respiration and closed-chest cardiac massage, performed by either one or two rescuers on a patient who is pulseless and non-breathing. When promptly and properly applied, CPR has been shown to be an effective method for preventing deterioration of vital organs in patients who are without natural circulation and respiration. This rescue technique is generally recognized as a "holding action" which merely sustains the patient until advanced life support measures can be applied to restore natural pulse and breathing. Where large numbers of citizens in a community have been trained to perform CPR, statistical evidence

shows substantial improvement in the long-term survival of persons who suffer from out-of-hospital cardiac arrest.

Advanced life support: All basic life support measures, plus invasive medical procedures, including: intravenous therapy; cardiac defibrillation; administration of antiarrhythmic medications and other specified drugs, medications, and solutions; use of adjunctive ventilation devices; and other procedures which may be authorized by state law and performed under medical control.

Basic life support: Generally limited to airway maintenance, ventilatory (breathing) support, CPR, hemorrhage control, splinting of fractures, management of spinal injury, protection and transportation of the patient in accord with accepted procedures.

EMT (emergency medical technician): A generic term referring to at least three emergency care positions: (1) EMT (sometimes known as EMT-

was officially approved by the American Red Cross.) Also, during this period, resuscitation equipment was made more compact and portable. At the same time, public demand for fire department first aid services was steadily, if slowly, increasing.

In the mid-1960s medical journals reported the dramatic results of a mobile coronary care program in Belfast, Northern Ireland.[3] That revolutionary program reversed the traditional approach of emergency care and instead took the medical team from the hospital to the location of patients suffering from acute heart attacks. A few pioneering physicians began developing similar systems in several locations across the United States. Almost without exception, firefighters were chosen to be trained as the specialized paramedic technicians to serve on those early units.[4]

In Miami, Columbus, Los Angeles, Seattle, and Jacksonville, fire department paramedics quickly earned the vocal support of their medical mentors as they jumped from the basic first aid level of service to sophisticated medical care. One of the pioneering physicians referred to Miami firefighter paramedics as practitioners of "gutter medicine."

By 1971, there were at least twenty-four mobile intensive care units in operation in the United States.[5] That year, a popular television series opened depicting the adventures of a team of Los Angeles County fire department paramedics. Fire departments showed new interest in EMS as citizens began to ask why their local fire department did not provide the sort of services depicted in the television series. By 1977, advanced life support systems (using paramedics) were operational in at least 310 American communities. It was estimated that 33 percent were operated by local fire departments.[6]

Ambulance), a person who has been trained in a program of at least eighty-one hours in length and who has been appropriately certified as proficient in basic life support; (2) EMT-Paramedic (sometimes known as EMT-P), a person who has been trained in a program which includes, as a minimum, all fifteen modules of the U.S. Department of Transportation's National Training Course for the EMT-Paramedic, and who has been appropriately certified as proficient in advanced life support; (3) EMT-Defibrillation (sometimes known as EMT-D), a person who is trained and authorized to use portable cardiac monitors and defibrillators, to analyze certain cardiac rhythms, and to apply defibrillation where appropriate. (Prompt defibrillation is the key factor for survival of many heart attack victims. Where these specially trained EMTs are available and can arrive at the scene in six minutes or less, EMT-Defibrillation programs have been effective in resuscitating a significant percentage of patients for whom death was certain without this intervention.)

Medical control: A planned approach to the provision of advanced life support services in an out-of-hospital setting. Under this approach paramedic personnel are viewed as surrogates of a designated resource hospital and a designated medical director in that hospital (regardless of other employer-employee relationships).

Triage: A military term referring to the process of sorting the sick and wounded on the basis of severity of condition and urgency. In modern EMS systems triage occurs as calls are screened by a dispatcher, as first-responders determine the need for basic and/or advanced life support personnel, as basic life support units determine whether advanced life support personnel will be needed, and where decisions are made concerning transportation (emergency or nonemergency; private or public).

New services, training, and equipment

In subsequent years, first-response and basic life support services have been developed and upgraded throughout the fire service. A national survey conducted in 1977 reported that more than 56 percent of all U.S. fire departments were providing some level of emergency medical services.[7] Since then, there have been no national surveys to measure this activity. However, a study conducted by the California Fire Chiefs Association in 1986 revealed that fire departments serve 90 percent of that state's population with some level of EMS, and that 67.5 percent of all emergency calls answered by California fire departments are EMS-related.[8]

The prehospital care and transportation components of an EMS system often involve not only a variety of services but also a variety of resources. For example, a fire department may provide first-response basic life support with pumper, ladder, or special rescue companies while relying on a private ambulance service for advanced life support (paramedic) services and ambulance transportation. In other instances police and fire agencies may provide first-response services, with fire department paramedics providing advanced life support and private ambulances providing patient transportation. One study revealed twenty-five different profiles involving fire, police, volunteer ambulance, private ambulance, separate municipal ambulance, and hospital-operated ambulance services.[9]

A significant advance in prehospital care has been the evolution of a new classification of emergency medical technician, EMT-Defibrillation (EMT-D). Research conducted in King County, Washington, and in the state of Iowa indicates that very prompt defibrillation is the most effective therapy in cases of cardiac arrest (ventricular fibrillation).[10] Also, research has shown that basic life support EMTs can be trained to recognize lethal arrhythmias and defibrillate patients through training programs of ten hours or less. New automated defibrillators have been created and have added to the relative safety of the EMT-D concept.

Trauma care systems have been a subject of substantial development and conflict throughout the United States. Inspired by the federal EMS program and by more recent documented cases of life-saving performance by organized trauma care systems in several locales, trauma care has become a symbol of medical accomplishment while also feeding competition for patients and prestige among hospitals. Intensifying the competition has been the rapid growth of hospital-based helicopter ambulance programs.

Accompanied by ample publicity, these developments in emergency medical services have elevated public expectations. Along with other segments of the EMS community, fire service EMS providers generally have responded with improvements in training, equipment, and operational procedures. In many instances, changes and improvements in fire service EMS programs have been a response to increasingly competitive and businesslike local and private ambulance companies.

Organizational responsibility

The tradition of an organized response to individual medical emergencies is rooted in military history. As early as the Napoleonic wars, special conveyances were committed to the task of moving the injured from the battlefront to treatment areas behind the lines. In the United States, early ambulance services were operated by hospitals. As time passed, the function became the province of funeral directors, police and fire departments, private ambulance operators, and volunteers.

A number of factors, including major changes in the traditional practice of medicine, contributed to public expectations for emergency medical services and ambulance transportation. When physicians stopped making house calls, the need for specialized transport to a hospital increased. Also, as Americans became more mobile, long-term relationships with a family physician became a rarity. The hospital emergency room became the primary location of medical care for more and more citizens. A growing tendency to depend on government for services emerged in the field of ambulance transportation with a consequent increase in local government involvement, including financial subsidies to private services and outright assumption of ambulance service responsibility by some public agencies.

The local fire department often seemed a natural source of medical aid responsibility, because it had a sizable body of reliable, trained, and disciplined personnel, operating within an existing command structure, possessing vehicular and communications resources, operating from structural facilities located throughout the community, and holding the confidence of the public. Also affecting this trend was the fact that most firefighting personnel were actually engaged in emergency activity for only a small percentage of their total available on-duty time.

Fire departments have not always been willing to assume this new and greater responsibility, however. In a number of communities fire officials resisted efforts to utilize their personnel and other resources for EMS. In most of those locations, the primary responsibility for prehospital emergency medical care and transportation has been assumed by private ambulance companies, hospital organizations, or new and independent public EMS agencies.

With a few exceptions, development of the early mobile coronary care units in the late 1960s and early 1970s occurred in areas where the local fire departments were willing to expand their traditional services. These departments seemed to attract the attention of doctors who hoped to create pilot programs in advanced prehospital life support. Many of them concluded that firefighters were ideal for the role of physician surrogates in taking advanced life support to the streets in the critical early stages of a medical emergency. In many cases, the local fire department's personnel resources could be utilized without any significant cost to the pilot advanced life support project.

Although most local governments have experienced severe financial difficulties since the early 1970s, public support for local government-operated paramedic services generally has been consistent. With public support, availability, trainability, and tradition in its favor, the fire service has steadily moved toward a dual function—provision of fire protection services and provision of some form of prehospital emergency medical care and/or transportation.

Planning for EMS

As local government decisionmakers well know, when services expand, problems inevitably follow, especially if the new and expanded service differs significantly from the traditional functions of the organization, both in size and in the services provided. Fire service involvement in EMS presents an array of potential problems that have tested the management skills of many municipal officials.

Actually, fire departments became involved in comprehensive EMS systems (during the federal EMS funding era) at a time when planning as a management function was finding new acceptance in the fire service in general. Health care planning, as a discipline, has a long history flowing from federal initiatives intended to increase the availability of health care while reducing its cost. To the extent that prehospital care is a part of the total health care system, organized planning of fire service involvement is basic to the endeavor.

Planning considerations

Among the essential planning considerations are the staffing and organizational requirements of the fire department's prehospital component—in other words, organizing and implementing the service for the most cost-effective use of existing personnel. Alteration of the department's staffing patterns and response profiles may be necessary to meet the need for the shortest possible response times at all hours, including periods of peak demand. Training programs for basic, intermediate, or advanced life support personnel require advance planning to budget and arrange for adequate staffing during training. Changes in a department's recruiting standards may be necessary to reflect the special requirements of emergency medical training programs. Planning also should take into account the fact that skills need to be maintained and personnel need to replace or refresh the knowledge, skills, and abilities they lose to attrition. A concentrated effort to gather planning data should include seeking information from other agencies and programs to make certain that there is no "reinvention of the wheel."

Labor-management relations are critical to the planning process, as they provide a forum for efforts to anticipate and overcome possible resistance to changes in work load and responsibility. Where new organizational structures, staffing patterns, compensation arrangements or working conditions can be anticipated, employee consensus should be pursued through the planning process.

Involvement in an EMS system requires ongoing coordination with other community agencies, services, and institutions. The first step toward this coordination can be made through the planning process. Thus, the local medical community, hospitals, other public safety agencies, training facilities, and the program's medical director should be included in the planning process from the beginning.

The planning process

Figure 14-1 shows a continuous, cyclical planning process. The process starts with general goals. (What do we want to accomplish?) It then proceeds to the development of specific objectives. (How are we going to do it?) In developing these objectives, management should put together a *planning data base*. This is a compilation of all relevant information needed to formulate practical and achievable objectives. (What do we have to work with and what potential obstacles do we face?) A detailed example of a planning data base is given in Figure 14–2.

In planning to achieve a goal, a single approach can seldom be agreed upon. Two or more alternative approaches may be developed as objectives. Implementers of the program then have to choose from among the alternatives and developing programs based on the selected objectives (Figure 14–1). After implementation, the service will produce reported information (data) that can be referred to as *system outcomes*. These data should be evaluated continuously. If evaluation discloses excessive deviation from the original objectives, these objectives should be revised to correct the deviation or performances should be modified as needed. It is the evaluation of system outcomes and the revision of objectives that make planning continuous and cyclical. Without this evaluation, deviations are likely to go undetected until a crisis occurs. Continuous and cyclical planning provides an opportunity to monitor the activity and prevent a crisis: It is a practical method of controlling events rather than being controlled by them.

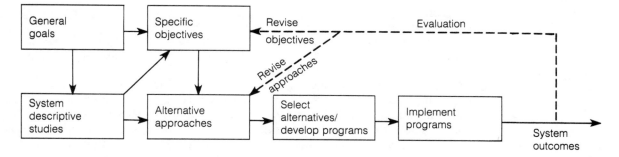

Figure 14–1   EMS planning as a continuous, cyclical process.

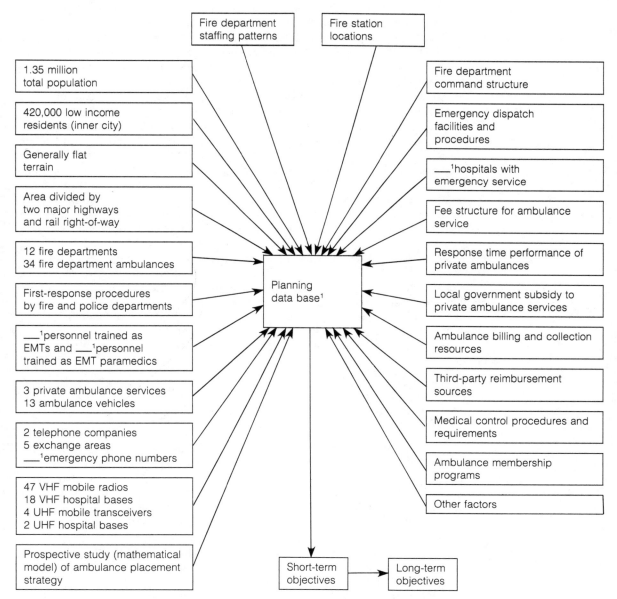

Figure 14–2   Example of a planning data base used in an EMS cyclical planning process.

[1]Input factors not fully developed: intended for illustrative purposes only

Responsibility for planning

In planning, implementing, upgrading, or expanding a fire department, EMS operation fire officials do not work alone. EMS is a part of the larger health care system, and the health care system in any community can be likened to an artist's suspended mobile: Touch it here and it jiggles over there. Thus it is important to distinguish the EMS *system* (as part of the health care system) from the various EMS *services* (including the fire department's prehospital care operations) that make up the system.

In the early years of EMS, various federal programs created a national network of health planning organizations. Each of those organizations employed professional staff members who were involved in every aspect of planning, implementing, or changing health care services on a regional basis. These "community planners" often became deeply involved in making basic decisions on how local communities could best provide prehospital EMS.

The decline in federal enthusiasm and funding for traditional health care planning greatly reduced the size and effect of regional health planning agencies. In the case of EMS, however, every state has developed a structure of regulation and approvals under which EMS regulatory officials at the state, regional or county levels in many ways have replaced the professional health care planners who earlier functioned under federal funding and authority. Whether they are based in a state government agency, a state-subsidized regional EMS organization, or a county or local health department, these EMS regulatory officials must be involved in any effort to create or modify a fire department's EMS operation. The persons staffing that organization or agency are most familiar with laws and regulations governing the EMS system, they are aware of the experience of other locales, and they can be very helpful in estimating costs of the new or modified operation. For the purposes of this discussion and to illustrate planning responsibilities (Figure 14–3), these persons are called "EMS regulators."

The ability and willingness of EMS regulators to participate in planning with fire officials will vary from location to location, depending on the legal responsibilities and staffing levels of the regulatory agency, that agency's leadership and staff competence, and the prior relationship between the fire department and the EMS regulatory agency. In any event, the EMS regulatory agency should be invited to participate in any effort to plan for upgrading or changing a fire department's involvement in providing prehospital emergency care services.

The fire official who is responsible for planning an EMS program or for altering an existing program is called a "program planner." In order to avoid conflict, the responsibilities of the EMS regulator should be clearly separated from those of the program planner. This division is shown in Figure 14–3. As it indicates, problem identification falls within the province of the EMS regulator. In reality, however, it may be necessary for the fire department (program planner) to apprise the EMS regulator of the fact that the community's emergency care resources are less than adequate, or unreliable, or too costly. For example, a local ambulance service with excessive response times may mean that some survivable patients are not surviving, or that poorly maintained ambulance vehicles and equipment are having frequent breakdowns, or that high fees for ambulance service may be keeping some patients from using an ambulance when they need it. Even a competent basic life support system that lacks the backup of advanced life support (paramedic) services, or intermediate-skills EMT services, suggests that improvements could be made.

By the nature of their responsibilities, EMS regulators generally serve a large geographic area and oversee many EMS providers. Most of their time and attention is spent on reacting to problems; thus, it may be necessary for the fire

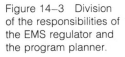

Figure 14–3 Division of the responsibilities of the EMS regulator and the program planner.

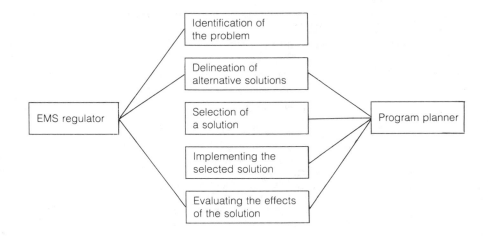

department (program planner) to document the local problems (need for improvement) in such a way as to involve EMS regulators in the planning process.

Once the problem has been identified (e.g., excessive response times, frequent breakdowns of ambulances or patient care equipment, or relatively high ambulance service fees) and once the EMS regulator has been involved in the planning process, the EMS regulator and the fire official/program planner should collaborate on delineating alternative solutions to the problem. However, selecting and implementing solutions should be the province of the program planner, provided those solutions do not conflict with existing law, regulations, contracts, or ordinances.

Finally, to make the process continuous and cyclical (through evaluation and possible modification of objectives), the EMS regulator and the program planner should work in concert.

Alternative operational profiles

Fire departments throughout the United States have identified and developed many diverse approaches to the delivery of EMS. In the planning process alternative approaches need to be identified, and the program planner will need to select from among these alternatives (or select features from several alternatives).

Figure 14–4 lists program characteristics for six distinct operational profiles. The factors illustrated are not intended as a complete list. They may, however, be used by managers as a basis for planning and designing a fire department EMS program or for modifying or expanding an existing service. The six profiles represent composites of actual fire service experiences in a number of locations in the United States. None of them describes a specific fire department, but each is close enough to actual experiences to produce some valuable lessons.

Profile A

Profile A is based on the assumption that no other qualified emergency service in the community can reach the scene of most medical emergencies faster than the nearest engine or truck company can. Thus, at least two members of each of these companies are trained to the level of *first responder* or *emergency medical technician (EMT)* (both training programs developed by the National Highway Traffic Safety Administration, U.S. Department of Transportation).

When the emergency medical dispatcher receives and confirms a report of a medical emergency, the nearest unit (engine or truck company, whether located

Figure 14–4 Six sample operational profiles for fire department EMS programs.

Program characteristics	A	B	C	D	E	F
Level of service/training						
First-response	X	X	X	X	X	X
Basic life support	X	X	X	X	X	X
Intermediate skills						X
Advanced life support	X	X		X	X	
Operational profile						
Engine companies	X	X	X	X	X	X
Truck companies	X	X				X
Rescue vehicles (nontransporting)	X		X			
Rescue ambulances (transporting)		X		X		
Paramedic pumper/truck	X					
"Medic company"					X	
EMS personnel						
Civilian employees of fire department				X		
Firefighters (dual-role)	X	X	X		X	X
Volunteer members						X
Patient transport						
Transport all cases						X
Transport only emergencies		X		X	X	
Nontransport	X		X			
Dispatch locations						
Respond from hospital				X		X
Respond from fire stations or field	X	X	X	X	X	X
Supervision of EMS personnel						
Designated field EMS supervisors				X		
Fire company officers	X	X	X	X	X	X
EMS units dispatched by						
Fire department dispatcher			X	X	X	X
911 or public safety dispatcher	X	X	X			X
Hospital			X			X
Dispatchers trained as EMDs	X	X			X	
Cooperation with ambulance service						
Private ambulance service(s)	X	X	X	X	X	
Municipal (government) ambulance			X			
Volunteer ambulance						X
Training of EMS personnel						
Fire department training staff		X	X	X		X
College or university	X		X	X	X	X
Hospital	X	X		X	X	X
Finance						
Fire department budget only	X	X	X	X	X	X
Fees charged for service		X		X		X
Membership (subscription) program		X				
Community fund-raising						X

in a fire station or available by radio in the field) is dispatched simultaneously with the nearest available mobile intensive care (paramedic) unit. In the hypothetical department described here, a number of paramedic firefighters have been promoted to driver or company officer positions. By assigning these individuals to districts with high frequencies of medical emergencies and by equipping their fire apparatus with paramedic equipment and supplies, the department has been able to ease the burden on its busy rescue units. Thus, in some cases the first-response unit may actually be a paramedic pumper or truck.

The first crew to arrive at the scene of the medical emergency immediately assesses the situation and determines the need for the paramedic rescue unit (which usually responds from a more distant location). If it can be determined that the paramedic rescue unit will not be needed, the first-response unit can cancel the paramedic unit by radio or telephone contact with the dispatcher. This action makes the paramedic rescue unit immediately available for another emergency (fire or medical). It is important that any such medical *triage* decision be made by individuals adequately trained in basic life support (EMT training and certification, as a minimum). Where there is any doubt as to the seriousness of the patient's condition, the paramedic rescue unit is allowed to continue to the scene to assess the patient.

In this profile firefighters are used in a dual role. That is, first-response, basic life support, and advanced life support (paramedic) personnel are fully qualified firefighters who have been specially trained for emergency medical care functions after completing a period of service as firefighters. These paramedic personnel respond to fire alarms as well as to medical emergencies. In firefighting operations, their assignments can range from search and rescue, forcible entry, and salvage operations to actual fire suppression functions and overhaul of the fire scene. Obviously, their presence at the scene of a fire is valuable in the event of casualties. In most cases they are employed in fire operations in such a manner as to maintain reasonable readiness to respond to a medical emergency if necessary.

Many jurisdictions have utilized the dual-role concept successfully; under this profile, advanced life support services can be implemented with minimal increases in total personnel. There have been no reports that either function has been compromised by using the same personnel in both roles. However, the willingness of individuals to serve in both capacities seems to depend on such factors as the history and tradition of the organization, the quality and style of the department's management, and the relative work load of the department.

In Profile A all units respond from fire stations or by radio from field assignments. All personnel, including the paramedics, are supervised by fire company officers. This supervision never extends to medical judgments, however, as they are the responsibility of the medical control hospital and its authorized staff. Even where the company officer is certified as a paramedic or formerly served as a paramedic, the advanced life support program is viewed as a hospital outreach program, and medical judgments are made by the hospital emergency staff in consultation with paramedics over communications linkages. Although this split in supervisory responsibility has been troublesome for some departments in the early stages of their programs, it has proven to be workable and tends to smooth out with frequent contact and coordination between department officials and hospital personnel.

Nearly all calls for assistance in Profile A are received by the fire department's emergency communications center via the 911 or other emergency telephone number. The calls then are communicated to department units by dispatch personnel who may have been specially trained as emergency medical dispatchers (EMDs). By virtue of their EMD training, the dispatchers are capable of using medically approved protocol cards for selecting and dispatching emergency medical resources to match the patient's medical needs. Also, they are capable of providing pre-arrival rescue instruction to the caller while emergency units are responding to the scene.

An important element in Profile A is that private ambulance services are used to provide patient transportation where needed. Originally, as fire departments began to implement paramedic rescue services, the use of private ambulance transport was viewed as essential to dual-role (firefighter-paramedic) staffing. The ability to "hand off" noncritical patients to basic life support ambulance crews allows the fire department's paramedic unit to be available for service quicker. Also, the use of a nontransporting rescue vehicle allows for a vehicle design that can carry heavy rescue, extrication, salvage and overhaul, and lighting equipment for use on fires.

Training of EMS personnel in Profile A is conducted by the medical control hospital, which is affiliated with a university medical school. This training function is the primary responsibility of a qualified emergency physician (referred to as the *medical director*) and of the medical education staff of the hospital. Training is continuous for paramedics, with regular reviews of medical incidents and run reports, and monthly continuing education programs. By constantly monitoring performance, the medical director can detect instances of serious skill decay. In those cases, he can mandate retraining—which can cause extra salary expenses for the fire department. Or he may determine that an individual's attitude is inappropriate and will probably never change and may order that person removed from active service as a paramedic. Under a contract between the fire department and the hospital, such a decision is the sole responsibility of the medical director and requires immediate compliance by the fire department.

Financing for Profile A comes from the fire department budget. The dual-role personnel feature of this profile allows the service to operate without a significant increase in expenses beyond what would be required for fire protection services alone. Although the fire department pays a fee to the hospital for training personnel as paramedics, actual training costs are subsidized by the hospital and university and the fees paid by the fire department do not represent actual training costs.

Disadvantages of the Profile A approach include the medical and legal risks of the patient "hand-off" to a lesser-trained ambulance crew. In cases where paramedic-level care is needed, at least one of the fire department's paramedics must accompany the patient to the hospital in the private ambulance, and the paramedic rescue vehicle must follow. Thus, the fire department vehicle is not readily available for another emergency. If a firefighter from the first-response fire company is used to drive the rescue vehicle to the hospital (and retrieve the paramedics), the first-response company will have to operate at reduced strength until all personnel and vehicles are back in service.

Regardless of whether the fire department provides its paramedic services to the patient without direct fee, the patient will receive a bill from the private ambulance provider for scene-to-hospital transportation. If the fire department does charge for its paramedic services, the patient will receive a second bill from the fire department.

A large percentage of citizens is covered by health insurance, health care plans, Medicare, or Medicaid. Thus, if the fire department's charges for paramedic services are nonexistent or do not cover full costs, the department is, in essence, subsidizing the health insurance carriers or federal and state health care financing programs. Since most fire departments are hard pressed to maintain minimum levels of service within their budgets, it is questionable whether those agencies should be subsidizing private insurance carriers and state and federal health care financing programs.

These and other factors have caused many fire service managers to rethink the issue of ambulance transportation. (See Profile B for an example of a fire department emergency paramedic ambulance service.)

Whether or not the fire department transports emergency patients, a well-run private ambulance service may be required to meet a community's total health care needs. In the absence of this service, a public agency is obligated to provide all nonemergency medical transportation, including convalescent transfers, interhospital transfers, and transportation of nonambulatory outpatients for periodic clinic appointments.

A few fire departments have elected to provide the full range of ambulance transportation services (emergency and nonemergency) and have used these services as a source of revenue to supplement the fire department budget. However, unless a fire department is staffed and equipped for all these functions, its ability to handle its emergency responsibilities may suffer.

Although the quality and reliability of private ambulance services continually improve, few private ambulance providers can match the resources and capabilities of a well-run fire department in delivering prehospital care. (Features of modern private ambulance systems are further discussed in Profile D.)

Profile B

Most of the features of Profile A are present in Profile B, the main difference being that Profile B includes transporting rescue ambulance vehicles. This feature has an impact on the entire service.

Although the department discussed in this profile provides first-response and basic life support services in addition to rescue ambulances staffed by paramedics, the average "out-of-service" time tends to be longer (in that none of the emergency patients are handed off to a private ambulance service at the scene). Each of the department's rescue ambulances is staffed by two firefighter-paramedics. Thus, in critical cases where both paramedics are needed to care for the patient(s) en route to a hospital, a firefighter is borrowed from the first-response fire company to drive the ambulance. Later, the paramedics must return the firefighter to the fire company, increasing their out-of-service time.

The availability of public ambulance service initially encouraged greater public use of the system (including some degree of calculated abuse). Although Profiles A and B cover nearly identical population bases, the department in Profile B receives nearly double the number of calls for assistance. However, a moderate fee for service has been implemented to discourage abuse of the system. The fee is less than half the Medicare reimbursement rate for ambulance service in the region, and the collection rate of the city's finance department is less than 50 percent.

The hypothetical Profile B department described here has examined these problems through the planning processes described earlier in this chapter. To assist in that planning process—adding technical information to the planning data base, and defining alternative solutions—a private health care consultant has been employed. Following several of the alternative solutions defined in the planning process, the fire department in Profile B has doubled its fee for service and has contracted with a professional billing service to collect ambulance fees (it now receives about 70 percent of billed amounts, less billing and collection fees). Further, it has created an ambulance membership program whereby local residents can purchase annual memberships for $35 per family and thus avoid any direct charge for using the emergency paramedic ambulance service during a membership year. As a part of the membership program, the fire department reserves the right to access members' third-party reimbursement sources, if any (private insurance, Medicare, Medicaid, etc.). Close to 20 percent of all families in the city are program members.

These changes have created a revenue base out of which the fire department in Profile B has added paramedic units, improved vehicles and equipment, and supplemented firefighter staffing on first-response engine companies. Rather than discourage use of the system, the department has developed an ongoing marketing program that encourages all persons needing emergency ambulance service to utilize it. In many ways, it is operating as a business.

Before creating the new revenue source and before adding to its paramedic fleet and personnel resources, the fire department in Profile B was often unable to keep up with public demand. This caused delayed responses and extended out-of-service time for first-response units—while waiting for the first available fire department ambulance or a back-up private ambulance. These problems have been alleviated by selective medical dispatch by trained emergency medical dispatchers and the availability of a larger number of paramedic ambulance units.

As in Profile A, the paramedics used in Profile B are firefighters who have been certified as paramedics; they receive a salary incentive or bonus while certified and assigned as paramedics. In Profile B, the firefighter-paramedics are assigned in teams of three per platoon per rescue ambulance. This allows each of them to rotate off the ambulance (and work on the engine company) every third duty shift, on a continuous basis.

Also, paramedics in Profile B are eligible to compete for promotion within the fire suppression ranks. As a result, new paramedic personnel have to be trained to replace those who are promoted. However, this system avoids career deadends and the attendant attitude and morale problems. Further, personnel who have been promoted from firefighter-paramedic to company officer, for example, carry their paramedic experience with them into their new roles as first responders.

In Profile B, the fire department training staff has trained and certified all uniformed members of the department as basic life support EMTs. The training staff is also responsible for refresher training and periodic recertification of all EMTs. The medical control hospital assists with this program and assumes all responsibility for paramedic training and retraining under a contract with the fire department. As in Profile A, a medical director oversees the program. As indicated, the fire department's ambulance service is staffed with dual-role personnel. Costs that are incurred as a direct result of the EMS program are offset by fees for service, third-party reimbursements, and ambulance membership program revenues.

Profile C

In this third profile the fire department does not provide advanced life support (paramedic) services; instead, it complements a municipal ambulance service and private ambulance services through immediate response by fire department units when a call for emergency medical assistance is received.

The limited nature of the services provided by this hypothetical fire department is a product of local history. Until recent years the fire department was headed by a fire chief who had spent many years in the department and was approaching retirement. During his tenure, he had not added EMS to his department's responsibilities, and the voters approved an election referendum to provide tax resources for the development of a separate municipal ambulance service that would include the training and implementation of paramedics. The municipal ambulance service was established as a separate branch of local government.

The municipal ambulance service is operational at the advanced life support level, and it provides only emergency care and transportation. Thus, private ambulance services continue to provide nonemergency medical transportation. Further, the number of available units is not adequate to provide consistent response times of five minutes or less to all sections of the jurisidiction.

With a change in fire department leadership came a greater interest in EMS and the new chief has recommended that the department supplement the municipal ambulance service with first-response and basic life support services. Through mutual planning, an effective system of dual agency response has evolved.

In Profile C most calls for emergency medical assistance are received by the countywide public safety communications center (which utilizes the 911 or other emergency telephone number as well as seven-digit emergency numbers). The dispatcher simultaneously sends out the municipal ambulance service and notifies the fire dispatcher. The latter, in turn, notifies the fire station closest to the address of the emergency. Where the reported information suggests the need for extra personnel or special equipment, the fire department's special rescue vehicle also is dispatched.

In a majority of cases, the local engine company arrives first at the scene of the emergency. At least two members of each company have been trained to the level of basic life support EMT. Where needed, basic life support is initiated by these personnel pending the arrival of the municipal paramedic ambulance. Through a common radio frequency the fire unit can communicate with the responding paramedics to advise them of conditions at the scene. If the patient is stable and an emergency response is not warranted, the paramedics proceed to the scene at normal traffic speeds.

If the first arriving engine company determines that the case is nonemergency, the company officer is authorized to cancel the response of the paramedic unit. In such instances a private ambulance is called to the scene and transportation must be paid for by the patient or the patient's insurer. A majority of cases are in fact nonemergency, and company officers have received special training to assist them in diplomatically handling those who may be distressed by the refusal to provide public ambulance service. If there is any question concerning the patient's true medical condition, the municipal ambulance paramedics continue to the scene and make a medical evaluation in communication with the medical control hospital.

Fire department personnel are trained through an arrangement with a local community college. Fire department training officers are trained and certified as EMT instructors and as community college instructors. Thus, although the training is conducted on-duty in fire department facilities (except for a ten-hour hospital internship), firefighters trained as EMTs in this program also receive college credit.

Since the fire department provides its first-response and basic life support services with dual-role personnel, it has not had to expand its staff or its personnel budget. However, alarm activity has increased threefold since the cooperative program began. This has had some impact on vehicle replacement, vehicle maintenance, and operating budgets. All necessary basic life support equipment is purchased and maintained through the fire department budget.

In this particular department, many of the younger firefighters have expressed an interest in operating at the advanced life support (paramedic) level and resent the former chief's failure to pursue this possibility during his tenure. Although they realize that the municipal ambulance service (and its paramedic staff) is permanently in place, they continue to push to have their role in EMS expanded. In the early stages of the program this morale problem produced some personal confrontations between employees of the respective municipal agencies. Circumstances have improved, however, through skillful personnel management by administrators of both agencies.

Many of the firefighters have welcomed the gradual expansion of their training and skills to permit their active involvement in life-threatening medical emergencies. Training exercises conducted by the municipal ambulance paramedics at fire stations have been a major factor. Consequently, in most instances of cardiac arrest, severe trauma, or other serious emergencies, the basic life support firefighters tend to serve as adjuncts to the paramedics, setting up intravenous equipment, staffing the radiotelemetry unit, operating suction units, retrieving equipment, and so on.

Profile D

This fourth example is the only fire department in the six profiles to use civilian (nonfirefighter) employees. The decision to establish an EMS service in the fire department was made by the mayor and the city council. The fire chief, responding to the mandate, recommended that a separate civilian-staffed EMS service be established within the department.

The fire chief's recommendation was based largely on the department's high rating by the insurance industry. This rating was grounded on relatively heavy staffing standards. The chief was reluctant to otherwise use those personnel committed to fire protection and proposed that additional personnel—either additional firefighters or civilians—be employed to operate the ambulance service. Cost became the major factor in the ultimate decision. The chief concluded that he could employ civilians, have them trained to the paramedic level, and compensate them at a rate somewhat less than his paid firefighters. His recommendations were accepted by the fire commission and the city council.

Exceptionally high-quality recruits were obtained after a period of advertising and selection. Their initial training included a period of orientation conducted by the fire department's training staff. This was followed by a community college training program leading to certification as basic-level EMTs. Finally, the trainees were committed to an extensive paramedic training program conducted by a university medical center hospital.

In the new arrangement, existing fire stations are utilized as dispatch locations, and the civilian paramedics are assigned to be supervised by fire company officers in those stations. Several veteran paramedics also have been recruited and employed as field EMS supervisors, although their roles have never been clearly defined.

In Profile D all alarms are transmitted to the paramedics by the fire dispatcher, although some may originate with other public safety agencies that have telephone contact with the fire dispatcher. The paramedics operate rescue ambulances with patient transport capability. They respond from their respective fire station bases or in response to radio assignments if they are in the field and available for calls.

If one of the paramedic ambulances is as close to the location of a reported emergency as the local engine company, or closer, then that ambulance is dispatched alone. If it is unavailable for a response or if a local engine company is closer to the scene, then the engine company is dispatched. However, engine company personnel are trained only as first-aiders. Although they have been trained in cardiopulmonary resuscitation, their skills in initial management of most critical cases are highly limited.

The dispatch profile of this department creates difficulty for the paramedic teams. For example, when they respond to a case of cardiac arrest without additional assistance, they have great difficulty in carrying out the steps required in the initial stages of the rescue effort. Recommendations for a universal medical emergency response by engine companies have not been accepted.

As with the early stages of the Profile B experience, the availability of public ambulance service in Profile D has tended to encourage greater public use (and abuse) of the service. Here, too, a minimal fee is charged for use of the ambulance service. It is referred to the city's finance department for billing and collection. Due to the relatively small charge and poor collection experience, revenue derived from this charge recovers less than 30 percent of the costs of operating the service.

High demand for this department's EMS service produces frequent instances when an ambulance is not available for immediate dispatch. This leaves the patient in the custody of the local engine company personnel, with their limited emergency care training, until a fire department ambulance arrives or a private ambulance is called by the fire dispatcher. Until then, the engine company is unavailable for other fire or medical emergency calls.

In this hypothetical case, the salary savings expected from the hiring of civilians have been erased by subsequent events. The civilian paramedics complained that their work load was considerably greater than that of their firefighter counterparts, and that their paramedic training was longer and more demanding than the recruit training of the firefighters, who were compensated at a higher rate. At the same time, the fire department afforded paramedic equipment repairs a low priority. Paramedic grievances went without answer. Frustration rose as morale plummeted. In desperation and anger the paramedics formed their own union, which eventually negotiated salaries exceeding those of the firefighters.

In the meantime financial pressure has caused the city council to order across-the-board cuts in departmental budgets. In setting budget priorities, the fire chief is aware that no cuts can be made in the overworked paramedic ambulance service. On the other hand, his heavily staffed fire companies are limited to the primary function of fire protection and are occupied by emergency activity for less than 5 percent of their on-duty time. As financial pressure increases, political enthusiam for insurance rating designation weakens, and eventually the chief may be forced to reduce his staffing standards as the only means of balancing a reduced budget.

This department and its EMS service have experienced deficiencies in design, political and financial planning, and management of human resources, particularly the lack of an ''escape route'' for overworked paramedics. Although sophisticated planning was undertaken to determine appropriate numbers and locations of paramedic ambulances, the planners made a political miscalculation in presuming that the city council would accept the limitation of service to true emergencies. In practice, council members get angry when a constituent is denied service, so the service is forced to operate beyond its designed capacity. Inadequate numbers of ambulances and personnel are attempting to handle an excessive number of calls.

Failure to plan for the special management problems of an EMS service has contributed to the poor morale and labor-management turmoil in this example. It has been assumed that the EMS service can be managed as the fire protection function has been for generations. But nonstop emergency activity tends to limit the individual and collective tolerance and motivation of the paramedics. Their attitudes can affect their handling of the public and encourage lawsuits against the municipality for perceived negligence. Since they are civilian employees, they cannot transfer to a firefighting assignment. In essence, they have no escape route other than resignation from the department or disability retirement.

Profile E

The fifth profile combines fire protection and emergency medical services in a blend of personnel and vehicle resources. A selected number of fire stations are designated to house *medic companies*. Each of these companies consists of a four-person crew, with at least two trained and certified as advanced life support paramedics and the remaining members trained to the basic life support level. Each medic company has a standard fire pumper and a fully equipped paramedic ambulance vehicle. One of the four serves as the company officer while another serves as the assigned driver (classed as *engineer*).

All alarms received by medic companies are transmitted through the fire department dispatcher, although some calls are forwarded to the dispatcher by a public safety communications center. In the event of a fire alarm all four members of a medic company respond on the pumper, leaving the ambulance in the station unstaffed. In the event of a medical emergency, they respond on the paramedic ambulance. During the period of unavailability, any fire or medical emergencies occurring within the medic company's first-in district are handled by adjacent companies.

This profile has several advantages. For example, it provides a full four-person crew for handling medical emergencies (which outnumber fire alarms three to one), and it can be implemented without hiring additional personnel. It allows paramedics to achieve promotions without leaving the advanced life support (paramedic) service. It is possible for the company officer and the driver of a medic company to be paramedics (having been promoted from the firefighter ranks).

The medic company approach may be limited in its application to locales with dense populations and compact boundaries, because it depends on the availability of prompt response by fire companies in adjacent districts. To avoid overuse it should be limited to emergency cases. Private ambulance services should be available to transport nonemergency cases, to allow prompt availability of medic companies at the conclusion of a medical emergency response.

This hypothetical city also operates a number of standard fire companies. When medical emergencies occur in the districts of those companies, the medic company must respond from a distant location. To accommodate cases in which the medic company response is likely to take more than four minutes, the standard fire company crews have been trained as basic EMTs and equipped to serve in a first-response role. Upon arrival of the medic company, the first-response unit becomes immediately available for other calls. With personnel of the first-response companies trained to the EMT level, they are capable of triage, which enables them to cancel the response of the medic company if the case does not require emergency assistance.

Personnel in this system are trained in a program conducted by a local hospital that is affiliated with a university medical center. The physician who supervises the training is on the faculty of the medical school and serves as the fire department's medical advisor. His authority to monitor paramedic skills and correct apparent deficiencies is informal but is readily acknowledged by the administration of the fire department.

Budgetary requirements related to the EMS service include the salaries of individuals working in the place of trainees during the paramedic training program. Otherwise, no additional personnel have been hired. Purchase, maintenance, and replacement of vehicles and EMS equipment costs are borne by the fire department budget. Training costs (other than trainee salaries) are absorbed by the medical school, which is funded by the state government. Overall, the cost of the EMS service is less than 5 percent of the total fire department budget.

Profile F

This last example is the only one of the six profiles to use the services of volunteers. In this particular community the volunteer ambulance service is steeped in local tradition and community pride, enjoying the respect and financial support of the community. It has provided ambulance service for nearly thirty-five years and has expanded that service to include some invasive medical procedures administered by certain of its members who have been trained to the "EMT-Intermediate" level. Until recently, the fire department was a separate and distinct volunteer entity in this community. However, with the rapid growth of the population and tax base, this department has been converted to a paid fire service, supplemented by volunteers in cases of major fires.

Until the volunteer service was upgraded to the paramedic level, there was no cooperative arrangement between that group and the fire department. Calls for medical assistance were handled exclusively by the ambulance service, which provided both emergency and nonemergency medical transportation.

As the ambulance service became more sophisticated its medical advisor recognized the need for basic life support first response as an adjunct to the intermediate skills available from the ambulance volunteers. Because all of the volunteer service's ambulances respond from a single central location, however, response times to some locations in the community exceed eight minutes. Consequently, the medical advisor proposed that the fire department's units be used for a first-response function in cooperation with the volunteers.

The fire department responded positively and has trained its entire staff to the level of basic life support EMT. Dispatch procedures have been revised to provide for an immediate response by the nearest engine or truck company at the same time that the volunteer ambulance service is dispatched. On arrival at the scene, firefighter EMTs begin basic life support actions where necessary. Since the volunteers transport both emergency and nonemergency cases, the fire companies cancel the ambulance response only in the event of a false alarm.

To maintain their skills, volunteers who trained as EMT-Intermediate are required to engage in continuing education programs at the medical control hospital. While engaged in these programs, volunteers are available for response from that location. First-response fire companies, however, are dispatched from their fire stations or from the field when notified by radio.

The volunteers are dispatched by a public safety communications center that is accessible through a 911 or other emergency telephone number. Since the fire department began its first-response function, citizens have increasingly tended to call the fire dispatcher to report medical emergencies. Cooperative arrangements have been developed to relay calls immediately and dispatch appropriate units without delay.

Training of the firefighters to the EMT level has been conducted jointly by the fire department training staff and a local community college. The medical control hospital provides a ten-hour clinical experience for the trainees and has developed a continuing education program to prepare the firefighter EMTs for periodic recertification, as required by state law. Training of the firefighter EMTs has been complemented by programs available from the state EMS agency. Those programs include special extrication courses and refresher training for EMTs. These programs are mobile and are conducted while firefighters are on duty.

The fire department's EMS component has required no additional personnel. Although the state EMS agency provided the original patient care equipment for the fire department's first-response program, the fire department has since borne the cost of maintaining that equipment and replacing it as it wears out or becomes obsolete.

In the early stages of the program the firefighters and the volunteer ambulance personnel experienced occasional conflict over their respective roles. Some of the younger firefighters were frustrated by the limits of their basic life support service. Later, however, they were given the opportunity to join the volunteer unit and train in the intermediate skills program in their off-duty time. Several accepted the offer. When these firefighters are on duty with the fire department their role is limited to basic life support, but their specialized knowledge and skills are valuable to the volunteer ambulance personnel when both agencies are present at the scene of a life-threatening medical emergency.

Many volunteer organizations have shown a strong interest in providing intermediate or advanced life support skills with specially trained volunteer personnel. However, several real-world factors need to be considered. For example, most volunteer fire or ambulance organizations must maintain a large roster of members in order to provide adequate emergency response coverage. Volunteer services usually exist in rural or suburban areas, some of which have a relatively low volume of calls for emergency services. When this is the case, the combination of large numbers of volunteers and a relatively low call volume results in a limited number of actual emergency events for each volunteer member.

Initial training of volunteers in advanced skills is another limiting factor. Despite some early training programs that were short in duration and limited to cardiac problems, a national standard for paramedic training has evolved that calls for in-depth training in a variety of medical emergency disciplines. Deviation from the standard presents the potential for serious legal problems.

The national experience with EMT-Intermediates and paramedics has demonstrated that the important skills of advanced life support diminish quickly without frequent involvement in significant medical emergency situations. The typical demographic environment in which volunteers work may not present opportunities for frequent involvement. Furthermore, a large number of trained volunteers must share these infrequent opportunities, with the result that individual experience is limited. Although less desirable than actual field experience, ongoing training in a hospital is used to counter skill decay among underutilized intermediate-skills and advanced life support personnel in some locations. However, since most volunteers are already committed to their primary employment—not to mention responsibilities to home and family—the burden of such training is unacceptable in many cases. Finally, the stability of a volunteer organization is affected by extraneous factors: For example, transfers or changes of employment can remove a trained volunteer from the community after considerable time and resources have been devoted to his or her training.

All in all, it is an extraordinary achievement for a volunteer organization to implement an intermediate-skills program and make that program function smoothly over the long term. Further, it is a rare community that can implement an advanced life support (paramedic) service with volunteers. On the other hand, however, enough communities have succeeded in this task to prove that it is possible.

An assessment of the sample operational profiles

From the foregoing analysis of six distinct profiles of EMS involvement for fire departments, managers will recognize that there is no single set of features that is appropriate for all agencies. Community history and tradition tend to affect the design of EMS within a local fire department. Other organizations and agencies may have preempted the field of service or parts of it. Design may be affected by the availability of ancillary services such as dispatching by a public safety communications center. The size, shape, and function of a fire department EMS component may be affected by the size, strength, and affiliation of local hospitals. Political influences are likely to affect the design where decisions must receive the sanction of a city council or other policymaking body. The nature and availability of supplemental funding is yet another influential factor.

While the six profiles represent composites of actual fire service experiences, the profiles come close enough to actual experiences to furnish some valuable lessons.

Ambulance membership programs

One method of financing fire department ambulance services—while meeting the needs of residents with limited or fixed incomes—is an ambulance membership program. Typically, these programs allow residents to purchase a one-year family membership at a moderate price. If any person covered by the membership requires the fire department's ambulance service during the membership year, the program covers the uninsured portion of the ambulance bill.

The concept of ambulance membership started in 1939 with a volunteer service in Pennsylvania, and subsequently programs have been developed in many areas of the United States. For example, a private company offers an ambulance membership program to residents of about one-third of the state of Louisiana. In central Oregon, a network of fire departments offers a membership program known as FireMed to about 1 million residents. In the neighboring cities of Eugene and Springfield, Oregon, 18 percent of all families have joined.

In the United States, fire department EMS membership fees range from $12 per year (for nontransporting paramedic rescue service) to $35 per year (for emergency and nonemergency paramedic ambulance service). The presumption, of course, is that most members will not need to use the service during a membership year. Further, the membership fees give the fire department's EMS program a fairly predictable revenue base, along with fees for service charged to nonmembers and nonresidents, and third-party reimbursements from Medicare, Medicaid, and health or auto insurance carriers.

Probably the most important aspect of membership programs is their ability to serve limited- or fixed-income residents with state-of-the-art EMS—without causing financial hardship for the patient and family. For example, if an elderly member requires emergency paramedic ambulance service, he or she will receive no direct bill after service is rendered. However, in most programs, the fire department (or its billing contractor) will file a claim with Medicare for reimbursement of the amount charged to nonmembers for the same service. Generally, the department will accept as payment in full the amount that Medicare reimburses.

Before setting up a membership program, it is important to research any possible limitations of state law. There may be licensing requirements, or it may be necessary to establish that the proposed membership program is not an insurance coverage.

Ambulance membership programs, though excellent bargains for many families, do not often sell themselves. To make the program successful, it may be necessary for the department to establish a marketing budget, to advertise and promote the program widely, and to enlist on-duty fire companies in a door-to-door informational campaign to local residents. All in all, these efforts often have improved departments' relationship with the community.

As ambulance membership programs grow and mature, additional features and benefits are being offered. Several fire departments have arranged for citizens to pay their membership fees through an assessment to their regular water bills, thus securing a continuous source of revenue until the resident moves, stops paying the water bill, or asks to be removed from the program. In at least one program, a member's personal medical history can be entered into the department's computer for use if a medical emergency occurs.

The EMS Committee of the International Association of Fire Chiefs can provide information on fire department EMS or ambulance membership programs. In some states, networks of fire departments are undertaking areawide marketing of membership programs and sharing of information and resources.

Level of service/training It should be noted that each of the six examples provides first-response and basic life support services. This factor is related to location and mobility of fire department resources. Although some police agencies have trained and equipped their officers and patrol units for this function, a paid fire department is difficult to match in its ability to deliver trained personnel to the scene of a medical emergency within a very few minutes.

In all but two of the examples, fire departments provide advanced life support (paramedic level) services. As a result of widespread adoption of EMS by the fire service and ongoing upgrades and improvements in those services, this probably is a reflection of actual national ratios. However, as the examples illustrate, this move changes the entire complexion of a fire department's EMS responsibilities. Inherent in this move is the requirement for medical control (discussed in greater detail later in this chapter).

The private sector In the past, private ambulance services had full freedom to open shop and compete against other existing companies in a city or county. At its worst, this competition involved monitoring police radios, jumping calls, and racing competitors to accident scenes. A temporary but fragile solution has been to create ambulance zones or a rotation system.

In recent years, local governments have made a concerted effort to create exclusive operating areas in which a single ambulance company acquires exclusive rights. Bidders prepare detailed proposals and compete for the right to serve a city or county government entity exclusively for a period of several years. The winning competitor is subject to financial incentives and disincentives to meet or exceed established standards for level of care and response time performance.

The intense competition forces competitors to bid low, which can save the local government money on ambulance service. However, the successful bidder must then deliver without going bankrupt. The new generation of private ambulance executives accomplish that with something called "high-performance" prehospital care and transportation.

High-performance private ambulance systems use a process called "system status management"—an efficient deployment of ambulances from different parts of the service area at different times of the day and night and days of the week—to meet guaranteed response times with the least possible number of ambulances and personnel.

Other features of high-performance private ambulance systems include staffing ambulances with one paramedic and one EMT, the use of all ambulances in the system for both emergency and nonemergency medical transportation (to extract additional revenues from periods of low demand for emergency calls), and an eight-minute response time standard.

These developments offer many important lessons to fire service managers. While the so-called high-performance ambulance services may achieve economies through partial paramedic staffing and clinically questionable response times, many elected officials are attracted by the private sector's package of nonsubsidized, trouble-free ambulance service with self-enforcing performance controls.

The fire service's grasp on prehospital EMS has forced the private sector to compete on a higher plane. The private sector has risen to the challenge and is now forcing its fire service competitors to innovate, to explore the intricacies of EMS delivery and finance, and to deliver more convincing, businesslike proposals for the right to serve as ambulance providers. A process of natural selection is under way and in the end, despite some casualties, both sides of the competition will benefit from it.

Response vehicles The use of fire apparatus (pumpers and trucks) for EMS response has increased greatly in recent years. As indicated in Profile A, paramedic pumpers are a feasible approach. In several metropolitan areas of the United States, fire departments have completely replaced their small rescue vehicles with paramedic pumpers, and they report success with the concept. However, in this and other nontransporting modes cooperative arrangements with local private ambulance services are necessary.

The issue of patient transportation is critical to every EMS operation. As indicated by the examples, a fire department's assumption of patient transport responsibility has far-reaching implications. Although previously viewed as a burden to be avoided, some fire service managers have begun to view the issue as an opportunity to make their departments more productive, to relate to the community through a wider range of services, and to generate revenues through ambulance fees. As reflected in Profile B, financing arrangements can include a membership program that (a) generates revenues through a voluntary subscription arrangement, and (b) meets the needs of limited income residents for quality emergency ambulance service without the burden of ambulance service fees.

The fire department assumption of emergency ambulance service requires clearly articulated policy from the local body of elected policymakers. In seeking a statement of policy, the department and the city or county manager should be very candid as to the nature and intent of the service and the potential for constituent complaints when transportation service is denied in nonemergency cases. A lack of political commitment signals the potential for an overused service that will produce innumerable management and operational problems.

In five of the six profiles, private ambulance services are used (in varying degrees) for patient transportation. Such a cooperative arrangement can serve a variety of needs although the response pattern may appear uncoordinated. In addition to the advantages of cooperation with private ambulance services, there are a number of problems to be anticipated.

Traditionally, private ambulance services have been marginal business enterprises. A "new breed" of private ambulance executive, however, has begun to make important changes that affect the entire industry (see accompanying sidebar). Even so, the intense competition for the right to serve exclusive operating areas within stringent performance requirements and often without local government subsidies has created pressure on these companies. Inasmuch as labor costs are the single greatest expense for any ambulance enterprise, economic pressures resulting from the competition have kept wages for private ambulance EMTs and paramedics somewhat lower than typical firefighter salaries. The private companies generally attract young people who tend to leave when an opportunity for higher income appears. Personnel turnover remains high, as it has traditionally. Although many fire departments and private ambulance companies have developed cooperative working relationships, those relationships are tenuous in many cases.

Through legislative and other efforts at the state and national levels, the private ambulance industry has opposed fire service involvement in EMS. These efforts have intensified now that fire departments have begun to explore and implement membership or subscription ambulance service programs. Unfortunately, the animosity in some cases has carried into the working environment, resulting in confrontations while the parties have been engaged in patient care and transportation.

While many fire service administrators continue to strive for better working relationships with private ambulance providers despite periodic eruptions, some elected bodies have approached the problem by creating exclusive authority for either the private or the public sector to provide the service. Despite these either/ or solutions, national experience by and large indicates that the public is best served by a cooperative arrangement between the fire service and the private ambulance sector, and that the problems that arise in a public-private cooperative arrangement are surmountable.

Civilian employees   Among the examples presented, the most perplexing set of difficulties is to be found in Profile D, the only example to use civilian employees of the fire department. Although the use of civilian employees is not universally unwise, several problems arise from such a situation.

One problem is that there is little justification for limiting full-time paid firefighters to the single role of firefighting. Contemporary economics in local government require that optimum use be made of public employees' available time. There is abundant evidence that properly trained and motivated firefighters can be trained to provide both fire protection and EMS services without compromise to either. Where EMS activity is specifically assigned to a separate body of civilian personnel, questions remain concerning justification for the unproductive time of the single role force of firefighters.

In some locations the proponents of civilian EMS employees have argued that a career ladder is needed. Presumably, a new administrative structure within the fire department would provide promotional opportunities for the civilian employees while maintaining their occupational involvement in the emergency care service. In reality, however, supervisory vacancies would occur only in the event of death, discharge, or retirement. The vast majority of personnel would remain at the working level throughout their career.

Paramedics   Long-term assignment to an advanced life support unit has special significance for a paramedic operating in an urban environment. Growing public awareness and demand for advanced life support services means that most urban paramedics are engaged in nonstop emergency activity during almost every duty shift. The realities of this duty involve high levels of stress for most paramedics. It is believed that this stress is the product of frequent operation of an EMS vehicle under emergency conditions, operation in the undisciplined and emotional environment of an emergency scene under the watchful eyes of numerous observers, the need for uncommon skill in dealing with distraught patients and their families, and the requirement for immediate life or death judgments in

Figure 14–5   This Type III modular ambulance is equipped for advanced life support services. It is staffed by cross-trained, dual-role firefighter-paramedics, and it is partially financed by a community ambulance membership program.

handling serious medical emergencies. Stress is compounded where paramedics are subject to physical abuse and injury when dealing with drug and intoxication cases or while operating amid crowds of unruly spectators. Stress is aggravated when fire department administration fails to be sensitive to paramedics' special needs, or when their medical control hospital is unresponsive.

During the late 1970s, urban paramedics began to display symptoms referred to as paramedic burnout. For those paramedics so affected who are committed to a dual role, an escape route exists through reassignment to a firefighting role. Others escape the rigors of their paramedic assignment through successful competition in promotional exams. Civilian paramedics employed by a fire department, on the other hand, seldom have an effective escape route other than resignation from the department.

Where paramedics are removed from their emergency care role (by promotion or reassignment), the question will occur as to the relative wisdom of expensive training programs in preparation for short tenure. In some cases, the cost of training replacement paramedics may be regarded as a cost of doing business. In others, however, it is an investment that pays off in future benefits to the department. For example, when a firefighter paramedic is promoted to an officer's position, assignment is likely to be made to a local fire company. If that company is involved in first-response activities the promoted paramedic will bring an extra degree of skill and experience to the job. Those skills and that experience will have relevance to the provision of basic life support pending arrival of a paramedic unit, and they will be helpful in the form of another set of trained hands to assist paramedics after their arrival at the scene. The same benefits can accrue in the case of paramedics who have burned out and are reassigned to fire companies.

As evidenced by Profiles A and E, there exists an opportunity in some departments to reorganize in an effort to retain the value of paramedic training and experience after promotions occur. This can occur through assignment of promoted paramedics to paramedic pumper/truck companies or to a medic company. In considering profiles for optimum use of skill and experience, it is important to note that most fire departments with EMS find that medical emergencies represent the majority of alarms received. Although the agency may be officially designated as a fire department, the community sees its service role as being much broader. Many of the EMS implementation and management difficulties experienced by fire departments relate to a lack of relevant background on the part of fire department administrators. The situation is analogous to that of fire protection services that are organized and managed by a physician who has no background in firefighting. In the future, however, if promotional opportunities are afforded to firefighter EMTs and paramedics, they will become the next generation of fire chiefs and they will bring to their position relevant experience in both fire protection and emergency medical care.

Management issues

Three major issues challenge the manager of EMS in the fire service: direction and control, coordination of the diverse elements that make up the system, and program evaluation.

Direction and control

Direction of a fire department's EMS function is one of the most sensitive issues to be dealt with by local government decisionmakers. In many instances direction is split between medical considerations and operational prerogatives. This split is most significant with regard to advanced life support services delivered by paramedics. In order to understand the points of division it is necessary to clearly recognize prehospital advanced life support services as an outreach function of the medical control hospital. This perception should be distinguished from the view of paramedic services as a local government or private ambulance function that merely uses a hospital for guidance.

The concept of medical control The concept of medical control in EMS has grown from the actual experience of paramedic operations throughout the country. Many early programs were established without the advantage of clear conceptual understanding. Medical and operational problems growing out of those operations resulted in federal and state requirements for medical control of paramedic operations. Subsequently, most such operations have been developed as hospital outreach programs, using employees of another agency (such as a fire department) as surrogates of a designated physician at the medical control hospital (or as that physician's authorized representatives).

The concept of medical control has created some discomfort for fire officials, hospitals, and physicians. In essence, fire chiefs are required to relinquish some degree of control over their employees. The physician at the medical control hospital (often referred to as the medical director) is required to assume responsibility for someone else's employees in certain situations. The hospital itself may be required to stand behind the fire department's paramedics and even insure against any possible negligence in their medical performance. In addition, the hospital may find it necessary to devote some of its personnel and resources to training paramedics who are not on the hospital's payroll.

Despite its unorthodox aspect, the concept of medical control has proved itself in locations throughout the United States. Moreover, it is a reflection of long-established legal principles. Legal precedents dating back to 1826 have dealt with the issues of vicarious liability,[11] respondeat superior (employer responsibility for employee negligence),[12] and the "borrowed servant" (borrowed employee; discussed later in this section)[13] situations found in the concept of medical control.

The medical control hospital A major element in the modern concept of medical control is the designation of one or more hospitals in a community to serve as medical control hospitals (often referred to as resource hospitals or base hospitals). Given the responsibilities attached to such a designation, it is important that a hospital be so designated solely on the basis of its ability and willingness to carry out those responsibilities. In some of the early EMS programs excessive numbers of hospitals were equipped with radio and telemetry gear and were then presumed to be fulfilling their role by merely communicating with EMTs and paramedics during the management of medical emergencies. The flaws in this arrangement were revealed as it became obvious that no single hospital or medical professional had the ultimate responsibility for training, skill maintenance, continuing education, medical auditing, and system coordination. Moreover, in such a situation no single hospital had come to grips with the issue of legal and financial indemnification of paramedics who might be charged with negligence by civil litigants.

Designation as a medical control hospital tends to carry a degree of prestige, even though the burdens of the designation generally outweigh any benefits. Thus, in most communities there is intense competition among hospitals for this role. The actual designation process should be conducted by a regional or community EMS coordinating agency, using appropriate criteria. The final designation of one or more hospitals should be made by a broad-based health-related committee or council after review of written proposals submitted by each of the competing hospitals. This final designation should be based entirely on the relative ability of the hospital or hospitals to meet or exceed the criteria established for the medical control function.

The medical director   Another major element in the medical control concept is the designation of a fully qualified physician to serve as medical director at the medical control hospital. In this regard, qualifications should include un-questionable competence and experience in all phases of emergency medicine. Preferably this person should be a full-time emergency physician and should have department head status over the emergency department at the medical control hospital.

The medical director needs to be armed with sufficient authority to effect necessary changes in the hospital's operations, including the mandating of improved emergency care skills on the part of physicians and nurses working in the emergency department. The authority should extend to coordination with other hospitals in the community to ensure that patients treated by paramedics and transported to these other hospitals receive appropriate care in all cases.

The medical director will need full access to the resources necessary for initial training of EMTs and paramedics, and for skill maintenance and continuing education programs. Through daily reviews of run reports and medical records, the medical director needs to make every effort to detect faulty care or defective skills or judgment on the part of prehospital and in-hospital personnel, and he or she should have the authority to call for such a review and to correct any deficiencies.

Through formal contracts with prehospital provider agencies (such as the local fire department), the medical director should be given authority to direct EMTs and paramedics into retraining programs where these are necessary. Such contracts should also authorize the director to mandate the removal of personnel from emergency care positions where their skills, knowledge, attitudes, or performances are deemed medically inappropriate to the responsibilities.

The legal principles   Under the concept of medical control, service providers and the medical control hospital are governed by the legal principles referred to above (vicarious liability, respondeat superior, the "borrowed servant"). One authoritative source has described the basic principle as follows:

> A servant (employee) directed or permitted by his master (employer) to perform services for another may become the servant (employee) of such other in performing the services. He may become the other's servant (employee) as to some acts and not as to others.[14]

Restated in contemporary terms, it may be said that the medical control hospital desires to improve its service to the community by providing prehospital care in the form of advanced life support performed by paramedics. However, since the hospital lacks the resources to actually deliver those prehospital services, it must rely on another agency to provide the necessary personnel, dispatching, vehicle, and structural resources (such as the local department). When the employees of that other agency are engaged in patient evaluation and care functions they are performing as "servants" (employees) of the hospital. Thus, as with all of its own agents and employees, the hospital has a need to protect its patients and itself against negligent or otherwise defective performance. This reality supports the medical control hospital's right to assert its standards of quality through the training, monitoring, and continuing education of paramedics employed by another agency.

The guiding legal principles, then, hold that one may become the "servant" of another as to some acts and not others. It is obvious that fire department paramedics would not be under appropriate control of the medical control hospital other than when they were in direct contact with patients, or during preparation for their patient care role (training). At all other times these personnel should be viewed as being within the operational control of their principal employer (the fire department).

Supporting the applicable legal principles is the persuasive fact of community reliance on its hospitals as the focal point of health care quality. Certainly no informed citizen would expect the fire department or private ambulance service to make judgments as to the relative quality of emergency health care performance. Similarly, a firefighters' labor organization that might be offended by the power of the medical director should be reminded that the physician and the hospital he or she is responsible to have the ultimate legal, moral, and professional responsibility for health care quality. No other public agency, committee, community organization, or employee representative group is qualified to make judgments as to the quality of medical professional or paraprofessional performance. Even if such an entity were to assert itself in this role of monitoring quality, it undoubtedly would not wish to be in the role of civil defendant when a performance defect results in injury or death.

Management and supervision In the six profiles presented in this chapter, the operational direction of the fire department paramedics is delegated to the company officer. There is abundant evidence that company officers—even without paramedic training—can adequately perform this supervisory task.

Traditional approaches to fire department and fire company supervision may need to be altered to some degree to meet the special requirements of an EMS program. The nature of most fire department EMS operations will tend to reduce the traditional close contact between company officers and their subordinates. This factor together with the division of loyalties between the fire department and the medical control hospital may prove a disturbing experience for company officers and their supervisors.

Overall, it would appear that operational difficulties have been generated by one or the other of two extreme approaches. In one such approach there is an effort to oversupervise the EMS personnel: For example, an officer may interfere in patient care situations for which the officer is neither qualified nor trained. Occasionally such an attitude manifests itself in the restrictive tethering of EMS personnel to the fire company: Refusing to allow paramedics to leave the station with their vehicle to attend a continuing education program at the hospital would be an example. Another example would be making paramedics responsible for station maintenance chores despite their obligation to answer many more alarms than their firefighter counterparts answer.

The other extreme approach appears to be an attitude of official insulation from those personnel assigned to the EMS function. This attitude was inherent in the problems discussed in Profile D. Where the department's administrators fail to communicate the importance of the EMS component, disregard and contempt are likely to filter down through the ranks. In such instances the EMS personnel tend to feel rejected by their department and an imbalance of loyalties is a common result.

Despite such difficulties the national experience suggests that the majority of fire departments involved in EMS have succeeded in mastering appropriate direction of the operational aspects of the program. As more firefighter EMTs and paramedics rise through the promotional ranks, it is likely that their supervisory and management techniques will reflect their background and experience in both aspects of their department's mission.

Coordination

EMS involves a diverse set of individuals, agencies, organizations, and institutions. There is no single organizational umbrella that employs and directs every person who must serve the immediate needs of an emergency patient throughout the sequence of emergency care and transportation. For example, a public utility telephone company may be responsible for establishing and maintaining an emergency telephone system. Calls generated by that service may be received by employees of a public agency not affiliated with the telephone company. That public agency may, upon receipt of a call for assistance, activate the response of one or more other organizations (such as a fire department, a police department, and a private ambulance company). The roles of the respective response agencies must be predetermined and the employees of those agencies must be adequately skilled in those roles.

Training of the prehospital emergency personnel may be the assigned role of still another organization or institution. Medical direction of these personnel, as well as monitoring of their medical performance, is likely to be the responsibility of a private physician who may be bound by contract to a hospital. That hospital is still another entity in the scenario. Its roles are likely to be multiple and can encompass provision of acute emergency care, ambulatory care for the less-than-acute emergency patient, long-term care for the seriously ill or injured, and rehabilitation services for those who survive their medical crises.

To the extent that local government perceives a responsibility in EMS, elected officials may assert their collective will on the system from time to time. In addition, they may be expected to provide financial resources to support certain segments of the EMS system.

EMS regulatory agencies at the county or state levels may be still another element to consider in designing, implementing, and operating an EMS program. Depending on the locale and the authority of the regulatory agency, its involvement may include licensure or certification of personnel and vehicles and even influence on the size, shape, and functions of the local system and its many elements.

In most communities there is little chance that so many diverse elements will ever come under a single management entity—nor is there any valid reason to believe that long-term benefits would result from such a consolidation. EMS, in the context of a comprehensive emergency care system, usually involves some reorganization of existing roles, territories, and procedures. The comfort and security of tradition and status quo are often disturbed by the organizational and operational needs of an EMS system. It is all the more important, then, that these various elements be coordinated toward the essential focal point— the needs of the emergency patient. In most cases the relative success of such coordination will determine the relative success of the EMS system in reaching its performance goals.

Cooperation in EMS is fragile and requires constant attention. When it is a planned endeavor, pursued on a regular basis, coordination can become a method of controlling events rather than being controlled by them. But when coordination is viewed merely as a response to crisis, it is likely to affect emergency care services adversely while continually diverting key policymakers and managers from the goals of creativity and stability.

In smaller fire departments coordination of the department's EMS functions within the community is likely to be the responsibility of the chief or one of the chief's key subordinates. In many larger departments the coordination function may be assigned to an EMT or paramedic who has been promoted to the rank of officer. Although it is not absolutely necessary, it has proved of value to assign the coordination function to individuals who have served (or are currently serving) in an actual patient care role. Such experience in the system lends credibility to the individual in his or her efforts to coordinate with other service providers.

Where a fire department assigns one of its members to coordinate its EMS function with the rest of the EMS community, it is essential that that individual possess authority commensurate with responsibility. Diligent commitment to planning is of great help in this regard. Where a department's EMS planning is thorough and continuous, all potential policy conflicts will be anticipated and strategies can be devised in advance for use by the EMS coordinator. On the other hand, a crisis-oriented approach to EMS coordination will leave the fire department's coordinator without any guidance in dealing with the day-to-day ebb and flow of organizational interrelationships; instead, the coordinator will be obligated to serve as a messenger of crisis and reaction between the fire department and the other elements of the system.

One of the key roles of the fire department's EMS coordinator stems from the department's unique relationship with the medical control hospital and the medical director. The potential problems of perception and cooperation are endless. To compound the difficulties, the medical director may take a possessive stance with regard to fire department employees trained as paramedics. In such circumstances the paramedics often become pawns in a battle for loyalty and operational prerogatives. Where this situation is not appropriately managed, the fire department may tend to step into the arena of medical judgments and the medical director may tend to venture into operational policy. A most effective means of preventing such a dilemma lies in role sharing.

In some of the more successful EMS programs emergency physicians are given frequent opportunities to spend periods of duty with paramedics in their operational environment. For an emergency physician concerned with fire department paramedics, this experience should include spending time at fire stations between alarms, as well as watching dual role paramedics performing as firefighters in actual situations. After such experience a physician may find most of the fire department's policy prerogatives reasonable and acceptable.

Where a fire department's EMS personnel must rely on emergency nurses in their relationships with hospitals, these nurses should also be given the opportunity to join the paramedics in their environment. In addition to contributing to mutual understanding, the "ride-along" programs provide an opportunity for physicians and nurses to assess their own skills in the real world of prehospital care.

Fire service administrators may also find their relations with medical control hospitals and medical professionals strained by mandates issued by those sources. Those fire service administrators would do well to orient themselves to the operational environment of the hospital emergency department and its staff. Basic level EMTs must spend at least ten hours in an emergency department internship as part of their training. Paramedic trainees often spend hundreds of hours in their clinical internship. Their fire department superiors would benefit from such firsthand observation, and could gain a better understanding of the circumstances that produce conflicting views on how best to deliver services.

Where EMS is a solid commitment of a fire department, and where that commitment is clearly communicated from the top, coordination of the function within the department should operate as a matter of course.

Once again, planning is an essential ingredient. If used before implementation of the EMS service and on a continuous basis after implementation, planning can identify potential conflicts within the agency and strategies can be effected to minimize or prevent such conflicts. This is largely a matter of organizational attitude. In nearly every fire department there will be personnel who strongly believe that a fire department's role should be limited to fire protection. Unless there is strong and consistent evidence of top level policy to the contrary, pockets of resistance and interference will surface to produce problems that could have been prevented.

While some of the most vocal opponents of fire department EMS programs have been found within the fire service, experience has shown that such resistance can be penetrated and that equally strong supporters can arise from the ranks of the original opponents. Such a conversion can result from a program of internal orientation. The command structure of a fire department can serve as the most effective mechanism for such orientation. (It may be necessary to conduct training programs for management employees to prepare them for the orientation task.) It is important for managers to always keep in mind the fact that support and clarity will have to flow from the top if the program is to function successfully.

Program evaluation

One of the words heard most frequently in the EMS field is *evaluation*. In essence, it merely means the examination of a specific function to determine whether that function is producing the desired results. It is obvious, then, that *the desired results* must be identified. These results will have been stated as goals (What do we want to accomplish?) in the initial stages of the planning process. Also, it is obvious that reported information (data) will be necessary to measure performance. When the data (in the form of system outcomes) are measured against the goals (and the objectives formulated under those goals), there will be an opportunity to evaluate the program and its performance. Evaluation is represented by the broken lines in Figure 14–1.

The primary goal of a comprehensive EMS system is to reduce unnecessary death and disability through improved emergency care and transportation. The measurement of performance against this goal is referred to as *patient outcomes*: that is, How many patients survived who would have died without the proper functioning of the system? There are many sophisticated variables in this form of system evaluation and they tend to be beyond the scope of a fire department's effort to evaluate its components of the system.

Factors for evaluation in the fire department's EMS component would include response times for EMS units, relative availability of units to respond when needed, safety and maintenance factors in the operations of department vehicles in EMS activity, relative performance of department employees in EMS training programs, and relative durability of department employees in their respective EMS-related roles. However, for purposes of evaluation these and other factors must be stated in terms of measurable goals and objectives from the outset. An end product or result cannot be measured without a starting-point reference. For example, if a fire department's goal is to arrive at the scene of 80 percent of all medical emergencies in six minutes or less, that goal should be identified from the outset. Then, if a one-year experience discloses that the six-minute standard was accomplished in only 78 percent of all responses, either the objective or the approach to achieving that objective should be revised. Or if a department's goal is to graduate 80 percent of all paramedic trainees from the paramedic training program, that goal should be identified and stated prior to initiating the program. If the experience discloses that only 75 percent of all trainees are graduating, it may be a sign that admission criteria need to be strengthened or that the department's recruitment standards are inappropriate to its full range of emergency services. On the other hand, such a disclosure may indicate defects in the training program or in its testing procedures. In any event, either the objective or the approach to achieving the objective must be revised as a planning function.

Conclusion and outlook

The role of the American fire service has expanded to meet community needs for improved emergency medical services. This development coincides with and is related to advancements in emergency medical technology and the philosophy of delivering sophisticated life support services at the scene of the medical emergency and during transportation of the patient to a medical facility. The expansion of the fire service role also coincides with growing economic pressure to use the available time of fire protection personnel more effectively.

Although numerous problems arise in this evolutionary process, skillful planning and good management can produce optimum results in improved public service.

The future is not likely to hold any relief from the pressure of limited municipal finances. Public demand for increased services is likely to continue, placing responsibility on local government to make cost-effective use of public employees, including the production of revenues through the delivery of ambulance service.

A new generation of fire service managers can be expected to emerge as dual-role personnel rise through the ranks with broadened expectations and abundant practical experience in service delivery. Properly managed, the merger of EMS with traditional fire service responsibilities can contribute to a healthy future for tomorrow's fire departments.

1   Editorial, *Journal of Emergency Medical Services* 9, no. 6 (June 1984):4.

2   The Emergency Medical Services Systems Act of 1973 (Public Law 93-154) and regulations promulgated by the U.S. Department of Health, Education and Welfare (later known as the Department of Health and Human Services).

3   J. Frank Pantridge, "A Mobile-Intensive Care Unit in the Management of Myocardial Infarction," *Lancet* 2 (1967): 217–73.

4   James O. Page, "Why Fire Fighters?" *Fire Command*, August 1972, pp. 28–31.

5   Leonard B. Rose and Edward Press, "Cardiac Defibrillation by Ambulance Attendants," *Journal of the American Medical Association* 219 (3 January 1972):64.

6   *Emergency Care News* (published by Public Technology, Inc., Washington, D.C., for the Emergency Medical Services Technical Assistance Program, October 1977), p.1.

7   Research report prepared by the Harold Hayes Research Organization for *Fire Chief* magazine, 1977. See "Fire Department EMS—A Nationwide Survey," *Fire Chief*, November 1977, 34–35.

8   California Fire Service/EMS Survey and Directory, published by California Fire Chiefs Association, Emergency Medical Services Section, Southern Division, 1986.

9   Ibid.

10 Mickey S. Eisenberg, et al., "Treatment of Ventricular Fibrillation: Emergency Medical Technician Defibrillation and Paramedic Services," *Journal of the American Medical Association* 251, no. 13 (1984): 1723–26; Kenneth R. Stults et al., "Pre-Hospital Defibrillation Performed by Emergency Medical Technicians in Rural Communities," *New England Journal of Medicine* 310 (1984): 219–23.

11 Laugher v. Pointer (1826, King's Bench) 5 B.&C.547, 108 Eng. Repr. 204.

12 McFarland v. Dixie Machinery & Equipment Company, 348 Mo. 341, 153 S.W.2d. 67 (1953).

13 Mature v. Angelo, 373 Pa. 593, 97 A2d. 59, 60 (1953).

14 American Law Institute, *Restatement of Agency* (Philadelphia: American Law Institute), sec. 227.

15 Comprehensive fire prevention and code administration

To provide a comprehensive prevention program that protects the lives and property of citizens is a formidable challenge for today's fire departments. In the first place, the term *fire department* has become a misnomer. The fire service is often the first responder to emergencies caused not only by fire but also by other environmental hazards—floods, building collapses, wind storms, hazardous materials incidents, and so on. Consequently, a department's prevention efforts need to focus not only on fires but also on this expanded range of concerns.

This chapter describes the elements of a comprehensive prevention program. Among the major tools used to achieve comprehensive prevention are the codes and ordinances adopted by the community, and a major responsibility of the fire department is to ensure that the codes relating to fire and environmental safety are enforced. The second part of the chapter therefore covers comprehensive code administration, which serves a major purpose of the prevention program. The two topics are interrelated, of course, the ultimate goal being to protect life and property from fire and other hazards.

Prevention

Most governments do not have the luxury of organizing a comprehensive prevention program from the ground up. Pieces of a program generally are in place, but they are often firmly entrenched within various departments or divisions, and each serves only one function in the total prevention program.

Fire prevention is the responsibility of every member of a fire service organization. In addition, it is often formalized and consolidated into a fire prevention bureau or fire marshal's office in a medium-sized or large department. In small places, fire prevention functions may be assigned to individuals, depending on their particular skills and on scheduling considerations.

The fire prevention bureau is responsible for the key elements of a comprehensive fire prevention program: public education, fire investigation, enforcement of fire codes and ordinances, preconstruction plans review and issuance of permits, property inspection, evaluating built-in fire protection, training, and program analysis to monitor progress. Many bureaus or divisions do not have the organizational authority or the resources to carry out a total fire prevention program, and a large part of their job consists of coordinating the efforts of the fire department with those of the planning, building, zoning, health, police, and other departments; with operators of schools, hospitals, factories, and commercial buildings; and with the public. Limitations on personnel and budgetary resources and emphasis on other programs may limit fire prevention efforts. Despite such limits, however, any department with a true commitment to fire prevention can maintain a workable program.

Public education

The United States is consistently at or near the top of the list of modern industrial nations that have a major problem with fire. This is true whether the measure

Public education in fire protection

Public fire education efforts date back at least to the 1930s. Early programs were directed at educating the public on the role of the fire service, then at swaying public opinion about provisions of the fire code. Public education today is much more externalized—focusing on the "consumers" rather than the "producers" of fire protection. It is viewed essentially as an intervening strategy to prevent fires from occurring or help control them at the incipient stage.

There is a saying in the fire service that there are three causes of fires—men, women, and children—and changing their attitudes and behavior with respect to fire conditions can have a significant impact on the incidence of fire. Public education frequently covers technological advances, such as sprinkler systems and smoke detectors; specific hazards, such as kerosene heaters, fireworks, and hazardous household wastes; exit drills; and disaster preparedness.

In terms of fire protection planning, public education is a "soft" program, because its results are difficult to measure and the public may be apathetic about it unless a major fire has occurred. Faced with competition from other departmental programs, therefore, public education and prevention programs may not be adequately funded. It is difficult to demonstrate that dollars allocated to education may go further in the long run than dollars allocated to suppression.

The U.S. Fire Administration recommends a five-step planning process for public education programs:

1. Identification of the most important local fire risks and hazards

2. Selection of program objectives that meet the community's needs for fire education and utilize the resources available

3. Design of the specific content and format of the program for delivery to the community

4. Implementation through producing and distributing materials, training personnel, and involving members of the target population

5. Evaluation of the program by comparing new data with baseline information on fire incidents and losses and on community knowledge and behavior.

In practice, many public education programs are staffed by civilians, or education is a collateral duty for someone in the fire prevention bureau or for the training officer. Education may be combined with the function of public information—an evolution that occurred as a result of the need to be responsive to media coverage in the event of a major emergency. Public information officers often develop considerable expertise in the behaviors that contribute to loss of life and property, and public education becomes a natural use of this knowledge base. The most successful public education programs are those that enjoy the support of line firefighters, address specific community priorities, and link education with code enforcement.

Resources for public education include the U.S. Fire Administration, which has developed residential sprinkler demonstration trailers as well as the planning process described above; the International Society of Fire Service Instructors, which has an entire subgroup of public educators; the International Association of Fire Chiefs, which maintains a resource center in Washington, D.C.; the National Fire Protection Association, which has developed, printed, and distributed a great deal of information designed for the public; the Tobacco Institute, which has developed programs for elderly and hearing impaired citizens; private-sector vendors that market such products as puppets, robots, and audio-visual materials; and, in many places, the state fire marshal's office and/or the state fire chiefs' association.

is property loss, deaths and injuries, or fires per capita.[1] Among the contributing factors to these statistics are a general lack of knowledge of the destructive nature and costs of fire, vast quantities of material goods that can be discarded and/or replaced easily, and institutionalized methods of recouping financial losses through insurance claims and tax write-offs.

Attempts at reducing the fire losses associated with the material aspects of U.S. society are carried out through codes and ordinances, testing laboratories, and inspections of properties for hazards. Yet these efforts have not produced a solution to the problem. The reality is that, in most cases, buildings and material goods do not start fires—people do.

The basis of a good fire prevention program, therefore, is the attitude and concern of individuals toward fire. Programs and activities that constantly remind the public to avoid careless activities and teach the proper methods for individual response to fire help to develop that concern. Probably the most influential group of citizens to reach are children. Not only are they the most receptive to elementary fire education programs, but they also influence adult behavior. Tomorrow, they will be the community leaders who can see to it that sound prevention programs are continued. Other target populations include the elderly, who, like children, are frequently the victims of fire, and disabled individuals, who often have special communication or mobility needs. Programs that involve members of these groups can be very effective in creating awareness and widespread support.

Public education programs in fire prevention can include the following:

1. Voluntary home inspections, in which fire suppression and/or fire prevention personnel identify hazards and give suggestions to help citizens reduce the risk of fire
2. Talks and demonstrations at meetings of civic groups—fraternal organizations, scout troops, and community associations
3. School visits by fire prevention personnel and employment of such programs as the Learn Not to Burn curriculum of the National Fire Protection Association
4. Parades, fairs, and other organized events designed to create awareness
5. Formal public information programs, including printed materials, radio broadcasts and public service announcements, mobile information vans, fire safety clinics, and other publicity efforts (see Figure 15–1)
6. Discounted (or free) fire protection equipment, such as smoke detectors, and free installation.

Figure 15–1   A flyer from the Learn Not to Burn campaign, a long-term national public education effort of the National Fire Protection Association.

Some of these public education efforts require skills not normally available within small or medium-sized fire departments. The expertise of trained educators is just as important here as it is in the teaching of math or science, and, where possible, the department should draw on local educators as part of the prevention effort.

Fire investigation

A second important element of a fire prevention program is a thorough understanding of fires in the community. Fire investigators seek to determine the cause of fires by looking at what burns, when, where, how, and possibly by whom. The answers to these questions in turn provide feedback to other aspects of the prevention program.

In general, all fires can be classified as accidental or intentional. Once the cause of a fire has been determined, the findings can be put to their best use. If a fire is accidental in origin, it may provide lessons for the public education program, the inspection program, and the process used to revise and adopt codes and standards.

If the fire is intentional in origin—if it results from arson—it may have an effect on public education and inspection programs. If the community has a severe arson problem and the department has the ability to analyze its incidence, the prevention program may need to concentrate education and/or inspection efforts on specific types of businesses or segments of the community. Findings of arson may also have an effect on the criminal justice system by causing a revision of arson-related laws as a preventive measure.

Fire and arson investigators need thorough training if they are to accurately determine causes of fires from both the technical and legal perspectives. Personnel policies that encourage long-term dedication to this effort are essential.

Some communities have arson awareness or prevention programs that are intended to ensure that the general public is informed of the problem and to provide a means for people with information to be reimbursed for their assistance. For example, the department may immediately placard a building damaged or destroyed by an arson fire with information about the effect of the fire on the community:

1. Loss of revenue due to removal of the property from the tax rolls
2. Number of jobs lost (for *X* number of people and *X* number of family members they support)
3. The sequential number of this fire as counted since the beginning of the year or other appropriate point in time
4. Estimated cost of extinguishing and investigating the fire.

The Arson Resource Center The Arson Resource Center, created by the U.S. Fire Administration, collects and makes available data and information about the incidence, nature, and prevention of arson. The center answers questions and responds to requests made in person, by mail, by telephone, and through its electronic mail system. It can supply local departments with a limited amount of photocopied material (journal articles, research reports, and other documents) and suggest further resources as needed. Information is available through area libraries via interlibrary loan or on line through an electronic bulletin board.

General information can be obtained by calling 301/447-1032. The bulletin board number is 301/447-2787. Information on borrowing materials can be obtained toll free: 800/638-1821.

Enforcement of fire codes and ordinances

Fire prevention codes regulate building construction, electrical wiring, and heat sources; hazardous materials and processes; fire exits; fire protection equipment; and public assembly. They specify acceptable construction methods and materials, require inspection of potentially dangerous sites, mandate the installation of such safety devices as alarms and sprinklers, and set limits on occupancy.

The intent of fire codes is to provide a means for ensuring that protection features are built in and maintained properly. Occasionally, codes mandate the addition or retrofitting of equipment or features that were not originally required. For example, with the advent of inexpensive, easy-to-install smoke detectors, ordinances across the country are requiring them in existing facilities that previously had no smoke detection equipment.

The enforcement of fire prevention regulations has traditionally been accomplished primarily by relying on voluntary compliance. "Selling" fire prevention has been effective and continues to be the preferred method of enforcement. In terms of personnel resources, it is the most cost-effective method of achieving compliance. Still, the inspector and the department must have some alternative method of persuasion when voluntary compliance does not work.

Procedures for code enforcement vary considerably and are usually outlined in state statutes and local charters. If the enforcement function is to be taken seriously, the inspector needs the legal authority to issue a ticket and fine if an imminent fire hazard is present or, in more serious cases of noncompliance, to issue a summons to appear in court.

The regulation of fire protection is recognized as a state and national necessity. The proliferation of state fire marshals' rules and the trend toward creating model fire codes by national code-making organizations are evidence of this recognition. The uniformity of these codes and their encouragement of progressive fire protection regulations can be of great assistance to enforcement personnel in local fire departments. It is essential that fire administrators stay abreast of national and state trends in regulations and, whenever possible, have a voice in how they are codified.

No program of enforcement can be effective without properly trained personnel to carry it out. The ability to sell compliance can be taught along with technical skills if personnel with the right traits and background are selected for this type of work. Likewise, personnel can be trained to prepare a case for legally ordered compliance.

Preconstruction planning and permitting

Most fire prevention programs incorporate program activities to ensure that fire protection is planned into new construction projects. From the viewpoint of developers and designers of construction projects, safety is only one consideration. They must provide a product that sells at an affordable price. This means that construction design must be functional and cost effective as well as safe. A sensitivity to these considerations, particularly costs, must be conveyed by fire prevention personnel through their attitudes and through their willingness to help resolve problems related to fire protection.

There is no substitute for early involvement to help prevent future problems. The sooner a problem is recognized, the more easily and economically it can be resolved. Fire service input at this stage can allow changes that would be very difficult to achieve after public hearings have taken place and other agencies have given their approvals. Once construction has begun, it may be too late to incorporate protection features if they were missing from the plans. Therefore, involvement in the construction process must begin as soon as possible after the developer has an idea. Preconstruction meetings should take place well before construction plans are submitted. This means forging new relationships with other agencies that deal with developers and designers. Such preconstruction meetings have traditionally been the realm of planners, community development specialists, zoning specialists, the building department, the public works department, and land use attorneys, but this initial stage of the development process is vitally important to overall fire protection as well.

Once construction plans are submitted, fire service involvement in the review process must be thorough and consistent and must be coordinated with the work of the technical construction trades: structural (fire resistivity), plumbing (sprinkler system piping), electrical (alarm system wiring), mechanical (smoke removal systems), and so on (see Figure 15–2). The fire prevention personnel must step back and determine if all of the built-in requirements come together to create a total protection system. Fire prevention sign-off authority on the

Figure 15–2 A check-off form used by plans examiners in Miami, Florida.

CITY OF MIAMI–BUREAU OF FIRE PREVENTION–EXAMINATION FORM

Address: _____ Building Name (use): _____
_____ Sq. ft.
___New/Add/Rev _____ Sq. ft. _____ Alter. _____ (Occ. Change) _____ Tenants _____Type Const. _____ Const. Req'd ____# Stories

____Hgt. _____Basement ___ Covered Parking _____ Fire Zone _____ Fire Alarm _____ Standpipe _____ Sprinkler Sys. _____ # Floor

The plans submitted with the attached application have been examined. The items marked below were either omitted or do not conform to Code requirements. The original tracings must be corrected and the plans re-submitted for approval.

MEANS OF EGRESS:

_____ Additional required _____	_____ Panic hardware_____
_____ Not remote _____	_____ Door swing _____
_____ Travel distance _____	_____ Exit signs _____
_____ Width inadequate_____	_____ Exit enclosure_____
_____ Dead end _____	_____ Smoke enclosure_____
_____ Exit discharge _____	_____ Other _____
_____ Self-closer _____	_____ Other _____

FIRE RESISTIVE PROTECTION

_____ Exterior elev. _____	_____ Ceilings_____
_____ Wall openings _____	_____ Floors _____
_____ Corridors_____	_____ Rated assemblies _____
_____ Corridor openings _____	_____ Other _____

FIRE SEPARATION

_____ Fire Division _____	_____ Floors _____
_____ Occupancies _____	_____ Other _____
_____ Tenants _____	_____ Other _____

FIRE SUPPRESSION & LIFE SAFETY SYSTEMS:
(Schematic and Sequence of Operations Required)

_____ Sprinkler_____	_____ Smoke control_____
_____ Standpipe_____	_____ Emergency systems_____
_____ Fire alarm_____	_____ Exits_____
_____ Fire detection_____	_____ Other _____
_____ Central control_____	_____ Other _____
_____ Voice Communications_____	_____ Other _____

DETAILED VERTICAL SECTIONS REQUIRED:

_____ Trash chute_____	_____ Curtain wall_____
_____ Laundry chute_____	_____ Partitions _____
_____ Other shafts_____	_____ Other _____

MISCELLANEOUS:

_____ Elevators_____	_____ Schedules required _____
_____ Ventilation _____	_____ Flow test (Ord. 74-96) _____
_____ Combustible materials_____	_____ Admin._____
_____ Spec. extinguishing equip. _____	_____ Other _____
_____ Interior Finishes_____	_____ Other _____

COMMENTS:

_____
_____
_____
_____
_____
_____
_____
_____
_____
_____
_____

Date: _____/_____/_____ Rejected   Date _____ Approved

By: _____ For: _____   By: _____ For: _____

This approval does not relieve the permit holder from complying with all Code requirements that are not specifically covered by this examination form

PERMIT FILE — WHITE   PLANS FILE — CANARY   CONSTRUCTION FILE — PINK

construction permit is vital. This sign-off carries the responsibility of ensuring that the fire protection features required are indicated on the construction plans and that the end result will be a fire protection system for the building.

The plans review process requires special training and the development of personal and professional skills. Where possible, fire departments should employ fire protection engineers as a part of this process.

Once the plans review process is complete and construction begins, it is equally important to ensure that the fire protection that was designed and reviewed is built into the project. For this reason, it is desirable for plans reviewers to participate in field inspections. In all cases, a close relationship between the plans reviewers and the field inspection personnel must be maintained.

Property inspection

A property inspection program carried out by trained personnel is the backbone of a total fire prevention program. Nothing can take the place of an on-site visit and one-on-one discussion with a property owner or manager to eliminate potentials for fire. Organizationally, the inspection function resides in the fire department and/or the building or public works department.

A total inspection program will cover both existing properties and new construction. The approaches to the resolution of problems associated with existing properties are significantly different from those for new construction. In addition, some types of occupancies require specialized inspections, owing to the hazards associated with materials used on the site, industrial or commercial processes, or number of occupants.

All available personnel resources should be utilized to assist the inspection programs. Each person should receive specialized training in the types of properties to be inspected. Equally important is the availability of material resources such as code books, reference standards, and data collection forms (see Figure 15–3). Periodic refresher courses and technical assistance to resolve difficult issues help sustain interest and keep the program on track.

Evaluating built-in fire protection

Built-in fire protection that reacts immediately to an emergency condition is the best possible response to the emergency. Some protection features are passive, such as concrete designed to provide one or more hours of protection from fire spread. Other features are active, such as heat and smoke sensors that constantly monitor the environment for signs of trouble. Built-in fire protection encompasses devices with a range of capabilities. Some, such as overload protection on electric motors, actually prevent fires. Others, including fire dampers, prevent the spread of fire. Alarm systems detect and alert building occupants, and water sprinklers and halogenated vapor systems actually suppress fire.

All these forms of protection are equally important; each must be in place and fully functional to complement the others. Determining the proper built-in protection for a specific occupancy or building requires extensive knowledge of the codes and standards that regulate the fire service and the construction industry. These features and their intended purposes must be fully understood by both plans examiners and field inspection personnel. When possible, active fire protection features should be tested as part of the inspection process.

Today, any community can become the site of a high-rise building, a multi-level shopping mall covering several city blocks, or a large industrial plant. In some cases, such proposed construction projects pose problems beyond the capabilities of the existing program. A successful fire prevention program must recognize its capabilities and its limitations and be prepared to contract out to other government agencies or private industry for the necessary expertise.

Figure 15–3 An inspection form used in Miami, Florida.

```
         MIAMI FIRE DEPARTMENT INSPECTION FORM          901 ZONE: ___

OCCUP ADDR: _____ __ _____ ____   NO: _____   DIST: _-__-_-__
BUS: _____ HOLDER: _____  _____
BILLING ADDRESS:




CU NUMBER: _____   EMERG PH: _____   DATE: __/__/__   FEE: _____

USAGE CODE: __                                                 UNITS: _____

PROP CLASS: ___                        NIGHT?: _    OCCUPANT LOAD: _____

# FLOORS:      CU EXEMPT?: _   BAL-DUE: _____   CU STAT:
ANNUAL FIRE ALARM TEST REPORT NEEDED?: _


    VIOLATIONS
01 [ ] EXIT DOORS LOCKED          19-169(D), 19-173
02 [ ] MEANS OF EGRESS OBSTRUCTED      19-169(A)(B), 19-42(5)
03 [ ] STAIRWAY/FIRE ESCAPE DOORS PROPPED OPEN    19-172, 19-30(E)(F)(G)
04 [ ] STAIRWAY DOORS SWING IN WRONG DIRECTION    19-28(D)
05 [ ] LIGHTING INADEQUATE FOR MEANS OF EGRESS    19-171
06 [ ] EXIT/DIRECTIONAL SIGNS MISSING/NOT ILLUMINATED   19-170(B)(C)
07 [ ] FIRE EXIT PLANS NOT PROVIDED    19-170(D)
08 [ ] F.D. EMERGENCY SERVICE ELEVATOR KEY NOT PROVIDED    19-193
09 [ ] HAZARDOUS STORAGE IN TRASH CHUTE ROOM/METER ROOM/BASEMENT    19-42(3)
10 [ ] EXCESS COMBUSTIBLE TRASH-EXTERIOR    19-538
11 [ ] COMMUNITY KITCHEN NOT PROTECTED    19-42(6), 19-173
12 [ ] EXCESS STORAGE CLASS 1-A OR 1-B FLAMMABLE LIQUID    19-260(1)
13 [ ] FLAMMABLE LIQUID STORED NEAR MEANS OF EGRESS    19-283(A)
14 [ ] FLAMMABLE LIQUID MAINTENANCE SUPPLY NON-CONFORMING    19-283(B)(2)
15 [ ] FIRE ALARM SYSTEM REQUIRED    19-196(5)(A)(B)
16 [ ] ANNUAL FIRE ALARM TEST REPORT REQUIRED    19-196(5)(A)(B)
17 [ ] NO SEPARATION BETWEEN FLOORS    19-29(A)
18 [ ] UTILITY SHAFTS OR OTHER VERTICAL OPENINGS NOT SEALED   19-30(A), 19-42(6)
19 [ ] REQUIRED SELF-CLOSER/LATCHING DEVICES INOPERATIVE/MISS   19-30(F), 19-42(6)
20 [ ] HORIZONTAL SEPARATION NON-CONFORMING    19-29(B)
21 [ ] GAS SERVICE DEFICIENCIES    19-439, 19-42(2)
22 [ ] SPRINKLER OR STANDPIPE SYSTEM NEEDS MAINTENANCE    19-193
23 [ ] EXTENSION CORD VIOLATION    19-626
24 [ ] FIRE EXTINGUISHERS MISSING OR NEED SERVICE    19-606, 19-605
99 [ ] OTHER VIOLATIONS


REINSPECTION DATES: __/__/__  __/__/__  __/__/__  __/__/__  __/__/__  __/__/__
          INSPECTOR: _____  _____  _____  _____  _____  _____


DATE REFERRED TO FPB: __/__/__
REASON (FIRE, PLUMBING, ELECTRICAL, MECHANICAL, STRUCTURAL, ZONING, OTHER):

_____

_____


DATE COMPLETED: __/__/__       FPB INSPECTOR: _____

NAME: _____ COMPANY: _____   SHIFT/FPB: ___   INSP MONTH: __
```

Training

A comprehensive fire prevention program must include provisions for ongoing training and development of personnel; both prevention and suppression personnel need training in fire prevention. The main program resource is people. To ensure that they have the mental tools and the professional qualifications necessary to accomplish their tasks, the training program must address each special skill need.

In practice, especially in small communities, much training is done on the job, but specialized training can be accomplished through other organizations. For example, community colleges and universities offer training courses for plans examiners and field inspectors. Fire investigators can attend police training programs for investigative techniques and criminal law. The National Fire Academy at Emmitsburg, Maryland, offers courses in virtually every aspect of fire prevention. Specific instruction in the building code and other ordinances of the particular municipality must be a part of the training program. Wherever possible, in-the-field instruction should be utilized to ensure that the fundamentals are fully understood and the necessary skills can be applied.

Program analysis

A program also needs a method of self-analysis, and the fire prevention manager needs to ensure that such analysis takes place.

The first step in program analysis is to collect all relevant data on number and types of fires and trends over time. Some departments or local governments employ personnel primarily for data analysis, and their perspectives are helpful when it comes to displaying data for review by other officials such as the budget director or city manager. Analysis of data can be used most effectively to monitor progress toward goals if those goals can be quantified. Chapter 6 discusses useful data relating to fire prevention efforts and shows how they can be collected, stored, and used to quantify the effectiveness of fire prevention programs and to identify problems that need additional attention.

Comprehensive code administration

To protect the health, safety, and welfare of their citizens, local governments enact and adopt a multitude of codes and ordinances. In doing so, governments take on added responsibility for ensuring that the rules are followed, both by providing information and assistance to facilitate compliance with the codes and ordinances and by enforcing their provisions.

Depending on the priorities of a particular community, enforcement programs may develop around a variety of regulations—building construction, fire prevention, health and sanitation, housing, land use, business and commercial property, animal control, and environmental pollution. Often, the responsibility for enforcement is scattered among various government departments.

Recognizing that such decentralization of responsibility may lead to duplication of effort and poor coordination among related functions, many local governments have brought these functions together into a comprehensive code administration program.

A comprehensive code administration program can be defined as a program that groups code enforcement responsibilities, including budget and personnel, under the authority of one administrator. Since one major objective of a comprehensive code administration program is to protect life and property from the hazards associated with the physical (or built) environment, this section is written from the perspective of a code administration program with this objective. Size of jurisdiction and other constraints may dictate that two or more major objectives be combined into a comprehensive program. The same methods and concepts discussed here can be adapted for such circumstances.

A comprehensive code administration program with the objective of protecting life and property from hazards associated with the physical environment requires a clear commitment from the fire and building departments, the administrative leadership, and the elected officials of the city.

The best course is to design a program that provides a cost-effective way to deliver the services that logically could be the responsibility of a multipurpose safety-oriented agency. If the program is devised so that it can be implemented incrementally, one part at a time, it allows for a period of evaluation and adjustment to ensure success. Flexibility in implementing the program also makes it possible to adjust to any unforeseen road blocks.

Organization

How the components necessary for the protection of life and property are organized depends on local administrative and political realities. The size of the various departments or divisions, the ability of an existing department to shoulder the burden, the feasibility of creating a new department drawing personnel and other resources from existing departments, and how much can be saved by each approach are examples of concerns a city administrator must evaluate in order to make a decision.[2]

Once the commitment is made to consolidate various programs, the implementation is likely to encounter the difficulties that often accompany change— anxiety over turf, reporting relationships, and new office space; confusion over consolidation of records and support staff; and unfamiliarity with new assignments. No one method or approach is always successful. Each program has its unique political, legal, and internal administrative problems to overcome. Variables such as the scope of the consolidation program, the existing division of responsibilities, and the capabilities of personnel, particularly top managers, whose commitment to the process is vital, determine how the program should be structured.

In many local governments, comprehensive code administration is a responsibility of the fire service. Most modern fire departments already provide a variety of programs under one administrative umbrella, and they already have the management capability to assume new responsibilities. One possible organizational structure is shown in Figure 15–4. Furthermore, code administration is closely related to traditional fire service responsibilities in prevention and emergency response. The costs associated with emergency response can be contained, and in some cases reduced, by sound administration of the code process.

A strong administrative argument for this choice is the desire to use fire-fighters' nonemergency time more efficiently. Parts of the code administration program, particularly some field inspections, can be successfully carried out by in-service fire suppression personnel. The ability to provide these personnel resources at little or no additional cost automatically enhances the code administration program.

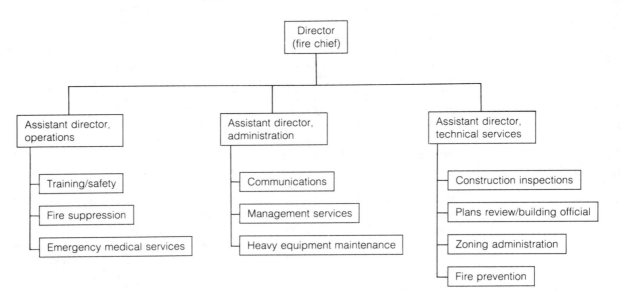

Figure 15–4 Organizational option showing comprehensive code administration as part of the fire department.

Elements of a program

The first order of business is to determine which adopted codes and ordinances (or parts) pertain to the goals of the comprehensive program. Codes and ordinances that relate to the protection of life and property from the built environment vary from community to community, but typically, the following will be on the list: fire codes, building codes and adopted standards, housing codes,

---

Cross-training for fire prevention and code enforcement   The fire department in Pampa, Texas, population 24,000, responded to 295 fires in 1987, a substantial reduction from the annual figure of 415 before the fire prevention program began in July 1985. The department's functions include fire prevention (fire marshal and assistant fire marshal), fire suppression (fire chief, assistant fire chief, and thirty-four firefighters), and code enforcement (building, health, and code inspections).

The Fair Labor Standards Act permits the cross-training of personnel and the utilization of personnel outside the narrow scope of fire suppression services. With this in mind, the department implemented a cross-training program with four primary objectives: (1) to reduce the incidence of fires; (2) to increase the productivity and utilization of fire personnel; (3) to improve the service delivery of building inspections; and (4) to improve the overall appearance of the community.

Initially, twelve fire personnel were selected to cross-train in four broad areas:

Fire inspections—personnel were trained to inspect public buildings to ensure that they met applicable fire codes.

Health inspections—personnel were trained to inspect food-handling businesses, in particular, restaurants.

Building inspections—personnel were trained and certified to conduct structural, plumbing, electrical, and mechanical inspections.

Police/arson training—firefighters were required to attend the police academy and become certified as peace officers; additional training and certification were required to investigate arson.

Personnel work for and are assigned to the Fire Prevention and Code Enforcement departments. They leave the fire station to work in City Hall from 9:00 a.m. until 5:00 p.m. during their twenty-four hour shift.

Cross-training has proven to have many advantages. For instance, firefighters conduct fire inspections and health inspections simultaneously. On building inspections, the city's objective is to respond to a request within thirty minutes, and because of twenty-four-hour shifts, personnel are available to conduct these inspections in the evening and on weekends in the event of emergencies, or the need for follow-up work. This has improved the working relationship with contractors and has helped reduce expensive inspection waiting time.

All cross-trained personnel carry portable radios and firefighting clothing at all times. In the event of a fire, personnel assigned to the fire stations respond to the scene of the fire. Cross-trained personnel return to the fire station to serve as backup personnel. In the event of a major fire, they respond directly to the fire scene.

Firefighters receive a base pay. Additional pay is granted upon successful completion, certification, and demonstration of proficiency in the areas of fire inspection, health inspection, building inspection (with subcategories of structural, plumbing, electrical, and mechanical), certification as a peace officer, and certification as an arson investigator.

water supply ordinances, zoning ordinances, and occupational license ordinances.

Many other codes can assist and do occasionally have an impact on physical environment regulations. However, since their main objectives are different from the above codes, they are not included here.

Fire codes Fire codes and regulations are directly related to the objectives of the comprehensive code administration program. Primarily aimed at maintenance of protection features, such as alarm systems, sprinkler systems, occupancy limits, and means of egress, fire codes have fostered ongoing inspection routines by fire departments. Most other codes and standards are concerned with installation or construction, not maintenance. Thus, once the provisions of a particular code have been met, no additional inspections are required.

The uniqueness of a fire code in this regard also makes it one of the most valuable. By constantly monitoring a community's overall condition, code inspectors not only ensure that fire protection is maintained but also may observe that aspects of other codes bearing on the built environment may be adversely affecting the overall condition. For example, an interior wall of a building may have been removed during remodeling. If not done correctly, this change can affect the structural stability of the building and its potential for collapse.

Building codes and adopted standards A major portion of the provisions of most nationally accepted building codes applies to fire safety, with much of the remainder relating to structural safety. Thus, the building code is the cornerstone of protection for the citizens who live, work, and play in a community's buildings.

The fire code is intended to work in concert with the building code to ensure that built-in fire protection is maintained properly, but the building code goes beyond fire safety in determining what is built in and how.

As noted earlier, the most cost-effective way to protect life and property from fire and other environmental hazards is to prevent their occurrence by ensuring that the essential elements are covered in the building code or its adopted standards and then by monitoring the construction process to make certain the provisions of the building code are followed.

The training and expertise of fire inspectors apply to portions of the building code, but additional specialized training and experience are required to properly review construction plans and, through field inspection, to see that the total building code and its adopted standards are complied with. In addition, the building codes and adopted local ordinances generally specify that personnel involved in such specialties must be licensed or certified before they can hold particular positions.

Personnel involved in the enforcement of the building code normally come from the construction industry—architects, engineers, contractors, electricians, plumbers, heating and air-conditioning specialists, gas and boiler specialists, elevator specialists, and more. Their technical background and experience provide a large resource for achieving better protection of life and property.

Housing codes Housing codes commonly reflect a need to ensure that living conditions meet certain minimum standards. Their range is very broad in scope, covering quality of life, health, maintenance, and safety. The personnel who enforce this code require a broader, more generalist approach than those responsible for the building or fire codes. They become arbitrators in landlord, tenant, and neighbor disputes. As representatives of the government, they frequently bear the brunt of citizens' various frustrations and thus should have the personality traits, education, and experience usually expected of a social worker or public relations agent. When technical assistance is needed, housing code

Figure 15–5 Structural collapse is a constant danger to firefighters. Building codes and fire codes, used properly, can reduce this threat.

personnel should be able to draw on other code experts from building, fire, health, sanitation, and other specialties.

Particularly as it relates to fire safety, the housing code can greatly assist in achieving protection of life and property, as the majority of fire deaths occur in residences, mostly in the victims' own homes.[3] Attention to cooking and heating appliances, requirements for smoke detection and alarm devices, and basic exiting capability are the types of items that can be included in a housing code.

Water supply ordinances A primary tool of the fire service is water. To ensure that an adequate and reliable supply is available for hydrants, standpipes, sprinklers, and other emergency equipment, communities establish standards that can be applied to all parts of the water supply system. The demands for both domestic and fire flow requirements are considered in the standards.

Some water supply ordinances relate more to reliability of supply by the water utility than to determination of hydrant spacing, gallons per minute required for protection of various types of occupancies, and other fire service concerns. Consistent practical standards on water for fire protection must be enforced by ordinance if fire protection goals are to be achieved. Otherwise the door remains open for authorities to approve new construction projects that will not be adequately protected.

Equally important is the upgrading of existing water supply systems, particularly in older communities where zoning changes have allowed more intense development or new types of land use. Commonly, older residential districts are rezoned to commercial use, while the water supply infrastructure was originally designed to handle only the needs of family units. To determine whether the system is capable of handling increased demands, personnel must have a thorough knowledge of the existing system and a method of field testing so that delivery levels can be maintained at the necessary gallons per minute.

The water supply ordinance must address the question of responsibility for upgrading the water system to meet the required demand. When large areas are rezoned, the responsibility may fall to the city or county or its costs may be shared by the municipality, the water utility, and the property owners.

To ensure that the water requirements for fire flow are met, someone knowledgeable in this field should be required to review current levels and sign off before building construction permits are issued.

Zoning ordinances　The purpose of zoning is to regulate the use of land. Zoning is one of the most flexible tools available to municipalities. It is the first to reflect the changing needs of the community. It is constantly subject to public scrutiny and political concern. A developer must be certain that zoning requirements can be met *before* deciding to invest money in a construction project. Master plans for communities create needs for changes in zoning. Because of its impact on every segment of the community, a zoning ordinance is one of the most difficult to administer.

Enforcing the zoning ordinance is quite different from enforcing the fire and other codes. For one thing, an ordinance has several logical interpretations, with the result that many issues can be resolved in more than one way. This means that personnel must be capable of determining the proper application of the ordinance in each case. Furthermore they must be able to confer with professionals from a variety of fields such as planning, law, construction, and development. They must also be able to deal with neighbor disputes and a variety of community nuisance problems that seem to relate to zoning questions.

Zoning has an impact on fire codes, building codes, and practically every other primary code. It is easy to overlook its importance to protection of life and property because the public emphasis in zoning issues is mainly on enhancing the quality of life. An argument often proffered in support of a change in zoning, for example, is that it will serve the best interests of the community because it will create more jobs or housing.

It is very important for fire service managers to stay abreast of proposed changes in zoning to ensure that emphasis is also placed on the protection of life and property. As suggested in the discussion on water system infrastructure, zoning changes can affect other safety considerations. For example, a change to higher-density apartment buildings may have an impact on the numbers and location of firefighting and emergency medical personnel because of increased demands for service.

Occupational license ordinances　Ordinances that regulate business licenses are relevant to a comprehensive code administration program because they serve as a checkpoint. They present an opportunity for a regular inspection routine, verification of property data, and control over legal and illegal business activity.

Many communities charge a fee for business licenses and employ inspectors whose primary function is to verify occupational license information. Often the data on specific addresses collected through occupational licensing programs is the most accurate and comprehensive information base to use for a systematic inspection program.

Problems with enforcement of any of the primary codes can be alleviated by proper coordination with an occupational licensing program. In particular, those with an annual renewal requirement allow periodic inspection for code compliance and the maintenance of reliable data.

Other codes and ordinances   City and county governments have a variety of additional regulations. Many of them were not adopted primarily for reasons of public safety, but they may contain elements that pertain to physical environment hazards. Some communities adopt ordinances specifically designed to regulate a safety problem unique to that community. For example, a large industrial plant or storage facility for hazardous materials may require special regulations. Health codes are a good example of regulations that can be extremely important in some aspects of physical environment hazard prevention. Health codes regulate storage and use of toxic substances, which can become dangerous environmental hazards affecting large areas of a community. It is necessary to have a broad understanding of these other codes and ordinances and know which agency is responsible for enforcing them in order to administer a comprehensive program.

Interagency relationships

Typically, because of the breadth and scope of safety-related codes, these codes take up the largest share of a local government's code enforcement budget. But size of budget alone does not determine a community's priorities. Other concerns such as health, sanitation, maintenance of public properties, architectural aesthetics, and general appearance are all important to a community and its citizens. Those responsible for a fire department's code administration function need to understand the roles of other regulating agencies and the possible interactions among departments.

For example, the parks and recreation and police departments may propose closing off a public street to vehicular traffic to create a safer pedestrian access route to a public park. The public works department may be responsible for making a traffic survey, assessing the impact on traffic flow for the surrounding neighborhood, and then erecting barriers. Unless the government has in place a process whereby the public works department (the controlling agency) notifies the fire service of such proposals, the result may be an inaccessible fire hydrant or an inadequate response route for emergency vehicles.

Similarly, the sanitation department may need assistance in alleviating a recurring problem with trash and debris accumulation. Both health and fire code violations may be involved, and thus several agencies may be able to jointly enforce the code and resolve the problem.

When enforcement programs with different missions interact and assist each other, an atmosphere of teamwork develops and agencies avoid needless duplication of effort. The result is that goals and objectives of each coincide with the overall needs of the community in a more cost-effective manner.

Political aspects

Like all activities of local government, comprehensive code administration occurs in the context of local politics. Elected representatives constantly monitor their constituents and respond to their desires and concerns through policies and directions to government administrators.

A consistent frustration to both citizens and politicians is the lag time between the formulation and adoption of public policy and results. The ability of a governmental system to adjust, shift resources, and change programs rapidly is limited. These frustrations and limitations need to be recognized and constantly monitored by administrators of a comprehensive code enforcement program. Because aspects of the program touch on zoning, development, and other central local activities, frictions are bound to develop, and it will take political and technical savvy to handle them.

If the program is to succeed and constructive changes are to take place, elected representatives must feel comfortable with the way the program is being administered, technical explanations must be accurate and consistent, and alternatives must be provided whenever possible.

An example can be constructed from the previous discussion of zoning. A proposed zoning change to allow higher-density apartment buildings may be politically desirable in order to respond to public demands for more housing. A direct technical response from the fire department may be that such a change will increase demands for service and emergency response times, and that the solution is to hire more emergency service personnel and relocate or build a fire station to reduce emergency response times. Such a solution may be politically unacceptable because of its impact on the local budget.

A creative manager often can devise a politically acceptable alternative that does not conflict with goals of protection of life and property. In this case, an objective analysis of minimum building and fire code requirements for such a project can be conducted. A proposal can then be formulated that calls for additional built-in protection beyond the minimum code requirements. The additional built-in protection can be an acceptable technical alternative to increasing personnel or relocating a fire station to attain protection goals, and it does not require budget increases. Depending on the government's involvement with the project, a one-time subsidy to the developer for all or part of the costs of the additional requirements may be politically acceptable.

In some cases, of course, no technically or politically acceptable alternative is available. When an elected representative must tell a constituent that nothing can be done, the reasons must be explained fully and evidence shown that potential alternatives were explored. If the elected officials have gained confidence in the code administration program because of its previous assistance in resolving problems, they will be more inclined to accept the difficult answers.

Legal aspects

Codes and ordinances, like traffic laws and criminal laws, are laws of the land. The legal role of code administration officials is twofold. First, they must explain the laws. Second, if there is resistance to the laws, they must take the proper administrative and, if necessary, legal steps to ensure compliance.

Explaining the law Explaining the law is not a simple task when the law is a technical construction code, fire code, or zoning ordinance. Often, the people who receive the explanation are professionals in applying the law in question, such as architects, engineers, and zoning attorneys. Explanations must be logical and consistent with a practical rationale for applying the law to the specific circumstance. "Because I said so" or "Because I am the authority having jurisdiction" *is not acceptable*.

Since most of the people who work in related private industries are licensed to practice in their fields, there is a built-in incentive through training and ethical standards to follow the codes. These factors ensure that, most of the time, people can be convinced to comply with the code if given a reasonable explanation of the rationale used to arrive at a particular conclusion.

The preconstruction meeting and the plans review and permitting process are the critical factors in resolving differences. Consistent and sustained effort that produces quality review and approval of construction projects is the most cost-effective service a government can provide in its code administration program. Deficiencies noted while actual construction is under way require careful explanation and an open mind if a different interpretation or alternative is offered. Common sense and flexibility in decision making are required in these circumstances.

Once a construction project is finished and it becomes an existing facility, the approach to resolving code deficiencies must change accordingly. The owner generally feels that once the building receives authorization for occupancy, it also signifies that *all* code provisions have been satisfied. The longer a facility is occupied (before a deficiency is noted) the more difficult it becomes to gain voluntary compliance with the code.

The impact on the property owner must be considered when methods for resolving the deficiency are being considered. When deficiencies are minor—for example, when additional railings need to be installed for disabled persons or portable fire extinguishers are required—resistance may not be great. When deficiencies are major—for example, when a building does not meet zoning setback requirements or have the required fire alarm system—the costs will be high, and the natural reluctance to make the requested changes will be hard to overcome. In these circumstances, the ability to explain the law and "sell" the necessary changes is extremely important.

The real value of a comprehensive code administration program becomes evident in the process of settling disputes. When the enforcement officials responsible for the various codes are called upon to evaluate alternatives together, there is a greater chance that disputes will be settled without having to resort to formal legal action.

Resolving disputes A major difference between most laws and the codes and ordinances discussed here is that the latter commonly rely on arbitration to resolve disputes. Some states call for the establishment of arbitration boards or panels to assess technical arguments and formulate consistent policies for the enforcement of various codes. Even where this is not the case, local governments have established such processes as a logical method for ensuring all sides of a dispute are considered. Such processes can be nonjudicial or quasi-judicial in scope.

Nonjudicial arbitration processes provide an impartial administrative appeal for any party in a dispute as it relates to a specific code or ordinance. In practice, such arbitration processes commonly include legal as well as technical arguments. The boards and panels themselves commonly have legal counsel available at hearings. On the other side of the table, it is not uncommon for attorneys who specialize in the particular code to present arguments that tend to direct matters as much to a legal conclusion as they do to a technical conclusion. These realities must be considered when code administrators are preparing their cases for hearings.

Most arbitration boards and panels are made up of a cross section of the community. Commonly, recognized authorities on the particular code are mixed with citizens who represent various industries affected by the code and sometimes those who represent citizen groups such as property owners and/or tenant associations.

The major codes discussed here are subject to such processes, and each requires a different representative group and functions under separate rules and guidelines. The building code, for example, generally requires a large and active board owing to the dynamic nature of the construction industry and the wide range of technical issues that call for representative expertise. Code administrators must recognize that the method for preparing a case for a zoning board is much different from the method required for a fire code board.

A building code board of rules and appeals   The Metropolitan Dade County (Miami), Florida, Board of Rules and Appeals is responsible for interpreting and recommending changes to the South Florida Building Code by serving as a technical guide to the community on construction matters, approving new products for construction industry use, and certifying building officials and trade inspectors as qualified to enforce the code. The South Florida Building Code is the mandated construction code for Metropolitan Dade County and its municipalities.

The board has twenty-five members, all appointed by the Dade County Commission. They represent a cross section of the construction industry, including the American Institute of Architects, Florida Engineering Society, Associated General Contractors, Construction Industry Advisory Council, Dade County Fire Chiefs Association, mechanical and electrical engineers, the plumbing industry, handicapped persons associations, and the home builders association.

The county provides an executive secretary and staff, which includes code enforcement field personnel who investigate and report on issues as directed by the board.

Metropolitan Dade County covers 1,998 square miles and includes 27 municipalities with a combined population of approximately 1,750,000. There are 26 building officials and 5 civilian government fire service agencies, each responsible to their respective governments for proper application of the building code.

Without the arbitration process provided by the board, the multitude of enforcement authorities and the wide scope of code administration programs being carried out by the various governments would give rise to inconsistent applications of the building code, which would work to the detriment of the governments, their citizens, and the construction industry at large.

Quasi-judicial arbitration boards have the ability to provide some form of sanction, generally a fine or assessment levied against the person who violates the code. Such assessment does not preclude an individual from taking the matter to a court of law for a final legal determination.

The general makeup of the boards is similar to that of nonjudicial boards. The intent of such boards is generally to relieve an overburdened judicial legal system from minor types of infractions. Disputes involving violation of zoning ordinances or sanitation or housing codes, for example, can generally be successfully arbitrated by quasi-judicial boards.[4]

Once a code enforcement dispute is formally taken to a court of law for resolution, the opportunity for resolving it on technical merit alone is gone. The arguments of law become more important than those based on technical considerations or moral concern. This is not to imply that the legal system does not listen to technical and moral arguments and weigh them in the decision-making process, but the basis for decision making is changed to a more restrictive and different set of rules than those that the code administrators use to further their goals. This simple fact must be understood and accepted before a decision to seek a legal resolution of a problem is attempted.

Knowing through experience or past interpretation that compliance with a particular provision of the code is in the best interests of the community is not enough in court. Before a case can even be accepted, those bringing suit must be able to show that the individual charged is the person legally responsible and that the specific charges relate directly to a specific property. Cases can be thrown out if property ownership of the individual charged began after the violation first occurred, or if the adoption date of a specific code provision does not correspond to the adoption date of the codes under which a building was permitted. Code administration managers must ensure that the department has a consistent method of gathering essential information to present a case in court.

At best, the legal process is cumbersome and slow. The time and effort expended on it generally do not produce the same results as other methods of gaining compliance. Nevertheless, the judicial system must be a working part of a code administration program.

Besides considering questions of moral responsibility and legal liability, a code enforcement program must make use of the judicial/legal system or it will soon degenerate into a "paper tiger" program. Enforcement personnel will perceive that they have no real authority to enforce, inspection routines will become vague and superficial, and in the end the goals of the overall program will become more difficult to achieve.

To ensure that the method and approach to presenting cases for legal action are workable, assistance and guidance must be obtained from trained legal counsel. Generally, this assistance is provided by the legal staff of the city or county. Wherever possible, a specific individual should be identified to work as the legal counsel to the code administration program. Expertise in zoning, building, fire, and housing codes is just as difficult to attain as expertise in criminal law, municipal finance, and other fields in which attorneys are specifically trained and assigned, and the commitment of a trained, dedicated attorney goes a long way toward ensuring success with this aspect of code administration.

Adoption and modification of codes

Generally, the adoption and modification of codes is a process whose full impact and complexity are not clearly understood by local political leaders and administrators. Because codes are detailed, technical, and difficult to understand, the advice of code administrators and groups with an interest in various aspects of a code is required in the process.

Codes that relate specifically to the community, such as a local zoning or housing ordinance, are usually reviewed by such groups as tenant associations, planners, zoning officials, private consultants, and city attorneys. This attention ensures that controversial portions can be modified or eliminated. Equally important, the attention helps ensure that application and interpretation by those involved in enforcement will be consistent.

Specialized codes do not generally receive as much overall attention in the adoption or modification process. Building and fire codes fall into this category and are good examples of codes that have important long-range impacts on a community, but receive relatively little attention outside of the industries affected by them.

Model codes and national standards   Model codes and national standards are available for both building construction and fire prevention, and many communities adopt them. The main advantage to adopting model codes and national standards is that it eliminates the need to reinvent the wheel. In addition, the organizations that create these codes and standards are able to provide the sustained resources necessary to ensure that modifications, new criteria, and changes in construction technology are considered and adopted in a timely fashion.

Consistency of application and interpretation over a state, a group of states, and even nationally is a benefit to citizens, industries, and code enforcement personnel. Citizens are assured of high standards in codes and their enforcement; industries are able to mass-produce products that meet code requirements; and code enforcement personnel have a resource for answers to questions. Model codes and national standards formalize processes for technical interpretations to resolve disputes and sponsor training programs and seminars in an effort to assure the code or standard is consistently applied.

Examples of model codes and national standards widely adopted include the national building and fire codes produced by the American Insurance Association; the standard building, mechanical, plumbing, gas, and fire prevention codes produced by the Southern Building Code Congress, International; the uniform building code and other codes produced by the International Conference of Building Officials; and the basic building and fire codes produced by the Building Officials and Code Administrators International.

The National Fire Protection Association produces standards on a broad range of subjects, including a fire prevention code, the national electric code, and many more. The American Society of Mechanical Engineers and the American Society of Heating, Refrigerating and Air Conditioning Engineers produce standards related to their industry, which are extremely important to life safety, health, and other considerations.

Mini/max codes   Since the 1950s the United States has become an increasingly mobile society. The ability to reach new markets and achieve economic goals has resulted in a hopscotch pattern of development across the nation. Traditional patterns of development that expanded out from central population cores usually allowed time for local areas to adopt adequate codes and standards to regulate construction and growth. As soon as populations were able to hopscotch, the orderly regulation of development broke down. Large industrial complexes, residential communities, and resort facilities began to spring up in areas with no effective standards or codes to protect public safety, health, and welfare.

To solve this problem, states have adopted minimum (mini) codes and standards that must be applied consistently throughout the state. When a mini code is adopted, areas with no local standards have to meet the state minimum standards, and areas with adopted standards have to apply the state minimum standards if the local ones are less stringent. Local governments, however, are free to adopt standards more stringent or broader in scope than the state minimums.

Local communities adopt more stringent requirements for a variety of reasons. Some are intended to provide a higher standard of protection. Examples are fire sprinkler and fire-resistive construction requirements. Others are intended to ensure that the distinct character or general makeup of a community is maintained. Examples are special architectural requirements or restrictions that make it prohibitive to construct certain types of occupancies.

As growth continues, conflicts sometimes surface when developers must meet stringent and costly local standards. As a result, some states have adopted maximum (max) codes, which preclude local governments from adopting standards more stringent than the state standards. The mini/max building code concept is intended to provide some uniformity throughout the adopting state.

Although consistency of standards has considerable value, strict uniformity is not always ideal, as the geographical diversity of some states can result in different regulatory needs. For example, a state with both mountains and a coastline may require different standards to accommodate temperature extremes, flooding potential, and wind storm conditions for the same type of structure in different parts of the state. Furthermore, a community may desire to provide additional fire or other life safety protection either because of physical vulnerability to a potential threat or the general makeup of the citizenry, such as large numbers of elderly people.

Another difficulty with maintaining strict uniformity through the mini/max concept is the administrative rule-making authority of various state agencies. Such agencies as the Department of Public Education, the State Fire Marshal, and the Department of Health and Rehabilitative Services commonly have the authority to create rules to govern their specific areas of responsibility. The rules may include construction requirements different from those mandated in the state's mini/max building code. For example, a public school may be constructed according to the rules of the department of public education. Several blocks away, a private school may be constructed following the state mini/max code. Which one is better constructed and provides a safer environment depends on the intent of the administrative rule-making body on one hand and the provisions of the mini/max code on the other. When rule-making authority is separate from a state mini/max code, a multitude of minimum and maximum standards arise that undermine efforts to obtain uniformity.

Figure 15–6   Personnel representing various functions work together in a comprehensive code enforcement program.

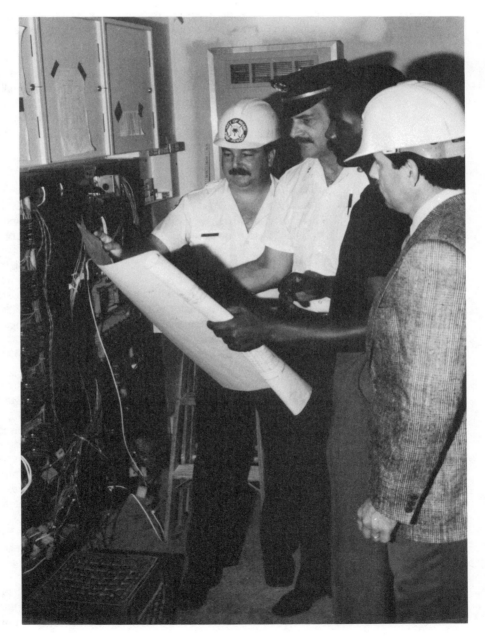

Training

One of the most essential, yet frequently overlooked elements of a comprehensive code administration program is training. Training is taken for granted as necessary for emergency service personnel. To reduce the emphasis on training for personnel working to prevent the emergencies from occurring is false economy and detrimental to the overall goal of protecting life and property.

The types of training required for a code administration program are extremely varied and complex. Clerical personnel need training in telephone etiquette and a clear understanding of who is responsible for what in the organization. Plans processors and field personnel need to understand their duties and responsibilities as enforcement officials as well as their technical specialties. Supervisors and managers must be capable of professionally arbitrating disputes between citizens and enforcement personnel, preparing technical reports, and representing the code administration program in a variety of intergovernment and public forums. Training in the legal processes must not be neglected for anyone who may be called upon to participate.

Most code administration programs do not have a dedicated person or staff responsible for training; consequently, supervisory and management personnel often attempt to fill this need. In addition, most community-supported universities and junior colleges offer courses related to the technical expertise needed, as well as to human behavior and other subjects designed to train people for work requiring heavy public contact. For management personnel, supervisory and public administration courses are generally available through institutions for higher education.

Program analysis

With the availability of user-friendly centralized computer systems, the tools necessary to develop comprehensive code administration programs are available. The old stumbling blocks created by hand-processed records and data collection techniques no longer stymie efforts toward effective organization analysis. Chapter 6 covers computer use and management information systems in detail.

The merging of records kept by a variety of separate code enforcement programs into a centralized system should coincide with the merging of the programs themselves. Until a centralized record-keeping system is set up, accurate analysis from a total administrative perspective will not be possible. This means that, at best, the program would only be equipped to achieve some of its goals.

Computers are now available to fit every need, so even small organizations can use electronic record-keeping equipment. Large organizations require personnel trained and experienced in computer programming and systems analysis to help create useful data collection and analysis programs.

No facet of the comprehensive program should be neglected in the data collection system. This includes hand-held equipment for field inspectors, desk top equipment for clerical personnel, sophisticated equipment that can recreate construction blueprints and maps of underground utilities, and, of course, the central equipment necessary to collect and store useful information for management decisions.

With a modern centralized record-keeping system, program analysis can be a continuous process that helps personnel avoid "management by crisis" decisions. Automatic indicators to alert supervisory personnel when their program responsibilities are not being met provide an opportunity for proactive planning and adjustments. This is particularly important for a local government code administration program in which personnel are often required to shift resources and emphasis on short notice to meet a temporary community need. Thus, management must be able to quickly assess the impact of such actions on other parts of the program and the overall goals in order to determine the least disruptive method of accomplishing a temporary task.

Obviously, a centralized record-keeping system of this scope will take time to develop. The first steps should coincide with the commitment to create a comprehensive code administration program. The initial expense for equipment and personnel resources to create the system may seem high, but these costs will be quickly recovered if the system is used to improve the productivity and effectiveness of the program.

Summary

In summary, the establishment of a fire prevention program within a fire department is an important first step toward achieving better protection of life and property. The establishment of a comprehensive code administration program is a second important step toward that same goal. By taking the second step, the community, elected officials, government administrators, and employees all make an important contribution to better protection of life and property. Fire service managers who welcome these contributions and are willing to change their organizations can take full advantage of the opportunities they bring.

1   Philip S. Schaenman and Edward F. Seitz, *International Concepts in Fire Protection—Ideas from Europe That Could Improve U.S. Fire Safety* (Arlington, Va.: TriData Corporation, 1982), 11–13.

2   See Institute for Local Self Government, *Public Safety Inspection Consolidation*, Alternatives to Traditional Public Safety Delivery Systems, no. 3 (Berkeley, Calif., 1977).

3   U.S. Fire Administration, National Fire Data Center, *Fire in the United States* (Washington, D.C.: Government Printing Office, 1978), iv.

4   A description of a quasi-judicial board system appears in Remar M. Harvin, "Florida's Code Enforcement Boards," in *Code Administration and Enforcement: Trends and Perspectives*, Management Information Service Special Report no. 10 (Washington, D.C.: International City Management Association, August 1982), 79–82.

Part four:
Managing for
the future

16 Managing innovation

Since change brought about by technological and other developments is commonplace in our socioeconomic system, and since its impact on the work environment is increasing, every command officer in the fire service should become familiar with the process of managing innovation. This chapter presents a brief overview of the subject. It defines innovation, explores organizational and personal incentives for innovation, points out common barriers to innovation, and suggests ways to create an environment for innovation. Finally, it shows how to manage the innovation process itself, discussing the role of the leader and the other participants in the administration and implementation of change.

Throughout their careers, all fire service managers will be confronted with change and therefore must be able to manage innovation. They must also recognize that innovation is an ongoing process. Modest examples in the form of ''innovation briefs'' are scattered throughout the chapter to show how departments have adopted changes—not necessarily as permanent solutions to problems, but at least as interim solutions that may later be replaced by newer, more effective ones.

As used in this chapter, the term *innovation* encompasses anything that is perceived as new, regardless of its objective newness. Innovation includes the use of new technology, but it also includes new ideas, new concepts, and new methods and procedures. An innovation may be a new and better computer program or the use of quality circles, task forces, or any process that employs a problem-solving idea that has not been utilized by the organization before.[1] Because innovation implies the capacity to change or adapt, the terms *innovation* and *change* will be used interchangeably throughout this chapter.

Incentives for innovation

The fire protection system usually reflects the experience and recommendations of national, state, and local fire officials and quasi-public organizations. These recommendations are formalized in codes, statutes, and ordinances, which reflect the fire protection standards of the community or the fire district and in many ways guide the day-to-day operations of the fire department.

Incentives for innovation originate both inside and outside the organization. Each fire service manager is responsibile for directing and operating the fire protection delivery system and therefore has the obligation to constantly review those standards and to inform the governing body or the chief administrative officer of any problem or development that can have an impact on the fire service delivery system or the safety of the public. To fulfill this mandate effectively, fire service officials must be alert to changes that are needed in all parts of the system, both inside and outside the department.

The incentive for innovation may also originate with employees. When managing or performing a particular task, they may perceive a better way of accomplishing it and request or recommend a change. A change brought about under these circumstances is likely to succeed because those who suggested the change are involved in its formulation and implementation and therefore are accountable for its success. Successful implementation has a positive impact on the individuals involved and can create a climate that further facilitates change. On the other hand, the same individuals can contribute to the failure of a mandated change in which they had no opportunity to participate.

Technology also spurs change. The development of large air carriers and new toxic substances, for example, has changed the nature of the potential emergencies to which the fire department must respond. Advances in electronics, equipment, and chemicals all affect the capabilities and practices of the fire department. These are examples of external forces that have a direct impact on the adequacy of a fire defense system and that can be used to motivate an organization to review its posture, to analyze its effectiveness, and to search for different, more simplified ways to meet demands for service.

Smoke detectors are an example of a technological innovation that produced a greater public awareness of the dangers of fire. Their rapid acceptance led many communities to amend fire codes to call for automatic sprinklers for new residences. This development, in turn, focused attention on materials being used in the construction of homes and multifamily dwellings. The advent of low-cost automatic fire protection systems has also altered the demand for fire suppression services.

Pressure from another level of government (i.e., state or federal) can provide an incentive to undertake an innovation. Such pressure often takes the form of monetary grants that can be used to hire additional personnel, purchase apparatus and equipment, or qualify departmental personnel for certain training programs. Conversely, if the department fails to react to this pressure, the granting agency can withhold funds.

Pressure from citizens often leads officials to adopt an innovation. This pressure may originate with a special interest group that feels the service being provided is inadequate or is inferior to that being provided for other segments of the community. If this situation is ignored, the issue often escalates in importance and creates political pressures that could have an impact on the fire delivery service.[2] Citizen interest has an extraordinary ability to encourage innovation or to permit potential innovations to emerge and operate, and the diversification of services delivered to the public by fire personnel will, in itself, precipitate changes in the delivery system. We have witnessed an expansion of the role of the firefighter to that of paramedic. In many departments the number of fire calls is being equaled and even surpassed by requests for emergency

---

Innovation brief   FLASH (Fire Loss Awareness for Safer Homes) is a home safety inspection program sponsored by the Wichita (Kansas) Fire Department and the Wichita Red Cross. After the occurrence of a house fire, Red Cross volunteers go into the neighborhood and, when invited, into the house to do a complete survey. If no one is home, material is attached to the front door.

An inspection form is provided for the homeowner to complete, and the data are entered into a computer and used to measure the change in fire loss in the area the next year.

Worn-out batteries found in residential smoke alarms are exchanged for new ones, and smoke alarms purchased with contributions from local merchants are furnished to homes not so equipped.

The initial outlay costs for the program were low, and maintenance costs are moderate. The Red Cross furnishes uniforms and transportation.

medical services. This diversification has brought about changes in training, deployment of apparatus, and staffing. The same changes are occurring in the field of hazardous materials.

Emergency medical service is one of the few innovations accepted by the fire service in recent years that have modified the traditional value system of the fire service. It is one of the few services that the public has supported for additional funding—even advocating special fees and charges to ensure that it continues to expand. More change can be expected in this area because of the public's increasing awareness of its availability.

Unionization has been recognized as yet another social force that has brought about change.

Who, then, are the ideal people to minimize or eliminate the effects of external developments that cause problems for the department? The first option is to utilize the knowledge of those who are a part of the organization and who are most familiar with its problems. Among the most effective agents of change are the talent, the imagination, and the combined skills of an organization's employees. No one knows the problems or difficulties that impinge on the effectiveness of an organization as well as those who are a part of it.

Quite often, change can be attributed to the abilities of single individuals who, when successful, will be emulated by others.[3] These changes (designed to solve a particular problem) may affect the organizational structure, the operations, or the procedures of a fire department. Sometimes these changes have a secondary effect in that they improve the climate for introducing additional innovations. This result is similar to the public's reaction to the introduction of the smoke detector. For example, a program to develop standard performance and design specifications for a fire pumper would have as primary goals cost savings and improved operational capabilities; secondary effects of such a program could include the reexamination of firefighting strategy and tactics, the number of firefighters required, and a range of equipment associated with the pumper.[4]

Departmental resources cannot be used to bring about change, however, without preparation. Appropriate training must be employed to prepare the members of the organization to analyze, plan for, and implement change. These tasks are discussed later in the chapter.

The responsibility for creating an environment for change rests with the chief administrative officer and the departmental managers. In a local government, that means the city manager or mayor and the department heads. Among other things, these leaders must talk—incessantly—about innovation.[5] In other words, if the fire service organization is to become creative, the chief must talk about creativity.

Whatever forces advocate change, innovation will not occur without leadership that provides encouragement, positive reinforcement, direction, and timely follow-through.[6]

Barriers to innovation

Just as leadership can stimulate change, so the lack of leadership can create a barrier to change. Often leaders of an organization become complacent after achieving some initial goals and, not realizing the need for constant and consistent goal setting, may decide to maintain the status quo and may offer the following excuses for not initiating a project: "We tried that ten years ago"; "We don't need to change"; "That wouldn't be acceptable to the employees." The fire official who recognizes these barriers and avoids them, or who can turn them to an advantage, will be the more effective manager.

Innovation brief In St. Petersburg, Florida, at any given time, three flying fire squads made up of six firefighters per squad are available for assignment.

The increase in firefighters at fire scenes is apparent, and in some cases the flying fire squads have been the first to arrive at the scene.

Source: Product Information Service Advisory Report, *Mini-Pumpers* (New York: McGraw-Hill, December 1981), 13.

Many who have this attitude also fail to comprehend the accelerating rate of change confronting society in general—and the fire service is no exception. This effort to ignore the inevitability of change is one barrier to innovation.

"Conservatism" associated with the bureaucratic structure and the cost of proposed innovations are also cited as factors that inhibit innovation. However, they too can be overcome if there is a sincere desire to do so. Too often incumbents think that new solutions threaten their power and status within the organization.

The modern fire department is traditionally organized in a quasi-military form. It has been argued that this results in greater inequality of social standing and abilities, and in a corresponding inequality in contribution and awards. Also, since promotion within the system is often predicated on a person's ability to conform, the more success an individual achieves, the more vague and subjective become the standards by which that individual is judged. Eventually the only safe posture is conformity.[7]

Here are some other barriers to innovation:

1. The fire service is exempt from the sanction of economic failure faced by private businesses.
2. Innovations hold few personal rewards for participants, and there are few penalties for failure to adapt to a changing environment.[8]
3. People fear failure, which can result in termination, peer ridicule, or loss of influence.[9]
4. Promotion is often based on seniority or on examination scores, not on an individual's contribution.

Although many of these barriers may be present in an organization, they do not show up in every organization. In any case, a change that challenges current beliefs is almost certain to meet with resistance if employees are not involved in the change process. If an individual feels that a contemplated change will result in a loss of self-esteem or that it will threaten his or her status or sense of competency, expose a weakness, or affect the person's influence with the peer group, a high level of resistance can be expected. Unions may well participate in opposing change perceived to be detrimental to their membership or to the union itself.

People also resist changes when they do not understand them or when the reasons for change are not clearly defined. Many organizations resist any change that can be categorized as "not invented here" or any change that is introduced by force.

Rosabeth Moss Kanter in *The Change Masters* lists ten "rules" for stifling innovation (see the accompanying sidebar). These rules place the responsibility for removing the barriers to innovation not on the unknown "they" or on "external factors" but on the top management of an organization. If these rules—even though they may be unwritten and undocumented—are in place, it is likely that the organization supports the status quo by blaming others for

Ten rules for stifling innovation

1. Regard any new idea from below with suspicion—because it's new, and because it's from below.

2. Insist that people who need your approval to act first go through several other levels of management to get their signatures.

3. Ask departments or individuals to challenge and criticize each other's proposals. (That saves you the job of deciding; you just pick the survivor.)

4. Express your criticisms freely, and withhold your praise. (That keeps people on their toes.) Let them know they can be fired at any time.

5. Treat identification of problems as signs of failure, to discourage people from letting you know when something in their area isn't working.

6. Control everything carefully. Make sure people count anything that can be counted, frequently.

7. Make decisions to reorganize or change policies in secret, and spring them on people unexpectedly. (That also keeps people on their toes.)

8. Make sure that requests for information are fully justified, and make sure that it is not given out to managers freely. (You don't want data to fall into the wrong hands.)

9. Assign to lower-level managers, in the name of delegation and participation, responsibility for figuring out how to cut back, lay off, move people around, or otherwise implement threatening decisions you have made. And get them to do it quickly.

10. And above all, never forget that you, the higher-ups, already know everything important about this business.

Source: Rosabeth Moss Kanter, *The Change Masters* (New York: Simon & Schuster, 1983), 101.

their reluctance to innovate or accommodate needed changes within the organization.[10]

Creating an environment for innovation

Regardless of the "incentives" and "barriers" to innovation, the organizational environment must be such that employees become willing to accept mistakes—and even failure—or nothing is going to happen. This type of environment is particularly important in the high-tech age. Tomorrow's managers will have to be skilled not just in the operational aspects of their jobs but also in the application of technology. This high-tech world will require "high-touch" executives, who are adept at communicating new concepts and leading workers into uncharted waters. At the very least, future executives must learn to make projections for a variety of different scenarios, either personally, using a microcomputer, or through other persons in the organization. What is even more important, managers will need to know how to manage technology so that they can take advantage of scientific advances, reduce costs, and increase the effectiveness of the organization.[11] Since it is clear that the fire service will not be bypassed by the "information revolution," public service agencies must equip themselves accordingly if they are to successfully innovate and accommodate to change.

To create a climate for innovation, top management must lead the way in fostering risk taking within an organization. This attitude must be adopted by the entire staff. Once employees recognize that their input is desired, an aura of excitement develops in the organization. The president and CEO of a suc-

---

Innovation brief The city of Vancouver, Washington, is saving a substantial amount annually on certain fire hydrant parts by contracting with a local plastics firm to manufacture main shutoff valve seals at a fraction of the manufacturer's price. Vancouver has also stopped going to manufacturers for the break-away bolts on fire hydrants. With this arrangement, Vancouver pays less than half of the usual costs.

Source: Product Information Network Bulletin, vol. 4, no. 14.

---

cessful high-tech company is quoted as follows: "If you think about it, people love others not for who they are, but for how they make us feel. We willingly follow others for much the same reason. It makes us feel good to do so. . . . This business of making another person feel good in the unspectacular course of his daily comings and goings is, in my view, the very essence of leadership."[12]

Leaders with positive self-regard rarely, if ever, have to rely on criticism or negative sanctions. They focus instead on the positive. Having a group of individuals think well of themselves—individually and collectively—is the most important element in achieving excellence.[13] Therefore, an innovating organization needs a work force that has not become so stuck in the rhythm of routine jobs that it cannot easily adapt to a new drumbeat. If change is to be a way of life rather than an occasional traumatizing shock, workers at all levels must be engaged in change making and change mastery—while still doing their necessary jobs.

An environment that is conducive to innovation combines the necessity for routine jobs with the possibility for employee participation beyond those jobs. Individuals at all levels of the organization deserve an equal chance to innovate. This encourages an integrative culture rather than isolating the production and support ranks.[14]

The innovation process

The innovation process can be viewed as having three stages: recognition and exploration, research and development, and acceptance and implementation.

Recognition and exploration

The innovation process consists of a series of events starting with the recognition by someone inside or outside the fire department of a need to alter a method now in use or to overcome a shortcoming in an operating procedure. This need can stem from any development that affects the work of the department. The initial perception might give rise to ideas that could fulfill the need or correct the oversight. Most often, a series of ideas is explored. The ideas could be generated by fire personnel within the organization in search of a solution, through inquiries to other fire departments that have resolved a similar problem, or through information and data discovered in trade journals, texts, or other reference materials.

Personal contacts are a prime source of ideas. It has been said that, in the public sector, individual relationships constitute one of the best communication networks. It follows that many of the ideas adopted by fire officials originate through this informal and haphazard network among fire chiefs, fire training officers, fire prevention personnel, and members of affiliated unions.

Professional organizations serving members of the fire service also serve as repositories of ideas. Individuals associated with a state university, a regional fire academy, a community college, a local industry, or a state municipal organization might be sources of ideas that could be of benefit to the fire chiefs or their staffs.

Research and development

Out of an idea an invention may come. The invention may be nothing more than a combination of several ideas, or a modification of another idea through the addition or deletion of subcritical elements.[15] Although the "not invented here" syndrome has not afflicted all fire departments, all too many are reluctant to undertake a program or to initiate a process that another community has found to be successful. The fact that most local fire agencies formulate specifications for new apparatus suggests that they are reinventing the wheel. A greater sharing of ideas could maximize the limited resources available to the fire service. Any modification that improves the process or procedure should nevertheless be encouraged.

During this research and development stage the invention is refined and its potential application expanded.[16] It will undergo close scrutiny by those on whom it will have an impact. Each party will try to determine to what extent the innovation threatens the individual and the group, will ascertain the advantages to be accrued from its use, and, subsequently, will accept or reject it.

Some innovations are tried on a pilot basis, an approach that gives the user an opportunity to test its acceptability and preview the consequences of full adoption. Trying out an innovation on a small scale helps minimize possible unanticipated consequences—noneconomic as well as economic.[17]

Acceptance and implementation

The final step in the innovation process is to accept the innovation and implement it as part of the ongoing operations of the department. The true test of the successful implementation of an innovation is its institutionalization.

Several factors bear on the acceptance or rejection of the innovation. They include visibility, credibility, and complexity. The more visible the innovation—the easier it is to see its results—the more likely it is that it will be adopted and accepted. An innovation is also more likely to be accepted by fire officials if one of the early adopters is recognized as a leader in the fire service profession. Complexity, as perceived by fire personnel, will determine whether a change will be adopted throughout the fire service and, if so, how rapidly. Some innovations are less easily understood by potential users than are others

Information sources   Several organizations are available to provide advice and information that can be of great help in finding a solution to various problems. Among them are Public Technology, Inc., 1301 Pennsylvania Avenue, N.W., Washington, D.C. 20004; Management Information Center, International Association of Fire Chiefs, 1329 18th Street, N.W., Washington, D.C. 20036; and United States Fire Administration, Federal Emergency Management Agency, 16825 South Seton Avenue, Emmitsburg, Maryland 21727.

Several state and regional innovation groups, formally organized to service local government, now operate in many areas of the country. In addition, the federal laboratories will provide local officials with the results of research conducted within their facilities on fire-related matters.

and, consequently, will be adopted more slowly. In general, ideas that the implementer finds easy to pick up will be accepted earlier.[18]

An examination of acceptance of innovation by firefighters has verified that some innovations seem to catch on more quickly than others.[19] Those that were accepted most readily by the group studied had an effect on the efficiency of the individual (e.g., newer, lighter breathing apparatus; and power saws to replace hatchets) rather than the organization of fire attack.

Managing the change process

The difference between a successful innovation and an unsuccessful attempt to innovate quite often lies in the capabilities (or lack of them) of management personnel within a particular fire department.

The role of the fire chief

The importance of strong leadership has already been mentioned, but it is well to reemphasize the role of the chief fire officer in bringing about change. In a change-oriented environment the fire chief will devote more time and will direct a substantial part of the organization's effort toward adjusting to rapidly evolving technologies. Therefore, fire agency officials will need to make a commitment to long-range planning.

In many respects the fire chief will need to "market" the program of change and, for example, remind other chief officers that they bear the responsibility of showing others the advantages of future changes. In other words, the leadership style of the chief executive should include a sales component. Although others will be in charge of implementing change, the fire chief should maintain a coordinating role in the total change effort to ensure that maximum improvement is achieved, that the original objective is kept intact, that those in charge of the program are both responsive and responsible—and that, in addition to performing well, they are expanding their capacity to implement change.

In this context, the fire chief, when making appointments to top administrative posts, should consider carefully each individual's capability to support change.

The role of middle management

While it remains the chief executive's responsibility to motivate top management, the assistant deputy or battalion chiefs should, in turn, influence middle management personnel by providing them with an environment in which they can achieve greater influence, both upward and downward, and in which they can become key implementers and communicators.

Middle management personnel, in turn, are responsible for increasing opportunities for nonmanagerial employees to participate in the change process. Nonmanagerial employees should be fully advised as to the details of the contemplated change, the reasons for the change, the expected alterations in the work program, and the advantages to be gained throughout the organization.

Choosing the change group

No change can be initiated without the participation of key people in the organization. One of the responsibilities of the fire chief in implementing change is to evaluate the strengths and weaknesses of key personnel whose talents will be needed to carry out the program successfully. Members of the change group or task force should be selected on the basis of their involvement in and knowledge of the area in which change is to be considered and should include

1. Representatives of the functions that will be implementing any change
2. Representatives of organizations (both inside and outside the government) whose support and cooperation would help ensure the success of a change
3. Representatives of groups whose work could be altered by a change (including such people helps to prevent the feeling that change is being imposed without consulting those affected or that there is a "hidden agenda" that will reveal itself when it is least expected).

The chairperson of the change group must be creative and change-oriented, must be a good listener, and must be able to organize the other members of the task force into a team. Otherwise, any initiative undertaken by the group will be short-lived, and the overall endeavor will suffer.

This undertaking has two objectives—a short-range objective and a long-range one. The first is to achieve defined goals through the implementation of change, at least on a pilot basis. The second is to develop the managerial capabilities of the participants.

The people selected to initiate the project should be given the opportunity to express their opinions on programs or projects that could solve the problem or meet the need that has been identified. Through discussion, the group should select a proposed course of action that can directly affect the organization and that can be achieved through the use of resources presently available to the

---

Innovation brief In 1981 the Industrial Emergency Council, whose membership represents approximately 100 organizations mainly in San Mateo and Santa Clara counties in California, began to develop a hazardous materials response system for San Mateo County. This jurisdiction was selected because of the high concentrations of hazardous materials among Silicon Valley manufacturers. The South County Fire District was selected as the lead agency for this project.

The first step was to identify the problem by conducting research and surveys. Once the data had been gathered, the next step was to convince twenty cities and one county of the need for a regional approach to solve the problem.

After four years of intensive effort, the system was operational. Key fire people have had over 200 hours of specialized training in response to chemical emergencies and industrial people have been trained in a 144-hour course on hazardous materials.

A fully equipped vehicle is in service to respond throughout San Mateo County. Joint agreements have been made with each of eighteen fire agencies to work together in emergency response.

organization. In other words, the initial project should be selected not only because it fills a need, but also because it can be achieved. Group members will then be enthusiastic about undertaking a new, different, and more difficult project, and other members of the organization, though not directly participating in the project, will share in the feeling of accomplishment.

Committing the plan to writing

Once a recommendation is made, its details should be committed to writing. A program seldom proceeds as anticipated, and people often have differing perceptions of the decisions and commitments that have been made. For these and other reasons, it is prudent to have the details of a program transcribed and distributed to all task force members.

The written plan should include information concerning individual responsibilities for each task, anticipated date of completion for each assignment, and ways in which the individual can measure progress in accomplishing specific objectives. To ensure that these tasks are being completed in a timely manner, a review process should be incorporated into the procedure. This step also serves to coordinate the work of the different participants and to ensure that they are not working at cross-purposes.

Providing direction

Although the term *change* implies adventure, excitement, and exploration, change is a tedious and exacting process. Yet it is the rigor of the process that brings each detail into focus and thereby avoids unsatisfactory or substandard results. The more often the change process is implemented and the more closely the plan is followed, the greater the chance that each undertaking will achieve success.

Even if a task force is appointed, the chief will have to provide the ongoing direction needed to complete the mission successfully. Periodically, the chief should call a meeting at which each participant reports on his or her activities

---

Innovation brief In 1982 information was compiled by the San Mateo (California) Fire Department on large-diameter hose. The chief formed a task force, and vendors were contacted and invited to demonstrate their products.

During this period, some of the surrounding cities had purchased new equipment. However, there was no consistency in the size or type of couplings. Everyone realized that problems in compatibility would arise. Therefore a one-day workshop was conducted for mayors, city council members, city managers, and fire chiefs to discuss standardization concerning large-diameter hose. Engines were on hand, and demonstrations carried out.

Fire chiefs of nineteen departments subsequently agreed on a standard size hose with compatible couplings for future purchases. The change was effected by educating firefighter personnel rather than using the "bulletin board" approach to announce that a change would be effected on a certain day. In fact, this project was successful because of the participation and contribution of many people.

Since this project had potential emotional overtones, and since it was essential to gain the support of all sworn personnel, it had to be approached slowly and intelligently. It was also vital to establish communication linkages throughout the organization and with other organizations whose activities would be affected by this equipment conversion. Finally, equipment was not used until all members of the department were trained and certified.

since the last meeting. At these gatherings the chief will be apprised of the continuing efforts of each individual and, in turn, top management will demonstrate its enthusiasm and support.

Generating enthusiasm

Without support from the chief, the project is probably doomed to failure. Optimism and enthusiasm are contagious, and a "win" attitude can counter temporary setbacks. People tend to perform best in an optimistic environment, and, since both enthusiasm and pessimism are easily communicated, it is important for the chief to give positive signals personally and to consider the attitudes of others when selecting them for the task force.

On the other hand, if a proposed change would be disadvantageous to the mission of the organization, or if it would adversely affect the organization's service capabilities, the chief should redirect the efforts of the task force to another program. This situation arises more often during the early undertakings. A negative conclusion to a change should not be tagged a failure but must be viewed as part of learning how to manage change. Instead, the basic factors that led the group to select the project should be reevaluated.

Communicating successfully

It is important to keep people informed as the project progresses. Good communication can generate enthusiasm and excitement among those who might otherwise be skeptical and nonreceptive. As questions arise from those not directly involved in the project, they should be answered thoroughly, honestly, and as quickly as possible. Communications should flow both ways. In addition to dispensing answers, the chief needs to be receptive to ideas that may help the task force avoid certain pitfalls that might otherwise go unnoticed.

Once two-way communication has been established, it should be used to provide rapid feedback on employees' recommendations. If suggestions have been favorably received and are being considered for the plan or for implementation, the individual should be told and given an approximate date as to when to expect to see some results of the suggestion. If a recommendation offered by an individual or a group is to be rejected for any reason, it is just as important—if not more important—to communicate the reasons. The more thorough and complete the reasons cited for the rejection of offered suggestions, the easier it is for those who made the recommendations to understand why they were not applicable—and the more confident they will feel about making additional suggestions (suggestions that might prove more appropriate because of the knowledge they have gained).

Employees who have taken the time and made the effort to communicate with the task force, and whose suggestions have been accepted, should be recognized for their contributions. In addition, the team members themselves might receive letters of commendation and be cited publicly for their contribution.

Recognition should not be given, however, until a suggestion has been implemented and has proven worthwhile. If employees believe that recognition is used only to stimulate interest in the project and not to reward a genuine contribution, the effort will lose credibility. If this happens, the pilot project may fail completely and the entire change program may be adversely affected.

Activating and evaluating

The fire chief and other command officers, along with members of the task force, may find that they are unable to choose a project that meets the established criteria. Only then will they realize that selecting a first-phase assignment is more difficult than might be expected. Some departments faced with such a situation have gone through a needs assessment to identify the most important steps that should be undertaken in each division. Many projects can be identified through this procedure, and the results can be put in priority order by a task force; decisions can then be made about which projects to address.

Once an initial project has been completed, the participants should critique the selection of the task, the procedure used, the detailed assignments, and the schedule with a view to improving the process and making the project more interesting for future participants. Each participant should look upon the first project as a learning experience. Several projects will have to be initiated and completed before project members will come to realize that the process is becoming easier, that things are becoming clearer, and that the participants are becoming more adept at seeing the intricacies of the total problem.

As the tasks become more complex, additional time will be required to develop a suitable work plan. Also, as the projects are expanded in scope, the impact on various work groups will tend to increase.

Dealing with obstacles

As projects become more complex and involve more people from various divisions, the need for effective project management becomes greater. Chapter 10 discusses project management in detail.

Sometimes information and data essential to the project are not available to the task force members because key people will not provide the data or the authority to obtain it, possibly because they feel threatened by potential changes. Task force members then lose their momentum and begin to doubt their ability to accomplish the goals. To overcome these and similar obstacles, sometimes the chief has to step in and see that the required information is forthcoming. It is important that these obstacles, whether natural or contrived, not be allowed to obscure the reasons for the project. The obstacle may be the very reason why progress has been slow within the organization.

Learning from the process

Managing the change process is part of change itself. Certainly it is a learning experience for anyone who has undertaken its management. By incorporating this process into the department, the chief begins to realize the undeveloped potential that exists within the organization. The change process becomes a tool for developing managers: The better the job they do, the better managers they

Figure 16–1 Innovations in fire service delivery often come from local firefighting agencies. This "portable sprinkler system" was an early attempt to improve the delivery of water to attic fires.

become. Thus, the change process has short-term and long-term benefits for the individual members of the group implementing the change—for the chief responsible for the change process, for members of the fire service delivery organization, and, most important, for the citizens they are to serve.

Conclusion

Although the management of change is a complex task, it is a critical responsibility that fire service managers must undertake as well as understand if they are to meet the increasing demands that will be placed upon them in the future by elected and appointed officials, professional groups, special interest groups, and individual citizens. Fire service managers can expect to receive more and more requests from groups who are critical of the quality, the timeliness, and the adequacy of the services supplied. Representatives of the same groups will also inquire about the possibility of new or expanded services. At the same time, others will complain about the cost associated with the current level of service.

As these demands increase, fire service managers will need to be aware of and receptive to change. They will need to use new technology such as computer modeling techniques for locating fire response facilities, for providing up-to-date analyses of the performance of the fire agency, and for projecting staff, apparatus, and equipment requirements for the future. Fire apparatus and equipment will also change, becoming increasingly self-contained, requiring minimal attention during operation. Scarce, valuable, and expensive personnel will be employed to supervise the automated and semiautomated tools that will handle many routine situations.

This sets the stage for the fire service managers of tomorrow, who may find that confidence in their own capability to manage change will be the critical element in helping them understand and control the future.

1 Rosabeth Moss Kanter, *The Change Masters* (New York: Simon & Schuster, 1983), 20.

2 Norman I. Fainstein and Susan S. Fainstein, "Innovation in Urban Bureaucracies: Clients and Change," *American Behavioral Scientist* 15 (March–April 1972), 519.

3 Ibid., 528.

4 John W. Lawton, *A National Agenda for Programs to Increase the Introduction of Innovations in the Fire Services* (Washington, D.C.: Public Technology, Inc., 1973), 9.

5 Thomas J. Peters and Nancy Austin, *A Passion for Excellence* (New York: Random House, 1985), 177.

6 Edward M. Glaser, "Knowledge Transfer and Institutional Change," *Professional Psychology* 4 (November 1973): 439.

7 Victor A. Thompson, "Bureaucracy and Innovation," *Administrative Science Quarterly* 10 (June 1965): 3, 6.

8 Fainstein and Fainstein, "Innovation in Urban Bureaucracies," 516.

9 Ibid.

10 Kanter, *The Change Masters*, 101.

11 Costis Toregas, preface, in Costis Toregas, ed., *Managing New Technologies* (Washington, D.C.: International City Management Association, 1985).

12 Irwin Federman, Monolithic Memories, Inc., quoted in Warren Bennis and Burt Nanus, *Leaders* (New York: Harper & Row, 1985), 62–63.

13 Louis Tice, *Investment In Excellence* Application Guide (Seattle: Pacific Institute, 1983), 8A-1.

14 Kanter, *The Change Masters*, 181.

15 E. M. Rogers and John D. Eveland, "Diffusion of Innovations Perspectives on National R&D Assessment: Communication and Innovation in Organizations," paper prepared for the National Science Foundation National R&D Assessment Program, n.d., 41.

16 Ibid.

17 Public Affairs Counseling, *Factors Involved in the Transfer of Innovations: A Summary and Organization of the Literature*, prepared for the U.S. Department of Housing and Urban Development, Office of Policy Development and Research (Washington, D.C.: U.S. Department of Housing and Urban Development, January 1976), 49.

18 Ibid.

19 Malcolm Getz, "The Economics of Fire Departments," in *Research Report from the M.I.T.–Harvard Joint Center for Urban Studies* (Cambridge, Mass.: Joint Center for Urban Studies, 1978), 5.

17 Alternative delivery systems

Faced with tight budgets and other pressures, elected and appointed officials frequently ask how their local governments can deliver fire services more effectively and efficiently. A city or county may consider changing the way it provides fire protection services for many reasons. The following catalysts for change tend to be the most influential:

1. Growth in demand for services, especially ambulance and rescue services
2. Municipal budget constraints and/or contractual labor demands
3. Not enough volunteers available during daylight hours
4. Pressures to improve the productive use of paid firefighter "downtime"
5. The complexity of modern firefighting and the length of training volunteers require to meet community fire-safety standards
6. Economies of scale (some cities are served by as many as six fire departments).

The factors that eventually induce a change in the way fire protection is provided are related to a number of variables, including the type of organization that is currently providing the service for the community.

This chapter discusses the types of fire protection delivery systems that are most common in the United States and describes the pressures for change to alternative systems. It then treats responses to these pressures, starting with improvements in existing delivery systems and moving on to six alternatives—private-sector fire services, consolidated police and fire services, combination (career/volunteer) departments, intergovernmental contracts, and, briefly, joint service agreements and regional consolidation. In addition, it reviews local sprinkler ordinances, particularly for residences, because they represent a kind of alternative that complements any delivery system.

Fire protection delivery systems

Three basic types of fire protection delivery systems are used in the United States: volunteer, combination (career/volunteer), and fully paid departments. A study sponsored by the National Science Foundation further subdivided combination departments into mostly volunteer and mostly paid departments. The study identified the following four kinds of departments:

1. Volunteer (members are paid some token amount but no full-time fire protection personnel are employed)
2. Mostly volunteer (full-time personnel make up less than half the membership)
3. Mostly paid (full-time personnel make up more than half but less than 100 percent of the membership)
4. Fully paid.[1]

By this classification, 35 percent of fire departments in the study were fully volunteer and served approximately 13 percent of the protected population; 24 percent were mostly volunteer and protected 14 percent of the population; 12

percent were mostly paid and protected 9 percent of the population; and only 29 percent of the sample were fully paid but protected 64 percent of the population. Most volunteer departments are found in small places, which take in a large proportion of the cities in the United States but a small proportion of the population.[2]

The type of fire service a city or county employs appears to be influenced by such factors as community size, geographic region, metropolitan status, and form of government, as indicated by a 1980 survey of cities under 50,000 conducted for the U.S. Fire Administration (USFA) by the International City Management Association (ICMA) in cooperation with the National Volunteer Fire Council (NVFC) (see Figure 17–1).[3] The study sponsored by the National Science Foundation also suggested that, in a very general sense, a different type of fire department predominates in each major geographic area of the country: the Northeast tends to have fully volunteer departments, the North Central region mostly volunteer departments, the West mostly paid departments, and the South fully paid departments.[4]

Pressure for change

The pressure for change in delivery systems has been most evident in municipalities that are served by fully volunteer departments. A principal reason for this has been the comparatively high fire loss that these communities tend to experience.[5] In addition, volunteer departments have suffered a decline in membership, simultaneous increases in service demands (especially for ambulance services), and tougher training requirements mandated by more stringent community fire-safety standards.

Figure 17–1 Types of fire departments serving cities with differing characteristics.

Classification	No. of cities reporting (A)	Fully volunteer No.	Fully volunteer % of (A)	Mostly volunteer No.	Mostly volunteer % of (A)	Mostly paid No.	Mostly paid % of (A)	Fully paid No.	Fully paid % of (A)	Don't know No.	Don't know % of (A)
Total, all cities	2,133	801	37.6	433	20.3	670	31.4	198	9.3	31	1.5
Population group											
25,000–49,999	279	14	5.0	181	64.9	38	13.6	46	16.5	0	0.0
10,000–24,999	597	104	17.4	187	31.3	188	31.5	106	17.8	12	2.0
5,000– 9,999	550	224	40.7	42	7.6	234	42.5	36	6.5	14	2.5
2,500– 4,999	567	353	62.3	20	3.5	183	32.3	8	1.4	3	0.5
Under 2,500	140	106	75.7	3	2.1	27	19.3	2	1.4	2	1.4
Geographic region											
Northeast	542	310	57.2	57	10.5	153	28.2	16	3.0	6	1.1
North Central	691	256	37.0	157	22.7	208	30.1	61	8.8	9	1.3
South	576	162	28.1	146	25.3	187	32.5	71	12.3	10	1.7
West	324	73	22.5	73	22.5	122	37.7	50	15.4	6	1.9
Metro status											
Central	65	0	0.0	46	70.8	6	9.2	13	20.0	0	0.0
Suburban	1,098	412	37.5	210	19.1	361	32.9	102	9.3	13	1.2
Independent	970	389	40.1	177	18.2	303	31.2	83	8.6	18	1.9
Form of government											
Mayor-council	885	428	48.4	138	15.6	255	28.8	56	6.3	8	0.9
Council-manager	1,065	292	27.4	274	25.7	346	32.5	133	12.5	20	1.9
Commission	37	12	32.4	7	18.9	16	43.2	2	5.4	0	0.0
Town meeting	122	61	50.0	8	6.6	48	39.3	2	1.6	3	2.5
Rep. town meeting	24	8	33.3	6	25.0	5	20.8	5	20.8	0	0.0

Fully paid departments are under pressure as well. In these departments tight finances and contract demands by professional firefighter unions have led citizens and local officials to question traditional fire service operations. Citizen pressure for higher levels of service, reductions in the percentage of calls to structural fires, and competition from other city departments for budget funds leave elected and appointed officials hard pressed to find a way to improve firefighter productivity.

Historically, most communities with an all-volunteer force introduced paid personnel into their delivery system when fire protection services had to be changed. As the population of a jurisdiction increases, for example, the de-

---

Volunteers   Once the social knot that united isolated farms and rural communities, volunteer fire companies are suffering sharp membership declines. They have become victims of Americans' peripatetic way of life and the social and economic pressures that have changed the fabric of Main Street.

In the Northeast, the problem has been exacerbated by the decline in manufacturing industries. Blue-collar employees have traditionally been the heart of volunteer departments in many communities. The number of active firefighters in one New York department has dropped to forty from fifty in five years, making it difficult to run trucks during the day, according to an example in a survey conducted by the National Volunteer Fire Council, a nonprofit association that represents volunteer departments in thirty-eight states.

The survey, which identified respondents only by their state, found that membership in one Nevada department had dropped to twenty from thirty in five years. The council says there are about 1.5 million volunteer firefighters in the country, the same number as twenty years ago. But since there are more communities, the average number of members in a company is down.

Volunteer ambulance corps have also lost members, and for many of the same reasons.

"In the past, many departments had people knocking their doors down," said E. James Monihan, chairman of the council, who is deputy chief of the fire department in Lewes, Delaware. "They were fat and happy. They had a ceiling on membership. They'd put applicants on waiting lists, and if somebody died, OK, they'd take somebody in. But now departments that have always had plenty of manpower all of a sudden are waking up and having trouble."

Small boys and girls still dream of becoming firefighters and ambulance drivers. But the children's fathers are less likely to volunteer their time.

In large part, the authorities say, that is because firefighting has changed. A popular pastime has evolved into an unpaid profession. Twenty years ago, volunteers had to do little more than sign up and pass a 12-hour first-aid course. Now many departments require recruits to undergo 110 hours of training. And paramedics in many communities must take several hundred hours of medical courses.

The problem for volunteer ambulance corps is aggravated by the shrinking pool of nonworking women.

Simultaneously, demand for service is quickly climbing in fast-growing bedroom communities near major cities. Caught in the squeeze, officials near Back Mountain, Pennsylvania, in an area that is becoming a favorite region of vacation homes for well-to-do New Yorkers, are considering hiring full-time chiefs and drivers to make sure that trucks reach fires.

Source: Lindsey Gruson, "Ranks of Volunteer Firefighters Thinned by Changing Society," *New York Times*, April 19, 1987.

partment may supplement the volunteer force with a career maintenance worker who could respond with the apparatus as soon as the alarm sounds, or a full-time fire marshal who could inspect commercial property. Once a department has become fully paid, however, volunteers are seldom added, except in private-sector fire services, where it has been the norm to add volunteers as auxiliary personnel. There are a few notable exceptions, as the accompanying sidebar shows.

An advantage of combination departments with both career and volunteer personnel is that they keep fire protection costs low and yet are able to solve many of the problems faced by fully volunteer departments. But because combination departments differ from strictly volunteer and career departments they require special leadership skills. Conflicts between career and volunteer personnel, for example, are not uncommon. Full-time career firefighters may believe that they are better decisionmakers on the fireground than volunteer lieutenants who may be less experienced. In a profession that requires a high level of team integrity and cooperation, this can sometimes lead to serious management problems.

An example of a combination career/volunteer fire department with a long record of service can be found in Montgomery County, Maryland. Eighteen independent volunteer fire departments and two rescue departments provide suppression and EMS services to 670,000 residents across 506 square miles. Career personnel fill 714 positions to supplement the work of approximately 1,200 volunteers. About 60 persons work for the Department of Fire and Rescue Services itself, providing countywide communications, training, fire prevention, and fire investigation services. The remaining career personnel are employed by independent volunteer fire departments, and the arrangements vary from regular, round-the-clock company staffing to straight days during the normal working hours when few volunteers are available. Only a few chief officers are career personnel, the vast majority being volunteers elected to their positions from within the individual departments.

One example of the pressures on the Montgomery County department was the replacement of the fire board, which was composed of representatives of the individual volunteer departments, by a fire commission appointed by the county executive. Another was a lawsuit filed by the firefighters' union in May 1986 against fifteen of the eighteen volunteer departments. The career fire-

---

Using volunteers in a paid department Houston, Texas, has a successful nonprofit volunteer fire safety education program, the Cease Fire Club, with over 300 members. The club helps the Houston fire marshal's office in fire education activities and engages in fund raising as well.

Among the club's projects is the Citizen's Fire Prevention Training Center, which has displays on home fire hazards, home fire prevention, and residential sprinkler systems. It also has a library, a classroom, and audiovisual facilities. Outside the center is a fire extinguisher training area where actual fires are lighted and then extinguished by students. Scout groups and others are encouraged to visit the center and use its facilities.

The Cease Fire Club also created a juvenile firesetters prevention program. This activity has an annual budget of over $200,000 and employs seven psychologists solely to work with juvenile firesetters.

Other activities of the club have included seminars on fire prevention and life safety and fund raising for lab equipment for Houston's arson squad.

Source: E. A. Corral, "Houston's Center for Fire Prevention," *International Fire Chief,* August 1984.

fighters contended that, under the Fair Labor Standards Act (FLSA), they were entitled to overtime pay if they worked in excess of 40 hours per week and asked the court to extend overtime pay retroactively to May 1983. Their argument was that they were working for private, independent membership organizations, not public agencies. (Under the provisions of FLSA, described in more detail in Chapter 9, publicly employed firefighters are not due overtime pay until they work in excess of 53 hours per week.) The U.S. District Court in Baltimore ruled in favor of the career firefighters, most of whom worked an average 48 hours per week.[6] Faced with an estimated $6.1 million in overtime pay for the next year, the county subsequently made the volunteers into county employees.

Whenever alternative systems are proposed, proponents and opponents build their cases for or against change. Many arguments for and against various alternative delivery systems are reviewed later in the chapter.

Improving existing departments

Short of replacing an entire system of fire service delivery, what are some steps that local officials can take to preserve and strengthen the systems they already have?

Volunteer departments

Improving the management of a fully or mostly volunteer fire department is clearly the most important step the chief executive of a municipality can take to keep these delivery systems as viable options. Without sound management, the quality of volunteer fire protection is difficult to control.[7] A key conclusion of the study conducted by ICMA for USFA was that municipal officials could no longer afford to continue the "time-honored laissez-faire policy toward their volunteer fire organizations."[8] The study also concluded that

1. A community's level of fire service is not solely the responsibility of the fire department, but of the entire community.
2. The volunteer fire service is built on a sense of pride and professionalism. CAOs should support the volunteer fire service in order to increase its effectiveness and improve its community image.
3. The CAO and the volunteer fire service must work together to
   a) establish and implement mutually acceptable performance standards
   b) improve management skills within the volunteer fire service
   c) define mutual problems and agree on mutual priorities
   d) establish and implement a recruitment and recruit training program (including selection, retention, and promotion requirements)
   e) develop guidelines for fire department administration, including financial management and reporting requirements to ensure credibility and accountability to the community.
4. CAOs and volunteer fire departments need to examine the expansion of cooperative intergovernmental agreements.
5. When appropriate, CAOs should consider the volunteer fire service a municipal department and extend the support services it would give to other municipal departments.[9]

Recruitment and personnel management are a constant challenge in the volunteer fire service, as the department is dependent on persons who volunteer their time.[10] Volunteers are frequently motivated by a sense of duty or public service, an interest in developing a new skill, or the congeniality of working with other volunteers. Departmental managers who tailor incentives to such motivations find this approach helps to sustain motivation. Suggested incentives include

1. Training and staff development (with paid staff)
2. Formal awards or recognition
3. Insurance coverage while on the job
4. Letters of recommendation for future employment as career firefighters
5. Reimbursement for out-of-pocket expenses
6. A structured career ladder to allow volunteers to accept increasing responsibility commensurate with their abilities
7. An active role in planning and goal setting for the organization.[11]

The city of Bloomington, Minnesota (85,000), is an example of a community that has kept its all-volunteer department a practical alternative in protecting the 38 square miles it covers. The department is staffed by 150 paid-on-call members operating out of six fire stations. Three full-time paid civilians, a fire investigator, and two fire prevention officers are employed by the city's building and inspections department. The task of receiving alarms and dispatching fire equipment is handled by the police communications center.

Bloomington maintains a set of rigorous training and performance standards coupled with a reward system. The volunteers are recruited, accepted, and trained on the understanding that their hours of emergency service will fit their daily schedules. An applicant who works from 9:00 A.M. to 5:00 P.M. many miles away, or who is otherwise unable to respond to alarms during normal daytime working hours, is assigned to a group expected to respond during evenings or deep night hours. As is the case with many other volunteer fire departments, Bloomington finds it difficult to recruit volunteers who would be available to respond to alarms during the daylight hours, Monday through Friday. In addition to night workers, real estate agents and on-duty city employees are two occupational groups that have provided a number of daytime volunteers. Bloomington volunteers must respond to 30 percent of all alarms, must back their automobiles into their driveways or garages to facilitate rapid response, and can be fired for missing three scheduled training sessions. (Every Monday is training day, with drills held at noon, 4:30 P.M., and 6:30 P.M. to accommodate the various work schedules of the volunteers.)

Bloomington volunteers are rewarded with a pension equivalent to one-third of a police officer's salary upon successfully completing twenty years of service and upon reaching fifty years of age. In addition, the volunteers conduct a variety of fund-raising projects during any given year, and volunteers who retire during that year receive severance pay from the pot (which is not city money), which may amount to several thousand dollars. Indicative of their performance is the city's fire rating. Surveyed in 1985 by the Insurance Services Office (ISO), the city was awarded a class 3.[12] Although the ISO schedule was developed for insurance rating purposes and not for fire protection planning, it provides one standard by which to judge this city's fire protection system.

Volunteer fire protection cannot be viewed as a free service, but it can be a cost-effective fire service delivery option. The key to its success lies in active community commitment. Service-level decisions are total community decisions. Once the level and standard of service are agreed upon, the community must also share the responsibility of identifying and allocating resources and participating in program policy decisions.

Paid departments

Fully paid departments that have to deal with local officials who are increasingly reluctant to spend more money on fire protection face a different dilemma. How can efficiency be improved without affecting performance? Part of the difficulty of answering this question is that there is no comprehensive system of determining what level of fire protection is adequate for a community. Many local policymakers have stopped using the ISO system as a stimulus for spending more money on fire services.

A further difficulty is quantifying the total cost of fire to a community, which will cover both the dollars expended to deliver fire services and the costs associated with fire losses. Included in these costs are fire insurance, productivity lost due to the effects of fire, and the unquantifiable costs associated with injuries and the loss of human life. The efficient delivery of fire protection to a community therefore depends not only on the cost-effectiveness of the delivery system itself, but also on how effective the system is in reducing fire losses.

Three methods of improving the efficiency of fully paid departments are to develop standards, add civilians to the department, and emphasize fire prevention, especially through public education.

Standards If fire chiefs do not have an accepted, comprehensive system by which to evaluate fire services, they are forced to justify ever-increasing expenditures without clear standards linked to the fire safety needs of the community. The states of Michigan and Texas have attempted to set standards for evaluating fire protection by establishing criteria for judging a fire department's effectiveness. Adopted in 1982 by Michigan's legislature, Act 494 provides for the following:

1. Development of a method of evaluating a fire service delivery system (defined as all the equipment, personnel, procedures, and resources that are utilized in the prevention and suppression of fire)
2. Establishment of a fire service classification scale (defined as the criteria by which a fire service delivery system is evaluated)
3. Review of each fire service delivery system every eight years and the establishment of a grade (defined as the fire protection level a fire service delivery system achieves on the fire service classification scale)
4. Provision of assistance, upon request of a municipality, for the purpose of improving the capabilities of the fire service delivery system so as to improve life safety and reduce fire losses
5. Establishment of an appeal process for municipalities or insurance companies involving the criteria used on the grade assigned in the fire service classification scale
6. Utilization of the fire service classification system by an insurance company.

In addition, the act provides for the establishment of a municipal fire service classification board that would develop the grading system, administer it, set a schedule of fees to be charged to municipalities requiring assistance in evaluating their fire protection systems, and provide reports to the state legislature and the commissioner of insurance on its activities and recommendations.

The proposed grading system is voluntary. Thus any fire department not wishing to be classified would be given an *X*, indicating "grade undetermined" under the system. Fire departments that do wish to be graded would need to meet a set of minimum standards before beginning the classification system's self-evaluation and grading process. Any department that meets these minimum criteria would be given a grade of *M*. One of the minimum requirements would be that the department is recognized by the governing authority. Other requirements relate to written policies, rules, and procedures; records (including maps, personnel records, incident reports, maintenance records, and fire prevention activity records); minimum personnel; protective clothing and equipment; training; facilities; communications; pumping capacity; and investigations.[13]

Once the department met the minimum criteria, it would have three years in which to complete the self-evaluation and grading or be assigned a grade *X*. The grading process itself is based on the types of occupancy hazards and the subsequent water-flow requirements that exist in the community and the prevention and suppression capabilities of the department for each category of occupancy hazard.

Civilianization Civilians or nonsworn personnel are still rarely used by fully paid departments. ICMA, which collects data each year on police and fire personnel practices, has found that police departments use far more civilians to perform such duties as record keeping, dispatching, and prevention activities than fire departments. Certain fire service activities, however, could easily be performed by civilian personnel. Among the areas in which lower-paid civilians can readily replace uniformed personnel are fire department administration, fire prevention, public education, and code enforcement.

Fire prevention Innumerable studies have shown that fire prevention, especially through public education, is the most effective way to reduce fire losses. Yet most fully paid departments across the United States continue to spend only a fraction of their total budget on this endeavor. A 1980 survey by the U.S. Conference of Mayors found that 86 percent of fire departments had a fire prevention function, but over a third had no full-time public education staff. Yet 94 percent of the cities responding said that public fire education rated highest as an effective fire prevention activity, higher than inspections, code enforcement, and arson investigation.[14]

Guidelines for improvement

Too often the possibilities for improving the way a fire service is delivered are ignored, often because of resistance from the fire department. Resistance is a natural reaction to any innovation. Even a minor change such as the way time sheets are filled out will cause employees to grumble. Stakeholders tend to see radical changes, such as a restructuring of the delivery system, as a direct assault on "a way of life" and therefore can be expected to put up organized resistance. Nevertheless, local officials should explore ways to improve the current method of providing fire protection before examining an alternative. Changes in the current system are likely to be less disruptive than a wholesale restructuring. (Chapter 16 discusses the management of change in the fire service.)

Harry Hickey has suggested that local government officials need to ask four questions when contemplating alternative systems of fire service delivery:

1. What level of risk is the city or county willing to accept—in terms of both life safety and property safety?
2. Who benefits and who is deprived under each proposed alternative? To ensure social equity, officials should consider what effects a given change will have on property owners, persons of various income levels, and other groups in the community.
3. What are the scope, objectives, and methods of providing a fire safety delivery system? The scope and level of fire services exert a wide-ranging influence on the functions of fire protection, fire prevention, fire suppression, rescue services, emergency medical care, life support services, and large-scale disaster services.
4. What can realistically be implemented given the local political climate, budgetary resources, and legal constraints? Answers to this question will indicate both limitations and opportunities.[15]

Private-sector fire services

The private sector offers fire services either by contract (to local government) or by subscription (to property owners). In the former case, the private agency becomes the service provider for the government under a formal agreement, and in the latter, the agency collects annual fees in exchange for the protection of specific properties.[16] Contract services may be arranged on a *fixed-price* or a *cost* basis. In a fixed-price contract, the contractor agrees to deliver a specific level and quality of service for a set price. The contractor is responsible for any cost overruns, but also receives the benefit of any cost savings.[17] Under a cost contract, the local government assumes all costs up to a predetermined amount. Cost contracts are generally undesirable because the local government assumes most of the financial risk.

Private-sector fire services are found principally in the Southeast and the West. In a study of alternative fire protection services for the U.S. Fire Administration, John Bennett, writing for Centaur Associates, Inc., theorized that several factors play a role in the geographical distribution of private-sector services. Subscription services are found in states where local governments are not required to provide fire protection to unincorporated areas, where there is no strong tradition of volunteer service, and where union opposition to private services is poorly organized.[18] He suggests that subscription-type services may experience a decline as unincorporated areas are annexed or incorporated.[19]

At the time of the Centaur study, seventeen communities were employing private subscription services, which they obtained from nine private corporations. Figure 17–2 shows the community, the 1985 population protected, the service provider, and the year the subscription service was instituted. Figure 17–3 provides the same information for twenty communities with contract services. As the figures show, Rural/Metro Corporation and Wackenhut Services, Inc., serve the greatest populations.

The Private Sector Fire Association, which represents the seven largest private-sector fire services, claims that private services can provide comparable fire protection for 10 to 50 percent less cost than a public fire department, with a typical savings of 25 percent. Private services are able to realize such savings by using reserve firefighters (who are paid only while they are on call), by manufacturing their own equipment, and by taking advantage of technology.[20]

The Centaur study, too, found that communities contracting with private-sector fire services typically incurred lower costs per capita for fire protection than nearby communities with public fire departments. In 1985 the cost per capita for fire protection, excluding fire insurance rates and fire loss, was typically $30 to $35 in most of the communities served by private-sector fire services. The national average per capita cost for public fire services as of January 1985 was $61.66.[21]

Hall County, Georgia, is an example of a jurisdiction with private fire protection services. The county first contracted with Rural/Metro in 1979. As of 1985, the county was served by Wackenhut. The contractor provides fire protection services throughout the county except in Gainesville, the county seat, and in the town of Flowery Branch. It provides emergency medical services to the entire county.[22] Hall County is mostly rural, covers about 427 square miles, and has a population (excluding Gainesville and Flowery Branch) of approximately 66,000.

The county commission began investigating private-sector fire services in late 1978 as a result of citizen opposition to increased government spending and taxation, the discontinuation of CETA funds for thirteen firefighters, and the termination of free countywide ambulance service by local funeral home operators. After visiting Scottsdale, Arizona, and reviewing Rural/Metro's operations there, the commission contracted with Rural/Metro to study the county's

Figure 17–2
Communities using
private subscription fire
services.

Community	1985 Population protected under subscription	Private subscription fire service	Year instituted
Carefree City, AZ	—[a]	Rural/Metro Corp.	—
Maricopa County, AZ	—[a]	Rural/Metro Corp.	—
Oro Valley, AZ	—[a]	Rural/Metro Corp.	—
Paradise Valley, AZ	13,000	Rural/Metro Corp.	—
Pima County, AZ	—[a]	Rural/Metro Corp.	—
Pinal County, AZ	—[a]	Rural/Metro Corp.	—
Yuma County, AZ	—[a]	Rural/Metro Corp.	—
Chatham County, GA	20,000	Southside Fire Dept.	1961
Yellowstone County, MT	7,500	O'Donnell Fire Service & Equipment Company	1954
Josephine County, OR	18,000	Grant's Pass Rural Fire Dept. & Ambulance Service	1957
		Valley Fire Service	1979
Umatilla County, OR	2,500	Milton-Freewater Rural Fire District	1982
Brentwood, TN	9,431	Brentwood Fire Dept. Inc.	1954
East Ridge, TN	21,236	East Ridge Fire Dept. Inc.	1946
Knox County, TN	100,000	Rural/Metro Corp.	1972
La Vergne, TN	5,495	La Vergne Fire Dept. Inc.	1965
Rutherford County, TN	—	La Vergne Fire Dept. Inc.	1965
Williamson County, TN	2,500	Brentwood Fire Dept. Inc.	1954

Note: Detailed source notes for the information in this figure appear in the original: Centaur Associates, Inc., "Alternative Methods of Providing Fire Protection," report submitted to the U.S. Fire Administration, May 1986.

[a]Although numbers are not available for most of the Arizona communities, Rural/Metro estimates that it protects 200,000 persons in the state on a subscription basis.

Figure 17–3   Communities contracting with private-sector fire services.

Community	1985 population	Private-sector fire service	Year instituted
Colonia Verde F.D., AZ	360	Rural/Metro Corp.	
Flowing Wells F.D., AZ	20,000	Rural/Metro Corp.	
Fountain Hills F.D., AZ	3,500	Rural/Metro Corp.	
Gilbert, AZ	12,200	Rural/Metro Corp.	
Green Valley F.D., AZ	11,000	Rural/Metro Corp.	
Laveen F.D., AZ	3,100	Rural/Metro Corp.	
Northwest F.D., AZ	23,000	Rural/Metro Corp.	
Sabino Vista F.D., AZ	2,400	Rural/Metro Corp.	
Scottsdale, AZ	108,400	Rural/Metro Corp.	1951
Sun City F.D., AZ	43,000	Rural/Metro Corp.	
Sun City West F.D., AZ	4,600	Rural/Metro Corp.	
Tonopah, AZ	1,200	Rural/Metro Corp.	
Tuscon County Club Estates, AZ	7,500	Rural/Metro Corp.	
Youngstown, AZ	2,285	Rural/Metro Corp.	
Hall County, GA	65,615	Wackenhut Services, Inc.	1979
Savannah, GA	25,000	Southside Fire Dept.	1979
Vernonberg, GA	100	Southside Fire Dept.	
Elk Grove Township, IL	8,000	American Emergency Services	1979
Grants' Pass, OR	N.A.[a]	Valley Fire Service	
Ridgeside, TN	500	East Ridge Fire Department, Inc.	

Notes: F.D. means *fire district*.
  Detailed source notes for the information in this figure appear in the original: Centaur Associates, Inc., "Alternative Methods of Providing Fire Protection," report submitted to the U.S. Fire Administration, May 1986.

[a]The Valley Fire Service provides first truck response for a limited area of the city. The population of that area is not available, but the 1980 population of the city was 14,997.

fire department. In its report, Rural/Metro was critical of the department and proposed to provide fire services to the county for less than the department's budget for the previous year.

Opponents of the proposal claimed that the change would lower the county's ISO rating, which had improved during the mid-1970s from class 9 to class 8. Nevertheless, the county commission, without a formal request for proposals or public hearings, voted unanimously to disband the county fire department and contract with Rural/Metro. A citizens group immediately sprang up and initiated a recall vote for the five county commissioners. They were recalled, but their successors voted to continue with the contractual arrangement after a county-wide referendum overwhelmingly supported such a decision.

By 1985, under a three-year, fixed-fee contract, the contractor was responsible for the Hall County Fire Department, which provides fire and ambulance services under the department of public safety. The public safety department is responsible only for all emergency services in the county, including communications, the emergency management agency, the county marshals, animal control, and the correctional institution.[23] The equipment, fire apparatus, and stations are owned by the county and leased to the contractor. The contractor is responsible for

1. Hiring, firing, and compensating the personnel for fire prevention/suppression and ambulance services (minimum wages and cost-of-living increases are specified in the contract)
2. Operating fire prevention and inspection programs, including a public education program
3. Maintaining mutal-aid agreements and fire and ambulance records, and completing an annual study of the fire and ambulance system
4. Training employees to meet state standards, using a training director/officer (all departmental personnel are cross-trained as firefighters and EMS technicians)
5. Repairing fire apparatus with reimbursement by the county (major repairs are undertaken at the discretion of the county administration).[24]

Work schedules and minimum employees per shift are outlined in the contract, which provides for a reduction in payment to the contractor if proper staffing is not maintained at all times. The fire department is managed by a fire chief employed by the contractor under the general supervision of the department of public safety, which also handles planning for the fire department in close consultation with the fire chief.

In 1986 the fire department abandoned its two-shift work schedule and went to a new schedule of 24 hours on duty and 48 hours off, versus the old 24-on 24-off schedule. It has about 100 employees, plus 25 volunteers. The organization is charted in Figure 17–4.

Despite the fears of early opponents, the county's ISO rating actually improved after the contract arrangement was implemented. In 1987, for commercial and residential properties, it was 6 in one portion of the county and 7 in another.[25] The costs for fire department and ambulance service from 1979 to 1987 are presented in Figure 17–5. After being adjusted for inflation, the contract cost actually declined slightly.[26]

The use of auxiliary personnel accounts in part for the success of private-sector fire service protection in Hall County. The department is very active in training industrial fire brigades, a strategy that has helped ease the pressure on the fire department, since fires at industrial facilities are frequently extinguished or contained by members of these brigades before the fire department arrives. The department also trains private security guards in basic firefighting and life-support techniques.[27]

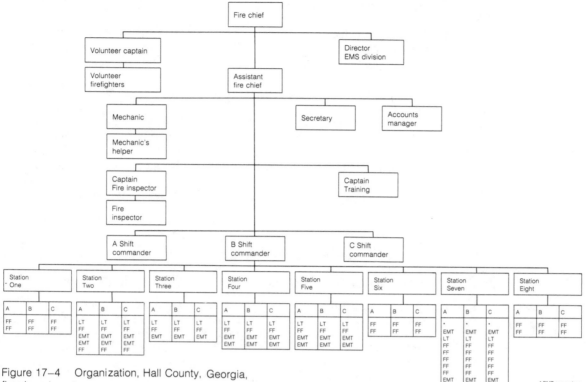

Figure 17–4   Organization, Hall County, Georgia,
fire department.

Figure 17–5   Fire department and ambulance service costs, Hall County, Georgia, 1979 to 1987.

Period	Fire	Ambulance	Total	Contractor
3/79 – 3/80	$ 862,464	$180,000	$1,042,464	Rural/Metro
3/80 – 3/81	N.A.	N.A.	$1,015,000	Fire Suppression Management
3/81 – 3/82	N.A.	N.A.	$1,090,000	Fire Suppression Management
3/82 – 3/83	$ 794,000	$356,000	$1,150,000	Wackenhut
3/83 – 3/84	$ 818,000	$367,000	$1,185,000	Wackenhut
3/84 – 3/85	$ 842,000	$378,000	$1,220,000	Wackenhut
3/85 – 7/86	$1,113,000	N.A.	N.A.	Wackenhut
7/86 – 7/87	$1,213,200 (estimated)	N.A.	N.A.	Wackenhut

Notes: N.A. indicates *not available*.

Detailed source notes for the information in this figure appear in the original: Centaur Associates, Inc., "Alternative Meth-ods of Providing Fire Protection," report submitted to the U.S. Fire Administration, May 1986.

In a case study of the Hall County experience, the county administrator made several recommendations to other communities that were considering contracting for private-sector fire services:

1. Proceed slowly.
2. Consult elected officials about their support for contracted services and talk to the fire chief to explain the rationale for contracted services.
3. Contact potential bidders for general information and assistance in preparing detailed bid specifications.

4. Be sure the fire chief and the county attorney review the bid specifications.
5. Have the elected body approve the final bid specifications and the bidding process.
6. Issue a prepared statement explaining the rationale for contracting to educate the public.
7. Prepare for criticism from fire department employees, their relatives, and friends.
8. Advertise for bids and explain how to qualify as a bidder, which may include attending a pre-bid conference and submitting a final bid within 60 days.
9. Establish a special committee to review bids and make recommendations.
10. Expect a large critical audience at the final meeting to approve contracted services.[28]

Consolidated police and fire services

The consolidation of police and fire services can take five basic forms:

1. Full consolidation, in which the police and fire services are fully combined into a department of public safety. Officers perform both public safety functions and are usually identified as public safety officers (PSOs). A minimum number of PSOs are assigned to duty in the fire station while the remaining officers patrol, performing both fire prevention activities and police patrol duties.
2. Partial consolidation, in which the identities of the police and fire services are retained and a special patrol is created to perform combined police-fire duties. This special patrol is usually composed of personnel recruited from both departments. Such officers are also called PSOs and when not engaged in firefighting activities are supervised by the police department.
3. Selected area consolidation, in which the police and fire services function separately except for specially trained police-firefighters assigned to combined duties in a specific geographical area.
4. Functional consolidation, in which separate police and fire services are retained, but one or more duties normally performed by one department are assigned to members of the other. For example, firefighters may help with administrative tasks in the police station or police officers may prepare hydrants for hoses at the fire scene before fire apparatus arrives. (Another kind of functional consolidation is the consolidation of building and fire plan review and inspections, as discussed in Chapter 15.)
5. Nominal or administrative consolidation, in which both services retain individual and distinct identities operationally (and sometimes administratively) but are under one public safety director.[29]

The basic principle of the public safety concept is that fewer personnel can be assigned to fire stations because public safety officers on police patrol are trained in two disciplines and can supplement fire companies at the scene of a fire. Proponents of public safety departments cite statistics showing that only a small percentage of firefighters' time is actually spent responding to emergencies. The nonproductive "downtime" can be better used to augment police patrol activities. Police-fire consolidation, they say, can significantly increase the number of on-duty staff available for police patrol or fire response and the number of off-duty personnel who can be recalled in the event of a major emergency.[30] Furthermore, costs can be reduced by combining operational functions that police and fire services have in common (such as dispatching) as well as administrative activities (budgeting, office staff, records, and so on).

Opponents of consolidation counter that

1. When firefighters are not responding to fires, they typically perform a wide range of important duties—for example, station and equipment repair and maintenance and fire prevention activities.
2. Patrol personnel meet apparatus manned by skeleton crews at the fire site. Patrol personnel may be located far from the fire and/or engaged in police duties that delay their arrival. These personnel lose additional time while changing from dress uniform to protective firefighting gear.
3. Much of the training given to personnel in consolidated departments is not adequate to prepare the fire-police officer to perform either the police or firefighting component of his or her duties.
4. A major fire can temporarily leave a community with inadequate police protection, just as a major police emergency can temporarily leave a community with inadequate fire protection.[31]

Approximately 188 U.S. communities have been identified as having one form of consolidation or another.[32] The large majority (153) of these communities have a population of 25,000 or less, and half are in cities of 10,000 or less. Of the cities in which the type of consolidation could be identified, 60 percent had either functional or nominal consolidation. Forty-six cities had fully consolidated departments.

Sunnyvale, California, is the largest city with a fully consolidated public safety department. Before it adopted the public safety system in 1950, the city was served by a police department and a volunteer fire department. At the time, the city had a population of 9,829, incorporated 6 square miles, and employed 23 public safety employees.

By 1983, the city's population had increased to 108,600 and the incorporated territory had expanded to 24 square miles. The total number of departmental personnel per 1,000 population was 2.23; when civilians (just police and fire personnel) were excluded, it was 1.88.[33] This compares favorably with the 1983 national average of police alone, which was 2.45 per 1,000 population.[34]

The public safety department is organized into three units: support services, police services, and fire services (see Figure 17–6). Each service is under the direction of a commanding officer who reports to the public safety director.

The support services section consists of staff services, planning and research, training, emergency communication, and emergency preparedness. Specialists and administrative staff work a standard 40-hour week, Monday through Friday.

The police services program is organized into two patrol teams, each under the direction of a patrol team captain with ten public safety lieutenants who serve as shift supervisors. The city is divided into six beats, or geographical areas, that are determined by the level of demand for service. PSOs assigned to patrol respond to emergencies, engage in crime prevention, provide assistance for the public, and supplement firefighting efforts. PSOs on police duty work four 10-hour shifts for a 40-hour work week and perform some unique activities. "Neighborhood resource officers," for example, are responsible for addressing the special problems and needs of a designated area of the city and report directly to the police staff services captain.[35]

The objectives of the fire services program are to provide on-scene services to emergency requests within an average of 4 minutes and to conduct fire and life-safety inspections of apartments and commercial establishments an average of twice a year. The second objective applies to both suppression and prevention divisions.

A complement of 86 PSOs, lieutenants, and captains are assigned to twelve companies, which are responsible for suppression activities, inspections, and

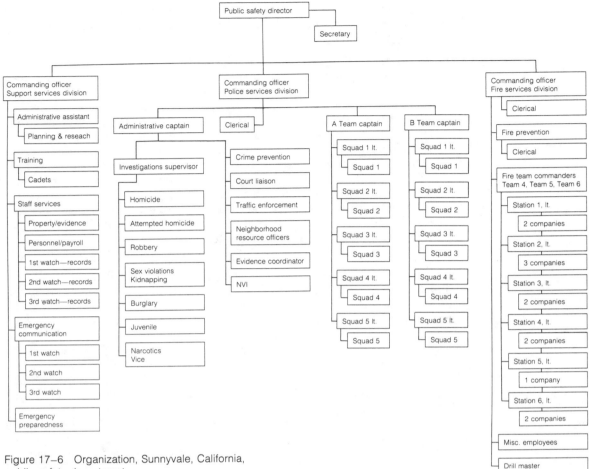

Figure 17–6   Organization, Sunnyvale, California,
public safety department.

enforcement of fire- and life-safety regulations in commercial structures and multiple family dwellings in their districts. Figure 17–7 shows how suppression personnel and fire apparatus are assigned.[36] Public safety officers assigned to fire duty work a 56-hour week in 24-hour shifts.

The fire prevention bureau provides for

1. Coordinating all fire prevention activities
2. Inspecting all properties having complex fire hazards
3. Checking building and development plans for fire- and life-safety features
4. Conducting public education campaigns
5. Providing technical advice on matters related to fire prevention and
6. Managing a comprehensive hazardous materials storage permit program to identify the location of hazardous materials.[37]

The responsibility for investigation also lies with the bureau, assisted by patrol and detective personnel.

Training is a key element in Sunnyvale's public safety system. Basic training for PSOs includes 480 hours of basic fire science instruction, 640 hours of instruction in police science, and 320 hours of field training. After being assigned to the police division, each officer receives 130 hours of in-service training each year on such topics as fire training, range qualification, first aid, and CPR. Fire-based personnel receive 298 hours of refresher training during

Figure 17–7 Fire station apparatus and personnel complement, Sunnyvale, California.

Fire station	Apparatus	Personnel on duty
1	1500 GPM pumper	1 Lt. and PSO
	75' aerial platform w/1500 GPM pump	2 PSO
2	1500 GPM pumper	1 Lt. and 1 PSO
	75' aerial ladder telesquat w/ 1500 GPM pump	2 PSO
	Chemical light air rescue apparatus	2 PSO
3	1000 GPM pumper	1 Lt. and 1 PSO
	1000 GPM pumper	2 PSO
4	1500 GPM pumper	1 Lt. and 1 PSO
	65' aerial platform w/1250 GPM pump	2 PSO
5	1000 GPM pumper	1 Lt. and 1 PSO
6	1000 GPM pumper	1 Lt. and 1 PSO
	1000 GPM pumper	2 PSO
	Reserve apparatus	
1	1000 GPM pumper	
5	1000 GPM pumper	

scheduled weekly drills. Each officer assigned to the police division also receives 40 hours of advanced officer training each year.[38]

Every one to three years an officer may expect to rotate duties, from police to fire or vice versa. Because they perform both police and fire functions, public safety officers have always been paid a rate higher than prevailing wage scales in the area. In 1982, the differential was set at 8 percent over police salaries in comparable jurisdictions.[39]

A major criticism of public safety departments is that their performance does not equal the level of conventional delivery systems. Figure 17–8, which reports work load and performance indicators for the Sunnyvale fire services program, suggests that lower public safety system costs do not necessarily imply inferior fire protection for a community.

Combination (career/volunteer) departments

Historically, most combination fire departments originated as fully volunteer departments. As the communities they served grew in population or became more mobile, they added career personnel to complement the all-volunteer force.[40] Combination departments are found mainly in mid-sized cities (population 10,000 to 50,000).[41] What little research has been done on these departments usually focuses on other types of delivery systems and refers to combination departments only for comparison. This research shows, however, that combination departments often exhibit several advantages over fully volunteer and fully paid fire departments:

1. Response times tend to be faster in combination departments than in fully volunteer departments (although they are slower than in fully paid departments).
2. The resources allocated for fire prevention and public education activities are higher in combination departments than in fully volunteer departments.
3. The per capita cost of delivering fire services is generally lower in combination fire departments than in fully paid departments.[42]

Because of their organization, many combination departments also have some inherent disadvantages. The special requirements of systems using both career and volunteer fire personnel have been expanded since the U.S. Supreme Court ruled that the Fair Labor Standards Act (FLSA) can constitutionally be applied to state and local governments. For example, it is not unusual for career personnel in combination departments to volunteer their time to the same department on off-hours. Under the regulations promulgated by the Department of Labor (DOL) to implement the FLSA, these individuals must now be compensated. The DOL regulations specifically state that "a [career] firefighter cannot volunteer as a firefighter for the same public agency." The regulations do, however, allow a career firefighter to volunteer his or her time to a neighboring department and to retain his or her volunteer status with that neighboring department even if it has a mutual-aid agreement with the first community.

Critics of combination departments also argue that friction can easily develop between career and volunteer personnel who work together. When volunteers are scarce, for example, it is difficult to maintain the same professional standards

Figure 17–8 Community condition indicators, Sunnyvale, California.

Indicator	FY 1980–81	FY 1981–82	FY 1982–83	FY 1983–84	Projected FY 1984–85
Total number of calls for fire services	4,096	3,940	3,776	4,356	4,076
Number of calls per 1,000 population	38.6	37.2	34.8	40.1	36.1
Average response time to emergency calls in minutes[a]	—	3.4[a]	3.1[a]	3.2[a]	4.2
Percentage of emergency calls within 5 minutes or less response time	—	—	—	—	85%
Fire services and support cost per capita	$43.57 (21.80)[b]	$47.97 (22.26)[b]	$49.77 (21.65)[b]	$55.19 (22.60)[b]	—
Number of building fires per 1,000 population	2.2	1.9	1.7	1.8	1.8
Median dollar loss per building fire			300	400	300
Number of fire-related deaths	1	0	1	0	1
Number of fire-related injuries	25	24	14	13	19
Total dollar amount fire loss	3,504,833 (1,753,293)[b]	1,084,084 (503,055)[b]	860,549 (374,314)[b]	896,912 (367,286)[b]	
Number of hazardous materials responses	—	48	38	69	80
Number of emergency medical service calls	2,508	2,562	2,512	2,603	2,586
Percentage of fire causes identified	—	90%	93%	92%	92%
Number of building inspections	15,124	10,500	12,544	13,037	10,900
Number of hazards detected	10,353	7,460	9,478	8,292	9,200
Number of corrections achieved	9,133	6,377	8,582	7,204	7,800
Number of building plans reviewed	2,145	937	1,100	1,181	1,105
Number of hazardous storage permits issued	—	—	—	—	—
Number of operational permits issued	776	785	1,162	1,219	1,470
Number of leaks identified					

[a]Method of response time measurement was changed in 1985 to include time necessary to dispatch the assignment upon receipt of the call.
[b]Adjusted for inflation.

for volunteers as for career personnel. Because of lower training requirements for volunteers, fireground operations tend to be less effective, as some career regulars are reluctant to take orders from or even to work with volunteers.

However, proponents argue that many interpersonal problems associated with combination departments can be solved with strong, effective leadership and sound management. They point to such departments as those in the cities of Kettering, Ohio (see accompanying sidebar), and Mt. Lebanon, Pennsylvania, where these problems were identified and successfully dealt with.

The Mt. Lebanon Fire Department has managed to sidestep most of the disadvantages of a combination department while benefiting from the many advantages. The department attributes its success to several key factors: (1) strict control through rules and regulations, (2) comprehensive screening and testing of all applicants, and (3) mandatory professional training requirements for both career and volunteer personnel.

Mt. Lebanon has been served by a combination fire department for over fifty years.[43] The city has a population of about 37,000 and an area of 6 square miles

---

Professional management of volunteers Kettering, Ohio (population 62,000), has a combination fire department of about 100 volunteer and 40 career firefighters. When the department found itself having difficulty recruiting and retaining volunteers, the city manager appointed a professional manager to maintain the volunteer force.

The volunteer manager is a civilian with specialized skills in recruitment, interviewing, placement, recognition, and evaluation. Her objectives are to (1) recruit new volunteers through publicity, special campaigns, and promotional activities; (2) retain existing volunteers by building morale through recognition and improved intradepartmental communication; and (3) build public awareness by enhancing the image of volunteer firefighters through positive publicity and by educating the public about the fire department's structure, including the responsibilities and skill levels of volunteers, as well as the city's need for additional volunteer firefighters.

The most significant obstacle to implementing this change was the anticipated reluctance of the volunteers to accept an "outsider." To help overcome potential resistance, a popular, recently retired veteran of the volunteer force was hired part-time to help ease the transition.

A review of the program has shown progress on all its objectives. The department succeeded in maintaining a viable volunteer force in the city. Exit interviews indicated that persons who left the force were leaving for personal or professional reasons, not because they were dissatisfied with the department. Recognition of volunteers was increased through gestures of appreciation to firefighters and their families. And intradepartmental communication was improved through a retreat for both career and volunteer firefighters along with the city manager's top staff, the personnel director, and the fire department administration. Among the concrete outcomes was a management seminar on interpersonal communications and supervisory techniques for officers. City officials also reported that they perceived an increase in public awareness.

This innovation was based on the belief that, as economic and social trends discourage citizens from volunteering their time, volunteer management requires a level of knowledge and sophistication that was not necessary in the past.

Source: Laima Rastikis, "A Combination Department Breaks with Tradition," *Fire Command*, January 1987, 34–36

that it protects through one centrally located fire station housing three engines, one truck, one rescue squad, a mobile command post, and a reserve engine.

The department is organized into two subgroups to minimize potential friction between full-time paid and volunteer personnel: (1) a paid subgroup that consists of fourteen personnel who work a 10-on 14-off shift and 42-hour workweek and (2) a volunteer subgroup that consists of these fourteen career personnel plus thirty-eight volunteers.

The volunteer organization elects its own executive officers, conducts regular business meetings, and is funded by the city of Mt. Lebanon. The volunteers have no fire officers and take all fireground orders from the paid officers and firefighters. In order to retain membership, a volunteer must respond to at least 33 percent of the full alarms. A minimum of two paid personnel are on duty at all times.

Six of the career officers have staff functions in addition to their suppression responsibilities. They are the chief, an equipment officer, a communications officer, a fire prevention officer, an adjutant, and a training officer. Career personnel must be residents of Mt. Lebanon.

Mandatory training is a critical feature of Mt. Lebanon's department. Every member of the department must attend at least 50 percent of the regular drills for the year. Anyone failing to make these percentages is called before the executive board and may be dismissed. In addition to regular drills, the department holds specialized drills to practice preplanned hookups at target hazards and to practice emergency rescue techniques.

The department's response procedures are tailored to its structure. The department receives calls directly from the person reporting the emergency, whereupon one of two types of alarm is issued: (1) a full alarm, consisting of the complete activation of the on-duty paid personnel, a recall of off-duty paid personnel (reporting to the station), and the calling of volunteers, or (2) a still alarm, which is answered by the on-duty firefighters with some assistance from volunteers. Still alarms, which represent 89 percent of all calls, cover automobile fires, investigations, gas leaks, small brush and rubbish fires, and other miscellaneous calls. The average response time for both full and still alarms is 4 minutes.

In 1986, the Mt. Lebanon fire department had 2,473 calls for service. Of these, 638 were emergencies and 1,835 were nonemergency calls. The department's performance in both suppression and prevention is clearly shown in its five-year average fire loss statistics. As an indicator of suppression effectiveness, Mt. Lebanon's fire loss per capita of $5.11 compares favorably with the figure of $6.83 per capita for cities with a population of 25,000 to 100,000.[44] Fire prevention effectiveness is shown by the number of fires per 1,000 population protected, which is 2.14 in Mt. Lebanon, compared with 4.97 nationally in mostly volunteer departments.[45]

Intergovernmental contracts

Prior to the introduction of motorized fire apparatus, fire services were rarely available to areas outside a municipality's borders. To assist neighboring jurisdictions was impractical because of the distance involved, the lack of an adequate water supply, and the difficulty of reaching a fire scene quickly. But as the response capabilities of fire departments improved and as suburban populations surrounding cities increased, requests for assistance outside the borders of municipalities also tended to rise. Eventually the frequency of these requests became a matter of concern to local government officials, and communities started adopting ordinances forbidding the provision of fire services outside the municipal borders unless a conflagration threatened the community itself. Finding their free fire services withdrawn, groups of citizens or individuals in unprotected areas started to contract with municipalities to provide fire protection for a fee. As suburban areas incorporated, some continued to contract for fire protection services.

Intergovernmental service contracts can be defined as "agreements (formal and informal) between two units of government in which one pays the other for the delivery of a service to the inhabitants in the jurisdiction of the paying government."[46] Intergovernmental fire service contracts should not be confused with mutual-aid agreements. Mutual-aid agreements are formal or informal reciprocal arrangements by which the fire departments agree to assist each other in case of need and usually without compensation, except perhaps to replace damaged equipment.

In a survey on the use of intergovernmental service contracts completed by ICMA and the Advisory Commission on Intergovernmental Relations in 1983, 159 cities and counties of the 2,069 that responded indicated that they had contracted with another government to provide fire services. Governments listed seven reasons for using this means of delivering services:

1. To make use of qualified personnel
2. To make use of existing facilities
3. To achieve economies of scale (this was the most frequently cited reason)
4. To eliminate service duplication
5. To organize services in the most logical way, rather than have them constrained by jurisdictional or areal limits
6. To take politics out of service delivery
7. To meet citizen demand.[47]

Municipalities with written contracts outnumbered those with unwritten or informal arrangements by two to one. This is not surprising, especially in fire protection. Considering the risks to life and property that are involved in firefighting, it would be exceedingly risky for a municipality to provide fire protection to another community on a regular basis without a standard contract specifying the extent of its liability.

Charges for fire service can be established by a number of methods. The question of what is a fair share of fire service costs has led to the development of many different kinds of formulas, which usually take into consideration one or more of the following factors:

1. Fire department operating costs
2. Money paid to support pensions
3. Cost of apparatus and major equipment depreciated over a specific time period
4. Cost of the physical plant over a given time
5. Percentage of fire department use by the contracting municipality over a given time period
6. Percentage of assessed valuation of the contracting municipality to the total assessed valuation of all areas protected.[48]

Examples of popular methods used to assess a fair share of costs are the following:

1. Fixed formula. Fees are determined on the basis of a formula designed to include as many of the costs of providing fire services as possible.
2. Ratio of calls. Fees are determined by taking the calls of the contracting area as a proportion of the total calls received by the fire department and then applying that percentage to all fire department costs.
3. Per unit cost. Fees are determined by counting the number of structural units being protected and then dividing the department's operating costs

by the total number of units in all areas protected to determine a per unit cost.

4. Assessed valuation. The assessed valuation of the contract service area serves as the basis for proportionately sharing fire service costs.

5. Population. Since the number of fire responses are fairly reflective of the size of a community's population, this becomes the method for proportionately determining costs.

6. Flat fee or standard rate. The fee is based on the ratio of fire calls but a flat fee is levied only when a fire call occurs.[49]

In addition to specifying the method and amount of payment, an intergovernmental fire service contract will also usually include the following provisos:

1. Identification of the area. This is usually a map or description of the area to be protected.

2. Duration of the contract. The period covered is frequently one year.

3. Waiver of liability. Under this provision, the contracting municipality waives any action against the providing jurisdiction for damages or injuries when responding to a fire as well as liability for a failure to respond.

4. First duty. Many contracts require that the first priority for fire response be given to the citizens of the jurisdiction providing the fire service and that the secondary responsibility be given to those who contract for fire protection outside of the municipality.

5. Minimum provider responsibilities. Some contracts specify the number and type of equipment and firefighters that the providing municipality must have to deliver fire protection to those jurisdictions contracting for the service. Other agreements specify that the jurisdictions providing the fire service must become familiar with the property being protected or assume responsibility for dispatching or other functions.

6. Management of fire service. Frequently, a clause stipulates that the fire chief of the municipality providing the fire service is responsible for making decisions regarding management, level of response, or other such issues.

7. Arbitration board. Some contracts include a clause providing for a means to settle disputes.

8. Termination of agreement. Some contracts specify the amount of notice, usually 30 to 90 days, that either party must give before terminating the agreement.

The principal advantage of an intergovernmental service contract is that it usually allows both parties to receive a higher level of protection than they could provide on their own. One of the major difficulties with such agreements is that most communities do not have cost accounting systems that can fully and accurately track the actual costs of providing service. Without this ability, it is difficult to establish the appropriate fee to charge.[50]

Other alternative delivery systems

Two other alternative methods for delivering fire protection services are joint service agreements and regional consolidation.

Joint service agreements

The fire service has expanded beyond its original mission and moved into other service areas that previously did not exist or were provided by other public agencies or the private sector. These services include hazardous materials response, emergency medical services, emergency management, and code administration and enforcement. The fire service began to provide these other services because of public demand, frequently in areas where the fire department was well equipped and staffed to take on the new service. Many such services, however, are beyond the financial capability of most individual communities, or the number of incidents is too small to justify a full-response capability. Hazardous materials is a good example. Through a joint service agreement, two or more governments arrange for the joint planning, financing, and delivery of a service to all their inhabitants.[51] Joint service agreements allow jurisdictions to pool their resources so that they can provide these necessary public services and take advantage of economies of scale.

The city of Littleton, Colorado, and its neighbor, the Littleton Fire Protection District, entered into a joint service agreement with the city of Englewood and two other fire protection districts to become part owners of the South Metro Fire Training Center, the first cooperatively owned training center in Colorado. The facility contains a burn building, training tower, LPG burn pit, 5,000-gallon drafting pit, smoke maze, driving rodeo, and classroom. On their own, none of these jurisdictions could have afforded such a facility. Several other jointly owned projects in which the city participates are a hazardous materials van, a trench/heavy rescue vehicle, a swiftwater/dive vehicle, and a portable air supply vehicle. Although it is a small city (population about 29,000), Littleton has managed to develop the kind of comprehensive fire protection system for its citizens that even much larger urban communities would envy.

Regional consolidation

Communities in the South and West have frequently merged two or more fire departments into one regional department to deal with the rapid growth being experienced in those areas. Like some of the other alternatives discussed here, regional consolidation provides the potential advantages of (1) centralizing fire department management and reducing administrative costs, (2) centralizing the dispatching and communication network and other fire department support services, such as maintenance and training, (3) improving fire service capabilities because of increased resources and specialized equipment, (4) unifying fire prevention codes and, in some cases (5) reducing insurance premiums because of improvements in the ISO rating.

Cobb County, Georgia, which until 1971 was served by eight independent fire departments, realized many of these advantages through consolidation. Prior to consolidation the county had an ISO rating of 10; after consolidation the rating improved to 7, and the subsequent benefit passed on to homeowners was in the form of a 40 percent reduction in home insurance premiums. Some other examples of communities that have consolidated two or more fire departments are Pasco County, Florida; Contra Costa County, California; and Jacksonville, Florida.[52]

The primary disadvantage of consolidation is the perceived loss of local control, and this has been the reason why consolidation is frequently opposed by individual departments as well as by local politicians.

Built-in fire protection systems

No discussion of alternative fire service delivery systems would be complete without a brief review of built-in fire protection. Although sprinkler systems are not a substitute for an efficiently operated fire department, they are a critically important complement. Figure 17–9 illustrates that automatic suppression systems provide an immediate response to fire, whereas a manual system requires human detection, communication, decision, and response before suppression activities begin.[53]

Since 1872, when Henry S. Parmalee invented the fire sprinkler, these automatic suppression systems have become increasingly recognized as the most efficient and effective way to reduce property loss in commercial and industrial buildings. However, sprinklers designed for commercial and industrial use are inadequate for the protection of human life because they cannot react quickly enough to prevent high-intensity residential fires where the buildup of noxious gases can rapidly kill the occupants. In the mid-1970s the U.S. Fire Administration (at that time known as the National Fire Prevention and Control Administration) began funding a series of research and demonstration projects designed to extend the use of sprinkler systems to improve life safety. Along with the efforts of many fire chiefs and representatives of private industry, the result of these undertakings was a residential sprinkler technology that was not only quick to respond[54] but also reasonably priced and aesthestically acceptable.[55]

Innumerable studies have shown that automatic fire suppression systems are highly reliable and effective in reducing life and property loss,[56] yet only a few jurisdictions have adopted ordinances requiring or encouraging the sprinklering of buildings, especially single-family and two-family residences.[57] San Clemente, California, had a mandatory residential sprinkler ordinance—the first in the country—in 1978. In its study of alternative fire service delivery systems for the U.S. Fire Administration in 1986, Centaur Associates identified only 28 cities and 2 states that required or encouraged the installation of residential sprinkler systems. By the next year, Operation Life Safety, cosponsored by USFA and the International Association of Fire Chiefs, had identified 169 communities that either had or were considering residential sprinkler ordinances.

Cost has been the principal obstacle to the adoption of residential sprinkler ordinances by local government. In many communities developers have argued successfully that the costs related to the installation of sprinkler systems (estimated at $1,500 to $3,000 per residence) would make their new homes uncompetitive in the marketplace. Others have pointed out, however, that this averages about 95 cents per square foot—about the same as the cost of carpeting a new home. Other costs that builders contend would make residential sprinklers unpopular with homeowners are the fees that some water utilities levy for large-diameter water service lines.

Some communities that have successfully adopted residential sprinkler ordinances have overcome these objections by offering builders trade-offs that reduce their construction or up-front development carrying costs. For example, they might relax other building code requirements and zoning ordinances that have higher associated costs.[58] Cobb County, Georgia, has had voluntary sprin-

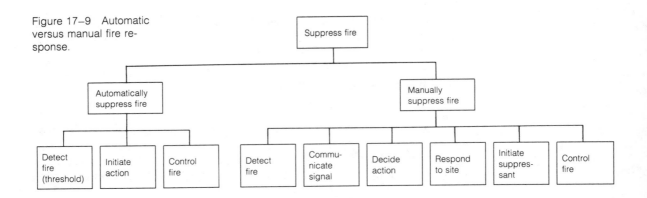

Figure 17–9 Automatic versus manual fire response.

kler ordinances for multi-family residences since 1982. Figure 17–10 illustrates code tradeoffs and the specific savings for builders.

Contributing to the success of Cobb County's voluntary sprinkler ordinance was the method by which the county fire department developed it. The department formed a fourteen-member consortium representing groups with an interest in residential sprinklers. The consortium included representatives of the county's fire, building, and water departments, along with developers, plumbers, sprinkler and piping manufacturers, sprinkler installers, hydraulic engineers, and the American Water Works Association. The consortium concentrated its efforts on identifying building code requirements that could be traded off to offset sprinkler installation costs without endangering life safety during a fire.

The county also conducted a series of sprinkler tests. The first series, monitored by the Factory Mutual Research Center, was held in a wood frame house. The second series, consisting of 218 test burns, was held in a 16-by-16-foot test building constructed with the voluntary assistance of local builders. Monitored by the Georgia Institute of Technology, these tests demonstrated the performance and the effectiveness of residential sprinklers in improving life safety. During one of the tests, four county commissioners were in the test

Figure 17–10 Typical cost offsets of building code tradeoffs allowed under Cobb County's sprinkler ordinance.

Without residential fire sprinklers	With residential fire sprinklers	Savings advantages
1. Tenant separation walls must be made of ⅝-inch type X fire-rated gypsum wallboard.	½-inch standard gypsum wallboard may be substituted.	$23.00 per 1,000 square feet
2. ⅝-inch type X fire-rated gypsum wallboard and ¾-inch plywood must be used in one-hour floor/ceiling assemblies.	½-inch standard gypsum wallboard and ⅝-inch plywood may be substituted in floor/ceiling assemblies.	$55.00 per 1,000 square feet
3. Fire stops are required in the attic at every unit.	Fire stops in attic required every 3,000 square feet.	$123 each fire stop
4. Maximum tenant travel to a fire exit must not exceed 20 feet.	Exit travel may be extended to a maximum of 35 feet.	Design freedom
5. Tenants may not travel by other tenants' windows or doors unless those doors are ¾-hour fire-rated doors in 20-minute frames with 3 U.L.-listed spring hinge closers.	Windows may be placed along travel paths, standard doors and frames with no closers may be used.	Design freedom $111.70 each door
6. One-hour rating on walls and door of hazardous areas.	No one-hour rating of walls and doors of hazardous areas.	$23.00 per 1,000 square feet (walls) $111.70 each door
7. All buildings must have a 4-hour masonry wall every 6,000 square feet.	Only a 2-hour wall is required at 8,000 square feet and 4-hour wall not required until 10,000 square feet.	$8,345 each 4-hour wall (Note: Cost of 2-hour sheetrock wall = $750.00)
8. Fire department access must not exceed 50 feet from back of the parking area to the front of the building.	Fire department access can be extended to 125 feet. This allows freedom in design; makes it possible to place building in more aesthetic surrounding.	Design freedom
9. Two-hour rated party walls are required between fee simple townhouses.	One-hour rated party walls can be used.	$300 per wall

building to observe the effectiveness of the sprinklers firsthand. The ordinance passed without opposition in 1982.

In 1985, the county began developing a similar but mandatory ordinance for sprinklering new single-family residences. Once again, the effort included a consortium of interested parties and a search for various tradeoffs to offset the cost of installation. Several tradeoffs that came under discussion were

1. Reducing local fire tax millage
2. Allowing increased density in single-family residential developments
3. Increasing the spacing of fire hydrants from 500 to 1,200 feet
4. Reducing water mains from 8 inches to 6 inches in diameter
5. Decreasing street width from 28 to 26 feet
6. Allowing longer cul-de-sacs
7. Reducing curb and gutter size.[59]

The city of Salinas, California, used similar methods in the development of its single- and multi-family residential sprinkler ordinance, which became law in 1985. The city used a self-built test-burn trailer to publicly demonstrate the effectiveness of sprinklers. It also offered tradeoffs to reduce the impact of installation costs.

Other cities that have successfully adopted residential sprinkler ordinances have also used carefully orchestrated approaches to educate the public and special interest groups. Some additional incentives discussed by local officials to make the adoption of residential sprinkler ordinances more palatable are tax incentives[60] and lower home insurance premiums. Neither, however, has had much impact on the level of acceptance.

Advances in built-in fire protection technology have made these systems a necessary complement to any fire service delivery system, yet acceptance has been slow. The model code organizations have not adopted single-family residential sprinklers, for example. This has greatly hampered the adoption of sprinkler ordinances in municipalities. As more cities adopt residential sprinkler ordinances, evidence of their reliability and effectiveness will no doubt increase and perhaps encourage still other communities to follow suit.

Figure 17–11
Experimental fires in Cobb County, Georgia; Marina del Rey, California; and San Clemente, California, led to the adoption of residential sprinkler ordinances in many communities.

Conclusion

This chapter has outlined the strengths and weaknesses of various fire protection delivery systems. Its purpose has been not only to suggest alternatives that can help a community respond to pressures on its department, but also to give fire service managers a benchmark for making sure that their departments are providing the best protection possible.

Each community in the United States is unique. Because each has a distinct heritage, politics, and social/cultural environment, it is impossible to prescribe a universal formula for the effective delivery of fire services. What works for Sunnyvale, California, is instructive but not necessarily applicable nationwide. Every community must carefully assess its own circumstances in order to determine what works best locally.

If the current system in a community is not working effectively, the orchestration of change will be critically important. Unless those involved in the planning and implementation can introduce incremental change, building on the strengths and weaknesses of the current system, radical change may be inevitable. Sometimes, however, a community does not have the luxury of adjusting slowly over time. Populations shift, local economies change, and cultural norms and fashions come and go. The fire service cannot afford to ignore these variables or to reject an alternative simply because it does not fit with current practice or suit various stakeholders. Such resistance to change usually leads to inferior fire service delivery and in the long run is detrimental to the entire community.

1   Research Triangle Institute, International City Management Association, and National Fire Protection Association, *Evaluating the Organization of Service Delivery: Fire*, Technical report to the National Science Foundation, 1977. The study, completed in 1977, involved a survey of some 1,400 fire jurisdictions in 50 standard metropolitan statistical areas (SMSAs) across the United States—jurisdictions protecting a population of over 43 million people. Results of the study can also be found in the *Municipal Fire Service Workbook*, published by the U.S. Government Printing Office.

2   The 1982 Census of Governments reported a total of 19,076 cities in the United States; those under 2,500 in population represent 65 percent of all cities but only 7 percent of the population.

3   Gerard J. Hoetmer and Amy Cohen Paul, *Municipalities and the Volunteer Fire Service*, Urban Data Service Reports, vol. 12, no. 9 (Washington, D.C.: ICMA, September 1980), 3. Other statistics on types of fire organizations are available from the National Fire Protection Association and the U.S. Fire Administration.

4   Research Triangle Institute et al., *Municipal Fire Service Workbook*, 72.

5   Ibid., 94.

6   *Washington Post*, August 14, 1987.

7   Lawrence Davis, "Where Is the Volunteer Fire Service Headed?" *ISFSI Volunteer Section News* 1, issue 3 (July 1980), 1. Davis writes that the volunteer department "is pretty unique in that it functions as a monopoly over which there is virtually no control. This generally happens because no one in the community is smart enough or cares enough to find out what a good department should do."

8   Hoetmer and Paul, *Municipalities and the Volunteer Fire Service*, 1.

9   Ibid., 7, 10.

10 Colin A. Campbell, *Personnel Management for Volunteer Fire Departments* (Washington, D.C.: International Association of Fire Chiefs Foundation, 1980), 4.

11 Amy Cohen Paul, *The Volunteer Fire Department: Personnel Management and the Local Government Connection*, Management Information Service Reports, vol. 12., no. 10 (Washington, D.C.: International City Management Association, October 1986), 9.

12 Insurance Services Office, Inc., *The Fire Suppression Rating Schedule* (New York, 1980). The ISO states explicitly that the document should not be used for purposes other than insurance rating.

13 National Fire Protection Association, *Self Evaluation and Grading of Fire Service Delivery System*, Basic Minimum Fire Department Evaluation, June 1987 Proposed.

14 U.S. Conference of Mayors, *Fire Prevention Project 1980*, final report, U.S. Fire Administration, March 1981. Quoted in Philip Schaenman et al., *Overcoming Barriers to Public Fire Education in the United States* (Arlington, Va.: TriData Corporation, 1987), 3.

15 Harry E. Hickey, "Management Options in Fire Protection," in *Managing Fire Services* (Washington, D.C.: International City Management Association, 1979), 41.

16 Centaur Associates, Inc., "Alternative Methods of Providing Fire Protection," report submitted to the U.S. Fire Administration, Federal Emergency Management Agency, May 1986, 1-6.

17 Other variations in fixed-price contracting are firm fixed price, fixed price with escalation, and fixed price with incentive. See Carl F. Valente and Lydia D. Manchester, *Rethinking Local Services: Examining Alternative Delivery Approaches*, Management Information Services Special Report (Washington, D.C.: International City Management Association, March 1984), 3–4.

18 Centaur Associates, "Alternative Methods," 1-10, 1-12.

19 Ibid., 1-18, 1-19.

20 Ibid., 1-6.

21 Gregg B. Jackson, *Police, Fire, and Refuse Departments*, Baseline Data Reports, vol. 17, no. 7 (Washington, D.C.: International City Management Association, July 1985), 12.

22 Centaur Associates, "Alternative Methods," 2-41.

23 Ibid., 2-49, 2-50.

24 Valente and Manchester, *Rethinking Local Services*, 171.

25 Centaur Associates, "Alternative Methods," 2-45.

26 Ibid., 2-51.

27 Ibid., 2-50.

28 Valente and Manchester, *Rethinking Local Services*, 172-73.

29 Marie Hayman, *Public Safety Departments: Combining the Police and Fire Functions*, Management Information Service Reports, vol. 8, no. 7 (Washington, D.C.: International City Management Association, July 1976), 1.

30 Kalamazoo, Michigan, Public Safety Study Committee, *The Consolidation of Fire and Police Services*, July 1981, 2.

31 Centaur Associates, "Alternative Methods," 1-67.

32 International Association of Fire Fighters, *Consolidation of Fire and Police Departments*, 1980 (continuously updated).

33 City of Sunnyvale, California, *Public Safety Concepts and Practices*, n.d., 2.

34 Gerard J. Hoetmer, *Police, Fire and Refuse Collection and Disposal Departments*, Baseline Data Reports, no. 14 (Washington, D.C.: International City Management Association, 1983).

35 City of Sunnyvale, California, *Public Safety Concepts*, 11.

36 Ibid., 13–14.

37 Ibid., 14.

38 Ibid., 6–7.

39 Ibid., 6.

40 "Residential instability appears to be the community characteristic most consistently associated with whether a town has one type of fire department organization or another. If there is great residential stability in a town, its residents apparently are likely to maintain a volunteer fire department. As residential turnover increases, residents add some call or paid personnel to their largely volunteer departments. Finally in towns with considerable residential turnover, residents apparently prefer a full paid department." Research Triangle Institute et al., *Municipal Fire Service Workbook*, 58.

41 Hoetmer and Paul, *Municipalities and the Volunteer Fire Service*, 3.

42 Research Triangle Institute et al., *Municipal Fire Service Workbook*.

43 The information presented on Mt. Lebanon was gathered principally from a presentation made by Stephen Walther, fire chief, Mt. Lebanon Fire Department, to the International Society of Fire Service Instructors, November 2, 1980, Virginia Beach, Virginia, and the 1986 Mt. Lebanon Fire Department annual report.

44 Research Triangle Institute et al., *Municipal Fire Service Workbook*, 33. Per capita fire loss of $3.84 in 1977 dollars recalculated as $6.83 in 1986 dollars.

45 Mt. Lebanon Fire Department annual report, 1986.

46 Lori M. Henderson, "Intergovernmental Service Arrangements and the Transfer of Functions," *The Municipal Year Book 1985* (Washington, D.C.: International City Management Association, 1985), 194.

47 Ibid., 196

48 Bill Bruen, "Fire Department Contracts in Minnesota," *Minnesota Township News*, May–June 1987, 7.

49 Ibid., July–August 1987.

50 Kyland Howard, *Determining Appropriate User Fees*, Management Information Service Reports, vol. 19, no. 9 (Washington, D.C.: International City Management Association, September 1987).

51 Henderson, "Intergovernmental Service Agreements," 194.

52 Centaur Associates, "Alternative Methods," 1-4.

53 Geoffrey S. Bogart, *Residential Fire Sprinkler Ordinances*, Management Information Service Reports, vol. 19, no. 3 (Washington, D.C.: International City Management Association, 1987), 2.

54 Underwriters Laboratory (UL) standard 199 requires commercial and industrial sprinklers to activate in 6 minutes and 30 seconds in an air atmosphere where heated gases are not circulating. Residential sprinklers are designed to meet the requirement of UL 1626, which requires response in a minimum of 6 seconds and a maximum of 13 seconds in a circulating air atmosphere.

55 For a detailed and readable discussion of the history and development of modern residential sprinkler systems, see Ronny J. Coleman, *Alpha to Omega: The Evolution in Residential Fire Protection* (San Clemente, Calif.: Phenix Publications, 1985).

56 For example, "Automatic Sprinkler Performance Tables: 1970 Edition," *Fire Journal*, July 1970, shows a satisfactory performance rating of sprinkler systems of 96.2 percent. A Johns Hopkins University study completed in 1977 demonstrated that a combination of smoke detectors and built-in fire protection could reduce life and property loss by 97 percent. See Rolf Jensen, *Probable Impact of Residential Suppression Systems on Fire Loss Reduction*, Society of Fire Protection Engineers Technology Report 77-1.

57 The National Fire Protection Association (NFPA) estimates that during the period 1977–1981 an average of 5,814 civilian deaths occurred in residential structures; this was 81 percent of the average annual total of 7,175 civilian deaths from all fires.

58 As a result, some groups that manufacture special building construction material have opposed sprinkler ordinances because they have the potential to reduce the market for their products.

59 Centaur Associates, "Alternative Methods," 2-22.

60 Gordon E. Brunton, "Alaska Tries an Incentive Approach," *International Fire Chief*, April 1985.

Training and professional development

The fire service of today is markedly different from the service that existed 100, 50, or even 10 years ago. Not only have the apparatus and techniques changed, but also the personnel and role of the fire service. With the advent of formalized education programs, the status of the firefighter has been elevated from that of a mere doer to that of a technician. Increased demands for service have expanded the role of the fire service into areas beyond fire protection. At the same time, an appreciation of the fact that fires must be prevented as well as controlled has caused the fire service to place greater emphasis on prevention. Simultaneously, firefighting and its associated activities have emerged as true professional partners in the public service spectrum. This chapter gives an overview of the elements of professionalism in the fire service, with an emphasis on developing training programs.

Professionalism

In order to appreciate the fire service as a professional organization, one must first decide what professional means. A profession has been defined as

[an] occupation requiring specialized knowledge that can only be gained after intensive preparation. Professional occupations tend to possess three features: (1) a body of erudite knowledge which is applied to the service of society; (2) a standard of success measured by accomplishments in serving the needs of society rather than purely serving personal gain; and (3) a system of control over the professional practice which regulates the education of its new members and maintains both a code of ethics and appropriate sanctions. The primary characteristic that differentiates it from a vocation is its theoretical commitment to rendering a public service.[1]

The elements of a profession

The main characteristics of a profession are a certain base of knowledge, competent application of knowledge, social responsibility, and self-regulation. Each of these areas is addressed by the fire service.

Knowledge base The field of fire science provides the scientific base for modern fire suppression methods. Continued fire research in such areas as material burn characteristics, suppression techniques, and protection of firefighters provides the necessary base for the firefighting profession.

Competent application To ensure competent application of the skills and knowledge of fire protection, the fire service has established a qualifications system through the National Professional Qualifications Board of the Joint Council of National Fire Service Organizations.

Portions of this chapter are based on ''Education and Training'' by Warren E. Isman from the 1979 edition of *Managing Fire Services*.

Social responsibility   The increased awareness of the social responsibility of the fire service is evident from the greater emphasis on prevention, expanded work in arson control, and extension of the service into areas such as education, emergency medical services, and hazardous materials control.

Self-regulation   Self-regulation has been the rule in the fire service for many years. The National Fire Protection Association, working with the fire service, has established standards for all areas of the fire service. Many national and international organizations have been formed to promote the exchange of information and to establish standards of performance and behavior within the fire service.

The chief as a professional

If the fire service is to continue developing as a profession, the fire service manager must be dedicated to the ideals of the profession. In the past, the fire chief was often appointed on the basis of length of service. Chiefs were expected to know about all aspects of firefighting and fire apparatus. It was not uncommon to see the chief clamber under a piece of apparatus and fix it, or to man a hose line at a large fire. The chief was "one of the boys."

Increasingly, the fire chief is a manager, skilled not only in the art of fire suppression, but in such areas as fiscal administration, public relations, human resource development, and labor negotiations. A typical national chief's conference offers workshops on such topics as management by objectives (MBO), federal labor standards, equipment rehabilitation, physical fitness, and assessment centers. The fire chief can no longer prepare for the role of manager by merely progressing through the ranks. The chief also needs to strive to foster those aspects of the fire service that lead to true professionalism and to cultivate the knowledge and skills of good management through involvement in fire service organizations, specialized education, internships both within and outside the department, and continued reassessment of the fire chief's role.

Ethics and the fire officer

A major aspect of professionalism in the fire service is ethics. Most professions abide by some "code of ethics" that expresses their members' agreement as to what constitutes acceptable behavior. Often the code is a formal statement, such as medicine's Hippocratic oath.

Ethical questions in the fire service are complex, as they involve code enforcement, resource allocation, affirmative action, conflict of interest, and misuse of position. Historically the code of ethics has been informal and simple. However, the International Association of Fire Chiefs publishes a formal code of ethics (see accompanying sidebar), and individual departments sometimes create their own codes based on the IAFC or another model.

Aside from formal codes, a simple application of some guidelines based on common sense can serve as a foundation for professional conduct:

1.   Obey the law.
2.   Tell the truth.
3.   Show respect for people.
4.   Stick to the "golden rule."
5.   Practice participation, not paternalism.
6.   Act when it is your responsibility to do so.
7.   Above all, do no harm.[2]

For the fire service professional to revert to the basic goal of protection of life and property is to closely identify with the Greek root of the word ethics,

Fire chiefs' code of ethics The fire chiefs' code of ethics published by the International Association of Fire Chiefs reads as follows:

The purpose of the International Association of Fire Chiefs is to actively support the advancement of the fire service which is dedicated solely to the protection and preservation of life and property against fire and other emergencies coming under the jurisdiction of the fire service. Towards this endeavor, every member of the International Association of Fire Chiefs shall with due deliberation live according to ethical principles consistent with professional conduct and shall:

1. Maintain the highest standards of personal integrity, be honest and straightforward in dealings with others, and avoid conflicts of interest.

2. Place the public's safety and welfare and the safety of firefighters above all other concerns; be supportive of training and education which promote safer living and occupational conduct and habits.

3. Ensure that the lifesaving services offered under the member's direction be provided fairly and equitably to all without regard to other considerations.

4. Be mindful of the needs of peers and subordinates and assist them freely in developing their skills, abilities, and talents to the fullest extent; offer encouragement to those trying to better themselves and the fire service.

5. Foster creativity and be open to consider innovations that may better enable the performance of our duties and responsibilities.

ethos, which means the character or custom of the community.[3] What does the community reasonably expect of our public servants in the protection of life and property?

Professionalism through associations

Another obligation of the fire chief and the fire service as a profession is to foster communication and the exchange of ideas and concerns. The profession of fire protection must also be capable of speaking with one voice and addressing the issues that affect its ability to carry out its mission. This can be accomplished in part through local, state, regional, national, international, and special interest organizations.

Major organizations within the fire service include the National Fire Protection Association (NFPA), International Association of Fire Chiefs (IAFC), International Society of Fire Service Instructors (ISFSI), and the International Fire Service Training Association (IFSTA).

National Fire Protection Association (NFPA) The National Fire Protection Association is an independent, voluntary, nonprofit membership organization that was organized in 1896. The activities of the NFPA are technical and educational. Technical activities include development, publication, and dissemination of consensus standards related to life safety and fire protection. Over 2,600 individuals serve as members of technical committees responsible for approximately 260 standards. The organization also publishes *Fire Journal*, *Fire Command*, and *Fire Technology* magazines. In its educational activities, the NFPA attempts to inform the general public about all aspects of fire safety. Most notable in this area is the "Learn Not to Burn" school program for grades K through 8.

International Association of Fire Chiefs (IAFC) The International Association of Fire Chiefs was founded in 1873 to raise the professional status of the fire service and to ensure and maintain protection of life and property from fire. This mission is carried out on an international scale. The members are primarily chief officers of volunteer and paid fire departments. The IAFC is active in applied research geared toward improving local government fire departments. The IAFC also serves as an information exchange medium for chief officers.

International Society of Fire Service Instructors (ISFSI) The International Society of Fire Service Instructors, founded in 1960, is concerned with fire service education and the training and the professionalization of instructors. Members of ISFSI are divided into special interest sections, including one for municipal instructors. ISFSI conducts educational seminars throughout the year and sponsors the Fire Department Instructors Conference (FDIC), a yearly meeting of fire service instructors from across the United States.

International Fire Service Training Association (IFSTA) The International Fire Service Training Association was founded in 1933 for the purpose of developing training materials for the fire service. The association has its offices at Oklahoma State University. Members represent training agencies for the states, provinces, and countries adopting IFSTA publications. Each year committees meet to review and validate the many training manuals published by IFSTA. The overall goal of IFSTA is to improve the fire service through training.

Other associations Examples of special interest and regional organizations are the International Association of Black Professional Fire Fighters, International Association of Arson Investigators, International Municipal Signal Association, and the Fire Marshals Association of North America. Regional organizations include the Metropolitan Committee of the IAFC as well as the regional divisions of the IAFC.

At the local and state level, many jurisdictions have chiefs' associations and state firefighters' associations. These organizations provide a forum for the discussion of local concerns and foster cooperation among the member jurisdictions. Some also provide training, scholarships, and legislative input. An example of one such organization formed to address training concerns among a group of metropolitan departments is the Maryland Council of Fire Rescue Academies, which is made up of training academies or persons responsible for training in departments in the Baltimore/Washington metropolitan area. The council's objective is to foster cooperation, information interchange, and shared resources among its members through such activities as research and development. It also encourages members to share lesson plans and instructional information by adopting a uniform lesson guide, and to sit on state boards affecting fire service operations or activities.

Other professional development opportunities

For chiefs, other fire service managers, and aspiring firefighters, there are other opportunities for pre-service and in-service training as well. They include internships, exchange programs, and formal education and training sessions. Whereas other professions in areas of government service have required, or actively participated in such activities, internships and exchange programs have not been widely used in the fire service.

Internships Interning involves bringing in potential department candidates for a period of time, usually four months to a year, and allowing them to work in the organization in order to gain experience and insight into the fire service. One type of internship that has been effectively employed in some departments has personnel within the department spend a period of time in another section or division; for example, suppression personnel may be assigned to training or prevention for one or two days a month.

Other systems have developed cadet programs in order to provide high school students with an opportunity to view the fire service as a potential career. This activity generally includes some type of on-the-job training that may approximate interning.

Apprentice training Since 1982, Buena Park, California (population 65,000), has been operating a three-year apprentice firefighter program that combines practical experience with technical studies in fire science.

The apprentice program is grounded in a clearly articulated set of beliefs about the purpose and value of an apprenticeship. The department defines an apprenticeship as training in an occupation that requires "a . . . diverse range of skills as well as maturity and independence of judgment." The apprenticeship program is designed to ensure that participants, under close supervision, are given the opportunity to acquire both the necessary skills and the judgment to apply them.

Mastery of a trade, as defined by the department, occurs through the achievement of four goals: (1) acquiring all or most of the requisite skills; (2) perfecting the use of each skill; (3) bringing each skill up to the level of speed and accuracy required on the job; and (4) learning to use specific skills in combination with other skills.

As part of its planned program of job skill development, the department places apprentices on a regular schedule of job rotation. Although participants in the program perform nearly all the tasks assigned to regular firefighters, apprentices are not used to meet the required complement of firefighters; they are considered supplemental staff only. However, an apprentice who has completed six months in the program is permitted to serve as a regular firefighter for a maximum of three shifts per year. These shifts provide an opportunity to evaluate the apprentice's progress.

To qualify, participants must be high school graduates, accredited by a California Fire Academy as Firefighter I, and be in good physical health. Upon completion of a two-week basic training course, apprentices are assigned to a company on a twenty-four-hour shift. They are paid at minimum wage for all hours worked for the first year and at minimum plus one dollar thereafter. Participants receive holiday, vacation, and sick leave benefits at one-half the rate granted regular, full-time employees; health and accident insurance is identical to that provided for regular employees.

Vacancy permitting, apprentices may be promoted to the position of regular probationary firefighter under three conditions: (1) a minimum of six months satisfactory performance as an apprentice; (2) successful completion of a promotional examination including both academic and practical elements; and (3) a favorable recommendation from supervisors. Regular firefighters are hired only from the ranks of the apprentice program.

The program has four advantages for the participant: the opportunity to develop job skills; a guaranteed wage during training; eligibility for consideration as an entry-level firefighter in the Buena Park service; and the chance to evaluate the position of firefighter. The program also provides a number of advantages for Buena Park: for example, it helps the city meet affirmative action goals; provides a steady supply of skilled, locally recruited and trained firefighters; enables the city to pay recruits at a level that is commensurate with their experience; permits unsatisfactory employees to be terminated before extensive investment has been made in their training; and reduces overtime for regular firefighters.

Exchange programs   Now that the technology of firefighting is rapidly changing and expanding, there is a limit to what the fire chief or fire officer can learn within the confines of one department. To facilitate increased exposure, exchange programs may be arranged with another department, branch of government, or organization.

Exchange programs may have an even more limited application but perhaps offer a greater opportunity for department enhancement. Traditionally the fire service professional has received the sum of his or her education, training, and experience within one organization. This has tended to institutionalize department procedures and prejudices, while excluding constructive ideas and innovations that may have been developed in another department. To avoid this problem, some educational institutions limit or refuse to appoint their own Ph.D. graduates to faculty positions. Although it is probably unnecessary to suggest such a radical step in the fire service, there seems to be ample opportunity for individuals with similar education and experience to be exchanged among various departments for limited periods of time. Such exchanges may in the future lead to permanent or periodic transfers and opportunities for lateral entry.

Resources for formal education and training   The most important means of accomplishing professionalism is education and training. Because this area is so important, the remainder of this chapter focuses on education and training in the fire service. Fire departments can obtain information on training programs and materials from various sources. At the national level, the National Fire Academy, part of the National Emergency Training Center of the Federal Emergency Management Agency, has developed numerous train-the-trainer packages. It provides complete courses, including student materials and visual aids.

Many of the national fire service organizations conduct regular conferences as well as professional development programs. The International Association of Fire Chiefs, the International Society of Fire Service Instructors (ISFSI), and the National Fire Protection Association (NFPA) hold one or two conferences a year.

The International Fire Service Training Association publishes a series of fire service training manuals which are internationally validated on a regular basis. IFSTA also provides visual aids to supplement many of the manuals.

Almost every state has a fire training program. Although the scope and size of such programs vary, they provide training courses at the local level and/or at a central campus. Some state programs emphasize skills training, whereas others cover such advanced subjects as staff and command, instructor training, management techniques, and special response units.

The National Fire Academy   The National Fire Academy (NFA) offers a wide range of training programs in fire service technology, fire incident management, fire prevention and risk management, and fire service organizational management, designed to improve students' abilities to protect their communities from the threat of fire.

The NFA, located in Emmitsburg, Maryland, is part of the National Emergency Training Center established by the Federal Emergency Management Agency. Through programs delivered in Emmitsburg and through an extensive off-campus outreach effort, the NFA offers courses at the college and university levels for command and staff officers, technical specialists, and executive fire officers. A special "train-the-trainer" program is designed to prepare state and local training personnel to use the academy's course offerings in their local jurisdictions.

Information and catalogs are available from the National Emergency Training Center, 16825 S. Seton Avenue, Emmitsburg, Maryland 21727-8995.

In many areas, vocational or trade schools provide courses for fire service personnel. The particular classes vary, but in many states there is a highly developed delivery system to bring firefighter training into the field.

The various trade journals contain many advertisements from training services and consultants. Although the quality and expertise of the service may not be apparent, this may be another source of training programs, especially in highly technical or specialized areas such as driver training and advanced rescue techniques.

The training officer should also look at other departments in the area and review their training programs. It is not necessary or useful for each department to "reinvent the wheel." The formation of a training officers' group or committee at the county or regional level is an effective means of promoting mutual cooperation among departments on a regular basis.

Developing a training program

Whether the actual training is to be conducted inside or outside the department, the department needs to develop a training program. The idea of developing a training program may seem overwhelming at first, especially in view of the many variables that must be considered. However, a comprehensive program planning process will enable departments both large and small to accomplish this task. This section reviews the program development process. Many of the steps required for program development are applicable to other phases of department operations and may have already been addressed by the department.

Before the program development process can begin, even before a training officer or coordinator can be assigned to the program, the department administration must be convinced that the department needs a training section and must make a commitment to support a departmental training program. Then the program planning process can begin.

The program planning process is the means by which a defined, workable program of activities is developed to meet a department's training objectives. Program planning

1. Is a teaching and learning process
2. Is continuous
3. Provides for continuity as well as flexibility
4. Is based on determined and perceived needs
5. Must consider the people involved
6. Is based on realistic and definable objectives
7. Provides a definite plan of action to meet objectives
8. Includes evaluation to show measurable changes in departmental and personnel actions.

There are five major steps to the program planning process: needs assessment, formulation of objectives, program selection/development, program delivery, and evaluation (see Figure 18–1).

Needs assessment

The purpose of program planning is to develop a plan of action to bring about change that will move an organization or individual to a defined level or state. A department's goals and objectives are set through a planning process (Chapter 4) and monitored through constant evaluation (Chapter 5). The training program should further the mission of the department as a whole. A needs assessment is the means by which the goals or objectives of a training program are identified and defined. It should consider organizational needs, learner needs, and environmental needs.

Figure 18–1　The program planning process.

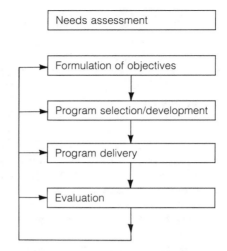

Organizational needs　The department should answer the question "What level when?" To what level of training should personnel be taken and when should they reach this level? What are the future plans of the department and how will these affect training? Will the department be establishing a hazardous materials team in the near future? Will the ambulance service be upgraded to advanced life support? Questions like these must be considered during the needs assessment. It is important that the training supervisor be aware of departmental plans and activities.

Learner needs　Learner needs are the gaps between what a firefighter knows and what he or she needs to know in order to do the job as required by the department. An example of a gap would be requiring an engine company to respond to medical calls without providing emergency medical training. This gap would be translated into the objective of providing such training for engine company personnel.

　Learner needs may include needs expressed or perceived by the individuals in the department. Learner needs also include such personal concerns as safety, security, and sense of worth and belonging. If an individual perceives a training activity as threatening to his or her well-being or security, the training will not be effective.

Environmental needs　Environmental needs are those related to the environment or conditions under which a firefighter must function. The need for training in the use of protective breathing apparatus or effective emergency vehicle operation are examples of environmental needs. Also included in this category may be special needs germane to a particular locality or condition.

　A needs assessment can be carried out in different ways. It may be advisable in some cases to enlist an outsider to perform the assessment so as to obtain an unbiased view. Approaches to needs assessment may include

1. Reviewing requests for training from field personnel and officers
2. Interviewing personnel on their perceptions of what the job entails
3. Reviewing department job descriptions and comparing them to current training activities
4. Reviewing accident reports for common causes that could be addressed through training
5. Reviewing the fire service literature for job analyses performed by other fire departments
6. Conducting surveys of personnel to determine areas of interest for training

7. Reviewing goals and objectives established for the department
8. Reviewing national standards for relevant positions.

Formulation of objectives

One of the more difficult tasks facing the program developer is to translate identified needs into a curriculum. This task involves three steps—screening, grouping, and prioritizing.

Screening is a matter of scrutinizing each need at three levels. First, is the expressed need consistent with departmental goals and objectives? Second, can the need be met with the available resources? Is it feasible within the scope of the department's operation? Third, are the needs consistent with learner and environmental considerations?

Once the needs have been screened, those that need to be addressed are grouped into like areas. For example, all those related to engine company activities, all those related to officer training, and so on, are grouped together. The objectives in each group are then prioritized. This priority may be based on frequency of the need being expressed during the needs assessment, immediate departmental goals, availability of resources, necessity to address one need before being able to address others. Once the needs have been prioritized, they can be translated into program objectives.

The key to a successful training program lies in establishing clear, concise objectives. As R. F. Mager notes, without them, there will be no basis for selecting training methods and materials or for evaluating progress.[4] The basic reason for establishing objectives is to state the desired outcome of the course in specific terms. This outcome should be carefully stated in writing, so that the desired intent is clear to all readers and means the same thing to each one.

Trainers should also exercise care in distinguishing between course content and specific objectives. For example, the statement, ''Practice with ladders will be conducted,'' is a description of one of the activities of the course. Contrast that with the objective that might say, ''The student shall demonstrate how to raise and place a 35-foot ladder in 30 seconds as part of a two person team.''

It takes three steps to prepare an objective:

1. Determine the specific behavior that the student will actually exhibit as evidence of having learned the skill. In the example above, the specific behavior is to demonstrate the action. Other key words that could be used include *write, compare, list, identify,* and *construct.*
2. Determine the conditions under which the student will exhibit the skills that have been learned. Again, using the example above, the conditions require that the student raise the 35-foot ladder, place the ladder, and be part of a two-person team. If a department had both wooden and aluminum ladders, the objective would specify that both kinds must be raised and placed.
3. Determine the measures of performance. The example used a time limit of 30 seconds. Other measures could include the ability to answer written or oral questions or to make comparisons against a standard performance list.

It is important to remember that all three steps must take place in preparing most objectives. If there is a clear objective, the answer to the following questions will be yes:

1. If a fire training supervisor is given the objective and a student to perform it, do the supervisor and the objective writer both agree that the student gave a competent performance?

2. If the student performed the objective more than once in exactly the same manner, is the evaluation consistent?

Finally, it is not necessary to include the entire objective in a single sentence. As the skills become more complex, it will take additional sentences to describe the objective desired. The final criterion for the acceptability of an objective is its clarity.

Program selection/development

If no program is conveniently available to meet the department's training needs, the training officer will have to develop one. The question then is what to include as the contents of the course. The objectives developed through the needs assessment will serve as the basis for the curriculum. The steps of the curriculum development process are task analysis, development of performance objectives, determination of evaluation method, determination of the instructional sequence, and selection of the instructional technique. Throughout the curriculum development process, the training officer must continually evaluate what is being planned against available resources. There is no point in developing a sophisticated training program using computer-aided instruction if the department does not have access to computer hardware.

Task analysis   Task analysis is the process of breaking down the various things necessary to accomplish an objective into specific, defined parts or steps.

A job is a composite of the operations performed by an individual. A job has a specific beginning and end and produces a specific result or product. A task is defined as "a logically related set of actions required for the completion of a job objective. A task is a complete job element."[5]

Each task to be performed should be listed. The analyst should observe an individual perform the job correctly and list the tasks involved and the order in which they occur. Information needed by the student to complete the task must also be noted. Figure 18-2 is an example of a task analysis work sheet.

Development of performance objectives   After the task analysis has been completed, the training officer develops performance objectives. Performance objectives can be defined as the least acceptable performance by a student at the end of an instructional period.

The main difference between the task analysis and the preparation of the performance objectives is that the task analysis covers all the steps necessary to accomplish the job, including anything learned earlier on the job or in the course. On the other hand, the performance objectives relate specifically to the outcome of the training.

Determination of evaluation method   Next the training officer needs to determine how students' performance will be evaluated. The method selected to evaluate the students should match the objectives and be consistent with the instructional method. The instructor should evaluate skill-related objectives that contain terms such as *demonstrate, perform*, or similar action words by observing the student doing the skill, perhaps comparing student performance against a check sheet. An objective that requires the student to "discuss," "integrate," or "describe" would be evaluated by means of a written test or oral report. If the evaluation fails to consider the proper objectives, it will be inaccurate and unfair.

To avoid this pitfall, the training officer must have an understanding of the three domains of learning: psychomotor, affective, and cognitive. Each performance objective will fall into one of these domains. The psychomotor domain encompasses physical skills learning—things we do with our hands and body. Most basic fire service training is in the psychomotor domain. The affective domain relates to the emotions or feelings. Objectives in the affective domain are rare because of the difficulty in measuring performance. Cognitive domain objectives deal with thinking, synthesis, integration, and application or extrapolation. A course in tactics or fireground command would contain cognitive objectives. Cognitive subject material is most often presented in lecture or discussion groups with no ''hands-on'' activities, and students are evaluated by means of written tests.

Determination of the instructional sequence   Having developed the performance objectives and determined an evaluation method, the training officer can now determine the sequence of the instruction. The material for each course must be taught in a logical sequence. The training officer should prepare the outline so that basic material is taught first, before proceeding to the more complex subjects. In general, the course should begin with an overview of the

Figure 18–2 Task analysis work sheet.

UNIVERSITY OF MARYLAND	
COLLEGE PARK, MARYLAND	

MARYLAND FIRE AND RESCUE INSTITUTE

OCCUPATIONAL ANALYSIS FORM

Analyst George E. Thomas, Jr.	**DATE** April 12, 1988
OCCUPATION Fire Service	**BLOCK** Suppression
UNIT Engine Company 34	**TASK** Hydrant Man
JOB Properly Operate the Hydrant	

REFERENCE MFRI Basic Manual, SOP for Westminster Fire Engine & Hose Company No. 1

	What the Student Does (Operations Listed in the Order in Which Done)	**What the Student Must Know** (Key Points, Factors that Must Be Known, Condition or Influence)
1.	Unbuckle safety strap and step off tail board with hydrant wrench	Where the hydrant wrench is located; how to unbuckle safety strap
2.	Go to the hydrant and remove the steamer cap by turning it counterclockwise using the hydrant wrench	Where hydrant is located; how to use hydrant wrench; how to remove steamer cap
3.	Open the hydrant by turning the nut on top of the hydrant slowly counterclockwise until completely open using the hydrant wrench	How to use hydrant wrench; how to open the hydrant properly
4.	Close the hydrant by turning the nut on top of the hydrant slowly clockwise until completely closed using the hydrant wrench	How to use hydrant wrench; how to close the hydrant properly
5.	Replace the steamer cap by turning it clockwise until hand tight	How to replace steamer cap properly
6.	Return to the tail board, replace the hydrant wrench and buckle safety strap	Where hydrant wrench came from; what happens if not replaced; how to buckle safety strap

Hazardous materials training Fridley, Minnesota (population 30,000), has approached training and preparation of hazardous materials incidents and spills using a four-part program.

The city's fire department of five career firefighters and thirty paid on-call firefighters handles an average of twelve to fourteen potentially serious hazardous materials incidents a year. To prepare its firefighters, the department sends them to hazardous materials incident schools throughout the nation and to state and regional programs.

The department also has asked industry to help it identify potential problems and to provide on-site resources that can help it identify the products and tactics needed to safely and successfully mitigate the incident.

Twice each year simulated incidents are staged to involve the industry, medical support systems, and the fire department mutual aid capability. These simulations are generally videotaped and critiqued by the participants. During these drills, any member may be the incident commander or be assigned any other role. Thus, all members of the department develop a better insight into the total management of a hazardous materials incident or spill.

Finally, the department has developed and continually updates a brief hazardous materials incident guide for officers and incident commanders. This guide includes basic and required actions as to notification and call lists; it also includes resource call lists of specialized equipment and personnel.

---

entire subject or job, then move on to the various parts of the job, and conclude by putting the parts together as a whole. Mager describes five techniques to use when determining the sequencing of material:

1. General to specific. Present the overall view first, gradually working down to specific procedures.
2. By interest. The first topic to be covered is the one the student is most interested in. Then work toward areas that are of least interest but that the student is required to know.
3. By logic. Begin with the material that needs to be used as the foundation and build up to more complex information.
4. By skill. Teach the material by skill so that groups of subject areas can be mastered separately.
5. By frequency. Cover the skills that are needed most frequently first, working down to those least used.[6]

Program delivery

The selection of delivery techniques will also be guided by the performance objectives. Some material can be presented only in one way, whereas other material can be approached from various angles. The instructor should select a technique that will do the job and will also maintain interest in the subject and be feasible with resources available. Among the techniques instructors can use are lectures, demonstrations, discussion, case studies, role playing, simulations, games, and programmed instruction.

Lectures The lecture method is the technique used most frequently. Here, the instructor merely stands in front of the students and speaks. For the most part, it is a one-way conversation, and the only interruptions are questions.

The most serious drawback to the lecture technique is that it cannot take into account the different capabilities, attitudes, and interests of students, which can vary so widely that the lecture may not reach them all. If it does not, the student's mind will wander from the subject. The best thing that can be said for the lecture is that it is inexpensive and is easy to prepare.

Demonstrations   The demonstration technique is an excellent means of teaching manipulative skills. This process consists of three steps:

1. The instructor demonstrates the skill.
2. Students practice the skill under the supervision of the instructor.
3. The students are tested to determine that the skill has been learned.

Discussion   The discussion method is used when interaction is necessary. There is not usually an instructor as such, but a leader who guides the discussion and keeps it on track. This method is an effective way of getting students to understand concepts and to change their attitudes.

Since there is a great deal of interaction, material that is unclear can be amplified and explained. This is the greatest advantage of the discussion over the lecture method. The students are able to ask questions, discover possible answers, and evaluate such answers as solutions. This helps them understand and remember material.

The success of the discussion technique depends largely on the leader. This individual must be able to keep the interest up, promote a learning atmosphere, and keep the conversation going. The leader must take care not to turn the discussion into a lecture by dominating the conversation. The leader must do a great deal of preparation if the discussion is to accomplish its goal.

Case studies   The trainer can prepare in writing an actual or a fictitious case history problem in the subject area to be studied. The case study method enables the student to develop an understanding of the principles being taught. Instead of looking for a single, simple answer, the student learns that there are several ways to attack a problem, each with its advantages and disadvantages. The student learns to weigh these before deciding on a course of action. Since each student will look at the problem in a different way, a number of alternative solutions can be explored by the group.

Role playing   One of the best ways to learn how to deal with a situation is to observe an event actually occurring and then to decide on a course of action. In this method, the drama is brought to the classroom. Role playing involves preparing a script and using the trainees to play out the roles.

Usually the students chosen to participate are given sketchy information about the overall problem and the types of personalities involved. From this they improvise the script to play out what might happen. The remaining students then discuss the outcome.

As with other teaching techniques there are major advantages and disadvantages. Role playing is not suitable for all types of subject material. In addition, the skill of the students in spontaneously developing the script is important. They should not overact, make facetious comments, or ridicule other personnel outside the context of the problem. Specific advantages are that the technique simulates the real world, the students participate, they get practice in interpersonal skills, and receive immediate feedback.

Simulation   Training officers in fireground command is difficult, because a large-scale fire is hard to reproduce in the classroom. As a result, simulation techniques have become increasingly popular. There are basically two kinds of simulation: visual and live.

With a combination of slide and overnead projectors and special equipment, it is possible to produce a visual simulation of a fire. The fire actually appears to be burning the building and can be increased or decreased in size. Communications equipment can be used along with a dispatching system to add to the realism. Some departments project different views of the same incident in which the personnel coordinating the incident are unable to see the other views. This forces the officers to utilize the communications system.

A simulated exercise can be an excellent means of training individuals to handle a large-scale incident. A staged hazardous materials accident with victims made up to simulate various injuries can provide training for firefighting as well as for emergency medical services. And officers can learn about the problems of command as well as the need for a central operating post.

The success of each of these two techniques, however, depends on the realism of the exercise. As the students become involved, the pace picks up and the tension builds. The instructors and evaluators need to prepare the problems very carefully to maintain the realism.

Games   Games are structured exercises designed to teach specific principles or ideas. They can be as simple as putting information on a sheet of paper, or as complex as interacting with a computer. Games can vary in length from an hour to as long as a week. Subjects range from management styles to personnel management and teamwork.

The major advantage of this technique is that the student becomes involved in the problem solving and the conclusions. Games can also be used to illustrate various management tools under active conditions.

One of the best games to use in training fire service supervisors is the in-basket exercise. Each student is given an in-basket containing written materials such as incoming letters, memoranda, procedures, grievances, and meeting notices. The student then must decide how to deal with all of these pieces of paper. Some of these matters will be delegated to subordinates. In some cases the student will prepare a reply for some other staff member and in others will prepare a direct answer.

Again, the instructors will need to review many possible alternatives and establish some expected, standardized responses. The students can then discuss their solutions and the reasons they were chosen.

Programmed instruction   Programmed instruction provides step-by-step procedures and gives the student immediate feedback concerning his or her understanding of the material. The programmed media are designed so that students must respond to questions after some information has been provided. On the basis of the answers to the questions, the students receive a tailored instructional program. If they give the wrong answer, further explanation is provided. If they answer correctly, they move on to more complex material.

A variation of programmed instruction is computer-aided instruction (CAI). Information is displayed on a computer screen and the student responds to questions through keyboard entry. The computer not only directs the student to the proper material in the presentation, but can also record frequency of wrong responses and provide the student and training officer with a profile of the student's performance.

Evaluation

The final step in the program planning process is a critical one—evaluation of the training program. After investing a great deal of staff time and funds, fire service administrators need to have a way of determining whether the program is accomplishing its objectives. If the evaluation is to be of any use, it must provide feedback for the program development and revision process. After a program has been presented, the training officer, course instructor, and course developer (these may be the same person) should review the information obtained through the evaluation process and make the necessary changes in the program, both at the delivery level and at the curriculum level. Evaluation is a continuous and dynamic process.

The criteria and method of evaluation should be determined during the program planning process so that the evaluator will be forced to look at all areas of the program, not just those that indicate positive results. There are two broad approaches to program evaluation: evaluation of outputs and evaluation of outcomes.

Outputs are the end products of the training process. These would include class statistics such as number of students completing, total student hours, cost per student hour, number of personnel eligible for promotion, and so on. *Outcomes* are more extrinsic factors relating to the results of training. They are not directly quantifiable in some instances, but are evaluated in terms of other measures. Examples of outcomes would be a reduced fire loss since the training program has begun, reduction in reported back injuries as a result of a program on proper lifting techniques, increased morale, or reduced operating cost.

Student evaluations of a training program and instructor can also help point out the strengths and weaknesses of a program. If students can provide their responses anonymously, they are more likely to give a frank evaluation, especially if the instructor was of higher rank in the department. Student evaluations have both advantages and disadvantages. Advantages are that the evaluations

1. Reflect students' perceptions of the course and the instruction
2. Indicate areas students had trouble understanding or mastering and areas students liked or found most useful
3. If used with experienced students, provide a means of comparing course to others
4. May make the instructor aware of unknown habits or shortcomings
5. Allow students to feel they have made a contribution to the training process.

Disadvantages are that

1. Students may lack the experience base to evaluate program, especially recruits.
2. Students may be influenced by instructor's personality and camaraderie developed over the course of instruction.
3. Students may be afraid of reprisal for a negative evaluation.
4. Evaluations may be influenced by student interest in the subject matter or by the final grade—poor grade, poor evaluation; good grade, good evaluation.

Administering a training program

To administer a training program, the training officer and departmental managers need to consider a number of practical questions. These include scheduling, personnel qualifications and selection, record keeping, and physical training facilities.

Scheduling

Training must be scheduled so that the training identified in the department's needs analysis is provided for all members in a timely and efficient manner. Care must be taken to ensure that those tasks that are essential or subject to rapid degradation receive proper attention and are repeated. Proper scheduling involves more than simply rotating through a predetermined list of basic skills.

Scheduling is affected by a number of considerations:

1. Will the training be held at a central location or a field delivery site? While formal classes may be held at a central facility, in-service drills must be scheduled in coordination with the availability of field sites.
2. Is this training directed to the company as a whole or to individuals of a specific rank?
3. Can the company remain in service during the training session, or will the nature of the training make it necessary to keep the apparatus and personnel out of service during the entire session?

These and other factors should be considered in scheduling department training. Flexibility in scheduling provides several benefits. Since not all emergency activities take place in daylight hours, training should be scheduled accordingly. Further, departments with both career and volunteer personnel can greatly enhance the spirit of cooperation by ensuring that both groups of personnel train together. This means that some, if not all, of the career personnel training will have to be conducted on evenings or weekends. Volunteers who are available during the day should be encouraged to attend regularly scheduled career training programs and in-service drills.

Despite all efforts to provide appropriate scheduling, adjustments will be necessary, and contingency plans should be developed. The need to provide realistic training conditions should never compromise safety. The schedule should allow for adjustments whenever training conditions may be unsafe. This may be during inclement weather or when there are insufficient numbers of personnel, when equipment or apparatus is inadequate or inoperative, and, most important, when trained and prepared instructors are not available.

Qualifications for training personnel

A good training program is the key to an efficient fire department. The personnel selected for the training division should therefore be of high caliber.

The policy in many departments that have a promotional vacancy in training is to give the job to the next person on the eligibility list. In many cases, this person wants the promotion, but is not really interested in training. Consequently, this person requests a transfer back to the field. This lack of experience and interest on the part of training personnel can lower morale and create problems within the program. Very little training will be accomplished and the efficiency of the department will drop.

Now that training personnel are required to meet professional standards and be certified, it has become essential to have a highly qualified cadre of instructors. The Fire Service Instructor Professional Qualifications (NFPA 1041)[7] were developed by the Fire Service Instructor Certification Qualifications Committee as one of four committees of the National Professional Qualifications System established by the Joint Council of National Fire Service Organizations.

The purpose of the qualifications system is to establish standards that can be used to determine levels of competency within the fire service. The standards set forth in NFPA 1041 are minimal performance standards for instructors. The NFPA publication lists entrance requirements for all levels of instructors specified in the standard:

2-1 General. The fire service instructor candidate for Instructor I shall be a qualified Fire Fighter III as defined in NFPA 1001.

2-2 Physical Requirements. Instructors at each level of progression shall possess the physical ability to perform all tasks associated with their instructor assignment.[8]

Instructor training literature for the fire service contains little information on instructor criteria or selection. In the *Fire Service Instructor's Guidebook*, Anthony R. Granito presents a series of questions for the instructor to ponder to discover his or her own level of competence in those areas in which the improvement is needed (see accompanying sidebar). The questions in this checklist cover the behavior of a good instructor, stressing administrative and procedural activities.

There is little discussion, however, of the personality of a good instructor. Perhaps the best-known textbook on emergency services instructor training is *Fire Service Instructor* by the International Fire Service Training Association (IFSTA).[9] This text, designed for teaching instructors in accordance with NFPA 1041, lists eight qualities of a good instructor, which are similar to those suggested by Strother and Klus for adult educators.[10] The qualities are a desire to teach, mastery of teaching techniques, ingenuity, competence in subject, an ability to understand and work with people, motivation, empathy, and enthusiasm.[11] There is no reference to a schema for selecting instructors. It is assumed that instructors will be appointed from within the ranks of the emergency service, as this has been customary.

Administrators should ensure that those persons responsible for their department's training have appropriate qualifications. Some states insist that persons instructing fire service personnel be certified, but this is the exception rather than the rule. Although it may not be necessary for the person ultimately responsible for the training activity in a department to be a qualified instructor, persons delivering training sessions should be qualified.

The National Professional Qualifications System The National Professional Qualifications System was begun in 1972 by the Joint Council of National Fire Service Organizations. At that time the council established committees to develop national standards of professional competence within the fire service and an independent National Professional Qualifications Board (NPQB) to oversee and validate the standards in a continuing professional development program.

Working with the National Fire Protection Association, the board and committees have developed standards for all levels of the fire service. To implement the standards nationwide, the board reviews state and local testing procedures and accredits certification agencies or organizations that meet the standards. These accredited agencies or organizations can, in turn, give national certification to members of the fire service who have demonstrated that they have acquired the skills and knowledge necessary to meet a particular standard of professional competence.

To become accredited as a certifying agency, an organization needs to apply to the NPQB, which sends in a team to examine the state certification program administered by the organization and determine whether it meets the criteria set by the board. Accreditation is granted for one year and must be renewed annually.

Accreditation is based on certification on the following standards: NFPA 1001, Fire Fighter; NFPA 1002, Driver/Operator; NFPA 1003, Airport Fire Fighter; NFPA 1004, Medical Technician; NFPA 1021, Fire Officer; NFPA 1031, Fire Inspector; NFPA 1033, Fire Investigator; NFPA 1035, Public Fire Educator; and NFPA 1041, Fire Instructor.

Information on certification, accreditation, and standards may be obtained from the National Professional Qualifications Board Secretariat, Batterymarch Park, Quincy, Massachusetts 02269.

Criteria of a good instructor   A good instructor does the following:

Understands why he or she became an instructor

Has a real commitment to teaching and gets satisfaction from the intangible accomplishments of teaching

Understands students' motivation and knows how to foster it

Shows enthusiasm and knows the subject matter thoroughly

Imparts a sense of professionalism to students

Avoids subjective reactions to students but is capable of empathy

Employs sound teaching principles

Uses performance standards to measure behavior and ensures that students measure up to departmental standards

Attends to practical aspects of instruction: the physical environment of the classroom, personal introductions and attention, conscientious preparation of lesson plans, and clear presentation of lesson material.

These and other guidelines for instructors are discussed by Anthony R. Granito in *Fire Service Instructor's Guidebook* (Boston, Mass.: National Fire Protection Association, 1976), 5–12.

At a minimum, persons responsible for formalized training sessions in course development should meet NFPA 1041, Level II. Fire officers and others who conduct in-service training should be qualified NFPA 1041 Level I instructors.

Training records

With the evolution of local, statewide, and national certification systems that require initial and perhaps subsequent documentation, training records must be complete, clear, and readily available. Although record-keeping systems need not be elaborate or computerized, they must be accurate.

Basically two types of records should be kept. Each fire department member should have a permanent record of the courses taken, as well as any that the individual may have taught. In addition, records should be kept of the training conducted daily.

Individual records   An individual's training records become a permanent source of information for that person as long as he or she is associated with the fire department. Items that should appear in this record include the person's name and social security number, date of appointment, ranks held, courses taken (with class hours and dates completed), grade (if applicable), name of instructor, and also the instructor's comments.

Individual training records should be kept confidential, but members should be permitted to inspect their own training records if they wish to do so. Departments should comply with the appropriate laws for the protection of privacy, particularly the Family Education Rights and Privacy Act (Buckley Amendment). Personal information should not be disclosed unless the member has given prior written consent, and the member should be able to have the training records corrected, where appropriate.

Daily training records   From an analysis of daily training records, administrators can determine which areas are being covered and which are being neglected. These records can provide a measure of the department's efficiency and may also indicate where changes are needed.

However, administrators should guard against developing a paper program that has field officers merely filling in the training forms without actually attending the classes. The fire department then looks good on paper, but probably does not perform well in practice. This situation can be avoided if the training staff monitors in-service classes on a random basis and if each company performs a series of evolutions against an established department standard.

The information on the daily training records should include subject taught, date, time of start and finish of class, instructor, equipment used, and personnel attending.

Data processing of records   Regardless of size, today's fire departments can make effective use of electronic data processing equipment. This equipment can greatly increase a department's ability to keep training records of all kinds up to date and can be used to integrate these records in other department activities.

Administrators should ensure that information requested and compiled in training as well as in all record keeping is needed and utilized. The greatest disincentive to an effective and efficient record keeping system is not to use the data collected. Chapter 6 discusses information systems in detail.

Physical facilities

The best fire service training programs are not necessarily those that have the most outstanding or elaborate training facilities. However, an effective training program must have appropriate facilities and support space to accommodate the training program designed for the department. Quite often the training division shares space with other activities and functions or is assigned equipment and physical space that has been declared surplus by the department or other agencies.

These challenges do not, in themselves, render a program unsuccessful. Many departments have developed excellent support for their programs from renovated facilities and rehabilitated equipment.[12] (See the accompanying sidebar on the Miami Fire Department.)

The key to success lies in the continued commitment of the department to, and the appropriate development of, the department's training program.

Whenever practical, department training, both in-service and formal training classes, should be offered as close to the station as possible. This is particularly important wherever departments utilize volunteer personnel, since travel can complicate schedules that are already tight.

At a minimum, it will be necessary to provide for classroom instruction, outside drill activities, storage, office and other support space. Facilities for specialized training, including such things as flammable liquids, flammable gases, high-rise, confined space rescue, and aircraft firefighting may be necessary.

Local departments operating under fiscal restraints will find that sharing facilities is an excellent way to provide for these needs. While most departments cannot justify building a special purpose training facility for the limited times it may be in use, a regional training effort may provide such justification for a building shared with others who are providing the same type of service. Regional planning groups or area fire chiefs' associations offer an excellent framework in which to begin discussing and implementing the shared facilities concept.

Fixed versus mobile facilities   In an attempt to provide quality support for training needs, many organizations, especially state or regional training agen-

Figure 18–3   The Miami Fire-Rescue Training Center,
which was adapted from an abandoned city incinerator.

Miami Fire-Rescue Training Center   In 1977, the Miami Fire Department began searching for property on which to construct a new Fire-Rescue Training Center to replace the fifty-year-old building that was no longer suitable for training. A $10 million bond program had been approved in 1976, and funds were available for a new, modern facility. A 3- to 5-acre site was needed and it had to be near the inner city. All sites evaluated proved to be too costly or unavailable for this specific purpose.

It was suggested that the department evaluate the city's abandoned incinerator in Coconut Grove, a residential neighborhood. The site was approximately 4 acres and the building interior measured over 60,000 cubic feet (much more space than the depart-

ment could afford to build). An architect was hired to develop a feasibility study comparing several options for new construction and for retrofitting the incinerator as a fire-rescue training facility. The cost to retrofit the existing incinerator was considerably less than constructing a new facility of comparable size, and that option was selected.

The incinerator had some unique features: a ramp leading to the tipping room where the garbage was dumped created an interesting, aesthetically pleasing entrance to the building; large, open spaces on the ground floor were easily converted into an apparatus room for two pumpers, a 100-foot aerial apparatus, and a rescue unit; and a 30-foot deep pit with a sump and piping for drainage could be converted into a rescue diving pool. Be-

cies, have designed and built facilities that can be transported to the local department, training center, or fire station. The development of these mobile training labs (MTLs) has greatly assisted small and medium-size departments that find it difficult to assign companies out of their primary service area for training (see Figure 18–5). The Maryland Fire and Rescue Institute and the University of Maryland have pioneered many mobile training lab props, and others are available commercially.

Figure 18–4 Firefighter training should be as realistic as possible. This training prop was designed to simulate crawling through an attic while wearing breathing apparatus.

cause of its 87-foot height, the building proved to be an excellent radio antenna site as well.

The vast interior could accommodate six levels, which housed a fire museum, a 100-seat auditorium, a TV production studio, an elevator with fireman service, a fire alarm system, a smoke detection system, emergency dispatcher training (computers), air mask training, a 1,200-square-foot maze, a human performance lab (fully equipped strength facility), a fireground tactics simulator, and an emergency medical services open learning center. This facility was designed to provide complete training for all personnel from recruits to chiefs.

Before getting public approval for the necessary zoning changes, department

representatives held several meetings with the neighbors, as well as open public hearings before the local zoning board to answer questions and try to dispel rumors that fire trucks would be racing up and down the streets with sirens screaming while fire and smoke belched from every window of the building. Ultimately, the city commission approved rezoning. Construction of the new facility began July 8, 1981, and was completed March 21, 1983.

By creatively utilizing available resources that the city was unable to use, the fire department was able to develop a training center, at a cost considerably less than anticipated, that has become a model for fire-rescue training centers around the country.

Figure 18–5 A mobile training facility used in Prince George's County, Maryland.

Some types of training lend themselves more appropriately to mobile units or props than others. Effective structural firefighting training has not, to date, been successfully transported to the local fire station. Some of the training props that have been mobilized include breathing apparatus, maze, flammable gas, sprinklers (residential, commercial and industrial), tactical simulation, drill towers, and pressurized vessel patching (chlorine).

Structural firefighting facilities   Special attention should be given to structural firefighting facilities as many programs emphasize the need to provide entry-level firefighters initial training and in-service personnel continued training in the techniques of structural firefighting.

The use of buildings scheduled for demolition for the purpose of interior structural fire attack is usually discouraged by professional emergency services training personnel, except as a last resort. Whenever these types of buildings are to be used for training purposes, strict adherence to a formalized safety and procedure policy is imperative. NFPA Standard 1403 addresses live fire training evolutions in structures. The purpose of this standard is to provide for ''aggressive, coordinated, interior fire suppression operations with a minimum exposure to risk for the participants.'' Whenever possible, structural firefighting training should be conducted in a facility designed for that purpose so that instructors can concentrate on the techniques and procedures to be introduced, reinforced, or evaluated without having to be concerned about the safety of the students and themselves owing to the unpredictability of fire behavior within the structure.

Conclusion

Professional development is a continuous and complex responsibility for the fire service manager. Among its many facets are a recognition that the fire service constitutes not only a job but a profession, with its own unique body of knowledge, an orientation toward community service, and a commitment to a set of ethical standards. Professional development also involves the promotion of growth and development opportunities through professional associations and meetings, internships and exchange programs, and formal education and training curricula.

A large portion of this chapter has focused on the development and delivery of departmental training programs, which are a major professional development tool within any department. Taken together, professional development and training are the cornerstone of an effective and well-managed fire service organization.

1 Jay M. Schafritz, *Dictionary of Personnel Management and Labor Relations* (Oak Park, Ill.: Moore, 1980), 275.

2 Chris Lee, "Ethics Training: Facing the Tough Questions," *Training*, March 1986, 32.

3 Ibid.

4 Robert F. Mager, *Preparing Instructional Objectives* (Belmont, Calif.: Fearon, 1964), 3.

5 Robert F. Mager and Kenneth M. Beach, Jr., *Developing Vocational Instruction* (Belmont, Calif.: Fearon, 1967), 10.

6 Ibid., 59–61.

7 National Fire Protection Association, *Standard for Fire Service Instructor Professional Qualifications*, NFPA 1041 (Quincy, Mass.: 1981).

8 Ibid., 5.

9 International Fire Service Training Association Committee, *Fire Service Instructor*, 4th ed., Gene Carlson, ed. (Stillwater, Okla.: Fire Protection Publications, Oklahoma State University, 1981), 5–22.

10 George B. Strother and John B. Klus, *Administration of Continuing Education* (Belmont, Calif.: Wadsworth, 1982).

11 International Fire Service Training Association Committee, *Fire Service Instructor*, 5–22.

12 K. E. McCullough, "Trash to Training," *Fire Engineering*, December 1984, 62, 64.

19 The future of the fire service

Beginning about 1960 the United States became preoccupied with the future. In popular books, authors such as Alvin Toffler, John Diebold, and John Naisbitt highlighted past and present trends and projected them forward.[1] Beginning with Toffler's book *Future Shock,* and continuing through Naisbitt's *Mega-Trends,* the literature reminds us that there always has been and always will be change. The best evidence for that is the past.

Fire protection services have often been characterized as "traditional" and resistant to change. History suggests otherwise, however, and Chapter 1 demonstrated that the fire service has been constantly changing in mission, methodology, and technology for the last century. It is important to understand the history of the fire service in order to comprehend its future, for the forces that will shape the delivery of fire protection services tomorrow came from the past and are present today. It is also important to understand the process of change, for change is inevitable and forms the link between the past and the future.

Models of change

Two models provide some insight into change. Figure 19–1, for example, identifies four areas in which change occurs—knowledge, attitudes, individual behavior, and group behavior—and describes for each the difficulty (low to high) and time frame (short to long) involved in introducing change. For example, it takes a relatively short time and is not very difficult to achieve a change in knowledge. Participating in a fire service training course or a community college program or even reading a text or other professional literature can increase an individual's knowledge. New knowledge, in turn, may render old attitudes obsolete. As the figure shows, changes in attitudes are more difficult and take longer to bring about. If a person acquires new knowledge but does not accept it, change at the next levels—individual and group behavior—will not occur. A classic example is incident command training. Many have learned about incident command theory and put it to use right away. Others have been informed but are reluctant to adopt it. Attitude is the difference in the rate of change in the methodology of handling incidents.

Individual behavior is the outward expression of acceptance, meaning a change in the way a person acts. Early in their fire service career, for example, recruits acquire new knowledge about the paramilitary structure of the fire service. Shortly, they begin to accept the fact that they are expected to conform to rules and regulations as set forth in operations and procedures manuals. Subsequently, they change their behavior, at least when they are dealing with others inside the fire service. Those who do not conform to these required changes in individual behavior are generally screened out at that point.

As the model suggests, group behavior is the most difficult to change, and change at this level takes a relatively long time. Changes in group behavior depend on changes in knowledge, attitudes, and individual behavior, but they also go further, encompassing the performance of the organization as a whole. For example, if an organization goes through a hazardous materials training

Figure 19–1   Change model.

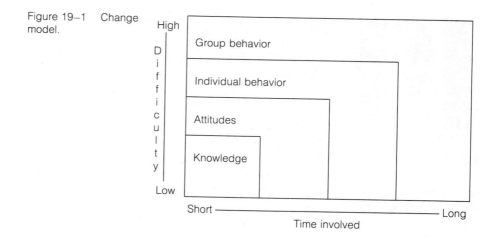

program, each individual will gain new knowledge, will almost certainly change his or her attitudes toward the hazardous materials problem, and will begin to behave differently when handling hazmat incidents. Then the engine company, the shift, and, ultimately, the whole fire department will begin to handle hazardous materials problems in a more sophisticated and complex fashion. This is a change in group behavior. It is an evolutionary process.

The second model, illustrated in Figure 19–2, suggests that people can more or less be placed in a standard distribution curve in terms of their orientation toward change. Individuals on one end of the curve are extremely change-oriented and actively seek out new ways to do things. Those at the other end resist change at all costs. The remainder are distributed in the middle, with different degrees of receptivity and commitment.

The distribution curve is further divided into three main segments: state of the art, mainstream, and obsolescence. Persons falling into the "state-of-the-art" segment have an orientation toward the future. They are creators, innovators, and early adopters. The attitude of this group is one of identifying, classifying, and utilizing new concepts, technologies, and methodologies as quickly as they can be acquired.

The middle of the chart reflects the mainstream, those who adopt an innovation after it has become more or less established. Those who represent the "bandwagon" and those who are late adopters tend to be cautious about change and oriented toward predictability and control of results.

Finally, "obsolescence" is reflected by the late adopters, the resistors, and the refusers of change. These individuals are oriented toward the past and accept change only when it is forced upon them.

The individuals, departments, and local governments that make up the fire service fall all along the continuum represented by the distribution curve. Furthermore, acceptance of change varies with the specific innovation. For example, few firefighters today would defend the use of canister gas masks to fight hazardous materials incidents. The new technology that has been adopted has had a positive influence on the physical safety of firefighters. Nonetheless, there are still those who resist the use of computers, sprinkler systems, and other innovations in fire protection methodology.

One of the greatest problems in understanding change is that it is a process, not an event. However, change is brought about as a result of events—decisions or actions that ultimately change an individual, an organization, and a profession. An organization that is in the process of change is always in a transitional state. It is always moving on a continuum that reflects incremental change. A

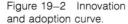

Figure 19–2 Innovation and adoption curve.

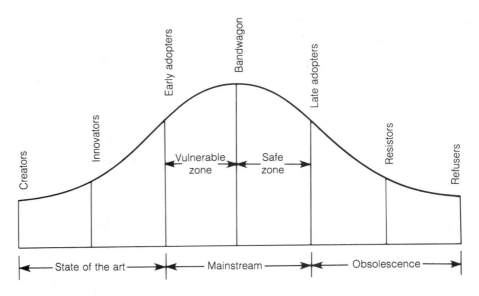

fire department is always moving from the state of stability created by its past toward a new way of doing things—the future. This process often creates stress and conflict. For example, one can observe a great deal of difficulty in an organization that is moving from a totally volunteer force to a combination or totally paid force. Another more subtle example might be the adoption of a company fire inspection program in a department that has no fire prevention program. The new role of ''fire inspector'' may be difficult for a firefighter to fulfill. A change in roles can create anxiety.

Initially, there is resistance to a new way of doing things, but this book has shown how, with skillful management, change can become accepted.

Impediments to change

Given the range of attitudes toward change, no smooth transition or predictable outcome can be projected from the patterns emerging in the fire service profession. Instead, a range of ''futures'' can be predicted, each based on the behavior of an organization and the individuals in it as they attempt (or neglect to attempt) to predict and control events.

The future—or futures—of the fire service can be viewed at four levels:

1. The personal future of each individual who is part of the service, encompassing career opportunities, personal innovation and contribution, and the individual's changing role in a complex organization
2. The organizational future that grows out of the individual and collective actions of the members of the organization
3. The professional future, or the overall direction in which the profession will move as a result of collective attitudes, beliefs, and acceptance of new ideas by its leadership
4. The societal future, or the impact of economic conditions, community attitudes, and social values on the public perception of the contribution of fire protection to the quality of life.

Change is frequently hindered by inherent conflicts among the needs of individuals, organizations, professions, and society as a whole. For example, individual needs for growth and change may be incompatible with organizational needs for stability and continuity. Conversely, organizational needs for change may threaten individual job security. And conflicting goals may affect what society expects from the fire service. In its concern for quality of life, society may believe it wants a "risk-free" society, yet that desire may be at odds with what society is willing to pay to protect itself from risks.

Change is also hindered by the tendency of a profession to place limits on itself. In his book *The Structure of Scientific Revolutions,* Thomas S. Kuhn finds that most systems are subject to a "paralysis of paradigm syndrome."[2] Kuhn says that in almost every scientific or professional setting there is a tendency to establish a paradigm, or limit of knowledge.

The paradigm can be a limitation to predicting the future. If an individual, an organization, or a society believes there are limits to its knowledge, that tends to be a self-fulfilling prophecy. Further, Kuhn states that often some type of "anomaly" occurs to challenge the validity of the "facts." This anomaly challenges the status quo and suggests a "new truth." Evidence of this type of challenge appears throughout history in the form of breakthroughs in fields of human behavior, aerospace, electronics, medicine, and so forth. Historically, breakthroughs in the fire service have occurred in fire apparatus, fire protection engineering, and personnel practices that have changed the fire service knowledge base.

Dealing with new areas of knowledge will be one of the challenges for the fire service. Breaking out of its own paradigm and challenging the status quo of existing technologies, methods, and attitudes regarding fire protection will create stress and conflict. And it will surely result in the evolution of a new fire service.

Finally, change is frequently limited by artificial time frames. Although change is ongoing, people and organizations need defined time frames or targets for achieving and measuring change. Thus, they set goals and deadlines that are some distance in the future but close enough to allow them to measure the outcomes of individual performances or decisions. This time frame is called a *horizon*.

Many firefighting organizations operate on a horizon of approximately one year, which is the normal budget cycle. By developing an annual budget, departments have some degree of influence over what things will look like over the next twelve months as the day-to-day activities of the organization unfold in accordance with a financial plan. For purposes of definition a tactical or limited horizon for most fire service organizations is three to five years. A tactical horizon is the limit to which one can reasonably predict the effects of *changes*. A strategic or visionary horizon is five to ten years. A strategic horizon is the limit to which one can anticipate the impact of new *goals*. Tactical horizons are often shaped by economic constraints. Strategic horizons are often shaped by philosophical orientation.

One-year horizons are very limiting and may fail to deal with changing conditions. For example, many communities have suffered gradual population losses. In some of these communities the local fire department budget has continued to grow even as the tax base and population base have been eroding. Ultimately, there comes a point at which the fire department, as well as other local services, are drastically affected by the community's inability to pay, and there is a traumatic reduction in force.

Some techniques are available to change that horizon. For example, the concept of master planning was designed to help fire departments move their horizon to some five to ten years in the future. The emerging concept of strategic planning, used in the private sector, does the same thing. Both planning techniques are intended to allow the leadership and management of an organization to start planning for changing conditions in the community. Communities that have developed such planning mechanisms have tended to be successful in spite of changes in local conditions. Many communities that have ignored this need have faced unforeseen problems.

Terms and definitions

To deal with the future, fire administrators should become familiar with the vocabulary of futurism. Among these terms are *information half-life*, *technological obsolesence*, *technology transfer*, *deviation amplification*, *synergy*, and *synthesis*.

Information half-life is the time it takes for approximately 50 percent of a particular knowledge base to become obsolete. A classic example of information half-life can be observed in the field of computers. A group of engineers who went to school in 1950 and learned everything they could learn about computer technology would have been noncompetitive by 1960 if they had not kept up with changes. Computer technology changed so rapidly during that period that over 50 percent of the previous knowledge became useless.

Examples of the same phenomenon occur in the area of fire protection, not so much in fire combat operations as in the fields of information systems, human resources management, fire prevention codes and ordinances, and communications, where the half-life of the information has diminished each year.

Technological obsolescence is exactly what it sounds like—a gradual out-dating of technology, so that a technique or piece of equipment no longer serves the purpose for which it was originally intended. Steam fire apparatus became technologically obsolete when gasoline-powered fire equipment became available, and gasoline equipment is being replaced by diesel.

The space race introduced the term "technology transfer" into the vocabulary of change. Technology transfer is the application of a technology designed in one frame of reference for use in another. During the NASA moon flights and, subsequently, the space shuttles, technologies identified for that effort were used in the fields of medicine and information. Some visible examples of technology transfer in the fire service have been the use of fire-resistant materials for protective clothing and the development of infrared heat-seeking technology as instrumentation for fireground operations. Public Technology, Inc., has sought to foster technology transfer in the fire service.

"Deviation amplification" refers to the tendency of an organization to go more and more off course if it once deviates from its accepted plan. To prevent this from happening, managers need to constantly monitor the path of an organization and make corrections as needed, but not overcompensate by going off course in another direction. The term comes from rocketry where navigational equipment is set to make sure that if a rocket goes five degrees off course, a five-degree course adjustment is made—not a ten-degree adjustment. In the fire service the analogy applies to crisis administration. When an organization is faced with an emergency, it may overreact in an attempt to restore stability, and the effect may be negative instead of positive.

Finally, "synthesis" and "synergy" are related to the combination of elements. Synthesis is the combination of separate elements to create a new entity. For example, a community may choose to use its fire combat arm not only as a suppression force but to add public education and fire prevention activities to the role of fire companies. This synthesis of two functions can make the individual fire company more effective in handling emergencies. By increasing their knowledge of occupancies and the demographics of the community, the fire companies can become more than mere firefighters and take more responsibility for the resolution of the fire problem.

Synergy is the combined action of elements that are greater in their total effect than the sum of their parts. Synergy may be evident in fire prevention efforts. That is, if behavior in a community is modified through public education at the same time that code enforcement activities are increased, the result may be a greater decrease in fire losses and loss of life than could be effected by each change implemented separately.

Forces for change

The fire service does not exist in a vacuum. Although it is often accused of being parochial and inward-oriented, the fire service is in many ways a reflection of the society it serves. When society changes, the fire service changes. It follows that, as society continues to change in the future, the fire service will evolve on a parallel course. Although literature on the future is very limited within the fire profession, books such as those cited earlier provide a considerable insight into the directions in which society—and by implication the fire service—is moving. While they do not treat the technical side of fire protection, they do discuss the environment in which fire protection will be delivered in the future. And the mere existence of such futuristic thinking has stimulated a renaissance of concern about direction, goal orientation, and "quality-of-life" issues.

The future of the fire service will be shaped by decisionmakers in various roles within the fire profession. The levels at which these decisions are made will determine the speed with which change occurs. For example, a local fire chief probably has more to say about the community's fire problem and can make changes in it more quickly than the state fire marshal. In turn, the state fire marshal can have a more rapid effect on the modification of a fire problem in one part of the country than can legislation at the national level. The reason is the difference in lead time or reflex time between the enactment of legislation and its actual implementation and evaluation at the local level. It is interesting to note that the majority of life-safety legislation enacted in the 1970s and 1980s was first enacted on a local level, then supported at the state and, later, at the national level with public education programs.

Fire professionals, government professionals, and other management professionals must fulfill a variety of roles at the local, regional, and national levels. And these various decisionmakers can be entrusted with a wide variety of missions that will ultimately shape the fire service. Over the last several decades, however, there has been considerable controversy over exactly who is responsible for what role and for what mission. The development of the Joint Council of National Fire Service Organizations was an attempt to resolve this problem.

As a leader or manager in the fire service, each organization has a role to fulfill as a change agent, a catalyst that promotes actions that will "make the future." Classic examples of change agents are states that have developed certification programs for fire officers, thereby shaping the working environment for many individuals entering the fire service in the future or moving up through the professional ranks by way of promotion. As state, regional, and federal organizations take positions on various issues, they begin to modify the future.

Future changes

Over the last fifty years, there have been gradual changes in most fire departments in the United States. These changes can be classified in three categories: mission, methodology, and technology.

A change of mission has occurred since the early days when fire departments were viewed essentially as combat organizations, focusing an inordinate amount of resources, time, attention, and training on fire suppression operations. Although the need to maintain a strong combat capability has never diminished, especially in densely populated areas, the mission has slowly evolved in the direction of providing overall fire protection, not just suppression. The addition of duties such as emergency medical services in many communities has modified firefighter training and even the type of individual who seeks fire service as employment. The addition of fire prevention duties and the expansion of the role of code enforcement has changed the mission of many organizations to a proactive instead of reactive one. The rapid increase in hazardous materials incidents has shifted the focus in the combat arm away from fire to dealing with a highly technical field of hazardous materials containment. Sometimes the mission statement of the organization has not been modified to reflect such changes. As a result, many fire service employees find themselves doing a job that is totally different from what they hired on to do.

Changes in methodology in the fire service include increased emphasis on human resources and the strengths of individual employees instead of compliance with rules and regulations. Authority in many fire service organizations has been considerably decentralized and increased emphasis has been put on professional competency in the promotion process.

Perhaps the most significant technological change affecting the fire service has been the introduction of the computer. Other technological changes have been in the field of communications and the use of chemicals as additives to water. Still others are having synergistic effects. For example, the development of smoke detector technology in the 1960s and 1970s, together with the development of residential sprinkler technology in the 1970s and 1980s, are having a major effect on fire losses in many communities.

Changes and trends can often be spotted by a careful reading of fire protection and local government publications and popular national magazines. Articles published in these sources not only describe the past and the state of the art, but also reflect the trends that will shape the future of the fire service. For example, fire case studies basically reflect past conditions, while articles dealing with new materials and new methodologies are directed toward the future. The amount of space devoted to new concepts in any given issue will vary.

Initially, when a new trend or pattern begins to emerge, it is usually "reported on" in the news section of the publication, often as a study or research report. The second stage of acceptance is signaled by the appearance of an article describing the concept in a practical application. The third stage occurs when the concept is used to define a success story somewhere.

The evolution can be illustrated by an incident command system project called FIRESCOPE, an acronym for Fire Fighting Resources of Southern California Organized for Potential Emergencies. Initially, FIRESCOPE was a joint project of the national, state, and local governments designed to respond to the problems of dealing with massive wildland fires. Then, within a decade or so, the concept was applied to other major fires and found to be workable. Retitled the National Interagency Incident Management System (NIIMS), the concept was embraced by the Federal Emergency Management Agency (FEMA) and subsequently became the backbone of most emergency management delivery systems.

It remains for the readers and practitioners in any profession to identify those innovations that are not only acceptable, but workable. These will form the foundation for future changes.

Current trends in the fire service seem to fall into a number of categories: consolidation and regionalization of resources, conflict between generalization and specialization of personnel, less rigid management approaches, technological improvements, and continuing emphasis on built-in fire protection. The chapters of this book have reflected these trends.

Consolidation and regionalization are evidenced by the increasing number of fire service organizations that are engaged in mergers and regional consolidations to compensate for increased costs of personnel and equipment. These arrangements often improve the efficiency and effectiveness of fire services in the region.

The dichotomy between generalization and specialization is reflected in the need to develop fire suppression personnel on one hand and highly specialized personnel such as fire protection analysts and public educators on the other. In some departments, staff positions, even the fire chief's position, are being filled with civilians.

In the areas of organization and management the use of "participative" management styles, task force management, matrix management, project management, and team building are relatively new to the fire service's administrative language. Increased emphasis on human behavior and utilizing strengths and weaknesses of individuals in the organization is being reflected in the journals also.

Technological trends include miniaturization in radios and communications equipment; increased use of infrared and chemical water additives; use of "attack" pumpers and specialized response apparatus to defer wear and tear on larger, more expensive apparatus; and redesign of both apparatus and equipment to make them safer.

Finally, a concept readily identifiable in professional publications is financial responsibility in the fire service and a renewed focus on the use of built-in fire protection equipment as an alternative to manual firefighting forces.

These trends and patterns will find their way into fire departments at various rates. Some will be rejected, at least initially, and others may be embraced too quickly and consequently may fail.

Research and development

To assure a healthy future, fire service professionals need to seek a happy medium between an adoption that is too late and an experiment that is too early. One way to do this is to actively pursue a research and development function as part of managing the organization. This R&D effort, in turn, needs to be grounded in sound data and forecasting.

Of all the tools used in private industry, these two—forecasting and R&D—have traditionally been the weakest in the fire service. The 1973 report of the National Commission on Fire Prevention and Control, *America Burning,* noted a serious lack of information concerning America's fire problem. Although there have been significant strides in data collection, especially with the establishment of the National Fire Incident Reporting System and various statewide fire reporting systems, there is still a need for data bases on the community's total fire problem and identification of effective resources for dealing with it. This is especially true at the local level.

Dealing with the future depends on predictions, but fire statistics are based on the past and may encourage a department to react to the past instead of looking ahead and proactively planning for the future that those past statistics predict.

One future need that deserves the attention of the fire administrator, then, is the development of an adequate data base to allow management to identify trends and patterns that will affect the future of the department. In the area of finance, for example, if the data support a prediction of increased costs accompanied by increased revenues, that may mean a sound future for the department. If they suggest increased costs and decreased revenues, the picture is entirely different. Using knowledge of the past, the administrator then needs to initiate an ongoing R&D program. R&D is not necessarily a large assignment, and it can be conducted on an ad hoc basis. It consists of having someone in the organization committed to the task of maintaining surveillance of trends and patterns as they emerge in professional conferences and literature and in the field. That person should also have the responsibility of evaluating new concepts as quickly as possible, once they have been found acceptable in a practical setting, to determine a potential use in the local organization.

Research and development is the responsibility of top management. In most fire service agencies this means the fire chief. It can be delegated, but it should not be discounted, for it requires a commitment from the highest levels if it is to be meaningful and relevant to the long-range success of the organization. Failure to provide for R&D can, and often does, lead the organization toward obsolescence, and, in the worst case, toward eventual decline or demise.

A fire service organization that fails to carry out R&D may not feel the consequences in the short run. The inertia of many fire service functions may obscure the impact of slowly eroding methodologies and technologies. In the long run, however, change occurs whether or not the department plans for it. The only positive way to deal with the future is to anticipate and act on changes. What many consider to be fate is more often the result of failure to take action than a random convergence of bad luck or timing.

Summary

The future of the fire service, then, is most likely going to be determined by the actions of its managers and leaders today. Those leaders will need to be alert to new possibilities, and creativity will become a necessity instead of a desirable qualification for future fire officials. Most important, the future of each individual, each fire department, and the fire service as a whole is going to depend on having a vision of the future. That is the challenge for the fire service: to define a vision of what the future can hold, to explore potential methods and technologies to achieve that outcome, and then to accept the changes that will make that vision a reality.

1   Alvin Toffler, *Future Shock* (New York: Random House, 1970); Alvin Toffler, *The Third Wave* (New York: Morrow, 1980); John Diebold, *Making the Future Work* (New York: Simon & Schuster, 1984); and John Naisbitt, *Megatrends* (New York: Warner Books, 1982).

2   Thomas S. Kuhn, *The Structure of Scientific Revolutions*, 2nd ed. (Chicago: University of Chicago Press, 1970).

Bibliography and resource guide

This bibliography is highly selective and represents informed judgments about basic materials of managerial interest in the proliferating area of fire services. It is intended to supplement the material cited in the endnotes to individual chapters in this book with a selection of basic books and research reports on the many specific subjects within fire services management. The bibliography and resource guide is arranged by chapter for the convenience of the reader, although some items will of course cover several of the many functional divisions of the text. Such references will, therefore, be shown in each applicable chapter.

To help readers supplement the materials set out in the chapter listings of the bibliography, the following synopsis identifies some of the standard reference sources and information available in journals, yearbooks, and association publications with application generally to the fire services management field.

A fundamental reference source for statistics of concern to fire service managers is the *Statistical Abstract of the United States*, published annually by the U.S. Bureau of the Census and obtainable from the U.S. Government Printing Office, Washington, D.C. 20402, or through any U.S. Department of Commerce district office. The annual appendix titled *Guide to Sources of Statistics* is an invaluable guide to the many specialist statistical reference sources applicable to the fire services. *The Municipal Year Book*, published annually by the International City Management Association, Washington, D.C., is an authoritative reference source, containing detailed guides to further sources of information—organizations as well as bibliographic materials—in local government management, including fire services. *The Fire Protection Handbook*, published by the National Fire Protection Association, Quincy, Massachusetts (revised about every five years), contains data on loss of life and property from fire, information on the behavior of materials under fire conditions, and many other facts on

changes in fire protection techniques, systems, and equipment.

Several specialist fire service organizations have been described in Chapter 18 of this book. The major organizations presented immediately below are sources for a large variety of useful information about fire services management in general.

The National Fire Protection Association (Batterymarch Park, Quincy, Massachusetts 02269) publishes numerous codes, standards, recommended practices, and manuals in all areas of fire protection; the *Fire Protection Handbook*; *Fire Journal* (the bimonthly membership magazine); *Fire Command* (a monthly magazine for fire service leadership); *Fire Technology* (a quarterly journal); and various books, as well as educational and audiovisual materials.

The United States Fire Administration (16825 S. Seton Avenue, Emmitsburg, Maryland 21727) publishes numerous reports, many brochures on public education, and *Public Fire Education Today*, a listing of fire training programs across the United States (updated every two or three years).

The International Association of Fire Fighters (1750 New York Avenue, N.W., Washington, D.C. 20006) publishes the bimonthly magazine *International Fire Fighter*. The "Death and Injury Report," published in one issue annually, attracts national interest.

The International Association of Fire Chiefs (1329 18th Street, N.W., Washington, D.C. 20036) publishes a variety of information and educational materials about fire protection, including a twice-monthly newsletter, *IAFC On Scene*, and *International Connections*, published six times a year.

The International Society of Fire Service Instructors (20 Main Street, Ashland, Massachusetts 01721) conducts seminars on fire service education and the training of instructors and publishes several monthly publications, a biennial directory, and *Rural Firefighting Operations*.

The International Fire Service Training Association (Fire Protection Publications, Oklahoma State University, Stillwater, Oklahoma 74078) develops and publishes training materials for the fire service, including two quarterly publications, *Speaking of Fire. . .* and *Training Bulletin*.

FIREDOC, at the Center for Fire Research, National Bureau of Standards (301-975-6862), is the bibliographic data base to the Fire Research Information Services collection.

National Organization of Women in Fire Suppression, 18 West Hudson Avenue, Dayton, Ohio 45405.

The Joint Council of Fire Service Organizations (% National Fire Protection Association, Batterymarch Park, Quincy, Massachusetts 02269) holds quarterly meetings for its eleven member organizations:

> Fire Marshals' Association of North America
> International Association of Arson Investigators
> International Association of Fire Chiefs (IAFC)
> International Association of Fire Fighters
> International Fire Service Training Association
> International Municipal Signal Association
> International Society of Fire Service Instructors
> Metropolitan Committee of the IAFC
> National Fire Protection Association
> International Association of Black Professional Fire Fighters
> National Volunteer Fire Council

The International City Management Association (1120 G Street, N.W., Washington, D.C. 20005) publishes *The Municipal Year Book*. Fire service management topics are covered frequently in ICMA reports.

Public Technology, Inc. (PTI; 1301 Pennsylvania Avenue N.W., Washington, D.C. 20004) is the technical arm of the International City Management Association and the National League of Cities. PTI researches and publishes technical solutions to widespread and urgent problems facing local governments.

In addition to the association journals, fire service periodicals on general topics include the following: *Fire Chief*, monthly (307 N. Michigan Avenue, Chicago, Illinois 60601); *Firehouse*, monthly, and *Chief Fire Executive*, bimonthly (both published by Firehouse Communications, Inc., 33 Irving Place, New York, NY 10003); *Fire Engineering*, monthly (250 Fifth Avenue, New York, NY 10011); and *American Fire Journal*, monthly (9072 E. Artesia Boulevard, No. 7, Bellflower, California, 90706-6299). There are many different periodicals on special subjects, for example, arson investigation, communications, and labor relations; some of these are cited in the endnotes to the appropriate chapters. Those cited, and other special periodicals, can be obtained from the appropriate organizations.

1 The evolution of fire services

Bare, William K. *Introduction to Fire Science and Fire Protection*. New York: John Wiley & Sons, 1978.

Bond, Horatio, ed. *Fire and the Air War*. Manhattan, Kan.: Kansas State University, Military Affairs/Aerospace Historian, 1974.

Bush, Loren S., and McLaughlin, James. *Introduction to Fire Science*. Beverly Hills, Calif.: Glencoe Press, 1970.

Cannon, Donald J., ed. *Heritage of Flames: The Illustrated History of Early American Firefighting*. New York: Doubleday, 1977.

Ditzel, Paul C. *Fire Engines, Firefighters*. New York: Crown, 1976.

Lyons, Paul R. *Fire in America!* Boston: National Fire Protection Association, 1976.

Smith, Dennis. *Dennis Smith's History of Firefighting in America*. New York: The Dial Press, 1978.

2 Overview of the fire protection system

Carlsen, Robert D., and James A. Lewis. *The Systems Analysis Workbook*. 2d ed. Englewood Cliffs, N.J.: Prentice-Hall, 1979.

Churchman, C. West. *The Systems Approach*. New York: Dell Publishing Co., 1983.

Emery, F. E. *Systems Thinking*. Harmondsworth, England: Penguin Education, 1969.

Federal Emergency Management Agency. U.S. Fire Administration. *Public Fire Education Today: Fire Service Programs from Across America*. Emmitsburg, Md., 1986.

Hickey, Harry E. *Public Fire Safety Organization: A Systems Approach*. Quincy, Mass.: National Fire Protection Association, 1973.

Johnson, Richard A., Fremont E. Kast, and James E. Rosenzweig. *The Theory and Management of Systems*. 3d ed. New York: McGraw-Hill, 1973.

Optner, Standford L. *Systems Analysis for Business and Industrial Problem Solving.* Englewood Cliffs, N.J.: Prentice-Hall, 1965.

Silvern, Leonard C. *Systems Engineering Applied to Training.* Houston, Tex.: Gulf Publishing Co., 1972.

---

3 Organization and management

Buchele, Robert. *The Management of Business and Public Organizations.* New York: McGraw-Hill, 1977.

Casey, James F. *The Fire Chief's Handbook.* New York: Technical Publishing Co., 1978.

Coleman, Ronny J. *Management of Fire Service Operations.* North Scituate, Mass.: Duxbury Press, 1978.

Denhardt, Robert B. *Theories of Public Organization.* Monterey, Calif.: Brooks/Cole, 1984.

Didactic Systems, Inc. *Management in the Fire Service.* Ed. K. Tower and A. E. Dean. Quincy, Mass.: National Fire Protection Association, 1977.

Drucker, Peter F. *Management: Tasks, Responsibilities, Practices.* New York: Harper & Row, 1973.

Groening, William. *The Moderate Corporate Manager.* New York: McGraw-Hill, 1981.

Hershey, Paul, and Kenneth H. Blanchard. *Management of Organizational Behavior: Utilizing Human Resources.* Englewood Cliffs, N.J.: Prentice-Hall, 1982.

Kanter, Rosabeth Moss. *The Change Masters.* New York: Simon & Schuster, 1983.

Massie, Joseph, and John Douglas. *Managing.* 4th ed. Englewood Cliffs, N.J.: Prentice-Hall, 1985.

Megginson, Leon, David C. Mosley, and Paul H. Pietri. *Management: Concepts and Applications.* 2nd ed. New York: Harper/Colophon, 1985.

Nigro, Felix A., and Lloyd G. Nigro. *Modern Public Administration.* New York: Harper & Row, 1980.

Peters, Thomas J., and Robert H. Waterman, Jr. *In Search of Excellence.* New York: Harper & Row, 1980.

Schermerhorn, John R., Jr., James G. Hunt, and Richard N. Osborn. *Managing Organizational Behavior.* New York: John Wiley & Sons, 1982.

Steiner, George. *Strategic Planning: What Every Manager Must Know.* New York: The Free Press, 1979.

Yukl, Gary A. *Leadership in Organizations.* Englewood Cliffs, N.J.: Prentice-Hall, 1981.

---

4 Planning for community fire protection

Ewing, David W. *Human Side of Planning: Tool or Tyrant?* New York: Macmillan, 1969.

Gaudette, John J., Jr., and Joseph J. Harrington. *Information Systems for Urban Fire Protection Planning: A Case Study.* Cambridge: Harvard University, 1977.

Federal Emergency Management Agency. U.S. Fire Administration. *Master Planning Report to Congress.* Washington, D.C.: Government Printing Office, 1981.

Institute for Local Self Government. *A Tale of Two Cities: Master Planning, an Alternative to the Practice of Incremental Decision Making.* Alternatives to Traditional Public Safety Delivery Systems, no. 4, Berkeley, Calif., 1977.

Multijurisdictional Fire Protection Planning. Washington, D.C.: National Association of Counties Research, Inc., 1979.

National Commission on Fire Prevention and Control. *America Burning.* Washington, D.C.: Government Printing Office, 1973.

U.S. Department of Commerce. National Fire Prevention and Control Administration. *A Basic Guide for Fire Prevention and Control Master Planning.* Prepared by the Office of the Oklahoma State Fire Marshal and Mission Research Corp. Washington, D.C.: Government Printing Office, 1978.

———. *Urban Guide for Fire Prevention and Control Master Planning.* Prepared by the Mountain View Fire Department, Los Angeles City Fire Department, and Mission Research Corporation. Washington, D.C.: Government Printing Office, 1977.

---

5 Evaluating community fire protection

Adams, Donald L., et al. *Utilization of Technological Equipment to Reduce Manning.* Emmitsburg, Md.: National Fire Academy Executive Development III Program, October 27–November 7, 1980.

Alley, Steven, et al. *Evaluation of the Impact of Response Time and Company Staffing on First Alarm Capability: A Decision Making Process.* Emmitsburg, Md.: National Fire Academy Executive Development III Program, March 12–23, 1984.

Backoff, Robert W. *Measuring Firefighting Effectiveness: A Preliminary Report.* Columbus: Ohio State University, School of Public Administration, 1986.

Barrett, Jim, et al. *Alternatives to Reduced Manning in the Fire Service.* Emmitsburg, Md.: National Fire Academy Executive Development III Program, July 25–August 5, 1983.

Chaiken, Jan M., and Edward J. Ignall. *Analysis of Fire Company Staffing Policies.* Concept paper. Santa Monica, Calif.: The Rand Corporation, 1977.

Chaiken, Jan M., Edward J. Ignall, and Warren E. Walker. *Deployment Methodology for Fire Departments: How Station Locations and Dispatching Practices Can Be Analyzed and Improved.* Santa Monica, Calif.: The Rand Corporation, 1975.

A Fire Service Demand Charge Study. City of Tacoma, Wash., January 1976. Funded by the National Science Foundation.

Fire Station Location Package: Fire Chiefs Report. Washington, D.C.: Public Technology, Inc., 1971.

Getz, Malcolm. *The Economics of the Urban Fire Department.* Baltimore, Johns Hopkins University Press, 1979.

Granito, John A. "Evaluation and Planning of Public Fire Protection." In *Fire Protection Handbook.* 16th ed. Quincy, Mass.: National Fire Protection Association, 1986.

Hickey, Harry E. *A Comparative Analysis of Resource Allocation Plans for Urban Fire Safety.* FPP-B-77-1. Laurel, Md.: Johns Hopkins University, August 1977.

Lotz, David T. *The Development and Application of a Modeling System for the Measurement of Service Levels in Fire Suppression Operations: The Seattle Experience–1976.* © David T. Lotz, 1982. Copies may be obtained from David T. Lotz, Corporate Budget Manager, Vitro Corporation, 14000 Georgia Avenue, Silver Spring, Md. 20910.

Research Triangle Institute, International City Management Association, and National Fire Protection Association. *Municipal Fire Service Workbook.* Washington, D.C.: Government Printing Office, 1977.

Schaenman, Philip S., John R. Hall, Jr., Alfred H. Schainblatt, Joseph A. Swartz, and Michael J. Kartner. *Procedures for Improving the Measurement of Local Fire Protection Effectiveness.* Quincy, Mass.: National Fire Protection Association, 1977.

Variable Manning and Deployment. Unpublished study. San Jose, Calif.: San Jose Fire Department, 1977.

6   Management information systems and data analysis

Eichelberger, Peirce. "New Technologies and Old Friends: The Geographic-Based Management Information System." *Fire Journal* 79, no. 1 (January 1985), 39–43.

Icove, David J., and M. Osama Soliman. "Computer-Assisted Arson Information Management." *International Fire Chief* 49, no. 12 (December 1983), 28–31.

McNabb, Robert L. "Affordable Data Management Solutions." *Fire Command*, July 1985, 38–39.

National Fire Protection Association. *Uniform Coding for Fire Protection*, NFPA no. 901, and *Fire Reporting Field Incident Manual*, NFPA no. 902M. Boston: National Fire Protection Association, 1976.

Thomas, Jan. "The New Wave in Computers for the Fire Service." *International Fire Chief*, March 1985, 14–16.

U.S. Fire Administration. National Fire Data Center. *Fire in the United States in 1978.* 2d ed. Emmitsburg, Md.: Federal Emergency Management Agency, 1982.

7   Resource management

Beach, Dale S. *Personnel: The Management of People at Work.* 4th ed. New York: Macmillan, 1980.

Gay, William, et al. *Fire Station Location: Analysis and Technology.* Management Information Service Reports, vol. 19, no. 7. Washington, D.C.: International City Management Association, July 1987.

Killian, Ray A. *Human Resource Management: An ROI Approach.* New York: AMACOM, 1976.

Schaenman, Philip S., and Joe Swartz. *Measuring Fire Protection Productivity in Local Government.* Boston: National Fire Protection Association, 1974.

Sklar, Peggy D. "Work Scheduling: The Basics." In *Police and Fire Work Scheduling.* Management Information Service Reports, vol. 17, no. 12. Washington, D.C.: International City Management Association, December 1985.

8   Budgeting, finance, and cost containment

Anthony, Robert N., and Regina E. Herzlinger. *Management Control in Nonprofit Or-*

ganizations. Homewood, Ill.: Richard D. Irwin, 1975.

Aronson, J. Richard, and Eli Schwartz, eds. *Management Policies in Local Government Finance.* 3d ed. Washington, D.C.: International City Management Association, 1987.

Ayres, Douglas W. *Integrative Budgeting System: A New Approach from Old Failures.* Working paper no. 19. Long Beach: University of Southern California, School of Public Administration. In cooperation with The Center for Public Affairs.

Governmental Accounting Standards Board. *Governmental Accounting and Financial Reporting Standards.* Chicago: Government Accounting Research Foundation, 1985.

Lynch, Thomas D. *Public Budgeting in America.* 2d ed. Englewood Cliffs, N.J.: Prentice-Hall, 1985.

Moak, Lennox L., and Albert M. Hillhouse. *Concepts and Practices in Local Government Finance.* Chicago: Municipal Finance Officers Association, 1975.

National Council on Governmental Accounting, Richard J. Haas, primary author. *Governmental Accounting, Auditing, and Financial Reporting.* Chicago: Governmental Finance Officers Association, 1980.

9 Legal aspects of fire department management

Banovetz, James M., ed. *Small Cities and Counties: A Guide to Managing Services.* Washington, D.C.: International City Management Association, 1984. A handbook on local government management, including a particularly enlightened chapter on the legal structure of local governments and the legal aspects of daily government operations.

McQuillin Municipal Corporations. 22 vols. Chicago: Callaghan and Co., 1967. One of the prime sources available to city and county attorneys.

Sands, C., and Michael Libonati. *Local Government Law: 1981.* 4 vols. Wilmette, Ill.: Callaghan and Co., 1981. An in-depth discussion and analysis of local government law; less detailed than *McQuillin* but a thoughtful critique of the legal problems facing local government managers.

10 Program management

Baker, N. Bruce, Dalmar Fisher, and David C. Murphy. "Project Management in the Public Sector: Success and Failure Patterns Compared to Private Sector Projects." In *Project Management Handbook.* Ed. David I. Cleland and William R. King. New York: Van Nostrand Reinhold, 1983, 686–99.

Bozeman, Barry. *Public Management and Policy Analysis.* New York: St. Martin's Press, 1979.

Didactic Systems, Inc. *Management in the Fire Service.* Ed. K. Tower and A. E. Dean. Quincy, Mass.: National Fire Protection Association, 1977.

Dinsmore, Paul C. *Human Factors in Project Management.* New York: American Management Association, 1984.

Favreau, Donald F. *Fire Service Management.* New York: Reuben H. Donnelley Corp., 1969.

Gray, Clifford, F. *Essentials of Project Management.* Corvallis, Or: Petrocelli Books, 1981.

International Fire Service Training Association. *Chief Officer.* Ed. Gene Carlson. Stillwater, Okla.: Oklahoma State University, 1985.

Lawrence, John, and Barry Pasternack. *An Introduction to Management Science.* Los Angeles: West Publishing Co., 1985.

Martin, Charles C. *Project Management: How to Make It Work.* New York: AMACOM, 1976.

Rosenau, Milton D., Jr. *Successful Project Management.* Belmont, Calif.: Lifetime Learning Publications, Wadsworth Publishing Co., 1981.

Silverman, Melvin. *The Technical Manager's Survival Book.* New York: McGraw-Hill, 1984.

Stallworthy, E. A., and O. P. Kharbanda. *Total Project Management.* Hants, England: Gower Publishing Co., 1983.

11 Personnel management

Federal Emergency Management Agency. U.S. Fire Administration. *The Role of Women in the Fire Service.* Washington, D.C.: Government Printing Office, 1980.

Feldstein, Lee M. *Fire Personnel Practices, 1986.* Baseline Data Reports, vol. 19, no. 1. Washington, D.C.: International City Management Association, January/February 1987.

Henry, Kenneth C., and Morton D. Shurtleff, eds. *Managing People.* Fire Officer Series.

Ashland, Mass.: International Society of Fire Service Instructors, 1987.

Kramer, William M., et al. *Personnel Management for the Fire Service*. 2d ed. Lexington, Mass.: Open Learning Fire Service Program, Ginn Press, 1985.

Matzer, John, Jr. *Creative Personnel Practices*. Washington, D.C.: International City Management Association, 1984.

Powell, Pam. *Managing Your Fire Department: Managing People*. Quincy, Mass.: National Fire Protection Association, 1984.

Sayles, Leonard R., and George Strauss. *Managing Human Resources*. 2d ed. Englewood Cliffs, N.J.: Prentice-Hall, 1981.

12 Labor-management relations

Baird, James R., Theordore Clark, Jr., and Michael J. Rybicki. *Maintaining Public Services: The NPELRA Strike Planning Manual*. Washington, D.C.: National Public Employer Relations Association, 1978.

Elkouri, Frank, and Edna Asper Elkouri. *How Arbitration Works*. 4th ed. Washington, D.C.: Bureau of National Affairs, 1985.

Feville, Peter. *Final Offer Arbitration*. Chicago: International Personnel Management Association, 1975.

Fisher, Roger, and William Ury. *Getting to Yes*. Boston: Houghton Mifflin, 1981.

Jackson, Gordon E. *How to Stay Union Free*. Memphis, Tenn.: Management Press, 1978.

Koven, Adolph M., and Susan L. Smith. *Just Cause: The Seven Tests*. San Francisco: Coloracre Publications, 1985.

Morris, Charles J. et al., eds. *The Developing Labor Law*. 2 vols. 2d ed. Washington, D.C.: Bureau of National Affairs, 1983.

Morse, Bruce. *How to Negotiate the Labor Agreement*. Farmington Hills, Mich.: Trends Publishing Co., 1984.

Rynecki, Steven B., Douglas A. Cairns, and Donald J. Cairns. *Firefighter Collective Bargaining Agreements: A National Management Survey*. Washington, D.C.: International Association of Fire Chiefs Foundation and National League of Cities, 1979.

13 Emergency management

Academy for Contemporary Problems. *What to Do When a Disaster Strikes: Advice to Local Chief Executives from Eau Claire, Wisconsin*. Washington, D.C., 1981.

Drabek, Thomas E., et al. *Managing Multiorganizational Emergency Responses: Emergent Search and Rescue Networks in Natural Disaster and Remote Area Settings*. Monograph no. 33. Institute of Behavioral Science, Program on Technology, Environment, and Man. Boulder, Colo.: University of Colorado, 1981.

Federal Emergency Management Agency. Emergency Management Institute. *Formulating Public Policy in Emergency Management: A Course Book and Resource Manual for Public Officials*. Emmitsburg, Md., 1984.

————. *Guide for Development of State and Local Emergency Operations Plans: Interim Guidance*. CPG1-8. Emmitsburg, Md., October 1985.

————. *Hazard Identification, Capability Assessment, and Multi-Year Development Plan*. Vols. 1–3. Washington, D.C.: Government Printing Office, 1985.

Hessel-Garten, Rebecca, and Eugene R. Russell, Sr. *Manual for Small Towns to Develop a Hazardous Material Emergency Plan*. Washington, D.C.: U.S. Department of Transportation, 1986.

Hoetmer, Gerard J., and Cindy Herrera. *Assessing Local Government Emergency Management Needs and Priorities*. Final Technical Report. Washington, D.C.: International City Management Association, 1983.

————. *Emergency Management*. Baseline Data Reports, vol. 15, no. 4. Washington, D.C.: International City Management Association, 1983.

Johnson, Quinten. *Comprehensive Emergency Management: A Guide for County Officials*. Washington, D.C.: National Association of Counties Research, Inc., 1982.

National Governors Association. NGA State Emergency Management Series. Various titles.

Quarantelli, Enrico L. *An Annotated Bibliography on Disaster and Disaster Planning*. Columbus: Ohio State University, Disaster Research Center, 1980.

————. *Delivery of Emergency Medical Services in Disasters: Assumptions and Realities*. New York: Irvington, 1983.

Rubin, Claire B. *Disaster Mitigation: Challenge to Managers*. Washington, D.C.: Academy for Contemporary Problems, 1979.

————. *Managing the Recovery from a Natural Disaster*. Management Information Service Reports, vol. 14, no. 2. Washington,

D.C.: International City Management Association, 1982.

14 Emergency medical and rescue services

Barton, George K. "The Wait for an Ambulance." *Journal of Emergency Medical Services* 11 (December 1986): 67–70.

Clawson, Jeff J. "The Maximal Response Disease." *Journal of Emergency Medical Services* 12 (January 1987): 28–31.

Clawson, Jeff J., and Kate B. Dernocoeur. *Emergency Medical Dispatching.* Bowie, Md.: Brady Communications, 1987.

Dernocoeur, Kate B. *Streetsense: Communication, Safety and Control.* Bowie, Md.: Brady Communications, 1985.

"EMS in the U.S.'s 150 Most Populous Cities." Staff report. *Journal of Emergency Medical Services* 12 (January 1987): 47–56.

Fitch, Joseph J. *Beyond the Street: A Handbook for EMS Leadership and Management.* Washington, D.C.: Jems Publishing Co., 1988.

Frank, Michael, M. D. "Fire Chief vs. Medical Director." *Journal of Emergency Medical Services* 9 (June 1984): 46–55.

Morris, Gary P. "Common Errors in Mass Casualty Management." *Journal of Emergency Medical Services* 11 (February 1986): 34–38.

Page, James O. "Understanding the Fire Service." *Journal of Emergency Medical Services* 9 (June 1984): 30–37.

"Service of the Year: Exceptional EMS in Oregon." *Journal of Emergency Medical Services* 11 (January 1986): 38–45.

Stout, Jack. "Why Subscription Programs?" *Journal of Emergency Medical Services* 11 (October 1986): 71–75.

Stults, Kenneth. *EMT-D Prehospital Defibrillation.* Bowie, Md.: Brady Communications, 1985.

15 Comprehensive fire prevention and code administration

Bancroft, Raymond L. *Municipal Fire Service Trends.* Washington, D.C.: National League of Cities, 1972.

Brannigan, Francis L. *Building Construction for the Fire Service.* Quincy, Mass.: National Fire Protection Association, 1982.

The Committee on Fire Research and The Fire Research Conference. *Methods of Studying Mass Fires.* National Academy of Sciences–National Research Council publication 569. Washington, D.C.: Government Printing Office, 1958.

Hatry, Harry P., et al. *How Effective Are Your Community Services? Procedures for Monitoring the Effectiveness of Municipal Services.* Washington, D.C.: The Urban Institute and International City Management Association, 1977.

Institute for Local Self Government. *Civilians in Public Safety Services.* Alternatives to Traditional Public Safety Delivery Systems, no. 5. Berkeley, Calif., 1977.

———. *Public Safety Inspection Consolidation.* Alternatives to Traditional Public Safety Delivery Systems, no. 3. Berkeley, Calif., 1977.

International City Management Association. *Code Administration and Enforcement: Trends and Perspectives.* Management Information Service Special Reports, no. 10. Washington, D.C.: International City Management Association, August 1982.

International Fire Service Training Association. *Fire Prevention and Inspection Practices.* IFSTA-110. Stillwater, Okla.: Oklahoma State University, 1981.

———. *Private Fire Protection and Detection.* IFSTA-210. Stillwater, Okla.: Oklahoma State University, 1979.

National Fire Protection Association. *Life Safety Code Handbook.* Quincy, Mass., 1981.

Schaenman, Philip S., and Edward F. Seitz. *International Concepts in Fire Protection— Ideas from Europe That Could Improve U.S. Fire Safety.* Arlington, Va.: TriData Corp., 1982.

The Urban Institute and International City Management Association. *Measuring the Effectiveness of Basic Municipal Services:* Initial Report. Washington, D.C.: The Urban Institute and International City Management Association, 1974.

16 Managing innovation

Bennis, Warren, and Burt Nanus. *Leaders.* New York: Harper & Row, 1985.

Drucker, Peter F. *Innovation and Entrepreneurship.* New York: Harper & Row, 1985.

Kanter, Rosabeth Moss. *The Change Masters.* New York: Simon & Schuster, 1983.

McCormack, Mark H. *What They Don't Teach You at Harvard Business School.* New York: Bantam Books, 1984.

Naisbitt, John, and Patricia Aburdene. *Reinventing the Corporation.* New York: Warner Books, 1985.

Pascarella, Perry. *The New Achievers: Creating a Modern Work Ethic.* New York: The Free Press, 1984.

Peters, Thomas J., and Nancy Austin. *A Passion for Excellence: The Leadership Difference.* New York: Random House, 1985.

Peters, Thomas J., and Robert H. Waterman, Jr. *In Search of Excellence.* New York: Harper & Row, 1982.

von Oech, Roger. *A Whack on the Side of the Head: How to Unlock Your Mind for Innovation.* New York: Warner Books, 1983.

17 Alternative delivery systems

Bogart, Geoffrey S. *Residential Fire Sprinkler Ordinances.* Management Information Service Reports, vol. 19, no. 3. Washington, D.C.: International City Management Association, 1987.

Campbell, Colin A. *Personnel Management for Volunteer Fire Departments.* Washington, D.C.: International Association of Fire Chiefs Foundation, 1980.

Coleman, Ronny J. *Alpha to Omega: The Evolution in Residential Fire Protection.* San Clemente, Calif.: Phenix Publications, 1985.

Hayman, Marie. *Public Safety Departments: Combining the Police and Fire Functions.* Management Information Service Reports, vol. 8, no. 7. Washington, D.C.: International City Management Association, July 1976.

Hoetmer, Gerard J. *Police, Fire and Refuse Collection and Disposal Departments.* Baseline Data Reports, no. 14. Washington, D.C.: International City Management Association, 1983.

Hoetmer, Gerard J., and Amy Cohen Paul. *Municipalities and the Volunteer Fire Service.* Urban Data Service Reports, vol. 12, no. 9. Washington, D.C.: International City Management Association, September 1980.

Paul, Amy Cohen. *The Volunteer Fire Department: Personnel Management and the Local Government Connection.* Management Information Service Reports, vol. 12, no. 10. Washington, D.C.: International City Management Association, October 1986.

Schaenman, Philip, et al. *Overcoming Barriers to Public Fire Education in the United States.* Arlington, Va.: TriData Corporation, 1987.

Valente, Carl F., and Lydia D. Manchester. *Rethinking Local Services: Examining Alternative Delivery Approaches.* Management Information Service Special Report. Washington, D.C.: International City Management Association, March 1984.

18 Training and professional development

Andrews, Kenneth R. "Toward Professionalism in Business Management." *Harvard Business Review*, March–April 1969.

Boatner, J. W. "Higher Education for the Fire Service." *Fire Chief*, July 1982.

Boyle, P. G. *Planning Better Programs.* New York: McGraw-Hill, 1981.

Didactic Systems, Inc. *Management in the Fire Service.* Ed. K. Tower and A. E. Dean. Quincy, Mass.: National Fire Protection Association, 1977.

Education and Training Officer: Vol. 4. Supervision and Management. Manual no. 7504 04 0169. United States Air Force, Sheppard Air Force Base, Texas, 1985.

Garner, D. P. *The Adult Learner, the World of Work, and Career Education.* Dubuque, Iowa: Kendall/Hunt Publishing Co., 1978.

Granito, Anthony R. *Company Leadership and Operations.* Boston: National Fire Protection Association, 1975.

———. *Fire Service Instructor's Guidebook.* Boston: National Fire Protection Association, 1976.

Hawk, Curtis L. "Training Leadership for a Small Department." *Fire Chief*, October 1983.

International Fire Service Training Association Committee. *Fire Service Instructor.* 4th ed. Ed. Gene Carlson. Stillwater, Okla.: Oklahoma State University, 1981.

Johnson, E. I., and C. Ulmer. *Developing Programs for Adults in Public Service and Other Fields.* Englewood Cliffs, N.J.: Prentice-Hall, 1972.

Knowles, Malcolm S. *The Modern Practice of Adult Education: From Pedagogy to Andragogy.* Rev. ed. New York: Cambridge Book Co., 1980.

Lee, Chris. "Ethics Training: Facing the Tough Questions." *Training*, March 1986.

Mager, Robert F. *Preparing Instructional Objectives.* 2d, rev. ed. Belmont, Calif.: Pitman Learning, 1984.

McCullough, K. E. "Trash to Training." *Fire Engineering*, December 1984.

National Fire Protection Association. *Standard for Fire Service Instructor Professional Qualifications*. NFPA 1041. Quincy, Mass., 1981.

Peters, John M., et al. *Building an Effective Adult Education Enterprise*. San Francisco: Jossey-Bass, 1980.

Randleman, Bill. "NVFC Holds Stonebridge III." *Fire Chief*, November 1984.

Strother, George B., and John P. Klus. *Administration of Continuing Education*. Belmont, Calif.: Wadsworth Publishing Co., 1982.

Walsh, Charles V., and Leonard G. Marks. *Firefighting Strategy and Leadership*. 2d ed. New York: McGraw-Hill, 1977.

List of contributors

Persons who have contributed to this book are listed below with the editors first and the chapter authors following in alphabetical order. A brief review of experience and training is presented for each author. Since many of the contributors have published extensively, books, monographs, articles, and other pubications are omitted.

Ronny J. Coleman (Editor and Chapter 19) is fire chief for Fullerton, California. He holds degrees from Santa Ana College and California State University–Fullerton, and he is currently doing graduate work for a master's degree in organizational development at California State University–Long Beach. He is an executive board member of the International Association of Fire Chiefs, and he serves on the editorial advisory board for publications of the International Association of Fire Chiefs as well as on numerous committees relating to the fire service. Chief Coleman is recognized as a master instructor in the fire service field. He has published over one hundred articles and five textbooks and is consulting editor for *Fire Chief* Magazine. He has lectured worldwide on the fire service.

John A. Granito (Editor and Chapter 19) is professor and vice president emeritus of the State University of New York. He has a doctoral degree in psychological theories of leadership. He is a consultant and writer on fire protection, public safety, and emergency management and is associate editor of *Chief Fire Executive* magazine. He has served as supervisor of fire training for New York State and as a fire and public safety advisor throughout North and South America and in Europe.

Douglas W. Ayres (Chapter 8) is president of Management Services Institute, a diversified management company. He has been a professor in the School of Public Administration at the University of Southern California; at California State University–Long Beach; and at the University of California–Irvine. He has served as city manager of Inglewood, California; Salem, Oregon; and Melbourne, Florida, as staff consultant with Public Administration Service in Chicago, and as general manager of Leisure World in Laguna Hills, California. Mr. Ayres received a bachelor's degree in political science from the University of North Carolina and a master's degree in public aministration from Syracuse University.

Joseph N. Baker (Chapter 16) is president of Joseph N. Baker Enterprises, Inc., which markets video training tapes to government and business organizations. Before forming this company, he was city manager of Orange, California. Prior to that, he was regional vice president of Public Technology, Inc., and city manager of Burbank, California, and Gladstone, Missouri. He holds a bachelor's degree from the University of Missouri–Kansas City and a master's degree from the University of Kansas.

Robert B. Burns (Chapter 4) is a fire protection consultant and president of Fire Loss Management Systems, a fire protection consulting firm. He served in the fire service for thirty-two years and retired as chief of the Mountain View City Fire Department, California. He participated in the preparation of the presidential commission report *American Burning* as the principal author of Chapter 4, "Master Planning." He has assisted over forty public agencies in the development of long-range fire protection plans and for the past eight years, has taught long-range fire protection planning at the California State Fire Academy. Mr. Burns lectures throughout the United States on fire protection planning and management. He has been active in the development and implementation of advanced fire protection systems, including fire protection data systems, residential sprinklers, and fire retardant roofing.

Stephen Chapple (Chapter 9) is an assistant attorney general of Virginia. A

1973 graduate of the University of Minnesota Law School, Mr. Chapple served for ten years as the general counsel of the United States Conference of Mayors. He has practiced law in Chicago and in Arlington, Virginia, and has served as an assistant to the mayor of St. Paul, Minnesota. He has authored numerous articles on the legal aspects of federalism and intergovernmental relations and is admitted to practice law in Illinois, Minnesota, the District of Columbia, and Virginia and before the U.S. Supreme Court. Mr. Chapple received his bachelor's degree in history from the University of Illinois–Urbana.

John M. Dionne (Chapter 5) has been chief of the Burlington, Vermont, Fire Department since 1984, following retirement from the New York City Fire Department. He holds a bachelor's degree in fire service administration from John Jay College and is completing the master of public administration degree at the University of Vermont. He has served as a consultant to the public and private sectors in the area of fire protection.

Douglas P. Forsman (Chapter 7) is chief of the Champaign, Illinois, Fire Department, a position he has held since 1980. He holds degrees in fire protection technology and in trade and industrial education from Oklahoma State University. He was formerly employed by the National Fire Protection Association as senior fire service specialist. He has also served as the volunteer fire chief of Wabash Township, Indiana, and Norfolk, Massachusetts. He is executive secretary of the International Fire Service Training Association and is a member of the National Professional Qualifications Board for the Fire Service. In Champaign, Chief Forsman is responsible for emergency management functions and all code enforcement activities in addition to more traditional fire service activities.

Thomas M. Hawkins, Jr. (Chapter 13) was appointed fire chief in Arlington County, Virginia, in 1978. Previously he was program manager for the Executive Development curriculum with the National Fire Academy. For seven years he served as associate professor of fire science at Northern Virginia Community College. Chief Hawkins has been involved with the fire service for more than twenty-five years, in both a career and a volunteer capacity. He was president of the State Fire Chiefs Association of Virginia and served as chairperson of the National Advisory Committee for the Integrated Emergency Management System. He has been a speaker at national forums on emergency management and fire service management. He holds bachelor's and master's degrees from George Washington University and has done post-graduate work at Virginia Polytechnic Institute.

Gerard J. Hoetmer (Chapter 17) is director of public safety programs with the International City Management Association (ICMA). Since 1978 he has managed over 3 million dollars in grants and contracts dealing with a wide range of subjects including fire service productivity improvement, local government emergency management, the use of microcomputers in municipalities, and the design of a scientific technical information system for the Federal Emergency Management Agency (FEMA). With FEMA he designed a training course attended by nearly 2,000 local chief executives and emergency management personnel. Prior to his tenure at ICMA, Mr. Hoetmer was an assistant to the fire chief and aide to the city manager in Aurora, Colorado. He holds a master's degree in public administration from the University of Colorado.

James R. Korom (Chapter 12) is an attorney with the Milwaukee law firm of von Briesen and Purtell. He received his law degree from the University of Wisconsin–Madison and served as an intern with the Wisconsin Employment Relations Commission. He practices labor law full time, representing management and emphasizing the public sector. He has authored numerous articles for the International Association of Fire Chiefs, the Wisconsin Police Chiefs Association, and other organizations, and he lectures frequently on public-sector labor issues.

Kenneth R. Lavoie (Chapter 2) is chief of the Needham, Massachusetts, Fire Department. He holds an AA degree in fire science, a bachelor's degree in public administration, and a master's degree in education. Chief Lavoie has served as an adjunct instructor in both the resident and field programs division of the National Fire Academy. Prior to his assignment in Needham, he served with the Hampton, Virginia, and Los Angeles County fire departments. He serves on the National Fire Protection Association's 1301 committee on fire department organization and operation.

Leonard G. Marks (Chapter 8) is fire chief of Bremerton, Washington. He has served as instructor of fire science at Santa Ana

College, California; senior instructor at the Maryland Fire and Rescue Institute at the University of Maryland; assistant professor at San Jose State University; and deputy fire chief of San Jose, California. He received a bachelor's degree in business (accounting) from San Jose State University and master's and doctoral degrees in public administration from the University of Southern California. He was elected treasurer of San Clemente, California.

F. Patrick Marlatt (Chapter 18) is an administrator with the Maryland Fire and Rescue Institute at the University of Maryland, where he manages the delivery of education and training to over 12,000 emergency services students annually. After completing undergradute studies in fire protection, education, and management, Mr. Marlatt worked in the insurance industry. Later he joined the faculty of a local community college, and in 1977 he moved to the Maryland Fire and Rescue Institute. His graduate stuides have been in public administration, with a concentration in state and local emergency services organizations. Mr. Marlatt has served as a consultant to numerous public and private organizations. A former career firefighter and officer, he remains active today in a volunteer organization.

John Matzer, Jr. (Chapter 11) is a consultant to local government. Previously he was city administrator of San Bernardino, California; distinguished visiting professor at California State University–Long Beach; deputy assistant director of the U.S. Office of Personnel Management; city manager of Beverly Hills, California; village manager of Skokie, Illinois; and city administrator of Trenton, New Jersey. Mr. Matzer has taught graduate courses in public administration at a number of universities. He received bachelor's and master's degrees from Rutgers University.

Hugh McClees (Chapter 13)   Biography unavailable.

Chester A. Newland (Chapter 10) is professor of public administration at the University of Southern California in Sacramento and in Washington, D.C. He is also editor-in-chief of the *Public Administration Review*. From 1971 to 1973 he was a professor at the Federal Executive Institute (FEI); he served as director of the FEI from 1973 to 1976 and from 1980 to 1981. Dr. Newland was the initial director of the Lyndon Baines Johnson Library, from 1968 to 1970. Since 1966 he has been associated with the University of Southern California when not in other

service. He is a past president of the American Society for Public Administration, is a member of the National Academy of Public Administration, and was elected to honorary membership in the International City Management Association in 1980.

Don W. Oaks (Chapter 10) is chief officer with the Santa Barbara County Fire Department and is a practicing California attorney. His law practice is a blend of administrative law and liability management. He holds a bachelor's degree in public administration from California State University–Long Beach and a doctorate in law from the California Law Institute in Santa Barbara. Dr. Oaks represents the California Fire Chiefs Association (CFCA) and the State Fire Marshal's Office on state-level committees and is past president of the CFCA Fire Prevention Officers. He is a member of the adjunct faculty of the National Fire Academy and is a lecturer for academies of California, Arizona, Hawaii, Wyoming, Montana, and Alaska.

James O. Page (Chapter 14) is fire chief for the city of Monterey Park, California. He is also publisher of a national monthly emergency medical services (EMS) journal. A member of the California bar since 1971, he is instructor of fire science at a community college in Los Angeles and adjunct assistant professor of emergency health services at the University of Maryland in Baltimore County. He holds a J.D. degree from Southwestern University of Law and has served as a consultant to local and state governments in the areas of fire protection and EMS.

Philip Schaenman (Chapter 6) is president of TriData Corporation, a fire protection consulting firm in Arlington, Virginia. An authority on national fire statistics, he holds advanced degrees in engineering from Columbia and Stanford universities. From 1976 to 1981 Mr. Schaenman was associate administrator of the U.S. Fire Administration, where he directed the National Fire Data Center during the development of the National Fire Incident Reporting System. He has served as consultant to local, state, and federal governments, private companies, and trade associations in the areas of fire data, prevention, and policy.

Jack W. Snook (Chapter 3) is chief/administrator of consolidated fire services in Washington County, Oregon, where he has been employed since 1986. He also is president of Management Development

Institute Inc. He has authored several fire service publications and has consulted and lectured in most of the United States. He holds an associate degree in fire science and a bachelor's degree in fire administration. He is currently completing a master's degree in public administration.

David H. Teems (Chapter 15) is assistant director of the Fire, Rescue, and Inspection Services Department in Miami, Florida. He administers fire suppression, emergency medical, training, and fire prevention divisions. From 1981 to 1986 he managed the building and zoning and fire prevention programs for the city of Miami. He holds an associate degree in fire administration from Miami Dade Community College and a bachelor's degree in professional studies from Barry University in Miami.

B. J. Thompson (Chapter 1) is a professor in the School of Engineering and Technology at California State University–Los Angeles. His area of specialization is fire protection administration, and he serves as the advisory for that program. During his career, Dr. Thompson has served as administrator of the U.S. Fire Administration (a presidential appointment); superintendent of the National Fire Academy; fire chief in Atlanta, Georgia; city manager of Santa Ana, California; fire chief in Santa Ana, California; and fire chief in

Santa Fe Springs, California. Dr. Thompson holds bachelor of arts and master of science degrees from California State University–Long Beach and a doctor of philosophy degree from Union Graduate School in Cincinnati, Ohio. He is a registered professional engineer in California.

Bruce J. Walz (Chapter 18) is assistant professor of emergency health services at the University of Maryland in Baltimore County. Previously he worked as manager of the Institute Development Division of the Maryland Fire and Rescue Institute of the University of Maryland, and he is currently active as an emergency services provider and educator. He holds a doctorate in adult education from the University of Maryland.

Paul M. Whisenand (Chapter 11) is president of PMW Associates, a firm specializing in public-sector recruitment, selection, and assessment centers. He is also full professor at California State University–Long Beach. He holds bachelor's, master's, and doctoral degrees in public administration from the University of Southern California. Dr. Whisenand has authored or coauthored fourteen textbooks on public management, human resource development, and personnel administration and has consulted with government agencies nationwide on the use of assessment centers and team building.

Illustration credits

Chapter 1   Figure 1–1: From *Great Fires of America*, by the editors of *Country Beautiful* (Waukesha, Wisconsin: Country Beautiful Corporation, 1973), 29; Figures 1–2, 1–3, 1–5, 1–7, 1–9, and 1–10: Courtesy of the National Fire Protection Association; Figure 1–4: The Fine Arts Museums of San Francisco, Achenbach Foundation for Graphic Arts, photo by Arnold Genthe, Grand View of Earthquake and Fire, looking down Sacramento Street; Figure 1–6: Chicago Tribune photograph, courtesy of the National Fire Protection Association; Figure 1–8: Las Vegas Metropolitan Police Department; Figure 1–11: The New Haven Colony Historical Society.

Chapter 2   Figure 2–1: Ira Sharkansky, *Public Administration: Policy-Making in Government Agencies* (Chicago: Rand McNally, 1978), 8; Figure 2–2: Ronny J. Coleman, *Management of Fire Service Operations* (North Scituate, Mass.: Duxbury Press, 1978); Figure 2–4: Courtesy of Fairfax County, Virginia, Fire and Rescue Services.

Chapter 3   Figure 3–6: Courtesy of The Village, Oklahoma, fire department; Figure 3–7: Courtesy of the Dover, New Hampshire, fire department; Figure 3–8: Courtesy of the Portage, Michigan, fire department; Figure 3–9: Courtesy of the Howard County, Maryland, fire department; Figure 3–10: Courtesy of the Wallingford, Connecticut, fire department; Figure 3–11: Courtesy of the Park Ridge, Illinois, fire department; Figure 3–12: Courtesy of the Tucson, Arizona, fire department.

Chapter 4   Figure 4–3: Adapted from National Fire Prevention and Control Administration, National Fire Safety and Research Office, *Urban Guide for Fire Prevention and Control Master Planning* (Washington, D.C.: Government Printing Office, 1977), 3–4; Figure 4–6: Robert Burns and Kenneth McAllister, *Fire Management 2D, Master Planning,* curriculum materials for California State Fire Academy.

Chapter 5   Figure 5–1: Arthur J. Swersey, Edward J. Ignall, et al., *Fire Protection and Local Government: An Evaluation of Policy-Related Research*, New York City-Rand Institute Report R-1813-NSF (Santa Monica, Calif.: Rand Corporation, 1975), 4; Figure 5–2: Courtesy of the Glendale, Arizona, fire department.

Chapter 6   Figures 6–1, 6–2, and 6–3: Courtesy of the National Fire Incident Reporting System; Figure 6–5: Robert L. McNabb, "Affordable Data Management Solutions," *Fire Command,* July 1985, 38–39.

Chapter 7   Figure 7–2: Adapted from Institute for Public Program Analysis, *Work Schedule Design Handbook: Methods for Assigning Employees' Work Shifts and Days Off* (St. Louis, August 1978), 75–77; Figure 7–5: Courtesy of the Champaign, Illinois, fire department; Figure 7–7: Adapted with major revisions from National Center for Productivity and Quality of Working Life, *Improving Productivity: A Self-Audit and Guide for Federal Executives and Managers* (Washington, D.C.: Government Printing Office, 1978).

Chapter 10   Figure 10–2: Courtesy of the Fullerton, California, fire department; Figure 10–4: Program information courtesy of the Flagstaff, Arizona, fire department, based on forms developed for the Phoenix, Arizona, fire department.

Chapter 13   Figures 13–1, 13–2, and 13–4: Federal Emergency Management Agency.

Chapter 15   Figure 15–1: Courtesy of the National Fire Protection Association; Figures 15–2, 15–3, and 15–6: Courtesy of the Department of Fire, Rescue and Inspection Services, Miami, Florida.

Chapter 17   Figure 17–1: Gerard J. Hoetmer and Amy Cohen Paul, *Municipalities and the Volunteer Fire Service,* Urban Data Service Reports, vol. 12, no. 9 (Washington, D.C.: International City Management Association, September 1980), 3; Figure 17–4: Wackenhut Services, Inc., *Report on the*

Operation of the Hall County Fire Department (Coral Gables, Fla., 1986), 12; Figure 17–6: City of Sunnyvale, California, *Public Safety Concepts and Practices,* n.d., 17; Figure 17–7: Ibid., 14.; Figure 17–8: City of Sunnyvale, California, *Fire Services Sub-Element of the General Plan,* 1985, 118; Figure 17–9: Geoffrey S. Bogart, *Residential Fire Sprinkler Ordinances,* Management Information Service Reports, vol. 19, no. 3 (Washington, D.C.: International City Management Association, 1987), 2; Figure 17–10: "Building Trade Offs Slash Sprinkler System Costs," *Size Up,* February 1986.

Index

Municipal Management Series

**Managing
Fire
Services
Second Edition**

Text type
Times Roman, Helvetica

Composition
Harper Graphics
Waldorf, Maryland

Printing and binding
Kingsport Press
Kingsport, Tennessee

Design
Herbert Slobin